Beginning Algorithms

Beginning Algorithms

Simon Harris and James Ross

Wiley Publishing, Inc.

Beginning Algorithms

Published by
Wiley Publishing, Inc.
10475 Crosspoint Boulevard
Indianapolis, IN 46256
www.wiley.com

Published 2006 by Wiley Publishing, Inc., Indianapolis, Indiana

Published simultaneously in Canada

ISBN-13: 978-0-7645- 9674-2
ISBN-10: 0-7645-9674-8

Manufactured in the United States of America

10 9 8 7 6 5 4 3 2

1MA/RS/RQ/QV/IN

Library of Congress Cataloging-in-Publication Data:

Harris, Simon, 1972-
Beginning algorithms / Simon Harris and James Ross.
p. cm.
Includes index.
ISBN-13: 978-0-7645-9674-2 (paper/website)
ISBN-10: 0-7645-9674-8 (paper/website)
1. Computer algorithms. I. Ross, James, 1968- II. Title.
QA76.9.A43H376 2005
005.1--dc22
2005022374

Credits

Executive Editor
Carol Long

Consulting Editor
Jon Eaves

Development Editors
Ami Frank Sullivan
Sydney Jones

Production Editor
William A. Barton

Copy Editor
Luann Rouff

Editorial Manager
Mary Beth Wakefield

Production Manager
Tim Tate

Vice President & Executive Group Publisher
Richard Swadley

Vice President and Executive Publisher
Joseph B. Wikert

Project Coordinators
Erin Smith
Ryan Steffen

Media Development Specialists
Angela Denny
Kit Malone
Travis Silvers

Graphics and Production Specialists
Jonelle Burns
Lauren Goddard
Denny Hager
Joyce Haughey
Jennifer Heleine
Barbara Moore
Melanee Prendergast
Alicia South

Quality Control Technicians
John Greenough
Leeann Harney

Proofreading
TECHBOOKS Production Services

Indexing
Valerie Haynes Perry

About the Authors

Simon Harris started writing animated sprites on a Commodore 64 in primary school. After a break of many years, he taught himself 80x86 and IBM System/370 assembler and started working professionally. Since then he has moved from assembler to C, C++, and, of course, Java. He believes a fundamental understanding and appreciation of algorithms is essential to developing good software; and since starting his own company, RedHill Consulting, he has managed to make a living discussing and demonstrating software development practices and techniques to anyone who will listen.

In his more than 15 years of development experience, **James Ross** has ranged from building packaged products to large enterprise systems to research into compilers and languages. In recent years, he has become a code quality fanatic and agile methods specialist, particularly with test-driven development. He works as a consultant for ThoughtWorks, the world's leading agile software development company. He is currently leading the development of a large J2EE project in the insurance industry in Melbourne, Australia. He lives with his wife and family in Melbourne.

Acknowledgments

From Simon Harris: First and foremost, a mighty big thank-you to Jon Eaves for handing us this opportunity, and to James, whose skill and professionalism never cease to amaze me. I certainly couldn't have finished this book without either of you.

Many thanks also to all those who read the draft chapters and provided feedback: Andrew Harris, Andy Trigg, Peter Barry, Michael Melia, and Darrell Deboer (I'm sure I've missed some). I hope you find the final product does justice to your efforts.

I also want to acknowledge my brother Tim for listening to my ranting at all hours of the night and day, and Kerri Rusnak and her family for feeding me waffles and cups of tea, not to mention my Aikido students for continuing to turn up and practice during my various absences.

Finally, I'd like to extend my sincerest gratitude to everyone at Wiley who persisted with the book and to all of my other friends and family who continued to prod and encourage me, especially when I thought the sky was falling. It's certainly been a learning experience.

From James Ross: First of all, I'd like to thank Simon for letting me come along for the ride on his first book. It was a great opportunity to write seriously for the first time and it's always a pleasure and an education to work with Simon. We heard a lot of stories about author teams who destroy their relationship while collaborating on a book, but I'm glad to say we avoided that trap.

I'd also like to thank all the folks at Wiley who were extremely understanding with two newbie authors and guided us unerringly towards the goal—especially Ami Sullivan and Carol Long. It is much appreciated.

To all the supergeeks at ThoughtWorks who have made my professional life such a pleasure over the past few years, especially Andy Trigg, who's been my programming pal since we wrote our first unit tests together, and who reviewed all the chapters I wrote with incredible attention to detail and insight, and Jon Eaves, the technical editor on this book, who never fails to make me laugh and teach me something. Simon Stewart also helped with great feedback on early drafts, and Gregor Hohpe and Martin Fowler provided the encouragement and inspiration to actually keep typing all those long nights.

Speaking of the long nights, I can honestly say that this book would not have been possible (at least my chapters!) without the love and understanding of the ladies in my life—Catherine, who is the sun in our little solar system; Jessica; Ruby; and little Ella, who was six months old when I signed on for this project and who slept at least 12 hours every single night while it was being written. You may never read it, baby, but I'll always think of you when I pick it up!

Contents

Introduction

Welcome to *Beginning Algorithms*, a step-by-step introduction to computing algorithms for the real world.

Developers use algorithms and data structures every day of their working lives. Having a good understanding of these algorithms and knowledge of when to apply them is essential to producing software that not only works correctly, but also performs efficiently.

This book aims to explain those algorithms and data structures most commonly encountered in day-to-day software development, while remaining at all times practical, concise, and to the point, with little or no verbiage to distract from the core concepts and examples.

Who Should Read This Book

The ideal reader of this book is someone who develops applications, or is just starting to do so, and who wants to understand algorithms and data structures. This might include programmers; developers; software engineering students; information systems students; and computer science students.

While this book assumes you have an understanding of computer programming in general, it is also hoped that if you took away the code, you could still read the book cover to cover and follow along—albeit at a largely conceptual level. For this reason, team leaders, architects, and even business analysts might also benefit.

Prerequisite Knowledge

As the code examples are all written in the Java programming language, a working knowledge of Java is likely necessary, as is a familiarity with the standard Java libraries—and with the `java.lang` package in particular. Also necessary is an understanding of arrays, loops, and so on, and, of course, how to create, compile, and run Java classes.

Over and above the prerequisites mentioned, there is no particular requirement that you have any knowledge of the data structures or the algorithms contained herein.

What You Will Learn

In these pages, you will find detailed explanations, some implementations, example uses, and exercises, all designed to build your understanding to a point where you can use this knowledge in the real world. The examples given are rarely, if ever, academic in nature. Very careful consideration has been given in each chapter to present you with code that, in most cases, could be used in real-world applications, immediately.

We tried very hard to adhere to many of the most commonly accepted software development practices. These include the use of Design Patterns [Cormen, 2001], coding conventions, quality checks, and fully automated unit tests. We hope that in addition to an understanding of algorithms and their importance in problem-solving, you will come away with a deeper appreciation for how to build robust, extensible, and, of course, functional software.

For those of you who are more familiar with the Java language, you may notice a certain overlap between the classes described in this book and those found in the `java.util` package. This book is not concerned with the specific implementations found in the Java libraries. Rather, we hope to give you an insight into why the designers of the Java language felt that it was so important to include specific implementations of certain algorithms and data structures, including how they work and when to use them.

As already noted, this book is not designed to teach you the basics of computer programming in general or Java programming in particular. It does not explain how to use the standard Java libraries, for that is not the intent. While the code examples may use any classes from the `java.lang`, and in some cases the `java.io`, packages, all other Java packages were off limits. Instead, throughout the course of this book, you will build all the necessary classes by hand, which will enable you to experience the satisfaction that comes with discovering algorithms for yourself.

Although significant emphasis is placed on unit testing in each chapter, this book is not a study of, or even a guide to, unit testing. Rather, it is hoped that by exposing you directly to unit test code, you will gain an understanding of basic unit testing techniques.

How to Use This Book

For the most part, this book is intended to be read from beginning to end. It guides the reader through the basics of algorithms, data structures, and performance characteristics through to specific algorithms for sorting, searching, and so on. To this end, the book is divided into four main sections:

- The first five chapters explain the basics of algorithms, such as iteration, recursion, and so on, before introducing the reader to some fundamental data structures such as lists, stacks, and queues.
- Chapters 6 through 10 deal with various sorting algorithms, as well as some prerequisite topics such as keys and ordering.
- Chapters 7 through 15 cover efficient techniques for storing and searching by way of hashing, trees, sets, maps, and so on.
- Chapters 16 through 19 include several specialized, more advanced topics, as well as a general discussion on common performance pitfalls and optimization techniques.

Each chapter introduces concepts that build on previous chapters and provides the necessary background for subsequent ones. That said, it should still be possible to open the book at any chapter and, with a bit of thumbing between chapters, attain a sufficient understanding of the subject matter. In any event, we recommend that you carefully work through all of the sample implementations, example code, and exercises in each chapter in order to gain a solid understanding of the concepts and principles covered. Finally, at the very end, you can check out the appendixes for our suggestions for further reading, resources, and the bibliography.

Principles of the Approach

Often, the most difficult part of understanding code is coming to grips with the often unwritten assumptions and principles that guided the decision-making process. For this reason, we felt it was important to explain in some detail the approach we have taken. We would like to give you some insight into the rationale behind what we consider to be the fundamental development practices that guided us when writing this book. Among other things, we hope you will come to appreciate why we believe the following:

- Simplicity leads to better code.
- Don't optimize prematurely.
- Interfaces promote flexibility of design.
- All production code should be covered by automated unit and functional tests.
- Assertions are a developer's best friend.

Keep It Simple

How often have you heard "Oh, it's too complex. You wouldn't understand." or "Our code is too difficult to test." Dealing with complexity is the essence of software engineering.

If you've managed to build a system that does the job but is too hard to explain or too difficult to test, then your system works by coincidence. You may think you've deliberately implemented a solution in a particular way, but the fact that it works is more dependent on probability than pure determinism.

If it seems too complex, first break the problem down into smaller, more manageable chunks. Start solving the smaller problems. Then start refactoring and abstracting based on common code, common solutions, etc. In this way, large systems become complex arrangements of simple things.

In keeping with the Keep-It-Simple-Stupid (KISS) motto, all the examples in this book have been kept as simple as possible, but no simpler. Because this book is intended to be a practical guide to algorithms, the code examples provided are as close as possible to what we would produce for a real-world application. However, in some cases we have had to make methods a little longer than we might otherwise like, as this is, after all, a book intended to teach—not an exercise in writing the smallest number of lines of code.

Don't Pre-optimize

It is often tempting to try to make your code as fast as possible right from the start. The interesting thing about optimization and performance is that the bottlenecks are almost never where you expect them, nor of the nature you first suspected. Preempting where these hot-spots might be is a costly exercise. It is much better to get the design of your code right and leave performance improvement as a separate task requiring separate skills, as explained in Chapter 19.

Throughout this book, whenever a trade-off needs to be made between performance and clarity, we err on the side of clarity. We think it is much more important that you understand the design and intent of the code than it is to shave milliseconds from the running time.

A good design is much easier to profile and optimize than the spaghetti that results from "clever" code, and in fact our experience is that simple designs actually result in code that performs well with little optimization required.

Use Interfaces

Many data structures and algorithms have the same extant (outward) functionality even though the underlying implementation may be quite different. In real-world applications, it is often necessary to choose between these various implementations based on processing or memory constraints. In many cases, these constraints may not be known in advance.

Interfaces enable us to define the contract without regard to the underlying implementation. Because of this, they give us flexibility in our design by facilitating pluggability of implementation. Therefore, it is imperative that we code to interfaces as much as possible to allow substituting different implementations.

Throughout this book, all example implementations begin by first translating the functionality defined into operations on an interface. In most cases, these operations fall into one of two groups: core and optional.

The core operations provide the base functionality required for a given interface. The implementations of these are usually derived from first principles and are thus largely independent of one another.

The optional operations, conversely, can usually be implemented on top of the core operations, and are generally considered to be provided as a convenience to the developer. That is, you could quite easily implement them yourself on an as-needed basis in your own application code. However, as they are all commonly used in practice, we consider them part of the core API, and we do not finish a discussion on a given topic without implementing each of them in detail.

Employ Testing

Modern development practices demand that our software be rigorously united and functionally tested to ensure the ongoing integrity of the code. In keeping with this approach, after defining the interface, but before defining any concrete implementation, we translate our functional requirements into test cases, ensuring that every assumption has been covered and confirmed.

The tests are written using JUnit, the de facto standard testing framework for Java, and they exercise each functional aspect of the implementation.

Tests are written based on the defined interfaces, rather than any concrete implementation. This enables you to use the same tests for each implementation, thereby ensuring consistent quality. In addition, it demonstrates the different performance characteristics. This is important when choosing between different implementations for use in your application.

Testing purists may argue that the tests are sometimes a little too long for their liking, and that they test too many things in one method. We would tend to agree with them, but to keep things as simple as possible in order to facilitate understanding, we occasionally found it necessary to take the liberty of combining some scenarios into one test method.

The important point is that we write our tests first, i.e., before we have written any implementation code. This approach, also known as *test-driven development (TDD)*, forces us to concentrate on the contract, the published behavior, of our classes, rather than the implementation. It enables us to treat the test cases almost as requirements or use cases for our code; and in our experience, it keeps the design of our classes much simpler. As demonstrated in the examples, the fact that we code our tests to the interfaces makes TDD a breeze.

Be Assertive

Given the rigor of our testing, we might get complacent, believing that because our code is fully tested it is therefore bug-free. The problem is that tests don't necessarily prove that the software does what it's supposed to. Rather, tests prove that software works for the given scenarios and the assumptions made, but these do not always match reality. We may have the greatest, most comprehensive test suite in the world, but if it's testing the wrong things, it matters little.

In keeping with the fail-fast motto, we urge you to program defensively; check for null pointers; assert that objects are in the correct state at the start of a method, and so on. Experience has shown us that this kind of programming catches all manner of strange bugs much earlier than waiting for a `NullPointerException`.

Anytime you make an assumption about the state of an object or the nature of a parameter, validate your assumption in code with an assertion. Anytime you find yourself saying, "This will never happen so I don't have to worry about it," put in a code-level assertion.

For example, imagine you have a monetary field in a database that you "know" will "never" have a negative value. If you turn assertions off, someday, somehow, a negative value *will* creep in. It may be days, months, or even years before you notice the effects. Maybe it has been affecting other parts of the system during calculations. If the amount were -0.01 cents, you may hardly even notice. However, by the time the problem is discovered, you may have no way of determining all the adverse side effects, let alone devise a way to fix them. If you had only enabled that code-level assertion, the software would have failed in an entirely predictable way at the very instant the problem arose, most likely with all the diagnostic information you would need to track down the problem. Instead, the data in your system has been corrupted, possibly beyond repair.

Assertions in production code enable your software to fail in predictable ways, ways that will ultimately help you identify the nature and cause of a problem as easily and quickly as possible. They also incur negligible overhead. Don't presume for a moment that assertions will somehow cause your software to perform badly. Chances are good that all the assertions in your code combined probably don't compare to the time taken inside a remote procedure call or a database query. We strongly recommend that you leave assertions turned on in production code.

What You Will Need

Getting up and running couldn't be simpler. If you want to give yourself a quick head start, you can download a fully working project with all the source code, tests, and an automated command-line build from the Wrox website (refer to the "Source Code" section below).

If you prefer the do-it-yourself approach, you're in luck, because we have minimized the number of dependencies. To get started, all you need is the following:

- A copy of the Java Development Kit (JDK) version 1.4 or later, which includes everything you need to compile and run your code
- The JUnit library, consisting of a single jar file made available on your classpath if you wish to compile and run the unit tests
- A text editor or Integrated Development Environment (IDE) for working on the code itself

The first two (JDK and JUnit) are freely available and can be downloaded from the Internet (see Appendix B, "Resources"). As for the last requirement, well, we'd rather not start an IDE war so that's up to you. No doubt you already have a favorite, so stick with it. However, in the event that you don't have something with which to edit your code, try asking friends, fellow students, lecturers, or work colleagues. We're pretty sure they won't be shy about giving you their opinion.

Being Java, the code will compile and run on just about any operating system. We wrote and developed this book on a combination of Apple Macintosh and Windows-based machines. None of the code is particularly CPU intensive either, so whatever hardware you are using for your usual software development will most likely be just fine.

Conventions

To help you get the most from the text and keep track of what's happening, we've used a number of conventions throughout the book.

Try It Out Hands-on Practice

The Try it Out section is an exercise you should work through, following the text in the book.

1. Each Try it Out usually consists of coded steps.
2. The steps are not always be numbered, and some are very short, while others are a series of small steps that lead to a final, larger accomplishment.

How It Works

After each Try It Out, the step that each block of code accomplishes is explained in detail in a How It Works section. The particular topic of this book, algorithms, is less suited to hands-on numbered exercises and more suited to hands-on examples, so you'll find that the Try it Out and How it Works sections have been altered accordingly. The idea is still to engage you in applying what you're learning.

> **Boxes like this one hold important, not-to-be forgotten information that is directly relevant to the surrounding text.**

Tips, hints, tricks, and asides to the current discussion are offset and placed in italics like this.

As for styles in the text:

- We *italicize* important words when we introduce them.
- We show keyboard strokes like this: Ctrl+A.
- We show filenames, URLs, and code within the text like so: `persistence.properties`.
- We present code in two different ways:

```
In code examples, we highlight new and important code with a gray background.
```

```
The gray highlighting is not used for code that's less important in the present
context or has been shown before.
```

Source Code

As you work through the examples in this book, you may choose either to type in all the code manually or to use the source code files that accompany the book. All of the source code used in this book is available for download at `www.wrox.com`. Once at the site, simply locate the book's title (either by using the Search box or by using one of the title lists) and click the Download Code link on the book's detail page to obtain all the source code for the book.

Because many books have similar titles, you may find it easiest to search by ISBN; for this book the ISBN is 0-7645-9674-8 (changing to 978-0-7645-9674-2 as the new industry-wide 13-digit ISBN numbering system is phased in by January 2007).

Once you download the code, just decompress it with your favorite compression tool. Alternately, you can go to the main Wrox code download page at `www.wrox.com/dynamic/books/download.aspx` to see the code available for this book and all other Wrox books.

Errata

We made every effort to ensure that there are no errors in the text or in the code. However, no one is perfect, and mistakes do occur. If you find an error in the book, such as a spelling mistake or a faulty piece of code, we would be very grateful for your feedback. By sending in errata, you may save another reader hours of frustration, and at the same time you will be helping us provide even higher quality information.

To find the errata page for this book, go to `www.wrox.com` and locate the title using the Search box or one of the title lists. Then, on the book details page, click the Book Errata link. On this page, you can view all errata submitted for this book and posted by Wrox editors. A complete book list, including links to each book's errata, is also available at `www.wrox.com/misc-pages/booklist.shtml`.

If you don't spot "your" error on the Book Errata page, go to `www.wrox.com/contact/techsupport.shtml` and complete the form there to send us the error you have found. We'll check the information and, if appropriate, post a message to the book's errata page and fix the problem in subsequent editions of the book.

p2p.wrox.com

For author and peer discussion, join the P2P forums at `p2p.wrox.com`. The forums are a Web-based system for you to post messages relating to Wrox books and related technologies and interact with other readers and technology users. The forums offer a subscription feature to e-mail you topics of interest of your choosing when new posts are made. Wrox authors, editors, other industry experts, and your fellow readers are present on these forums.

At `http://p2p.wrox.com` you will find a number of different forums that will help you not only as you read this book, but also as you develop your own applications. To join the forums, just follow these steps:

1. Go to `p2p.wrox.com` and click the Register link.
2. Read the terms of use and click Agree.
3. Complete the required information to join as well as any optional information you wish to provide and click Submit.
4. You will receive an e-mail with information describing how to verify your account and complete the joining process.

You can read messages in the forums without joining P2P, but in order to post your own messages, you must join.

Once you join, you can post new messages and respond to messages other users post. You can read messages at any time on the Web. If you would like to have new messages from a particular forum e-mailed to you, click the Subscribe to this Forum icon by the forum name in the forum listing.

For more information about how to use the Wrox P2P, be sure to read the P2P FAQs for answers to questions about how the forum software works as well as many common questions specific to P2P and Wrox books. To read the FAQs, click the FAQ link on any P2P page.

Getting Started

This journey into the world of algorithms begins with some preparation and background information. You'll need to know a few things before learning the many algorithms and data structures in the rest of the book. Although you're keen to get going, reading this chapter will make the rest of the book more useful for you, as it includes concepts that are prerequisites for understanding the explanations of all the code and the analyses of the algorithms themselves.

This chapter discusses:

- What an algorithm is
- The role of algorithms in software and everyday life
- What is meant by the complexity of an algorithm
- Several broad classes of algorithm complexity that enable you to distinguish quickly between different solutions to the same problem
- "Big-O" notation
- What unit testing is and why it is important
- How to write unit tests with JUnit

Defining Algorithms

Perhaps you already know that algorithms are an important part of computing, but what exactly are they? What are they good for? And should you even care?

Well, as it turns out, algorithms aren't just limited to computing; you use algorithms every day of your life. In simple terms, an *algorithm* is a set of well-defined steps required to accomplish some task. If you've ever baked a cake, or followed a recipe of any kind, then you've used an algorithm.

Algorithms also usually involve taking a system from one state to another, possibly transitioning through a series of intermediate states along the way. Another example of this from everyday life is simple integer multiplication. Although most of us memorized multiplication tables back in grade school, the actual process of multiplication can also be thought of as a series of additions. The expression 5×2, for example, is really a shorthand way of saying $2 + 2 + 2 + 2 + 2$ (or $5 + 5$ for that matter). Therefore, given any two integers *A* and *B*, we can say that multiplying *A times B* involves adding *B* to itself, *A* times. This can be expressed as a sequence of steps:

1. Initialize a third integer, *C*, to zero.
2. If *A* is zero, we're done and *C* contains the result. Otherwise, proceed to step 3.
3. Add the value of *B* to *C*.
4. Decrement *A*.
5. Go to step 2.

Notice that unlike a recipe for baking a cake, the multiplication-using-addition algorithm loops back on itself at step 5. Most algorithms involve some kind of looping to repeatedly apply a calculation or other computation. *Iteration* and *recursion*—the two main types of looping—are covered in detail in the next chapter.

Quite often, algorithms are described in pseudo-code, a kind of *made-up* programming language that is easy to understand, even for nonprogrammers. The following code shows a function, `Multiply`, that takes two integers—*A* and *B*—and returns $A \times B$ using only addition. This is pseudo-code representing the act of multiplying two integers using addition:

```
Function Multiply(Integer A, Integer B)
    Integer C = 0

    While A is greater than 0
        C = C + B
        A = A - 1
    End

    Return C
End
```

Of course, multiplication is a very simple example of an algorithm. Most applications you are likely to encounter will involve algorithms that are far more complex than this. The problem with complex algorithms is that they are inherently more difficult to understand and therefore are more likely to contain bugs. (In fact, a large part of computer science involves proving that certain algorithms work correctly.)

Coming up with algorithms isn't always easy. In addition, more than one algorithm may solve a given problem. Some solutions will be simple, others will be complex, and some will be more efficient than others. The simplest solution isn't always the most obvious either. While rigorous, scientific analysis is always a good starting point, you can often find yourself stuck in *analysis paralysis*. Sometimes a bit of good old-fashioned creativity is needed. Try different approaches, and investigate hunches. Determine why your current attempts at a solution work for some cases and not for others. There is a reason why one of the seminal works on so-called computer *science* and software *engineering* is called *The* Art *of Computer Programming* (authored by Donald E. Knuth). Most of the algorithms in this book are *deterministic*—the result of any algorithm can be determined exactly based on the inputs. Sometimes, however, a problem is so difficult that finding a precise solution can be too costly in terms of time or resources. In this case, a *heuristic* may be a more practical approach. Rather than try to find a perfect solution, a heuristic uses certain well-known characteristics of a problem to produce an approximate solution. Heuristics are often used to sift through data, removing or ignoring values that are irrelevant so that the more computationally expensive parts of an algorithm can operate on a smaller set of data.

A rather lighthearted example of a heuristic involves crossing the street in different countries of the world. In North America and most of Europe, vehicles drive on the right-hand side of the road. If you've lived in the United States your whole life, then you're no doubt used to looking left and then right before crossing the street. If you were to travel to Australia, however, and looked left, saw that the road was clear, and moved onto the street, you would be in for quite a shock because in Australia, as in the United Kingdom, Japan, and many other countries, vehicles drive on the left-hand side of the road.

One simple way to tell which way the cars are traveling irrespective of which country you're in is to look at the direction of the parked cars. If they are all lined up pointing left-to-right, then chances are good you will need to look left and then right before crossing the road. Conversely, if the parked cars are lined up pointing right-to-left, then you will need to look right and then left before crossing the street. This simple heuristic works *most* of the time. Unfortunately, there are a few cases in which the heuristic falls down: when there are no parked cars on the road, when the cars are parked facing in different directions (as seems to happen quite a lot in London), or when cars drive on either side of the street, as is the case in Bangalore.

Therefore, the major drawback with using a heuristic is that it is usually not possible to determine how it will perform all of the time — as just demonstrated. This leads to a level of uncertainty in the overall algorithm that may or may not be acceptable depending on the application.

In the end, though, whatever problem you are trying to solve, you will undoubtedly use an algorithm of some kind; and the simpler, more precise, and more understandable you can make your algorithm, the easier it will be to determine not only whether it works correctly but also how well it will perform.

Understanding Complexity in Relation to Algorithms

Having come up with your new, groundbreaking algorithm, how do you determine its efficiency? Obviously, you want your code to be as efficient as possible, so you'll need some way to prove that it will actually work as well as you had hoped. But what do we mean by efficient? Do we mean CPU time, memory usage, disk I/O, and so on? And how do we measure the efficiency of an algorithm?

One of the most common mistakes made when analyzing the efficiency of an algorithm is to confuse *performance* (the amount of CPU/memory/disk usage) with *complexity* (how well the algorithm scales). Saying that an algorithm takes 30 milliseconds to process 1,000 records isn't a particularly good indication of efficiency. While it is true that, ultimately, resource consumption is important, other aspects such as CPU time can be affected heavily by the efficiency and performance of the underlying hardware on which the code will run, the compiler used to generate the machine code, in addition to the code itself. It's more important, therefore, to ascertain how a given algorithm behaves as the size of the problem increases. If the number of records to process was doubled, for example, what effect would that have on processing time? Returning to our original example, if one algorithm takes 30 milliseconds to process 1,000 records while another takes 40 milliseconds, you might consider the first to be "better." However, if the first algorithm takes 300 milliseconds to process 10,000 records (ten times as many) and the second algorithm only takes 80 milliseconds, you might reconsider your choice.

Generally speaking, complexity is a measure of the amount of a particular resource required to perform a given function. While it is therefore possible—and often useful—to measure complexity in terms of disk I/O, memory usage, and so on, we will largely focus on complexity as it affects CPU time. As such, we will further redefine complexity to be a measure of the number of computations, or operations, required to perform a particular function.

Interestingly, it's usually not necessary to measure the precise number of operations. Rather, what is of greater interest is how the number of operations performed varies with the size of the problem. As in the previous example, if the problem size were to increase by an order of magnitude, how does that affect the number of operations required to perform a simple function? Does the number remain the same? Does it double? Does it increase linearly with the size of the problem? Does it increase exponentially? This is what we mean when we refer to algorithm complexity. By measuring the complexity of an algorithm, we hope to predict how it will perform: Complexity affects performance, but not vice versa.

Throughout this book, the algorithms and data structures are presented along with an analysis of their complexity. Furthermore, you won't require a Ph.D. in mathematics to understand them either. In all cases, a very simple theoretical analysis of complexity is backed by easy-to-follow empirical results in the form of test cases, which you can try for yourself, playing around with and changing the inputs in order to get a good feel for the efficiency of the algorithms covered. In most cases, the average complexity is given—the expected average-case performance of the code. In many cases, a worst-case and best-case time is also given. Which measure—best, worst, or average—is most appropriate will depend on the algorithm to some extent, but more often than not it is a function of the type of data upon which the algorithm will operate. In all cases, it is important to remember that complexity doesn't provide a precise measure of expected performance, but rather places certain bounds or limits on the achievable performance.

Understanding Big-O Notation

As mentioned earlier, the precise number of operations is not actually that important. The complexity of an algorithm is usually defined in terms of the *order of magnitude* of the number of operations required to perform a function, denoted by a capital `O` for *order of*—hence, big-O—followed by an expression representing some growth relative to the size of the problem denoted by the letter N. The following list shows some common orders, each of which is discussed in more detail a little later:

- `O(1)`: Pronounced "order 1" and denoting a function that runs in constant time
- `O(N)`: Pronounced "order N" and denoting a function that runs in linear time
- $O(N^2)$: Pronounced "order N squared" and denoting a function that runs in quadratic time
- `O(log N)`: Pronounced "order log N" and denoting a function that runs in logarithmic time
- `O(N log N)`: Pronounced "order N log N" and denoting a function that runs in time proportional to the size of the problem and the logarithmic time
- `O(N!)`: Pronounced "order N factorial" and denoting a function that runs in factorial time

Of course, there are many other useful orders besides those just listed, but these are sufficient for describing the complexity of the algorithms presented in this book.

Figure 1-1 shows how the various measures of complexity compare with one another. The horizontal axis represents the size of the problem — for example, the number of records to process in a search algorithm. The vertical axis represents the computational effort required by algorithms of each class. This is not indicative of the running time or the CPU cycles consumed; it merely gives an indication of how the computational resources will increase as the size of the problem to be solved increases.

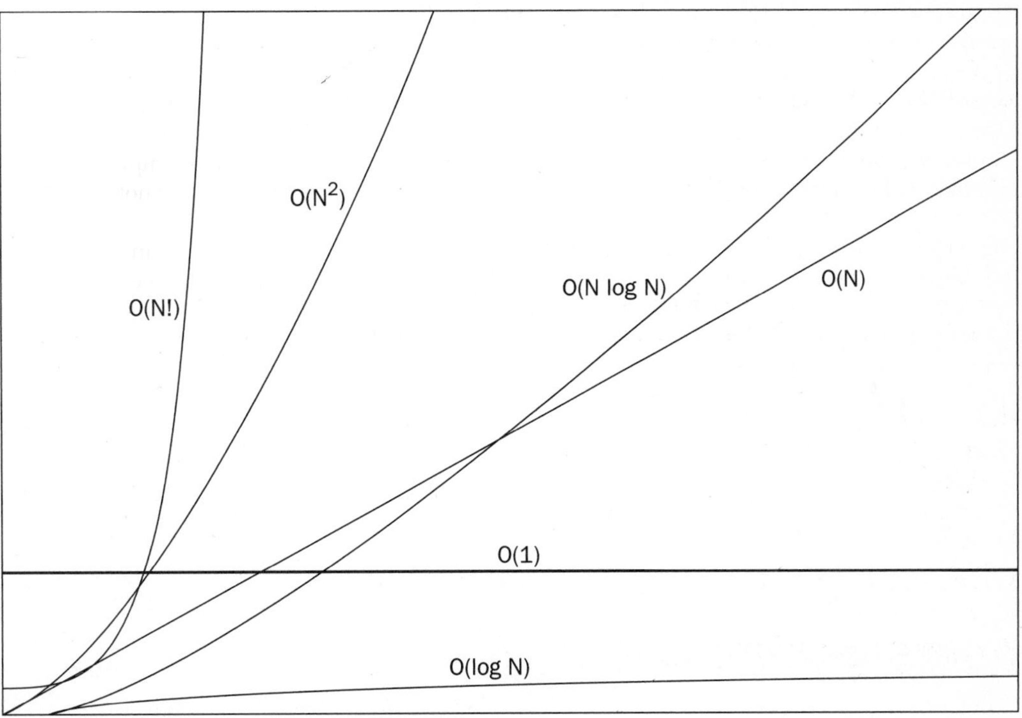

Figure 1-1: Comparison of different orders of complexity.

Referring back at the list, you may have noticed that none of the orders contain constants. That is, if an algorithm's expected runtime performance is proportional to `N`, `2×N`, `3×N`, or even `100×N`, in all cases the complexity is defined as being `O(N)`. This may seem a little strange at first — surely `2×N` is better than `100×N` — but as mentioned earlier, the aim is not to determine the exact number of operations but rather to provide a means of comparing different algorithms for relative efficiency. In other words, an algorithm that runs in `O(N)` time will generally outperform another algorithm that runs in `O(N²)`. Moreover, when dealing with large values of N, constants make less of a difference: As a ration of the overall size, the difference between 1,000,000,000 and 20,000,000,000 is almost insignificant even though one is actually 20 times bigger.

Of course, at some point you will want to compare the actual performance of different algorithms, especially if one takes 20 minutes to run and the other 3 hours, even if both are `O(N)`. The thing to remember, however, is that it's usually much easier to halve the time of an algorithm that is `O(N)` than it is to change an algorithm that's inherently `O(N²)` to one that is `O(N)`.

Constant Time: O(1)

You would be forgiven for assuming that a complexity of `O(1)` implies that an algorithm only ever takes one operation to perform its function. While this is certainly possible, `O(1)` actually means that an algorithm takes constant time to run; in other words, performance isn't affected by the size of the problem. If you think this sounds a little too good to be true, then you'd be right.

Granted, many simple functions will run in `O(1)` time. Possibly the simplest example of constant time performance is addressing main memory in a computer, and by extension, array lookup. Locating an element in an array generally takes the same amount of time regardless of size.

For more complex problems, however, finding an algorithm that runs in constant time is very difficult: Chapter 3, "Lists," and Chapter 11, "Hashing," introduce data structures and algorithms that have a time complexity of `O(1)`.

The other thing to note about constant time complexity is that it still doesn't guarantee that the algorithm will be very fast, only that the time taken will always be the same: An algorithm that always takes a month to run is still `O(1)` even though the actual running time may be completely unacceptable.

Linear Time: O(N)

An algorithm runs in `O(N)` if the number of operations required to perform a function is directly proportional to the number of items being processed. Looking at Figure 1-1, you can see that although the line for `O(N)` continues upward, the slope of the line remains the same.

One example of this might be waiting in a line at a supermarket. On average, it probably takes about the same amount of time to move each customer through the checkout: If it takes two minutes to process one customer's items, it will probably take 2 × 10 = 20 minutes to process ten customers, and 2 × 40 = 80 minutes to process 40 customers. The important point is that no matter how many customers are waiting in line, the time taken to process each one remains about the same. Therefore, we can say that the processing time is directly proportional to the number of customers, and thus `O(N)`.

Interestingly, even if you doubled or even tripled the number of registers in operation at any one time, the processing time is still officially `O(N)`. Remember that big-O notation always disregards any constants.

Algorithms that run in `O(N)` time are usually quite acceptable. They're certainly considered to be as efficient as those that run in `O(1)`, but as we've already mentioned, finding constant time algorithms is rather difficult. If you manage to find an algorithm that runs in linear time, you can often make it more efficient with a little bit of analysis—and the occasional stroke of genius—as Chapter 16, "String Searching," demonstrates.

Quadratic Time: O(N^2)

Imagine a group of people are meeting each other for the first time and in keeping with protocol, each person in the group must greet and shake hands with every other person once. If there were six people in the group, there would be a total of 5 + 4 + 3 + 2 + 1 = 15 handshakes, as shown in Figure 1-2.

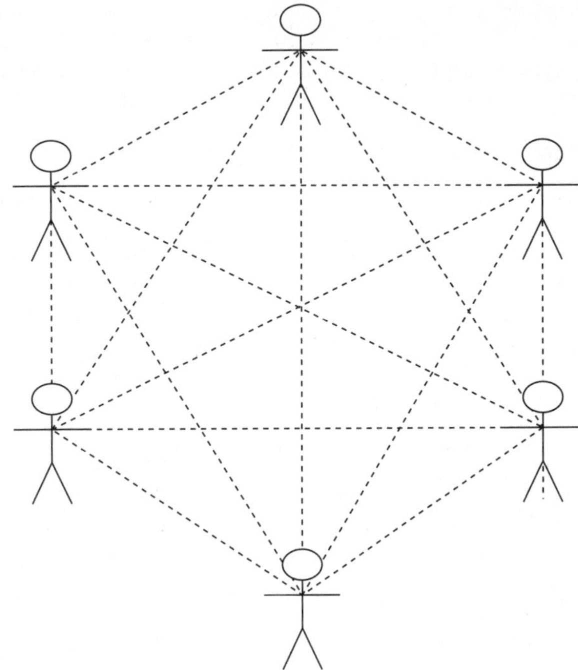

Figure 1-2: Each member of the group greets every other member.

What would happen if there were seven people in the group? There would be `6 + 5 + 4 + 3 + 2 + 1 = 21` handshakes. If there were eight people? That would work out to be `7 + 6 + . . . + 2 + 1 = 28` handshakes. If there were nine people? You get the idea: Each time the size of the group grows by one, that extra person must shake hands with every other person.

The number of handshakes required for a group of size N turns out to be $(N^2 - N) / 2$. Because big-O notation disregards any constants—in this case, the `2`—we're left with $N^2 - N$. As Table 1-1 shows, as `N` becomes larger, subtracting `N` from N^2 will have less and less of an overall effect, so we can safely ignore the subtraction, leaving us with a complexity of $O(N^2)$.

Table 1-1: Effect of Subtracting N from N^2 as N Increases

N	N^2	$N^2 - N$	Difference
1	1	0	100.00%
10	100	90	10.00%
100	10,000	9,900	1.00%
1,000	1,000,000	999,000	0.10%
10,000	100,000,000	99,990,000	0.01%

Algorithms that run in quadratic time may be a computer programmer's worst nightmare; any algorithm with a complexity of `O(N²)` is pretty much guaranteed to be useless for solving all but the smallest of problems. Chapters 6 and 7, on sorting, provide some rather interesting examples.

Logarithmic Time: O(log N) and O(N log N)

Looking at Figure 1-1, you can see that although `O(log N)` is better than `O(N)` it's still not as good as O(1).

The running time of a logarithmic algorithm increases with the log—in most cases, the log base 2—of the problem size. This means that even when the size of the input data set increases by a factor of a million, the run time will only increase by some factor of `log(1,000,000) = 20`. An easy way to calculate the log base 2 of an integer is to work out the number of binary digits required to store the number. For example, the log base 2 of 300 is 9, as it takes 9 binary digits to represent the decimal number 300 (the binary representation is 100101100).

Achieving logarithmic running times usually requires your algorithm to somehow discard large portions of the input data set. As a result, most algorithms that exhibit this behavior involve searching of some kind. Chapter 9, "Binary Searching," and Chapter 10, "Binary Search Trees," both cover algorithms that run in `O(log N)`.

Looking again at Figure 1-1, you can see that `O(N log N)` is still better than `O(N²)` but not quite as good as `O(N)`. Chapters 6 and 7 cover algorithms that run in `O(N log N)`.

Factorial Time: O(N!)

You may not have thought so, but some algorithms can perform even more poorly than `O(N²)`—compare the `O(N²)` and `O(N!)` lines in Figure 1-1. (Actually, there are many other orders that are far worse than even these but we don't cover any of them in this book.)

It's fairly unusual to encounter functions with this kind of behavior, especially when trying to think of examples that don't involve code, so in case you've forgotten what factorial is—or for those who never knew in the first place—here's a quick refresher:

> *The factorial of an integer is the product of itself and all the integers below it.*

For example, 6! (pronounced "six factorial") `= 6 × 5 × 4 × 3 × 2 × 1 = 720` and `10! = 10 × 9 × 8 × 7 × 6 × 5 × 4 × 3 × 2 × 1 = 3,628,800`.

Table 1-2 provides a comparison between N^2 and N! for the integers between 1 and 10.

Table 1-2: Comparison between N^2 and N! for Small Integers

N	N^2	N!
1	1	1
2	4	2
3	9	6
4	16	24

N	N^2	N!
5	25	120
6	36	720
7	49	5,040
8	64	40,320
9	81	362,880
10	100	3,628,800

As you can see, for values of `N` up to and including `N=2`, the factorial is less than the quadratic, after which point the factorial takes off and leaves everything else in its wake. As a consequence, even more so than with $O(N^2)$, you'd better hope that your code isn't `O(N!)`.

Unit Testing

Before continuing our journey into the realm of algorithms, we need to digress to discuss a topic that's very dear to our hearts: *unit testing*. Over the past several years, unit testing has become very popular among developers who place a high value on the quality of the systems they build. Many of these developers are not comfortable creating software without also creating an accompanying suite of automated tests that prove the software they've created does what they intend. As you may have guessed, we both hold this point of view. That's why for every algorithm we show you, we'll also show you how it works and what it does by providing unit tests for it. We strongly recommend that you adopt this habit in your own development efforts. It will greatly increase your odds of leaving work on time!

The next few sections provide a quick overview of unit testing in general and introduce the JUnit framework for unit testing Java programs. We use JUnit throughout the book, so you'll need to be familiar with it in order to make sense of the examples provided. Feel free to skip this section of the book if you're already a hardcore test-infected developer. Good for you!

What Is Unit Testing?

A *unit test* is simply a program that tests another program. In Java terms, it's usually a Java class whose purpose is to test another class. That's really it. Like most things, though, it's easy to learn but hard to master. Unit testing is an art as well as a science, and you can find many books just about testing, so we won't go into too much depth here. Check Appendix A for some good books with more detail on this topic.

The basic operation of a unit test is as follows:

1. Set up any objects that you need to support the test, such as sample data. This stuff is called *fixtures*.
2. Run your test by exercising the objects and ensuring that what you expected to happen did indeed happen. This is called making *assertions*.
3. Finally, clean up anything no longer needed. This is called *tearing down*.

The common convention when naming unit tests in this book is to create the test class using the class name, followed by `Test`. For example, if you are going to test a class called `Widget`, you create a new class called `WidgetTest` to act as the unit test for it. You will see many examples of this in the book. You should also notice a common convention for organizing source files. This involves placing unit tests in a parallel source tree with the same package structure as the main source files. For example, if the Widget lives in a package called `com.wrox.algorithms`, the source files are organized something like what you see in Figure 1-3.

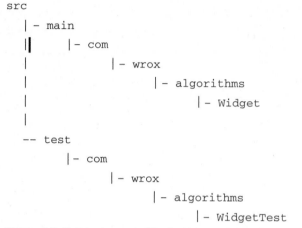

```
src
   | - main
   |      |- com
   |             |- wrox
   |                    |- algorithms
   |                           |- Widget
   |
   -- test
          |- com
                 |- wrox
                        |- algorithms
                               |- WidgetTest
```

Figure 1-3: Unit test source files live in a parallel package structure.

This means that the Java package statement at the top of each file would be exactly the same, but the files themselves live in different directories on the file system. This model keeps production code separate from test code for easy packaging and distribution of the main line of code, and makes it easy to ensure that production code doesn't rely on test code during the build process, by having slightly different classpath arrangements when compiling the two directories. Some people also like the fact that it can enable tests to access package-scoped methods, so that's something else to consider.

Before we finish describing unit testing, be aware that you may come across several other common types of testing. We'll provide some basic definitions here to give you some context and to avoid some unnecessary confusion. This book only makes use of unit testing, so check the references for additional information about other types of testing. Some of the terms you may encounter include the following:

- **Black-box testing:** Imagine you want to test your DVD player. All you have access to (without voiding your warranty) are the buttons on the front and the plugs at the back. You can't test individual components of the DVD player because you don't have access to them. All you have is the externally visible controls provided on the outside of the black box. In software terms, this is akin to only being able to use the user interface for a fully deployed application. There are many more components, but you may not have access to them.
- **Functional testing:** This is usually used interchangeably with black-box testing.
- **White-box testing:** This refers to testing that can get inside the overarching component organization of a system to a greater or lesser extent and test individual components, usually without the user interface.

- **Integration testing:** This is often used to describe the testing of an individual component of a large distributed system. These types of tests are aimed at ensuring that systems continue to meet their agreed contracts of behavior as they evolve independently from one another.

Unit testing is the most fine-grained of the testing techniques, as it involves usually a single class being tested independently of any other classes. This means unit tests are very quick to run and are relatively independent of each other.

Why Unit Testing Is Important

To understand why you're reading so much about unit testing in a book about algorithms, consider your Java compiler, which enables you to run your Java programs. Would you ever consider a program you wrote to be working if you hadn't compiled it? Probably not! Think of your compiler as one kind of test of your program — it ensures that your program is expressed in the correct language syntax, and that's about it. It cannot give you any feedback regarding whether your program does anything sensible or useful, and that's where unit tests come in. Given that we are more interested in whether our programs actually do something useful than whether we typed in the Java correctly, unit tests provide an essential barrier against bugs of all kinds.

Another benefit of unit tests is that they provide reliable documentation about the behavior of the class under test. When you've seen a few unit tests in action, you'll find that it's easier to work out what a class is doing by looking at the test than by looking at the code itself! (The code itself is where to look when you want to know *how* it does whatever it does, but that's a different matter.)

A JUnit Primer

The first place to visit is the JUnit website at `www.junit.org/`. Here you will find not only the software to download, but also information on how to use JUnit in your IDE, and pointers to the many extensions and enhancements to JUnit that have been created to address particular needs.

Once you've downloaded the software, all you need to do is add `junit.jar` to your classpath and you're ready to create your first unit test. To create a unit test, simply create a Java class that extends the `junit.framework.TestCase` base class. The following code shows the basic structure of a unit test written using JUnit:

```
package com.wrox.algorithms.queues;

import com.wrox.algorithms.lists.LinkedList;
import com.wrox.algorithms.lists.List;
import junit.framework.TestCase;

public class RandomListQueueTest extends TestCase {
    private static final String VALUE_A = "A";
    private static final String VALUE_B = "B";
    private static final String VALUE_C = "C";

    private Queue _queue;
    ...
}
```

Don't be concerned with what this unit test is actually testing; this particular unit test is one you'll understand during the discussion on queues later in the book. The main point here is that a unit test is just a regular class with a base class supplied by the JUnit framework. What this code does is declare the class, extend the base class, and declare some static members and one instance member to hold the queue you're going to test.

The next thing to do is override the `setUp()` method and add any code needed to get the objects ready for testing. In this case, this simply means calling the overridden `setUp()` method in the superclass and instantiating your queue object for testing:

Note the spelling of the `setUp()` *method. That's a capital "U" in the middle of it! One of Java's weaknesses is that methods are only overridden by coincidence, not by explicit intention. If you mistype the name of the method, it won't work as you expect.*

```
protected void setUp() throws Exception {
    super.setUp();

    _queue = new RandomListQueue();
}
```

Part of what is provided to you by the JUnit framework is the guarantee that each time a test method is run (you'll get to those shortly), the `setUp()` method will be called before each test runs. Similarly, after each test method is run, a companion `tearDown()` method provides you with the opportunity to clean up after yourself, as shown by the following code:

```
protected void tearDown() throws Exception {
    super.tearDown();

    _queue = null;
}
```

You might be wondering why you need to bother with setting the instance member field to `null`. While not strictly necessary, in very large suites of unit tests, neglecting this step can cause the unit tests to consume a lot more memory than they need to, so it's a good habit to acquire.

The following method of actual unit test code is designed to test the behavior of a queue when it is empty and someone tries to take an item off it, which is not allowed by the designer of the object. This is an interesting case because it demonstrates a technique to prove that your classes fail in expected ways under improper use. Here's the code:

```
public void testAccessAnEmptyQueue() {
    assertEquals(0, _queue.size());
    assertTrue(_queue.isEmpty());

    try {
        _queue.dequeue();
        fail();
    } catch (EmptyQueueException e) {
        // expected
    }
}
```

Note the following points about this code:

- The method's name begins with `test`. This is required by the JUnit framework to enable it to differentiate a test method from a supporting method.
- The first line of the method uses the `assertEquals()` method to prove that the size of the queue is zero. The syntax of this method is `assertEquals(expected, actual)`. There are overloaded versions of this method for all basic Java types, so you will become very familiar with this method during the course of this book. It is probably the most common assertion in the world of unit tests: making sure that something has the value you expect. If, for some reason, the value turns out to be something other than what you expect, the JUnit framework will abort the execution of the test and report it as a failure. This helps to make the unit test quite concise and readable.
- The second line uses another very common assertion, `assertTrue()`, which is used to ensure that Boolean values are in the expected state during the test run. In this case, we are making sure that the queue reports correctly on its empty state.
- The `try/catch` block surrounds a call to a method on our queue object that is designed to throw an exception when the queue is empty. This construct is a little different than what you'll be used to from normal exception handling in Java, so look at it carefully. In this case, it's considered *good* if the exception is thrown and *bad* if it is not thrown. For this reason, the code does nothing in the `catch` block itself, but in the `try` block, it calls the JUnit framework `fail()` method right after calling the method you're trying to test. The `fail()` method aborts the test and reports it as a failure, so if the method throws the expected exception, then execution will fall through to the end of the method and the test will pass. If no exception is thrown, then the test will immediately fail. If that all sounds a little confusing, read through it again!

Here is another example of a unit test method in the same class:

```
public void testClear() {
    _queue.enqueue(VALUE_A);
    _queue.enqueue(VALUE_B);
    _queue.enqueue(VALUE_C);

    assertEquals(3, _queue.size());
    assertFalse(_queue.isEmpty());

    _queue.clear();

    assertEquals(0, _queue.size());
    assertTrue(_queue.isEmpty());
}
```

The method name again starts with `test` so that JUnit can find it using reflection. This test adds a few items to the queue, asserts that the `size()` and `isEmpty()` methods work as expected, and then clears the queue and again ensures that these two methods behave as expected.

The next thing you'll want to do after writing a unit test is to run it. Note that your unit test does not have a `main()` method, so you can't run it directly. JUnit provides several *test runners* that provide different interfaces—from a simple text-based console interface to a rich graphical interface. Most Java development environments, such as Eclipse or IntelliJ IDEA, have direct support for running JUnit tests, but if all you have is the command line, you can run the preceding test with the following command (you will need to have `junit.jar` on your classpath, of course):

```
java junit.textui.TestRunner com.wrox.algorithms.queues.RandomListQueueTest
```

Running the graphical version is just as easy:

```
java junit.swingui.TestRunner com.wrox.algorithms.queues.RandomListQueueTest
```

JUnit can also be used from within many tools, such as Ant or Maven, that you use to build your software. Including the running of a good unit test suite with every build of your software will make your development life a lot easier and your software a lot more robust, so check out the JUnit website for all the details.

Test-Driven Development

All the algorithms and data structures we present in the book include unit tests that ensure that the code works as expected. In fact, the unit tests were written *before* the code existed to be tested! This may seem a little strange, but if you're going to be exposed to unit testing, you also need to be aware of an increasingly popular technique being practiced by developers who care about the quality of the code they write: *test-driven development*.

The term *test-driven development* was coined by Kent Beck, the creator of eXtreme Programming. Kent has written several books on the subject of eXtreme Programming in general, and test-driven development in particular. The basic idea is that your development efforts take on a rhythm, switching between writing some test code, writing some production code, and cleaning up the code to make it as well designed as possible (refactoring). This rhythm creates a constant feeling of forward progress as you build your software, while building up a solid suite of unit tests that protect against bugs caused by changes to the code by you or someone else further down the track.

If while reading this book you decide that unit testing is something you want to include in your own code, you can check out several books that specialize in this topic. Check Appendix A for our recommendations.

Summary

In this chapter, you learned the following:

- ❑ Algorithms are found in everyday life.
- ❑ Algorithms are central to most computer systems.
- ❑ What is meant by algorithm complexity.
- ❑ Algorithms can be compared in terms of their complexity.
- ❑ Big-O notation can be used to broadly classify algorithms based on their complexity.
- ❑ What unit testing is and why it is important.
- ❑ How to write unit tests using Junit.

Iteration and Recursion

Iteration and recursion are two fundamental concepts without which it would be impossible to do much, if anything, useful in computing. Sorting names, calculating credit-card transaction totals, and printing order line items all require that each record, each data point, be processed to achieve the desired result.

Iteration is simply the repetition of processing steps. How many repetitions are required can be determined by many different factors. For example, to calculate the total of your stock portfolio, you would iterate over your stock holdings, keeping a running total until each holding has been processed. In this case, the number of repetitions is determined by how many holdings you happen to have. *Recursion* is another technique for solving problems. Recursion can often, though not always, be a more natural way of expressing an algorithm than iteration. If you've done any programming at all, you probably already know what recursion is — you just didn't know you knew.

A recursive algorithm involves a method or function calling itself. It does this by breaking a problem into smaller and smaller parts, each looking very similar to the larger part yet finer grained. This can be a difficult concept to grasp at first.

You will find that algorithms tend to fall naturally into one category or the other; they are most easily expressed either iteratively or recursively. Having said this, it is fair to say that recursive algorithms are fewer and farther between than iterative ones for most practical applications. In this chapter, we assume you are familiar with how to construct loops, make method calls, and so on, and so we instead concentrate on how iteration and recursion are used to solve problems.

This chapter describes the following:

- How iteration is used to perform calculations
- How iteration is used to process arrays
- How to abstract the problem of iteration from simple arrays to more complex data structures
- How recursion is another technique for solving similar problems

Performing Calculations

Iteration can be used to perform calculations. Possibly one of the simplest examples of this is to raise one number (the *base*) to the power of another (the *exponent*): `baseexp` . This involves repeatedly multiplying the base by itself as many times as defined by the exponent. For example: `3^2 = 3 × 3 = 9 and 10^6 = 10 × 10 × 10 × 10 × 10 × 10 = 1,000,000`.

In this section, you'll implement a class, `PowerCalculator`, with a single method, `calculate`, that takes two parameters—an integer base and an exponent—and returns the value of the base raised to the power of the exponent. Although it's possible to use a negative exponent, for the purposes of this example you can assume that only exponents greater than or equal to zero will be used.

Try It Out Testing Calculations

The general case is pretty straightforward, but a few special rules should be considered, which are documented and codified as tests to ensure that the final implementation works as expected.

Begin by creating the test class itself, which does little more than extend `TestCase`:

```
package com.wrox.algorithms.iteration;

import junit.framework.TestCase;

public class PowerCalculatorTest extends TestCase {
    ...
}
```

The first rule involves raising the base to the power of zero. In all cases, this should result in the value of `1`:

```
    public void testAnythingRaisedToThePowerOfZeroIsOne() {
        PowerCalculator calculator = PowerCalculator.INSTANCE;

        assertEquals(1, calculator.calculate(0, 0));
        assertEquals(1, calculator.calculate(1, 0));
        assertEquals(1, calculator.calculate(27, 0));
        assertEquals(1, calculator.calculate(143, 0));
    }
```

The next rule involves raising the base to the power of one. In this case, the result should always be the base itself:

```
    public void testAnythingRaisedToThePowerOfOneIsItself() {
        PowerCalculator calculator = PowerCalculator.INSTANCE;

        assertEquals(0, calculator.calculate(0, 1));
        assertEquals(1, calculator.calculate(1, 1));
        assertEquals(27, calculator.calculate(27, 1));
        assertEquals(143, calculator.calculate(143, 1));
    }
```

Finally, you arrive at the general case:

```
public void testAritrary() {
    PowerCalculator calculator = PowerCalculator.INSTANCE;

    assertEquals(0, calculator.calculate(0, 2));
    assertEquals(1, calculator.calculate(1, 2));
    assertEquals(4, calculator.calculate(2, 2));

    assertEquals(8, calculator.calculate(2, 3));
    assertEquals(27, calculator.calculate(3, 3));
}
```

How It Works

The first rule makes a number of calculations, each with different values, and ensures that the calculation returns `1` in all cases. Notice that even `0` raised to the power of zero is actually `1`!

Also in the second rule, you perform a number of calculations with varying base values but this time using an exponent of `1`.

This time, the outcome of the calculation is tested using a number of different combinations of base and exponent.

Try It Out Implementing the Calculator

Having coded the tests, you can now implement the actual calculator:

```
package com.wrox.algorithms.iteration;

public final class PowerCalculator {
    public static final PowerCalculator INSTANCE = new PowerCalculator();

    private PowerCalculator() {
    }

    public int calculate(int base, int exponent) {
        assert exponent >= 0 : "exponent can't be < 0";

        int result = 1;

        for (int i = 0; i < exponent; ++i) {
            result *= base;
        }

        return result;
    }
}
```

How It Works

The `calculate()` method first checks to ensure that the exponent is valid (remember that you don't allow negative values) and initializes the result to `1`. Then comes the iteration in the form of a `for` loop. If the exponent was `0`, the loop would terminate without performing any multiplication and the result would still be 1 — anything raised to the power of zero is one. If the exponent was 1, the loop would make a single pass, multiplying the initial result by the base and returning to the caller — a number raised to the power of one is the number itself. For values of the exponent larger than this, the loop will continue, multiplying the result by the base as many times as specified.

A private constructor is used in order to prevent instances of the class from being constructed from outside the class itself. Instead, a single instance can be accessed via the constant INSTANCE. *This is an example of the Singleton design pattern [Gamma, 1995].*

Processing Arrays

Besides performing calculations, iteration is also used to process arrays. Imagine you wanted to apply a discount to a group of orders. The following code snippet iterates over an array of orders, applying a specified discount to each:

```
Order[] orders = ...;

for (int i = 0; i < orders.length; ++i) {
    orders[i].applyDiscount(percentage);
}
```

We first initialize our index variable with the position of the first element (`int i = 0`) and continue incrementing it (`++i`) until reaching the last element (`i < orders.length - 1`), applying the percentage. Notice that each iteration compares the value of the index variable with the length of the array.

Sometimes you may wish to process an array in reverse. For example, you may need to print a list of names in reverse order. The following code snippet iterates backward over an array of customers, printing the name of each:

```
Customer[] customers = ...;

for (int i = customers.length - 1; i >= 0; --i) {
    System.out.println(customers[i].getName());
}
```

This time, initialize the index variable to the position of the last element (`int i = customers.length - 1`) and continue decrementing (`--i`) until reaching the first (`i >= 0`), printing the customer's name each time through the loop.

Using Iterators to Overcome Array-based Problems

Although array-based iteration is useful when dealing with very simple data structures, it is quite difficult to construct generalized algorithms that do much more than process every element of an array from start to finish. For example, suppose you want to process only every second item; include or exclude specific values based on some selection criteria; or even process the items in reverse order as shown earlier. Being tied to arrays also makes it difficult to write applications that operate on databases or files without first copying the data into an array for processing.

Using simple array-based iteration not only ties algorithms to using arrays, but also requires that the logic for determining which elements stay, which go, and in which order to process them, is known in advance. Even worse, if you need to perform the iteration in more than one place in your code, you will likely end up duplicating the logic. This clearly isn't a very extensible approach. Instead, what's needed is a way to separate the logic for selecting the data from the code that actually processes it.

An *iterator* (also known as an *enumerator*) solves these problems by providing a generic interface for looping over a set of data so that the underlying data structure or storage mechanism—such as an array, database, and so on—is hidden. Whereas simple iteration generally requires you to write specific code to handle where the data is sourced from or even what kind of ordering or preprocessing is required, an iterator enables you to write simpler, more generic algorithms.

Iterator Operations

An iterator provides a number of operations for traversing and accessing data. Looking at the operations listed in Table 2-1, you will notice there are methods for traversing backward as well as forward.

Remember that an iterator is a concept, not an implementation. Java itself already defines an Iterator interface as part of the standard Java Collections Framework. The iterator we define here, however, is noticeably and deliberately different from the standard Java version, and instead conforms more closely to the iterator discussed in Design Patterns [Gamma, 1995].

Table 2-1: Iterator Operations

Operation	Description
previous	Positions to the previous item. Throws `UnsupportedOperationException` if not implemented.
isDone	Determines whether the iterator refers to an item. Returns `true` if the end has been reached; otherwise, returns `false` to indicate more items need to be processed.
current	Obtains the value of the current item. Throws `IteratorOutOfBoundsException` if there is no current item.

Most methods can potentially throw an `UnsupportedOperationException`. Not all data structures allow traversing the data in both directions, nor does it always make sense. For this reason, it is acceptable for any of the traversal methods—`first()`, `last()`, `next()`, and `previous()`—to throw an `UnsupportedOperationException` to indicate this missing or unimplemented behavior.

You should also leave the behavior of calling `current()` before either `first()` or `last()` has been called undefined. Some iterator implementations may well position to the first item, while others may require you to call `first()` or `last()`. In any event, relying on this behavior is considered to be *programming by coincidence* and should be avoided. Instead, when using iterators, be sure to follow one of the idioms described in the "Iterator Idioms" section, later in the chapter.

The Iterator Interface

From the operations just described, you can create the following Java interface:

```
package com.wrox.algorithms.iteration;

public interface Iterator {
    public void first();

    public void last();

    public boolean isDone();

    public void next();

    public void previous();

    public Object current() throws IteratorOutOfBoundsException;
}
```

As demonstrated, you have quite literally translated the operations into a Java interface, one method per operation.

You also need to define the exception that will be thrown if an attempt is made to access the current item when there are no more items to process:

```
package com.wrox.algorithms.iteration;

public class IteratorOutOfBoundsException extends RuntimeException {
}
```

Because accessing an iterator out-of-bounds is considered a programming error, it can be coded around. For this reason, it's a good idea to make `IteratorOutOfBoundsException` extend `RuntimeException`, making it a so-called *unchecked exception*. This ensures that client code need not handle the exception. In fact, if you adhere to the idioms discussed soon, you should almost never see an `IteratorOutOfBoundsException`.

The Iterable Interface

In addition to the Iterator interface, you'll also create another interface that provides a generic way to obtain an iterator from any data structure that supports it:

```
package com.wrox.algorithms.iteration;

public interface Iterable {
    public Iterator iterator();
}
```

The `Iterable` interface defines a single method — `iterator()` — that obtains an iterator over the data contained in whatever the underlying data structure contains. Although not used in this chapter, the `Iterable` interface enables code that only needs to iterate over the contents of a data structure to treat all those that implement it in the same way, irrespective of the underlying implementation.

Iterator Idioms

As with simple array-based iteration, there are two basic ways, or templates, for using iterators: either a `while` loop or a `for` loop. In either case, the procedure is similar: Once an iterator has been obtained—either by explicit construction or as an argument to a method—position to the beginning or end as appropriate. Then, while there are more items remaining, take each one and process it before moving on to the next (or previous).

Using a `while` loop enables you to perform quite a literal translation from the preceding text into code:

```
Iterator iterator = ...;
iterator.first();

while (!iterator.isDone()) {
    Object object = iterator.current();

    ...

    iterator.next();
}
```

This way is particularly useful when an iterator has been passed as a parameter in a method call. In this case, the method may not need to call `first()` or `last()` if the iterator has already been positioned to the appropriate starting point.

The use of a `for` loop, however, is probably more familiar to you as it closely resembles the way you would normally iterate over an array:

```
Iterator iterator = ...;

for (iterator.first();!iterator.isDone(); iterator.next()) {
    Object object = iterator.current();

    ...
}
```

Notice how similar this is to array iteration: The initialization becomes a call to `first()`; the termination condition is a check of `isDone()`; and the increment is achieved by calling `next()`.

Either idiom is encouraged, and both are used with more or less the same frequency in most real-world code you have seen. Whichever way you choose, or even if you choose to use both, remember to always call `first()` or `last()` before you call any other methods. Otherwise, results might be unreliable and depend on the implementation of the iterator.

Standard Iterators

In addition to the iterators provided by some of the data structures themselves later in this book, or even iterators you might create yourself, several standard implementations provide commonly used functionality. When combined with other iterators, these standard iterators enable you to write quite sophisticated algorithms for data processing.

Array Iterator

The most obvious iterator implementation is one that wraps an array. By encapsulating an array within an iterator, you can start writing applications that operate on arrays now and still extend easily to other data structures in the future.

Try It Out Testing the Array Iterator

The test for our array iterator will have the usual structure for a JUnit test case, as shown here:

```
package com.wrox.algorithms.iteration;

import junit.framework.TestCase;

public class ArrayIteratorTest extends TestCase {
    ...
}
```

One of the advantages of using iterators is that you don't necessarily have to traverse an array from the start, nor do you need to traverse right to the end. Sometimes you may want to expose only a portion of an array. The first test you will write, therefore, is to ensure that you can construct an array iterator passing in the accessible bounds—in this case, a starting position and an element count. This enables you to create an iterator over all or part of an array using the same constructor:

```
    public void testIterationRespectsBounds() {
        Object[] array = new Object[] {"A", "B", "C", "D", "E", "F"};
        ArrayIterator iterator = new ArrayIterator(array, 1, 3);

        iterator.first();
        assertFalse(iterator.isDone());
        assertSame(array[1], iterator.current());

        iterator.next();
        assertFalse(iterator.isDone());
        assertSame(array[2], iterator.current());

        iterator.next();
        assertFalse(iterator.isDone());
        assertSame(array[3], iterator.current());

        iterator.next();
        assertTrue(iterator.isDone());
        try {
            iterator.current();
            fail();
        } catch (IteratorOutOfBoundsException e) {
            // expected
        }
    }
```

The next thing you want to test is iterating backward over the array—that is, starting at the last element and working your way toward the first element:

```
    public void testBackwardsIteration() {
        Object[] array = new Object[] {"A", "B", "C"};
        ArrayIterator iterator = new ArrayIterator(array);

        iterator.last();
        assertFalse(iterator.isDone());
        assertSame(array[2], iterator.current());

        iterator.previous();
        assertFalse(iterator.isDone());
        assertSame(array[1], iterator.current());

        iterator.previous();
        assertFalse(iterator.isDone());
        assertSame(array[0], iterator.current());

        iterator.previous();
        assertTrue(iterator.isDone());
        try {
            iterator.current();
            fail();
        } catch (IteratorOutOfBoundsException e) {
            // expected
        }
    }
}
```

How It Works

In the first test, you begin by constructing an iterator, passing an array containing six elements. Notice, however, you have also passed a starting position of `1` (the second element) and an element count of `3`. Based on this, you expect the iterator to return only the values `"B"`, `"C"`, and `"D"`. To test this, you position the iterator to the first item and ensure that its value is as expected—in this case, `"B"`. You then call `next` for each of the remaining elements: once for `"C"` and then again for `"D"`, after which, even though the underlying array has more elements, you expect the iterator to be done. The last part of the test ensures that calling `current()`, when there are no more items, throws an `IteratorOutOfBoundsException`.

In the last test, as in the previous test, you construct an iterator, passing in an array. This time, however, you allow the iterator to traverse all the elements of the array, rather than just a portion of them as before. You then position to the last item and work your way backward, calling `previous()` until you reach the first item. Again, once the iterator signals it is done, you check to ensure that `current()` throws an exception as expected.

That's it. You could test for a few more scenarios, but for the most part that really is all you need in order to ensure the correct behavior of your array iterator. Now it's time to put the array iterator into practice, which you do in the next Try It Out.

Try It Out Implementing the Array Iterator

With the tests in place, you can now move on to implementing the array iterator itself. The iterator will need to implement the `Iterator` interface in addition to holding a reference to the underlying array.

If you assume that the iterator always operates over the entire length of an array, from start to finish, then the only other information you need to store is the current position. However, you may often wish to only provide access to a portion of the array. For this, the iterator will need to hold the bounds — the upper and lower positions — of the array that are relevant to the client of the iterator:

```
package com.wrox.algorithms.iteration;

public class ArrayIterator implements Iterator {
    private final Object[] _array;
    private final int _first;
    private final int _last;
    private int _current = -1;

    public ArrayIterator(Object[] array, int start, int length) {
        assert array != null : "array can't be null";
        assert start >= 0 : "start can't be < 0";
        assert start < array.length : "start can't be > array.length";
        assert length >= 0 : "length can't be < 0";

        _array = array;
        _first = start;
        _last = start + length - 1;

        assert _last < array.length : "start + length can't be > array.length";
    }

    ...
}
```

Besides iterating over portions of an array, there will of course be times when you want to iterate over the entire array. As a convenience, it's a good idea to also provide a constructor that takes an array as its only argument and calculates the starting and ending positions for you:

```
    public ArrayIterator(Object[] array) {
        assert array != null : "array can't be null";
        _array = array;
        _first = 0;
        _last = array.length - 1;
    }
```

Now that you have the array and have calculated the upper and lower bounds, implementing `first()` and `last()` couldn't be easier:

```
    public void first() {
        _current = _first;
```

```
    }

    public void last() {
        _current = _last;
    }
```

Traversing forward and backward is much the same as when directly accessing arrays:

```
    public void next() {
        ++_current;
    }

    public void previous() {
        --_current;
    }
```

Use the method `isDone()` to determine whether there are more elements to process. In this case, you can work this out by determining whether the current position falls within the bounds calculated in the constructor:

```
    public boolean isDone() {
        return _current < _first || _current > _last;
    }
```

If the `current` position is before the `first` or after the `last`, then there are no more elements and the iterator is finished.

Finally, you implement `current()` to retrieve the value of the current element within the array:

```
    public Object current() throws IteratorOutOfBoundsException {
        if (isDone()) {
            throw new IteratorOutOfBoundsException();
        }
        return _array[_current];
    }
```

How It Works

As you can see in the first code block of the preceding example, there is a reference to the underlying array as well as variables to hold the current, first, and last element positions (`0`, `1`, `2`, . . .). There is also quite a bit of checking to ensure that the values of the arguments make sense. It would be invalid, for example, for the caller to pass an array of length `10` and a starting position of `20`.

Moving on, you already know the position of the first and last elements, so it's simply a matter of setting the current position appropriately. To move forward, you increment the current position; and to move backward, you decrement it.

Notice how you ensure that there is actually a value to return by first calling `isDone()`. Then, assuming there is a value to return, you use the current position as an index in exactly the same way as when directly accessing the array yourself.

A Reverse Iterator

Sometimes you will want to reverse the iteration order without changing the code that processes the values. Imagine an array of names that is sorted in ascending order, *A* to *Z*, and displayed to the user somehow. If the user chose to view the names sorted in descending order, *Z* to *A*, you might have to re-sort the array or at the very least implement some code that traversed the array backward from the end. With a reverse iterator, however, the same behavior can be achieved without re-sorting and without duplicated code. When the application calls `first()`, the reverse iterator actually calls `last()` on the underlying iterator. When the application calls `next()`, the underlying iterator's `previous()` method is invoked, and so on. In this way, the behavior of the iterator can be reversed without changing the client code that displays the results, and without re-sorting the array, which could be quite processing intensive, as you will see later in this book when you write some sorting algorithms.

Try It Out — Testing the Reverse Iterator

The tests for the reverse iterator are straightforward. There are two main scenarios to test: forward iteration becomes backward, and vice-versa. In both cases, you can use the same test data and just iterate in the appropriate direction. Because you've just tested and implemented an array iterator, use it to test the reverse iterator:

```
package com.wrox.algorithms.iteration;

import junit.framework.TestCase;

public class ReverseIteratorTest extends TestCase {
    private static final Object[] ARRAY = new Object[] {"A", "B", "C"};

    ...
}
```

The test class itself defines an array that can be used by each of the test cases. Now, test that the reverse iterator returns the elements of this array in the appropriate order:

```
    public void testForwardsIterationBecomesBackwards() {
        ReverseIterator iterator = new ReverseIterator(new ArrayIterator(ARRAY));

        iterator.first();
        assertFalse(iterator.isDone());
        assertSame(ARRAY[2], iterator.current());

        iterator.next();
        assertFalse(iterator.isDone());
        assertSame(ARRAY[1], iterator.current());

        iterator.next();
        assertFalse(iterator.isDone());
        assertSame(ARRAY[0], iterator.current());

        iterator.next();
        assertTrue(iterator.isDone());
```

```
        try {
            iterator.current();
            fail();
        } catch (IteratorOutOfBoundsException e) {
            // expected
        }
    }
```

Notice that although you are iterating forward through the array from start to finish, the values returned are in reverse order. If it wasn't apparent before, it is hoped that you can now see what a powerful construct this is. Imagine that the array you're iterating over is a list of data in sorted order. You can now reverse the sort order without actually re-sorting(!):

```
    public void testBackwardsIterationBecomesForwards() {
        ReverseIterator iterator = new ReverseIterator(new ArrayIterator(ARRAY));

        iterator.last();
        assertFalse(iterator.isDone());
        assertSame(ARRAY[0], iterator.current());

        iterator.previous();
        assertFalse(iterator.isDone());
        assertSame(ARRAY[1], iterator.current());

        iterator.previous();
        assertFalse(iterator.isDone());
        assertSame(ARRAY[2], iterator.current());

        iterator.previous();
        assertTrue(iterator.isDone());
        try {
            iterator.current();
            fail();
        } catch (IteratorOutOfBoundsException e) {
            // expected
        }
    }
```

How It Works

The first test case ensures that when calling `first()` and `next()` on the reverse iterator, you actually get the `last` and `previous` elements of the array, respectively.

The second test makes sure that iterating backward over an array actually returns the items from the underlying iterator from start to finish.

The last test is structurally very similar to the previous test, but this time you're calling `last()` and `previous()` instead of `first()` and `next()`, and, of course, checking that the values are returned from start to finish.

Now you're ready to put the reverse iterator into practice, as shown in the next Try It Out.

Try It Out — Implementing the Reverse Iterator

Implementing the reverse iterator is very easy indeed: Just invert the behavior of calls to the traversal methods, `first`, `last`, `next`, and `previous`:

Because of this simplicity, we've chosen to present the entire class in one piece, rather than break it up into individual methods as we usually do.

```
package com.wrox.algorithms.iteration;

public class ReverseIterator implements Iterator {
    private final Iterator _iterator;

    public ReverseIterator(Iterator iterator) {
        assert iterator != null : "iterator can't be null";
        _iterator = iterator;
    }

    public boolean isDone() {
        return _iterator.isDone();
    }

    public Object current() throws IteratorOutOfBoundsException {
        return _iterator.current();
    }

    public void first() {
        _iterator.last();
    }

    public void last() {
        _iterator.first();
    }

    public void next() {
        _iterator.previous();
    }

    public void previous() {
        _iterator.next();
    }
}
```

How It Works

Besides implementing the `Iterator` interface, the class also holds the iterator to reverse its behavior. As you can see, calls to `isDone()` and `current()` are delegated directly. The remaining methods, `first()`, `last()`, `next()`, and `previous()`, then redirect to their opposite number — `last()`, `first()`, `next()`, and `previous()`, respectively — thereby reversing the direction of iteration.

A Filtering Iterator

One of the more interesting and useful advantages of using iterators is the capability to wrap or decorate (see the Decorator pattern [Gamma, 1995]) another iterator to filter the return values. This could be as simple as only returning every second value, or something more sophisticated such as processing the results of a database query to further remove unwanted values. Imagine a scenario whereby in addition to the database query selection criteria, the client was also able to perform some filtering of its own.

The filter iterator works by wrapping another iterator and only returning values that satisfy some condition, known as a *predicate*. Each time the underlying iterator is called, the returned value is passed to the predicate to determine whether it should be kept or discarded. It is this continuous evaluation of values with the predicate that enables the data to be filtered.

The Predicate Class

You begin by creating an interface that represents a predicate:

```
package com.wrox.algorithms.iteration;

public interface Predicate {
    public boolean evaluate(Object object);
}
```

The interface is very simple, containing just one method, `evaluate()`, that is called for each value, and returning a Boolean to indicate whether the value meets the selection criteria or not. If `evaluate()` returns `true`, then the value is to be included and thus returned from the filter iterator. Conversely, if the predicate returns `false`, then the value will be ignored, and treated as if it never existed.

Although simple, the predicate interface enables you to build very sophisticated filters. You can even implement predicates for AND (`&&`), OR (||), NOT (`!`), and so on, enabling the construction of any arbitrarily complex predicate you can think of.

Try It Out Testing the Predicate Class

You will now write a number of tests to ensure that your filter iterator performs correctly. All you really need to do is ensure that the filter returns any value from the underlying iterator the predicate accepts. You will perform four tests: two combinations of forward and backward iteration — one in which the predicate accepts the values, and one in which the predicate rejects the values:

```
package com.wrox.algorithms.iteration;

import junit.framework.TestCase;

public class FilterIteratorTest extends TestCase {
    private static final Object[] ARRAY = {"A", "B", "C"};

    ...
}
```

You want to know that the predicate is called once for each item returned from the underlying iterator. For this, you create a predicate specifically for testing purposes:

```
    private static final class DummyPredicate implements Predicate {
        private final Iterator _iterator;
        private final boolean _result;

        public DummyPredicate(boolean result, Iterator iterator) {
```

```
            _iterator = iterator;
            _result = result;
            _iterator.first();
        }

        public boolean evaluate(Object object) {
            assertSame(_iterator.current(), object);
            _iterator.next();
            return _result;
        }
    }

    ...
}
```

The first test is to ensure that the filter returns values the predicate accepts — `evaluate()` returns `true` — while iterating forward:

```
    public void testForwardsIterationIncludesItemsWhenPredicateReturnsTrue() {
        Iterator expectedIterator = new ArrayIterator(ARRAY);
        Iterator underlyingIterator = new ArrayIterator(ARRAY);

        Iterator iterator = new FilterIterator(underlyingIterator,
                new DummyPredicate(true, expectedIterator));

        iterator.first();
        assertFalse(iterator.isDone());
        assertSame(ARRAY[0], iterator.current());

        iterator.next();
        assertFalse(iterator.isDone());
        assertSame(ARRAY[1], iterator.current());

        iterator.next();
        assertFalse(iterator.isDone());
        assertSame(ARRAY[2], iterator.current());

        iterator.next();
        assertTrue(iterator.isDone());
        try {
            iterator.current();
            fail();
        } catch (IteratorOutOfBoundsException e) {
            // expected
        }

        assertTrue(expectedIterator.isDone());
        assertTrue(underlyingIterator.isDone());
    }
```

The next test is much simpler than the first. This time, you want to see what happens when the predicate rejects values — that is, `evaluate()` returns `false`:

```
    public void testForwardsIterationExcludesItemsWhenPredicateReturnsFalse() {
        Iterator expectedIterator = new ArrayIterator(ARRAY);
        Iterator underlyingIterator = new ArrayIterator(ARRAY);

        Iterator iterator = new FilterIterator(underlyingIterator,
                new DummyPredicate(false, expectedIterator));

        iterator.first();
        assertTrue(iterator.isDone());
        try {
            iterator.current();
            fail();
        } catch (IteratorOutOfBoundsException e) {
            // expected
        }

        assertTrue(expectedIterator.isDone());
        assertTrue(underlyingIterator.isDone());
    }
```

The remaining two tests are almost identical to the first two except that the order of iteration has been reversed:

```
    public void testBackwardssIterationIncludesItemsWhenPredicateReturnsTrue() {
        Iterator expectedIterator = new ReverseIterator(new ArrayIterator(ARRAY));
        Iterator underlyingIterator = new ArrayIterator(ARRAY);

        Iterator iterator = new FilterIterator(underlyingIterator,
                new DummyPredicate(true, expectedIterator));

        iterator.last();
        assertFalse(iterator.isDone());
        assertSame(ARRAY[2], iterator.current());

        iterator.previous();
        assertFalse(iterator.isDone());
        assertSame(ARRAY[1], iterator.current());

        iterator.previous();
        assertFalse(iterator.isDone());
        assertSame(ARRAY[0], iterator.current());

        iterator.previous();
        assertTrue(iterator.isDone());
        try {
            iterator.current();
            fail();
        } catch (IteratorOutOfBoundsException e) {
            // expected
        }

        assertTrue(expectedIterator.isDone());
        assertTrue(underlyingIterator.isDone());
```

```
    }

    public void testBackwardsIterationExcludesItemsWhenPredicateReturnsFalse() {
        Iterator expectedIterator = new ReverseIterator(new ArrayIterator(ARRAY));
        Iterator underlyingIterator = new ArrayIterator(ARRAY);

        Iterator iterator = new FilterIterator(underlyingIterator,
                new DummyPredicate(false, expectedIterator));

        iterator.last();
        assertTrue(iterator.isDone());
        try {
            iterator.current();
            fail();
        } catch (IteratorOutOfBoundsException e) {
            // expected
        }

        assertTrue(expectedIterator.isDone());
        assertTrue(underlyingIterator.isDone());
    }
```

How It Works

Besides the test cases themselves, the test class contains little more than some simple test data. However, in order to test the filter iterator adequately, you need to confirm not only the expected iteration results, but also that the predicate is being called correctly.

The `DummyPredicate` inner class that you created for testing purposes in the second code block holds an iterator that will return the values in the same order as you expect the predicate to be called with. Each time `evaluate()` is called, you check to make sure that the correct value is being passed. In addition to checking the values, `evaluate()` also returns a predetermined result—set by the test cases—so that you can check what happens when the predicate accepts values and when it rejects values.

Next, you create the actual tests. You started by creating two iterators: one for the items you expect the predicate to be called with, and the other to provide the items to the filter in the first place. From these, you construct a filter iterator, passing in the underlying iterator and a dummy predicate configured to always accept the values passed to it for evaluation. Then you position the filter iterator to the first item, check that there is in fact an item to obtain, and that the value is as expected. The remainder of the test simply calls `next()` repeatedly until the iterator is complete, checking the results as it goes. Notice the last two assertions of the first test (in the third code block from the preceding Try it Out) that ensure that both the underlying iterator and the expected iterator have been exhausted.

The next test begins much the same as the previous test except you construct the predicate with a predetermined return value of `false`. After positioning the filter iterator to the first item, you expect it to be finished straightaway—the predicate is rejecting all values. Once again, however, you still expect both iterators to have been exhausted; and in particular, you expect the underlying iterator to have had all of its values inspected.

In the last test, notice the use of `ReverseIterator`; the dummy iterator still thinks that it's iterating forward, but in reality it's iterating backward.

Try It Out Implementing the Predicate Class

With the tests in place, you can move straight into implementation. You've already defined the interface for predicates, so all you do now is create the filter iterator class itself:

```
package com.wrox.algorithms.iteration;

public class FilterIterator implements Iterator {
    private final Iterator _iterator;
    private final Predicate _predicate;

    public FilterIterator(Iterator iterator, Predicate predicate) {
        assert iterator != null : "iterator can't be null";
        assert predicate != null : "predicate can't be null";

        _iterator = iterator;
        _predicate = predicate;
    }

    public boolean isDone() {
        return _iterator.isDone();
    }

    public Object current() throws IteratorOutOfBoundsException {
        return _iterator.current();
    }

    ...
}
```

In the case of `first()` and `next()`, the call is first delegated to the underlying iterator before searching forward from the current position to find a value that satisfies the filter:

```
    public void first() {
        _iterator.first();
        filterForwards();
    }

    public void next() {
        _iterator.next();
        filterForwards();
    }

    private void filterForwards() {
        while (!_iterator.isDone() && !_predicate.evaluate(_iterator.current())) {
            _iterator.next();
        }
    }
```

Finally, you add `last()` and `previous()`, which, not surprisingly, look very similar to `first()` and `next()`:

```
    public void last() {
        _iterator.last();
```

```
        filterBackwards();
    }

    public void previous() {
        _iterator.previous();
        filterBackwards();
    }

    private void filterBackwards() {
        while (!_iterator.isDone() && !_predicate.evaluate(_iterator.current())) {
            _iterator.previous();
        }
    }
```

The `FilterIterator` can now be used to traverse any data structure supporting iterators. All you need to do is create an appropriate predicate to do the specific filtering you require.

How It Works

The filter iterator class implements the `Iterator` interface, of course, and holds the iterator to be wrapped and the predicate to use for filtering. The constructor first checks to make sure that neither argument is `null` before assigning them to instance variables for later use. The two methods `isDone()` and `current()` need do nothing more than delegate to their respective methods on the underlying iterator. This works because the underlying iterator is always kept in a state such that only an object that is allowed by the predicate is the current object.

The real work of the iterator is performed when one of the traversal methods is called. Anytime `first()`, `next()`, `last()`, or `previous()` is invoked, the predicate must be used to include or exclude values as appropriate while still maintaining the semantics of the iterator:

```
    public void first() {
        _iterator.first();
        filterForwards();
    }

    public void next() {
        _iterator.next();
        filterForwards();
    }

    private void filterForwards() {
        while (!_iterator.isDone() && !_predicate.evaluate(_iterator.current())) {
            _iterator.next();
        }
    }
```

When filterForwards is called, it is assumed that the underlying iterator will already have been positioned to an element from which to start searching. The method then loops, calling next() until either there are no more elements or a matching element is found. Notice that in all cases, you call methods on the underlying iterator directly. This prevents unnecessary looping, most likely resulting in abnormal program termination in extreme cases.

```
public void last() {
    _iterator.last();
    filterBackwards();
}

public void previous() {
    _iterator.previous();
    filterBackwards();
}

private void filterBackwards() {
    while (!_iterator.isDone() && !_predicate.evaluate(_iterator.current())) {
        _iterator.previous();
    }
}
```

As you did for first() and next(), last() and previous() call their respective methods on the wrapped class before invoking filterBackwards to find an element that satisfies the predicate.

Recursion

"To understand recursion, we first need to understand recursion." —Anonymous

Imagine a file system such as the one on your computer. As you probably know, a file system has a root directory with many subdirectories (and files), which in turn have more subdirectories (and files). This directory structure is often referred to as a *directory tree*—a tree has a root and branches (directories) and leaves (files). Figure 2-1 shows a file system represented as a tree. Notice how it is like an inverted tree, however, with the root at the top and the leaves at the bottom.

One of the interesting things about "trees" in the computing sense is that each branch looks just like another, smaller tree. Figure 2-2 shows the same tree as before, this time highlighting one of the branches. Notice how the structure is similar to the bigger tree.

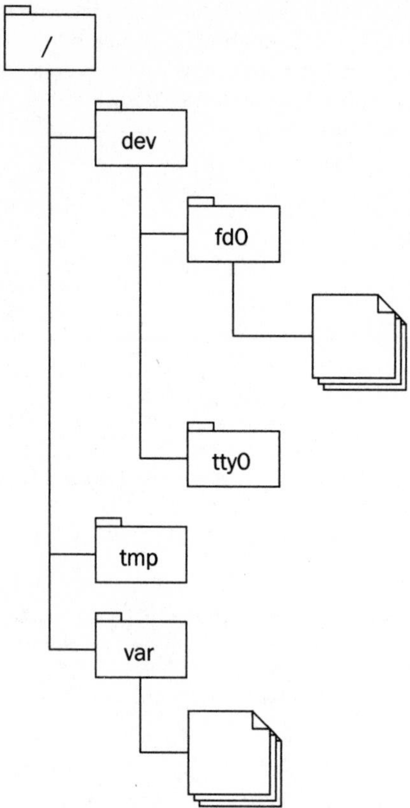

Figure 2-1: A directory structure represented as a tree.

This characteristic, whereby some things look the same at different granularities or magnifications, can be applied to solving problems as well. Anytime a problem can be broken down like this into smaller components that look just like the larger one (divide and conquer) is precisely when recursion comes into its own. In a sense, recursion is the ultimate re-use pattern: a method that calls itself.

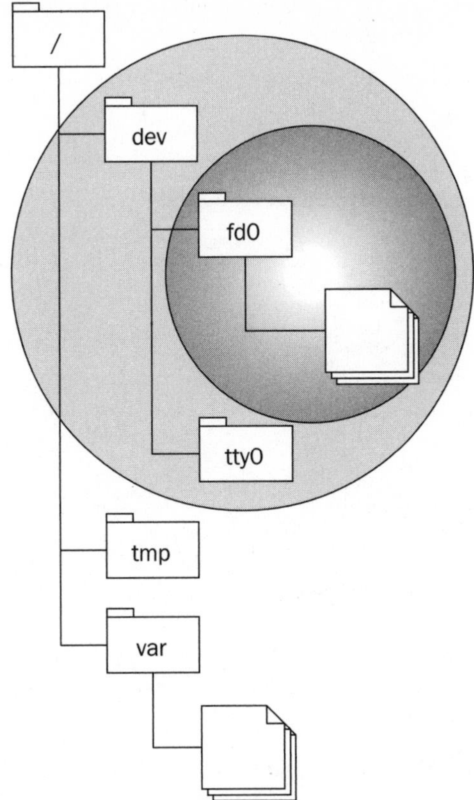

Figure 2-2: Branches of a tree are themselves trees.

Recursive Directory Tree Printer Example

Let's continue with the file system analogy and write a program to print the contents of an entire directory tree. More often than not, the examples used to demonstrate recursion involve finding prime numbers, fibonacci numbers, and possibly even solving mazes—hardly things you are likely to encounter on a daily basis.

Besides simply printing the names, let's also format the output so that each file and subdirectory is indented under its parent—like a text version of Windows Explorer or Mac OS X Finder. Given what you know about the structure of file systems, you should be able to construct a recursive algorithm to traverse the directory structure by breaking the problem down in such a way that the solution works at one level and then calls itself for each deeper level in the directory tree.

Naturally, you need to start with a class; and as you probably want to run this program from the command line, you will need a main method:

```
package com.wrox.algorithms.iteration;

import java.io.File;

public final class RecursiveDirectoryTreePrinter {
    private static final String SPACES = "  ";

    public static void main(String[] args) {
        assert args != null : "args can't be null";

        if (args.length != 1) {
            System.err.println("Usage: RecursiveDirectoryTreePrinter <dir>");
            System.exit(4);
        }

        print(new File(args[0]), "");
    }

    ...
}
```

Our program requires the name of a single directory (or file) to be passed on the command line. After performing some rudimentary checking, `main()` then constructs a `java.io.File` from the first argument and passes it to a `print()` method.

Notice that the second argument in the method call is an empty string. This will be used by `print()` to indent the output, but in this case, because it's the first level of the directory tree you are printing, you don't want any indenting at all, hence the `""`. The constant `SPACES` (defined as two spaces) will be used later to increase the indentation.

The `print()` method accepts a single `File` and a string that will be used when indenting the output:

```
    public static void print(File file, String indent) {
        assert file != null : "file can't be null";
        assert indent != null : "indent can't be null";

        System.out.print(indent);
        System.out.println(file.getName());

        if (file.isDirectory()) {
            print(file.listFiles(), indent + SPACES);
        }
    }
```

The code itself is straightforward. First the indentation is printed, followed by the name of the file and a new line. If the file represents a directory (in Java, `File` objects are used for both individual files and directories), you call a different `print()` method to process the list of files contained within and the indentation to use them.

Because you are about to nest another level down in the tree, you want to increase the amount of indentation—that is, print everything shifted a couple of spaces to the right. You can achieve this by taking the current indentation and appending the value of the constant SPACES. At first, the indentation would be an empty string, in which case it will increase to two spaces, then four spaces, then six, and so on, thereby causing the printed output to be shifted right each time.

Now, as indicated, the method `listFiles()` returns an array; and as you don't have a version of `print()` that accepts one of those yet, let's create one:

```
public static void print(File[] files, String indent) {
    assert files != null : "files can't be null";

    for (int i = 0; i < files.length; ++i) {
        print(files[i], indent);
    }
}
```

This method iterates over the array, calling the original `print()` method for each file.

Can you see how this is recursive? Recall that the first `print()` method—the one that takes a single file—calls the second `print()` method, the one that takes an array, which in turn calls the first method, and so on. This would go on forever but for the fact that eventually the second `print()` method runs out of files—that is, it reaches the end of the array—and returns.

The following code shows some sample output from running this program over the directory tree containing the code for this book:

```
Beginning Algorithms
  build
    classes
      com
        wrox
          algorithms
            iteration
              ArrayIterator.class
              ArrayIteratorTest.class
              Iterator.class
              IteratorOutOfBoundsException.class
              RecursiveDirectoryTreePrinter.class
              ReverseIterator.class
              ReverseIteratorTest.class
              SingletonIterator.class
              SingletonIteratorTest.class
  src
    build.xml
    conf
      build.properties
      checkstyle-header.txt
      checkstyle-main.xml
      checkstyle-test.xml
      checkstyle.xsl
      simian.xsl
    lib
```

```
        antlr-2.7.2.jar
        checkstyle-3.5.jar
        checkstyle-optional-3.5.jar
        commons-beanutils.jar
        commons-collections-3.1.jar
        getopt.jar
        jakarta-oro.jar
        jakarta-regexp.jar
        jamaica-tools.jar
        junit-3.8.1.jar
        simian-2.2.2.jar
      main
        com
          wrox
            algorithms
              iteration
                ArrayIterator.java
                Iterator.java
                IteratorOutOfBoundsException.java
                RecursiveDirectoryTreePrinter.java
                ReverseIterator.java
                SingletonIterator.java
```

As you can see, the output is nicely formatted with appropriate indentation each time the contents of a directory are printed. It is hoped that this has demonstrated, in a practical way, how recursion can be used to solve some kinds of problems.

Any problem that can be solved recursively can also be solved iteratively, although doing so can sometimes be rather difficult and cumbersome, requiring data structures that have not been covered yet, such as stacks (see Chapter 5).

Anatomy of a Recursive Algorithm

No matter what the problem, a recursive algorithm can usually be broken down into two parts: a base case and a general case. Let's reexamine the previous example and identify these elements.

The Base Case

In the example, when you encounter a single file, you are dealing with the problem at the smallest level of granularity necessary to perform whatever action the algorithm has been designed to do; in this case, print its name. This is known as the *base case.*

The base case, therefore, is that part of the problem that you can easily solve without requiring any more recursion. It is also the halting case that prevents the recursion from continuing forever.

A `StackOverflowException` *while executing a recursive algorithm is often an indication of a missing or insufficient termination condition, causing your program to make more and more nested calls until eventually it runs out of memory. Of course, it might also indicate that the problem you are trying to solve is too large for the computing resources you have available!*

The General Case

The general case, being what happens most of the time, is where the recursive call is made. In the example, the first recursive call occurs when you encounter a file that represents a directory. Having printed its name, you then wish to process all the files contained within the directory, so you call the second `print()` method.

The second `print()` method then calls back on the first `print()` method for each file found in the directory.

Using two methods that call each other recursively like this is also known as mutual recursion.

Summary

Iteration and recursion are fundamental to implementing any algorithm. In fact, the rest of this book relies heavily on these two concepts so it is important that you fully understand them before continuing.

This chapter demonstrated the following:

- Iteration lends itself more readily to solving some problems while for others recursion can seem more natural.
- Iteration is a very simple, straightforward approach to solving many common problems such as performing calculations and processing arrays.
- Simple array-based iteration doesn't scale particularly well in most real-world applications. To overcome this, we introduced the concept of an iterator and discussed several different types of iterators.
- Recursion uses a *divide-and-conquer* approach whereby a method makes repeated, nested calls to itself. It is often a better choice for processing nested data structures.
- Many problems can be solved using either iteration or recursion.

Exercises

You will find sample answers to these exercises (and all of the exercises from other chapters as well) in Appendix D, "Exercise Answers."

1. Create an iterator that only returns the value of every n^{th} element, where n is any integer greater than zero.
2. Create a predicate that performs a Boolean AND (&&) of two other predicates.
3. Re-implement `PowerCalculator` using recursion instead of iteration.
4. Replace the use of arrays with iterators in the recursive directory tree printer.
5. Create an iterator that holds only a single value.
6. Create an empty iterator that is always done.

Lists

Now that you are familiar with iteration and some of the basics of algorithms, it is time to move on to your first complex data structure. Lists are the most fundamental data structure upon which most other data structures are built and many more algorithms must operate.

It's not hard to find examples of lists in the real world: shopping lists, to-do lists, train timetables, order forms, even this "list of lists." Much like arrays, lists are generally useful in most applications you will write. In fact, lists make a great substitute for the use of arrays — it is usually possible (and more often than not desirable) to entirely replace your use of arrays with lists in all but the most memory-sensitive/time-critical applications.

This chapter starts by introducing the basic operations of a list. From there, it heads straight into the tests before covering two different list implementations: array lists and linked lists. Both implementations conform to a common interface but have quite different characteristics. These differences can affect how and when you use them in your applications. By the end of this chapter, you will be familiar with the following:

- What lists are
- What lists look like
- How lists are used
- How lists are implemented

Understanding Lists

A list is an ordered collection of elements supporting random access to each element, much like an array — you can query a list to get the value contained at any arbitrary element. Lists also preserve insertion order so that, assuming there are no intervening modifications, a given list will always return the same value for the same position. Like arrays, lists make no attempt to preserve the uniqueness of values, meaning a list may contain duplicate values. For example, if you had a list containing the values "swimming", "cycling", and "dancing" and you were to add "swimming" again, you would now find that the list had grown to include two copies of "swimming". The major difference between arrays and lists, however, is that whereas an array is fixed in size, lists can resize—growing and shrinking—as necessary.

As a minimum, a list supports the four core operations described in Table 3-1.

Table 3-1: Core Operations on a List

Operation	Description
`insert`	Inserts a value into a list at a specified position (0, 1, 2, . . .). The size of the list will increase by one. Throws `IndexOutOfBoundsException` if the specified position is outside the range (`0 <= index <= size()`).
`delete`	Deletes the value at a specified position (0, 1, 2, . . .) in a list and returns whatever value was contained therein. The size of the list will decrease by one. Throws `IndexOutOfBoundsException` if the specified position is outside the range (`0 <= index < size()`).
`get`	Obtains the value at a specified position (0, 1, 2, . . .) in the list. Throws `IndexOutOfBoundsException` if the specified position is outside the range (`0 <= index < size()`).
`size`	Obtains the number of elements in the list.

These operations are all that is absolutely necessary for accessing a list. That said, however, if the operations listed were the only ones available, then you would find yourself copying and pasting the same code repeatedly as you discovered more sophisticated ways to access your lists. For example, there is no specific method for changing the value of an existing element (as you might do with an array), although you can achieve the same thing by first deleting the element and then inserting a new one in its place. To prevent the unnecessary duplication of logic that comes from repeatedly using such a simple interface, you can choose to encapsulate this common behavior inside the list itself by implementing some convenience operations, as described in Table 3-2.

Table 3-2: Convenience Operations on a List

Operation	Description
`set`	Sets the value at a specified position (`0, 1, 2,...`) in the list. Returns the value originally at the specified position. Throws `IndexOutOfBoundsException` if the specified position is outside the range (`0 <= index < size()`).
`add`	Adds a value to the end of the list. The size of the list will increase by one.
`delete`	Deletes the first occurrence of a specified value from a list. The size of the list will decrease by one if the value is found. Returns `true` if the value is found, or `false` if the value doesn't exist.
`contains`	Determines whether a specified value is contained within a list.
`indexOf`	Obtains the position (`0, 1, 2,...`) of the first occurrence of a specified value within a list. Returns `-1` if the value is not found. Equality is determined by calling the value's `equals` method.

Operation	Description
isEmpty	Determines whether a list is empty or not. Returns true if the list is empty (size() == 0); otherwise, returns false.
iterator	Obtains an Iterator over all elements in a list.
clear	Deletes all elements from a list. The size of the list is reset to 0.

All of these operations can be implemented on top of the core operations described previously. However, by choosing to implement them as part of the list, you create a much richer interface, thereby greatly simplifying the job of any developer that uses a list.

The set() operation, for example, can easily be implemented using a combination of delete() and insert(), add() and insert(), isEmpty() and size(), and so on. However, again we stress that beyond the core operations, it is this richness, this encapsulation of common functionality and behavior, that makes a data structure such as a list so powerful.

Try It Out Creating the List Interface

Having described the operations in a general sense, it's time to create an actual Java interface that you will implement later in the chapter:

```
package com.wrox.algorithms.lists;

import com.wrox.algorithms.iteration.Iterable;

public interface List extends Iterable {
    public void insert(int index, Object value)
        throws IndexOutOfBoundsException;
    public void add(Object value);
    public Object delete(int index) throws IndexOutOfBoundsException;
    public boolean delete(Object value);
    public void clear();
    public Object set(int index, Object value)
                                            throws IndexOutOfBoundsException;
    public Object get(int index) throws IndexOutOfBoundsException;
    public int indexOf(Object value);
    public boolean contains(Object value);
    public int size();
    public boolean isEmpty();
}
```

How It Works

As you can see, you have quite literally taken the operations and converted them, one by one, into methods on an interface, with all the appropriate parameters, return types, and exceptions. It is by no means a trivial interface; there are numerous methods to implement. Once you get into the actual implementation, however, you will see that this extra functionality is quite simple to provide.

You'll also notice that the List interface extends the Iterable interface introduced in Chapter 2. This interface provides a single iterator() method and allows a list to be used anywhere you write code that need only iterate over the contents of a list.

With this interface in mind, have a look at the following two snippets of code. The first creates an array with three values and then iterates over it, printing each value in turn:

```
String[] anArray = ...;

anArray[0] = "Apple";
anArray[1] = "Banana";
anArray[2] = "Cherry";

for (int i = 0; i < anArray.length; ++i) {
    System.out.println(anArray[i]);
}
```

The second piece of code creates a list with three values and iterates over it, printing each value as it goes:

```
List aList = ...;

aList.add("Apple");
aList.add("Banana");
aList.add("Cherry");

Iterator i = aList.iterator()
for (i.first(); !i.isDone(); i.next()) {
    System.out.println(aList.current());
}
```

There isn't a lot of difference between the two—you could argue that in some ways, the version with the list is more readable. In particular, the use of `add()` and an iterator helps to convey the intent of the code.

Testing Lists

Even though you haven't yet implemented a single concrete list, you can still think about and describe in code the different scenarios your lists are likely to encounter. To ensure the correct behavior of the various list implementations, you need to create some tests that any implementation must satisfy. These tests will implement in code the requirements described in Tables 3-1 and 3-2 and become the definition of the list contract. Moreover, by working through each of the tests, you should gain a good understanding of the expected behavior of a list, which will make it much easier when it comes time to write your own implementation.

Try It Out — Creating a Generic Test Class

You already know there will be two list implementations. Ordinarily, you might think you would need to create an individual test suite for each, but it's possible to create a single test suite that can be re-used across all of your different implementations. To do this, create an abstract class containing the actual test cases along with some hooks for subclassing. To get started, you need to define the abstract base class that can be extended by concrete test classes specific for each implementation of a list:

```
package com.wrox.algorithms.lists;

import com.wrox.algorithms.iteration.Iterator;
import com.wrox.algorithms.iteration.IteratorOutOfBoundsException;
import junit.framework.TestCase;

public abstract class AbstractListTestCase extends TestCase {
    protected static final Object VALUE_A = "A";
    protected static final Object VALUE_B = "B";
    protected static final Object VALUE_C = "C";

    protected abstract List createList();

    ...
}
```

Apart from some common test data, you've defined an abstract method that returns an instance of a list. This will be used by your test methods to obtain a list to test. Anytime you wish to create a test suite for a new type of list, you can extend `AbstractListTestCase` and implement the `createList()` method to return an instance of the specific list class. In this way, you are able to re-use the same tests regardless of the actual implementation.

Now let's move on to testing the behavior of a list.

Try It Out — Testing Methods for Inserting and Adding Values

Insertion is probably the most fundamental function of a list—without it, your lists would remain empty. Here is the code:

```
    public void testInsertIntoEmptyList() {
        List list = createList();

        assertEquals(0, list.size());
        assertTrue(list.isEmpty());

        list.insert(0, VALUE_A);

        assertEquals(1, list.size());
        assertFalse(list.isEmpty());
        assertSame(VALUE_A, list.get(0));
    }
```

Next, you want to test what happens when you insert a value *between* two other values. You expect any elements to the right of the insertion point to shift position by one to make room:

```
    public void testInsertBetweenElements() {
        List list = createList();

        list.insert(0, VALUE_A);
        list.insert(1, VALUE_B);
        list.insert(1, VALUE_C);
```

```
        assertEquals(3, list.size());

        assertSame(VALUE_A, list.get(0));
        assertSame(VALUE_C, list.get(1));
        assertSame(VALUE_B, list.get(2));
    }
```

Now make sure you can insert *before* the first element of the list:

```
    public void testInsertBeforeFirstElement() {
        List list = createList();

        list.insert(0, VALUE_A);
        list.insert(0, VALUE_B);

        assertEquals(2, list.size());
        assertSame(VALUE_B, list.get(0));
        assertSame(VALUE_A, list.get(1));
    }
```

Also test inserting a value *after* the last element. This is fundamentally how you add to a list. (You will possibly find yourself doing this more often than any other type of insertion, so you need to get this right!)

```
    public void testInsertAfterLastElement() {
        List list = createList();

        list.insert(0, VALUE_A);
        list.insert(1, VALUE_B);

        assertEquals(2, list.size());
        assertSame(VALUE_A, list.get(0));
        assertSame(VALUE_B, list.get(1));
    }
```

Next you'll test that the list correctly handles an attempt to insert a value into a position that falls outside the bounds. In these cases, you expect an `IndexOutOfBoundsException` to be thrown, indicating an application programming error:

```
    public void testInsertOutOfBounds() {
        List list = createList();

        try {
            list.insert(-1, VALUE_A);
            fail();
        } catch (IndexOutOfBoundsException e) {
            // expected
        }

        try {
            list.insert(1, VALUE_B);
            fail();
        } catch (IndexOutOfBoundsException e) {
            // expected
        }
    }
```

Finally, you can test the `add()` method. Even though it is simple enough to add to a list using only the `insert()` method, it is more natural (and requires less coding) to express this intention with a specific method:

```
    public void testAdd() {
        List list = createList();

        list.add(VALUE_A);
        list.add(VALUE_C);
        list.add(VALUE_B);

        assertEquals(3, list.size());
        assertSame(VALUE_A, list.get(0));
        assertSame(VALUE_C, list.get(1));
        assertSame(VALUE_B, list.get(2));
    }
```

How It Works

The method `testInsertIntoAnEmptyList()` merely checks that when you insert a value into an empty list, the size of the list will increase by one and that you are then able to retrieve the value from the expected position.

The method `testInsertBetweenElements()` tests what happens when you attempt to insert a value between two others. The test starts off with a list containing two values—`A` and `B` in positions `0` and `1`, respectively, as shown in Figure 3-1.

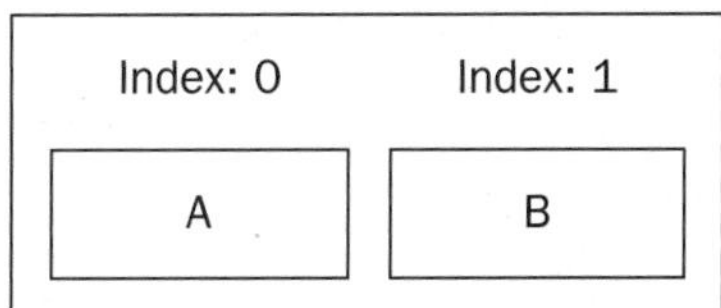

Figure 3-1: List prior to insertion.

It then inserts another value—`C`—between them at position 1. This should put the new value between the `A` and `B`, resulting in a list that looks like the one shown in Figure 3-2.

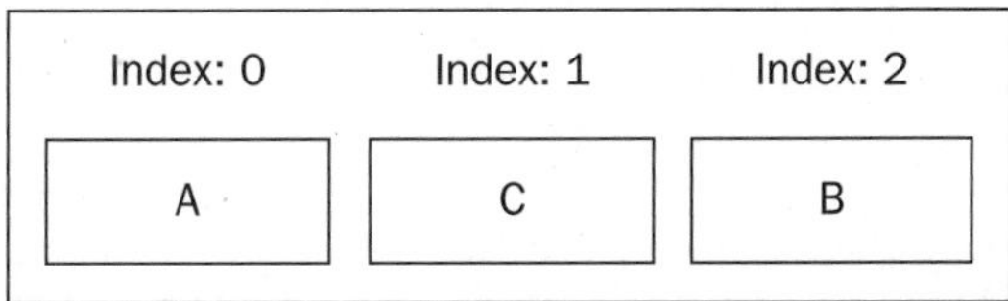

Figure 3-2: List after insertion between two elements.

As you can see, the `B` has shifted right one position to make room for `C`.

The method testInsertBeforeFirstElement() ensures that inserting a value into the first position shifts all existing values right one place. The test uses the same insertion point—position 0—each time insert() is called and confirms that the values end up in the correct order: The A should start off in position 0 and then move right one place to make room for the B.

The method testInsertAfterLastElement() ensures that you can add to the end of the list by inserting a value into a position that is one greater than the last valid position. If the list contained one element, inserting into position 1 would place the new value at the end. If the list contained three elements, inserting into position 3 would place the new value at the end. In other words, you can add to a list by inserting into a position that is defined by the size of the list.

The method testInsertOutOfBounds() checks that your list correctly identifies some common programming errors, such as using a negative insertion point or using an insertion point that is one greater than the size of the list (using an insertion point that is the size of the list adds to the end). The test code starts off with an empty list, meaning that the first position—position 0—is the only place into which a new value can be inserted. Any attempt to use a negative value or anything greater than zero should result in an IndexOutOfBoundsException.

Finally, the method testAdd() tests the behavior of the convenience method, add(). Three values are added to the list, which is then checked to ensure they end up in the correct order. As you can see from the relative simplicity of testAdd() versus testInsertAfterLastElement(), having a specific method for adding to the end of a list makes the code much more readable and requires slightly less code. More important, it requires less thinking to get it right. Calling add() is far more intuitive than calling insert(), passing in the value of size() as the insertion point!

Try It Out Testing Methods for Retrieving and Storing Values

Once you can place values into a list, the next thing you'll want to do is access them. For the most part, you have already tested the behavior of get() (and size() and isEmpty() for that matter) while testing insert() and add(), so you'll start by testing set():

```
public void testSet() {
    List list = createList();

    list.insert(0, VALUE_A);
    assertSame(VALUE_A, list.get(0));

    assertSame(VALUE_A, list.set(0, VALUE_B));
    assertSame(VALUE_B, list.get(0));
}
```

Another thing you haven't tested are the boundary conditions: What happens when you attempt to access a list before the start or beyond the last element? As with insert(), attempts to access a list beyond the boundaries should result in an IndexOutOfBoundsException:

```
public void testGetOutOfBounds() {
    List list = createList();

    try {
        list.get(-1);
        fail();
```

```
        } catch (IndexOutOfBoundsException e) {
            // expected
        }

        try {
            list.get(0);
            fail();
        } catch (IndexOutOfBoundsException e) {
            // expected
        }

        list.add(VALUE_A);

        try {
            list.get(1);
            fail();
        } catch (IndexOutOfBoundsException e) {
            // expected
        }
    }
```

You also want to test some boundary conditions when calling `set()`:

```
    public void testSetOutOfBounds() {
        List list = createList();

        try {
            list.set(-1, VALUE_A);
            fail();
        } catch (IndexOutOfBoundsException e) {
            // expected
        }

        try {
            list.set(0, VALUE_B);
            fail();
        } catch (IndexOutOfBoundsException e) {
            // expected
        }

        list.insert(0, VALUE_C);

        try {
            list.set(1, VALUE_C);
            fail();
        } catch (IndexOutOfBoundsException e) {
            // expected
        }
    }
```

How It Works

The method `set()` works in much the same way as setting the value of an element within an array, so after populating a list with a known value, `testSet()` replaces it and ensures that the new value is returned instead of the original.

The method `testGetOutOfBounds()` starts off with an empty list and attempts to access it using a negative position and then again using a position that is too large. Then, just to be doubly sure, it adds a value to the list, creating an element at position 0, and tries once again to access beyond the end of the list. In all cases, you expect an `IndexOutOfBoundsException` to be thrown.

The method `testSetOutOfBounds()` is basically the same as `testGetOutOfBounds()`, but instead of attempting to retrieve a value, you attempt to update its value by calling `set()`.

Try It Out Testing Methods for Deleting Values

The first type of deletion you'll test involves deleting the only element in a list. You expect that after the deletion, the list will be empty:

```
public void testDeleteOnlyElement() {
    List list = createList();

    list.add(VALUE_A);

    assertEquals(1, list.size());
    assertSame(VALUE_A, list.get(0));

    assertSame(VALUE_A, list.delete(0));

    assertEquals(0, list.size());
}
```

You also want to see what happens when you delete the first element of a list containing more than one element. All values should shift left one place:

```
public void testDeleteFirstElement() {
    List list = createList();

    list.add(VALUE_A);
    list.add(VALUE_B);
    list.add(VALUE_C);

    assertEquals(3, list.size());
    assertSame(VALUE_A, list.get(0));
    assertSame(VALUE_B, list.get(1));
    assertSame(VALUE_C, list.get(2));

    assertSame(VALUE_A, list.delete(0));

    assertEquals(2, list.size());
    assertSame(VALUE_B, list.get(0));
    assertSame(VALUE_C, list.get(1));
}
```

Now see what happens when you delete the last element of a list containing more than one element:

```
    public void testDeleteLastElement() {
        List list = createList();

        list.add(VALUE_A);
        list.add(VALUE_B);
        list.add(VALUE_C);

        assertEquals(3, list.size());
        assertSame(VALUE_A, list.get(0));
        assertSame(VALUE_B, list.get(1));
        assertSame(VALUE_C, list.get(2));

        assertSame(VALUE_C, list.delete(2));

        assertEquals(2, list.size());
        assertSame(VALUE_A, list.get(0));
        assertSame(VALUE_B, list.get(1));
    }
```

Next you test the behavior when deleting a value from between two others: All values to the right should shift left by one place:

```
    public void testDeleteMiddleElement() {
        List list = createList();

        list.add(VALUE_A);
        list.add(VALUE_C);
        list.add(VALUE_B);

        assertEquals(3, list.size());
        assertSame(VALUE_A, list.get(0));
        assertSame(VALUE_C, list.get(1));
        assertSame(VALUE_B, list.get(2));

        assertSame(VALUE_C, list.delete(1));

        assertEquals(2, list.size());
        assertSame(VALUE_A, list.get(0));
        assertSame(VALUE_B, list.get(1));
    }
```

You also need to ensure that attempts to delete from the list outside the bounds throw an `IndexOutOfBoundsException`:

```
    public void testDeleteOutOfBounds() {
        List list = createList();

        try {
            list.delete(-1);
            fail();
        } catch (IndexOutOfBoundsException e) {
```

```
            // expected
        }

        try {
            list.delete(0);
            fail();
        } catch (IndexOutOfBoundsException e) {
            // expected
        }
    }
```

You've tested what happens when you delete by position, but what about deleting by value? Deleting by value is not as straightforward as deleting by index—as you know, a list may contain the same value more than once, so you also need to ensure that in the event that there are duplicates, deleting by value only removes the first occurrence each time it is called:

```
    public void testDeleteByValue() {
        List list = createList();

        list.add(VALUE_A);
        list.add(VALUE_B);
        list.add(VALUE_A);

        assertEquals(3, list.size());
        assertSame(VALUE_A, list.get(0));
        assertSame(VALUE_B, list.get(1));
        assertSame(VALUE_A, list.get(2));

        assertTrue(list.delete(VALUE_A));

        assertEquals(2, list.size());
        assertSame(VALUE_B, list.get(0));
        assertSame(VALUE_A, list.get(1));

        assertTrue(list.delete(VALUE_A));

        assertEquals(1, list.size());
        assertSame(VALUE_B, list.get(0));

        assertFalse(list.delete(VALUE_C));

        assertEquals(1, list.size());
        assertSame(VALUE_B, list.get(0));

        assertTrue(list.delete(VALUE_B));

        assertEquals(0, list.size());
    }
```

How It Works

The first four tests exercise the basic functionality of deleting a specific element. Deletion is the inverse of insertion, so you can expect that when an element is deleted, the size of the list will decrease by one and that any elements to the right of the deleted element will shift left by one. The contract for "delete by index" also states that it must return the value just deleted, so this is also tested.

The method `testDeleteOutOfBounds()`—as with all the bounds-checking tests—attempts to access the list with an invalid position: first using a negative position, and then using a position that is too big. Each time, you expect an `IndexOutOfBoundsException` to be thrown to indicate an application programming error.

The method `testDeleteByValue()` ensures that you can delete a value from a list without knowing its exact location. The test inserts three values into the list, two of which are duplicates of one another. It then removes one of the duplicate values and ensures the other is still contained within the list. The same value is used again to ensure that the second occurrence is removed. Next, it attempts to delete a value that doesn't exist. This should have no effect on the list. Finally, it deletes the last known remaining value, leaving the list empty. Each time, you have checked that the value returned from `delete` is correct: Deleting a value that does exists should return `true`; and deleting an unknown value should return `false`.

Try It Out Testing Iteration

One of the most difficult parts of a list implementation to get right is iteration. Recall that the `List` interface extends the `Iterable` interface (from Chapter 2), requiring implementations to provide an iterator over the contents.

You will need to test three general scenarios: iteration over an empty list, iteration forward from the start, and iteration backward from the end.

Start by testing the behavior when iterating over an empty list:

```
public void testEmptyIteration() {
    List list = createList();

    Iterator iterator = list.iterator();

    assertTrue(iterator.isDone());

    try {
        iterator.current();
        fail();
    } catch (IteratorOutOfBoundsException e) {
        // expected
    }
}
```

Next you test forward iteration from the beginning of the list:

```
public void testForwardIteration() {
    List list = createList();

    list.add(VALUE_A);
    list.add(VALUE_B);
    list.add(VALUE_C);

    Iterator iterator = list.iterator();

    iterator.first();
```

```
        assertFalse(iterator.isDone());
        assertSame(VALUE_A, iterator.current());

        iterator.next();
        assertFalse(iterator.isDone());
        assertSame(VALUE_B, iterator.current());

        iterator.next();
        assertFalse(iterator.isDone());
        assertSame(VALUE_C, iterator.current());

        iterator.next();
        assertTrue(iterator.isDone());
        try {
            iterator.current();
            fail();
        } catch (IteratorOutOfBoundsException e) {
            // expected
        }
    }
```

Finally, you test reverse iteration beginning with the last element in the list:

```
    public void testReverseIteration() {
        List list = createList();

        list.add(VALUE_A);
        list.add(VALUE_B);
        list.add(VALUE_C);

        Iterator iterator = list.iterator();

        iterator.last();
        assertFalse(iterator.isDone());
        assertSame(VALUE_C, iterator.current());

        iterator.previous();
        assertFalse(iterator.isDone());
        assertSame(VALUE_B, iterator.current());

        iterator.previous();
        assertFalse(iterator.isDone());
        assertSame(VALUE_A, iterator.current());

        iterator.previous();
        assertTrue(iterator.isDone());
        try {
            iterator.current();
            fail();
        } catch (IteratorOutOfBoundsException e) {
            // expected
        }
    }
```

How It Works

When iterating over an empty list, you expect isDone() to always return true, indicating that there are no more elements.

The method testForwardIteration() creates a list containing three values and obtains an iterator. It then calls first() to start at the first element of the list and makes successive calls to next() and current(), checking that the values are returned in the expected order. The method isDone() should only return true after all of the elements have been visited.

Testing reverse iteration follows the same steps as testing forward iteration, except that you start at the last element and work your way backward by calling previous() instead of next().

In all cases, once the iterator has completed — isDone() returns true — an attempt is made to access the iterator by calling current(). This should throw an IteratorOutOfBoundsException.

Try It Out — Testing Methods for Finding Values

Lists enable searching for values via the indexOf() and contains() methods.

The indexOf() method returns the position (0, 1, 2, ...) of the value if found, and -1 if not found. In the event that a list contains duplicate values, indexOf() should only ever find the first occurrence:

```
public void testIndexOf() {
    List list = createList();

    list.add(VALUE_A);
    list.add(VALUE_B);
    list.add(VALUE_A);

    assertEquals(0, list.indexOf(VALUE_A));
    assertEquals(1, list.indexOf(VALUE_B));
    assertEquals(-1, list.indexOf(VALUE_C));
}
```

The method contains() returns true if a value is found; otherwise, it returns false:

```
public void testContains() {
    List list = createList();

    list.add(VALUE_A);
    list.add(VALUE_B);
    list.add(VALUE_A);

    assertTrue(list.contains(VALUE_A));
    assertTrue(list.contains(VALUE_B));
    assertFalse(list.contains(VALUE_C));
}
```

How It Works

Both tests populate a list with three values, one of which is a duplicate.

The method `testIndexOf()` then checks that the correct position is returned for existing values—`A` and `B`—and that `-1` is returned for a non-existing value—`C`. In the case of the duplicate value, the position of the first occurrence should be returned.

The method `testContains()` checks that `contains()` returns `true` for existing values and `false` for nonexisting ones.

Try It Out Testing What Happens When a List Is Cleared

Last but not least, you will test what happens when you reset a list by calling `clear()`. The list should be empty and its size reset to 0:

```
public void testClear() {
    List list = createList();

    list.add(VALUE_A);
    list.add(VALUE_B);
    list.add(VALUE_C);

    assertFalse(list.isEmpty());
    assertEquals(3, list.size());

    list.clear();

    assertTrue(list.isEmpty());
    assertEquals(0, list.size());
}
```

How It Works

The method `testClear()` populates the list with three values and then calls clear, after which the list is checked to ensure it no longer contains any values.

Implementing Lists

By now you should have a thorough understanding of list functionality. Having codified the expected behavior as tests, you can easily determine whether your implementations are working as expected. You can now dive into some well-earned production coding.

There are many ways to implement a list, but the two most common, and the two presented here, are an array-based implementation and a so-called *linked list*. As the name suggests, an array list uses an array to hold the values. A linked list, conversely, is a chain of elements in which each item has a reference (or link) to the next (and optionally previous) element.

You will begin with the simplest case, the array list, followed later by the more sophisticated linked list. Both have characteristics that make them more or less useful depending on the requirements of your application. For this reason, you will consider the specific pros and cons of each along with the explanation of the code.

In every case, we will make some assumptions about the type of data that can be stored within a list. Specifically, we will not allow lists to contain null values. Not allowing null values simplifies the code by removing many boundary conditions that tend to arise when dealing with null values. This restriction shouldn't cause you much concern because in most business applications, lists rarely, if ever, contain null values.

An Array List

As the name suggests, an array list uses an array as the underlying mechanism for storing elements. Because of this, the fact that you can index directly into arrays makes implementing access to elements almost trivial. It also makes an array list the fastest implementation for indexed and sequential access.

The downside to using an array is that each time you insert a new element, you need to shift any elements in higher positions one place to the right by physically copying them. Similarly, when deleting an existing element, you need to shift any objects in higher positions one place to the left to fill the gap left by the deleted element.

Additionally, because arrays are fixed in size, anytime you need to increase the size of the list, you also need to reallocate a new array and copy the contents over. This clearly affects the performance of insertion and deletion. For the most part, however, an array list is a good starting point when first moving away from simple arrays to using richer data structures such as lists.

Try It Out Creating the Test Class

First you need to define the test cases to ensure that your implementation is correct. Start by creating a class named `ArrayListTest` that extends the `AbstractListTestCase` class you created earlier:

```
package com.wrox.algorithms.lists;

public class ArrayListTest extends AbstractListTestCase {
    protected List createList() {
        return new ArrayList();
    }

    public void testResizeBeyondInitialCapacity() {
        List list = new ArrayList(1);

        list.add(VALUE_A);
        list.add(VALUE_A);
        list.add(VALUE_A);

        assertEquals(3, list.size());

        assertSame(VALUE_A, list.get(0));
        assertSame(VALUE_A, list.get(1));
        assertSame(VALUE_A, list.get(2));     }

    public void testDeleteFromLastElementInArray() {
```

```
        List list = new ArrayList(1);

        list.add(new Object());

        list.delete(0);
    }
}
```

How It Works

You already did most of the hard work when you created the AbstractListTestCase class earlier. By extending this class, you necessarily inherited all of the tests. Therefore, the only other one that was needed was to implement the createList() method in order to return an instance of an ArrayList class, which will be used by the tests. In addition to the standard tests, a couple of extras are needed due to the way array lists work internally.

The first method, testResizeBeyondInitialCapacity(), is needed because as the size of an array list increases, the underlying array is resized to accommodate the extra elements. When this happens, you want to make sure that the contents are correctly copied. The test starts by constructing an array list with an initial capacity of one. Three values are then added. This causes the underlying array to grow accordingly. As a consequence, the elements are copied from the original array to a new, larger one. The test then ensures that the size and contents have been copied successfully.

As the name implies, the second test method, testDeleteFromLastElementInArray(), checks what happens when you delete the last element in the list. As you will see in the code a bit later, this boundary condition can lead to ArrayIndexOutOfBoundsExceptions if not handled correctly.

Try It Out Creating the ArrayList Class

Now that you have created the test cases, you can safely proceed to creating the array list implementation. Start by creating the ArrayList class as shown here:

```
package com.wrox.algorithms.lists;

import com.wrox.algorithms.iteration.ArrayIterator;
import com.wrox.algorithms.iteration.Iterator;

public class ArrayList implements List {
    private static final int DEFAULT_INITIAL_CAPACITY = 16;

    private final int _initialCapacity;
    private Object[] _array;
    private int _size;

    public ArrayList() {
        this(DEFAULT_INITIAL_CAPACITY);
    }

    public ArrayList(int initialCapacity) {
        assert initialCapacity > 0 : "initialCapacity must be > 0";

        _initialCapacity = initialCapacity;
```

```
        clear();
    }

    public void clear() {
        _array = new Object[_initialCapacity];
        _size = 0;
    }
    ...
}
```

How It Works

The class itself is quite simple. All it needs is a few fields and, of course, to implement the `List` interface. You have created a field to hold the array of elements and a separate field to hold the size of the list. Be aware that the size of the list is not always the same as the size of the array: The array will almost always have "spare" capacity at the end, so the length of the array doesn't necessarily match the number of elements stored in the list.

There are also two constructors. The first is really a convenience—it calls the second with some default values. The second constructor takes as its only argument the size of the initial array, which is validated and saved before calling `clear()` to initialize the element array and reset the size of the list. (Technically, you could allow a value of 0, but that would require resizing the array the first time you inserted a value. Instead, force the caller to pass a value that is at least 1.)

Try It Out Methods for Inserting and Adding Values

The first method you will implement inserts values into a list at a specified position:

```
    public void insert(int index, Object value)
            throws IndexOutOfBoundsException {
        assert value != null : "value can't be null";

        if (index < 0 || index > _size) {
            throw new IndexOutOfBoundsException();
        }

        ensureCapacity(_size + 1);
        System.arraycopy(_array, index, _array, index + 1, _size - index);
        _array[index] = value;
        ++_size;
    }

    private void ensureCapacity(int capacity) {
        assert capacity > 0 : "capacity must be > 0";

        if (_array.length < capacity) {
            Object[] copy = new Object[capacity + capacity / 2];
            System.arraycopy(_array, 0, copy, 0, _size);
            _array = copy;
        }
    }
```

Once you can insert a value, adding a value to the end of the list follows naturally:

```
public void add(Object value) {
    insert(_size, value);
}
```

How It Works

The `insert()` method starts by validating the input. In the first instance, you need to check for `null` values, as these are explicitly not allowed. Second, as you may recall from the test cases, `insert()` is required to throw an `IndexOutOfBoundsException` if any attempt is made to insert before the first element or further than one beyond the last element of the list.

Next, because arrays are fixed in size but lists are not, it is also necessary to ensure that the underlying array has enough capacity to hold the new value. For example, say you had an array that was of length five and you wanted to add a sixth element. The array clearly doesn't have enough space, but it won't magically resize for you either, thus, the call to `ensureCapacity()` ensures that there is enough room in the array to accommodate another value. Once the call to `ensureCapacity()` returns, you know you have enough space, so you can safely shift the existing elements to the right by one position to make room for the new value. Finally, you store the value into the appropriate element, remembering to increase the size of the list.

The method `ensureCapacity()` handles the dynamic resizing of the underlying array. Anytime it detects that the underlying array is too small, a new array is allocated, the contents are copied over, and the old array is discarded, freeing it up for garbage collection. You could use any number of strategies for determining when and how big to allocate the new array, but in this particular example, the size of the array is increased by an additional 50 percent over what is actually required. This provides a kind of safety net that ensures the list doesn't spend most of its time allocating new arrays and copying the values across.

The `add()` method simply delegates to `insert`, passing the size of the list as the insertion point, thereby ensuring that the new value is added to the end.

Try It Out Methods for Storing and Retrieving Values by Position

Now you will create the two methods `get()` and `set()`, used for storing and retrieving values. Because this particular implementation is based on arrays, access to the contained values is almost trivial:

```
public Object get(int index) throws IndexOutOfBoundsException {
    checkOutOfBounds(index);
    return _array[index];
}

public Object set(int index, Object value)
        throws IndexOutOfBoundsException {
    assert value != null : "value can't be null";
    checkOutOfBounds(index);
    Object oldValue = _array[index];
    _array[index] = value;
    return oldValue;
```

```
    }

    private void checkOutOfBounds(int index) {
        if (isOutOfBounds(index)) {
            throw new IndexOutOfBoundsException();
        }
    }

    private boolean isOutOfBounds(int index) {
        return index < 0 || index >= _size;
    }
```

How It Works

After first checking that the requested position is valid, the `get()` method returns the value contained at the element for the specified index, while the `set()` method replaces whatever value was already there. Additionally, `set()` takes a copy of the value that was originally stored at the specified position before overwriting it. The original value is then returned to the caller.

As you can probably tell, an array list performs extremely well for indexed access. In fact, while indexed access to a list is generally considered to be `O(1)`, array lists come about as close as you will get to delivering on that promise with identical best, worst, and average case performance.

Try It Out Methods for Finding Values

As indicated in the discussion on `get()` and `set()`, lists are ideal for storing values in known positions. This makes them perfect for certain types of sorting (see Chapters 6 and 7) and searching (see Chapter 9). If, however, you want to determine the position of a specific value within an *unsorted* list, you will have to make do with the relatively crude but straightforward method of linear searching. The `indexOf()` method enables you to find the position of a specific value within a list. If the value is found, its position is returned; otherwise, `-1` is returned to indicate the value doesn't exist:

```
    public int indexOf(Object value) {
        assert value != null : "value can't be null";

        for (int i = 0; i < _size; ++i) {
            if (value.equals(_array[i])) {
                return i;
            }
        }

        return -1;
    }
```

Having provided a mechanism for searching the list via `indexOf()`, you can proceed to implement `contains()`:

```
    public boolean contains(Object value) {
        return indexOf(value) != -1;
    }
```

How It Works

The `indexOf()` method performs a linear search of the list to find a value. It achieves its goal by starting at the first position within the list and working its way through each element until either the value is found or the end is reached.

The `contains()` method calls `indexOf()` to perform a search on its behalf and returns `true` only if it is found (`indexOf >= 0`).

Although simple to implement, linear searching doesn't scale very well to large lists. Imagine a list containing the following values: `Cat`, `Dog`, `Mouse`, `Zebra`. Now imagine you were to search for each value in turn (first `Cat`, then `Dog`, and so on.) and count the number of comparisons needed to find each value. `Cat`, being the first in the list, will take one comparison. `Dog` will take two, `Mouse` three, and `Zebra` four. If you calculate the average number of comparisons required, `1 + 2 + 3 + 4 / 4 = 10 / 4 = 2.5`, you can see that for a list containing `N` items, the average number of comparisons required is around `N / 2`, or `O(N)`. This is the same as the worst-case time and therefore clearly not a very efficient method for searching.

Chapter 9, "Binary Searching," introduces a more efficient method for searching a list, but for now we will make do with this "brute force" approach to searching.

Try It Out Methods for Deleting Values

The `List` interface provides two methods for deleting values. The first of these enables you to delete a value by its position:

```
public Object delete(int index) throws IndexOutOfBoundsException {
    checkOutOfBounds(index);
    Object value = _array[index];
    int copyFromIndex = index + 1;
    if (copyFromIndex < _size) {
        System.arraycopy(_array, copyFromIndex,
                         _array, index,
                         _size - copyFromIndex);
    }
    _array[--_size] = null;
    return value;
}
```

You also need to support the deletion of a specified value without knowing its precise location. As with `contains()`, you can take advantage of the fact that you already have a mechanism for determining the position of a value using `indexOf()`:

```
public boolean delete(Object value) {
    int index = indexOf(value);
    if (index != -1) {
        delete(index);
        return true;
    }
    return false;
}
```

How It Works

After first checking the validity of the input, the first `delete()` method copies all values to the right of the deletion point left one position. Then the size of the list is decremented accordingly and the value in the last element of the array is cleared.

It is necessary to clear the last element of the array because you haven't actually moved the values left by one position, you've only copied them. If you didn't clear out what used to be the last element containing a value, you might inadvertently hold on to copies of deleted values, thereby preventing them from being garbage collected. This is more commonly referred to as a *memory leak.*

Notice the bounds checking to ensure you don't cause an `ArrayIndexOutOfBoundsException` when deleting from the last element of the array. In fact, you may like to try commenting out the entire block of code under the `if` statement and rerunning the tests to see what happens. Also notice you have been careful to take a copy of the value that was stored at the deleted position so that it can be returned to the caller.

It is worth noting here that the capacity of the underlying array never shrinks. This means that if the list grows very large and then shrinks significantly, there may be a lot of "wasted" storage. You could get around this problem by implementing the inverse of `ensureCapacity()`. Each time you delete an element from the list, you could check the new size against some percentage threshold. For example, once the size drops to 50 percent of the list capacity, you could reallocate a smaller array and copy the contents across, thereby freeing up the unused storage. However, for the sake of clarity, we have chosen not to do this.

> *As an aside, the code for the JDK implementation of* `ArrayList` *behaves in exactly the same way. Again, nothing to worry about in most cases, but something to keep in mind nevertheless.*

The second `delete()` works by first calling `indexOf()` to determine the position of the first occurrence of the specified value, calling the first `delete()` method if found. The performance of the first `delete()` method is `O(1)`—discounting the time taken to copy the values—whereas the second `delete()` is intrinsically tied to the performance of `indexOf()`, giving an average deletion time of `O(N)`.

Try It Out Completing the Interface

You're almost done with implementing the entire `List` interface. There are only a few more methods to cover:

```
public Iterator iterator() {
    return new ArrayIterator(_array, 0, _size);
}

public int size() {
    return _size;
}

public boolean isEmpty() {
    return size() == 0;
}
```

How It Works

The `iterator()` method is very simple—you already have the necessary code in the form of the `ArrayIterator` class from Chapter 2.

Implementing the `size()` method is even simpler. The `insert()` and `delete()` methods already maintain the size of the list, so you simply return whatever value is currently stored in the `_size` field.

Finally, `isEmpty()` returns `true` only if the size of the list is zero (`size() == 0`). Although trivial in implementation, `isEmpty()`—like all the convenience methods on the `List` interface—makes your application code more readable by reducing the amount of "noise."

A Linked List

Rather than use an array to hold the elements, a linked list contains individual elements with links between them. As you can see from Figure 3-3, each element in a linked list contains a reference (or link) to both the next and previous elements, acting like links in a chain.

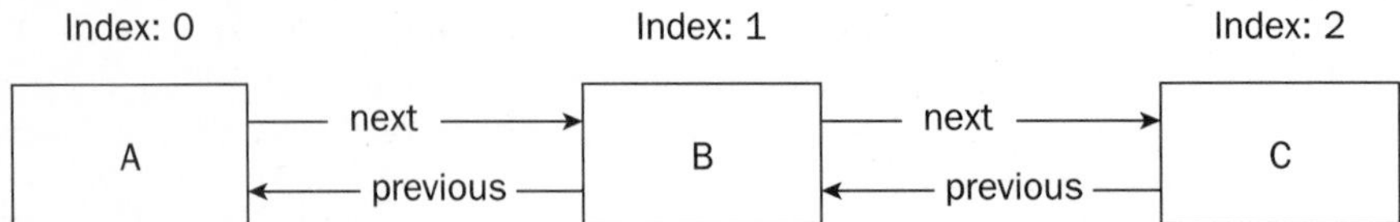

Figure 3-3: Elements of a doubly linked list have references in both directions.

More precisely, this is referred to as a *doubly linked list* (each element has two links), as opposed to a singly linked list in which each element has only one link. This double linking makes it possible to traverse the elements in either direction. It also makes insertion and deletion much simpler than it is for an array list.

As you might recall from the discussion on array lists, in most cases when deleting or inserting, some portion of the underlying array needs to be copied. With a linked list, however, each time you wish to insert or delete an element, you need only update the references to and from the next and previous elements, respectively. This makes the cost of the actual insertion or deletion almost negligible in all but the most extreme cases. For lists with extremely large numbers of elements, the traversal time can be a performance issue.

A doubly linked list also maintains references to the first and last elements in the list—often referred to as the head and tail, respectively. This enables you to access either end with equal performance.

Try It Out Creating the Test Class

Remember that the tests are the best way of validating that your implementation meets the requirements set out in Tables 3-1 and 3-2 at the beginning of the chapter. This time, create a class named `LinkedListTest` that extends `AbstractListTestCase`:

```
package com.wrox.algorithms.lists;

public class LinkedListTest extends AbstractListTestCase {
    protected List createList() {
        return new LinkedList();
    }
}
```

How It Works

As you did for your `ArrayListTest` class earlier, you extend `AbstractListTestCase` in order to take advantage of all the predefined test cases. This time, however, the `createList()` method returns an instance of `LinkedList`. Notice also that this time you haven't created any additional test cases because the tests already defined in `AbstractListTestCase` will be sufficient.

Try It Out Creating the LinkedList Class

Begin by creating the `LinkedList` class with all its fields and constructors:

```
package com.wrox.algorithms.lists;

import com.wrox.algorithms.iteration.Iterator;
import com.wrox.algorithms.iteration.IteratorOutOfBoundsException;

public class LinkedList implements List {
    private final Element _headAndTail = new Element(null);
    private int _size;

    public LinkedList() {
        clear();
    }

    ...
}
```

How It Works

As with any other list, the first thing you need to do is implement the `List` interface. Once again, you track the size of the list through the instance variable `_size`. (Theoretically, you could derive the size each time it's required by counting every element, but that really *wouldn't* scale!)

Not so obvious is why you have a single, unmodifiable, element `_headAndTail` instead of the two references discussed at the start of the section. This field is known as a *sentinel*. A sentinel—often referred to as the *null object pattern* or simply a *null object*—is a technique for simplifying an algorithm by adding a special element to one or both ends of a data structure to avoid writing special code that handles boundary conditions. Without the use of a sentinel, our code would be littered with statements that checked for and updated `null` references of the head and tail. Instead, use the next and previous fields of the sentinel point to the first and last elements of the list. Moreover, the first and last elements can themselves always refer back to the sentinel as if it was just another element in the chain. Sentinels can be a difficult concept to grasp, so don't worry too much if it seems a little strange at first. In fact, trying to formulate an algorithm that uses sentinels is not always a particularly intuitive process. However, once you become accustomed to using them, you will find that your algorithms become more elegant and succinct—try writing a doubly linked list without one and you will soon see what we mean.

Lastly, a constructor calls `clear()`. You'll create the `clear()` method later, so don't worry too much about what it does right now—suffice it to say that it resets the internal state of the class.

Try It Out Creating an Element Class

Unlike an array list, a linked list has no inherent place to store values, so you will need some other way of representing an element. For this, you create the aptly named `Element` inner class:

```
private static final class Element {
    private Object _value;
    private Element _previous;
    private Element _next;

    public Element(Object value) {
        setValue(value);
    }

    public void setValue(Object value) {
        _value = value;
    }

    public Object getValue() {
        return _value;
    }

    public Element getPrevious() {
        return _previous;
    }

    public void setPrevious(Element previous) {
        assert previous != null : "previous can't be null";
        _previous = previous;
    }

    public Element getNext() {
        return _next;
    }

    public void setNext(Element next) {
        assert next != null : "next can't be null";
        _next = next;
    }

    public void attachBefore(Element next) {
        assert next != null : "next can't be null";

        Element previous = next.getPrevious();

        setNext(next);
        setPrevious(previous);

        next.setPrevious(this);
        previous.setNext(this);          }

    public void detach() {
```

```
            _previous.setNext(_next);
            _next.setPrevious(_previous);
        }
    }
```

How It Works

For the most part, the inner class `Element` is quite straightforward. In addition to holding a value, each element also holds references to the next and previous elements, along with some simple methods for getting and setting the various fields.

At some point, however, your code will need to insert a new element into a list. This logic is encapsulated inside the method `attachBefore()`.

As the name suggests, this method allows an element to insert itself *before* another by storing the references to the next and previous elements and then updating them to refer to itself.

You also need to delete elements. For this, you created the method `detach()`, which allows an element to remove itself from the chain by setting the next and previous elements to point at one another.

Notice that at no point in all of this have you needed to check for `null` values or update references to the head or tail. This is only possible because you are using a sentinel. Because the sentinel *is itself* an instance of `Element`, there will *always be* a next and previous element to update.

Try It Out Methods for Inserting and Adding Values

Inserting into a linked list is conceptually simpler than it is for an array list because no resizing is involved. However, a little bit of logic is involved in finding the correct insertion point:

```
    public void insert(int index, Object value)
            throws IndexOutOfBoundsException {
        assert value != null : "value can't be null";

        if (index < 0 || index > _size) {
            throw new IndexOutOfBoundsException();
        }

        Element element = new Element(value);
        element.attachBefore(getElement(index));
        ++_size;
    }

    private Element getElement(int index) {
        Element element = _headAndTail.getNext();

        for (int i = index; i > 0; --i) {
            element = element.getNext();
        }

        return element;
    }
```

As for add(), you again simply delegate to insert(), passing the size of the list as the point for insertion:

```
public void add(Object value) {
    insert(_size, value);
}
```

How It Works

As always, insert() starts by first validating the input. You then create a new element with the specified value, find the insertion point, and attach it to the chain before finally incrementing the size of the list to reflect the change.

The getElement() method is really the workhorse of this linked list implementation. It is called by a number of methods and traverses the list in search of the element at the specified position. This brute-force approach gives insert() (and, as you will see later, delete()) an average and worst-case running time of O(N).

You can actually improve on the actual performance of getElement(). As the joke goes, "Q: How long is a linked list? A: Twice the distance from the middle to the end." Recall that our linked list implementation holds a reference to both ends of the list, not just the head. If the position we are searching falls in the first half of the list, we can start at the first element and work our way forward. Conversely, if the desired position falls in the second half of the list, we can start searching from the last element and work our way backward. This means we never traverse more than half the list to reach our destination. Although this has no effect on the magnitude of the search times, it does effectively cut the actual average running times in half. This has been left as an exercise at the end of the chapter.

Try It Out Methods for Storing and Retrieving Values

The way to go about setting and retrieving values from a linked list is almost identical to that for an array list except that instead of indexing into an array, you make use of the getElement() method you introduced for insert():

```
public Object get(int index) throws IndexOutOfBoundsException {
    checkOutOfBounds(index);
    return getElement(index).getValue();
}

public Object set(int index, Object value)
        throws IndexOutOfBoundsException {
    assert value != null : "value can't be null";
    checkOutOfBounds(index);
    Element element = getElement(index);
    Object oldValue = element.getValue();
    element.setValue(value);
    return oldValue;
}

private void checkOutOfBounds(int index) {
    if (isOutOfBounds(index)) {
        throw new IndexOutOfBoundsException();
    }
```

```
    }

    private boolean isOutOfBounds(int index) {
        return index < 0 || index >= _size;
    }
```

How It Works

In both cases, after first checking the validity of the position, you obtain the desired element and get or set the value as appropriate.

Because both `get()` and `set()` are tied to the implementation of `getElement()`, their running times are similarly constrained. This makes indexed-based retrieval of values from a linked list much slower on average than for an array list.

Try It Out Methods for Finding Values

Conceptually at least, searching a linked list is really no different from searching an array list. You have little choice but to start at one end and continue searching until you either find the value you are looking for or simply run out of elements:

```
    public int indexOf(Object value) {
        assert value != null : "value can't be null";

        int index = 0;

        for (Element e = _headAndTail.getNext();
                  e != _headAndTail;
                  e = e.getNext()) {
            if (value.equals(e.getValue())) {
                return index;
            }

            ++index;
        }

        return -1;
    }
```

The `contains()` method is identical in every way to the one found in `ArrayList`:

```
    public boolean contains(Object value) {
        return indexOf(value) != -1;
    }
```

How It Works

The difference between the linked list and array list implementations of `indexOf()` is really only in how you navigate from one element to the next. With an array list it's easy: You simply increment an index and access the array directly. With linked lists, on the other hand, you need to use the links themselves to move from one element to the next. If the value is found, its position is returned. Once the sentinel is reached, however, you have fallen off the end of the list, the loop terminates, and `-1` is returned to indicate that the value doesn't exist.

The `contains()` method calls `indexOf()` and returns `true`.

Try It Out — Methods for Deleting Values

Deletion from a linked list is almost trivial. You actually implemented most of the code inside your `Element` inner class earlier:

```
public Object delete(int index) throws IndexOutOfBoundsException {
    checkOutOfBounds(index);
    Element element = getElement(index);
    element.detach();
    --_size;
    return element.getValue();
}
```

And, of course, here's a method for deleting by value:

```
public boolean delete(Object value) {
    assert value != null : "value can't be null";

    for (Element e = _headAndTail.getNext();
                e != _headAndTail;
                e = e.getNext()) {
        if (value.equals(e.getValue())) {
            e.detach();
            --_size;
            return true;
        }
    }

    return false;
}
```

How It Works

After checking that the specified position is valid, the first `delete()` method obtains the appropriate element by calling `getElement()`, detaches it, and decrements the size of the list before returning its value.

The code for the second `delete()` method is almost the same as for `indexOf()`, the difference being that, rather than tracking and returning the position, upon finding the first matching element, you immediately delete it and return its value. (Don't forget to decrement the size of the list after calling `detach`!)

Try It Out — Creating an Iterator

Iteration for a linked list is somewhat more involved than for an array list. Like searching and deleting, however, it is simply a matter of following the links—in either direction—until you reach an end. For this you will create an inner class, `ValueIterator`, to encapsulate the iteration logic:

```
private final class ValueIterator implements Iterator {
    private Element _current = _headAndTail;

    public void first() {
        _current = _headAndTail.getNext();
    }

    public void last() {
        _current = _headAndTail.getPrevious();
    }

    public boolean isDone() {
        return _current == _headAndTail;
    }

    public void next() {
        _current = _current.getNext();
    }

    public void previous() {
        _current = _current.getPrevious();
    }

    public Object current() throws IteratorOutOfBoundsException {
        if (isDone()) {
            throw new IteratorOutOfBoundsException();
        }
        return _current.getValue();
    }
}
```

Having defined the inner class, you can return an instance from the `iterator()` method:

```
public Iterator iterator() {
    return new ValueIterator();
}
```

How It Works

The `ValueIterator` class is virtually identical to the `ArrayIterator` class from Chapter 2 except that, as was the case for searching and deleting, you use the `getNext()` and `getPrevious()` methods to traverse forward and backward, respectively, between the elements until you reach the sentinel.

Try It Out Completing the Interface

You have arrived at the last few methods of the interface: `size()`, `isEmpty()`, and `clear()`:

```
public int size() {
    return _size;
}

public boolean isEmpty() {
    return size() == 0;
}
```

```
public void clear() {
    _headAndTail.setPrevious(_headAndTail);
    _headAndTail.setNext(_headAndTail);
    _size = 0;
}
```

How It Works

Not surprisingly, the `size()` and `isEmpty()` methods are carbon copies of their array list counterparts.

The last method, `clear()`, is almost, but not quite, as simple as the array list implementation. In order to maintain the correct behavior while using the sentinel, you need to set its next and previous values to point to itself. This ensures that when you insert the first element into the list, its next and previous values will point to the sentinel, and, most important, the sentinel's next and previous values will point to the new element.

Summary

This chapter demonstrated that lists can be used as a replacement for the use of arrays in most real-world applications.

You learned that lists preserve insertion order and that they have no inherent concept of uniqueness.

You've also covered quite a lot of code in order to examine two of the most common list implementations and their relative performance characteristics. Both array lists and linked lists have similar search and iteration times. However, by their very nature, array lists have much better index-based access compared to linked lists. On the other hand, linked lists don't have the overhead of copying and resizing that array lists do, so they have generally better insertion and deletion times, especially at the ends.

Although lists as described here are useful in many situations, there are times when slightly different behavior is needed. The next two chapters discuss some variations on lists, known as *queues* and *stacks*, that help solve some very specific computing problems.

Exercises

1. Write a constructor for `ArrayList` that accepts a standard Java array to initially populate `List`.
2. Write an `equals()` method that will work for any `List` implementation.
3. Write a `toString()` method that will work for any `List` implementation that prints the contents as a single line with values surrounded by square brackets and separated by commas. For example, "`[A, B, C]`" or "`[]`" for an empty `List`.
4. Create an `Iterator` that will work for any `List` implementation. What are the performance implications?
5. Update `LinkedList` to traverse backward if, when inserting and deleting, the desired index is more than halfway along the list.
6. Rewrite `indexOf()` so that it will work for any list.
7. Create a `List` implementation that is always empty and throws `UnsupportedOperationException` if an attempt is made to modify it.

Queues

Queues are an essential part of algorithms that manage the allocation and scheduling of work, events, or messages to be processed. They are often used as a way of enabling different processes — either on the same or different machines — to communicate with one another.

In this chapter, you will learn the following:

- How queues differ from lists
- Characteristics and implementation of a first-in-first-out (FIFO) queue
- How to create a thread-safe queue
- How to create a bounded queue — one with a maximum size limit
- How to combine all of these queue types to build a multi-threaded simulation of a call center to see just how queues can be put to use

Understanding Queues

Customers line up in a bank waiting to be served by a teller and in supermarkets waiting to check out. No doubt you've been stuck waiting in a line to speak to a customer service representative at a call center. In computing terms, however, a queue is a list of data items stored in such a way that they can be retrieved in a definable order. The main distinguishing feature between a queue and a list is that whereas all items in a list are accessible — by their position within the list — the only item you can ever retrieve from a queue is the one at the *head*. Which item is at the head depends on the specific queue implementation.

More often than not, the order of retrieval is indeed the same as the order of insertion (also known as first-in-first-out, or FIFO), but there are other possibilities as well. Some of the more common examples include a last-in-first-out queue (see Chapter 5) and a priority queue (see Chapter 8), whereby retrieval is based on the relative priority of each item. You can even create a *random queue* that effectively "shuffles" the contents.

In this book, whenever we use the term "queue," we are not necessarily referring to a FIFO queue.

Queues are often described in terms of producers and consumers. A *producer* is anything that stores data in a queue, while a *consumer* is anything that retrieves data from a queue. Figure 4-1 shows the interactions between producers, consumers, and queues.

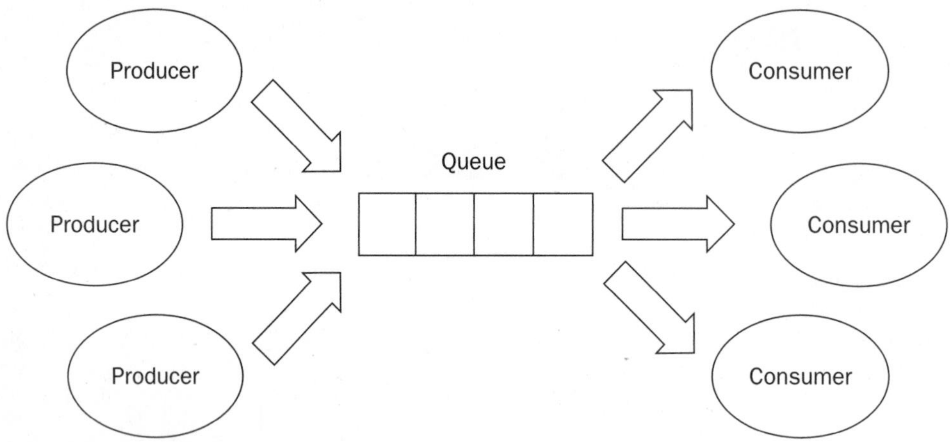

Figure 4-1: How producers and consumers interact with a queue.

Queues can be ether *bounded* or *unbounded*. Bounded queues have limits placed on the number of items that can be held at any one time. These are especially useful when the amount of available memory is constrained — for example, in a device such as a router or even an in-memory message queue. Unbounded queues, conversely, are free to grow in size as the limits of the hardware allow.

Queue Operations

This chapter describes several different queues used throughout the course of this book, all with slightly different retrieval order. Irrespective of their behavior, the various queues all share a common interface. Table 4-1 lists each of the queue operations along with a brief description.

Table 4-1: Queue Operations

Operation	Description
`enqueue`	Stores a value in the queue. The size of the queue will increase by one.
`dequeue`	Retrieves the value at the head of the queue. The size of the queue will decrease by one. Throws `EmptyQueueException` if there are no more items in the queue.
`clear`	Deletes all elements from the queue. The size of the queue will be reset to zero (0).
`size`	Obtains the number of elements in the queue.
`isEmpty`	Determines whether the queue is empty (`size() == 0`) or not.

As you can see, the queue interface is much simpler than that of the list: `enqueue()` is responsible for storing values, `dequeue()` for retrieving them. The remaining methods have the same behavior as those with the same names defined for lists. Notice also that there is no means for accessing all of the data items in a queue at once using an iterator (see Chapter 2), further reinforcing the idea that the only thing you can do is obtain the item at the head.

The Queue Interface

Any operations you have defined can be translated directly into a Java interface so that you can easily create pluggable implementations:

```
package com.wrox.algorithms.queues;

public interface Queue {
    public void enqueue(Object value);
    public Object dequeue() throws EmptyQueueException;
    public void clear();
    public int size();
    public boolean isEmpty();
}
```

Each operation has been translated directly into a method on the interface. The only other thing you need to define is the `EmptyQueueException` thrown by `dequeue()`:

```
package com.wrox.algorithms.queues;

public class EmptyQueueException extends RuntimeException {
}
```

We have chosen to make `EmptyQueueException` a runtime extension. This means you will not be forced to wrap `try-catch` blocks around calls to `dequeue()`. The primary reason for this is that we consider retrieval attempts from an empty queue to be a programming error; you can always call `isEmpty()` to check before calling `dequeue()`.

A First-In-First-Out Queue

This section describes the implementation of a first-in-first-out (FIFO) queue. You'll first learn about the characteristics of a FIFO queue. After that, you'll develop some tests and finally implement a very straightforward unbounded FIFO queue based on lists.

The name says it all really: The first value to go in is always the first value to come out. Calling `dequeue()` on a FIFO queue always returns the element that has been in the queue the longest.

If you were to call `enqueue()` with the values `Cat`, `Dog`, `Apple`, and `Banana`, for example, calling `dequeue()` would return them in the following order: `Cat`, `Dog`, `Apple`, `Banana`.

Although there are many ways to implement a FIFO queue (and other types of queues, for that matter), one of the simplest solutions, and the one presented here, is to use a list as the underlying storage mechanism. In many ways, this is a very natural fit: A queue can be thought of as a simplified list that includes some constraints on adding and removing items.

When you enqueue a value, it is added to the end of the list, as shown in Figure 4-2.

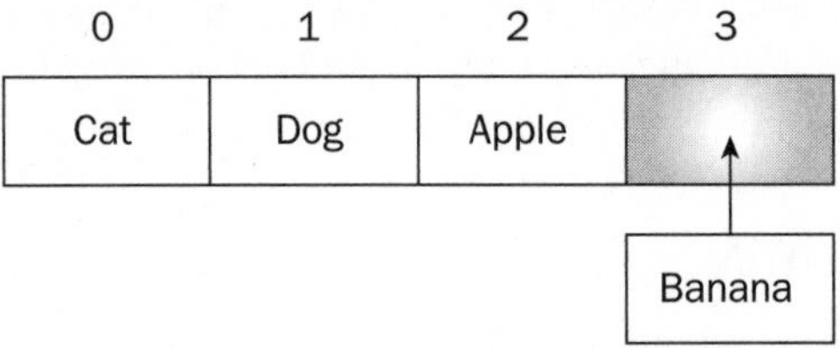

Figure 4-2: Calling `enqueue()` adds to the end of the list.

Conversely, when you dequeue a value, it is removed from the beginning of the list, as shown in Figure 4-3.

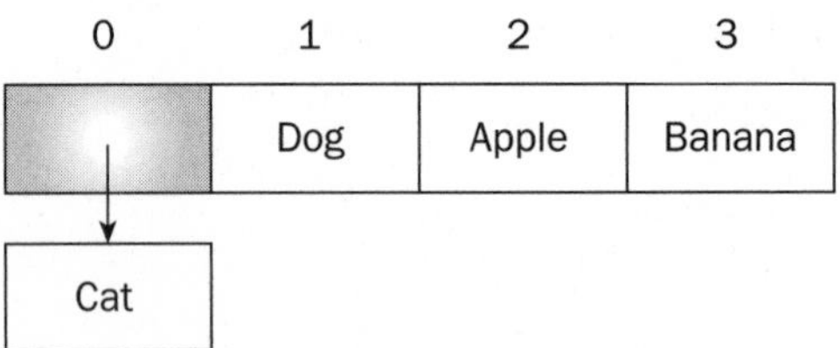

Figure 4-3: Calling `dequeue()` removes from the start of the list.

Of course, you could just as easily have chosen to add to the start and remove from the end. Either way will work, but in this instance we have chosen to add to the end and remove from the start because this seems to better fit our mental model of a queue.

Having discussed the design, it's time to write some code. As usual, you'll write some tests first and then the actual queue implementation.

Try It Out Testing the FIFO Queue

Although you're only going to examine one way to implement a FIFO queue, there are many others, so in keeping with our approach so far in this book, you'll develop a suite of tests that any FIFO queue should pass. These tests will be defined in an abstract class with some hooks, to enable you to extend them in order to test specific implementations later:

```
package com.wrox.algorithms.queues;

import junit.framework.TestCase;

public abstract class AbstractFifoQueueTestCase extends TestCase {
    private static final String VALUE_A = "A";
    private static final String VALUE_B = "B";
    private static final String VALUE_C = "C";

    private Queue _queue;

    protected void setUp() throws Exception {
```

```
        super.setUp();

        _queue = createFifoQueue();
    }

    protected abstract Queue createFifoQueue();

    ...
}
```

The first test is really a bit of bounds checking. You want to make sure that an empty list returns a size of zero, that `isEmpty()` returns `true`, and that attempting to dequeue something results in an `EmptyQueueException`:

```
    public void testAccessAnEmptyQueue() {
        assertEquals(0, _queue.size());
        assertTrue(_queue.isEmpty());

        try {
            _queue.dequeue();
            fail();
        } catch (EmptyQueueException e) {
            // expected
        }
    }
```

The next test is a little longer but still pretty straightforward. It checks to make sure that you can successfully enqueue and dequeue values:

```
    public void testEnqueueDequeue() {
        _queue.enqueue(VALUE_B);
        _queue.enqueue(VALUE_A);
        _queue.enqueue(VALUE_C);

        assertEquals(3, _queue.size());
        assertFalse(_queue.isEmpty());

        assertSame(VALUE_B, _queue.dequeue());
        assertEquals(2, _queue.size());
        assertFalse(_queue.isEmpty());

        assertSame(VALUE_A, _queue.dequeue());
        assertEquals(1, _queue.size());
        assertFalse(_queue.isEmpty());

        assertSame(VALUE_C, _queue.dequeue());
        assertEquals(0, _queue.size());
        assertTrue(_queue.isEmpty());

        try {
            _queue.dequeue();
            fail();
        } catch (EmptyQueueException e) {
```

```
            // expected
        }
    }
```

There is also one final test to ensure that when you call `clear()`, the queue is emptied as expected:

```
    public void testClear() {
        _queue.enqueue(VALUE_A);
        _queue.enqueue(VALUE_B);
        _queue.enqueue(VALUE_C);

        assertFalse(_queue.isEmpty());

        _queue.clear();

        assertEquals(0, _queue.size());
        assertTrue(_queue.isEmpty());

        try {
            _queue.dequeue();
            fail();
        } catch (EmptyQueueException e) {
            // expected
        }
    }
```

Having developed the abstract test class, we can now create a concrete test class for the actual FIFO queue implementation. Of course, we haven't yet defined the implementation class, but that won't stop us from defining the test case:

```
package com.wrox.algorithms.queues;

public class ListFifoQueueTest extends AbstractFifoQueueTestCase {
    protected Queue createFifoQueue() {
        return new ListFifoQueue();
    }
}
```

How It Works

The new test class, `AbstractFifoQueueTestCase`, defines some constants that will be used later in the actual tests. It also defines a local variable, `_queue`, for holding an instance of a FIFO queue for running the tests against. The `setUp()` method—called prior to running each individual test—ensures that the local variable always has a value. It achieves this by calling `createFifoQueue()`, an abstract method you will implement to return an instance of the specific FIFO queue class under test.

In the second and third tests, we ensure that each time a value is enqueued and dequeued, our actions are reflected accurately in the size of the queue, and, importantly, that when we retrieve values, they are returned to us in exactly the same order as they were stored. That is, of course, the definition of a FIFO queue.

The final test simply stores a number of values to the queue, calls `clear()`, and ensures that the queue is actually empty.

In the creation of the concrete class, the queue class will be named `ListFifoQueue`, in line with the fact that it is a FIFO queue and uses a list to store the data. Notice how easy it is to extend `AbstractFifoQueueTestCase` and implement the `createFifoQueue` method to return an instance of our concrete queue class.

Implementing the FIFO Queue

With the tests in place, you can safely start coding up your implementation class: `ListFifoQueue`:

```
package com.wrox.algorithms.queues;

import com.wrox.algorithms.lists.LinkedList;
import com.wrox.algorithms.lists.List;

public class ListFifoQueue implements Queue {
    private final List _list;

    public ListFifoQueue(List list) {
        assert list != null : "list can't be null";
        _list = list;
    }

    public ListFifoQueue() {
        this(new LinkedList());
    }


    ...
}
```

Besides implementing the `Queue` interface, this holds the underlying list and defines two constructors. The first constructor takes as its only argument a list to use for storing the data (naturally it is checked for `null`). The second—a default constructor—calls the first, passing in an instance of a linked list.

A linked list is perfectly suited for use with a queue, as it is capable of efficiently adding and removing elements from either end. Compare this to an array list, which you may recall incurs the overhead of continually moving elements as they are removed.

Now that you can construct a list-based FIFO queue, you need to be able to add things to the queue. For this there is `enqueue()`:

```
    public void enqueue(Object value) {
        _list.add(value);
    }
```

Pretty simple. As discussed earlier, all `enqueue()` does is add the value to the end of the underlying list.

Next you implement `dequeue()`, which enables you to retrieve items from the queue:

```
    public Object dequeue() throws EmptyQueueException {
        if (isEmpty()) {
            throw new EmptyQueueException();
```

```
        }
        return _list.delete(0);
    }
```

That wasn't much more complicated. Remember that `dequeue()` simply removes and returns the last element in the underlying list. The only extra action to do is a quick check to ensure that there is an element to remove. If there isn't (because the list is empty), you need to throw an `EmptyQueueException` as defined in the `Queue` interface.

You could argue here that because the `List` *interface throws an* `IndexOutOfBoundsException`*, you might simply catch the exception and throw an* `EmptyQueueException` *instead of checking for an empty list. However, as mentioned previously, if an* `IndexOutOfBoundsException` *was ever to be thrown, we would like it to propagate out as an indication of a programming error, and not something the caller has done wrong.*

The last few methods on the `Queue` interface are even easier to implement, as all of them (not coincidentally) have a corresponding method of the same name on the `List` interface:

```
    public void clear() {
        _list.clear();
    }

    public int size() {
        return _list.size();
    }

    public boolean isEmpty() {
        return _list.isEmpty();
    }
```

In all three cases, you need do nothing more than delegate the call to the underlying list.

Blocking Queues

Queues are often used in multi-threaded environments as a form of interprocess communication. Unfortunately, your `ListFifoQueue` is totally unsafe for use in situations where multiple consumers would be accessing it concurrently. Instead, a *blocking queue* is one way to provide a thread-safe implementation, ensuring that all access to the data is correctly synchronized.

The first main enhancement that a blocking queue offers over a regular queue is that it can be bounded. So far, this chapter has only dealt with unbounded queues—those that continue to grow without limit. The blocking queue enables you to set an upper limit on the size of the queue. Moreover, when an attempt is made to store an item in a queue that has reached its limit, the queue will, you guessed it, block the thread until space becomes available—either by removing an item or by calling `clear()`. In this way, you guarantee that the queue will never exceed its predefined bounds.

The second major feature affects the behavior of `dequeue()`. Recall from the implementation of `ListFifoQueue` presented earlier that an `EmptyQueueException` is thrown when an attempt is made to retrieve an item from an empty queue. A blocking queue, however, will instead block the current thread until an item is enqueued—perfect for implementing work queues where multiple, concurrent consumers need to wait until there are more tasks to perform.

By encapsulating all this behind the `Queue` interface, you free the consumers of the queue from the intricacies and subtleties of thread synchronization. There are two options for creating the blocking queue: *extend* an existing queue implementation (so far only `ListFifoQueue`), or try to wrap the behavior *around* another queue. The first option would lock you into one specific queue implementation, so instead you should use the second option—wrap another queue—as it gives you the flexibility to easily turn *any* queue implementation (such as the priority queues presented in Chapter 8) into a blocking queue.

Insofar as synchronization is concerned, we use a very common technique for ensuring that the code plays nicely in a multi-threaded environment: A lock object or, in more technical terms, a *mutual exclusion semaphore (mutex)*, will be used as the synchronization point for all the methods in the class. A mutex is one of the least error prone ways of ensuring that only one thread has access to the underlying queue at any given time.

Try It Out Using the BlockingQueue

This is usually the point at which we say something like "and of course we start with some tests." For this particular exercise, however, we are going to deviate from the norm and skip writing the tests altogether.

What!? No tests?

Actually, we did indeed write tests, but an explanation of testing multi-threaded applications is entirely beyond the scope of this book, so we chose to omit them from the text. Therefore, you're just going to have to trust us on this one. You can, of course, still run the tests by downloading the entire source code for the book.

> *If you would like to learn more about writing multi-threaded code, try starting with Doug Lea's* Concurrent Programming in Java: Design Principles and Patterns *(1999).*

The discussion of `BlockingQueue` code starts with the class declaration:

```
package com.wrox.algorithms.queues;

public class BlockingQueue implements Queue {
    private final Object _mutex = new Object();
    private final Queue _queue;
    private final int _maxSize;

    public BlockingQueue(Queue queue, int maxSize) {
        assert queue != null : "queue can't be null";
        assert maxSize > 0 : "size can't be < 1";

        _queue = queue;
        _maxSize = maxSize;
    }

    public BlockingQueue(Queue queue) {
```

```
        this(queue, Integer.MAX_VALUE);
    }

    ...
}
```

The BlockingQueue implements the Queue interface and holds a few instance variables. Two of the variables are pretty straightforward: the first, queue, holds a reference to the underlying queue in which the data will actually be stored; the second, _maxSize, holds the maximum allowable size of the queue. The third variable, _mutex, is the lock object described earlier.

There are also two constructors. The first takes a queue to be used for data storage and a maximum allowable size. This is the constructor that enables us to create a bounded queue. The second constructor only accepts a queue. It then calls the first constructor, passing in the largest possible integer value for the maximum queue size. Although there is still a limit, it is so large that you have effectively created an unbounded queue.

Now it's time to look at how to go about implementing the desired behavior, starting with enqueue(). It may look a little spooky at first, but it's really not that complicated:

```
    public void enqueue(Object value) {
        synchronized (_mutex) {
            while (size() == _maxSize) {
                waitForNotification();
            }
            _queue.enqueue(value);
            _mutex.notifyAll();
        }
    }

    private void waitForNotification() {
        try {
            _mutex.wait();
        } catch (InterruptedException e) {
            // Ignore
        }
    }
```

How It Works

The first thing that enqueue does (and all other methods, for that matter) is ensure that no other threads can access the queue at the same time. In Java, this is achieved by using synchronized to obtain a lock on an object—in this case, our mutex. If another thread already has a lock, the current thread will be blocked until that thread releases its lock. Once obtained, no other threads will be able to access the queue until the current thread falls out of the synchronized block. This enables you to manipulate the underlying queue without worrying about stepping on the actions of another thread, or another thread unexpectedly manipulating the underlying queue.

Having obtained sole access to the queue, the next thing to do is ensure that the bounds are respected. If the queue is already at the maximum allowable size, you need to allow another thread the opportunity to free up some space. This is achieved in our call to the waitForNotification() method. This method calls the mutex's wait() method, effectively putting the thread to sleep. In putting the thread to sleep, you temporarily give up the lock on the queue. The only way this thread can be woken from this sleep is for another thread to call the notifyAll() method on the mutex, at which time enqueue() will regain control and try again.

Eventually, enough space becomes available and the new value is stored in the underlying queue. You then call notifyAll() on the mutex so that any other threads that might have been asleep are woken.

Try It Out Implementing dequeue()

Implementing dequeue() is similar except that, of course, it retrieves from, rather than stores to, the queue:

```
public Object dequeue() throws EmptyQueueException {
    synchronized (_mutex) {
        while (isEmpty()) {
            waitForNotification();
        }
        Object value = _queue.dequeue();
        _mutex.notifyAll();
        return value;
    }
}
```

Just as was done for enqueue(), dequeue() obtains an exclusive lock to ensure that it is the only thread accessing the queue. It then waits until at least one item is available before calling dequeue() on the underlying queue.

How It Works

Again, as you did for enqueue(), once you're done, you call notifyAll(). Because dequeue() retrieves items, you need to notify any threads that may have been blocked while calling enqueue() (such as when the queue reaches its maximum allowable size).

Try It Out Implementing the clear() Method

The clear() method is even simpler:

```
public void clear() {
    synchronized (_mutex) {
        _queue.clear();
        _mutex.notifyAll();
    }
}
```

How It Works

After first obtaining a lock in the usual manner, the underlying queue is cleared and, just as you did for dequeue(), all threads are notified in case some were blocked waiting to store items in a queue that had reached its size limit.

Try It Out — Implementing the size() and isEmpty() Methods

Finally, here is the code for the last two methods, `size()` and `isEmpty()`:

```
    public int size() {
        synchronized (_mutex) {
            return _queue.size();
        }
    }

    public boolean isEmpty() {
        synchronized (_mutex) {
            return _queue.isEmpty();
        }
    }
```

How It Works

Both of these methods simply wrap the underlying queue's equivalent method inside some thread-safe synchronization code. In this case, however, no modification has been made to the underlying queue so there is no need to call `notifyAll()`.

Example: A Call Center Simulator

Now it's time to put our queues to use. This is where you get to take what you've learned so far and use it in a practical—if somewhat simplistic—context. You've already learned how queues can be used in allocating and prioritizing work, so in this section you're going to take one of the example scenarios, a call center, and build a simulator that uses a blocking queue.

The main idea is pretty simple: Develop a system whereby calls are randomly made to a call center and thereby queued, ready to be answered by the next available customer service agent. Figure 4-4 gives you an idea of the main concepts involved.

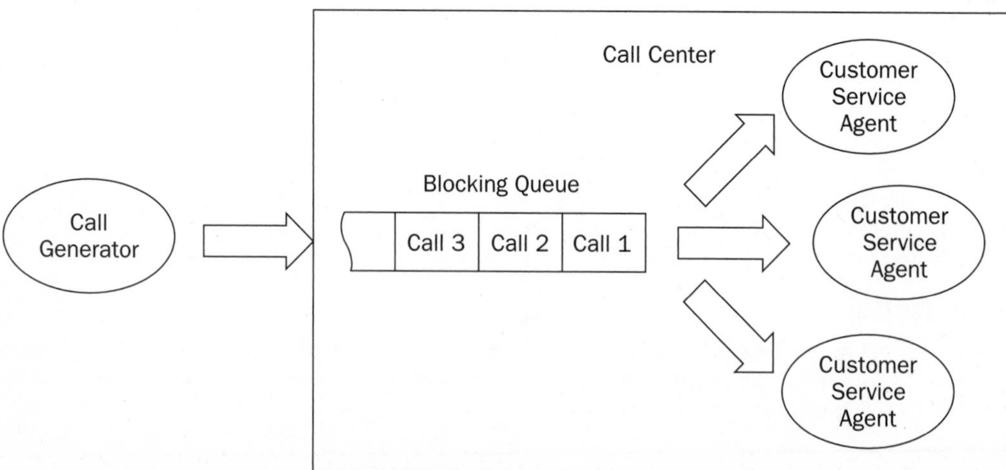

Figure 4-4: High-level design for a call center simulation.

A call generator creates calls that are sent to a call center. The call center then stores them in a blocking queue where they wait to be answered by the next available customer service agent. As each agent completes a call, it returns to the queue and attempts to retrieve another. If there are more calls to be processed, the queue returns immediately with the next one. If, however, the queue is empty, it will block until a new call appears. In this way, a customer service agent need never worry whether there are more calls to be answered; all that logic is handled by the blocking queue.

Notice that the queue, along with the customer service agents, live within the call center. Also notice that there are multiple customer service agents, all working at the same time — just like in the real world. Because of this concurrent execution, each customer service agent needs to run in its own thread. Thankfully, our blocking queue implementation was designed specifically with multi-threading in mind; and because the queue will be the only point of thread contention, in the context of this example, there's no need to worry about synchronizing any other parts of the application.

The simulator will be developed as a stand-alone application that will print log messages to the console as it runs so that you can see what is happening. The program enables you to run simulations under different scenarios based on the values of certain variables. These variables will be specified on the command line as follows:

- Number of customer service agents
- Number of calls
- Maximum call duration
- Maximum call interval

The number of customer service agents enables you to specify the number of threads consuming calls on the queue. The more agents (threads) you have, the faster the calls will be processed. The flip side to this is that depending on the rate of generated calls, the more threads you have, the more agents will be waiting for new calls to arrive if the queue is empty.

The number of calls determines how many calls in total to generate. This is purely a safety precaution to prevent the application from running forever. If you prefer, you can still set it to a very large number and see what happens.

The maximum call duration defines an upper limit on how long each call will take once answered. This enables you to simulate what happens when calls take longer or shorter amounts of time.

The maximum call interval defines an upper limit on how long to wait between generating each call.

The design itself is relatively straightforward — we've tried to keep it as simple as possible — and involves several classes in addition to using the `BlockingQueue` developed earlier. Each class is described fully in the next section.

Now that you have an idea of what we're trying to achieve, it's time to develop the application. Again, for reasons previously explained, we will forgo the usual tests and jump straight into the code. (Remember that tests are available with the downloadable source code, although we felt that an explanation within the text would confuse the issue.)

You'll start by creating a class for each of the concepts depicted in Figure 4-4 and finish with a simple simulator application that can be run from the command line.

So that you can monitor the behavior of a simulation as it runs, each class prints information to the console. When you run the application, you'll see a flood of messages showing you just what is happening inside the simulator. At the end of the section, we've included some example output to give you an idea of what this diagnostic information looks like.

Try It Out Creating the Call Class

The call represents a telephone call within the system. Calls are queued by a call center and subsequently answered by a customer service agent (both of which are discussed a little later):

```
package com.wrox.algorithms.queues;

public class Call {
    private final int _id;
    private final int _duration;
    private final long _startTime;

    public Call(int id, int duration) {
        assert duration >= 0 : "callTime can't be < 0";

        _id = id;
        _duration = duration;
        _startTime = System.currentTimeMillis();
    }

    public String toString() {
        return "Call " + _id;
    }

    ...
}
```

How It Works

Each call is assigned a unique id and a call duration. The id enables you to track the progress of a call through the system. The call duration determines how much time will be spent "answering" a call. Lastly, you record the time at which the call started. This will be used to determine how long each call has been waiting in the queue.

The only method in the call class is `answer()`. This method is used by a customer service agent to, you guessed it, answer the call:

```
    public void answer() {
        System.out.println(this + " answered; waited "
                + (System.currentTimeMillis() - _startTime)
                + " milliseconds");

        try {
            Thread.sleep(_duration);
        } catch (InterruptedException e) {
            // Ignore
        }
    }
```

Start by printing out the fact that the call was answered, along with the total time spent waiting in the queue. The method then goes to sleep for the duration specified when the call was constructed. In this way, the call is responsible for simulating the time taken to complete a call. Think of this as being like a customer who won't hang up until they're ready to do so.

Try It Out — Creating the CustomerService Agent Class

The next class is the `CustomerServiceAgent`—the consumer from Figure 4-1. This class is responsible for pulling calls off a queue and answering them:

```
package com.wrox.algorithms.queues;

public class CustomerServiceAgent implements Runnable {
    // Don't get hung on this just yet; it's described in more detail further on
    public static final Call GO_HOME = new Call(-1, 0);

    private final int _id;
    private final Queue _calls;

    public CustomerServiceAgent(int id, Queue calls) {
        assert calls != null : "calls can't be null";
        _id = id;
        _calls = calls;
    }

    public String toString() {
        return "Agent " + _id;
    }

    ...
}
```

Just like a call, an agent is also assigned a unique id. Again, this helps you identify which agent is doing what. Each agent also holds a reference to the queue from which to retrieve calls.

Notice that `CustomerServiceAgent` implements the `Runnable` interface. This enables each instance to be run in a separate thread, thereby enabling multiple agents to be run concurrently. `Runnable` specifies one method, `run`, that must be implemented; and this is where you'll put the code that pulls calls from the queue and answers them:

```
    public void run() {
        System.out.println(this + " clocked on");

        while (true) {
            System.out.println(this + " waiting");

            Call call = (Call) _calls.dequeue();
            System.out.println(this + " answering " + call);

            if (call == GO_HOME) {
                break;
            }

            call.answer();
```

```
        }

        System.out.println(this + " going home");
    }
```

How It Works

Each time a customer service agent is run, it prints a little message to say that it has started working. It then sits in a loop pulling calls from the queue and answering them. Each time a call is retrieved, a message is printed and the call is answered. Once the call has completed, the agent goes back to the queue for another.

You may have noticed there is no check to determine whether anything actually exists before calling `dequeue()`. You would be forgiven for thinking that because of this, it won't be long before you encounter an `EmptyQueueException`; this is where the blocking queue comes in. Recall that a blocking queue, besides being thread-safe, waits — as opposed to throwing an exception — when the queue is empty.

The other odd thing about this method is the following piece of code:

```
if (call == GO_HOME) {
    break;
}
```

Without this check, an agent would continue looping forever, waiting for more calls to arrive. Imagine what would happen when the call center closes for the day and stops accepting calls. As just discussed, the blocking queue will wait, leaving our poor customer service agent sitting there all night with nothing to do!

This is actually a fairly common problem when dealing with work queues. Fortunately, there is a very common solution as well. The idea is to create a special value that is understood to mean "stop processing." This example defined a constant, `GO_HOME`, right at the start of the class definition. Anytime this call appears on the queue, the customer service agent knows it's time to finish for the day.

Try It Out Creating the CallCenter Class

Now that you have your calls and customer service agents, you can finally create the call center. This class is responsible for managing — starting and stopping — the agents, and for placing calls on to a queue for the agents to process:

```
package com.wrox.algorithms.queues;

import com.wrox.algorithms.iteration.Iterator;
import com.wrox.algorithms.lists.ArrayList;
import com.wrox.algorithms.lists.List;

public class CallCenter {
    private final Queue _calls = new BlockingQueue(new ListFifoQueue());

    private final List _threads;
    private final int _numberOfAgents;

    public CallCenter(int numberOfAgents) {
```

```
        _threads = new ArrayList(numberOfAgents);
        _numberOfAgents = numberOfAgents;
    }

    ...
}
```

Before you can process calls, you must open the call center—just like in the real world. For this, you have the aptly named method `open()`:

```
    public void open() {
        assert _threads.isEmpty() : "Already open";

        System.out.println("Call center opening");

        for (int i = 0; i < _numberOfAgents; ++i) {
            Thread thread =
                        new Thread(new CustomerServiceAgent(i, _calls));

            thread.start();
            _threads.add(thread);
        }

        System.out.println("Call center open");
    }
```

Once a call center is open, it can begin accepting calls:

```
    public void accept(Call call) {
        assert !_threads.isEmpty() : "Not open";

        _calls.enqueue(call);

        System.out.println(call + " queued");
    }
```

Eventually, you need to close the call center and send all the customer service agents home:

```
    public void close() {
        assert !_threads.isEmpty() : "Already closed";

        System.out.println("Call center closing");

        for (int i = 0; i < _numberOfAgents; ++i) {
            accept(CustomerServiceAgent.GO_HOME);
        }


        Iterator i = _threads.iterator();
        for (i.first(); !i.isDone(); i.next()) {
            waitForTermination((Thread) i.current());
```

```
        }

        _threads.clear();

        System.out.println("Call center closed");
    }

    private void waitForTermination(Thread thread) {
        try {
            thread.join();
        } catch (InterruptedException e) {
            // Ignore
        }
    }
```

How It Works

The first thing `CallCenter` does is create a queue — more specifically, an instance of a `BlockingQueue`. This enables us to happily run multiple customer service agents, each in its own thread, all accessing the same queue. Note that because you are starting multiple threads, it must also stop them all as well. For this reason, you maintain a list of currently running threads. Lastly, you store the number of agents you will be starting.

The `open()` method is responsible for starting as many agents as were specified at construction. Each `CustomerServiceAgent` is constructed with an id — here you've just used the value of the iteration variable — and the call queue. Once created, it is started in its own thread and added to the list.

Each call, when you get around to placing it on the queue, waits to be answered by the "next available operator," which is not to say that your call isn't important to us, just that you won't be able to answer all the calls straightaway.

To send the agents home, the first thing you do is place a special call on the queue — one to tell all the customer service agents to finish for the day. For each agent you have running, place the special `GO_HOME` call onto the queue. Simply telling the agents to go home is not enough, however, as there may still be other calls waiting in the queue; you're a friendly sort of call center and you don't just hang up on your customers. After placing the `GO_HOME` call, you still need to wait for them to finish before turning off the lights and locking the doors.

The method `waitForTermination()` uses `Thread.join()` to effectively sleep until the thread finishes execution.

You're almost done now. Only two classes to go.

Try It Out — Creating the CallGenerator Class

A call generator, as the name suggests, is responsible for the actual generation of phone calls:

```
package com.wrox.algorithms.queues;

public class CallGenerator {
    private final CallCenter _callCenter;
    private final int _numberOfCalls;
```

```
    private final int _maxCallDuration;
    private final int _maxCallInterval;

    public CallGenerator(CallCenter callCenter, int numberOfCalls,
                         int maxCallDuration, int maxCallInterval) {
        assert callCenter != null : "callCenter can't be null";
        assert numberOfCalls > 0 : "numberOfCalls can't be < 1";
        assert maxCallDuration > 0 : "maxCallDuration can't be < 1";
        assert maxCallInterval > 0 : "maxCallInterval can't be < 1";

        _callCenter = callCenter;
        _numberOfCalls = numberOfCalls;
        _maxCallDuration = maxCallDuration;
        _maxCallInterval = maxCallInterval;
    }

    ...
}
```

Besides the constructor, there is only one other public method, which, as you might imagine, actually performs the call generation:

```
    public void generateCalls() {
        for (int i = 0; i < _numberOfCalls; ++i) {
            sleep();
            _callCenter.accept(
                    new Call(i, (int) (Math.random() * _maxCallDuration)));
        }
    }

    private void sleep() {
        try {
            Thread.sleep((int) (Math.random() * _maxCallInterval));
        } catch (InterruptedException e) {
            // Ignore
        }
    }
```

How It Works

The method `generateCalls()` sits in a loop and generates as many calls as configured. Each call is generated with a random duration before being sent to the call center for processing. The method then waits for a random interval between calls — again, all specified at construction time.

Try It Out — Creating the CallCenterSimulator Class

The last class is the call center simulator itself. This is a small application that can be run from the command line. It ties together a call center and a call generator. Most of the real simulation is performed by the classes already discussed. The `CallCenterSimulator` class is concerned primarily with reading and parsing command-line arguments:

```
package com.wrox.algorithms.queues;

public final class CallCenterSimulator {
```

```
    private static final int NUMBER_OF_ARGS = 4;
    private static final int NUMBER_OF_AGENTS_ARG = 0;
    private static final int NUMBER_OF_CALLS_ARG = 1;
    private static final int MAX_CALL_DURATION_ARG = 2;
    private static final int MAX_CALL_INTERVAL_ARG = 3;

    private CallCenterSimulator() {
    }

    public static void main(String[] args) {
        assert args != null : "args can't be null";

        if (args.length != NUMBER_OF_ARGS) {
            System.out.println("Usage: CallGenerator <numberOfAgents>"
                               + " <numberOfCalls> <maxCallDuration>"
                               + " <maxCallInterval>");
            System.exit(-1);
        }

        CallCenter callCenter =
            new CallCenter(Integer.parseInt(args[NUMBER_OF_AGENTS_ARG]));

        CallGenerator generator =
            new CallGenerator(callCenter,
                              Integer.parseInt(args[NUMBER_OF_CALLS_ARG]),
                              Integer.parseInt(args[MAX_CALL_DURATION_ARG]),
                              Integer.parseInt(args[MAX_CALL_INTERVAL_ARG]));

        callCenter.open();
        try {
            callGenerator.generateCalls();
        } finally {
            callCenter.close();
        }
    }
}
```

How It Works

The `main()` method is the entry point to the application and will be called by the Java interpreter, passing in an array of command-line arguments. These are then checked to ensure that all the required parameters have been provided:

- The number of agents to use
- The number of calls to generate
- The maximum call duration
- The maximum time to wait between generated calls

If parameters are missing, the application prints a message to this effect and terminates immediately. If all of the necessary parameters are there, the application constructs a call center and call generator. The call center is then opened, calls are generated, and finally the call center is closed to ensure that customer service agents are stopped correctly.

Running the Application

Before compiling and running the simulator, let's summarize the application you've just created: A `CallGenerator` creates `Calls` with a random duration. These calls are accepted by a `CallCenter` that places them onto a `BlockingQueue`. One or more `CustomerServiceAgents` then answer the calls until they are told to `GO_HOME`. All these are then tied together by a command-line application, `CallCenterSimulator`.

You ran the call center simulator with three customer service agents answering 200 calls. The maximum call duration was set at 1 second (1,000 milliseconds) and the maximum time to wait between generating calls was 100 milliseconds. Here is the output (with a large chunk removed for the sake of space):

```
Call center opening
Agent 0 clocked on
Agent 0 waiting
Agent 1 clocked on
Agent 1 waiting
Agent 2 clocked on
Agent 2 waiting
Call center open
Agent 0 answering Call 0
Call 0 answered; waited 1 milliseconds
Call 0 queued
Agent 1 answering Call 1
Call 1 answered; waited 1 milliseconds
Call 1 queued
Agent 2 answering Call 2
Call 2 answered; waited 1 milliseconds
Call 2 queued
Call 3 queued
Call 4 queued
Call 5 queued
Call 6 queued
Call 7 queued
Agent 2 waiting
Agent 2 answering Call 3
Call 3 answered; waited 203 milliseconds
Call 8 queued
Call 9 queued
Call 10 queued
Call 11 queued
Agent 1 waiting
Agent 1 answering Call 4
Call 4 answered; waited 388 milliseconds
...
Call 195 answered; waited 22320 milliseconds
Agent 1 waiting
Agent 1 answering Call 196
Call 196 answered; waited 22561 milliseconds
Agent 0 waiting
Agent 0 answering Call 197
Call 197 answered; waited 22510 milliseconds
Agent 0 waiting
Agent 0 answering Call 198
```

```
Call 198 answered; waited 22634 milliseconds
Agent 1 waiting
Agent 1 answering Call 199
Call 199 answered; waited 22685 milliseconds
Agent 2 waiting
Agent 2 answering Call -1
Agent 2 going home
Agent 0 waiting
Agent 0 answering Call -1
Agent 0 going home
Agent 1 waiting
Agent 1 answering Call -1
Agent 1 going home
Call center closed
```

This only shows the first and last five calls being answered, but you can still see the program in action. You can observe the call center opening, the three agents signing on, and then the calls being generated and waiting in the queue before being answered by the next available agent. Notice how the wait time starts at much less than a second, but by the time the last call is answered it's up to around 20 seconds (20,000 milliseconds)! Try playing with the input variables such as number of agents, time between calls, and so on, to see how that affects the results.

Although we have tried to keep the code relatively simple, it is hoped that you have an idea of how you might go about using queues. You might like to try gathering more statistics, such as average wait time for a call or for an agent, or perhaps even extending the code to allow different types of call generators to run against the same call center. In this way, you could simulate different types of calls, peak load times, and so on.

Summary

In this chapter, you learned the following key points about queues and their operation:

- Queues are similar to lists with a simpler interface and a defined order of retrieval.
- Queues can be optionally bounded such that limits are placed on the number of items in a queue at any one time.
- A linked list is an ideal data structure upon which to build a FIFO queue.
- You can implement a thread-safe wrapper that works with any queue implementation.
- You can implement a bounded queue — one with a maximum size limit.

Exercises

1. Implement a thread-safe queue that performs no waiting. Sometimes all you need is a queue that will work in a multi-threaded environment without the blocking.
2. Implement a queue that retrieves values in random order. This could be used for dealing cards from a deck or any other random selection process.

Stacks

Now that you are familiar with lists and queues, it's time to move on to describing stacks. You are probably familiar with some real-world examples of stacks: Plates are usually stacked — you place the first one on the shelf and add to the top. If you need a plate, you remove the top one first. The newspapers at your local convenience store are stacked, as are the books on your desk that you've been meaning to read.

Stacks can also be used to implement a simple Most-Recently-Used (MRU) cache and are often used for parsing programming languages.

This "everything stacks" chapter will familiarize you with the following topics:

- What stacks are
- What stacks look like
- How you use stacks
- How stacks are implemented

We start by introducing the basic operations of a stack. We then cover the tests required to validate the correctness of any stack implementation. Finally, you'll look at the most common form of stack, based on a list.

Stacks

A *stack* is like a list with access restricted to one end. Figure 5-1 shows a graphical representation of a stack.

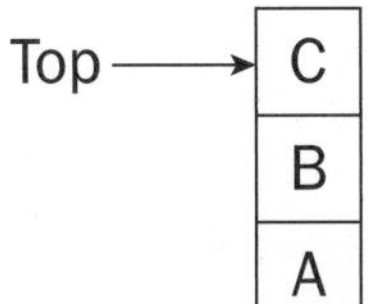

Figure 5-1: A stack is pictured vertically.

You'll notice that whereas lists and queues are usually thought of as running from left to right, stacks are pictured vertically—hence, the term "top" to refer to the first and only directly accessible element of a stack. A stack both inserts (pushes) and deletes (pops) from the top.

A stack is also known as a last-in-first-out (LIFO) queue, as it guarantees that the next element removed will be the one that has been on the stack for the least amount of time.

Table 5-1 describes the operations provided by a stack.

Table 5-1: Operations on a Stack

Operation	Description
`push`	Adds a value to the top of the stack. The size of the stack will increase by one.
`pop`	Deletes and returns the value at the top of the stack. The size of the stack will decrease by one. Throws `EmptyStackException` when there are no more elements on the stack.
`size`	Obtains the number of elements in the stack.
`peek`	Returns but does not delete the value at the top of the stack. Throws `EmptyStackException` when there are no elements on the stack.
`isEmpty`	Determines whether a stack is empty. Returns `true` if the stack is empty (`size() == 0`); otherwise, returns `false`.
`clear`	Deletes all elements from a stack. The size of the stack is reset to zero.

Pushing a value on a stack adds it to the top. Figure 5-2 shows what happens when the value `D` is pushed onto the stack shown in Figure 5-1.

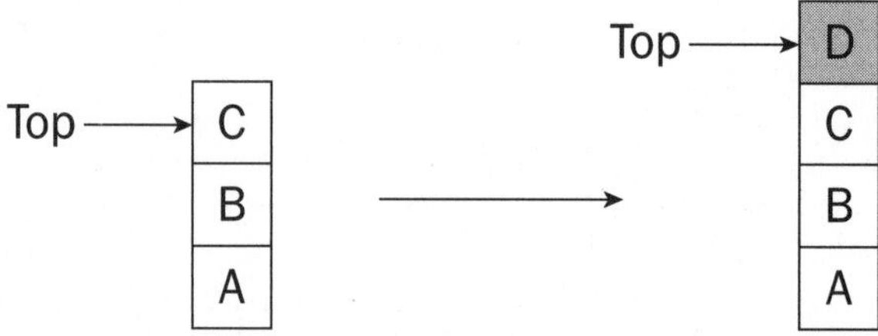

Figure 5-2: Pushing a value adds it to the top of the stack.

Popping a value from a stack removes it from the top. Figure 5-3 shows what happens when a value is popped from the stack shown in Figure 5-1.

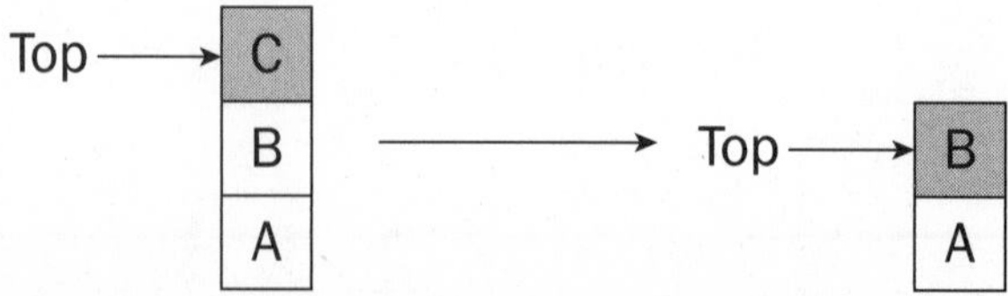

Figure 5-3: Popping a value removes it from the top.

The last three operations—`peek()`, `isEmpty()`, and `clear()`—are technically provided for convenience, as they can all be implemented on top of the first three.

Now take the operation definitions and convert these into a combination of Java interfaces and tests:

```
package com.wrox.algorithms.stacks;

import com.wrox.algorithms.queues.Queue;

public interface Stack extends Queue {
    public void push(Object value);
    public Object pop() throws EmptyStackException;
    public Object peek() throws EmptyStackException;
    public void clear();
    public int size();
    public boolean isEmpty();
}
```

The Java interface is quite simple because of the relatively small number of operations. The two methods `pop()` and `peek()` both declare that they throw an `EmptyStackException` anytime an attempt is made to access a stack that has no elements, so you also need to define this exception class as well:

```
package com.wrox.algorithms.stacks;

public class EmptyStackException extends RuntimeException {
}
```

> **Notice that, like the `EmptyQueueException` from Chapter 4, it has been defined as extending `RuntimeException`. This is because we consider it to be indicative of a programming error—an error in the application logic. There is no legitimate reason that one of these should ever occur during the normal course of application execution, and as such you don't want to force the developer to have to needlessly catch them.**

Lastly, note that the `Stack` interface extends the `Queue` interface. That's because, as previously discussed, a stack is really a LIFO queue (and you'd like it to be plug-compatible as such), with `enqueue()` and `dequeue()` acting as synonyms for `push()` and `pop()`, respectively.

The Tests

Now we can proceed to create the test cases necessary to ensure the correct operation of a stack. You will define separate test cases for each of the `push()`, `pop()`, `peek()`, and `clear()` methods. The `size()` and `isEmpty()` methods have no explicit tests of their own because they are tested as part of the others just mentioned.

Although we will only describe one stack implementation in this chapter, it is entirely possible to create your own variations. For that reason, you will create a generic test class that can be extended by concrete test classes specific to each implementation.

Try It Out — Creating a Generic Test Class

```
package com.wrox.algorithms.stacks;

import junit.framework.TestCase;

public abstract class AbstractStackTestCase extends TestCase {
    protected static final String VALUE_A = "A";
    protected static final String VALUE_B = "B";
    protected static final String VALUE_C = "C";

    protected abstract Stack createStack();

    ...
}
```

How It Works

The stack interface is very simple, as reflected in the small number of test cases. Still, it is important not to become complacent and presume that due to the simplicity, no testing is required.

Try It Out — Using the push() and pop() Methods

Besides `peek()`, which you will test next, the only way of accessing a stack is via the `push()` and `pop()` methods. It is, therefore, all but impossible to test one without the other:

```
    public void testPushAndPop() {
        Stack stack = createStack();

        stack.push(VALUE_B);
        stack.push(VALUE_A);
        stack.push(VALUE_C);

        assertEquals(3, stack.size());
        assertFalse(stack.isEmpty());

        assertSame(VALUE_C, stack.pop());
        assertEquals(2, stack.size());
        assertFalse(stack.isEmpty());

        assertSame(VALUE_A, stack.pop());
        assertEquals(1, stack.size());
        assertFalse(stack.isEmpty());

        assertSame(VALUE_B, stack.pop());
        assertEquals(0, stack.size());
        assertTrue(stack.isEmpty());
    }
```

You also need to ensure that any attempt to call `pop()` on an empty list results in an appropriate exception being thrown:

```
public void testCantPopFromAnEmptyStack() {
    Stack stack = createStack();

    assertEquals(0, stack.size());
    assertTrue(stack.isEmpty());

    try {
        stack.pop();
        fail();
    } catch (EmptyStackException e) {
        // expected
    }
}
```

How It Works

This test pushes the three values `B`, `A`, and `C` onto the stack and then pops them off one at a time, ensuring that they are removed in the correct order: `C`; then `A`; and finally `B`.

After first ensuring the stack is empty, you attempt to pop a value. If the call to `pop()` is successful, you fail the test because this is incorrect behavior—you shouldn't be able to pop from an empty stack. If instead an `EmptyStackException` is thrown, the stack is working as expected.

Try It Out Testing the peek() Method

In addition to pushing and popping values on and off the stack, the `peek()` method gives us a "sneak preview" of the topmost element, hence the name:

```
public void testPeek() {
    Stack stack = createStack();

    stack.push(VALUE_C);
    stack.push(VALUE_A);
    assertEquals(2, stack.size());

    assertSame(VALUE_A, stack.peek());
    assertEquals(2, stack.size());
}
```

To test peek, you push two values—`C` and then `A`—and ensure that not only does `peek()` return the last value pushed—in this case, an `A`—but also that nothing has been removed from the stack as a consequence:

```
public void testCantPeekIntoAnEmptyStack() {
    Stack stack = createStack();

    assertEquals(0, stack.size());
    assertTrue(stack.isEmpty());

    try {
        stack.peek();
        fail();
```

```
        } catch (EmptyStackException e) {
            // expected
        }
    }
```

Last but not least, you confirm that `clear()` performs as expected and removes all elements from the stack:

```
    public void testClear() {
        Stack stack = createStack();

        stack.push(VALUE_A);
        stack.push(VALUE_B);
        stack.push(VALUE_C);

        assertFalse(stack.isEmpty());
        assertEquals(3, stack.size());

        stack.clear();

        assertTrue(stack.isEmpty());
        assertEquals(0, stack.size());

        try {
            stack.pop();
            fail();
        } catch (EmptyStackException e) {
            // expected
        }
    }
}
```

How It Works

After initially filling the stack with some values, the stack is then cleared, after which the size is checked and an attempt is made to pop a value, which should fail: Popping a value from an empty stack should throw an `EmptyStackException`.

Implementation

Although you could try to implement a stack from first principles, there is really no need to. Instead, in the same way you did during the chapter on queues, you can take advantage of the fact that a list provides you with everything you need to implement a stack.

You'll see that it is trivial to implement a stack based on the methods already provided by a list. This being the case, anything you could implement with a stack could be done with a list instead. However, by using a specific construct for the purpose, you enforce a clean separation between the concept of a list and that of a stack. This separation of concerns is critically important when designing software.

Having chosen to use a list to implement the stack, you now need to decide how best this can be achieved. You have a few options here: Enhance an existing list implementation, extend an existing list implementation, or create a new class altogether.

Each of these solutions has pros and cons. Enhancing or extending an existing implementation would be trivial—you would simply have the class implement the `Stack` in addition to the `List` interface, and add the methods necessary to satisfy the requirements of a stack. However, this approach has one major drawback: Given that there are at least two known, and no doubt countless unknown, list implementations, you would need to repeat the process for each different type of list you wished to use. Clearly, this is not a particularly elegant solution.

Your other option, and the one discussed here, is to write an entirely new class, `ListStack`, that uses *composition*. That is, your new class will hold and wrap an instance of a list. This has a number of advantages, not the least of which is that, if implemented wisely, your stack should be capable of operating on top of any type of list you choose, with no code changes.

At this point in the book, it should be clear to you how important we deem tests to be, so as always, we need a concrete test class:

```
package com.wrox.algorithms.stacks;

public class ListStackTest extends AbstractStackTestCase {
    protected Stack createStack() {
        return new ListStack();
    }
}
```

Try It Out Implementing the ListStack Class

Next, you define the `ListStack` class itself, which, among other things, must implement the `Stack` interface defined earlier:

```
package com.wrox.algorithms.stacks;

import com.wrox.algorithms.lists.ArrayList;
import com.wrox.algorithms.lists.List;

public class ListStack implements Stack {
    private final List _list = new LinkedList();

    ...
}
```

Pushing a value onto the stack is as easy as adding to the end of the list:

```
    public void push(Object value) {
        _list.add(value);
    }

    public void enqueue(Object value) {
        push(value);
    }
```

How It Works

The only thing this class needs to hold is a list to use as the underlying data structure. A linked list has been used because it is very efficient at adding and removing items from the ends—something a stack does. Having said this, you could easily substitute an array list without much worry. The main thing to understand is that rather than extend a particular list implementation, you've instead used composition to "wrap" a list. This prevents the list methods from "leaking" out, which may cause users of your `ListStack` class to believe that they can use the methods on the list interface as well as those defined for the stack.

As you can see, `push()` just adds the value to the underlying list, while `enqueue()` simply delegates to `push()`.

Notice also that you haven't checked for a `null` value here because you can delegate that responsibility to the underlying list implementation.

Try It Out   Popping a Value from the Stack

Popping a value from the stack is almost as easy. You just need to remove the last element from the underlying list:

```
public Object pop() throws EmptyStackException {
    if (isEmpty()) {
        throw new EmptyStackException();
    }
    return _list.delete(list.size() - 1);
}

public Object dequeue() throws EmptyQueueException {
    try {
        return pop();
    } catch (EmptyStackException e) {
        throw new EmptyQueueException();
    }
}
```

The performance of `push()` and `pop()` as implemented here relies entirely on the performance of the underlying list's `add()` and `delete()` methods, respectively.

The `peek()` method allows access to the value at the top of the stack without removing it:

```
public Object peek() throws EmptyStackException {
    Object result = pop();
    push(result);
    return result;
}
```

To complete the class, you can delegate the remaining methods to the underlying list, as the expected behavior is identical:

```
public void clear() {
    _list.clear();
}

public int size() {
    return _list.size();
```

```
    }

    public boolean isEmpty() {
        return _list.isEmpty();
    }
```

How It Works

This time you are being a little more cautious. Without the defensive check, the list's `delete()` method might well throw an `IndexOutOfBoundsException`—not what the caller would have expected. Instead, you explicitly check the size of the stack and throw `EmptyStackException` as specified in the `Stack` interface, before removing and returning the last element in the underlying list.

Also notice that even though `dequeue()` can delegate most of its behavior to `pop()`, it still needs to convert an `EmptyStackException` into an `EmptyQueueException`.

Then, using the `peek()` method, you call `pop()` to retrieve the next item, record its value, and push it back on again before returning the value to the caller. In this way, you have effectively returned the value at the top of the stack without actually removing it.

You should now be able to compile and run the tests against the completed, list-based stack. As satisfying as this no doubt is, once all your tests are passing, you'll probably want to use your stack for something a bit more constructive.

Example: Implementing Undo/Redo

It is actually surprisingly difficult to find an example of using a stack that is not overly academic in nature. The usual examples involve solving the Towers of Hanoi puzzle, implementing a Reverse-Polish-Notation (RPN) calculator, reversing a list of values, and so on, none of which are particularly useful or relate particularly well to the applications with which you will likely be involved.

Some real-world examples that you are more likely to encounter include XML processing, screen flow management (such as the back and forward buttons in your browser), and undo/redo. It is this last item, undo, that is used in the example.

Imagine an application that holds a list—maybe a shopping list, a list of e-mail messages, or whatever. The user interface, which we will not detail here, displays this list and enables users to add, and possibly remove, items.

Now let's say that you wish to allow users to undo their actions. Each time the user performs an action, you would need to record some information about the state of the list (see Memento [Gamma, 1995]) that will allow us to undo the action sometime in the future. This state information could be pushed onto a stack. When the user requests to undo an action, you could then pop the information off the top of the stack and use it to restore the list to the state it was in just prior to the action being performed.

The most obvious way to implement this would be to store a copy of the list before each action is performed. While this works, it's not really an ideal solution. For one thing, you would need to make an entire copy of the list each time. Instead, you can take advantage of the fact that insert is the inverse of delete—if you insert an element at position 5, you can "undo" this by simply deleting the value at position 5. Conversely, if you delete an element from position 3, inserting the original value back into position 3 will have the effect of "undoing" the deletion.

Although a complete discussion is beyond the scope of this book, the example presented could easily be extended to support a single undo stack across multiple lists, or any data structure for that matter, by encapsulating the undo functionality in external classes.

Testing Undo/Redo

To demonstrate what we mean and at the same time build reliable production code, why not use some tests? Take the requirements described in the preceding section and turn them into test cases.

Try It Out — Creating and Running the Test Class

Because you want your undoable list to behave pretty much like any other list, you need to test a lot of functionality. Thankfully, though, if you implement the `List` interface, you can extend `AbstractListTestCase` and get all those predefined tests for free!

```
package com.wrox.algorithms.stacks;

import com.wrox.algorithms.lists.AbstractListTestCase;
import com.wrox.algorithms.lists.ArrayList;
import com.wrox.algorithms.lists.List;

public class UndoableListTest extends AbstractListTestCase {
    protected List createList() {
        return new UndoableList(new ArrayList());
    }

    ...
}
```

After a value is inserted into the list, you should be able to call `undo()` to restore the list to its original state:

```
    public void testUndoInsert() {
        UndoableList list = new UndoableList(new ArrayList());

        assertFalse(list.canUndo());

        list.insert(0, VALUE_A);
        assertTrue(list.canUndo());

        list.undo();
        assertEquals(0, list.size());
        assertFalse(list.canUndo());
    }

    public void testUndoAdd() {
```

```
        UndoableList list = new UndoableList(new ArrayList());

        assertFalse(list.canUndo());

        list.add(VALUE_A);
        assertTrue(list.canUndo());

        list.undo();
        assertEquals(0, list.size());
        assertFalse(list.canUndo());
    }
```

Neither of the two methods `undo` *and* `canUndo` *are part of the* `List` *interface. They are methods that you will add to the* `UndoableList` *class later.*

When you call `delete()` to remove a value, you should be able to call `undo()` to have the value restored to its original position:

```
    public void testUndoDeleteByPosition() {
        UndoableList list = new UndoableList(
            new ArrayList(new Object[] {VALUE_A, VALUE_B}));

        assertFalse(list.canUndo());

        assertSame(VALUE_B, list.delete(1));
        assertTrue(list.canUndo());

        list.undo();
        assertEquals(2, list.size());
        assertSame(VALUE_A, list.get(0));
        assertSame(VALUE_B, list.get(1));
        assertFalse(list.canUndo());
    }

    public void testUndoDeleteByValue() {
        UndoableList list = new UndoableList(
            new ArrayList(new Object[] {VALUE_A, VALUE_B}));

        assertFalse(list.canUndo());

        assertTrue(list.delete(VALUE_B));
        assertTrue(list.canUndo());

        list.undo();
        assertEquals(2, list.size());
        assertSame(VALUE_A, list.get(0));
        assertSame(VALUE_B, list.get(1));
        assertFalse(list.canUndo());
    }
```

Although calling `set()` doesn't change the size of a list, it does modify the contents. Therefore, you can expect that after changing the value of an element, a call to `undo()` should cause the same element to revert to its previous value:

```
public void testUndoSet() {
    UndoableList list = new UndoableList(new ArrayList(new Object[]
                                                            {VALUE_A}));

    assertFalse(list.canUndo());

    assertSame(VALUE_A, list.set(0, VALUE_B));
    assertTrue(list.canUndo());

    list.undo();
    assertEquals(1, list.size());
    assertSame(VALUE_A, list.get(0));
    assertFalse(list.canUndo());
}
```

For the purposes of this example, we have chosen to have `clear()` differ slightly from the other methods shown so far in that it won't record state for a subsequent undo. This decision was made purely on the grounds of simplicity. There is no reason you couldn't implement undo functionality for `clear()` yourself, possibly by taking an entire copy of the list prior to it being cleared:

```
public void testClearResetsUndoStack() {
    UndoableList list = new UndoableList(new ArrayList());

    assertFalse(list.canUndo());

    list.add(VALUE_A);
    assertTrue(list.canUndo());

    list.clear();
    assertFalse(list.canUndo());
}
```

So far, you've only tested individual actions and their corresponding undo behavior. If you only wanted to undo one level, you wouldn't need a stack. In fact, you want to be able to roll back any number of actions in the appropriate order. You should at least have a test to demonstrate that this actually works:

```
public void testUndoMultiple() {
    UndoableList list = new UndoableList(new ArrayList());

    assertFalse(list.canUndo());

    list.add(VALUE_A);
    list.add(VALUE_B);

    list.undo();
    assertEquals(1, list.size());
    assertSame(VALUE_A, list.get(0));
```

```
        assertTrue(list.canUndo());

        list.delete(0);

        list.undo();
        assertEquals(1, list.size());
        assertSame(VALUE_A, list.get(0));
        assertTrue(list.canUndo());

        list.undo();
        assertEquals(0, list.size());
        assertFalse(list.canUndo());
    }
```

How It Works

The tests first ensure that an empty list starts off with nothing to undo. A single value is then inserted in or added to the list. Because the test class itself extends `AbstractListTestCase`, you can be confident that the actual behavior of inserting a value into the list works. Therefore, all you need to ensure next is that calling undo removes the inserted value.

In both the undo and delete cases, the tests are relatively simple, as you need not concern yourself with the behavior of the actual `delete()` method — this has been tested by the methods in the superclass. The list is first initialized with some predefined values. Then, delete a value and, after calling `undo()`, ensure that it has reappeared in the expected location.

The final test starts off with an empty list and variously adds and removes values, invoking `undo()` along the way. In particular, you will see that the very first add is never undone until right at the end of the test, even though two other actions are undone in the meantime. This proves that the stack-based undo is working as expected.

Tests in place, it's time to actually implement the `UndoableList` class, as shown in the following Try It Out.

Try It Out Implementing the Undo Action with the UndoableList Class

Now that you've enshrined the requirements in code, implementing the undoable list is relatively straightforward. You will start by describing the `UndoableList` class itself, and then each of the list methods in turn. Take note how the design enables us to add the functionality with minimal coding effort. Given the chosen implementation, you need your undoable list to not only wrap a reference to the real, underlying list, but also to actually implement the `List` interface as well (see Decorator [Gamma, 1995]):

```
package com.wrox.algorithms.stacks;

import com.wrox.algorithms.iteration.Iterator;
import com.wrox.algorithms.lists.List;

public class UndoableList implements List {
    private final Stack _undoStack = new ListStack();
    private final List _list;

    public UndoableList(List list) {
        assert list != null : "list can't be null";
```

```
        _list = list;
    }

    private static interface UndoAction {
        public void execute();
    }

    ...
}
```

To get going, you need to start capturing state information each time a value is inserted in or added to the list by intercepting calls to `insert()`:

```
    private final class UndoInsertAction implements Action {
        private final int _index;

        public UndoInsertAction(int index) {
            _index = index;
        }

        public void execute() {
            _list.delete(_index);
        }
    }

    public void insert(int index, Object value) throws IndexOutOfBoundsException {
        _list.insert(index, value);
        _undoStack.push(new UndoDeleteAction(index));
    }

    public void add(Object value) {
        insert(size(), value);
    }
```

Next you need to intercept calls to `delete()` so that you can restore the deleted value at some later stage:

```
    private final class UndoDeleteAction implements Action {
        private final int _index;
        private final Object _value;

        public UndoDeleteAction(int index, Object value) {
            _index = index;
            _value = value;
        }

        public void execute() {
            _list.insert(_index, _value);
        }
    }

    public Object delete(int index) throws IndexOutOfBoundsException {
        Object value = _list.delete(index);
        _undoStack.push(new UndoInsertAction(index, value));
        return value;
```

```
    }

    public boolean delete(Object value) {
        int index = indexOf(value);
        if (index == -1) {
            return false;
        }

        delete(index);
        return true;
    }
```

The method first calls `indexOf()` to determine the position of the value within the list. Then, if the value isn't found, `false` is returned; otherwise, the `delete()` method that takes an index is called, which will record the necessary state to perform an undo operation later. Calling `set()` also modifies the state of the list, so you need a way to restore its effect as well:

```
    private final class UndoSetAction implements Action {
        private final int _index;
        private final Object _value;

        public UndoSetAction(int index, Object value) {
            _index = index;
            _value = value;
        }

        public void execute() {
            _list.set(_index, _value);
        }
    }

    public Object set(int index, Object value) throws IndexOutOfBoundsException {
        Object originalValue = _list.set(index, value);
        _undoStack.push(new UndoSetAction(index, originalValue));
        return originalValue;
    }
```

Now that you have defined the necessary infrastructure to record the undo state, you can write the code for the `undo()` method:

```
    public void undo() throws EmptyStackException {
        ((Action) _undoStack.pop()).execute();
    }
```

As a convenience, you might also enable callers to determine whether there are any more actions to undo. This would be handy, for example, if you wanted to enable/disable an undo button in a user interface:

```
    public boolean canUndo() {
        return !_undoStack.isEmpty();
    }
```

To determine whether there are any more actions to undo, you can just query the undo stack: If it's empty, then there is no more to undo and vice-versa.

Even though `clear()` modifies the list, it was decided that for this example, no undo state would be recorded and the list would be reset:

```
public void clear() {
    _list.clear();
    _undoStack.clear();
}
```

Besides clearing the underlying list, the undo stack is also cleared, thereby resetting the entire structure.

Completing the interface requirements for this class is somewhat of a formality:

```
public Object get(int index) throws IndexOutOfBoundsException {
    return _list.get(index);
}

public int indexOf(Object value) {
    return _list.indexOf(value);
}

public Iterator iterator() {
    return _list.iterator();
}

public boolean contains(Object value) {
    return _list.contains(value);
}

public int size() {
    return _list.size();
}

public boolean isEmpty() {
    return _list.isEmpty();
}

public String toString() {
    return _list.toString();
}

public boolean equals(Object object) {
    return _list.equals(object);
}
```

None of the remaining methods make any modifications to the state of the list, so it is sufficient that they simply delegate to the underlying instance.

How It Works

Aside from the underlying list, the class also holds the undo stack, which will hold instances of the inner interface `UndoAction` (also shown), which defines a single method, `execute()`, that will eventually be called to perform most of the work involved in implementing the undo functionality.

> *The* `UndoAction` *class is an example of the command pattern [Gamma, 1995]. In this case, the command pattern makes it simple to encapsulate all the undo behavior so that the action itself is responsible for performing whatever is needed to get the job done. An effective but rather less elegant—and much less extensible—alternative would be to use a* `switch` *statement, and route according to some constant defined for each action.*

The action `UndoDeleteAction` class implements the `UndoAction` interface and, of course, more important, the `execute()` method. To undo an insert is to delete, so when `execute()` is called, it uses the recorded position to delete a value from the underlying list.

The `insert()` method calls `insert()` on the underlying list and then pushes an undo action. The `add()` method can then call `insert()`. You could have created a special action to delete from the end of the list, but calling `insert()`, passing in the position, has exactly the same effect and requires much less code.

The `UndoDeleteAction` class implements the `UndoAction` interface and holds the recorded position and value for later use. To undo a deletion is to insert, so when `execute()` is called, the action reinserts the value into the underlying list.

The first `delete()` calls `delete()` on the underlying list and retrieves the deleted value before pushing an insert action and returning to the caller. Deleting by value is a little trickier. Because you have no way of knowing where in the list the value was deleted, you must re-implement delete by value based on delete by position—not a particularly efficient solution, but your only option.

A call to `set()` on the underlying list always returns the original value contained at the specified position, so in this case, the `UndoSetAction's execute()` method stores the old value, together with the position in order to perform the undo. Notice again that, as was the case for the previous two undo actions, the `execute()` method makes calls on the underlying list in order to prevent the undo from pushing additional undo action onto the stack.

As you can see, there's not a lot of code to actually write for the actual `undo()` method. All the hard work has already been done by each of the `UndoAction` classes, so making it all come together is a simple matter of popping the next action (if any) off the stack and calling `execute()`.

And there you have it. You now have a fully tested and implemented list that supports undo functionality.

Summary

Although conceptually very simple, stacks underpin the operation of most computers. In this chapter you've learned the following:

- Most CPUs, and therefore most programming languages, including Java, are stack-based.
- Stacks always add and remove from the top — thus, they are often referred to as FIFO queues.
- Stacks can easily be implemented on top of lists without constraining the implementation to one particular type of list.
- There are many possible uses for stacks. This chapter demonstrated how easy it is to augment another data structure — in this case, a list — with an undo feature.

Now that you have seen some simple algorithms for string searching, and are familiar with managing your data using basic data structures such as lists, queues, and stacks, it is time to move on to solving more complex problems.

Basic Sorting

Now that you understand some of the fundamental data structures used in today's software applications, you can use those data structures to organize the large amounts of data that your applications need to process. Sorting data into a logical order is a critical prerequisite for many of the algorithms in the chapters to come, and it is such a potential performance bottleneck that an enormous amount of research has been done over many decades to determine the most efficient way to sort various types of data. This chapter introduces three sorting algorithms that are easy to implement and are best suited to smaller sets of data, as their performance is $O(N^2)$. Chapter 7 covers more complex sorting algorithms with better performance characteristics for very large data sets.

This chapter discusses the following:

- The importance of sorting
- The role of comparators
- How the bubble sort algorithm works
- How the selection sort algorithm works
- How the insertion sort algorithm works
- The meaning of stability
- The pros and cons of the basic sorting algorithms

The Importance of Sorting

You already know from the real world how important sorting is when working with searching algorithms. To look up a word in a dictionary, you use an algorithm: You open the dictionary at a point roughly equivalent to the word's position in the sorted list of all the words in the dictionary. You then do a few quick narrowing searches until you find the page it's on, and then finally scan the page for the word. Now imagine the words in the dictionary were not sorted. You'd probably decide to give up because the time to search the unsorted data would be prohibitive, and you'd be right!

Without sorting, searching is impractical for very large sets of data. You could apply the same principle to many other types of data in the real world, such as the names in a phone book or the books on the shelves of a library. The problem with these examples is that you have never (I hope) had to deal with any of these types of data before they were sorted for you, so you've never had to create an efficient algorithm for sorting them. In the computer world, however, it is not uncommon to encounter sets of data just as large as these that arrive at your program unsorted, or in an order other than the one you need. A good grasp of the established algorithms helps you tackle this type of problem.

Sorting Fundamentals

Sorting data into some kind of meaningful order requires a data structure that is capable of maintaining the order of its contents. As you learned in Chapter 4, this is the distinguishing feature of a list, so we will be using lists as the data structure on which the sorting algorithms operate.

After the objects to be sorted are contained in a list, all of the sorting algorithms are built upon two fundamental operations:

- ❑ Comparing items to determine whether they are out of order
- ❑ Moving items into sorted position

The advantages and disadvantages of each sorting algorithm are based on how many times these fundamental operations need to be performed and how expensive these operations are in performance terms. The task of comparing objects to determine whether they are sorted is a larger topic than you might at first imagine, so we will deal with it in the following section on comparators. The list data structure supports several methods for moving the objects—namely, `get()`, `set()`, `insert()`, and `delete()`. These operations are covered in detail in Chapter 3.

Understanding Comparators

In Java, as in many other languages, when you wish to compare two integers, you can do something like the following:

```
int x, y;
...
if (x < y) {
    ...
}
```

This works fine for primitive types, but things get more difficult when dealing with more complex objects. For example, when you look at a list of files on your computer, you might typically look at them sorted by their filename. Sometimes, however, you might want to look at them in the order they were created, or the order in which they were modified, or even by the type of file they happen to be.

It is important to support different orderings without having to write a whole new algorithm. This is where comparators come in. A *comparator* is responsible for imposing a specific ordering on objects, so when you're trying to sort files, you might have one comparator for filenames, one for file types, and yet another for modification times. All these comparators would enable a single sorting algorithm to sort a list of file objects in different ways.

This is an example of an important design principle known as *separation of concerns*. In this case, you separate the concern of how to compare two individual objects (the comparator) from the concern of how to efficiently sort a large list of objects (the algorithm). This enables you to extend the usefulness of an algorithm by plugging in comparators that you had not imagined when creating it, and enables you to reuse a given comparator across multiple algorithm implementations to compare their performance.

Comparator Operations

A comparator consists of a single operation that enables you to compare two objects for relative order. It returns a negative integer, zero, or a positive integer, depending on whether the first argument is less than, equal to, or greater than the second, respectively. It throws a `ClassCastException` if the type of either object prevents them from being compared.

The Comparator Interface

A comparator is very simple—it has a single method that enables you to compare two objects to determine whether the first object is less than, equal to, or greater than the second object. The following code shows the `Comparator` interface:

```
public interface Comparator {
    public int compare(Object left, Object right);
}
```

The compare operation takes two arguments: `left` and `right`. We have chosen to label them as such because, in this context, they are conceptually rather like the left-side and right-side arguments when comparing primitive values. When calling `compare`, if left comes before right (left < right), the result is an integer less than zero (usually `-1`); if left comes after right (left > right), the result is an integer greater than zero (usually `1`); and if left equals right, the result of the comparison is zero.

Some Standard Comparators

In addition to the many custom comparators you will create, there are also a few standard comparators that will greatly simplify your application code. Each one is simple in concept and implementation yet quite powerful when used with some of the more complex algorithms discussed later in the book.

Working with the Natural Comparator

Many data types, especially primitives such as strings, integers, and so on, have a natural sort order: A comes before B, B comes before C, and so on. A natural comparator is simply a comparator that supports this natural ordering of objects. You will see that it is possible to create a single comparator that can sort any object that has a natural sorting order by basing it on a convention established by the Java language itself. Java has the concept of `Comparable`–an interface that can be implemented by any class you are using to provide a natural sort order.

The Comparable Interface

The `Comparable` interface is simple, consisting of the single method shown here:

```
public interface Comparable {
    public int compareTo(Object other);
}
```

Similar to a `Comparator`, it returns a negative integer, a positive integer, or zero to indicate that one object comes before, after, or is equal to another, respectively. The difference between a `Comparator` and a `Comparable` object is that a `Comparator` compares two objects with each other, whereas a `Comparable` object compares another object with itself.

Sometimes you may want to have your own classes implement `Comparable` to give them a natural sort order. A `Person` class, for example, may be defined as sorting by name. The fact that this concept is reflected in the standard Java language enables you to create a generic `Comparator` for sorting based on the natural ordering of a type. You can create a `Comparator` that will work for any class that implements `Comparable`. The fact that many of the commonly used classes in the java.lang package implement this interface makes it a handy comparator to start with.

When you think about the desired behavior of the `NaturalComparator`, you can see that there are three possible scenarios to handle, one for each of the three possible types of comparison result. You already know that strings in Java implement `Comparable`, so you can use strings as test data. In the next Try It Out, you test and then implement the `NaturalComparator`.

Try It Out Testing the Natural Comparator

You first test whether a negative integer results when the left argument falls before the right when sorting:

```
public void testLessThan() {
    assertTrue(NaturalComparator.INSTANCE.compare("A", "B") < 0);
}
```

Next, you determine whether a positive integer results when the left argument sorts after the right argument:

```
public void testGreaterThan() {
    assertTrue(NaturalComparator.INSTANCE.compare("B", "A") > 0);
}
```

Finally, when the two arguments are equal, you determine whether the result is zero:

```
public void testEqualTo() {
    assertTrue(NaturalComparator.INSTANCE.compare("A", "A") == 0);
}
```

How It Works

The test case contains one test method for each of the three cases we identified above. Each test method assumes that the `NaturalComparator` provides a single static instance that you can use without needing to instantiate it. Each test method uses two simple character strings as test data to validate that the `NaturalComparator` behaves as expected.

Try It Out — Implementing the Natural Comparator

Because the `NaturalComparator` has no state, you only need one instance of it:

```
public final class NaturalComparator implements Comparator {
    public static final NaturalComparator INSTANCE =
        new NaturalComparator();

    private NaturalComparator() {
    }
    ...
}
```

To ensure this, you mark the constructor as private to prevent instantiation and instead provide a publicly accessible static variable holding the single instance of the class. You must also be sure to mark the class as `final` to prevent it from being extended erroneously.

Next you implement `compare()`. Because you are implementing this on top of the `Comparable` interface, most of the actual work will be performed by the arguments themselves, making the implementation almost trivial:

```
    public int compare(Object left, Object right) {
        assert left != null : "left can't be null";
        return ((Comparable) left).compareTo(right);
    }
```

After first ensuring you haven't been passed a `NULL` argument, you cast the left argument to a `Comparable` and call the defined `compareTo()` method, passing the right argument.

You never check to see whether the left argument is actually an instance of `Comparable` because the `Comparator` interface specifically allows a `ClassCastException` to be thrown, meaning you can perform the cast without the additional check.

How It Works

The `NaturalComparator` is designed to compare two objects that implement the `Comparable` interface. Many built-in Java objects implement this interface, and classes you create are free to implement it as well. The code only needs to cast the left operand to the `Comparable` interface so that it can call the `compareTo()` method, passing in the right operand for the comparison to be performed by the left operand itself. The comparator here is not actually required to implement any comparison logic because it is all handled by the objects themselves.

Working with the Reverse Comparator

Often, you will want to sort things in reverse order. For example, when looking at a list of files on your computer, you may want to see the files from smallest to largest, or in reverse order from largest to smallest. One way to achieve a reverse version of the `NaturalComparator` described previously is to copy its implementation and reimplement the `compare()` method, as shown here:

```
    public int compare(Object left, Object right) {
        assert right != null : "right can't be null";
        return ((Comparable) right).compareTo(left);
    }
```

You swap the right and left arguments, confirming that the right argument is not `null` and then passing the left argument to its `compare()` method.

Although this approach works perfectly well in this particular case, it isn't very extensible. For each complex type, such as `Person` or `File`, you always end up creating two comparators: one to sort ascending, and one to sort descending.

A better approach, which you take in the next Try It Out, is to create a generic comparator that wraps (or "decorates") another comparator and reverse the result. This way, you only need one comparator for each complex type you wish to sort. You use the generic `ReverseComparator` to sort in the opposite direction.

Try It Out Testing the Reverse Comparator

As with `NaturalComparator`, there are three possible scenarios to handle, matching the three possible types of comparison result. For these tests, you use the previously defined `NaturalComparator` to enable you to compare simple string values.

If the left argument would normally sort before the right, you want the `ReverseComparator` to cause the opposite to occur; that is, if the underlying comparator returns a negative integer, indicating that the left argument is less than the right argument, you need to ensure that the result from the `ReverseComparator` is a positive integer:

```
public void testLessThanBecomesGreaterThan() {
    ReverseComparator comparator =
        new ReverseComparator(NaturalComparator.INSTANCE);

    assertTrue(comparator.compare("A", "B") > 0);
}
```

If the underlying comparator returns a positive integer, indicating that the left argument would normally sort after the right, the result should be a negative integer:

```
public void testGreaterThanBecomesLessThan() {
    ReverseComparator comparator =
        new ReverseComparator(NaturalComparator.INSTANCE);

    assertTrue(comparator.compare("B", "A") < 0);
}
```

If the two arguments are equal, then the result must be zero:

```
public void testEqualsRemainsUnchanged() {
    ReverseComparator comparator =
        new ReverseComparator(NaturalComparator.INSTANCE);

    assertTrue(comparator.compare("A", "A") == 0);
}
```

How It Works

The preceding code works by instantiating `ReverseComparator` objects and passing to them a `NaturalComparator` to which the comparison logic can be delegated. The first two test methods then make what look like nonsensical assertions: You know that A comes before B, but the opposite is true in this case, and the first test method makes sure this is the case. The second test method is similarly counterintuitive. The final test method ensures that objects that are equal remain equal when the `ReverseComparator` is used.

In the following Try It Out, you implement your `ReverseComparator`.

Try It Out Implementing the Reverse Comparator

Implement the generic `ReverseComparator` with a few lines of code:

```
package com.wrox.algorithms.sorting;

public class ReverseComparator implements Comparator {
    private final Comparator _comparator;

    public ReverseComparator(Comparator comparator) {
        assert comparator != null : "comparator can't be null";
        _comparator = comparator;
    }
    ...
}
```

You start, of course, by implementing the `Comparator` interface and defining a constructor that accepts the underlying `Comparator` to which you will eventually delegate the compare call.

Then comes the actual implementation of `compare`:

```
    public int compare(Object left, Object right) {
        return _comparator.compare(right, left);
    }
```

How It Works

At first glance, the code looks rather innocuous, simply delegating to the underlying comparator, but if you look carefully at the code, you will see that the two arguments are reversed before you pass them. If the `ReverseComparator` was called with (`A`, `B`), then the underlying comparator would be passed (`B`, `A`), thereby inducing the opposite result.

Because you don't actually need to access any of the attributes for either argument, this solution is completely generic; you need only implement it once to have a solution for all situations. You can now start to build your first sorting algorithm, the *bubble sort algorithm*.

Understanding Bubble Sort

Before implementing the bubble sort algorithm, you need to define some test cases for the implementation to pass. Because all of the sorting algorithms need to pass the same basic test (that is, prove that they actually sort objects correctly), you establish a base class for your unit tests to extend for each specific implementation. Each of the algorithms implements an interface so that they can be replaced easily. This means that you can use a single test case to prove any sorting algorithm's basic features, even one you haven't thought of yet!

Try It Out Performing a Bubble Sort

Imagine you are at a family gathering and you want to take a photograph of everyone there. You decide you'd like the family members to be arranged in age order, from youngest to oldest, but right now they're arranged randomly, as shown in Figure 6-1.

Figure 6-1: Randomly arranged family members.

To apply a bubble sort to this problem, turn your attention to the two people at the left of the line of family members. Ask them which one is older. If the one on the right of the pair is older, then do nothing, as they are sorted relative to each other. If the one on the left is older, then ask them to swap positions. In this case, the swap needed to happen. Figure 6-2 shows the family after this first swap has taken place.

Figure 6-2: The first swap has taken place.

Now move your attention along the line one place to address the second and third people in the line. The second person has just been compared with the first person and is now about to be compared with the third person. Repeat the same procedure as before, asking them which one is older and swapping them if they are out of order.

By the time you get to the last pair on the line of people and perform any necessary swaps, what will have happened? Figure 6-3 shows the family group after this first pass.

Figure 6-3: The family after the first pass—the oldest person is at the far right.

The group is by no means sorted, but the oldest person has bubbled up to the end of the line and is now in final sorted position. It probably seems like that was a lot of comparing and swapping just to get one person sorted, and that's true. Algorithms you'll see later have improved efficiency, but don't worry about that for now.

The next pass in the bubble sort algorithm is exactly the same as the first except you ignore the person at the right end of the line, as that person is already sorted. Starting at the far left again, do the same compare/swap process until the second oldest person is at the second rightmost position in the line, as shown in Figure 6-4.

Figure 6-4: The second oldest person is at the second rightmost position after the second pass.

Continue in this way, gradually sorting the smaller and smaller remaining groups until the whole group is sorted. Now you can take your picture (see Figure 6-5).

Figure 6-5: The entire group is sorted.

The ListSorter Interface

Like many interfaces, the `ListSorter` interface is extremely simple, consisting of a single operation to sort a list.

The `sort` operation accepts a list as its input and produces as its result a sorted version of the list. Depending on the implementation, the returned list might be the same as the provided list—that is, some implementations sort the list in place, whereas others create a new list.

Here is the code for the `ListSorter` interface:

```
public interface ListSorter {
    public List sort(List list);
}
```

Testing AbstractListSorter

Even though you have not yet written a single sorting algorithm, in the next Try It Out, you write a test that exercises any implementation of the `ListSorter` interface. This example uses an abstract test class, meaning that it can't be run until it has been extended for a specific sorting algorithm implementation. The actual implementation of the test for each specific algorithm will be trivial as a result.

`AbstractListSorterTest` performs the following tasks:

- Creates an unsorted list of strings
- Creates a sorted list of the same strings to act as an expected result for the test
- Creates a `ListSorter` (via an abstract method)
- Uses the `ListSorter` to sort the unsorted list
- Compares the sorted list with the expected result list

Try It Out Testing AbstractSorterTest

Begin the code by declaring the two lists and using a `setUp()` implementation to fill each of them with strings:

```
package com.wrox.algorithms.sorting;

import junit.framework.TestCase;
import com.wrox.algorithms.lists.List;
import com.wrox.algorithms.lists.LinkedList;
import com.wrox.algorithms.iteration.Iterator;

public abstract class AbstractListSorterTest extends TestCase {
    private List _unsortedList;
    private List _sortedList;

    protected void setUp() throws Exception {
        _unsortedList = new LinkedList();

        _unsortedList.add("test");
        _unsortedList.add("driven");
        _unsortedList.add("development");
        _unsortedList.add("is");
        _unsortedList.add("one");
        _unsortedList.add("small");
        _unsortedList.add("step");
        _unsortedList.add("for");
        _unsortedList.add("a");
        _unsortedList.add("programmer");
        _unsortedList.add("but");
        _unsortedList.add("it's");
        _unsortedList.add("one");
        _unsortedList.add("giant");
        _unsortedList.add("leap");
        _unsortedList.add("for");
        _unsortedList.add("programming");

        _sortedList = new LinkedList();

        _sortedList.add("a");
        _sortedList.add("but");
        _sortedList.add("development");
        _sortedList.add("driven");
        _sortedList.add("for");
        _sortedList.add("for");
        _sortedList.add("giant");
        _sortedList.add("is");
        _sortedList.add("it's");
        _sortedList.add("leap");
        _sortedList.add("one");
        _sortedList.add("one");
        _sortedList.add("programmer");
        _sortedList.add("programming");
```

```
        _sortedList.add("small");
        _sortedList.add("step");
        _sortedList.add("test");
    }
```

Next, implement `tearDown()`, which frees the references to the two `List` objects:

```
    protected void tearDown() throws Exception {
        _sortedList = null;
        _unsortedList = null;
    }
```

Finally, define the abstract method to create the specific sorting algorithm and the test itself:

```
    protected abstract ListSorter createListSorter(Comparator comparator);

    public void testListSorterCanSortSampleList() {
        ListSorter sorter = createListSorter(NaturalComparator.INSTANCE);
        List result = sorter.sort(_unsortedList);

        assertEquals(result.size(), _sortedList.size());

        Iterator actual = result.iterator();
        actual.first();

        Iterator expected = _sortedList.iterator();
        expected.first();

        while (!expected .isDone()) {
            assertEquals(expected.current(), actual.current());

            expected.next();
            actual.next();
        }
    }
```

How It Works

The first two lines of the test method create the sorting algorithm implementation and use it to sort the unsorted list. You pass a natural comparator because your expected results have been set up in the natural sequence of the strings themselves. The bulk of the test verifies that the result of the sort matches the expected result list. You do this by creating an iterator over the lists and comparing each item in turn to ensure an item-by-item exact match. Every one of your sorting algorithms must be able to pass this test or it will be of very little use in practice!

In the following Try It Out, you make a test that is specific to your bubble sort implementation.

Try It Out   Testing BubblesortListSorter

Extend the `AbstractListSorterTest` and implement the abstract `createListSorter()` method as shown here:

```
package com.wrox.algorithms.sorting;

public class BubblesortListSorterTest extends AbstractListSorterTest {
    protected ListSorter createListSorter(Comparator comparator) {
        return new BubblesortListSorter(comparator);
    }
}
```

That's all you need to do to complete the test for the `BubblesortListSorter`. Of course, the preceding code won't compile yet, as we don't have a `BubblesortListSorter` class; that's what we'll do now. In the next Try It Out, you implement your bubble sort.

How It Works

Despite the fact that you only implemented a single method with a single line of code, the key point here is that you are extending the `AbstractListSorterTest` class in the preceding code. The abstract class provides the test data and several test methods; all you need to do is provide the `ListSorter` implementation for these tests to use, and that's what you have done here.

Try It Out Implementing BubblesortListSorter

The implementation of the bubble sort algorithm must meet the following design criteria:

- Implement the `ListSorter` interface
- Accept a comparator to determine the ordering of objects
- Pass the unit test described in the preceding section

With these guidelines in place, you begin implementation with the constructor, as shown here:

```
package com.wrox.algorithms.sorting;

import com.wrox.algorithms.lists.List;

public class BubblesortListSorter implements ListSorter {
    private final Comparator _comparator;

    public BubblesortListSorter(Comparator comparator) {
        assert comparator != null : "comparator cannot be null";
        _comparator = comparator;
    }
    ...
}
```

You now need to implement the bubble sort algorithm itself. Recall from the description of the algorithm that it is comprised of a number of passes through the data, with each pass resulting in one item being moved into its final sorted position. The first thing to determine is how many passes are needed. When all but the last item have been moved into their final sorted position, the last item has nowhere to go and must therefore also be in its final position, so you need a number of passes that is one less than the number of items. The code that follows calls this the `outer loop`.

On each pass, you compare each pair of items and swap them if they are out of order (as determined by the comparator you have been given). Remember, however, that on each pass, one item is moved into final sorted position and can therefore be ignored on subsequent passes. Therefore, each pass deals with one less item than the previous pass. If N is the number of items in the list, then on the first pass, the number of comparisons you need to make is (N – 1), on the second pass it is (N – 2), and so on. This is why the inner loop in the following code has the condition `left < (size - pass)` to control how many comparisons are performed:

```
public List sort(List list) {
    assert list != null : "list cannot be null";

    int size = list.size();

    for (int pass = 1; pass < size; ++pass) {                    // outer loop
        for (int left = 0; left < (size - pass); ++left) {    // inner loop
            int right = left + 1;
            if (_comparator.compare(list.get(left), list.get(right)) > 0) {
                swap(list, left, right);
            }
        }
    }

    return list;
}
```

The preceding code uses the supplied comparator to determine whether the two items under scrutiny are out of order. If they are, then it calls the `swap()` method to correct their relative placement in the list. Here is the code for `swap()`:

```
    private void swap(List list, int left, int right) {
        Object temp = list.get(left);
        list.set(left, list.get(right));
        list.set(right, temp);
    }
}
```

When you compile and run this test, it passes with flying colors. Just to make sure, you can place a deliberate mistake in the test's expectation and run it again to see that it will indeed catch you if you slip up when implementing your next sorting algorithm.

Working with a Selection Sort

Imagine that you have a bookshelf filled with several books of varying sizes that are arranged haphazardly. Your mother is coming to visit, and to impress her with your housekeeping prowess, you decide to arrange the books neatly on the shelf in order from the tallest to the shortest. Figure 6-6 shows the bookshelf before you begin.

You'd be unlikely to use bubble sort in this case, because all that swapping would be a waste of time. You'd be taking each book out and putting it back on the shelf many times, and that would take too long. In this example, the cost of moving the items is relatively large when measured against the cost of comparing items. A selection sort is a better choice here, and you'll soon see why.

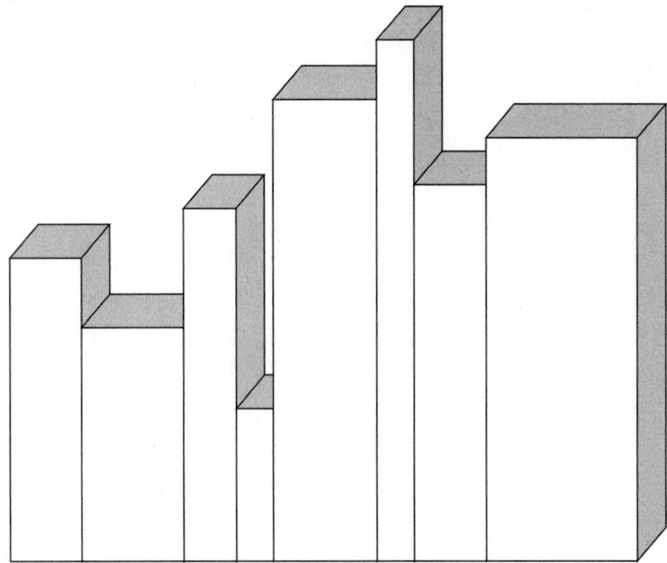

Figure 6-6: A haphazard bookshelf.

Start by scanning the shelf for the tallest book. Pull it out, as it needs to move to the far left of the shelf. Rather than move all the other books along the shelf to make room for it, just pull out the book that happens to be in the space where you want this one to go and swap them. Of course, the rest of the books will have to move a little because the books vary in thickness, but that won't matter in this software implementation, so just ignore that little issue. (Choosing to swap two books in this way, rather than slide all the books along, makes this implementation unstable, a topic covered later in this chapter, but don't worry about that for now.) Figure 6-7 shows how the shelf looks after your first swap.

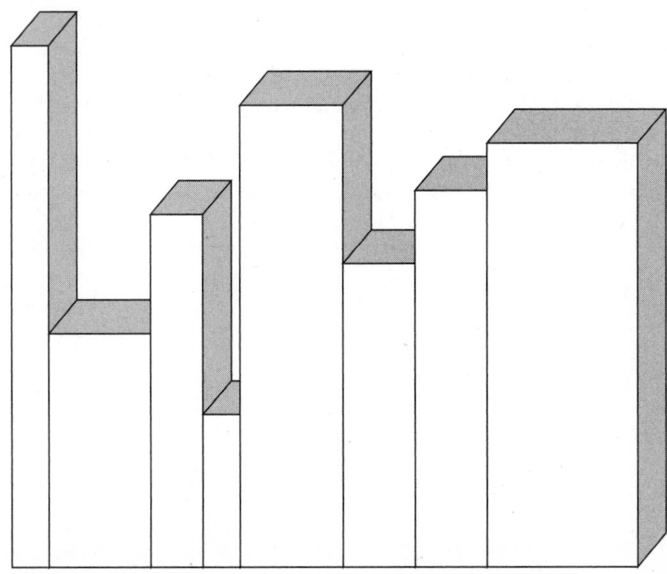

Figure 6-7: The tallest book is now at the far left position.

Leaving the tallest book where it is, scan the shelf for the tallest of the remaining books. Once you've found it, swap it with the book that happens to be just to the right of the tallest book. You now have sorted two books that you won't have to touch again. Figure 6-8 shows your shelf now.

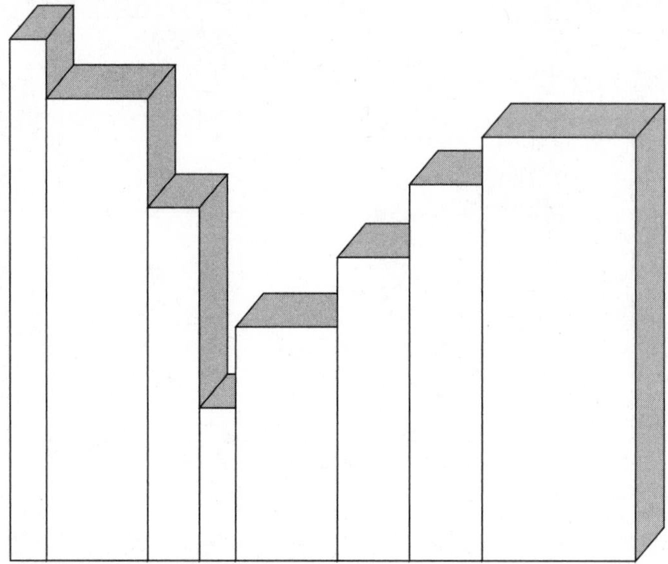

Figure 6-8: The second tallest book is now in the second position.

Leaving the largest books where they are, continue to scan the remaining books for the tallest among them, each time swapping it with the book that is just to the right of the already sorted books at the left end of the shelf. Each time you scan the shelf, you are selecting the next book in order and moving it into its final sorted position. That's why this algorithm is called selection sort. Figure 6-9 shows the shelf after each book is moved.

Sometimes, while scanning the unsorted books to find the tallest among them, you will find that it is already in position and no swap is required. You can see that after each book is moved, the set of sorted books grows, and the set of unsorted books shrinks until it is empty and the whole shelf is sorted. Each book is moved directly into its final sorted position, rather than taking small steps toward its final position (as in a bubble sort), which is a good reason to use this algorithm in this case.

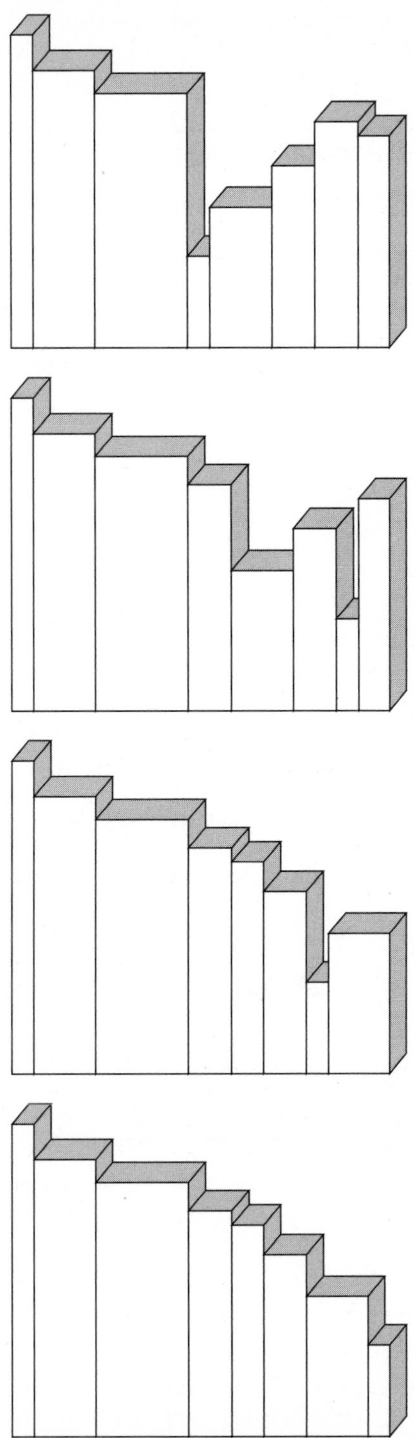

Figure 6-9: The shelf after each position is filled with the appropriate book.

You can re-use a lot of the work you did with the bubble sort algorithm to test your selection sort. In the next Try It Out, you start by creating a test case for it and then implementing the algorithm itself, making sure it passes the test to prove you implemented it correctly.

Try It Out Testing SelectionSortListSorter

The test for the `SelectionSortListSorter` is almost exactly the same as its bubble sort equivalent. You extend your abstract test case and instantiate the selection sort implementation:

```
package com.wrox.algorithms.sorting;

public class SelectionSortListSorterTest extends AbstractListSorterTest {
    protected ListSorter createListSorter(Comparator comparator) {
        return new SelectionSortListSorter(comparator);
    }
}
```

In the next Try It Out, you implement `SelectionSortListSorter`.

How It Works

Despite the fact that you only implemented a single method with a single line of code, the key point here is that you are extending the `AbstractListSorterTest` class described earlier in this chapter. The abstract class provides the test data and several test methods; all you need to do is provide the `ListSorter` implementation for these tests to use, which is what you have done here.

Try It Out Implementing SelectionSortListSorter

The implementation also shares much in common with its bubble sort counterpart. It too needs to implement the `ListSorter` interface, accept a `Comparator` to determine ordering, and pass the unit test described above. Create the following class declaration and constructor:

```
package com.wrox.algorithms.sorting;

import com.wrox.algorithms.lists.List;

public class SelectionSortListSorter implements ListSorter {
    private final Comparator _comparator;

    public SelectionSortListSorter(Comparator comparator) {
        assert comparator != null : "comparator cannot be null";
        _comparator = comparator;
    }
    ...
}
```

How It Works

The implementation has both an outer loop and an inner loop, like bubble sort, but there are subtle differences that might escape your attention if you don't look at this code closely. First, the outer loop index ranges between zero and (N – 2), rather than between 1 and (N – 1) in bubble sort. Note that this is still the same number of passes (N – 1), but it reflects your focus in the selection sort on filling a given "slot" with the right object on each pass. For example, on the first pass, your goal is to get the right object into position zero of the list. On the second pass, the goal is to fill position 1, and so on. Once again, you can get by with only (N – 1) passes because the last object naturally ends up in sorted position as a result of sorting every other object first.

No swapping occurs during the inner loop, as it did in bubble sort. During the inner loop, the only requirement is to remember the position of the smallest item. When the inner loop finishes, you then swap the smallest item into the slot you are trying to fill. This is slightly different from the earlier bookshelf example, in which the books were sorted from largest to smallest, but the algorithm would work just as well in that case. In fact, you simply plug in the `ReverseComparator` you created earlier in this chapter:

```
    public List sort(List list) {
        assert list != null : "list cannot be null";

        int size = list.size();

        for (int slot = 0; slot < size - 1; ++slot) {              // outer loop
            int smallest = slot;
            for (int check = slot + 1; check < size; ++check) {  // inner loop
                if (_comparator.compare(list.get(check), list.get(smallest)) < 0) {
                    smallest = check;
                }
            }
            swap(list, smallest, slot);
        }
        return list;
    }
```

There is also one small difference in the implementation of `swap()` for a selection sort when compared to a bubble sort. You add a *guard clause* to ignore requests to swap a slot with itself, which can occur quite easily with a selection sort, but not a bubble sort:

```
    private void swap(List list, int left, int right) {
        if (left == right) {
            return;
        }
        Object temp = list.get(left);
        list.set(left, list.get(right));
        list.set(right, temp);
    }
}
```

Understanding Insertion Sort

Insertion sort is the algorithm very commonly used by people playing cards to sort the hand they have been dealt. Imagine you have been given five cards face down and you want to sort them according to the following rules:

- Separate into suits in the following order: spades, clubs, diamonds, and hearts
- Within each suit, sort in ascending order: Ace, 2, 3, . . . , 9, 10, jack, queen, king

Figure 6-10 shows your hand of cards, face down. They are unsorted, although they may already be in just the order you need. (Even if they are, the algorithm will need to run its course.)

Figure 6-10: A hand of five cards.

You begin by turning over the first card. Nothing could be easier than sorting a single card, so you hold it in your hand on its own. In this case, it's the seven of diamonds. Figure 6-11 shows the current situation: one sorted card and four still unsorted cards lying face down.

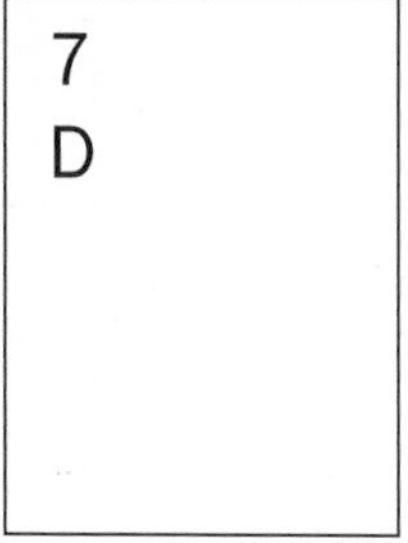

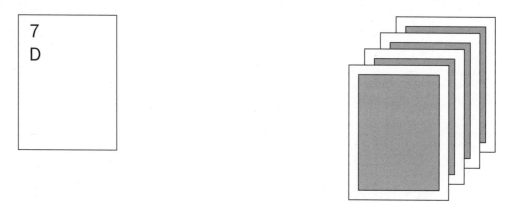

Figure 6-11: The first card is sorted by itself.

Pick up the second card. It's the jack of spades. Because you know spades come before diamonds, you insert it into your hand to the left of your current card. Figure 6-12 shows the situation now.

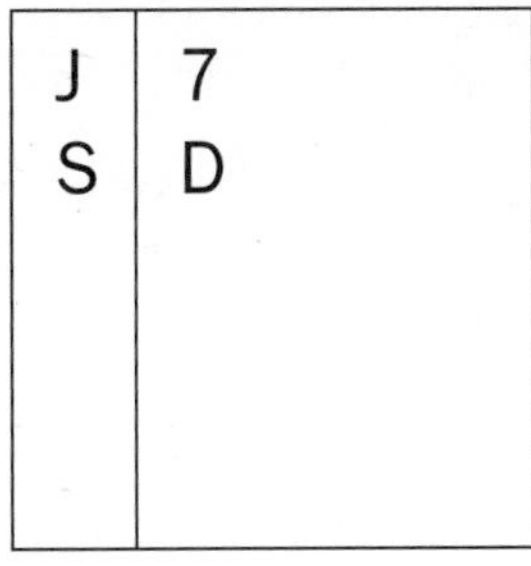

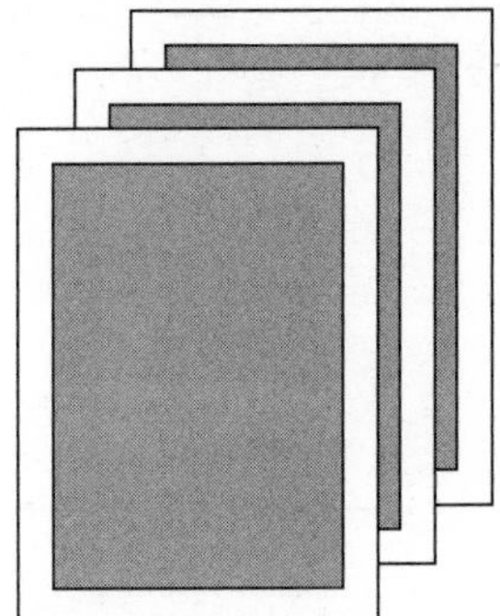

Figure 6-12: The second card is inserted before the first.

Pick up the third card. In the example it's the ace of clubs. Looking at your two already sorted cards, this new one needs to be inserted between them. Figure 6-13 shows the state of your hand now.

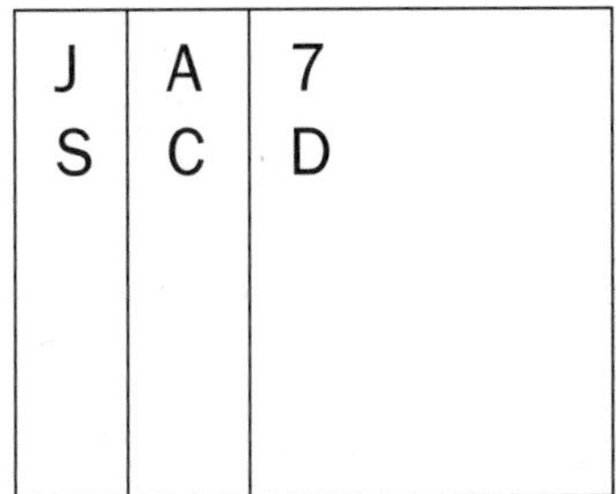

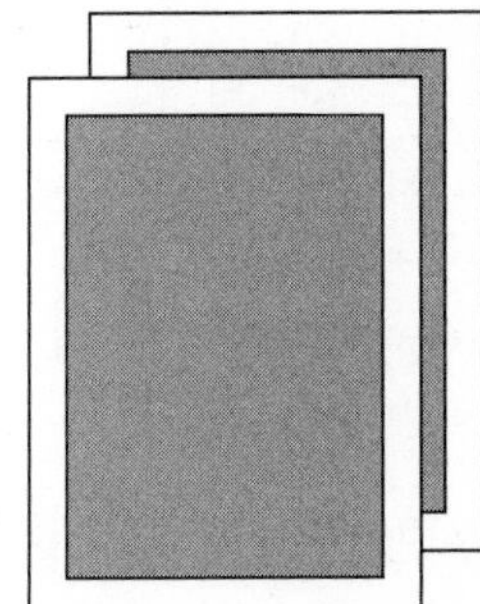

Figure 6-13: The third card is inserted in the middle.

An insertion sort works by dividing the data into two groups: already sorted items and unsorted items. Initially, the sorted group is empty and the unsorted group contains all the items. One by one, an item is taken from the unsorted group and inserted at the appropriate position in the growing group of sorted items. Eventually, all of the items are in the sorted group and the unsorted group is empty. Figure 6-14 shows what happens when you pick up the final two cards.

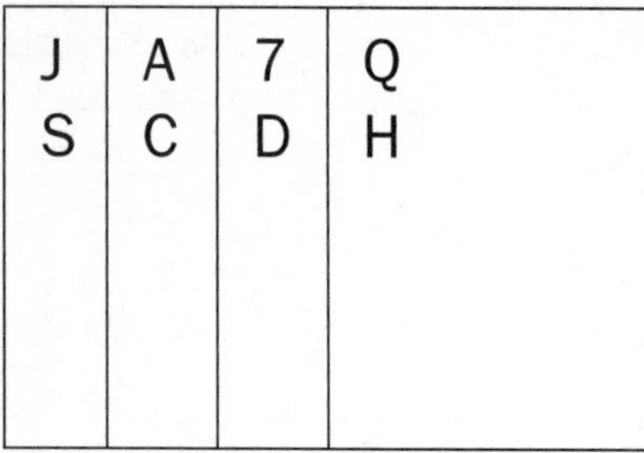

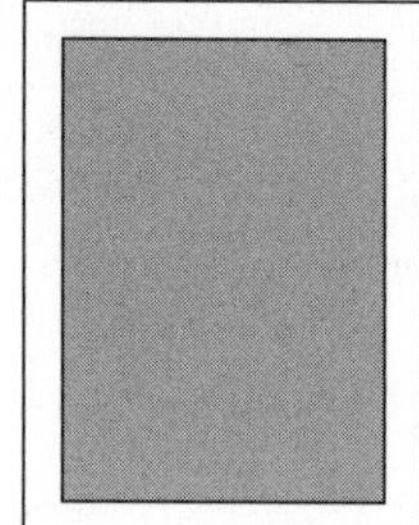

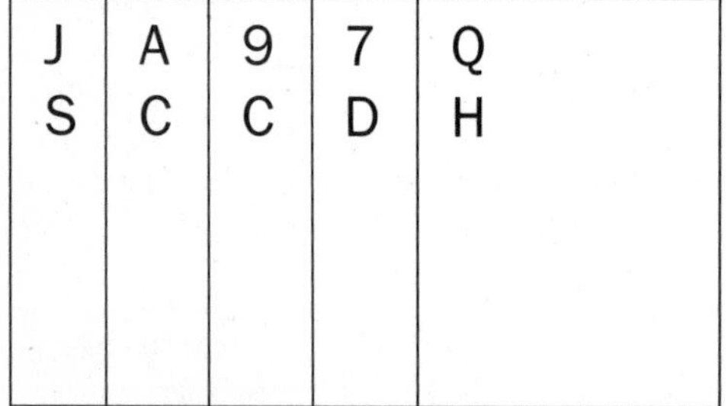

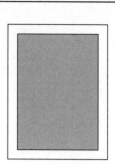

Figure 6-14: The last two cards are inserted.

In the next Try It Out, you start by creating a test case for the insertion sort algorithm. Then you implement it to complete the three basic sorting algorithms for this chapter.

Try It Out Testing InsertionSortListSorter

In the same way as you did for bubble sort and selection sort, you extend the `AbstractListSorter` test case for the insertion sort algorithm, as shown here:

```
package com.wrox.algorithms.sorting;

public class InsertionSortListSorterTest extends AbstractListSorterTest {
    protected ListSorter createListSorter(Comparator comparator) {
        return new InsertionSortListSorter(comparator);
    }
}
```

How It Works

Although you implemented a single method with a single line of code, the key point here is that you are extending the `AbstractListSorterTest` class described earlier in this chapter. The abstract class provides the test data and several test methods; all you need to do is provide the `ListSorter` implementation for these tests to use, and that's what you have done here.

Try It Out Implementing InsertionSortListSorter

By now you will be familiar with the basic structure of the sorting algorithm implementations. Use the following class declaration and constructor for `InsertionSortListSorter`:

```
package com.wrox.algorithms.sorting;

import com.wrox.algorithms.lists.List;
import com.wrox.algorithms.lists.LinkedList;
import com.wrox.algorithms.iteration.Iterator;

public class InsertionSortListSorter implements ListSorter {
    private final Comparator _comparator;

    public InsertionSortListSorter(Comparator comparator) {
        assert comparator != null : "comparator cannot be null";
        _comparator = comparator;
    }
    ...
}
```

How It Works

The implementation of the `sort()` method is very different from the two algorithms you have seen earlier in the chapter. This algorithm does not sort the objects in place by rearranging the order of the list it is given; rather, this algorithm creates a new, empty list and inserts each item from the original list into the result list in sorted order.

In addition, the original list is processed using an iterator instead of accessing the items by index because you have no need for direct access to the items in the original list. You simply process each one in turn, which is the natural idiom for an iterator:

```
    public List sort(List list) {
        assert list != null : "list cannot be null";

        final List result = new LinkedList();

        Iterator it = list.iterator();

        for (it.first(); !it.isDone(); it.next()) {
            int slot = result.size();
            while (slot > 0) {
                if (_comparator.compare(it.current(), result.get(slot - 1)) >= 0) {
                    break;
                }
                --slot;
            }
            result.insert(slot, it.current());
        }

        return result;
    }
```

Finally, notice that the inner loop is a `while` loop, rather than a `for` loop. Its task is to find the right position in the result list to insert the next item. After it finds the right position (or falls off the end of the result list), it exits the inner loop. The current item is then inserted into the result list. At all times, the result list is entirely sorted; each item is placed into position relative to those items already in the list, thereby maintaining the overall sorted sequence. This example uses a `LinkedList` for the result list because it is better suited to insertion operations.

Note also that the algorithm searches backwards through the result list looking for the right position, rather than forwards. This is a big advantage when it comes to sorting already sorted or nearly sorted objects, as demonstrated in the section "Comparing the Basic Sorting Algorithms," later in this chapter. It is also the reason why this algorithm is stable, which is the subject of the next section.

Understanding Stability

Some sorting algorithms share an interesting characteristic called *stability*. To illustrate this concept, examine the list of people sorted by their first names shown in Table 6-1.

Table 6-1: List Sorted by First Names

First Name	Last Name
`Albert`	`Smith`
`Brian`	`Jackson`
`David`	`Barnes`
`John`	`Smith`
`John`	`Wilson`
`Mary`	`Smith`
`Tom`	`Barnes`
`Vince`	`De Marco`
`Walter`	`Clarke`

Now imagine that you want to sort the same people by their last names. The list in Table 6-1 contains some common last names, such as Smith and Barnes. What would you expect to happen to the order of people with the same last name? You might expect that people with the same last name would be in the same relative order as the original list — that is, sorted by first name within the same last name group. This is stability. If a sorting algorithm maintains the relative order of items with a common sort key, it is said to be a *stable algorithm*.

Table 6-2 shows a stable last name sort of the people in this example.

Table 6-2: Stable Last Name Sort of Table 6-1

First Name	Last Name
`David`	`Barnes`
`Tom`	`Barnes`
`Walter`	`Clarke`
`Vince`	`De Marco`

First Name	Last Name
`Brian`	`Jackson`
`Albert`	`Smith`
`John`	`Smith`
`Mary`	`Smith`
`John`	`Wilson`

Two of the three implementations discussed so far — bubble sort and insertion sort — are stable. It is simple to make the selection sort implementation stable. Some of the more advanced sorting algorithms in later chapters may be faster than the three you have seen here, but they often fail to preserve stability, and you should take this into account if it is important to your particular application.

Comparing the Basic Sorting Algorithms

Now that you have seen a number of sorting algorithms in action, and how you can easily plug in any implementation that supports the `ListSorter` interface, you might be wondering when to use which algorithm. This section compares each algorithm using a practical approach, rather than a theoretical or mathematical approach. This is not intended to give you a definitive list of criteria for selecting an algorithm; rather, it provides an example of how comparative analysis can be put to use when you need to make implementation choices in the systems you build.

Recall from the introduction to this chapter that sorting algorithms perform two basic steps many times: comparing items and moving items around. This discussion assesses the behavior of the three sorting algorithms with regard to the first of these operations and puts the algorithms through their paces using much larger data sets than you used when implementing them. This is important because any divergence in their relative performance will be clearer on larger sets of data. It is also important that each algorithm receive input data in varying arrangements, as follows:

- Already sorted (the best case)
- Already sorted but in reverse order from our desired order (the worst case)
- Random order (the average case)

If you give each algorithm the same set of input data for each of these cases, then you can make an informed decision about the relative merits in a given real-world situation. The first task is to gather the information about how many times comparisons are made.

CallCountingListComparator

All comparisons in the sorting algorithms are performed by their respective comparator. To count the number of times the comparator's `compare()` method is called, you could alter the code for each comparator to specify that it remember the number of calls. Alternatively, you could make all the comparators extend a common base class and put the call counting behavior there. However, to re-use much of the code you've already written, you can add the call counting behavior by decorating any other comparator you already have, as you did with the ReverseComparator:

```
public final class CallCountingComparator implements Comparator {
    private final Comparator _comparator;
    private int _callCount;

    public CallCountingComparator(Comparator comparator) {
        assert comparator != null : "comparator cannot be null";

        _comparator = comparator;
        _callCount = 0;
    }

    public int compare(Object left, Object right) {
        ++_callCount;
        return _comparator.compare(left, right);
    }

    public int getCallCount() {
        return _callCount;
    }
}
```

Just like the ReverseComparator, the CallCountingComparator accepts any other Comparator in its constructor. The CallCountingComparator delegates the actual comparison check to this underlying comparator after incrementing the call count. All that is left is to provide the getCallCount() method to retrieve the call count when the sorting is complete.

With the help of the CallCountingComparator, you can now build a program to drive each of the sorting algorithms with best case, worst case, and average case test data and collect the results.

ListSorterCallCountingTest

Although this is not actually a unit test, the program is written to drive the algorithms as a JUnit test case because you need to do some setup and run several discrete scenarios for each algorithm. You begin by creating the test class, a constant for the size of the lists of data, and instance variables for the best, worst, and average case data sets. You also need an instance variable that holds a reference to the CallCountingComparator created in the previous section:

```
package com.wrox.algorithms.sorting;

import junit.framework.TestCase;
import com.wrox.algorithms.lists.List;
import com.wrox.algorithms.lists.ArrayList;

public class ListSorterCallCountingTest extends TestCase {
    private static final int TEST_SIZE = 1000;

    private final List _sortedArrayList = new ArrayList(TEST_SIZE);
    private final List _reverseArrayList = new ArrayList(TEST_SIZE);
```

```
    private final List _randomArrayList = new ArrayList(TEST_SIZE);

    private CallCountingComparator _comparator;
    ...
}
```

Next you set up the test data. For the best and worst cases, you fill the respective lists with `Integer` objects with values ranging between 1 and 1,000. For the average case, you generate random numbers within this same range. You also create the call counting comparator by wrapping a `NaturalComparator`. This works because `java.lang.Integer` supports the `Comparable` interface, just as the strings used in earlier examples do:

```
    protected void setUp() throws Exception {
        _comparator = new CallCountingComparator(NaturalComparator.INSTANCE);

        for (int i = 1; i < TEST_SIZE; ++i) {
            _sortedArrayList.add(new Integer(i));
        }

        for (int i = TEST_SIZE; i > 0; --i) {
            _reverseArrayList.add(new Integer(i));
        }

        for (int i = 1; i < TEST_SIZE; ++i) {
            _randomArrayList.add(new Integer((int)(TEST_SIZE * Math.random())));
        }
    }
```

To run each algorithm in the worst case, create the relevant `Listsorter` implementation and use it to sort the reverse-sorted list created in the `setUp()` method. The following code has a method to do this for each of our three algorithms. You might wonder how this works. If the reverse-sorted list is an instance variable and you first sort it using the bubble sort algorithm, how can it still be reverse-sorted when the next algorithm starts? This is one of the reasons you use JUnit to structure this driver program. JUnit creates a new instance of the driver class for each of the test methods, so each method in effect has its own copy of the reverse-sorted list, and `setUp()` will be run for each of them independently. This keeps the tests from interfering with one another:

```
    public void testWorstCaseBubblesort() {
        new BubblesortListSorter(_comparator).sort(_reverseArrayList);
        reportCalls(_comparator.getCallCount());
    }

    public void testWorstCaseSelectionSort() {
        new SelectionSortListSorter(_comparator).sort(_reverseArrayList);
        reportCalls(_comparator.getCallCount());
    }

    public void testWorstCaseInsertionSort() {
        new InsertionSortListSorter(_comparator).sort(_reverseArrayList);
        reportCalls(_comparator.getCallCount());
    }
```

To produce its output, each of these methods uses the `reportCalls()` method, described later in this section. Next are three similar methods for the best-case scenario, in which each algorithm is used to sort the already sorted list created in `setUp()`:

```
    public void testBestCaseBubblesort() {
        new BubblesortListSorter(_comparator).sort(_sortedArrayList);
        reportCalls(_comparator.getCallCount());
    }

    public void testBestCaseSelectionSort() {
        new SelectionSortListSorter(_comparator).sort(_sortedArrayList);
        reportCalls(_comparator.getCallCount());
    }

    public void testBestCaseInsertionSort() {
        new InsertionSortListSorter(_comparator).sort(_sortedArrayList);
        reportCalls(_comparator.getCallCount());
    }
```

You create three more methods to test the average case using the randomly generated list of numbers:

```
    public void testAverageCaseBubblesort() {
        new BubblesortListSorter(_comparator).sort(_randomArrayList);
        reportCalls(_comparator.getCallCount());
    }

    public void testAverageCaseSelectionSort() {
        new SelectionSortListSorter(_comparator).sort(_randomArrayList);
        reportCalls(_comparator.getCallCount());
    }

    public void testAverageCaseInsertionSort() {
        new InsertionSortListSorter(_comparator).sort(_randomArrayList);
        reportCalls(_comparator.getCallCount());
    }
```

Lastly, you define the `reportCalls()` method that produces the output for each scenario defined previously:

```
    private void reportCalls(int callCount) {
        System.out.println(getName() + ": " + callCount + " calls");
    }
```

This simple code contains one subtle point of interest. It uses the `getName()` method provided by the JUnit `TestCase` superclass to print the name of the scenario itself. The output produced by the program for the worst case is shown here:

```
testWorstCaseBubblesort: 499500 calls
testWorstCaseSelectionSort: 499500 calls
testWorstCaseInsertionSort: 499500 calls
```

As you can see, all three algorithms do exactly the same number of comparisons when tasked with sorting a completely reverse-sorted list! Don't take this to mean that they will always take the same amount of time to run; you are not measuring speed here. Always be careful to avoid jumping to conclusions based on simple statistics like those here. That said, this is a very interesting thing to know about these algorithms in this particular scenario.

The following numbers are produced for the best case:

```
testBestCaseBubblesort: 498501 calls
testBestCaseSelectionSort: 498501 calls
testBestCaseInsertionSort: 998 calls
```

Once again, the results are interesting. The bubble and selection sorts do the same number of comparisons, but the insertion sort does dramatically fewer indeed. You might want to review the insertion sort implementation now to see why this is the case.

The following numbers are produced in the average case:

```
testAverageCaseBubblesort: 498501 calls
testAverageCaseSelectionSort: 498501 calls
testAverageCaseInsertionSort: 262095 calls
```

Once again, the bubble and selection sorts performed the same number of comparisons, and the insertion sort required about half the number of comparisons to complete its job.

Understanding the Algorithm Comparison

You can draw a few conclusions from the comparative analysis just performed, but you must be careful not to draw too many. To really understand the difference in their behavior, you would need to run additional scenarios, such as the following:

- Quantifying how many objects are moved during the sort
- Using both `LinkedList` and `ArrayList` implementations for the test data
- Measuring running times for each scenario

Bearing the limitations of the analysis in mind, you can make the following observations:

- Bubble and selection sorts always do exactly the same number of comparisons.
- The number of comparisons required by the bubble and selection sorts is independent of the state of the input data.
- The number of comparisons required by an insertion sort is highly sensitive to the state of the input data. At worst, it requires as many comparisons as the other algorithms. At best, it requires fewer comparisons than the number of items in the input data.

Perhaps the most important point is that bubble and selection sorts are insensitive to the state of the input data. You can, therefore, consider them "brute force" algorithms, whereas the insertion sort is adaptive, because it does less work if less work is required. This is the main reason why the insertion sort tends to be favored over the other two algorithms in practice.

Summary

Highlights of this chapter include the following:

- You implemented three simple sorting algorithms — the bubble sort, the selection sort, and the insertion sort — complete with unit tests to prove they work as expected.
- You were introduced to the concept of comparators, and implemented several of them, including the natural comparator, a reverse comparator, and a call counting comparator.
- You looked at a comparative investigation of the three algorithms so that you can make informed decisions about the strengths and weaknesses of each.
- The idea of stability as it relates to sorting was also discussed.

Having worked through this chapter, you should understand the importance of sorting and the role it plays in supporting other algorithms, such as searching algorithms. In addition, you should understand that there are many ways to achieve the simple task of arranging objects in sequence. The next chapter introduces some more complex sorting algorithms that can sort huge amounts of information amazingly well.

Exercises

1. Write a test to prove that each of the algorithms can sort a randomly generated list of double objects.
2. Write a test to prove that the bubble sort and insertion sort algorithms from this chapter are stable.
3. Write a comparator that can order strings in dictionary order, with uppercase and lowercase letters considered equivalent.
4. Write a driver program to determine how many objects are moved by each algorithm during a sort operation.

7 Advanced Sorting

In Chapter 6, you learned about three sorting algorithms that were effective for small to medium problems. Although these algorithms are easy to implement, you need a few more sorting algorithms to tackle bigger problems. The algorithms in this chapter take a little more time to understand, and a little more skill to implement, but they are among the most effective general-purpose sorting routines you'll come across. One great thing about these algorithms is that they have been around for many years and have stood the test of time. Chances are good they were invented before you were born, as they date back as far as the 1950s. They are certainly older than both of the authors! Rest assured that the time you spend learning how these algorithms work will still be paying off in many years.

This chapter discusses the following:

- Understanding the shellsort algorithm
- Working with the quicksort algorithm
- Understanding the compound comparator and stability
- How to use the mergesort algorithm
- Understanding how compound comparators can overcome instability
- Comparing advanced sorting algorithms

Understanding the Shellsort Algorithm

One of the main limitations of the basic sorting algorithms is the amount of effort they require to move items that are a long way from their final sorted position into the correct place in the sorted result. The advanced sorting algorithms covered in this chapter give you the capability to move items a long way quickly, which is why they are far more effective at dealing with larger sets of data than the algorithms covered in the previous chapter.

Shellsort achieves this feat by breaking a large list of items into many smaller sublists, which are sorted independently using an insertion sort (see Chapter 6). While this sounds simple, the trick lies in repeating this process several times with careful creation of larger and larger sublists, until the whole list is sorted using an insertion sort on the final pass. As you learned in the previous chapter, an insertion sort is very effective on nearly sorted data, and this is exactly the state of the data on the final pass of a shellsort.

This shellsort example sorts the letters shown in Figure 7-1 alphabetically.

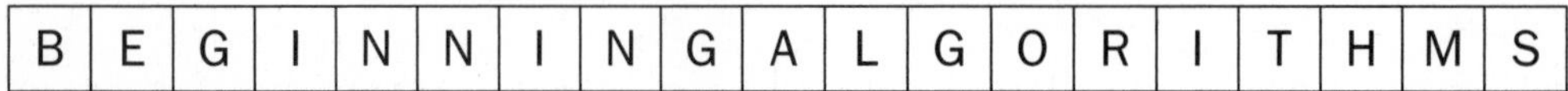

Figure 7-1: Sample data to demonstrate shellsort.

Shellsort is built upon the concept of *H-sorting*. A list is said to be H-sorted when, starting at any position, every H-th item is in sorted position relative to the other items. That concept will become clear as you work through an example. In the following Try It Out, you start by 4-sorting the list from Figure 7-1. In other words, you will consider only every fourth element and sort those items relative to each other.

Figure 7-2 shows every fourth item starting at position 0.

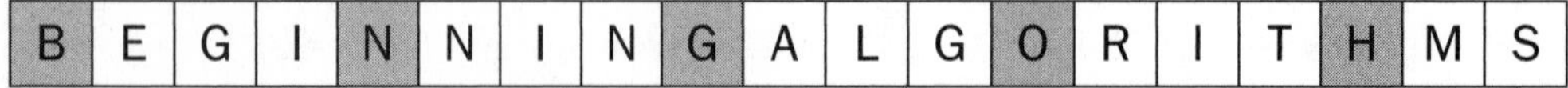

Figure 7-2: Every fourth item starting at position 0.

Ignoring all other items, you sort the highlighted items relative to each other, resulting in the list shown in Figure 7-3. The highlighted items now appear in alphabetical order (B, G, H, N, O).

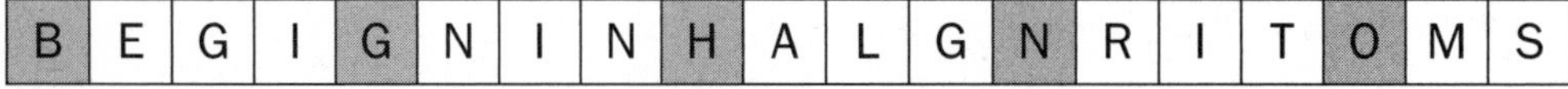

Figure 7-3: Every fourth item starting at position 0 sorted relative to each other.

You now consider every fourth item starting at position 1. Figure 7-4 shows these items before and after they are sorted relative to each other.

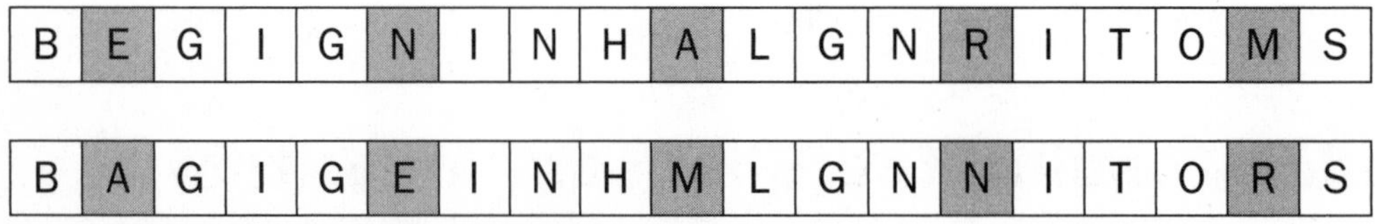

Figure 7-4: Sorting every fourth item starting at position 1.

Next you 4-sort starting at position 2, as shown in Figure 7-5.

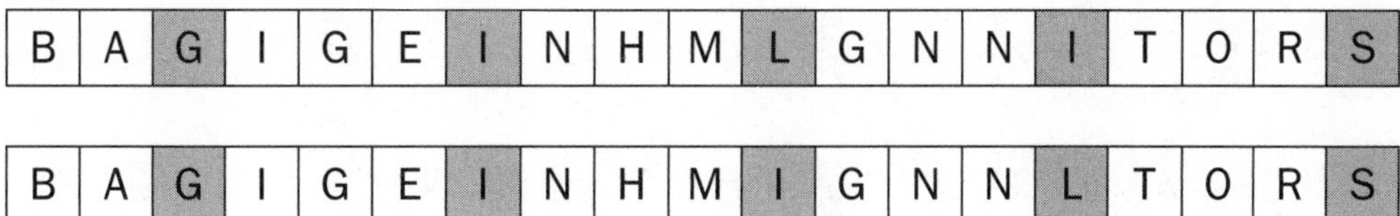

Figure 7-5: Sorting every fourth item starting at position 2.

Finally, you consider every fourth item starting at position 3. Figure 7-6 shows the situation before and after this step.

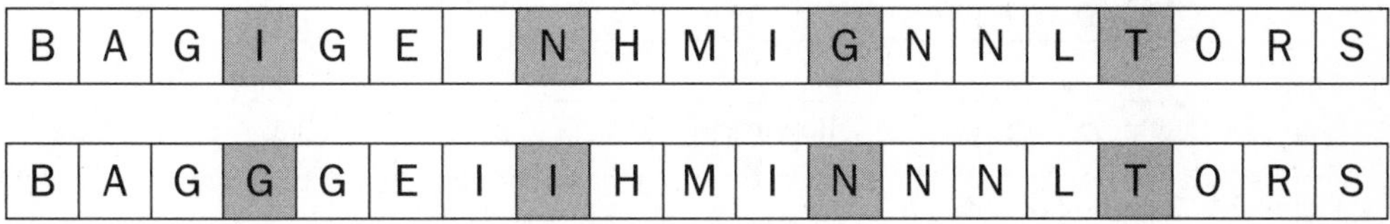

Figure 7-6: Sorting every fourth item starting at position 3.

There is no more to do to 4-sort the sample list. If you were to move to position 4, then you would be considering the same set of objects as when you started at position 0. As you can see from the second line in Figure 7-6, the list is by no means sorted, but it is 4-sorted. You can test this by choosing any item in the list and verifying that it is less than (or equal to) the item four positions to its right, and greater than (or equal to) the item four positions to its left.

The shellsort moves items a long way quickly. For very large lists of items, a good shellsort would start with a very large value of H, so it might start by 10,000-sorting the list, thereby moving items many thousands of positions at a time, in an effort to get them closer to their final sorted position quickly. Once the list is H-sorted for a large value of H, shellsort then chooses a smaller value for H and does the whole thing again. This process continues until the value of H is 1, and the whole list is sorted on the final pass. In this example, you 3-sort the list for the next pass.

Figure 7-7 shows every third item starting at position 0, both before and after being sorted relative to each other. By the way, notice the arrangement of the last four letters!

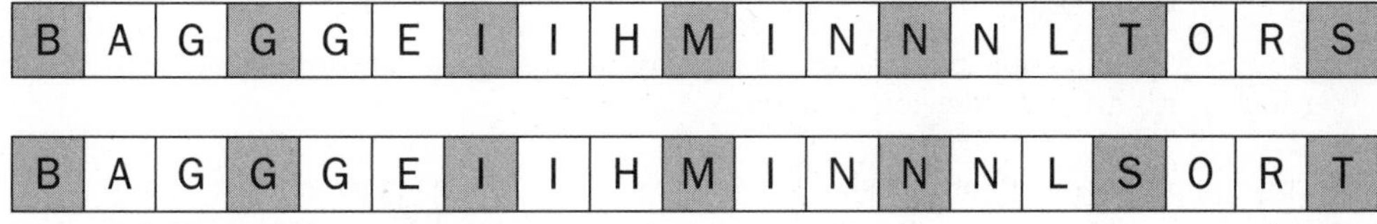

Figure 7-7: 3-sorting at position 0.

You move to position 1, and by coincidence there is nothing to do, as shown in Figure 7-8.

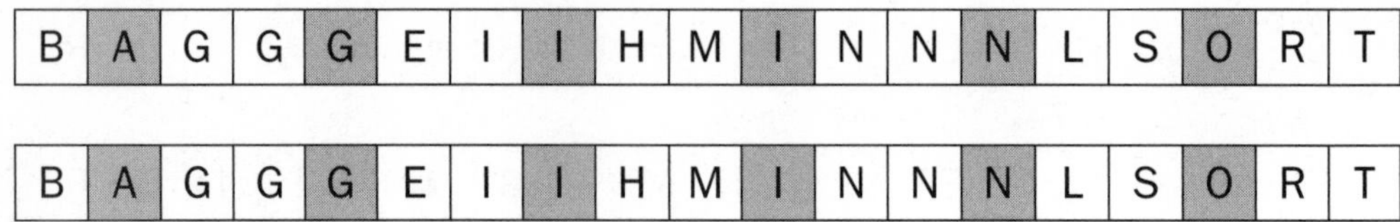

Figure 7-8: 3-sorting at position 1.

Finally, you sort every third item starting at position 2, as shown in Figure 7-9.

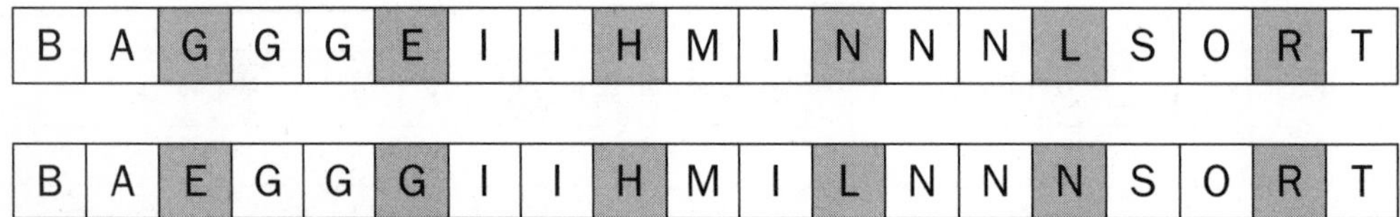

Figure 7-9: 3-sorting at position 2.

Notice how the list is now nearly sorted. Most items are only a position or two away from where they should be, which you can accomplish with a simple insertion sort. After a quick run over the list, you end up with the final sorted arrangement shown in Figure 7-10. If you compare this with the previous list, you will see that no item had to move more than two positions to reach its final position.

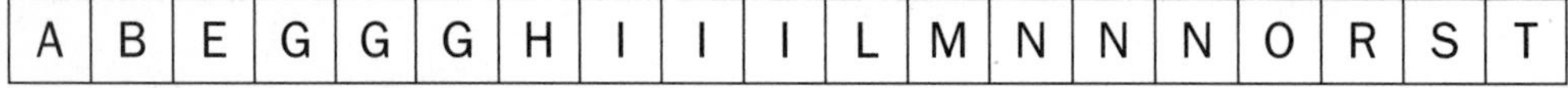

Figure 7-10: The final sorted list.

Much of the research into shellsort has revolved around the choice of the successive values for H. The original sequence suggested by the algorithm's inventor (1, 2, 4, 8, 16, 32, . . .) is provably terrible, as it compares only items in odd positions with items in odd positions until the final pass. Shellsort works well when each item is sorted relative to different items on each pass. A simple and effective sequence is (1, 4, 13, 40, . . .) whereby each value of `H = 3 × H + 1`. In the following Try It Out, you implement a shellsort.

Try It Out — Testing a Shellsort

In this section, you will implement the shellsort algorithm, using the same test data you used to drive the sorting algorithms in the previous chapter.

The test for your shellsort algorithm should look familiar by now. It simply extends `AbstractListSorterTest` and instantiates the (not yet written) shellsort implementation:

```
package com.wrox.algorithms.sorting;

public class ShellsortListSorterTest extends AbstractListSorterTest {
    protected ListSorter createListSorter(Comparator comparator) {
        return new ShellsortListSorter(comparator);
    }
}
```

How It Works

The preceding test extends the general-purpose test for sorting algorithms you created in Chapter 6. All you need to do to test the shellsort implementation is instantiate it by overriding the `createListSorter()` method.

In the following Try It Out, you implement the shellsort.

Try It Out Implementing the Shellsort

The implementation has a similar structure to those for the basic sorting algorithms. It implements the `ListSorter` interface, and requires a comparator to impose the order on the items. Create the implementation class with an instance field to hold the comparator to be used, and an array of integers representing the H-values to be used:

```
package com.wrox.algorithms.sorting;

import com.wrox.algorithms.lists.List;

public class ShellsortListSorter implements ListSorter {
    private final Comparator _comparator;
    private final int[] _increments = {121, 40, 13, 4, 1};

    public ShellsortListSorter(Comparator comparator) {
        assert comparator != null : "comparator cannot be null";
        _comparator = comparator;
    }
    ...
}
```

The `sort()` method, which you create next, simply loops through the increments defined in the previous array and calls `hSort()` on the list for each increment. Note that this relies on the final increment having a value of `1`. Feel free to experiment with other sequences, but remember that the final value has to be `1` or your list will only end up "nearly" sorted!

```
    public List sort(List list) {
        assert list != null : "list cannot be null";

        for (int i = 0; i < _increments.length; i++) {
            int increment = _increments[i];
            hSort(list, increment);
        }

        return list;
    }
```

Next, create the `hSort()` implementation, being careful to ignore increments that are too large for the data you are trying to sort. There's not much point 50-sorting a list with only ten items, as there will be nothing to compare each item to. You require your increment to be less than half the size of your list.

The rest of the method simply delegates to the `sortSubList()` method once for each position, starting at 0 as you did in the sample list:

```
private void hSort(List list, int increment) {
    if (list.size() < (increment * 2)) {
        return;
    }

    for (int i=0; i< increment; ++i) {
        sortSublist(list, i, increment);
    }
}
```

Finally, you create the method that sorts every H-th item relative to each other. This is an in-place version of insertion sort, with the added twist that it considers only every H-th item. If you were to replace every occurrence of `+ increment` and `- increment` in the following code with `+ 1` and `- 1`, you'd have a basic insertion sort. Refer to Chapter 6 for a detailed explanation of insertion sort.

```
private void sortSublist(List list, int startIndex, int increment) {
    for (int i = startIndex + increment; i < list.size(); i += increment) {
        Object value = list.get(i);
        int j;
        for (j = i; j > startIndex; j -= increment) {
            Object previousValue = list.get(j - increment);
            if (_comparator.compare(value, previousValue) >= 0) {
                break;
            }
            list.set(j, previousValue);
        }
        list.set(j, value);
    }
}
```

How It Works

The shellsort code works by successively sorting sublists of items that are evenly spaced inside the larger list of items. These lists start out with few items in them, with large gaps between the items. The sublists become progressively larger in size but fewer in number as the items are more closely spaced. The outermost loop in the main `sort()` method is concerned with H-sorting the sublists at progressively smaller increments, eventually H-sorting with H set to a value of `1`, which means the list is completely sorted.

The `hSort()` method is concerned with ensuring that all of the sublists that are made up of items separated by the current increment are correctly sorted. It works by looping over the number of sublists indicated by the current increment and delegating the actual sorting of the sublist to the `sortSublist()` method. This method uses an insertion sort algorithm (explained in Chapter 6) to rearrange the items of the sublist so that they are sorted relative to each other.

Understanding Quicksort

Quicksort is the first sorting algorithm discussed that uses recursion. Although it can be recast in an iterative implementation, recursion is the natural state for quicksort. Quicksort works using a divide-and-conquer approach, recursively processing smaller and smaller parts of the list. At each level, the goal of the algorithm is three-fold:

- To place one item in the final sorted position
- To place all items smaller than the sorted item to the left of the sorted item
- To place all items greater than the sorted item to the right of the sorted item

By maintaining these invariants in each pass, the list is divided into two parts (note that it is not necessarily divided into two halves) that can each be sorted independently of the other. This section uses the list of letters shown in Figure 7-11 as sample data.

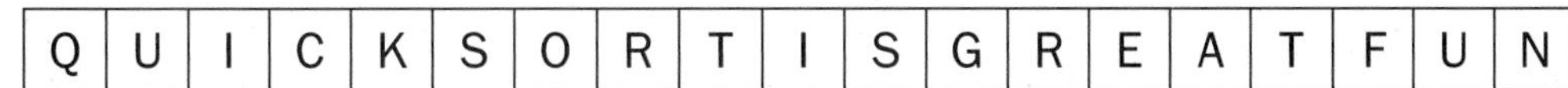

Figure 7-11: Sample list for quicksort.

The first step in quicksort is to choose the partitioning item. This is the item that ends up in its final sorted position after this pass, and partitions the list into sections, with smaller items to the left (arranged randomly) and larger items to its right (arranged randomly). There are many ways to choose the partitioning item, but this example uses a simple strategy of choosing the item that happens to be at the far right of the list. In Figure 7-12, this item is highlighted. You also initialize two indexes at the leftmost and rightmost of the remaining items, as shown in the figure.

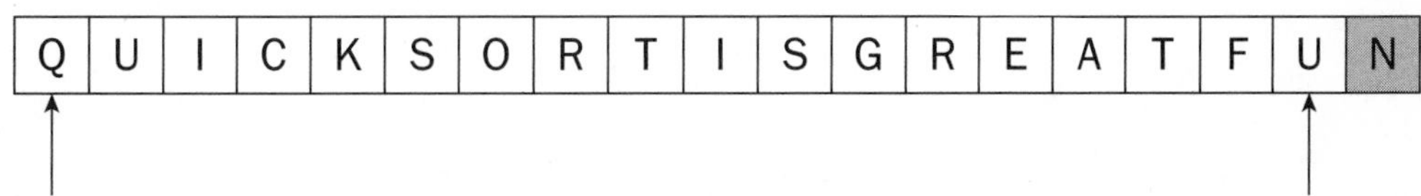

Figure 7-12: Starting position for the initial quicksort pass.

The algorithm proceeds by advancing the left and right indexes towards each other until they meet. As the left index proceeds, it stops when it finds an item that is larger than the partitioning item. As the right index proceeds, it stops when it encounters an item that is smaller than the partitioning item. The items are then swapped so that they are each in the appropriate part of the list. Remember that the idea is to have smaller items to the left and larger items to the right, although not necessarily in sorted order.

In the example shown in Figure 7-12, the left index is pointing to the letter Q. This is larger than the partitioning value (N), so it is out of place at the far left of the list. The right index was initially pointing at U, which is larger than N, so that's okay. If it moves one position to the left, it is pointing at the letter F, which is smaller than N. It is therefore out of place at the far right of the list. This situation is displayed in Figure 7-13.

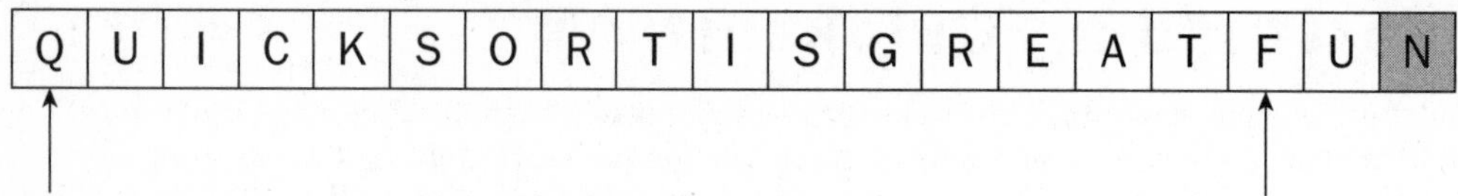

Figure 7-13: The first two out-of-place items have been found.

To get these two out-of-place items closer to their final sorted position, you swap them as shown in Figure 7-14.

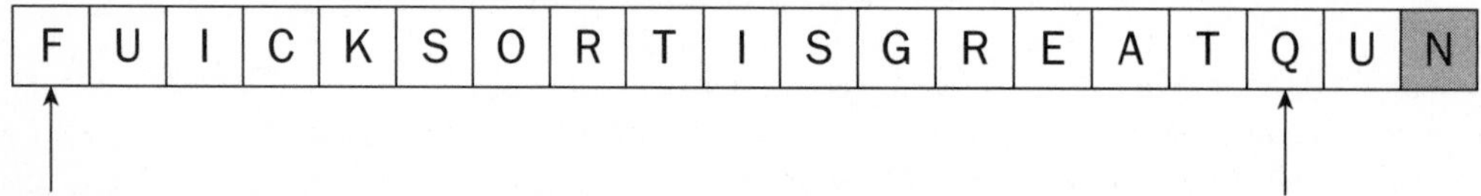

Figure 7-14: The first two out-of-place items are swapped.

The left index now continues moving to the right until it encounters an item that is larger than the partitioning item. One is found immediately in the second position (U). The right index then proceeds moving to the left and finds an A out of place, as shown in Figure 7-15.

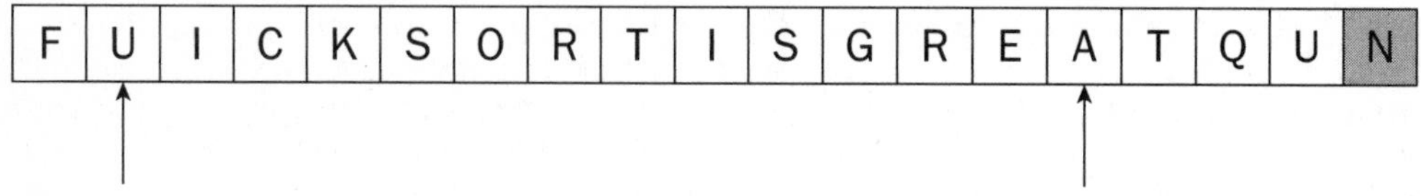

Figure 7-15: Two more out-of-place items are found.

Once again, the items are swapped, as shown in Figure 7-16.

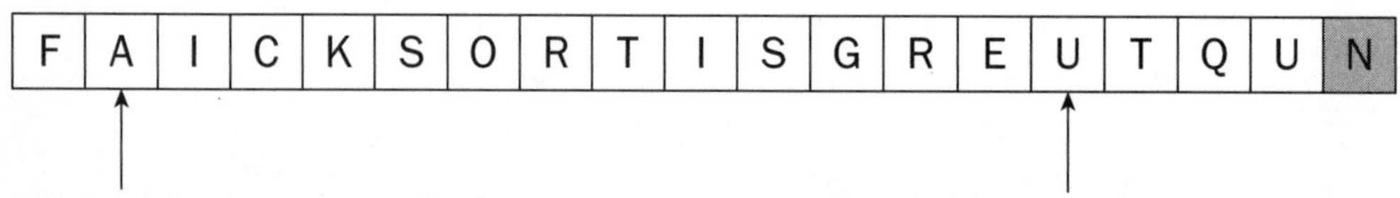

Figure 7-16: The second pair of out-of-place items are swapped.

The same procedure continues as the left and right indexes move toward each other. The next pair of out-of-place items are S and E, as shown in Figure 7-17.

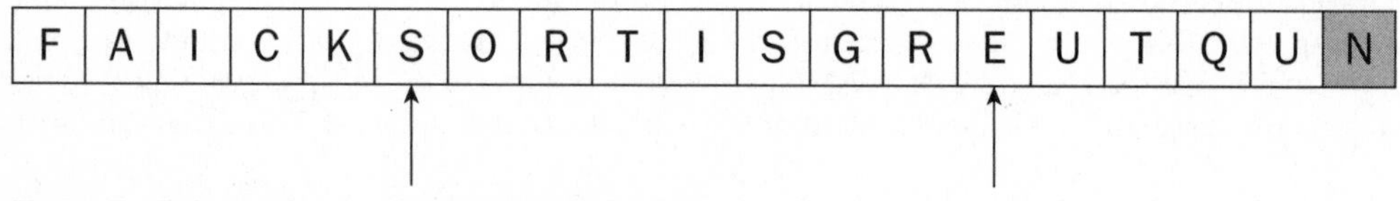

Figure 7-17: Two more out-of-place items are found.

You swap these items, leaving the list in the state shown in Figure 7-18. At this stage, every item to the left of the left index is less than the partitioning item, and every item to the right of the right index is larger than the partitioning item. The items between the left and right indexes still need to be handled.

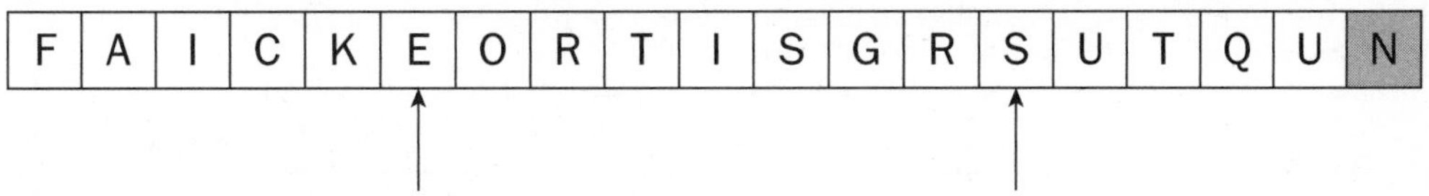

Figure 7-18: The letters E and S are swapped.

You continue with the same procedure. The next out-of-place items are shown in Figure 7-19.

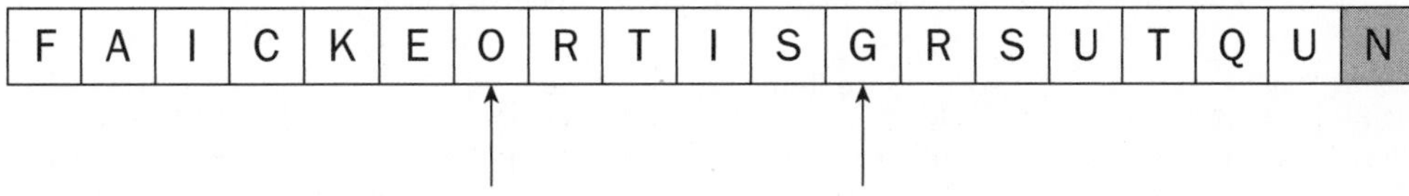

Figure 7-19: The letters O and G are out of place.

You swap them into the position shown in Figure 7-20.

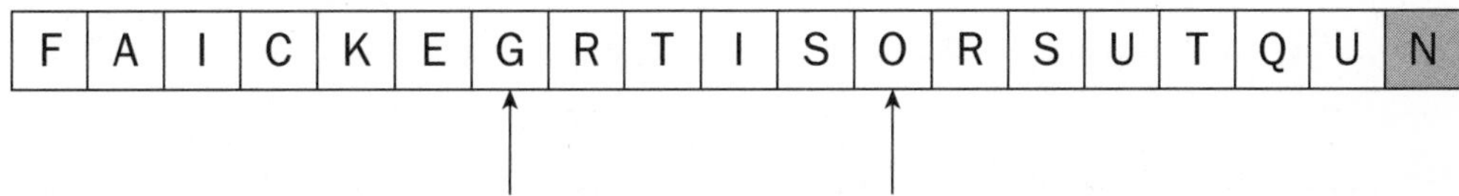

Figure 7-20: The letters O and G are swapped.

You are almost done for the first quicksort pass. Figure 7-21 demonstrates that one pair of out-of-place items remain.

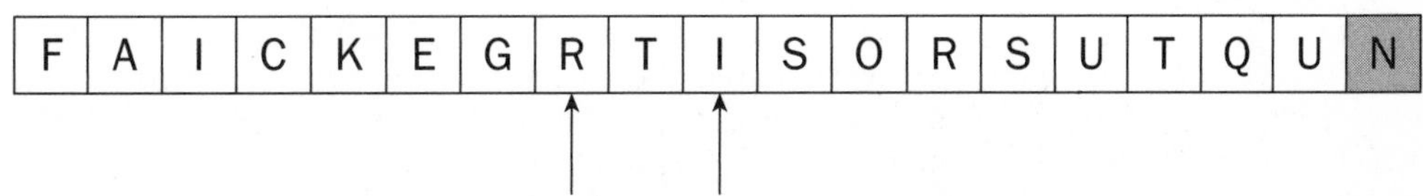

Figure 7-21: The letters R and I are out of place.

After you swap them, the list is in the state shown in Figure 7-22.

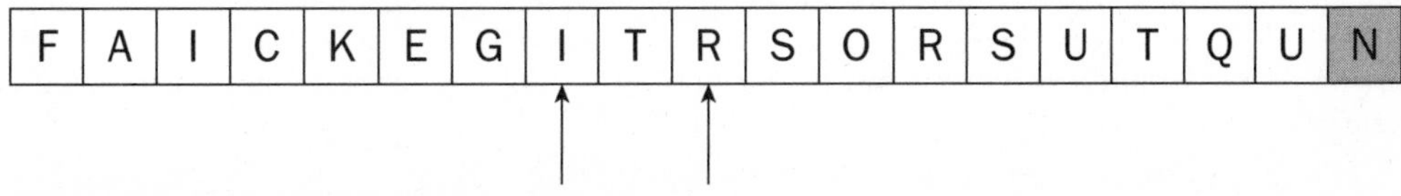

Figure 7-22: The letters R and I are swapped.

Now things get interesting. The algorithm proceeds as before, with the left index advancing until it finds an item larger than the partitioning item, in this case the letter T. The right index then advances to the left but stops when it reaches the same value as the left index. There is no advantage to going beyond this point, as all items to the left of this index have been dealt with already. The list is now in the state shown in Figure 7-23, with both left and right indexes pointing at the letter T.

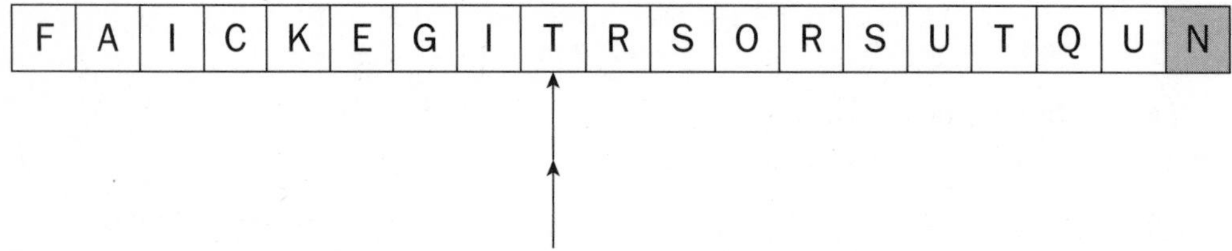

Figure 7-23: The left and right indexes meet at the partitioning position.

The point where the two indexes meet is the partitioning position—that is, it is the place in the list where the partitioning value actually belongs. Therefore, you do one final swap between this location and the partitioning value at the far right of the list to move the partitioning value into its final sorted position. When this is done, the letter N is in the partitioning position, with all of the values to its left being smaller, and all of the values to its right being larger (see Figure 7-24).

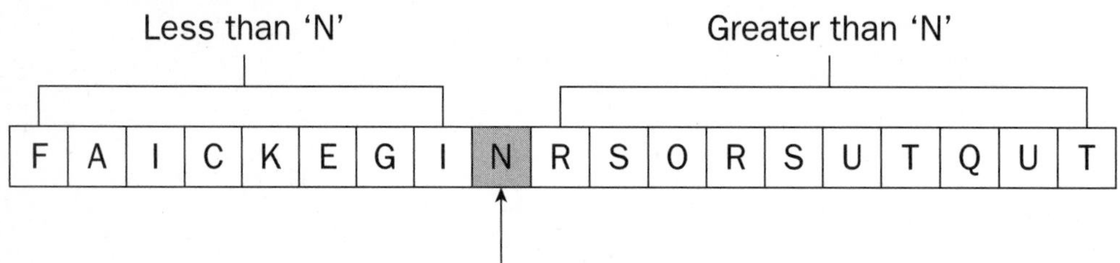

Figure 7-24: The partitioning item in final sorted position.

All the steps illustrated so far have resulted in only the letter N being in its final sorted position. The list itself is far from sorted. However, the list has been divided into two parts that can be sorted independently of each other. You simply sort the left part of the list, and then the right part of the list, and the whole list is sorted. This is where the recursion comes in. You apply the same quicksort algorithm to each of the two sublists to the left and right of the partitioning item.

You have two cases to consider when building recursive algorithms: the base case and the general case. For quicksort, the base case occurs when the sublist to be sorted has only one element; it is by definition already sorted and nothing needs to be done. The general case occurs when there is more than one item, in which case you apply the preceding algorithm to partition the list into smaller sublists after placing the partitioning item into the final sorted position.

Having seen an example of how the quicksort algorithm works, you can test it in the next Try It Out exercise.

Try It Out Testing the quicksort Algorithm

You start by creating a test case that is specific to the quicksort algorithm:

```
package com.wrox.algorithms.sorting;

public class QuicksortListSorterTest extends AbstractListSorterTest {
    protected ListSorter createListSorter(Comparator comparator) {
        return new QuicksortListSorter(comparator);
    }
}
```

How It Works

The preceding test extends the general-purpose test for sorting algorithms that you created in Chapter 6. All you need to do to test the quicksort implementation is instantiate it by overriding the `createListSorter()` method.

In the next Try It Out, you implement quicksort.

Try It Out Implementing quicksort

First you create the `QuicksortListSorter`, which will be familiar to you because its basic structure is very similar to the other sorting algorithms you have seen so far. It implements the `ListSorter` interface and accepts a comparator that imposes the sorted order on the objects to be sorted:

```
package com.wrox.algorithms.sorting;

import com.wrox.algorithms.lists.List;

public class QuicksortListSorter implements ListSorter {
    private final Comparator _comparator;

    public QuicksortListSorter(Comparator comparator) {
        assert comparator != null : "comparator cannot be null";
        _comparator = comparator;
    }
    ...
}
```

You use the `sort()` method to delegate to the `quicksort()` method, passing in the indexes of the first and last elements to be sorted. In this case, this represents the entire list. This method will later be called recursively, passing in smaller sublists defined by different indexes.

```
    public List sort(List list) {
        assert list != null : "list cannot be null";

        quicksort(list, 0, list.size() - 1);

        return list;
    }
```

You implement the quicksort by using the indexes provided to partition the list around the partitioning value at the end of the list, and then recursively calling `quicksort()` for both the left and right sublists:

```
    private void quicksort(List list, int startIndex, int endIndex) {
        if (startIndex < 0 || endIndex >= list.size()) {
            return;
        }
        if (endIndex <= startIndex) {
            return;
        }

        Object value = list.get(endIndex);

        int partition = partition(list, value, startIndex, endIndex - 1);
        if (_comparator.compare(list.get(partition), value) < 0) {
            ++partition;
        }

        swap(list, partition, endIndex);

        quicksort(list, startIndex, partition - 1);
        quicksort(list, partition + 1, endIndex);
    }
```

You use the `partition()` method to perform the part of the algorithm whereby out-of-place items are swapped with each other so that small items end up to the left, and large items end up to the right:

```
    private int partition(List list, Object value, int leftIndex, int rightIndex) {
        int left = leftIndex;
        int right = rightIndex;

        while (left < right) {
            if (_comparator.compare(list.get(left), value) < 0) {
                ++left;
                continue;
            }

            if (_comparator.compare(list.get(right), value) >= 0) {
                --right;
                continue;
            }

            swap(list, left, right);
            ++left;
        }

        return left;
    }
```

Finally, you implement a simple `swap()` method that protects itself against calls to swap an item with itself:

```
    private void swap(List list, int left, int right) {
        if (left == right) {
            return;
        }
        Object temp = list.get(left);
        list.set(left, list.get(right));
        list.set(right, temp);
    }
```

How It Works

The `quicksort()` method begins by bounds-checking the two indexes it is passed. This enables later code to be simplified by ignoring this concern. It next obtains the partitioning value from the far right end of the list. The next step is to obtain the partitioning position by delegating to the `partition()` method.

The `partition()` method contains a test to check whether the value at the partitioning location is smaller than the partitioning value itself. This can happen, for example, when the partitioning value is the largest value in the whole list of items. Given that you are choosing it at random, this can happen very easily. In this case, you advance the partitioning index by one position. This code is written such that the left and right indexes always end up with the same value, as they did in the explanation of the algorithm earlier in the chapter. The value at this index is the return value from this method.

Understanding the Compound Comparator and Stability

Before considering the third advanced sorting algorithm, this section elaborates on the discussion of stability, which was first brought to your attention in the previous chapter. Now is a good time because the two algorithms discussed so far in this chapter share the shortcoming that they are not stable. The algorithm covered next — mergesort — is stable, so now is a good opportunity to deal with the lack of stability in shellsort and quicksort.

As you learned in Chapter 6, stability is the tendency of a sorting algorithm to maintain the relative position of items with the same sort key during the sort process. Quicksort and shellsort lack stability, as they pay no attention at all to the items that are near each other in the original input list. This section discusses a way to compensate for this issue when using one of these algorithms: the *compound comparator*.

The example in Chapter 6 was based on a list of people that was sorted by either first name or last name. The relative order of people with the same last name is maintained (that is, they were ordered by first name within the same last name group) if the algorithm used is stable. Another way to achieve the same effect is to use a compound key for the `person` object, consisting of *both* the first name and last name when sorting by first name, and *both* the last name and first name when sorting by last name. As you saw in Chapter 6, it is often possible to create useful general-purpose comparators to solve many different problems. That is the approach taken in the next Try It Out, where you create a compound comparator that can wrap any number of standard single-value comparators to achieve a sort outcome based on a compound key.

Try It Out — Testing CompoundComparator

The tests for the compound comparator need the services of a dummy comparator that always returns a known value from its `compare()` method. Give this the obvious name of `FixedComparator`. The code is shown here:

```
package com.wrox.algorithms.sorting;

public class FixedComparator implements Comparator {
    private final int _result;

    public FixedComparator(int result) {
        _result = result;
    }

    public int compare(Object left, Object right) {
        return _result;
    }
}
```

You can now begin writing tests for the compound comparator. You have to cover three basic cases: it returns zero, it returns a positive integer, or it returns a negative integer from its `compare()` method. Each of these tests adds multiple fixed comparators to the compound comparator. The first of these is set up to return zero, indicating that the compound comparator must use more than the first element of the compound key to sort the items. The code for the three test cases is shown here:

```
package com.wrox.algorithms.sorting;

import junit.framework.TestCase;

public class CompoundComparatorTest extends TestCase {
    public void testComparisonContinuesWhileEqual() {
        CompoundComparator comparator = new CompoundComparator();
        comparator.addComparator(new FixedComparator(0));
        comparator.addComparator(new FixedComparator(0));
        comparator.addComparator(new FixedComparator(0));

        assertTrue(comparator.compare("IGNORED", "IGNORED") == 0);
    }

    public void testComparisonStopsWhenLessThan() {
        CompoundComparator comparator = new CompoundComparator();
        comparator.addComparator(new FixedComparator(0));
        comparator.addComparator(new FixedComparator(0));
        comparator.addComparator(new FixedComparator(-57));
        comparator.addComparator(new FixedComparator(91));

        assertTrue(comparator.compare("IGNORED", "IGNORED") < 0);
    }

    public void testComparisonStopsWhenGreaterThan() {
        CompoundComparator comparator = new CompoundComparator();
```

```
        comparator.addComparator(new FixedComparator(0));
        comparator.addComparator(new FixedComparator(0));
        comparator.addComparator(new FixedComparator(91));
        comparator.addComparator(new FixedComparator(-57));

        assertTrue(comparator.compare("IGNORED", "IGNORED") > 0);
    }
}
```

How It Works

The test relies upon being able to add any number of other comparators to the new `CompoundComparator` in sequence. The first test adds four comparators that all return zero when their respective `compare()` methods are called. The idea is that the `CompoundComparator` checks with each of its nested comparators in turn, returning as soon as one of them returns a nonzero value. If all of the nested comparators return zero, the overall comparison has determined that the objects are the same.

The second test sets up a series of nested comparators whereby the third one returns a negative value. The intended behavior of the `CompoundComparator` is that it should return the first nonzero value from its nested comparators. The test asserts that this behavior is correct. The final test does the same job but with a positive return value.

In the next Try It Out, you implement `CompoundComparator`.

Try It Out Implementing CompoundComparator

You start by creating the class to implement the `Comparator` interface, and give it a private `List` in which to hold the unknown number of comparators for each element of the compound sort key:

```
package com.wrox.algorithms.sorting;

import com.wrox.algorithms.iteration.Iterator;
import com.wrox.algorithms.lists.ArrayList;
import com.wrox.algorithms.lists.List;

public class CompoundComparator implements Comparator {
    private final List _comparators = new ArrayList();
    ...
}
```

You provide the `addComparator()` method to allow any number of comparators to be wrapped by the compound comparator:

```
    public void addComparator(Comparator comparator) {
        assert comparator != null : "comparator can't be null";
        assert comparator != this : "can't add comparator to itself";

        _comparators.add(comparator);
    }
```

Finally, implement `compare()` to use each of the wrapped comparators in turn, returning as soon as one of them returns a nonzero result:

```
public int compare(Object left, Object right) {
    int result = 0;
    Iterator i = _comparators.iterator();

    for (i.first(); !i.isDone(); i.next()) {
        result = ((Comparator) i.current()).compare(left, right);
        if (result != 0) {
            break;
        }
    }

    return result;
}
```

The `CompoundComparator` is extremely useful because it can re-use any existing comparators to overcome a lack of stability, or simply to sort on a compound key.

Understanding the Mergesort Algorithm

Mergesort is the last of the advanced sorting algorithms covered in this chapter. Like quicksort, it is possible to implement mergesort both recursively and iteratively, but we implement it recursively in this section. Unlike quicksort, mergesort does not sort the list it is provided in place; rather, it creates a new output list containing the objects from the input list in sorted order.

Merging

Mergesort is built upon the concept of merging. Merging takes two (already sorted) lists and produces a new output list containing all of the items from both lists in sorted order. For example, Figure 7-25 shows two input lists that need to be merged. Note that both lists are already in sorted order.

Figure 7-25: Two already sorted lists that we want to merge.

The process of merging begins by placing indexes at the head of each list. These will obviously point to the smallest items in each list, as shown in Figure 7-26.

Figure 7-26: Merging begins at the head of each list.

The items at the start of each list are compared, and the smallest of them is added to the output list. The next item in the list from which the smallest item was copied is considered. The situation after the first item has been moved to the output list is shown in Figure 7-27.

Figure 7-27: The first item is added to the output list.

The current items from each list are compared again, with the smallest being placed on the output list. In this case, it's the letter D from the second list. Figure 7-28 shows the situation after this step has taken place.

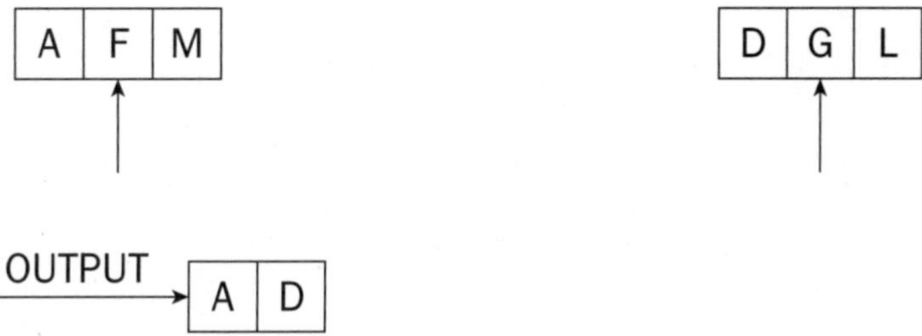

Figure 7-28: The second item is added to the output list.

The process continues; this time the letter F from the first list is the smaller item and it is copied to the output list, as shown in Figure 7-29.

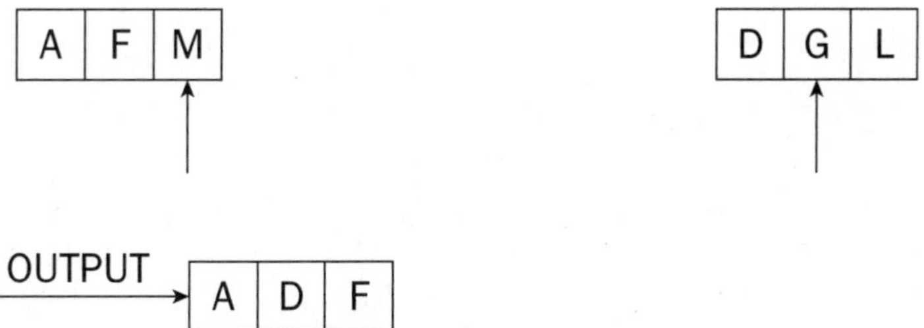

Figure 7-29: The third item is placed on the output list.

This process continues until both input lists have been exhausted and the output contains each item from both lists in sorted order. The final state is shown in Figure 7-30.

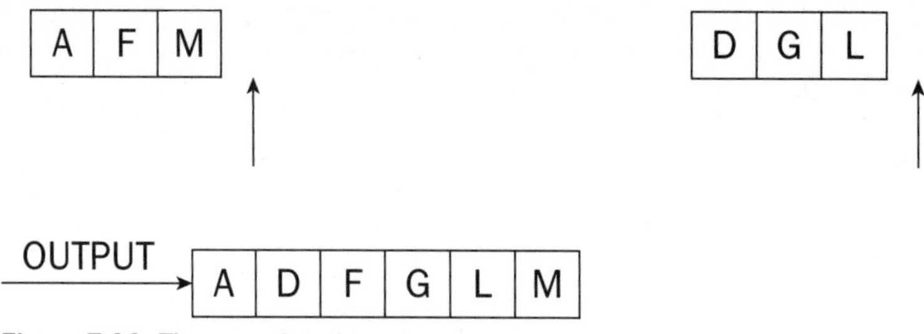

Figure 7-30: The completed merge process.

The mergesort Algorithm

The mergesort algorithm is based upon the idea of merging. As with the quicksort algorithm, you approach mergesort with recursion, but quicksort was a divide-and-conquer approach, whereas the mergesort algorithm describes more of a combine-and-conquer technique. Sorting happens at the top level of the recursion only after it is complete at all lower levels. Contrast this with quicksort, where one item is placed into final sorted position at the top level before the problem is broken down and each recursive call places one further item into sorted position.

This example uses the list of letters shown in Figure 7-31 as the sample data.

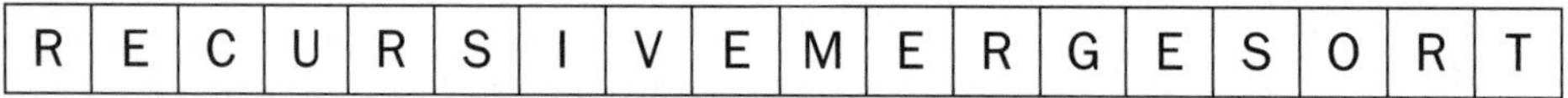

Figure 7-31: Sample list to demonstrate recursive mergesort.

Like all the sorting algorithms, mergesort is built upon an intriguingly simple idea. Mergesort simply divides the list to be sorted in half, sorts each half independently, and merges the result. It sounds almost too simple to be effective, but it will still take some explaining. Figure 7-32 shows the sample list after it has been split in half. When these halves are sorted independently, the final step will be to merge them together, as described in the preceding section on merging.

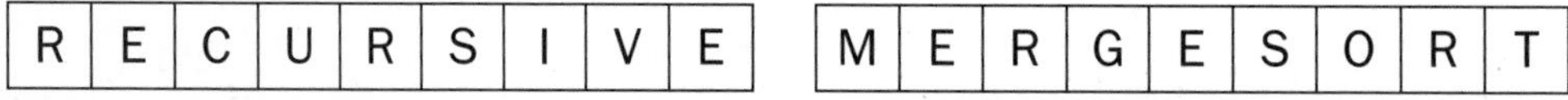

Figure 7-32: The sample list when split in half.

A key difference between mergesort and quicksort is that the way in which the list is split in mergesort is completely independent of the input data itself. Mergesort simply halves the list, whereas quicksort *partitions* the list based on a chosen value, which can split the list at any point on any pass.

So how do you sort the first half of the list? By applying mergesort again! You split that half in half, sort each half independently, and merge them. Figure 7-33 shows half of the original list split in half itself.

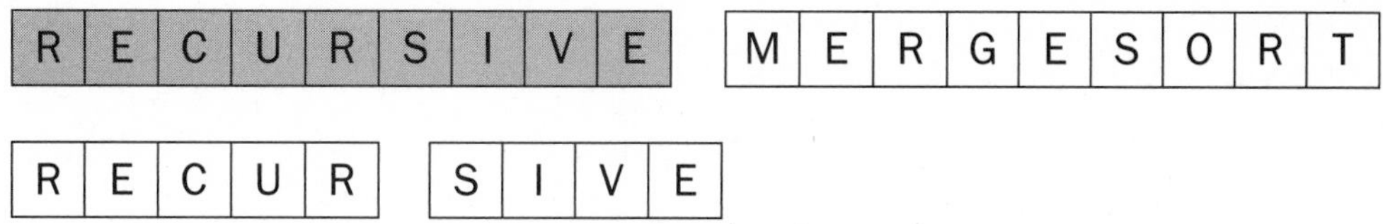

Figure 7-33: The first recursive call to mergesort the first half of the original list.

How do you sort the first half of the first half of the original list? Another recursive call to mergesort, of course. By now you will no doubt be getting the idea that you keep recursing until you reach a sublist with a single item in it, which of course is already sorted like any single-item list, and that will be the base case for this recursive algorithm. You saw the general case already — that is, when there is more than one item in the list to be sorted, split the list in half, sort the halves, and then merge them together.

Figure 7-34 shows the situation at the third level of recursion.

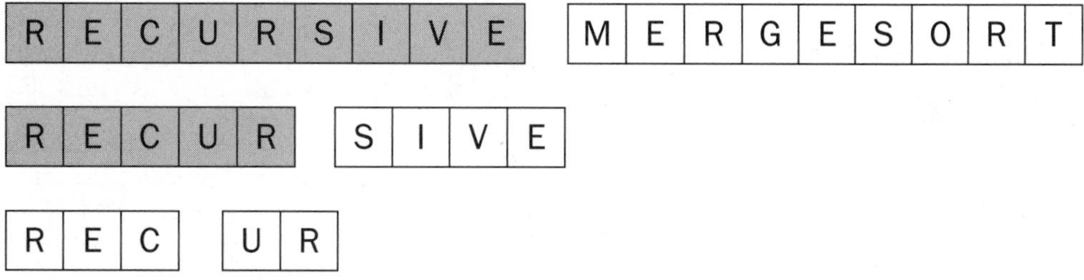

Figure 7-34: Third level of recursion during mergesort.

As you still have not reached a sublist with one item in it, you continue the recursion to yet another level, as shown in Figure 7-35.

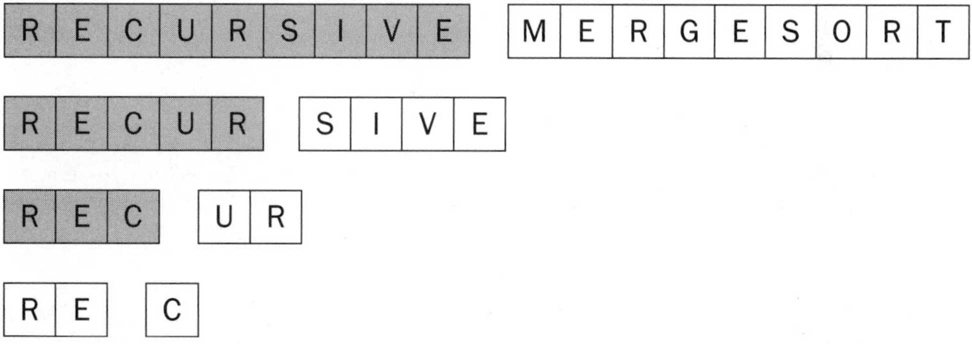

Figure 7-35: Fourth level of recursion during mergesort.

At the level of recursion shown in Figure 7-35, you are trying to sort the two-element sublist containing the letters R and E. This sublist has more than one item in it, so once more you need to split and sort the halves as shown in Figure 7-36.

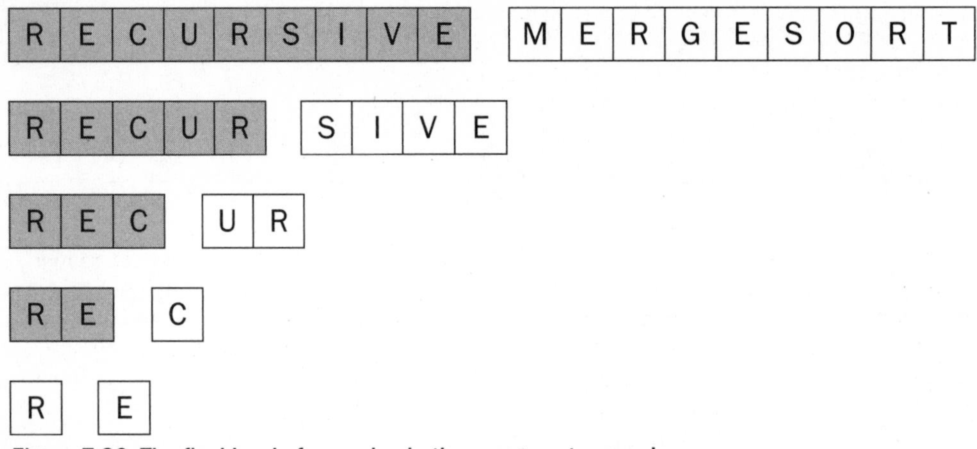

Figure 7-36: The final level of recursion in the mergesort example.

You have finally reached a level at which you have two single-item lists. This is the base case in the recursive algorithm, so you can now merge these two single-item sorted lists together into a single two-item sorted sublist, as shown in Figure 7-37.

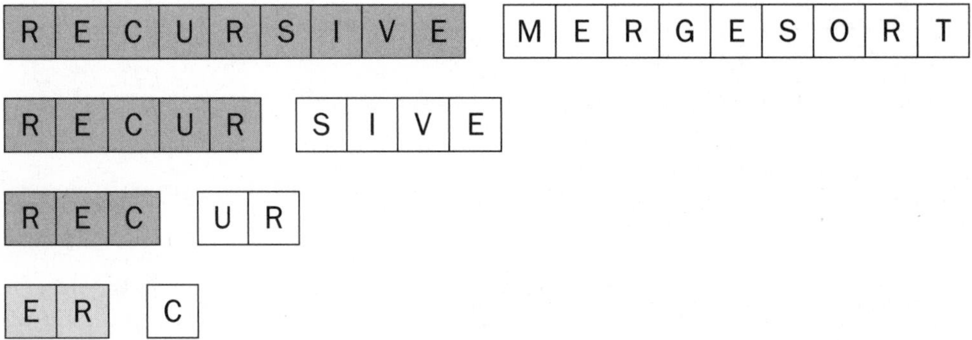

Figure 7-37: The first merge operation is complete.

In Figure 7-37, the two sublists of the sublist (R, E, C) are already sorted. One is the two-element sublist you just merged, and the other is a single-item sublist containing the letter C. These two sublists can thus be merged to produce a three-element sorted sublist, as shown in Figure 7-38.

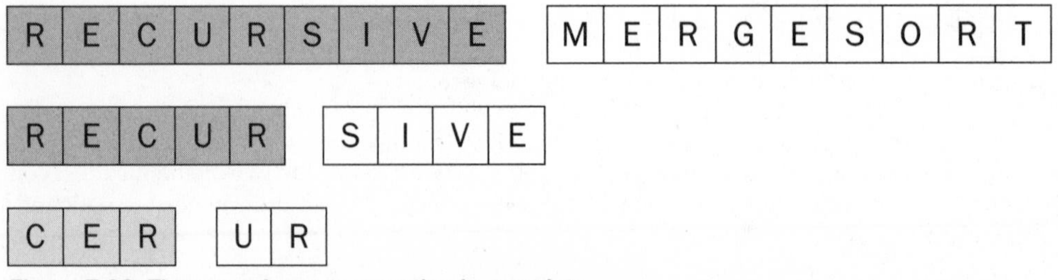

Figure 7-38: The second merge operation is complete.

The sublist (R, E, C, U, R) now has one sublist that is sorted and one sublist that is not yet sorted. The next step is to sort the second sublist (U, R). As you would expect, this involves recursively mergesorting this two-element sublist, as shown in Figure 7-39.

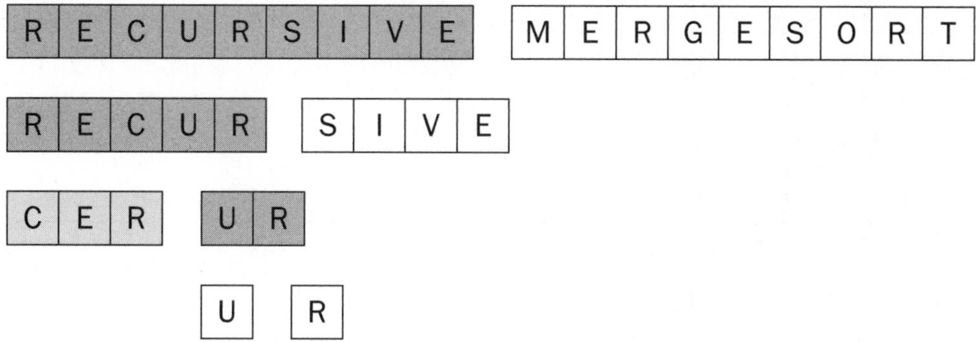

Figure 7-39: Recursively sorting the (U, R) sublist.

The two single-item sublists can now be merged as shown in Figure 7-40.

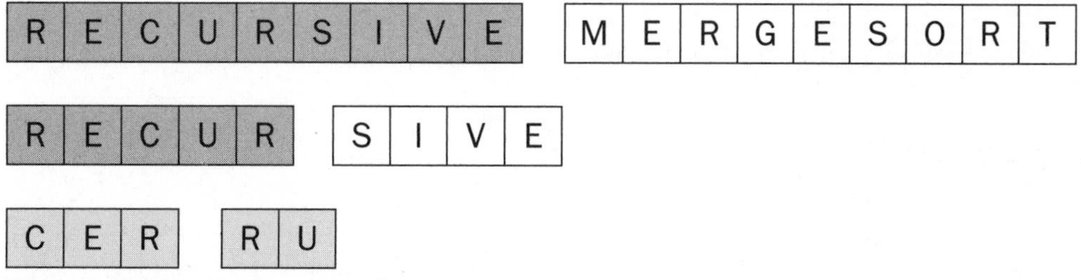

Figure 7-40: Merging the two single-item sublists.

Both sublists of the (R, E, C, U, R) sublist are sorted independently, so the recursion can unwind by merging these two sublists together, as shown in Figure 7-41.

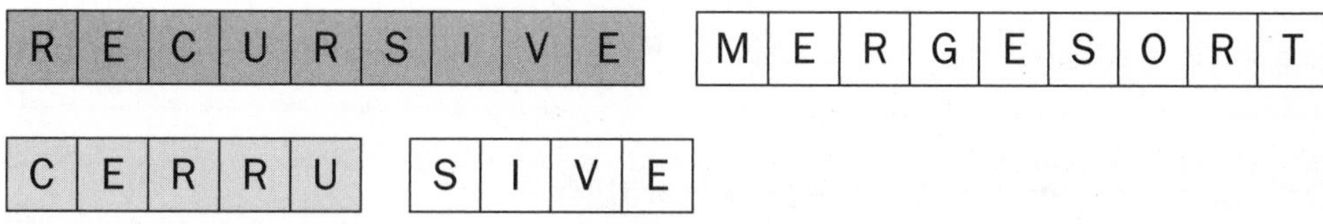

Figure 7-41: Unwinding the recursion by merging two sublists.

The algorithm continues with the (S, I, V, E) sublist until it too is sorted, as shown in Figure 7-42. (We have skipped a number of steps between the preceding and following figures because they are very similar to the steps for sorting the first sublist.)

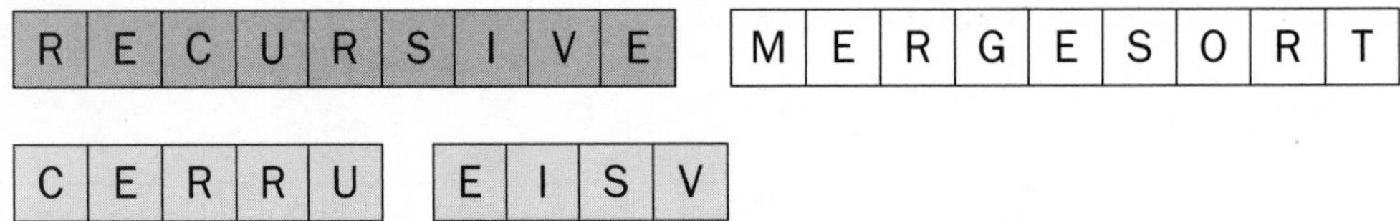

Figure 7-42: Ready to merge the first half of the original list.

The final step in sorting the first half of the original list is to merge its two sorted sublists, giving the result shown in Figure 7-43.

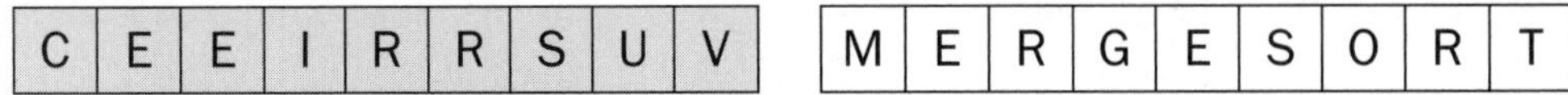

Figure 7-43: The first half of the list is now sorted.

The algorithm continues in exactly the same way until the right half of the original list is also sorted, as shown in Figure 7-44.

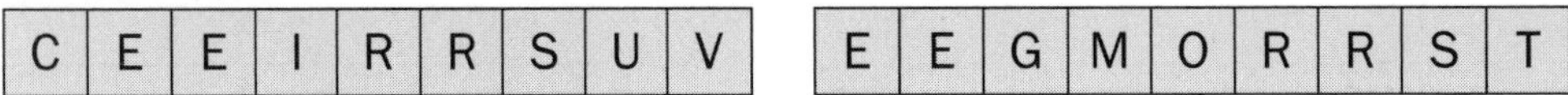

Figure 7-44: The right half of the original list is sorted.

Finally, you can merge the two sorted halves of the original list to form the final sorted list, as shown in Figure 7-45.

Figure 7-45: The final result.

Mergesort is an elegant algorithm that is relatively simple to implement, as you will see in the next Try It Out.

Try It Out — Testing the Mergesort Algorithm

The test for the mergesort algorithm is the same as each of the other tests in this chapter, with the only difference being that you instantiate the appropriate implementation class:

```
package com.wrox.algorithms.sorting;

public class MergesortListSorterTest extends AbstractListSorterTest {
    protected ListSorter createListSorter(Comparator comparator) {
        return new MergesortListSorter(comparator);
    }
}
```

In the next Try It Out, you implement the mergesort.

Try It Out Implementing Mergesort

Once again, the implementation follows the usual pattern: You implement the `ListSorter` interface and accept a comparator to impose order on the items to be sorted:

```
package com.wrox.algorithms.sorting;

import com.wrox.algorithms.lists.List;
import com.wrox.algorithms.lists.ArrayList;
import com.wrox.algorithms.iteration.Iterator;

public class MergesortListSorter implements ListSorter {
    private final Comparator _comparator;

    public MergesortListSorter(Comparator comparator) {
        assert comparator != null : "comparator cannot be null";
        _comparator = comparator;
    }
    ...
}
```

You use the `sort()` method from the `ListSorter` interface to call the `mergesort()` method, passing in the lowest and highest item indexes so that the entire list is sorted. Subsequent recursive calls pass in index ranges that restrict the sorting to smaller sublists:

```
    public List sort(List list) {
        assert list != null : "list cannot be null";

        return mergesort(list, 0, list.size() - 1);
    }
```

Create the `mergesort()` method that follows to deal with situations in which it has been called to sort a sublist containing a single item. In this case, it creates a new result list and adds the single item to it, ending the recursion.

If there is more than one item in the sublist to be sorted, the code simply splits the list, recursively sorts each half, and merges the result:

```
    private List mergesort(List list, int startIndex, int endIndex) {
        if (startIndex == endIndex) {
            List result = new ArrayList();
            result.add(list.get(startIndex));
            return result;
        }

        int splitIndex = startIndex + (endIndex - startIndex) / 2;

        List left = mergesort(list, startIndex, splitIndex);
        List right = mergesort(list, splitIndex + 1, endIndex);

        return merge(left, right);
    }
```

The following `merge()` method is a little more complicated than you might at first expect, mainly because it has to deal with cases in which one of the lists is drained before the other, and cases in which either of the lists supplies the next item:

```
    private List merge(List left, List right) {
        List result = new ArrayList();

        Iterator l = left.iterator();
        Iterator r = right.iterator();

        l.first();
        r.first();

        while (!(l.isDone() && r.isDone())) {
            if (l.isDone()) {
                result.add(r.current());
                r.next();
            } else if (r.isDone()) {
                result.add(l.current());
                l.next();
            } else if (_comparator.compare(l.current(), r.current()) <= 0) {
                result.add(l.current());
                l.next();
            } else {
                result.add(r.current());
                r.next();
            }
        }

        return result;
    }
```

How It Works

As with all recursive algorithms, the key part of the implementation is to cater to both the base case and the general case in the recursive method. In the preceding code, the `mergesort()` method separates these cases very clearly, dealing with the base case first and returning from the method immediately if there is only a single element in the sublist being considered. If there is more than one item, it splits the list in half, sorts each recursively, and merges the results using the `merge()` method.

The `merge()` method obtains an iterator on each sublist, as all that is required is a simple sequential traversal of the items in each sublist. The code is complicated slightly by the fact that the algorithm needs to continue when one of the sublists runs out of items, in which case all of the items from the other sublist need to be added to the end of the output list. In cases where both sublists still have items to be considered, the current items from the two sublists are compared, and the smaller of the two is placed on the output list.

That completes our coverage of the three advanced sorting algorithms in this chapter. The next section compares these three algorithms so that you can choose the right one for the problem at hand.

Comparing the Advanced Sorting Algorithms

As in Chapter 6, we compare the three algorithms from this chapter using a practical, rather than a theoretical or mathematical, approach. If you are interested in the math behind the algorithms, see the excellent coverage in *Algorithms in Java* [Sedgwick, 2002]. The idea behind this approach is to inspire your creativity when evaluating code that you or others have written, and to encourage you to rely on empirical evidence in preference to theoretical benefits as a general rule.

Refer to Chapter 6 for details on the `ListSorterCallCountingTest` class that was used to compare the algorithms from that chapter. Here you create code that extends this driver program to support the three advanced algorithms. The code for the worst-case tests is shown here:

```
public void testWorstCaseShellsort() {
    new ShellsortListSorter(_comparator).sort(_reverseArrayList);
    reportCalls(_comparator.getCallCount());
}

public void testWorstCaseQuicksort() {
    new QuicksortListSorter(_comparator).sort(_reverseArrayList);
    reportCalls(_comparator.getCallCount());
}

public void testWorstCaseMergesort() {
    new MergesortListSorter(_comparator).sort(_reverseArrayList);
    reportCalls(_comparator.getCallCount());
}
```

The code for the best cases is, of course, very similar:

```
public void testBestCaseShellsort() {
    new ShellsortListSorter(_comparator).sort(_sortedArrayList);
    reportCalls(_comparator.getCallCount());
}

public void testBestCaseQuicksort() {
    new QuicksortListSorter(_comparator).sort(_sortedArrayList);
    reportCalls(_comparator.getCallCount());
}

public void testBestCaseMergesort() {
    new MergesortListSorter(_comparator).sort(_sortedArrayList);
    reportCalls(_comparator.getCallCount());
}
```

Finally, look over the code for the average cases:

```
    public void testAverageCaseShellsort() {
        new ShellsortListSorter(_comparator).sort(_randomArrayList);
        reportCalls(_comparator.getCallCount());
    }

    public void testAverageCaseQuicksort() {
        new QuicksortListSorter(_comparator).sort(_randomArrayList);
        reportCalls(_comparator.getCallCount());
    }

    public void testAverageCaseMergeSort() {
        new MergesortListSorter(_comparator).sort(_randomArrayList);
        reportCalls(_comparator.getCallCount());
    }
```

This evaluation measures only the number of comparisons performed during the algorithm execution. It ignores very important issues such as the number of list item movements, which can have just as much of an impact on the suitability of an algorithm for a particular purpose. You should take this investigation further in your own efforts to put these algorithms to use.

Take a look at the worst-case results for all six sorting algorithms. We have included the results from the basic algorithms from Chapter 6 to save you the trouble of referring back to them:

```
testWorstCaseBubblesort:     499500 calls
testWorstCaseSelectionSort: 499500 calls
testWorstCaseInsertionSort: 499500 calls
testWorstCaseShellsort:        9894 calls
testWorstCaseQuicksort:      749000 calls
testWorstCaseMergesort:        4932 calls
```

Wow! What's up with quicksort? It has performed 50 percent more comparisons than even the basic algorithms! Shellsort and mergesort clearly require very few comparison operations, but quicksort is the worst of all (for this one simple measurement). Recall that the worst case is a list that is completely in reverse order, meaning that the smallest item is at the far right (the highest index) of the list when the algorithm begins. Recall also that the quicksort implementation you created always chooses the item at the far right of the list and attempts to divide the list into two parts, with items that are smaller than this item on one side, and those that are larger on the other. Therefore, in this worst case, the partitioning item is *always* the smallest item, so no partitioning happens. In fact, no swapping occurs except for the partitioning item itself, so an exhaustive comparison of every object with the partitioning value is required on every pass, with very little to show for it.

As you can imagine, this wasteful behavior has inspired smarter strategies for choosing the partitioning item. One way that would help a lot in this particular situation is to choose three partitioning items (such as from the far left, the far right, and the middle of the list) and choose the median value as the partitioning item on each pass. This type of approach stands a better chance of actually achieving some partitioning in the first place in the worst case.

Here are the results from the best-case tests:

```
testBestCaseBubblesort:     498501 calls
testBestCaseSelectionSort: 498501 calls
testBestCaseInsertionSort:    998 calls
testBestCaseShellsort:       4816 calls
testBestCaseQuicksort:     498501 calls
testBestCaseMergesort:       5041 calls
```

The excellent result for insertion sort will be no surprise to you, and again quicksort seems to be the odd one out among the advanced algorithms. Perhaps you are wondering why we bothered to show it to you if it is no improvement over the basic algorithms, but remember that the choice of partitioning item could be vastly improved. Once again, this case stumps quicksort's attempt to partition the data, as on each pass it finds the largest item in the far right position of the list, thereby wasting a lot of time trying to separate the data using the partitioning item as the pivot point.

As you can see from the results, insertion sort is the best performer in terms of comparison effort for already sorted data. You saw how shellsort eventually reduces to an insertion sort, having first put the data into a nearly sorted state. It is also common to use insertion sort as a final pass in quicksort implementations. For example, when the sublists to be sorted get down to a certain threshold (say, five or ten items), quicksort can stop recursing and simply use an in-place insertion sort to complete the job.

Now look at the average-case results, which tend to be a more realistic reflection of the type of results you might achieve in a production system:

```
testAverageCaseBubblesort:     498501 calls
testAverageCaseSelectionSort: 498501 calls
testAverageCaseInsertionSort: 251096 calls
testAverageCaseShellsort:       13717 calls
testAverageCaseQuicksort:       19727 calls
testAverageCaseMergeSort:        8668 calls
```

Finally, there is a clear distinction between the three basic algorithms and the three advanced algorithms! The three algorithms from this chapter are all taking about 1/20 the number of comparisons to sort the average case data as the basic algorithms. This is a huge reduction in the amount of effort required to sort large data sets. The good news is that as the data sets get larger, the gap between the algorithms gets wider.

Before you decide to start using mergesort for every problem based on its excellent performance in all the cases shown, remember that mergesort creates a copy of every list (and sublist) that it sorts, and so requires significantly more memory (and perhaps time) to do its job than the other algorithms. Be very careful not to draw conclusions that are not justified by the evidence you have, in this and in all your programming endeavors.

Summary

This chapter covered three advanced sorting algorithms. While these algorithms are more complex and more subtle than the algorithms covered in Chapter 6, they are far more likely to be of use in solving large, practical problems you might come across in your programming career. Each of the advanced sorting algorithms—shellsort, quicksort, and mergesort—were thoroughly explained before you implemented and tested them.

You also learned about the lack of stability inherent in shellsort and quicksort by implementing a compound comparator to compensate for this shortcoming. Finally, you looked at a simple comparison of the six algorithms covered in this and the previous chapter, which should enable you to understand the strengths and weaknesses of the various options.

In the next chapter, you learn about a sophisticated data structure that builds on what you have learned about queues and incorporates some of the techniques from the sorting algorithms.

Exercises

1. Implement mergesort iteratively rather than recursively.
2. Implement quicksort iteratively rather than recursively.
3. Count the number of list manipulations (for example, `set()`, `add()`, `insert()`) during quicksort and shellsort.
4. Implement an in-place version of insertion sort.
5. Create a version of quicksort that uses insertion sort for sublists containing fewer than five items.

Priority Queues

After studying a broad selection of sorting algorithms in the previous two chapters, you return to investigating data structures in this chapter. A priority queue is a special type of queue (see Chapter 4) that provides access to the largest element contained within it. This has many interesting applications, some of which you will see later in this book. We waited until we covered the sorting algorithms before discussing priority queues because the more complex priority queue implementations require you to understand the issues regarding sorting.

As an example of when you might use a priority queue, imagine a role-playing game in which you are making your way through hostile territory, with threatening characters all around you. Some of these characters are more lethal than others. Being able to quickly identify the largest threat to your health would be a good survival strategy! Notice that it is not necessary to maintain the list of threatening characters in full sorted order. Given that you can have only one fight at a time, all you need to know at any one time is which threat is the largest. By the time you've dealt with the biggest one, others may have arrived on the scene, so the sort would have been of little use.

This chapter covers the following topics:

- ❑ Understanding priority queues
- ❑ Creating an unordered list priority queue
- ❑ Creating a sorted list priority queue
- ❑ Understanding a heap and how it works
- ❑ Creating a heap-ordered list implementation of a priority queue
- ❑ Comparing the different priority queue implementations

Understanding Priority Queues

A *priority queue* is a queue that supports accessing items from the largest to the smallest. Unlike a simple queue that supports accessing items in the same order that they were added to the queue, or a stack, which supports accessing the items based on how recently they were added to the stack, a priority queue enables much more flexible access to the objects contained in the structure.

A priority queue allows a client program to access the largest item at any time. (Don't be concerned about the term *largest*, as a simple reverse comparator can switch that around to be smallest at no cost.) The point is that the priority queue has a mechanism to determine which item is the largest (a comparator) and provides access to the largest item in the queue at any given time.

A priority queue is a more general form of queue than an ordinary first-in, first-out (FIFO) queue or last-in, first-out (LIFO) stack. You can imagine a priority queue in which the comparator supplied to it was based on time since insertion (FIFO) or time of insertion (LIFO). A priority queue could be used in this way to provide exactly the same feature set as a normal stack or queue.

A Simple Priority Queue Example

Imagine you have a priority queue that contains letters. Your imaginary client program is going to insert the letters from a series of words into the queue. After each word is inserted, the client will remove the largest letter from the queue. Figure 8-1 shows the letters to use.

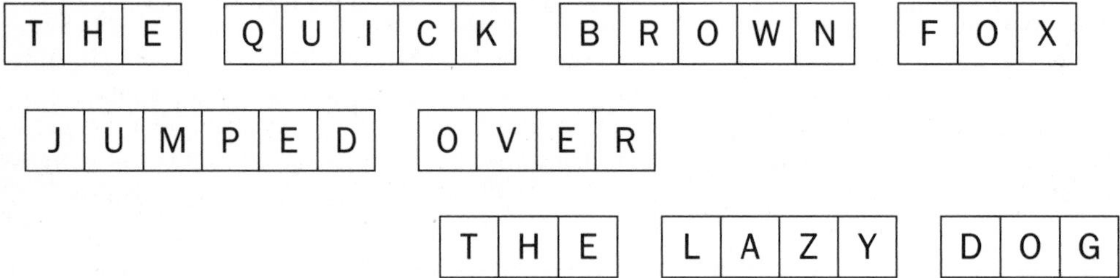

Figure 8-1: Input to the example priority queue.

You begin by adding the letters from the first word into the priority queue. Figure 8-2 shows the situation after you do this.

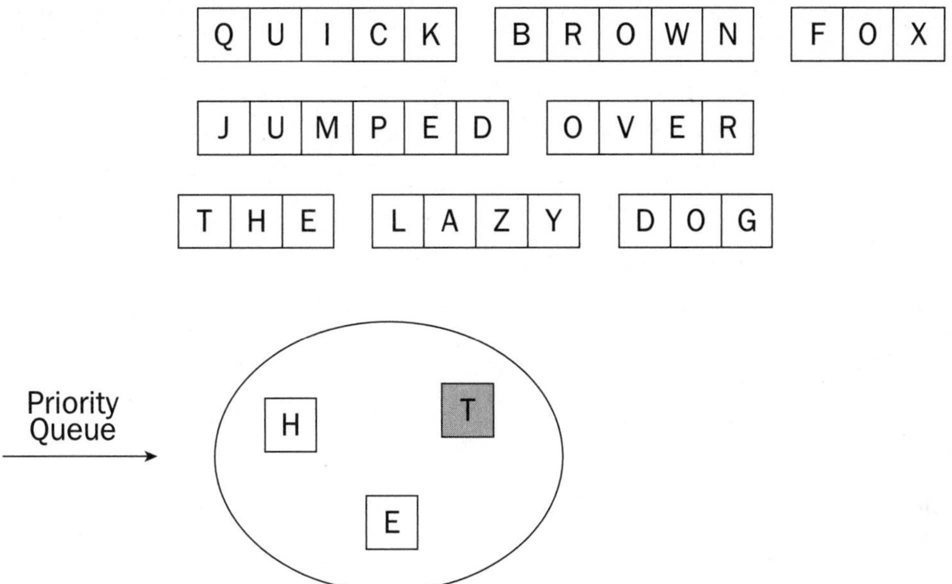

Figure 8-2: The letters from the first word have been added to the priority queue.

The largest letter in the priority queue is highlighted. When the client program removes the largest item, it becomes the item that is returned. We depicted the priority queue as a pool of letters, rather than as a list of letters with a specific order. Most priority queues hold their elements as a list, but it is important to understand that this is an implementation detail, and not part of the priority queue abstraction.

Figure 8-3 shows the situation after the client takes the largest item off the priority queue.

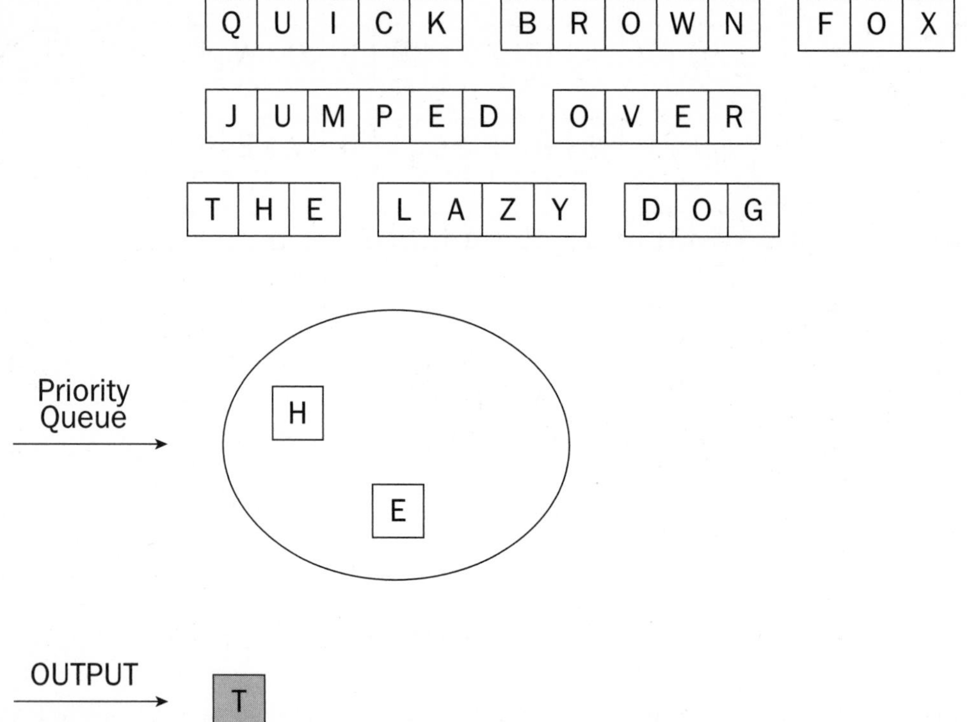

Figure 8-3: The largest letter is removed from the priority queue.

The client program adds all the letters from the second word into the priority queue; then it removes the largest one, leading to the situation shown in Figure 8-4.

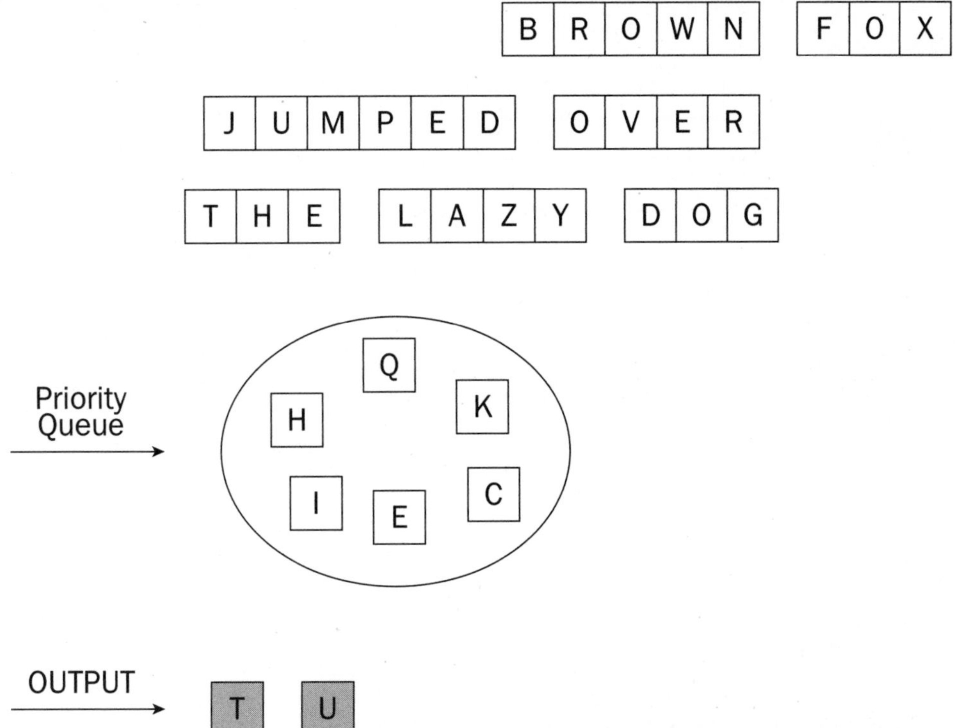

Figure 8-4: The second word is added to the queue and the largest letter is removed.

The process is repeated for the third word, as shown in Figure 8-5.

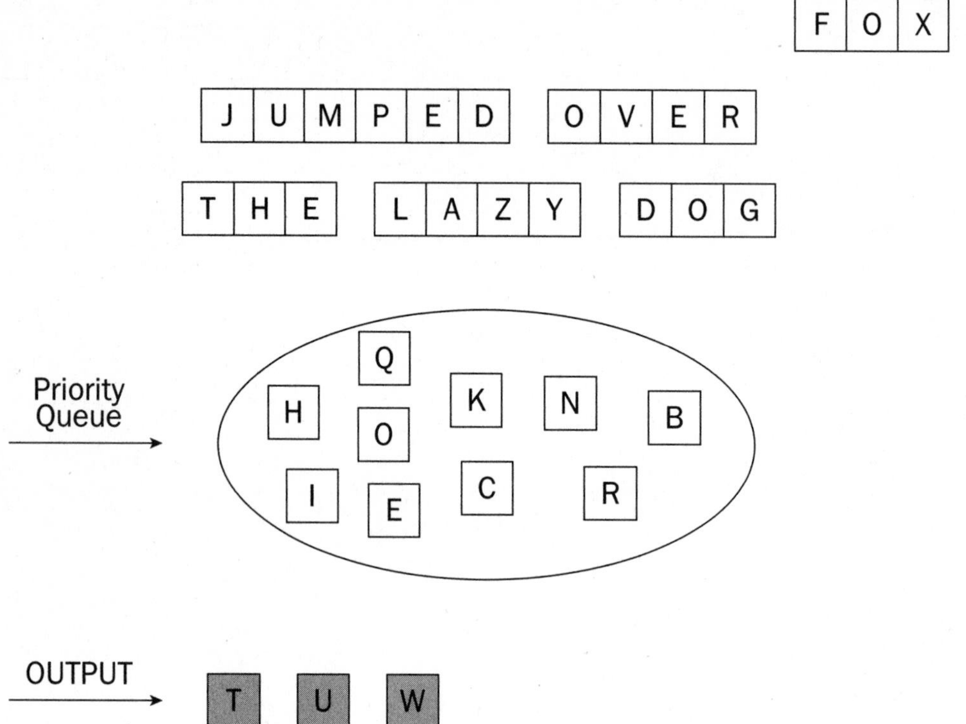

Figure 8-5: The third word in the example is processed.

By now, you'll be getting the idea of how the priority queue works, so we'll skip to the result in the example, after all the words have been processed in the same way (see Figure 8-6).

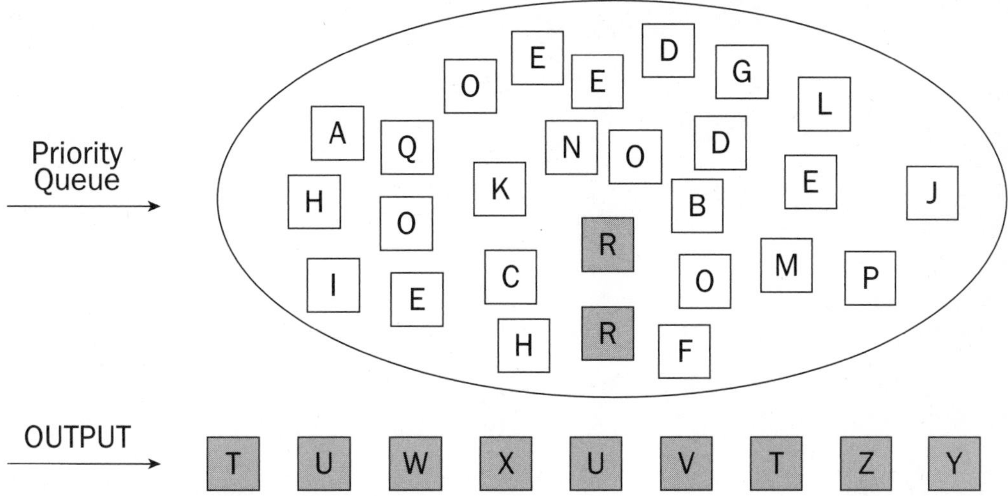

Figure 8-6: The final state of the example priority queue.

In this final state, two items that are the equal largest among the remaining items are highlighted in the priority queue. The next call by the client program to remove the largest item could remove either of these two items.

Working with Priority Queues

In the Try It Out examples that follow, you implement three priority queues. They all implement the `Queue` interface from Chapter 4, and vary from the very simple to a quite complex version based on a heap structure. There is no need to add operations to the `Queue` interface; all a priority queue does, in effect, is alter the semantics of the `dequeue()` method to return the largest item currently in the queue.

Try It Out Creating an AbstractPriorityQueue Test Case

First you define a test that your various priority queue implementations will need to pass. As you did with the sorting algorithms, you define the test itself in an abstract test case, leaving a factory method as a placeholder. When you want to test a specific implementation of a priority queue, you can extend this abstract class and implement the factory method to instantiate the implementation you want to test.

Start by declaring the test case with a few specific values to use and an instance member to hold the queue itself:

```
public abstract class AbstractPriorityQueueTestCase extends TestCase {
    private static final String VALUE_A = "A";
    private static final String VALUE_B = "B";
    private static final String VALUE_C = "C";
    private static final String VALUE_D = "D";
    private static final String VALUE_E = "E";

    private Queue _queue;
    ...
}
```

Next, you define the `setUp()` and `tearDown()` methods. `setUp()` calls the abstract factory method `createQueue()` that follows. This is the method that each specific test needs to implement:

```
    protected void setUp() throws Exception {
        super.setUp();

        _queue = createQueue(NaturalComparator.INSTANCE);
    }

    protected void tearDown() throws Exception {
        _queue = null;

        super.tearDown();
    }

    protected abstract Queue createQueue(Comparator comparable);
```

The first test establishes the behavior of an empty queue. This is exactly the same test shown in Chapter 4 for testing other types of queues. You could have avoided duplicating this code by having a more complex hierarchy of test cases, but we opted for simplicity and clarity. We do not recommend making this choice in production code!

```
    public void testAccessAnEmptyQueue() {
        assertEquals(0, _queue.size());
        assertTrue(_queue.isEmpty());

        try {
            _queue.dequeue();
            fail();
        } catch (EmptyQueueException e) {
            // expected
        }
    }
```

The next method is the major test of your priority queue behavior. You begin by adding three items to the queue and making sure that the `size()` and `isEmpty()` methods are working as expected:

```
    public void testEnqueueDequeue() {
        _queue.enqueue(VALUE_B);
        _queue.enqueue(VALUE_D);
        _queue.enqueue(VALUE_A);

        assertEquals(3, _queue.size());
        assertFalse(_queue.isEmpty());
```

Next, you make sure that the largest of the three items you added (in this case, the string `D`) is returned from the `dequeue()` method. In the preceding code that adds the items to the queue, this was the second of the three items, so a normal FIFO queue or LIFO stack fails this test straightaway. Having removed the item, you again verify that the other operations are still making sense:

```
        assertSame(VALUE_D, _queue.dequeue());
        assertEquals(2, _queue.size());
        assertFalse(_queue.isEmpty());
```

The string `B` is the largest of the two remaining items, so you make sure that it is returned from the next call to the `dequeue()` method:

```
        assertSame(VALUE_B, _queue.dequeue());
        assertEquals(1, _queue.size());
        assertFalse(_queue.isEmpty());
```

Add a couple more items to the queue. It is common in applications that use priority queues to have a mixture of `enqueue()` and `dequeue()` invocations, rather than simply building and then emptying the queue:

```
        _queue.enqueue(VALUE_E);
        _queue.enqueue(VALUE_C);

        assertEquals(3, _queue.size());
        assertFalse(_queue.isEmpty());
```

You now have three elements in your priority queue: the strings `A`, `E`, and `C`. They should come off the queue in order from largest to smallest, so your test completes by removing each one of them in turn, while also ensuring that `size()` and `isEmpty()` remain consistent with your expectations:

```
        assertSame(VALUE_E, _queue.dequeue());
        assertEquals(2, _queue.size());
        assertFalse(_queue.isEmpty());

        assertSame(VALUE_C, _queue.dequeue());
        assertEquals(1, _queue.size());
        assertFalse(_queue.isEmpty());

        assertSame(VALUE_A, _queue.dequeue());
        assertEquals(0, _queue.size());
        assertTrue(_queue.isEmpty());
    }
```

You complete the test case with another generic queue test to verify the behavior of the `clear()` method, as shown here:

```
    public void testClear() {
        _queue.enqueue(VALUE_A);
        _queue.enqueue(VALUE_B);
        _queue.enqueue(VALUE_C);

        assertFalse(_queue.isEmpty());

        _queue.clear();

        assertTrue(_queue.isEmpty());
    }
```

That's it for our general priority queue test. You can now move on to the first implementation, a very simple list-based queue that searches for the largest item when required.

Understanding the Unsorted List Priority Queue

The simplest way to implement a priority queue is to keep all of the elements in some sort of collection and search through them for the largest item whenever `dequeue()` is called. Obviously, any algorithm that uses a brute force search through every item is going to be `O(N)` for this operation, but depending on your application, this may be acceptable. If, for example, there are not many calls to `dequeue()` in your case, then the simple solution might be the best. This implementation will be `O(1)` for `enqueue()`, which is hard to beat.

In the next Try It Out, you implement a simple priority queue that holds the queued items in a list.

Try It Out Testing and Implementing an Unsorted List Priority Queue

You use a `LinkedList` in this case, but an `ArrayList` would also work, of course.

Begin by extending the `AbstractPriorityQueueTestCase` you created previously and implementing the `createQueue()` method to instantiate your (not yet created) implementation:

```
public class UnsortedListPriorityQueueTest extends AbstractPriorityQueueTestCase {
    protected Queue createQueue(Comparator comparator) {
        return new UnsortedListPriorityQueue(comparator);
    }
}
```

This implementation has a lot in common with the other queue implementations you saw in Chapter 4. We have chosen to reproduce the code in common here for simplicity.

Start by creating the class and declaring its two instance members: a list to hold the items and a `Comparator` to determine the relative size of the items. Also declare a constructor to set everything up:

```
public class UnsortedListPriorityQueue implements Queue {
    private final List _list;
    private final Comparator _comparator;

    public UnsortedListPriorityQueue(Comparator comparator) {
        assert comparator != null : "comparator cannot be null";
        _comparator = comparator;
        _list = new LinkedList();
    }
    ...
}
```

The implementation of `enqueue()` could not be simpler; you just add the item to the end of the list:

```
    public void enqueue(Object value) {
        _list.add(value);
    }
```

You implement `dequeue()` by first verifying that the queue is not empty. You throw an exception if this method is called when the queue is empty. If there is at least one item in the queue, you remove the largest item by its index, as determined by the `getIndexOfLargestElement()` method:

```
    public Object dequeue() throws EmptyQueueException {
        if (isEmpty()) {
            throw new EmptyQueueException();
        }
        return _list.delete(getIndexOfLargestElement());
    }
```

To find the index of the largest item in your list, you have to scan the entire list, keeping track of the index of the largest item as you go. By the way, the following method would be much better suited to an `ArrayList` than our chosen `LinkedList`. Can you see why?

```
    private int getIndexOfLargestElement() {
        int result = 0;

        for (int i = 1; i < _list.size(); ++i) {
            if (_comparator.compare(_list.get(i), _list.get(result)) > 0) {
                result = i;
            }
        }

        return result;
    }
```

To complete this class, you implement the remaining methods of the `Queue` interface. These are exactly the same as any other list-based `Queue` implementation:

```
public void clear() {
    _list.clear();
}

public int size() {
    return _list.size();
}

public boolean isEmpty() {
    return _list.isEmpty();
}
```

If you run the test, you will see that this implementation behaves exactly as expected. You can now move on to implementing a version of the priority queue that aims to eliminate all that brute-force searching!

How It Works

The unsorted list implementation of a priority queue is very simple. To enqueue an item, you simply use the internal list's `add()` method to append it to the list. To remove an item from the queue, you simply iterate through all the items in the member list, remembering which of those scanned so far is the largest. At the end of the iteration, you return the largest item, removing it from the list as you do so.

Understanding the Sorted List Priority Queue

One way to avoid a brute-force scan of the whole list of items in your queue whenever `dequeue()` is called is to make sure the largest item is available more quickly by keeping the items in sorted order. In this way, the `dequeue()` method will be very fast, but you have to sacrifice a little more effort during `enqueue()` to find the right position to insert the new item.

The approach you use in the next Try It Out is to use an insertion sort mechanism during calls to `enqueue()` to place newly added items into sorted position in the underlying list. Calls to `dequeue()` will then be extremely simple—merely remove the largest item at the end of the list.

Try It Out Testing and Implementing a Sorted List Priority Queue

In this section, we will implement a priority queue that uses an underlying list maintained in sorted order.

Extend `AbstractPriorityQueueTestCase` for our specific implementation, as shown here:

```
public class SortedListPriorityQueueTest extends AbstractPriorityQueueTestCase {
    protected Queue createQueue(Comparator comparator) {
        return new SortedListPriorityQueue(comparator);
    }
}
```

The basic structure of this implementation is very similar to the unsorted version described previously in this chapter. Use the same instance members and an identical constructor:

```
public class SortedListPriorityQueue implements Queue {
    private final List _list;
    private final Comparator _comparator;

    public SortedListPriorityQueue(Comparator comparator) {
        assert comparator != null : "comparator cannot be null";
        _comparator = comparator;
        _list = new LinkedList();
    }
    ...
}
```

Create the `enqueue()` method to scan backwards through the items in the list, finding the appropriate place to insert the new item:

```
    public void enqueue(Object value) {
        int pos = _list.size();
        while (pos > 0 && _comparator.compare(_list.get(pos - 1), value) > 0) {
            --pos;
        }
        _list.insert(pos, value);
    }
```

You implement `dequeue()` by removing the last item from the list. Remember to throw an exception when the list is empty, as there is nothing to return:

```
    public Object dequeue() throws EmptyQueueException {
        if (isEmpty()) {
            throw new EmptyQueueException();
        }
        return _list.delete(_list.size() - 1);
    }
```

You add a final few methods that are simple, with nothing different from the other `Queue` implementations you have seen:

```
    public void clear() {
        _list.clear();
    }

    public int size() {
        return _list.size();
    }

    public boolean isEmpty() {
        return _list.isEmpty();
    }
```

That's it for the sorted list implementation of a priority queue. Run the test and you will see that it meets the criteria you established for correct priority queue behavior. The next section addresses the most complex but most effective and practical version of a priority queue, based on a structure called a *heap*.

How It Works

The version of `enqueue()` you use in this implementation is a little more complex than your previous implementation. Its function is to find the appropriate position in the list where the new item should be inserted. It does this by scanning backwards through the items in turn until it either finds one that is smaller or comes to the beginning of the list. It then inserts the new item into the queue at this position. This ensures that at all times the largest item is at the end of the list.

The benefit of expending this extra effort is that the implementation of `dequeue()` has nothing to do except remove the last item from the list and return it.

Understanding Heap-ordered Priority Queues

A heap is a very useful and interesting data structure, so we will take our time in this section explaining how it works. After you grasp the concept, you can use a heap to implement an effective priority queue.

A *heap* is simply a binary tree structure in which each element is larger than its two children. This is known as *the heap condition*. In Figure 8-7, note that whichever node you look at, the element is larger than its children (if it has any).

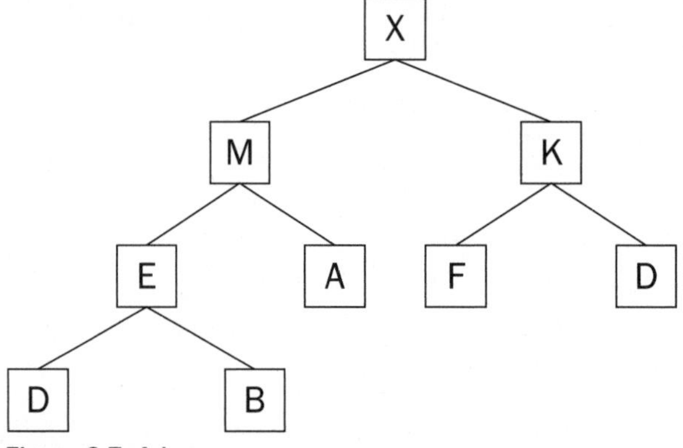

Figure 8-7: A heap.

Be careful not to think of a heap as being sorted, however, as it is not sorted at all. It does have a useful property that is of interest, however: By definition, in a heap, the largest item is sitting right at the top of the tree. The arrangement of the other items is of little interest to us. For example, notice that the smallest element in the heap (in this case, an A) is not on the bottom row of the tree as you might expect.

You might be wondering if there is a `Heap` interface or a `Tree` interface about to be defined and implemented. In this example, that won't be our approach. This case uses a simple list to contain the heap structure. Figure 8-8 demonstrates a technique of numbering the elements in the heap such that you can easily find them by their index. You start at the top of the tree with index zero, and work top to bottom and left to right, counting as you go.

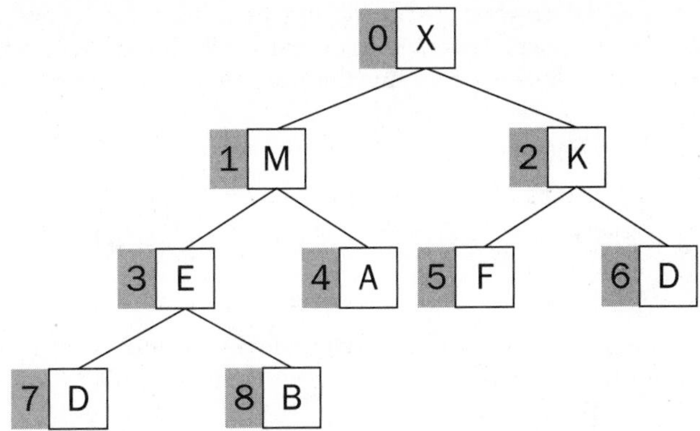

Figure 8-8: Numbering the items in a heap for storage in a list.

This approach enables you to have a mental model of a tree structure in an implementation in which no tree structure exists at all. Figure 8-9 shows what the list would look like that contains our sample heap structure.

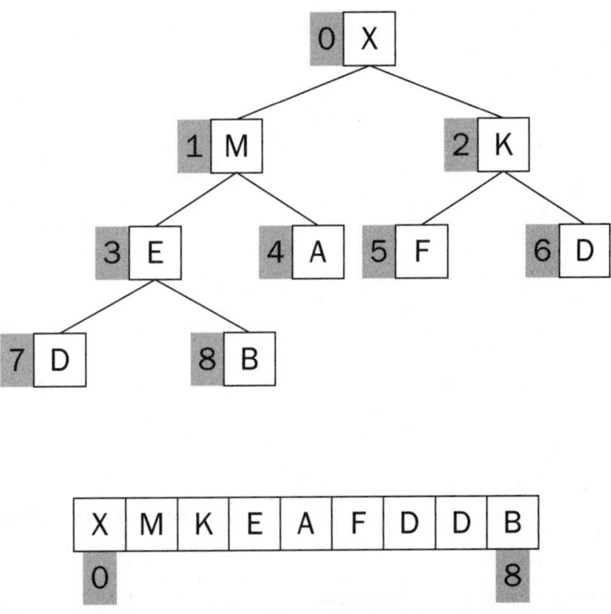

Figure 8-9: The heap structure contained in a list.

To use your heap, you must be able to navigate the structure upwards and downwards. Therefore, if you know the index of an item, you need to be able to determine the index of its left child item and its right child item. You also need to be able to determine the index of its parent item. Here's the way you do it:

- The left child of the item at index X is at index $(2 \times X + 1)$.
- The right child of the item at index X is at index $(2 \times X + 2)$.
- The parent of the item at index X is at index $((X - 1) / 2)$; the item at index 0 has no parent, of course!

Refer to the figures in this section to satisfy yourself that these formulas work as you expect. The formula for the parent index of an item relies upon truncation of the result if the item in question is the right child of the parent. You'll realize this if you try to access a list at index "3.5"!

Sink or Swim

To use the heap to build a priority queue, you need to be able to add items to it and remove items from it. That might sound obvious, but in order to perform each of those operations, you need to maintain the heap condition — that is, you need to make sure the heap is still a heap after you add or remove items from it.

Let's extend the sample heap by adding the letter P to it. You start by simply adding it to the bottom of the tree structure, as shown in Figure 8-10.

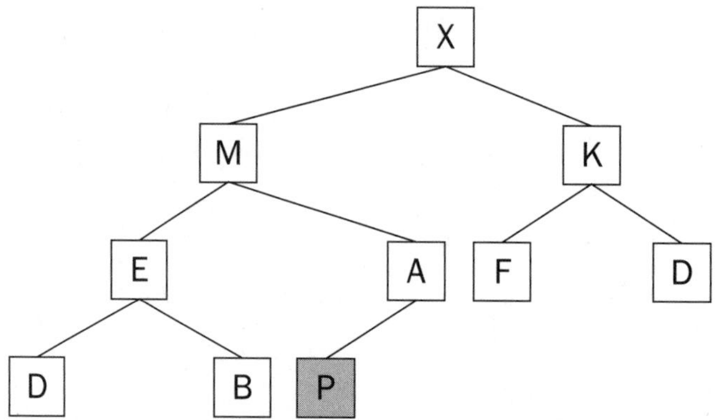

Figure 8-10: A new item is added to the heap, breaking the heap condition.

The heap is going to be stored as a simple list, so you just add the new item to the end. The problem is that now the heap is no longer a heap! This is because the parent (A) of the new item (P) is smaller than the item itself. To fix the heap and reestablish the heap condition, the new item must work its way up the tree structure until the heap condition is restored. This is called *swimming* to the top.

Swimming is a matter of exchanging an item with its parent if the parent is smaller, and continuing until the top of the heap is reached or a parent is found that is equal to or larger than the item doing the swimming. Figure 8-11 shows the situation after the new item has been swapped with its parent item.

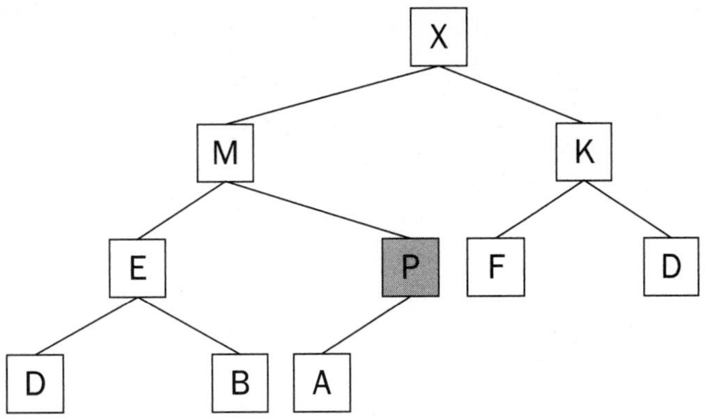

Figure 8-11: The new item is exchanged with its parent.

The heap condition is still not met because the new item (P) is larger than its parent (M). It needs to keep swimming. Figure 8-12 shows what happens when the new item is again swapped with its parent item.

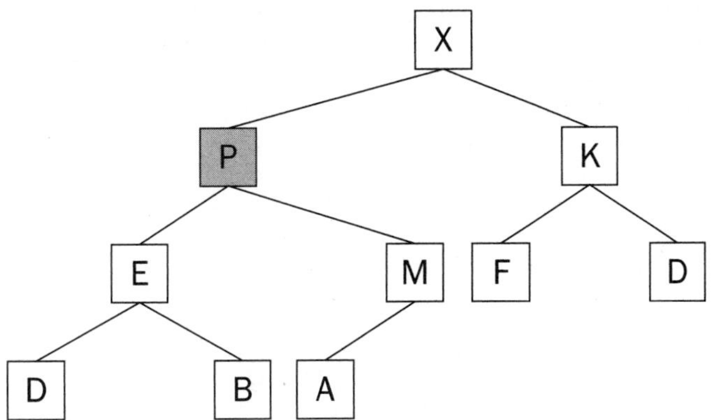

Figure 8-12: The new item moves into final position in the heap.

The heap condition is now restored, and the heap is one element larger than it was before you added an item and maintained the heap condition. The next challenge is to do the same when removing the largest item from the heap.

Locating the largest item is easy, but removing it is not so easy. If you just delete it from the underlying list, the tree structure is completely destroyed and you have to start again. (Feel free to try this as an experiment for your own enjoyment!) Instead, you can swap in the item at the bottom right of the tree, as shown in Figure 8-13.

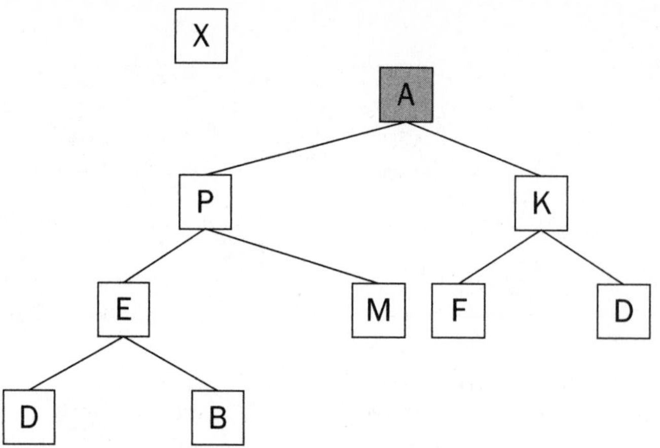

Figure 8-13: The largest item is removed and the last item is put at the top.

Although the tree structure itself is still intact, the heap condition is once again violated; the smallest item of all is now at the top of the tree. It is going to have to make its way down the tree until the heap condition is restored. This process is known as *sinking* to the bottom.

Sinking is the process of repeatedly exchanging an item with the larger of its children until the heap condition is restored or the bottom of the tree is reached. In this example, the larger of the children of the sinking item is P, so the A is exchanged with it. Figure 8-14 shows the state of the heap after this first exchange is made.

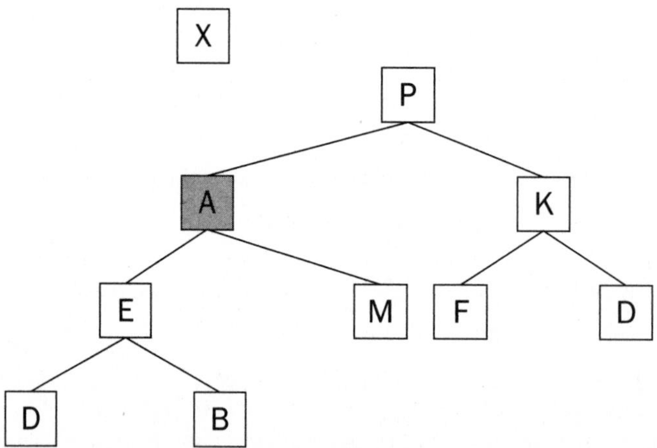

Figure 8-14: The top element has been sunk down one level.

The heap condition is still violated because the A is larger than both of its children. The larger of the children is M, so the swap is made with that item. Figure 8-15 shows the state of the heap after this exchange is made.

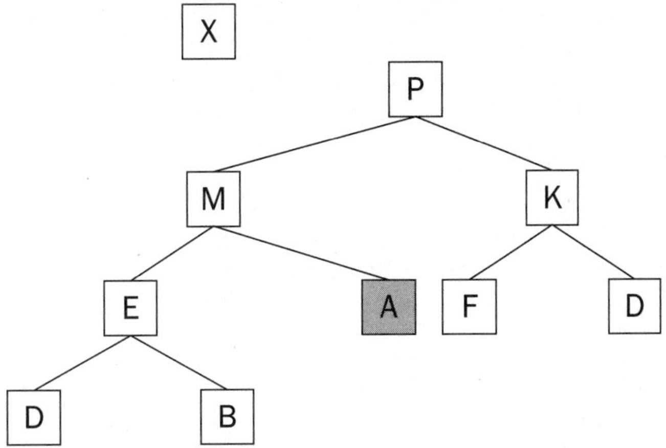

Figure 8-15: The heap condition is restored after sinking.

The heap condition has been restored and the largest item is removed, leaving the heap one item smaller than it was. Armed with your new understanding, you can now use this concept to implement a priority queue.

In the next Try It Out, you test and implement a priority queue that stores the elements in the queue in a heap-ordered list — that is, a list arranged logically as a heap. This is the most complex of the three implementations covered in this chapter.

Try It Out Testing and Implementing a Heap-ordered Priority Queue

First create a test case that is specific to your heap-ordered implementation, as shown here:

```
public class HeapOrderedListPriorityQueueTest extends AbstractPriorityQueueTestCase
{
    protected Queue createQueue(Comparator comparator) {
        return new HeapOrderedListPriorityQueue(comparator);
    }
}
```

You structure the implementation just as you did with the other two priority queues, with a list to hold the items and a `Comparator` to order them appropriately:

```
public class HeapOrderedListPriorityQueue implements Queue {
    private final List _list;
    private final Comparator _comparator;

    public HeapOrderedListPriorityQueue(Comparator comparator) {
        assert comparator != null : "comparator cannot be null";
        _comparator = comparator;
        _list = new ArrayList();
    }
    ...
}
```

You create the enqueue() method to add the new item to the underlying list and then swim it up the heap:

```
public void enqueue(Object value) {
    _list.add(value);
    swim(_list.size() - 1);
}
```

You create the swim() method, which accepts a parameter that is the index of the item that is swimming up the heap. You compare it with its parent (if it has one), swapping them if the parent is smaller. You call swim() recursively to continue the process further up the heap:

```
private void swim(int index) {
    if (index == 0) {
        return;
    }
    int parent = (index - 1) / 2;
    if (_comparator.compare(_list.get(index), _list.get(parent)) > 0) {
        swap(index, parent);
        swim(parent);
    }
}
```

You have seen numerous swap() methods before, so this should cause you no trouble:

```
private void swap(int index1, int index2) {
    Object temp = _list.get(index1);
    _list.set(index1, _list.get(index2));
    _list.set(index2, temp);
}
```

Next you create the dequeue() method. That returns the item at the front of the list. You then swap the item at the end of the list to the front of the list, and sink it down through the heap to restore the heap condition:

```
public Object dequeue() throws EmptyQueueException {
    if (isEmpty()) {
        throw new EmptyQueueException();
    }
    Object result = _list.get(0);
    if (_list.size() > 1) {
        _list.set(0, _list.get(_list.size() - 1));
        sink(0);
    }
    _list.delete(_list.size() - 1);
    return result;
}
```

Create the `sink()` method that is used to swap the item with the largest of its children. Be careful to cater to cases in which the item has two, one, or no children at all:

```
private void sink(int index) {
    int left = index * 2 + 1;
    int right = index * 2 + 2;

    if (left >= _list.size()) {
        return;
    }

    int largestChild = left;
    if (right < _list.size()) {
        if (_comparator.compare(_list.get(left), _list.get(right)) < 0) {
            largestChild = right;
        }
    }

    if (_comparator.compare(_list.get(index), _list.get(largestChild)) < 0) {
        swap(index, largestChild);
        sink(largestChild);
    }
}
```

You'll be exhausted after looking at that bit of code, so the good news is that the remaining methods are as simple as can be:

```
public void clear() {
    _list.clear();
}

public int size() {
    return _list.size();
}

public boolean isEmpty() {
    return _list.isEmpty();
}
```

How It Works

The `enqueue()` method is simple because it passes most of the hard work off to the `swim()` method after adding the new item to the underlying list. The parameter passed to the `swim()` method is the index of the item that needs to swim up the heap. The `swim()` method has the task of comparing the item at the index provided with its parent item in the heap, and exchanging it if the item is larger than its parent. If an exchange is required, the method calls itself recursively to continue the process higher up the heap. The method stops when the index is 0, as this means we are at the top of the heap. Notice also that the formula used to identify the index of the parent element matches the explanation given earlier in the chapter.

The implementation of `dequeue()` begins by locating the item to be returned, which is simple; it is already at index 0 in the list. Although this is the item you return, it is not necessarily the item you delete from the underlying list. The only item that ever gets deleted is the one at the very *end* of the list. If there is only one item in the queue, the item you return is the one you delete; in all other cases, you need to exchange the last item with the first item and sink it down through the heap to reestablish the heap condition.

`sink()` is unfortunately a lot more complex than `swim()` because there are a couple of interesting cases to consider. The item in question might have no children, or it may only have one child. If it has a right child, it must also have a left child, so having only a right child is one case we can ignore.

You start by calculating the index of your children. If these indices fall outside the valid range of items in the queue, you are done, as the item cannot sink any lower. Next, figure out which of your children (you have at least one child now) is the larger. It is the larger of the children that you exchange with the item in question if required. You start by assuming that the left child is the larger, and change your assumption to the right child only if you have a right child and it is larger than the left child.

At this point, you know which of your children is the larger one. All that remains is to compare the item itself with the larger of the children. If the child is larger, swap them and recursively call `sink()` to continue the process down the heap until the heap condition is restored.

The heap-ordered implementation of the priority queue is the final version included in this chapter. It is interesting because it adds items to the queue and removes them from the queue in a manner that is `O(log N)`. Any algorithm that is proportional to the depth of a binary tree of the elements in question has this characteristic, and has a great advantage over those that treat the items in a long linear fashion. In the next section, we will compare our three priority queue implementations to see how they stack up against each other.

Comparing the Priority Queue Implementations

As in previous chapters, we will opt for a practical, rather than a theoretical, comparison of the various implementations. Once again, we will use `CallCountingComparator` to gain an understanding of how much effort the various implementations take to achieve their results. Remember not to take this single dimension of evaluation as total or definitive. Rather, use it to gain insight and to inspire further investigation. Many theoretically sound comparisons are available, so check Appendix B for resources if you're interested in delving further into that area.

As when comparing sorting algorithms in the previous two chapters, this chapter considers best, worst, and average cases for each of the three priority queue implementations. We perform a mixed set of operations to add and remove items from the queues under test. The best case consists of adding data in sorted order. The worst case consists of adding the data in reverse sorted order, and the average case consists of adding randomly generated data to the queue.

The basic structure of the test driver class is shown here. You declare a constant to control the size of the tests, and then declare the lists for each of the best, worst, and average cases. Finally, you declare `CallCountingComparator` to collect the statistics:

```
public class PriorityQueueCallCountingTest extends TestCase {
    private static final int TEST_SIZE = 1000;

    private final List _sortedList = new ArrayList(TEST_SIZE);
    private final List _reverseList = new ArrayList(TEST_SIZE);
    private final List _randomList = new ArrayList(TEST_SIZE);

    private CallCountingComparator _comparator;
    ...
}
```

The `setUp()` method instantiates the comparator and fills the three lists with the appropriate test data:

```
    protected void setUp() throws Exception {
        super.setUp();
        _comparator = new CallCountingComparator(NaturalComparator.INSTANCE);

        for (int i = 1; i < TEST_SIZE; ++i) {
            _sortedList.add(new Integer(i));
        }

        for (int i = TEST_SIZE; i > 0; --i) {
            _reverseList.add(new Integer(i));
        }

        for (int i = 1; i < TEST_SIZE; ++i) {
            _randomList.add(new Integer((int)(TEST_SIZE * Math.random())));
        }
    }
```

Next are the three worst-case scenarios, all of which delegate to the `runScenario()` method:

```
    public void testWorstCaseUnsortedList() {
        runScenario(new UnsortedListPriorityQueue(_comparator), _reverseList);
    }

    public void testWorstCaseSortedList() {
        runScenario(new SortedListPriorityQueue(_comparator), _reverseList);
    }

    public void testWorstCaseHeapOrderedList() {
        runScenario(new HeapOrderedListPriorityQueue(_comparator), _reverseList);
    }
```

Now you define the three best-case scenarios, one for each of the priority queue implementations:

```
public void testBestCaseUnsortedList() {
    runScenario(new UnsortedListPriorityQueue(_comparator), _sortedList);
}

public void testBestCaseSortedList() {
    runScenario(new SortedListPriorityQueue(_comparator), _sortedList);
}

public void testBestCaseHeapOrderedList() {
    runScenario(new HeapOrderedListPriorityQueue(_comparator), _sortedList);
}
```

Finally, you have the three average-case scenarios:

```
public void testAverageCaseUnsortedList() {
    runScenario(new UnsortedListPriorityQueue(_comparator), _randomList);
}

public void testAverageCaseSortedList() {
    runScenario(new SortedListPriorityQueue(_comparator), _randomList);
}

public void testAverageCaseHeapOrderedList() {
    runScenario(new HeapOrderedListPriorityQueue(_comparator), _randomList);
}
```

The `runScenario()` method is shown next. It is provided with two parameters: a queue to test and a list of input data. Its approach is to iterate through the input data, adding the elements to the queue under test. However, every 100 items, it stops and takes 25 items off the queue. These numbers are entirely arbitrary and serve only to give you a mixture of both the `enqueue()` and `dequeue()` operations to better simulate how priority queues are used in practice. Before the method finishes, it completely drains the queue and calls `reportCalls()` to output a line summarizing the test:

```
private void runScenario(Queue queue, List input) {
    int i = 0;
    Iterator iterator = input.iterator();
    iterator.first();
    while (!iterator.isDone()) {
        ++i;
        queue.enqueue(iterator.current());
        if (i % 100 == 0) {
            for (int j = 0; j < 25; ++ j) {
                queue.dequeue();
            }
        }
        iterator.next();
    }

    while (!queue.isEmpty()) {
        queue.dequeue();
    }
    reportCalls();
}
```

The final method in the driver program is a simple dump of the number of comparisons made during the test run:

```
    private void reportCalls() {
        int callCount = _comparator.getCallCount();
        System.out.println(getName() + ": " + callCount + " calls");
    }
```

The following results of the comparison of the three priority queue implementations are for the worst case:

```
testWorstCaseUnsortedList:    387000 calls
testWorstCaseSortedList:      387000 calls
testWorstCaseHeapOrderedList: 15286 calls
```

The heap-ordered version is a clear winner here, with no difference at all between the two simpler versions. Next are the best-case results:

```
testBestCaseUnsortedList:    386226 calls
testBestCaseSortedList:         998 calls
testBestCaseHeapOrderedList: 22684 calls
```

That's interesting, although if you recall that insertion sort is excellent on already sorted data, you'll understand why these results show the sorted list version doing the least amount of work. The brute-force version is almost no different, and the heap version is performing about 50 percent more operations by this measure.

Finally, look at the results that most indicate what is likely to happen in the real world:

```
testAverageCaseUnsortedList:    386226 calls
testAverageCaseSortedList:      153172 calls
testAverageCaseHeapOrderedList: 17324 calls
```

You can see that the sorted list version is doing about half as many comparisons as the brute-force version, whereas the heap-ordered implementation remains a clear leader again. The implementation based on the heap structure is clearly the most effective based on this simple test; however, whether to use it depends on your specific circumstances. You need to balance the extra complexity with the extra efficiency to determine which implementation suits your application.

Summary

This chapter covered a few key points:

- You learned about a new data structure called a priority queue. This data structure is a more general form of the `Queue` that was covered in Chapter 4.
- A priority queue provides access to the largest item in the queue at any given time. A `comparator` is used to determine the relative size of the items in the queue.
- You implemented three different versions of a priority queue. The first simply added items to an underlying list and did a full scan of the items when required to return the largest. The second was an improvement on this, in that it kept the items in sorted order at all times, allowing rapid retrieval of the largest item at any time. The final version used a list arranged as a heap structure to achieve excellent performance for both add and remove operations. A thorough explanation of heaps and how they work was provided.
- The three implementations were compared and contrasted using a practical, rather than a theoretical, approach.

Exercises

To test your understanding of priority queues, try the following exercises:

1. Use a priority queue to implement a `Stack`.
2. Use a priority queue to implement a FIFO `Queue`.
3. Use a priority queue to implement a `ListSorter`.
4. Write a priority queue that provides access to the smallest item, rather than the largest.

Binary Searching and Insertion

So far, this book has discussed basic structures for storing and sorting your data, but it has only touched on some rudimentary approaches to searching the data.

Modern software applications often deal with enormous amounts of data, and being able to search that data efficiently is important. Being able to locate a particular patient's record quickly among tens of thousands of others can make or break an application. From now on, the chapters in this book focus largely on algorithms and data structures designed specifically for the efficient storage and searching of data.

Binary searching is one of the most basic techniques for efficiently searching through data in memory. Binary insertion is a variation on binary searching that enables you to maintain the data such that it can be efficiently searched.

This chapter discusses the following:

- How to perform binary searching
- Implementing a binary search using iteration and recursion
- Comparing binary searching with other search techniques
- Comparing binary insertion with other sorting techniques

Understanding Binary Searching

Binary searching is a technique for locating items in a sorted list. A binary search takes advantage of certain characteristics of sorted lists that a simple linear search doesn't. Indeed, whereas a brute-force linear search runs in `O(N)` time, a binary search runs in `O(log N)`, assuming the data to be searched is sorted.

As you saw in Chapter 2, the simplest way to search an unordered list is to start at the first item and continue forward until you either find a match or run out of items. This leads to an average-case running time of `O(N)`. The actual average running time is around `N/2`; that is, you would need to traverse, on average, half the items in the list before you found the one for which you were looking. For data that is sorted, however, you can do a lot better.

Binary searching gets its name from the fact that you continually divide the data in half, progressively narrowing down the search space until you find a match or there are no more items to process.

Take, for example, an English dictionary. If you were asked to look up the word *algorithm*, where would you start? You would probably open the book at the first page and start flipping through, one page at a time.

If you were asked to find the word *lama*, you would probably start somewhere towards the middle, but why? Why not start at the end of the book? The reason, of course, is because you know a dictionary is arranged in ascending alphabetical order (A–Z), so you can make a reasonably good guess as to where you should begin looking. When searching for *lama*, for example, if you open the book at *mandarin*, then you would know you had gone too far and you'd skip back a few pages. If, conversely, you first encounter *kangaroo*, then you would know you hadn't gone far enough and you would skip forwards some pages. Upon discovering that you are not yet at the page containing the word for which you are searching, the next question is, how far should you skip forwards or backwards?

In the specific example just given, you can probably guess how far to skip based on your knowledge of the language and the relative number of words beginning with each letter of the alphabet. But what if you had no idea about the contents? What if all you knew about the book was that it was sorted?

A binary search involves continually dividing the data in half —hence, binary—and searching the lower or upper half as appropriate. The steps involved in performing a binary search can be summarized as follows:

1. Start in the middle of the list.
2. Compare the search key with the item at the current location.
3. If the search key is at the current location, then you are done.
4. If the search key is less than the item at the current location, then it must be in the lower half of the data (if it exists at all) so divide the list in two and go to step 1, using the lower half.
5. Otherwise, it must be in the upper half of the list (again, if it exists at all), so go to step 1, using the upper half.

The following example demonstrates how to search for the letter K in the list of letters shown in Figure 9-1. This list contains nine letters in sorted order.

0	1	2	3	4	5	6	7	8
A	D	F	H	I	K	L	M	P

Figure 9-1: List containing nine letters in ascending sorted order.

You start the search in the middle of the list by comparing the search key with the letter I, as shown in Figure 9-2.

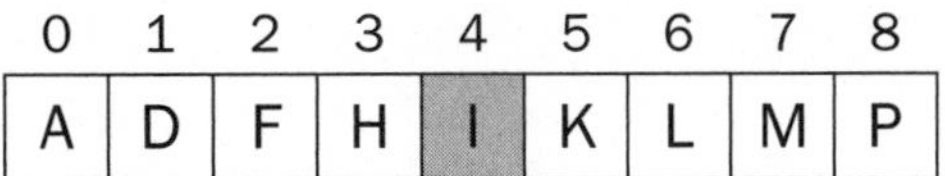

Figure 9-2: A search always begins with the middle item.

Because you haven't yet found a match, you divide the list in half. Then, because the search key, K, sorts higher than the current item, you concentrate your efforts on the upper half (see Figure 9-3).

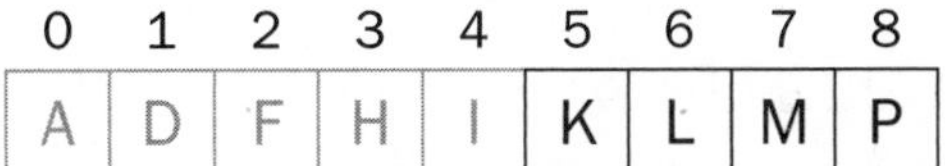

Figure 9-3: The search key must exist somewhere in the upper half of the list.

The new list consists of four letters: K, L, M, and P—an even number. Finding the middle item in a list containing an even number of items is clearly nonsensical. Luckily, though, it doesn't really matter whether the two halves are strictly equal, so you can arbitrarily choose one of the two middle items: L or M. This example uses L (see Figure 9-4).

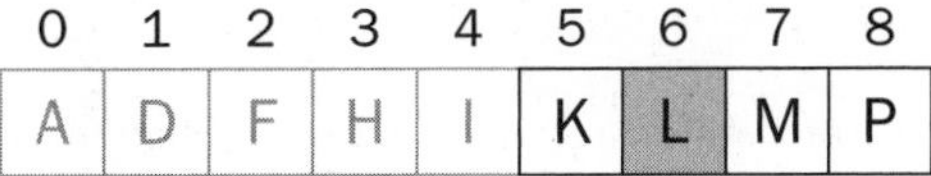

Figure 9-4: The search continues with the "middle" item.

Now you compare the search key with the chosen middle item—L. Once again, it's not the item you are looking for, so you divide the list in two and try again. This time, however, the search key sorts lower than the current item—K sorts before L—so you can assume that it will be found in the lower half, if indeed it exists at all.

Figure 9-5 shows that the search finally narrows to only one item, K, which in this case is the one you were looking for.

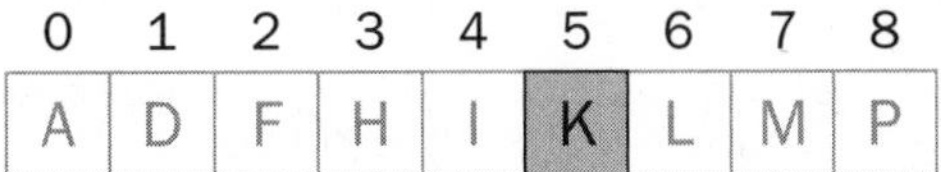

Figure 9-5: The search finally narrows to only one item.

The search is complete and you managed to locate the key in only three comparisons: the two intermediary comparisons with I and L, and the final comparison that resulted in the match. The same search using a brute-force approach would have taken six comparisons: first with the A, then D, F, H, I, and finally K.

You could argue that the search key used makes binary searching seem more efficient than it would have if the key had been at the start of the list. For example, if the letter A had been used as the search key, the brute-force approach would have found it in only one comparison, whereas the binary search would have taken four!

So it is fair to say that, in some very limited case, a brute-force search will do better than a binary search; however, in most cases, a binary search will do much better — a fact that is demonstrated concretely later in the chapter.

Binary Search Approaches

Now that you've observed how the algorithm works in principle, it's time to turn words into code. This section demonstrates two binary search approaches: one involving recursion and another using iteration. Each one has the same general performance characteristics, but you will see that one seems a little more intuitive than the other.

A List Searcher

In the following Try It Out, you define an interface that is common to the two approaches (recursive and iterative) you can take when implementing a binary search. This will enable you to plug in the different implementations for testing and performance evaluation.

A *list searcher* enables you to search a list (in this case, a sorted list) for a specified key via a single method, `search()`. This method uses a comparator to determine whether the search key matches any of the items in the list. If the key is found, `search()` returns its position (0, 1, 2, . . .). If the item is not found, `search()` returns a negative value corresponding to the point at which it would have been found had it existed. At this point, you're probably wondering how you can return the position information and at the same time indicate that the search key wasn't found.

Part of the answer is to use a negative value. That way, you can use positive return values to indicate searches that were successful, and negative values to indicate unsuccessful searches. However, if you simply take the negative value of the position (for example, 1 becomes –1, 2 becomes –2, and so on), what do you do with the first position in the list, 0? A value of –0 doesn't make sense.

The trick is to alter the return value so that a position of 0 becomes –1, 1 becomes –2, and so on. In this way, you can encode both the position *and* the fact that the search key wasn't found.

Try It Out Creating the List Searcher Interface

The first thing you need to do is to create the actual Java interface as follows:

```
package com.wrox.algorithms.bsearch;

import com.wrox.algorithms.lists.List;
```

```
public interface ListSearcher {
    public int search(List list, Object key);
}
```

How It Works

The interface has one method corresponding to the single `search()` operation discussed earlier. This method takes a list to search and a key to look for as arguments, and returns an integer corresponding to the position within the list.

Notice that you don't pass a comparator to `search()` even though you will need one. Instead, it is assumed that any searcher will have been constructed with a comparator already. This separation of concerns enables a list searcher to be passed around without code needing to know *how* the ordering is being performed. This should become more obvious when you write the actual test code.

Try It Out Writing the Tests

Now that you have an interface to work with, you write the tests. We've already identified at least two possible list searcher implementations, iterative and recursive, and you will end up with one more before the chapter is finished. We'll first create a suite of tests that any list searcher must satisfy. This way, you won't have to rewrite the tests for each different implementation.

Start by creating the test class itself:

```
package com.wrox.algorithms.bsearch;

import com.wrox.algorithms.lists.ArrayList;
import com.wrox.algorithms.lists.List;
import com.wrox.algorithms.sorting.Comparator;
import com.wrox.algorithms.sorting.NaturalComparator;
import junit.framework.TestCase;

public abstract class AbstractListSearcherTestCase extends TestCase {
    private static final Object[] VALUES = {"B", "C", "D", "F", "H", "I",
                                            "J", "K", "L", "M", "P", "Q"};

    private ListSearcher _searcher;
    private List _list;

    protected abstract ListSearcher createSearcher(Comparator comparator);

    protected void setUp() throws Exception {
        super.setUp();

        _searcher = createSearcher(NaturalComparator.INSTANCE);
        _list = new ArrayList(VALUES);
    }
}
```

How It Works

The AbstractListSearcherTestCase defines some test data, VALUES, a list searcher, of course, and a list to search. There's also an abstract method, createSearcher(), that subclasses of this test class implement to return the different list searcher implementations.

Then, during setUp(), you create a list searcher by calling createSearcher(), and finally construct a list from the array of values for the tests to work with.

Notice that the createSearcher() method takes a comparator as an argument. Recall that the search() method on ListSearcher makes no mention of a comparator, so the only time you need worry about one is at construction time.

In the next Try It Out, you can start writing some tests.

Try It Out Creating the Tests

Use the following simple test to ensure that when searching for existing values, you get back the correct position within the list:

```
public void testSearchForExistingValues() {
    for (int i = 0; i < _list.size(); ++i) {
        assertEquals(i, _searcher.search(_list, _list.get(i)));
    }
}
```

Create the next test, which searches for a value that doesn't exist in the list. Again, you need to ensure that the return value corresponds with the position at which the value would be located, had it existed:

```
public void testSearchForNonExistingValueLessThanFirstItem() {
    assertEquals(-1, _searcher.search(_list, "A"));
}
```

The next test searches for a non-existing value, but this time it belongs at the end of the list (position 12):

```
public void testSearchForNonExistingValueGreaterThanLastItem() {
    assertEquals(-13, _searcher.search(_list, "Z"));
}
```

Finally, you search for yet another non-existing value, this time belonging somewhere in the middle of the list:

```
public void testSearchForArbitraryNonExistingValue() {
    assertEquals(-4, _searcher.search(_list, "E"));
}
```

How It Works

The first test you created iterates through each value in the list (`_list.get(i)`) and performs a search for it. The result of each search is checked to ensure that it corresponds to the current position in the list. You could use an iterator here, but then you would have to track the current position independently. Instead, you use an integer position and call `get()`.

The second test searches for an A, which clearly doesn't exist. If it did exist, however, it would be found at the start of the list — position 0 — as it sorts before any of the other items. You therefore expect the return value to be `-(0 + 1) = -1`. Remember, values that are not found return –(`insertion point + 1`).

The third test searches for a Z and expects the result to indicate that it again wasn't found but that this time it belongs at the end of the list (position 12). Therefore, the return value should be `-(12 + 1) = -13`.

The last test searches for an E, which would be found at position 3 had it existed. Therefore, the search should return a value of `-(3 + 1) = -4` to indicate that it doesn't actually exist.

Recursive Binary Searcher

With the tests in place, you can implement the binary search algorithm. Binary searching is a process of continually dividing a problem into smaller and smaller pieces. This *divide-and-conquer* approach smacks of recursion, and the first implementation you develop indeed uses recursion.

Try It Out Testing and Creating the Recursive Binary Searcher

To ensure that your recursive binary search works properly, you first create a test class as follows:

```
package com.wrox.algorithms.bsearch;

import com.wrox.algorithms.sorting.Comparator;

public class RecursiveBinaryListSearcherTest extends AbstractListSearcherTestCase {
    protected ListSearcher createSearcher(Comparator comparator) {
        return new RecursiveBinaryListSearcher(comparator);
    }
}
```

Then create the list searcher itself:

```
package com.wrox.algorithms.bsearch;

import com.wrox.algorithms.lists.List;
import com.wrox.algorithms.sorting.Comparator;

public class RecursiveBinaryListSearcher implements ListSearcher {
    private final Comparator _comparator;

    public RecursiveBinaryListSearcher(Comparator comparator) {
        assert comparator != null : "comparator can't be null";

        _comparator = comparator;
    }
```

```
private int searchRecursively(List list, Object key,
                              int lowerIndex, int upperIndex) {
    assert list != null : "list can't be null";

    if (lowerIndex > upperIndex) {
        return -(lowerIndex + 1);
    }

    int index = lowerIndex + (upperIndex - lowerIndex) / 2;

    int cmp = _comparator.compare(key, list.get(index));

    if (cmp < 0) {
        index = searchRecursively(list, key, lowerIndex, index - 1);
    } else if (cmp > 0) {
        index = searchRecursively(list, key, index + 1, upperIndex);
    }

    return index;
}

public int search(List list, Object key) {
    assert list != null : "list can't be null";
    return searchRecursively(list, key, 0, list.size() - 1);
}
```

How It Works

Because you've already defined the tests in `AbstractListSearcherTestCase`, you simply extend this class and implement `createSearcher()` to return an instance of `RecursiveBinaryListSearcher`.

The `RecursiveListSearcher` class, in addition to implementing the `ListSearcher` interface, holds an instance of a comparator that is initialized in the constructor. Holding on to a comparator like this enables application code to perform searches without any knowledge of the comparison mechanism.

The method `searchRecursively()` is where the hard work is performed. Besides the list to search and the search key, `searchRecursively()` takes two addition arguments: `lowerIndex` and `upperIndex`. These mark the "bounds" of the search space. If you refer back to Figure 9-1 through Figure 9-5, you'll notice that each time the list is divided in half, you end up with a new range of elements to consider. The original list (refer to Figure 9-1) considered elements in positions 0 through 8 as potential locations for the search key. This was then pared down to positions 5 through 8 (refer to Figure 9-3). Ultimately, you ended up with only one possible element at position 5 (refer to Figure 9-5). These upper and lower bounds on the remaining search space correspond directly with the `upperIndex` and `lowerIndex` arguments.

Ignoring the termination condition for a while, the first step in the search process is to identify the "middle" element. This is done by subtracting the lower index from the upper index and dividing the result by 2, as follows:

```
int index = lowerIndex + (upperIndex - lowerIndex) / 2;
```

Now, starting with Figure 9-1, you can use this formula to calculate the middle element: `0 + (8 – 0) / 2 = 0 + 4 = 4`. In fact, as you can see from Figure 9-2, that is exactly where the example started. What may not be so obvious is why you also added the lower index. Refer to Figure 9-3. The lower and upper bounds are 5 and 8, respectively. When you run these numbers through the formula, you get: `5 + (8 – 5) / 2 = 5 + 3 / 2 = 5 + 1 = 6` (exactly as shown in Figure 9-4). If you don't add the lower index, then you end up with a position of `(8 – 5) / 2 = 3 / 2 = 1`! This is clearly incorrect. Subtracting the lower index from the upper index merely gives you the relative distance between the two, or, in other words, an offset *from* the lower index.

Next, you use the comparator to compare the key with the element at the position just calculated. The result of the comparison is then stored in the variable `cmp`:

```
int cmp = _comparator.compare(key, list.get(index));
```

A comparator returns a value that is equal to zero if the two arguments match; less than zero if the left argument sorts lower than the right argument; and greater than zero if the left argument sorts higher than the right argument. In the case of a binary search, this tells you everything you need to know about whether you have found the search key, or, if not, where to continue looking.

If the search key sorts before the current item, a recursive call is made to try searching in the lower half of the list: The lower half of the list always starts at the lower index and continues until just before the current position (`index - 1`):

```
if (cmp < 0) {
    index = searchRecursively(list, key, lowerIndex, index - 1);
}
```

If, conversely, the search key sorts after the current item, then a recursive call is made for the upper half of the list: The upper half of the list always starts just after the current position (`index + 1`) and continues until the upper index:

```
} else if (cmp > 0) {
    index = searchRecursively(list, key, index + 1, upperIndex);
}
```

Finally, if the search key matches the current item (the only other option), then no further searching is required and the code falls through to return the current position within the list. Now the only piece of code left is the termination condition—the bit we brushed over earlier.

Recall that every time there is a mismatch, the lower and upper bounds are incremented and decremented, and at some point the two cross—that is, the lower bound becomes greater than the upper bound. This only happens when the search encounters a mismatch with the final element.

Take another look at Figure 9-5, the point at which the search has narrowed to only one element, the K at position 5. This means that both the lower and upper index values will be 5. In the original example, a match was found, but if there had been a J in position 5, rather than a K, you would have had a mismatch; and because K sorts after J, you would have proceeded to search the upper half of the remaining elements.

In this case, a check is made to determine whether the `lowerIndex` and `upperIndex` variables have crossed. If so, this is the signal that you have run out of elements, and you terminate. At this point, the lower index always contains the position into which the search key would have been, had it existed in the list:

```
if (lowerIndex > upperIndex) {
    return -(lowerIndex + 1);
}
```

Finally, you created the `search()` method. It doesn't do much except pass the index to the first and last elements of the list to `searchRecursively()`.

Iterative Binary Searcher

In the next Try it Out, you test and create a recursive binary iterative searcher. The iterative version turns out to be quite simple once you understand the recursive version.

Try It Out Testing and Implementing the Iterative Binary Searcher

As with the recursive version, the iterative version needs its own test class. In addition, you do little more than extend the abstract test class:

```
package com.wrox.algorithms.bsearch;

import com.wrox.algorithms.sorting.Comparator;

public class IterativeBinaryListSearcherTest extends AbstractListSearcherTestCase {
    protected ListSearcher createSearcher(Comparator comparator) {
        return new IterativeBinaryListSearcher(comparator);
    }
}
```

This time, however, `createSearcher()` returns an instance of the `IterativeBinaryListSearcher` class, which you create as follows:

```
package com.wrox.algorithms.bsearch;

import com.wrox.algorithms.lists.List;
import com.wrox.algorithms.sorting.Comparator;

public class IterativeBinaryListSearcher implements ListSearcher {
    private final Comparator _comparator;

    public IterativeBinaryListSearcher(Comparator comparator) {
        assert comparator != null : "comparator can't be null";

        _comparator = comparator;
    }

    public int search(List list, Object key) {
        assert list != null : "list can't be null";
```

```
        int lowerIndex = 0;
        int upperIndex = list.size() - 1;

        while (lowerIndex <= upperIndex) {
            int index = lowerIndex + (upperIndex - lowerIndex) / 2;

            int cmp = _comparator.compare(key, list.get(index));

            if (cmp == 0) {
                return index;
            } else if (cmp < 0) {
                upperIndex = index - 1;
            } else {
                lowerIndex = index + 1;
            }
        }

        return -(lowerIndex + 1);
    }
}
```

How It Works

Like the recursive version, the `IterativeBinaryListSearcher` class implements `ListSearcher` and holds a comparator for later use. Besides the constructor, the only method in this class is the `search()` method itself, which is really a direct conversion from `RecursiveBinaryListSearcher`.

A close inspection of the recursive search code reveals that each time you recurse, you do little more than modify one of the upper and lower index variables. This may lead you to the realization that you can do away with recursion by using a `while` loop and simply modifying the upper and lower index variables as appropriate.

The iterative version of search, then, starts by initializing the lower and upper index variables to the positions of the first and last elements in the list, respectively:

```
int lowerIndex = 0;
int upperIndex = list.size() - 1;
```

This is analogous to the `search()` method passing in the positions of the first and last elements to `searchRecursively()` in the recursive implementation.

Next you enter a `while` loop as predicted:

```
while (lowerIndex <= upperIndex) {
    ...
}

return -(lowerIndex + 1);
```

As with the recursive version, at some point you can expect the values of the lower and upper index variables to cross if the search key doesn't exist. The loop therefore continues processing until this occurs (`lowerIndex <= upperIndex`). When this happens, the loop terminates and the position at which the search key would have been found, had it existed, will be returned (`-(lowerIndex + 1)`). Otherwise, while there are still values to search, you need to calculate the position of the middle and perform a comparison:

```
int index = lowerIndex + (upperIndex - lowerIndex) / 2;
int cmp = _comparator.compare(key, list.get(index));
```

If the comparison detects a match, the code can return immediately with the current position:

```
if (cmp == 0) {
    return index;
}
```

If, conversely, the search key sorts before the current item, you continue the search in the lower half of the list by adjusting the upper index down:

```
} else if (cmp < 0) {
    upperIndex = index - 1;
}
```

Finally, if the search key sorts after the current item, then you need to continue the search in the upper half of the list by adjusting the lower index up:

```
} else {
    lowerIndex = index + 1;
}
```

Assessing the List Searcher's Performance

In this section, you explore a number of scenarios that will gather statistics and enable you to determine which of the binary search algorithms performs significantly better than a brute-force, linear search. As when comparing the performance of the sorting algorithms in Chapters 6 and 7, this comparison will use a `CallCountingComparator` to count the number of comparisons made when a search is performed.

Linear Searching for Comparison

Before assessing the performance of the binary searchers, though, you need some way of comparing them with a linear search. One possibility might be to use the `indexOf()` method directly from the list interface, as you had originally implemented this as a brute-force, linear search. Unfortunately, `indexOf()` as defined doesn't use a comparator, nor does it provide any other convenient way to count the number of comparisons made. Therefore, in the next Try It Out, you'll create a list searcher that performs a linear search of a sorted list and uses a comparator to do so, thereby enabling you to collect some statistics for a thorough assessment.

Try It Out Testing and Implementing the Linear Searcher

Even though you will develop the linear list searcher purely for comparison with binary searching, you could hardly trust the results of such a comparison if there was a bug in any of the code, right? Therefore, as with all the code you have developed so far, you will start by creating a test suite:

```
package com.wrox.algorithms.bsearch;

import com.wrox.algorithms.sorting.Comparator;

public class LinearListSearcherTest extends AbstractListSearcherTestCase {
    protected ListSearcher createSearcher(Comparator comparator) {
        return new LinearListSearcher(comparator);
    }
}
```

Then create the searcher implementation class itself:

```
package com.wrox.algorithms.bsearch;

import com.wrox.algorithms.iteration.Iterator;
import com.wrox.algorithms.lists.List;
import com.wrox.algorithms.sorting.Comparator;

public class LinearListSearcher implements ListSearcher {
    private final Comparator _comparator;

    public LinearListSearcher(Comparator comparator) {
        assert comparator != null : "comparator can't be null";

        _comparator = comparator;
    }
    public int search(List list, Object key) {
        assert list != null : "list can't be null";

        int index = 0;
        Iterator i = list.iterator();

        for (i.first(); !i.isDone(); i.next()) {
            int cmp = _comparator.compare(key, i.current());
            if (cmp == 0) {
                return index;
            } else if (cmp < 0) {
                break;
            }

            ++index;
        }

        return -(index + 1);
    }
```

How It Works

Thankfully, because the outward behavior of the linear search is identical to every other list searcher implementation, you can once again take advantage of the abstract test class. All you need to do, of course, is have `createSearcher()` return an instance of `LinearListSearcher`.

The `LinearListSearcher` class implements `ListSearcher` and holds a comparator for later use, no doubt as expected.

For the `search()` method, you have essentially copied the code you developed for `indexOf()` in Chapter 2, except for a few minor changes. The first change is that instead of calling `equals()`, as you did for `indexOf()`, the code here uses the comparator. Then, after calling the comparator and recording the result in the local variable `cmp`, if the two values are equal you have found a match and can therefore return immediately:

```
int cmp = _comparator.compare(key, i.current());
if (cmp == 0) {
    return index;
}
```

The second difference between this code and that in Chapter 2 is an optimization. When the search key isn't found, the original implementation continues to the end of the list. In this case, however, you can take advantage of the fact that you know the list is sorted. (This seems reasonable, as it is an assumption upon which our binary search algorithms are predicated.) Therefore, you continue searching only while you believe there is still a chance that the search key might reasonably exist further along the list. When you reach a point in the list where the search key would sort before the current item, you can safely terminate the loop:

```
} else if (cmp < 0) {
    break;
}
```

Apart from these two changes, the rest of `search()` is identical to that found in the original `indexOf()` implementation.

Tests for Performance

Although you won't, strictly speaking, be creating tests in the real sense (you never make any assertions), because the JUnit framework makes an excellent harness for performance analysis, you will develop your performance tests in the form of test methods. These methods will perform the same sequence of searches using each of our three different list searchers.

As you have done previously, rather than use elapsed running times for measuring performance, you will instead count the number of comparisons made. For this you can re-use `CallCountingComparator` from Chapter 6.

Try It Out — Creating the Test Class

Start by creating a test class named `BinarySearchCallCountingTest`, which, as the name indicates, will be designed to count the number of comparison calls made:

```
package com.wrox.algorithms.bsearch;

import com.wrox.algorithms.lists.ArrayList;
import com.wrox.algorithms.lists.List;
import com.wrox.algorithms.sorting.CallCountingComparator;
import com.wrox.algorithms.sorting.NaturalComparator;
import junit.framework.TestCase;

public class BinarySearchCallCountingTest extends TestCase {
    private static final int TEST_SIZE = 1021;

    private List _sortedList;
    private CallCountingComparator _comparator;

    protected void setUp() throws Exception {
        super.setUp();

        _sortedList = new ArrayList(TEST_SIZE);

        for (int i = 0; i < TEST_SIZE; ++i) {
            _sortedList.add(new Integer(i));
        }

        _comparator = new CallCountingComparator(NaturalComparator.INSTANCE);
    }

    private void reportCalls() {
        System.out.println(getName() + ": "
                           + _comparator.getCallCount() + " calls");
    }

   ...
}
```

How It Works

The test class you created defines a constant, TEST_SIZE, which will be used shortly to populate and search the instance variable _sortedList and another instance variable, _comparator, to hold the call counting comparator that will be used for gathering the statistics.

In the setUp() method, you constructed an array list and populated it with integers in ascending order from 0 to TEST_SIZE. You then created a call counting comparator, for reporting, wrapped around a natural comparator. You can safely use a natural comparator because the Integer class implements the Comparator interface.

The reportCalls() method will be used by the individual tests to print the number of calls made to the comparator, in the following form:

```
test-name: #### calls
```

Now that you have a list containing sorted data, a comparator for gathering statistics, and a way to report those statistics, in the following Try It Out exercises you implement some tests to see how each of the list searchers perform.

Try It Out Implementing the Tests

The first set of tests you perform search for all values between `0` and `TEST_SIZE`, in order, and print the number of comparisons:

```
public void testRecursiveBinarySearch() {
    performInOrderSearch(new RecursiveBinaryListSearcher(_comparator));
}

public void testIterativeBinarySearch() {
    performInOrderSearch(new IterativeBinaryListSearcher(_comparator));
}

public void testLinearSearch() {
    performInOrderSearch(new LinearListSearcher(_comparator));
}

private void performInOrderSearch(ListSearcher searcher) {
    for (int i = 0; i < TEST_SIZE; ++i) {
        searcher.search(_sortedList, new Integer(i));
    }

    reportCalls();
}
```

The next set performs some random searches:

```
public void testRandomRecursiveBinarySearch() {
    performRandomSearch(new RecursiveBinaryListSearcher(_comparator));
}

public void testRandomIterativeBinarySearch() {
    performRandomSearch(new IterativeBinaryListSearcher(_comparator));
}

public void testRandomLinearSearch() {
    performRandomSearch(new LinearListSearcher(_comparator));
}

private void performRandomSearch(ListSearcher searcher) {
    for (int i = 0; i < TEST_SIZE; ++i) {
        searcher.search(_sortedList,
                        new Integer((int) (TEST_SIZE * Math.random())));
    }

    reportCalls();
}
```

How It Works

The in-order tests each construct one of the three different list searchers, which is then passed to `performOrderSearch()` to perform the in-order (0, 1, 2, . . .) search and finally report the number of comparisons made.

The random tests also construct an appropriate searcher with the counting comparator but pass them to `performRandomSearch()` to randomly generate some values to look up.

If you run the tests, depending on the tool you use, you will see something like the following:

```
testRecursiveBinarySearch: 9197 calls
testIterativeBinarySearch: 9197 calls
testLinearSearch: 521731 calls
testRandomRecursiveBinarySearch: 9197 calls
testRandomIterativeBinarySearch: 9132 calls
testRandomLinearSearch: 531816 calls
```

These results have been summarized in Table 9-1 to make it easier to make a comparison between the various search methods.

Table 9-1: Performance Comparison for 1021 Searches of a Sorted List

	Recursive Binary	Iterative Binary	Linear
Comparisons (In-Order)	9,197	9,197	521,731
Comparisons* (Random)	9,158	9,132	531,816
Comparisons* (Average)	9	9	515

* Actual results will vary due to the random nature of the test data.

The recursive and iterative implementations perform the same number of comparisons for the in-order search. (The difference between the number of comparisons for the random search for the recursive and iterative implementations is merely an artifact of the random nature of the test.) This is probably what you expected, but it's always nice to have your assumptions confirmed. It's also worth noting that the recursive version will suffer a slight penalty due to the overhead associated with the recursive method calls, but the difference will be negligible.

The important thing to observe, and the one of most interest to us, is the difference between the binary search and the linear search. In the case of the binary search, the average number of comparisons performed is approximately: `9,000 / 1,000 = 9`, whereas the average for the linear search is around `500,000 / 1,000 = 500`. These figures certainly confirm our original predictions about the performance characteristics of not only binary searching, but also linear searching. We expected our binary search to take, on average, `O(log N)` comparisons, and our linear search to take around `O(N)`.

Having said this, the actual performance of binary searching is excellent as long as you are using a data structure (such as an array list) that supports fast, indexed-based lookup. When using a linked list, for example, although the number of comparisons remains the same as for an array list, the continual traversal of the list to find the next item for comparison imposes considerable time penalties.

Understanding Binary Insertion

Binary insertion is a technique based on binary searching that enables you to maintain your data in sorted order. Clearly, you could use some of the sorting algorithms already covered in this book to keep your data in order, but as we will show, performing a sort after every insertion into a list can be very expensive. Indeed, performing a sort even after all of the data has been added to a list still turns out to be relatively more expensive than inserting the data in sorted order right from the start.

Binary insertion works pretty much like binary searching. In fact, the only difference between the two is that a binary search returns the position of the search key within the data, and a binary insert, as the name suggests, inserts the new key into the list at the appropriate position.

Imagine you wanted to add the letter G into the list of letters defined in the previous example. (Refer to Figure 9-1.) As with a binary search, you start at the middle item, I. Comparing the I with the new value, G, you determine that the insertion point must lie in the lower half of the list (I sorts lower than G).

Figure 9-6 shows that the next letter you compare against is the D. This time, the new value sorts higher than the current item, so you need to concentrate on the upper half of the remaining list.

0	1	2	3	4	5	6	7	8
A	D	F	H	I	K	L	M	P

Figure 9-6: The search moves to the lower half of the list.

You're now down to only two letters: F and H. Figure 9-7 shows that our new value sorts higher than the current item, F, so look to the H, as shown in Figure 9-8.

0	1	2	3	4	5	6	7	8
A	D	F	H	I	K	L	M	P

Figure 9-7: The search moves to the upper half of the remaining list.

The new value, G, sorts lower than the current item, H, but this time you have no more items to compare against; it's time to perform the insertion.

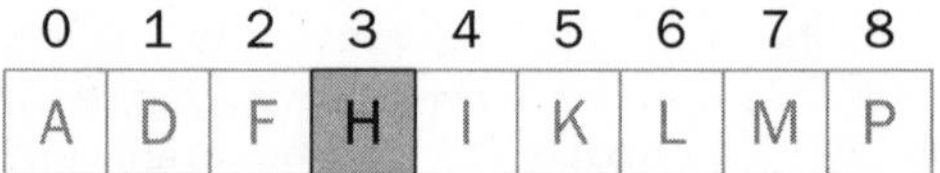

Figure 9-8: The search narrows to only one item.

The new value belongs before the last item, so you shift all the elements after and including the H to the right one position to make room for G, as shown in Figure 9-9.

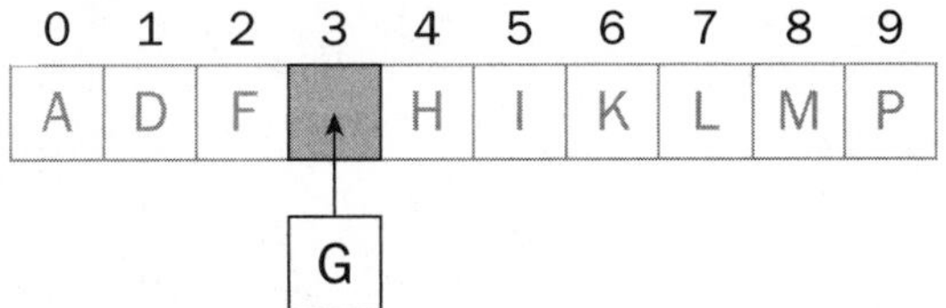

Figure 9-9: The key is inserted so as to maintain the correct ordering.

You can then insert the G into the correct position that ensures that the ordering of the list is maintained.

Now that you know how binary insertion works, you can write some code to actually perform a binary insertion into a list.

A List Inserter

In this section, you develop a very simple class that inserts a value into a list such that the ordering of the list is maintained. Rather than reinvent the wheel, though, you'll use a list searcher to find the insertion point.

Try It Out Creating the Tests

The tests themselves will use a binary insert algorithm to add numbers to a list. You add the numbers in sorted order and randomly. In all cases, expect the values to be inserted in the correct order.

Start by creating the test class as follows:

```
package com.wrox.algorithms.bsearch;

import com.wrox.algorithms.iteration.Iterator;
import com.wrox.algorithms.lists.ArrayList;
import com.wrox.algorithms.lists.List;
import com.wrox.algorithms.sorting.NaturalComparator;
import junit.framework.TestCase;

public class ListInserterTest extends TestCase {
    private static final int TEST_SIZE = 1023;

    private ListInserter _inserter;
    private List _list;

    protected void setUp() throws Exception {
        super.setUp();

        _inserter = new ListInserter(
                new IterativeBinaryListSearcher(NaturalComparator.INSTANCE));
```

```
        _list = new ArrayList(TEST_SIZE);
    }

    private void verify() {
        int previousValue = Integer.MIN_VALUE;
        Iterator i = _list.iterator();

        for (i.first(); !i.isDone(); i.next()) {
            int currentValue = ((Integer) i.current()).intValue();
            assertTrue(currentValue >= previousValue);
            previousValue = currentValue;
        }
    }

    ...
}
```

The first test involves inserting values into the list in ascending order. That is, add numbers starting at 0 followed by 1, 2, 3, and so on up to our specified maximum value, `TEST_SIZE`:

```
    public void testAscendingInOrderInsertion() {
        for (int i = 0; i < TEST_SIZE; ++i) {
            assertEquals(i, _inserter.insert(_list, new Integer(i)));
        }

        verify();
    }
```

The next test is really a variation on the first. Instead of inserting values in ascending order, this time you insert them in descending order. That is, start at your specified maximum and work your way down until you reach `0`:

```
    public void testDescendingInOrderInsertion() {
        for (int i = TEST_SIZE - 1; i >= 0; --i) {
            assertEquals(0, _inserter.insert(_list, new Integer(i)));
        }

        verify();
    }
```

The final test inserts random values into the list. Doing so ensures that the inserter isn't somehow working by coincidence when given values in order (as the previous two tests have done):

```
    public void testRandomInsertion() {
        for (int i = 0; i < TEST_SIZE; ++i) {
            _inserter.insert(_list,
                             new Integer((int) (TEST_SIZE * Math.random())));
        }

        verify();
    }
```

How It Works

The test class holds an instance of a ListInserter and a list into which each of the tests will insert values, both of which are initialized in the setUp() method.

The verify() method is called by each of the tests to ensure that the contents of the resulting list are in order. It does this by iterating over each item in the list. Each successive value (currentValue) is then checked to ensure that it is not less than the one before it (previousValue). Notice how you have initialized the previous value to Integer.MIN_VALUE. This guarantees that assertion will always succeed the first time through even though there was no previous value to speak of.

In the first test, a simple for loop enables you to add the values in ascending order, using an instance of the inserter. Each time a value is inserted, you also make sure that the return value accurately reflects the insertion point. In the case of this ascending insertion, the insertion point always matches the value inserted: 0 goes into position 0, 1 into position 1, and so on. Finally, after all the values have been added, you call verify() to ensure that they all actually went into the correct positions—just because insert() reported that they went into the correct positions doesn't actually mean that they did!

The second test used a for loop to add the values in descending order. This time, because you are inserting in descending order, you make sure that insert() reports that each value has been placed into position 0 (shifting all the existing values right by one spot). Finally, you call verify() to ensure that the insertion has actually worked as expected—again, trust that the return value accurately reflects the actual insertion point.

The final test still adds only TEST_SIZE integers to the list, but the value of each is determined randomly using Math.random(). Recall that Math.random() returns a double-precision floating-point number in the range 0.0 to 1.0—therefore, we multiply the result by TEST_SIZE to ensure that we obtain integers in the range 0 to TEST_SIZE. Notice that this time we make no assertions about the value returned from insert(). How could we? The values are being inserted in *random* order.

Your tests are in place. In the next Try It Out, you implement the actual inserter.

Try It Out — Implementing the Inserter

The code to perform binary insertion is quite simple. It involves creating the ListInserter class as shown here:

```
package com.wrox.algorithms.bsearch;

import com.wrox.algorithms.lists.List;

public class ListInserter {
    private final ListSearcher _searcher;

    public ListInserter(ListSearcher searcher) {
        assert searcher != null : "searcher can't be null";
        _searcher = searcher;
    }

   public int insert(List list, Object value) {
        assert list != null : "list can't be null";
```

```
            int index = _searcher.search(list, value);

            if (index < 0) {
                index = -(index + 1);
            }

            list.insert(index, value);

            return index;
        }
    }
```

How It Works

As you can see, the constructor for the `ListInserter` class takes as its sole argument a `ListSearcher`. This will be used to find the insertion point—most of binary insertion is the same as binary search, so why reinvent the wheel?

The `insert()` method then uses the list searcher to find the insertion point. If the search was successful, an element with the same value already exists. Not to worry, though, as you allow duplicates, so you simply insert the new value into this position and have the existing value move to the right one spot. If, however, the value wasn't found (`index < 0`), then you know from the discussion on searching that you can convert the return value into a valid position with `-(index + 1)`. Then, once you know where the new value should go, you insert it into the list and return the insertion point to the caller.

Assessing Performance

You now have a class that uses an efficient binary search mechanism for adding items to a list while at the same time maintaining the list in sorted order. Now the question is, what is the performance like? More specifically, how well does it stack up against the various sorting algorithms you developed in Chapters 6 and 7? Surely it would be better to just create an ordinary list, populate it with data and then sort it.

In the next Try It Out, you create a test suite that enables you to compare the performance of your binary insertion code with several of the sorting algorithms.

Try It Out Comparing the Binary Inserter with Other Sorting Algorithms

Just as you did when assessing the performance of the list searchers, you create a test suite that exercises the binary inserter and compares it with sorting a list using various sorting algorithms:

```
package com.wrox.algorithms.bsearch;

import com.wrox.algorithms.lists.ArrayList;
import com.wrox.algorithms.lists.List;
import com.wrox.algorithms.sorting.CallCountingComparator;
import com.wrox.algorithms.sorting.ListSorter;
import com.wrox.algorithms.sorting.MergesortListSorter;
import com.wrox.algorithms.sorting.NaturalComparator;
import com.wrox.algorithms.sorting.QuicksortListSorter;
```

```
import com.wrox.algorithms.sorting.ShellsortListSorter;
import junit.framework.TestCase;

public class BinaryInsertCallCountingTest extends TestCase {
    private static final int TEST_SIZE = 4091;

    private List _list;
    private CallCountingComparator _comparator;

    protected void setUp() throws Exception {
        super.setUp();

        _list = new ArrayList(TEST_SIZE);
        _comparator = new CallCountingComparator(NaturalComparator.INSTANCE);
    }

    ...
}
```

The first test you write exercises the binary inserter just developed to add a number of values to the list and count the number of comparisons made in the process:

```
    public void testBinaryInsert() {
        ListInserter inserter = new ListInserter(
                                    new IterativeBinaryListSearcher(_comparator));

        for (int i = 0; i < TEST_SIZE; ++i) {
            inserter.insert(_list,
                                new Integer((int) (TEST_SIZE * Math.random())));
        }

        reportCalls();
    }

    private void reportCalls() {
        System.out.println(getName() + ": "
                            + _comparator.getCallCount() + " calls");
    }
```

Now that you have a test for binary insertion, you create similar tests for some of the sorting alternatives. For this, you use the same sorting algorithms you used with binary searching earlier in this chapter:

```
    public void testMergeSort() {
        populateAndSortList(new MergesortListSorter(_comparator));
    }

    public void testShellsort() {
        populateAndSortList(new ShellsortListSorter(_comparator));
    }

    public void testQuicksort() {
        populateAndSortList(new QuicksortListSorter(_comparator));
    }
```

```
    private void populateAndSortList(ListSorter sorter) {
        for (int i = 0; i < TEST_SIZE; ++i) {
            _list.add(new Integer((int) (TEST_SIZE * Math.random())));
        }

        _list = sorter.sort(_list);

        reportCalls();
    }
```

How It Works

The test class holds a list into which values will be inserted, and of course a comparator to use when ordering and sorting. As in the previous performance tests, you use an array list and a call counting comparator to collect statistics necessary in order to evaluate the different approaches.

The method `testBinaryInsert()` first creates an iterative binary list searcher. (You could have used the recursive version instead but the iterative one doesn't have the overhead of the nested calls.) You then insert `TEST_SIZE` random integer values into the list. The method `reportCalls()` is then used to print the number of calls made to the comparator, in the following form:

```
test-name: #### calls
```

The final three tests each create a different sorting algorithm, which is then passed to `populateAndSortList()`, where all of the real work is done.

In `populateAndSortList()`, you add `TEST_SIZE` random integers to the list (using the same technique as used previously), sort it using the provided sorting algorithm, and finally report the number of calls made to the comparator. Again, you need to multiply the value obtained from `Math.random()` to ensure that the inserted value falls within the range `0` to `TEST_SIZE`.

If you run these tests, you should see output similar to the following:

```
testBinaryInsert: 41471 calls
testMergeSort: 43928 calls
testShellsort: 102478 calls
testQuicksort: 97850 calls
```

Table 9-2 summarizes what's going on.

Table 9-2: Performance Comparison for 4091 Random Inserts into a List

Sort Type	Comparisons*
Binary Insert	41,471
Mergesort	43,928
Shellsort	102,478
Quicksort	97,850

* Actual results will vary due to the random nature of the test data.

As Table 9-3 quite clearly shows, binary insert performs the best, with mergesort coming in a close second, and shellsort and quicksort way behind. Remember, however, that although the performance of mergesort is comparable, it requires another list for its results, whereas binary insert adds new values into the same list.

From these results, you can work out the average number of comparisons performed using a binary insert. The binary insert works by performing a binary search; and as you already know, binary search runs in `O(log N)` comparisons. Because the list starts off empty, there would initially be $\log_2 0$ comparisons required. The next insert would require $\log_2 1$ comparisons, followed by $\log_2 2$, and so on all the way to $\log_2 N$. A simplistic calculation would suggest performance around $N \log_2 N$, but actually it's better, much better, being more like $\log_2 N!$.

These comparisons have actually been a little unfair. Each time binary insert adds a new value, it goes directly into the correct position to maintain the ordering of values. This means that the list will *always* be in sorted order, no matter how many values you add or when you choose to add them. Conversely, these tests applied the three sorting algorithms only after *all* the values were inserted. This means that the list remains largely unsorted until the very end. What would happen if you instead sort the list after every insertion?

Table 9-3 summarizes the results obtained when changing `populateAndSort()` to sort after every insertion:

```
private void populateAndSort(ListSorter sorter) {
    for (int i = 0; i < TEST_SIZE; ++i) {
        _list.add(nextValue());
        _list = sorter.sort(_list);
    }


    reportCalls();
}
```

Table 9-3: Performance Comparison When Sorting after Every Insert

Sort Type	Comparisons*
Binary insert	41,481
Mergesort	48,852,618
Shellsort	44,910,616
Quicksort	N/A**

* Actual results will vary due to the random nature of the test data.

** After 5 minutes, we killed the process because it still hadn't completed.

Looking at these results, it's plain to see that sorting after each insertion is certainly not a viable option. If you want the data to remain in sorted order while inserting, binary insertion wins hands down, performing at least 1,000 times fewer comparisons!

One final point to note: Because you would preferably use an array list (or some other data structure that supports fast, index-based lookup) to achieve the desired performance, inserting new items can be relatively slow. (Recall that an array list must copy all data items one position to the right after the insertion point to make room.) With small data sets, the overhead is negligible. In larger data sets, however, this can have a noticeable impact on performance.

Summary

In this chapter, you have learned the following key points:

- Binary searching uses a divide-and-conquer approach to locating a search key and in doing so achieves an average number of comparisons that approaches `O(log N)`.
- Binary searching can be achieved efficiently using either recursion or iteration.
- Binary searching works best when used with a data structure that supports fast, index-based lookup.
- Binary insertion builds on binary searching to add items to a list while maintaining the sort order using `O(log N!)` comparisons.
- Binary insertion proves to be very efficient, performing as well as — and arguably better than — some of the sorting algorithms.

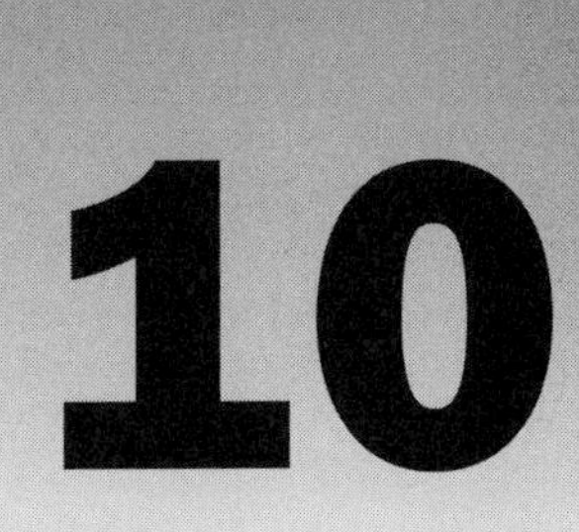

Binary Search Trees

Chapter 9 introduced a binary search algorithm that enables you to efficiently search a sorted array list. Unfortunately, a binary search algorithm suffers when it comes to insertions and deletions as elements are copied around. Binary search trees, on the other hand, can achieve the `O(log N)` average search/insert/delete time of the binary search algorithm without the associated overhead. By storing values in a tree structure — where values are linked together — it's easy to insert new values and remove deleted ones.

Unlike most other chapters, this chapter is largely theoretical. That is, you don't work through any practical examples because binary search trees actually form the basis for many other data structures. This chapter is confined to a discussion about how binary search trees work, rather than how you use them in practice. In later chapters on sets (Chapter 12), maps (Chapter 13), and B-Trees (Chapter 15), you'll see how these other data structures are built using the code in this chapter as a template.

This chapter discusses the following topics:

- Characteristics that make binary search trees so interesting
- Various binary search tree operations and how each works
- How the ordering of data can affect performance
- A simple technique for restoring the balance after insertion and deletion
- How to test and implement a nonbalancing binary search tree

Understanding Binary Search Trees

Chapter 2 mentioned how a file system is often referred to as a directory tree. More formally, though, a tree is a set of linked nodes whereby each node has zero or more children and at most one parent. One of the nodes is singled out as the root, and is the only node without a parent. Nodes without children are referred to as *leaf nodes*.

Just like a directory tree with any number of directories, subdirectories, and files, trees can have any number of children. However, a very common type of tree is a *binary tree*, so called because each node may have at most two children. (These children are often referred to as the left and right.)

A binary search tree is a binary tree with one more restriction: All children to the left of a node have smaller values, whereas all children to the right will have larger values.

Figure 10-1 shows an example of a binary search tree. Here, the letter I is the root node and the letters A, H, K, and P are all leaf nodes. The value of every child to the left of a node is smaller, and the value of every child to the right is larger, than the value of the node itself.

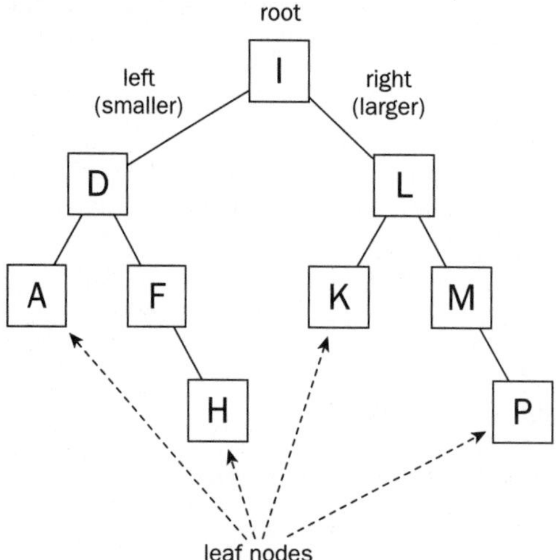

Figure 10-1: A simple binary search tree.

These properties allow very efficient searching, insertion, and deletion. In fact, the average search time for a binary search tree is directly proportional to its height: `O(h)`. In the case of the example shown in Figure 10-1, the height of the tree—the longest path from the root node to a leaf—is three, so you can expect the average search time to be in the order of three comparisons.

For a balanced tree—such as the one in Figure 10-1—the height of the tree is `O(log N)`. However, under certain circumstances, the height of the tree can degenerate, leading to a worst-case search time of `O(N)`.

Minimum

The *minimum* of a binary search tree is the node with the smallest value, and, thanks to the properties of a binary search tree, finding the minimum couldn't be simpler. Simply follow the left links starting from the root of the tree to find the one with the smallest value. In other words, the minimum is the leftmost node in the tree.

In the example shown in Figure 10-1, if you follow the left links starting from the root node, I, all the way down to a leaf node, you end up with the letter A — the smallest value in the tree.

Maximum

Whereas the minimum of a binary search tree is the node with the smallest value, the *maximum* is the node with the largest value. Finding the maximum is very similar to finding the minimum except that you follow the right links instead of the left. In other words, the maximum is the rightmost node in the tree.

To prove it, try following the right links starting from the root node in Figure 10-1 all the way down to a leaf node. You should end up with the letter P — the largest value in the tree.

Successor

A node's *successor* is the one with the next largest value in the tree. For example, given the tree shown in Figure 10-1, the successor of A is D, the successor of H is I, and the successor of I is K. Finding the successor is not that difficult, but it involves two distinct cases.

In the first case, if a node has a right child, then the successor is the minimum of that. For example, to find the successor of I, we see that it has a right child, L, so we take its minimum, K. The same holds for the letter L: It has a right child, M, so we find its minimum, which in this case happens to be M itself.

Conversely, if the node has no right child — as is the case with H — you need to search back up the tree until you find the first "right-hand turn." By this we mean that you keep looking up the tree until you find a node that is the left child, and then use its parent. In this example, you move up the tree moving left (that is, following right-hand links) from H to F and then left again to D, and finally you make a right-hand turn to I.

Predecessor

The *predecessor* of a node is the one with the next smallest value. For example, the predecessor of P is M, the predecessor of F is D, and the predecessor of I is H.

The algorithm for finding the predecessor is essentially the inverse of what you'd use for the successor, and it involves two similar cases. In the first case, if a node has a left child, then you take its maximum. In the second case — whereby the node has no left child — you work up the tree until you find a "left-hand" turn.

Search

When searching for a value in a binary search tree, you start at the root node and follow links left or right as appropriate until either you find the value you are looking for or there are no more links to follow. This can be summarized in the following steps:

1. Start at the root node.
2. If there is no current node, the search value was not found and you are done. Otherwise, proceed to step 3.
3. Compare the search value with the key for the current node.
4. If the keys are equal, then you have found the search key and are done. Otherwise, proceed to step 5.
5. If the search key sorts lower than the key for the current node, then follow the left link and go to step 2.
6. Otherwise, the search key must sort higher than the key for the current node, so follow the right link and go to step 2.

The following example shows how you would search for the letter K in the binary search tree shown in Figure 10-1.

Starting with the root node (step 1), you compare your search value, K, with the letter I, as shown in Figure 10-2.

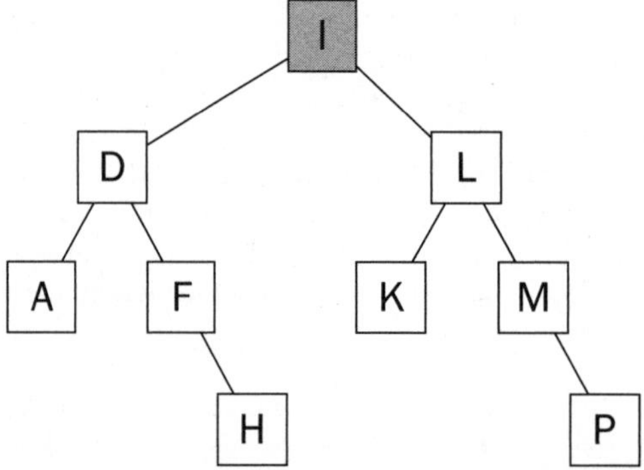

Figure 10-2: A search always starts with the root node.

Because K comes before I, you follow the right link (step 6), which leads you to the node containing the letter L (see Figure 10-3).

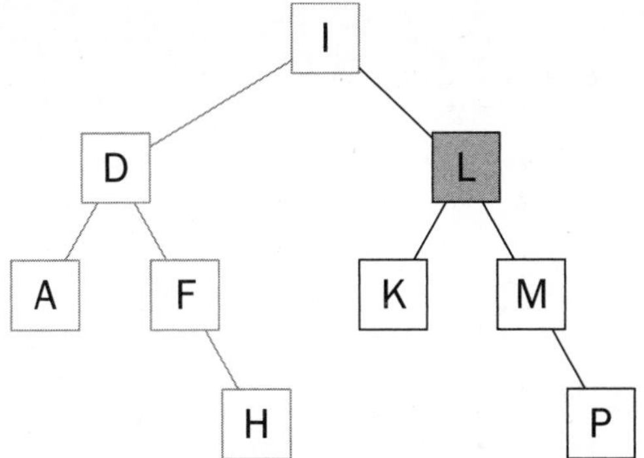

Figure 10-3: Follow the right link when the search key sorts after the key at the current node.

You still don't have a match, but because K is smaller than L, you follow the left link (step 5), as shown in Figure 10-4.

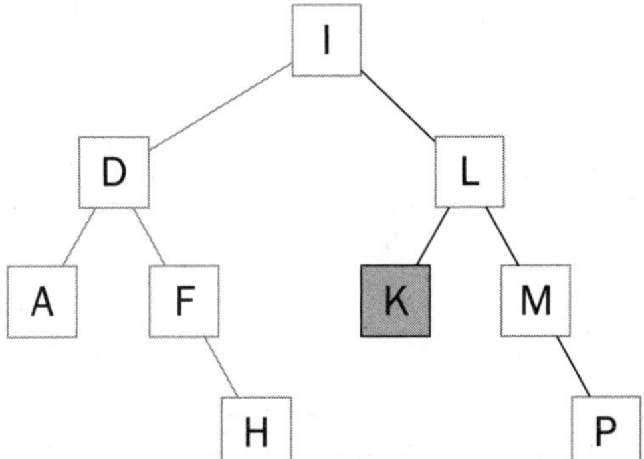

Figure 10-4: Follow the left link when the search key sorts before the key at the current node.

Finally, you have a match (see Figure 10-4): The search value is the same as the value at the current node (step 4), and your search completes. You searched a tree containing nine values and found the one you were looking for in only three comparisons. In addition, note that you found the match three levels down in the tree—`O(h)`.

Each time you move down the tree, you effectively discard half the values—just as you do when performing a binary search of a sorted list. In fact, given a sorted list, you can easily construct the equivalent binary search tree, as shown in Figure 10-5.

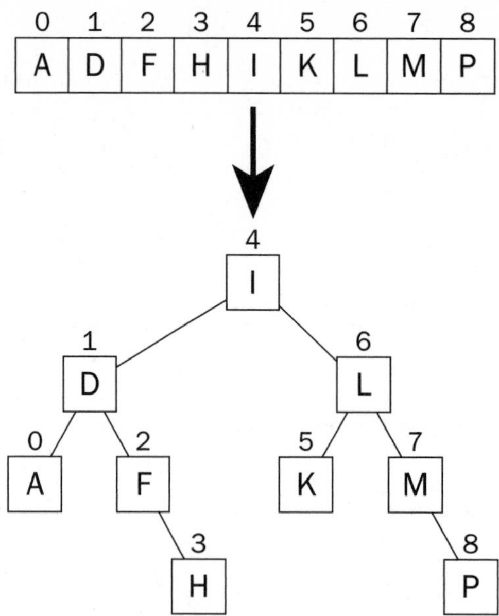

Figure 10-5: A sorted list depicted as a balanced binary search tree.

If you compare the search you just made with the examples in Chapter 9, you will find the order of comparisons to be identical. That's because a balanced binary search tree has the same performance characteristics as a sorted list.

Insertion

Insertion is nearly identical to searching except that when the value doesn't exist, it is added to the tree as a leaf node. In the previous search example, if you had wanted to insert the value J, you would have followed the left link from K and discovered that there were no more nodes. Therefore, you could safely add the J as the left child of K, as shown in Figure 10-6.

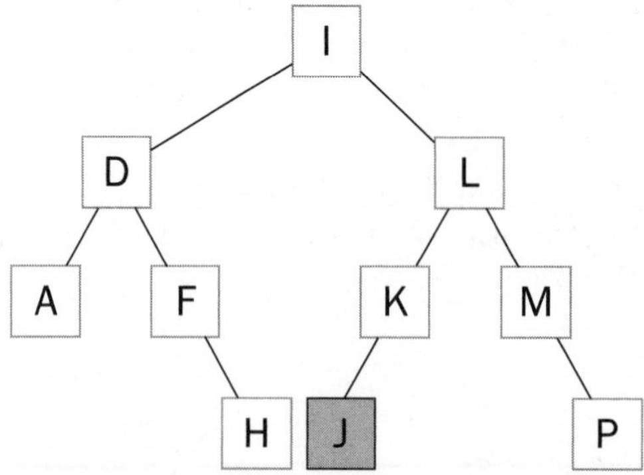

Figure 10-6: Insertion always involves creating a new leaf node.

The newly inserted value was added as a leaf, which in this case hasn't affected the height of the tree.

Inserting relatively random data usually enables the tree to maintain its `O(log N)` height, but what happens when you insert nonrandom data such as a word list from a dictionary or names from a telephone directory? Can you imagine what would happen if you started with an empty tree and inserted the following values in alphabetical order: A, D, F, H, I, K, L, M, and P?

Considering that new values are always inserted as leaf nodes, and remembering that all larger values become right children of their parent, inserting the values in ascending order leads to a severely unbalanced tree, as shown in Figure 10-7.

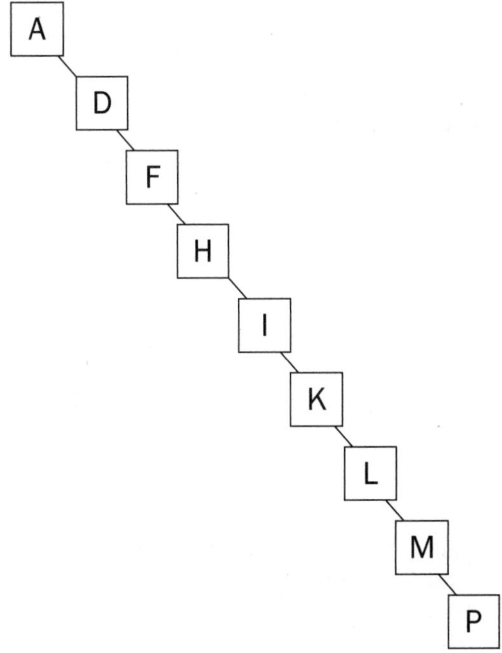

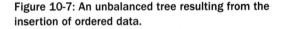

Figure 10-7: An unbalanced tree resulting from the insertion of ordered data.

In fact, whenever data is inserted in order, a binary search tree will degenerate into a linked list and the height of the tree—and with it the average search time—becomes `O(N)`.

Even if you do have ordered data, though, all is not lost. There are several variations on binary search trees that perform balancing, including Red-Black trees, AVL trees, Splay trees, and so on, all of which involve fairly complex restructuring to restore some balance to the tree. For this reason, they are not covered as part of this book. However, one novel yet fairly simple variation known as a *B-Tree* is introduced in Chapter 15.

Deletion

Deletion is a little more involved than searching or insertion. There are essentially three cases to consider. The node to be deleted will reflect one of the following conditions:

- No children (a leaf), in which case you can simply remove it.
- One child (either left or right), in which case you can replace the deleted node with its child.
- Two children, in which case you swap the node with its successor and try again with either case 1 or case 2 as appropriate.

We'll now discuss each of the cases in more detail, starting with the simplest case: deleting a leaf node. In all cases, assume you are starting with a tree that looks like the one shown in Figure 10-1.

The simplest case involves deleting a leaf node. Because a leaf node has no children, all you need to do is break the link with its parent. Figure 10-8 shows how to delete the value H from the tree.

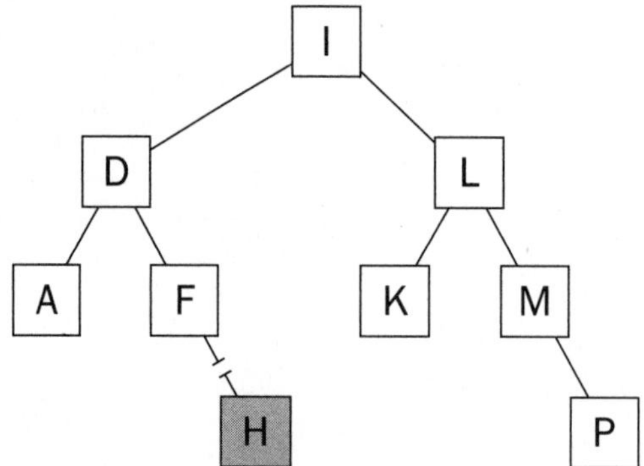

Figure 10-8: Leaf nodes are deleted by breaking the link with their parent.

The next simplest case involves deleting a node with only one child. When deleting a node with only one child, splice it out by making its parent point to its child. Figure 10-9 shows the tree after deleting the letter M.

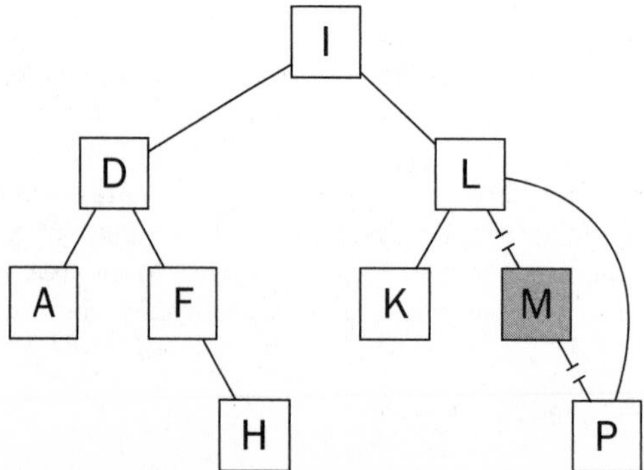

Figure 10-9: Nodes with only one child are spliced out.

Note how the links between M and its parent, L, and its child, P, have been replaced with a direct link between L and P.

Deleting a node with two children is somewhat trickier. For example, imagine you had to delete the root node I from the tree in Figure 10-1. Which node would you use as its replacement? Technically, you could use either of the two child nodes — D or L — and still maintain the properties of a binary search tree. However, both of these nodes already have two children each, making it difficult to simply splice out the deleted node.

Therefore, to delete a node with two children, the first thing you need to do is find the successor (you could just as easily choose the predecessor and it would work just as well) and switch the values. Figure 10-10 shows the result of switching the I with the K. Notice that this temporarily violates the properties of a binary search tree.

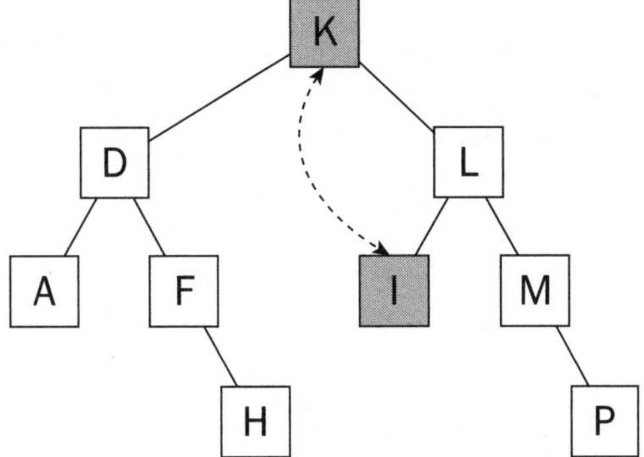

Figure 10-10: The value of the node to be deleted is swapped with its successor.

Now that the value has moved, rather than delete the original node, which now has the value K, you delete the node with which you switch values. This process is guaranteed to fall into either case 1 or case 2. How do you know this? Well, for a start, the node you originally wanted to delete had two children, meaning that it must have a right child. Furthermore, the successor of a node with a right child is the minimum (or the leftmost node) of the right child. Therefore, the successor can either be a leaf node (one with no children) or have at most a right child. If it had a left child, by definition it wouldn't be the minimum.

In the example, having swapped the values (see Figure 10-10), you can safely delete the leaf node containing the value I, as shown in Figure 10-11.

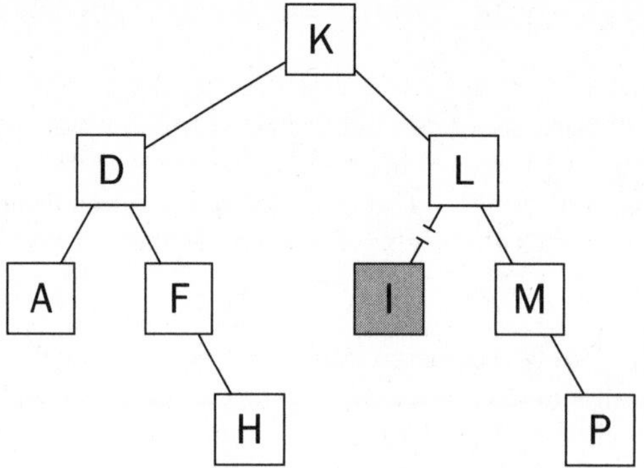

Figure 10-11: The successor node is deleted.

Deletion can unbalance a binary search tree, leading to a degradation in performance. Just like inserting ordered data into a tree can cause it to become unbalanced, deleting data in order causes it to become unbalanced. For example, Figure 10-12 shows the effect of deleting the values A, D, F, and H from the tree in Figure 10-1.

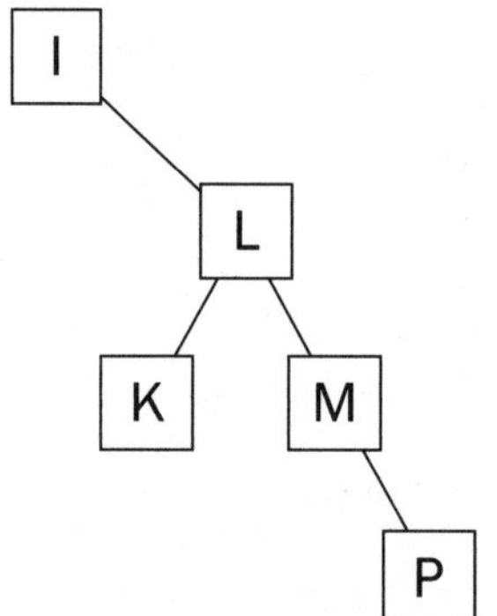

Figure 10-12: An unbalanced tree resulting from the deletion of ordered data.

Because all of the values listed are on the left-hand side of the tree (starting at the root), you end up with a lopsided tree.

In any event, whichever deletion case is required and regardless of whether, after deletion, the tree remains balanced, most of the time is actually spent finding the node to delete (and possibly finding its successor). Therefore, just like search and insert, the time to delete is still `O(h)`.

In-order Traversal

In-order traversal, as the name suggests, visits the values in a binary search tree in sorted order. This can be useful for printing out or otherwise processing the values in order. Again, given our example tree from Figure 10-1, an in-order traversal would visit the values in the following order: A, D, F, I, K, L, M, P.

There are two simple ways to perform in-order traversal: recursively and iteratively. To perform a recursive in-order traversal, starting with the root node:

1. Traverse the left subtree of the node.
2. Visit the node itself.
3. Traverse the right subtree.

To perform an iterative in-order traversal of a binary search tree, start with the minimum of the tree and visit it and each successor node until there are no more.

Pre-order Traversal

Pre-order traversal first visits the root node, then each of the subtrees. A pre-order traversal of the tree in Figure 10-1 would produce the following sequence of values: I, D, A, F, H, L, K, M, P.

Like in-order traversal, pre-order traversal can easily be defined recursively. To perform a pre-order traversal, starting with the root node:

1. Visit the node itself.
2. Traverse the left subtree.
3. Traverse the right subtree.

Unlike in-order traversal however, an iterative form is rather involved and requires the explicit use of a stack (see Chapter 5) in place of the implicit processor stack used when making recursive calls.

Post-order Traversal

Post-order traversal visits the root node *after* each of the subtrees. A post-order traversal of the tree in Figure 10-1 would visit the nodes in the following order: A, H, F, D, K, P, M, L, I.

To perform a post-order traversal, starting with the root node:

1. Traverse the left subtree.
2. Traverse the right subtree.
3. Visit the node itself.

Like pre-order traversal, an iterative form is rather involved and requires the use of a stack.

Balancing

The order in which data is inserted into and deleted from binary search trees affects the performance. More specifically, inserting and deleting ordered data can cause the tree to become unbalanced and, in the worst case, degenerate into a simple linked list. As mentioned, you can use *balancing* as a means of restoring the desired characteristics of the tree. Although the implementation is beyond the scope of this book, we still believe it is important to understand at least how the balancing algorithms work, even if we do not provide coded examples. To this end, we will present a short summary of one such tree: AVL.

One of the most difficult tasks in maintaining a balanced tree is detecting an imbalance in the first place. Imagine a tree with hundreds if not thousands of nodes. How, after performing a deletion or insertion, can you detect an imbalance without traversing the entire tree?

Two Russian mathematicians, G. M. Adel'son-Vel'skii and E. M. Landis (hence the name AVL), realized that one very simple way to keep a binary search tree balanced is to track the height of each subtree. If two siblings ever differ in height by more than one, the tree has become unbalanced.

Figure 10-13 shows a tree that needs rebalancing. Notice that the root node's children differ in height by two.

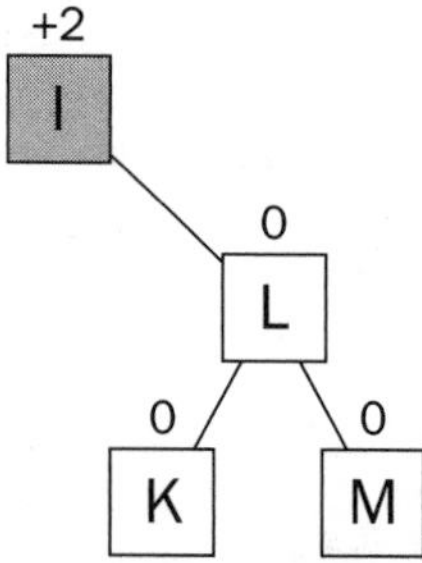

Figure 10-13: The difference in height between children of the root node is greater than one.

After an imbalance has been detected, you need to correct it, but how? The solution involves rotating nodes to remove the imbalance. You perform this rebalancing by working up the tree from the inserted/deleted node to the root, rotating nodes as necessary anytime a node is inserted or deleted from an AVL tree.

There are four different types of rotation depending on the nature of the imbalance: a single rotation and a double rotation, each with a left and right version. Table 10-1 shows you how to determine whether a single or a double rotation is required.

Table 10-1: Determining Rotation Number

Inbalanced	Child Is Balanced	Child Is Left-Heavy	Child Is Right-Heavy
Left-Heavy	Once	Once	Twice
Right-Heavy	Once	Twice	Once

In Figure 10-13, the root node I is right-heavy, and its right child, L, is also right-heavy. The information in Table 10-1 indicates that you only need to perform one rotation — to the left, to demote the I and promote the L, resulting in the tree shown in Figure 10-14.

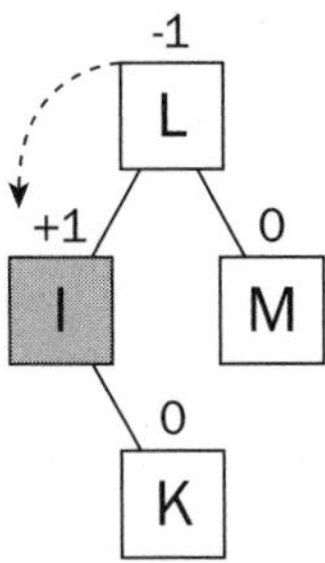

Figure 10-14: AVL height property restored by rotating the node once to the left.

If the tree looks like that shown in Figure 10-15, two rotations are required — the root node is right-heavy and its right child is left-heavy. This might happen if you had just inserted the K, for example.

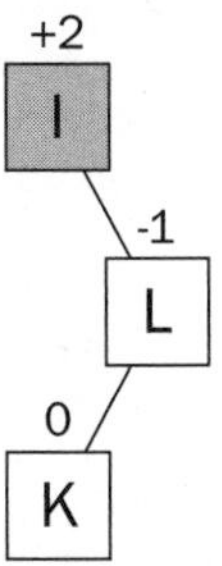

Figure 10-15: A tree requiring two rotations.

First you rotate L right once and then rotate the L left once, as shown in Figure 10-16.

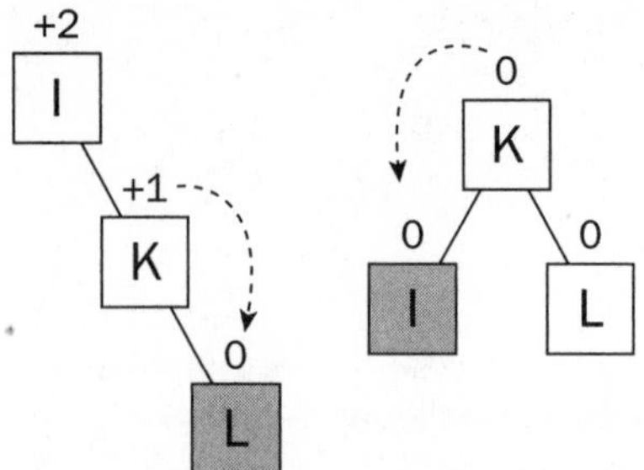

Figure 10-16: The first rotation moves the child node L to the right; the second rotates the unbalanced node I to the left.

Although AVL trees are not guaranteed to be perfectly balanced, they exhibit excellent performance characteristics. In fact, given a million nodes, a perfectly balanced tree will require around $\log_2 1000000 = 20$ comparisons, whereas the AVL tree requires around $1.44 \log_2 1000000 = 28$ comparisons. Certainly much better than the 500,000 comparisons required in the worst-case binary search tree!

Although not covered here, one more variation on self-balancing binary trees is the Red-Black tree. For more information on Red-Black trees, see *Introduction to Algorithms* [Cormen, 2001].

Testing and Implementing a Binary Search Tree

It's finally time to get into some code. As always, you're going to start by developing some tests. Once that's done, you write the implementation code. As part of the implementation, you create two main classes: `Node` and `BinarySearchTree`. `Node`, as the name suggests, will model the nodes in the tree, while `BinarySearchTree` will provide a wrapper around the root node and contain all the `search()`, `delete()`, and `insert()` code.

Because the `BinarySearchTree` class doesn't mean much without nodes, in the following Try it Out section you write some node tests. Following that, you'll write the node class itself.

Try It Out Testing a Node Class

Create the node tests as follows:

```
package com.wrox.algorithms.bstrees;

import junit.framework.TestCase;

public class NodeTest extends TestCase {
    private Node _a;
    private Node _d;
    private Node _f;
    private Node _h;
    private Node _i;
    private Node _k;
    private Node _l;
    private Node _m;
    private Node _p;

    protected void setUp() throws Exception {
        super.setUp();

        _a = new Node("A");
        _h = new Node("H");
        _k = new Node("K");
        _p = new Node("P");
        _f = new Node("F", null, _h);
        _m = new Node("M", null, _p);
        _d = new Node("D", _a, _f);
        _l = new Node("L", _k, _m);
        _i = new Node("I", _d, _l);
    }

    public void testMinimum() {
        assertSame(_a, _a.minimum());
        assertSame(_a, _d.minimum());
        assertSame(_f, _f.minimum());
        assertSame(_h, _h.minimum());
        assertSame(_a, _i.minimum());
        assertSame(_k, _k.minimum());
        assertSame(_k, _l.minimum());
        assertSame(_m, _m.minimum());
        assertSame(_p, _p.minimum());
    }

    public void testMaximum() {
        assertSame(_a, _a.maximum());
        assertSame(_h, _d.maximum());
        assertSame(_h, _f.maximum());
        assertSame(_h, _h.maximum());
        assertSame(_p, _i.maximum());
```

```
        assertSame(_k, _k.maximum());
        assertSame(_p, _l.maximum());
        assertSame(_p, _m.maximum());
        assertSame(_p, _p.maximum());
    }

    public void testSuccessor() {
        assertSame(_d, _a.successor());
        assertSame(_f, _d.successor());
        assertSame(_h, _f.successor());
        assertSame(_i, _h.successor());
        assertSame(_k, _i.successor());
        assertSame(_l, _k.successor());
        assertSame(_m, _l.successor());
        assertSame(_p, _m.successor());
        assertNull(_p.successor());
    }

    public void testPredecessor() {
        assertNull(_a.predecessor());
        assertSame(_a, _d.predecessor());
        assertSame(_d, _f.predecessor());
        assertSame(_f, _h.predecessor());
        assertSame(_h, _i.predecessor());
        assertSame(_i, _k.predecessor());
        assertSame(_k, _l.predecessor());
        assertSame(_l, _m.predecessor());
        assertSame(_m, _p.predecessor());
    }

    public void testIsSmaller() {
        assertTrue(_a.isSmaller());
        assertTrue(_d.isSmaller());
        assertFalse(_f.isSmaller());
        assertFalse(_h.isSmaller());
        assertFalse(_i.isSmaller());
        assertTrue(_k.isSmaller());
        assertFalse(_l.isSmaller());
        assertFalse(_m.isSmaller());
        assertFalse(_p.isSmaller());
    }

    public void testIsLarger() {
        assertFalse(_a.isLarger());
        assertFalse(_d.isLarger());
        assertTrue(_f.isLarger());
        assertTrue(_h.isLarger());
        assertFalse(_i.isLarger());
        assertFalse(_k.isLarger());
        assertTrue(_l.isLarger());
        assertTrue(_m.isLarger());
        assertTrue(_p.isLarger());
    }
```

```
    public void testSize() {
        assertEquals(1, _a.size());
        assertEquals(4, _d.size());
        assertEquals(2, _f.size());
        assertEquals(1, _h.size());
        assertEquals(9, _i.size());
        assertEquals(1, _k.size());
        assertEquals(4, _l.size());
        assertEquals(2, _m.size());
        assertEquals(1, _p.size());
    }

    public void testEquals() {
        Node a = new Node("A");
        Node h = new Node("H");
        Node k = new Node("K");
        Node p = new Node("P");
        Node f = new Node("F", null, h);
        Node m = new Node("M", null, p);
        Node d = new Node("D", a, f);
        Node l = new Node("L", k, m);
        Node i = new Node("I", d, l);

        assertEquals(a, _a);
        assertEquals(d, _d);
        assertEquals(f, _f);
        assertEquals(h, _h);
        assertEquals(i, _i);
        assertEquals(k, _k);
        assertEquals(l, _l);
        assertEquals(m, _m);
        assertEquals(p, _p);

        assertFalse(_i.equals(null));
        assertFalse(_f.equals(_d));
    }
}
```

How It Works

All the tests start with a node structure identical to the one shown in Figure 10-1. (Now might be a good time to refresh your memory.)

The `NodeTest` class defines some instance variables — one for each node shown in Figure 10-1 — and initializes them in `setUp()` for use by the test cases. The first four nodes are all leaf nodes (as in the examples) and as such need only the value. The remaining nodes all have left and/or right children, which are passed in as the second and third constructor parameters, respectively:

```
package com.wrox.algorithms.bstrees;

import junit.framework.TestCase;

public class NodeTest extends TestCase {
    private Node _a;
    private Node _d;
```

```
        private Node _f;
        private Node _h;
        private Node _i;
        private Node _k;
        private Node _l;
        private Node _m;
        private Node _p;

        protected void setUp() throws Exception {
            super.setUp();

            _a = new Node("A");
            _h = new Node("H");
            _k = new Node("K");
            _p = new Node("P");
            _f = new Node("F", null, _h);
            _m = new Node("M", null, _p);
            _d = new Node("D", _a, _f);
            _l = new Node("L", _k, _m);
            _i = new Node("I", _d, _l);

        }

        ...
    }
```

The design calls for the `minimum()` and `maximum()` methods (among others) to be part of the `Node` class. This enables you to find the minimum and maximum of a tree by querying the root node. It also makes testing much easier. The methods `testMinimum()` and `testMaximimum()` are pretty straightforward: You simply ensure that each node in the tree returns the correct value as its minimum or maximum, respectively:

```
        public void testMinimum() {
            assertSame(_a, _a.minimum());
            assertSame(_a, _d.minimum());
            assertSame(_f, _f.minimum());
            assertSame(_h, _h.minimum());
            assertSame(_a, _i.minimum());
            assertSame(_k, _k.minimum());
            assertSame(_k, _l.minimum());
            assertSame(_m, _m.minimum());
            assertSame(_p, _p.minimum());
        }

        public void testMaximum() {
            assertSame(_a, _a.maximum());
            assertSame(_h, _d.maximum());
            assertSame(_h, _f.maximum());
            assertSame(_h, _h.maximum());
            assertSame(_p, _i.maximum());
            assertSame(_k, _k.maximum());
            assertSame(_p, _l.maximum());
            assertSame(_p, _m.maximum());
            assertSame(_p, _p.maximum());
        }
```

Next are `successor()` and `predecessor()`. Again, you put these methods on `Node`, rather than have them as utility methods in `BinarySearchTree`.

The method `testSuccessor()`, for example, confirms that the successor for `"A"` is `"D"`, for `"D"` is `"F"`, and so on, just as in the earlier examples. Notice that because `"A"` has no predecessor and `"P"` no successor, you expect the result to be `null` in both cases:

```
public void testSuccessor() {
    assertSame(_d, _a.successor());
    assertSame(_f, _d.successor());
    assertSame(_h, _f.successor());
    assertSame(_i, _h.successor());
    assertSame(_k, _i.successor());
    assertSame(_l, _k.successor());
    assertSame(_m, _l.successor());
    assertSame(_p, _m.successor());
    assertNull(_p.successor());
}

public void testPredecessor() {
    assertNull(_a.predecessor());
    assertSame(_a, _d.predecessor());
    assertSame(_d, _f.predecessor());
    assertSame(_f, _h.predecessor());
    assertSame(_h, _i.predecessor());
    assertSame(_i, _k.predecessor());
    assertSame(_k, _l.predecessor());
    assertSame(_l, _m.predecessor());
    assertSame(_m, _p.predecessor());
}
```

You also create another pair of tests — `testIsSmaller()` and `testIsLarger()` — for methods that have thus far not been mentioned but come in very handy later. A node is considered to be the smaller child if it is the left child of its parent. Conversely, a node is considered to be the larger child only if it's the right child of its parent:

```
public void testIsSmaller() {
    assertTrue(_a.isSmaller());
    assertTrue(_d.isSmaller());
    assertFalse(_f.isSmaller());
    assertFalse(_h.isSmaller());
    assertFalse(_i.isSmaller());
    assertTrue(_k.isSmaller());
    assertFalse(_l.isSmaller());
    assertFalse(_m.isSmaller());
    assertFalse(_p.isSmaller());
}

public void testIsLarger() {
    assertFalse(_a.isLarger());
    assertFalse(_d.isLarger());
    assertTrue(_f.isLarger());
    assertTrue(_h.isLarger());
    assertFalse(_i.isLarger());
    assertFalse(_k.isLarger());
```

```
        assertTrue(_l.isLarger());
        assertTrue(_m.isLarger());
        assertTrue(_p.isLarger());
    }
```

Finally, you create some tests for `equals()`. The `equals()` method will be very important when it comes time to test the `BinarySearchTree` class, as it enables you to compare the structure produced when inserting and deleting nodes with the expected result. The implementation will start from the current node and compare the values as well as the left and right children all the way down to the leaf nodes.

In `testEquals()`, you construct a replica of the node structure. You then compare each of the instance variables with their local variable counterparts, as well as check some boundary conditions just to make sure you haven't hard-coded `equals()` to always return `true`!

```
    public void testEquals() {
        Node a = new Node("A");
        Node h = new Node("H");
        Node k = new Node("K");
        Node p = new Node("P");
        Node f = new Node("F", null, h);
        Node m = new Node("M", null, p);
        Node d = new Node("D", a, f);
        Node l = new Node("L", k, m);
        Node i = new Node("I", d, l);

        assertEquals(a, _a);
        assertEquals(d, _d);
        assertEquals(f, _f);
        assertEquals(h, _h);
        assertEquals(i, _i);
        assertEquals(k, _k);
        assertEquals(l, _l);
        assertEquals(m, _m);
        assertEquals(p, _p);

        assertFalse(_i.equals(null));
        assertFalse(_f.equals(_d));
    }
```

Now that you have the tests in place, you can create the node class itself in the next Try it Out section.

Try It Out   Implementing a Node Class

Create the node class as follows:

```
package com.wrox.algorithms.bstrees;

public class Node implements Cloneable {
    private Object _value;
    private Node _parent;
    private Node _smaller;
    private Node _larger;
```

```
    public Node(Object value) {
        this(value, null, null);
    }

    public Node(Object value, Node smaller, Node larger) {
        setValue(value);
        setSmaller(smaller);
        setLarger(larger);

        if (smaller != null) {
            smaller.setParent(this);
        }

        if (larger != null) {
            larger.setParent(this);
        }
    }

    public Object getValue() {
        return _value;
    }

    public void setValue(Object value) {
        assert value != null : "value can't be null";
        _value = value;
    }

    public Node getParent() {
        return _parent;
    }

    public void setParent(Node parent) {
        _parent = parent;
    }

    public Node getSmaller() {
        return _smaller;
    }

    public void setSmaller(Node smaller) {
        assert smaller != getLarger() : "smaller can't be the same as larger";
        _smaller = smaller;
    }

    public Node getLarger() {
        return _larger;
    }

    public void setLarger(Node larger) {
        assert larger != getSmaller() : "larger can't be the same as smaller";
        _larger = larger;
    }
```

```
    public boolean isSmaller() {
        return getParent() != null && this == getParent().getSmaller();
    }

    public boolean isLarger() {
        return getParent() != null && this == getParent().getLarger();
    }

    public Node minimum() {
        Node node = this;

        while (node.getSmaller() != null) {
            node = node.getSmaller();
        }

        return node;
    }

    public Node maximum() {
        Node node = this;

        while (node.getLarger() != null) {
            node = node.getLarger();
        }

        return node;
    }

    public Node successor() {
        if (getLarger() != null) {
            return getLarger().minimum();
        }

        Node node = this;

        while (node.isLarger()) {
            node = node.getParent();
        }

        return node.getParent();
    }

    public Node predecessor() {
        if (getSmaller() != null) {
            return getSmaller().maximum();
        }

        Node node = this;

        while (node.isSmaller()) {
            node = node.getParent();
        }
```

```
        return node.getParent();
    }

    public int size() {
        return size(this);
    }

    public boolean equals(Object object) {
        if (this == object) {
            return true;
        }

        if (object == null || object.getClass() != getClass()) {
            return false;
        }

        Node other = (Node) object;

        return getValue().equals(other.getValue())
                && equalsSmaller(other.getSmaller())
                && equalsLarger(other.getLarger());
    }

    private int size(Node node) {
        if (node == null) {
            return 0;
        }

        return 1 + size(node.getSmaller()) + size(node.getLarger());
    }

    private boolean equalsSmaller(Node other) {
        return getSmaller() == null && other == null
                || getSmaller() != null && getSmaller().equals(other);
    }

    private boolean equalsLarger(Node other) {
        return getLarger() == null && other == null
                || getLarger() != null && getLarger().equals(other);
    }
}
```

How It Works

Each node holds a value, a reference to a parent, a smaller (or left) child, and a larger (or right) child:

```
package com.wrox.algorithms.bstrees;

public class Node {
    private Object _value;
    private Node _parent;
    private Node _smaller;
    private Node _larger;

    ...
}
```

You've also provided two constructors. The first constructor is for creating leaf nodes—those with no children—so its only argument is a value:

```
public Node(Object value) {
    this(value, null, null);
}
```

The second constructor, however, is somewhat of a convenience, enabling you to create nodes that have children. Notice that if you specify a non-`null` child, the constructor conveniently sets that child's parent. This, as you may recall from the tests, makes it trivial to wire nodes together into a tree structure:

```
public Node(Object value, Node smaller, Node larger) {
    setValue(value);
    setSmaller(smaller);
    setLarger(larger);

    if (smaller != null) {
        smaller.setParent(this);
    }

    if (larger != null) {
        larger.setParent(this);
    }
}
```

Once constructed, you need access to the node's value, its parent, and any of its children. For this, you create some standard getters and setters. Nothing too strange there except that you've put in a few extra assertions—for example, checking to make sure that you haven't set both children to the same node:

```
public Object getValue() {
    return _value;
}

public void setValue(Object value) {
    assert value != null : "value can't be null";
    _value = value;
}

public Node getParent() {
    return _parent;
}

public void setParent(Node parent) {
    _parent = parent;
}

public Node getSmaller() {
    return _smaller;
}

public void setSmaller(Node smaller) {
    assert smaller != getLarger() : "smaller can't be the same as larger";
    _smaller = smaller;
}
```

```
public Node getLarger() {
    return _larger;
}

public void setLarger(Node larger) {
    assert larger != getSmaller() : "larger can't be the same as smaller";
    _larger = larger;
}
```

Next, follow some convenience methods for determining various characteristics of each node.

The methods `isSmaller()` and `isLarger()` return `true` only if the node is the smaller or larger child of its parent, respectively:

```
public boolean isSmaller() {
    return !isRoot() && this == getParent().getSmaller();
}

public boolean isLarger() {
    return !isRoot() && this == getParent().getLarger();
}
```

Finding the minimum or maximum is not much more complex. Recall that the minimum of a node is its smallest child, and the maximum is its largest (or itself if it has no children). Notice that the code for `maximum()` is almost identical to that of `minimum()`; whereas `minimum()` calls `getSmaller()`, `maximum()` calls `getLarger()`:

```
public Node minimum() {
    Node node = this;

    while (node.getSmaller() != null) {
        node = node.getSmaller();
    }

    return node;
}

public Node maximum() {
    Node node = this;

    while (node.getLarger() != null) {
        node = node.getLarger();
    }

    return node;
}
```

Finding the successor and predecessor of a node is a little bit more involved. Recall that the successor of a node is either the minimum of its largest child—if there is one—or the first node you encounter after a "right-hand" turn while moving up the tree.

Looking at successor(), you can see that if the node has a larger child, then you take its minimum. If not, you start moving up the tree looking for the "right-hand" turn by checking whether the current node is the larger of its parent's children. If it is the larger, then it must be to the right of its parent, and you would be moving to the left back up the tree. In essence, you are moving back up the tree looking for the first node that is the smaller (that is, left) child of its parent. Once found, you know you would then be making a "right-hand" turn to get to the parent—precisely what you were looking for.

Also notice that, as was the case with minimum() and maximum(), successor() and predecessor() are mirror images of each other: where successor() takes the minimum, predecessor() takes the maximum; when successor calls isLarger(), predecessor calls isSmaller():

```
public Node successor() {
    if (getLarger() != null) {
        return getLarger().minimum();
    }

    Node node = this;

    while (node.isLarger()) {
        node = node.getParent();
    }

    return node.getParent();
}

public Node predecessor() {
    if (getSmaller() != null) {
        return getSmaller().maximum();
    }

    Node node = this;

    while (node.isSmaller()) {
        node = node.getParent();
    }

    return node.getParent();
}
```

Finally, we have equals(). This method is a node's most complex (though still fairly straightforward), but it will be used extensively later to check the structure of the trees created by the BinarySearchTree class.

Besides the boilerplate code, the public equals() method compares three aspects of each node for equality: the value, the smaller child, and the larger child. Comparing values is simple: You know the value can never be null, so simply delegating to the value's equals() method is sufficient:

```
public boolean equals(Object object) {
    if (this == object) {
        return true;
    }
```

```
        if (object == null || object.getClass() != getClass()) {
            return false;
        }

        Node other = (Node) object;

        return getValue().equals(other.getValue())
                && equalsSmaller(other.getSmaller())
                && equalsLarger(other.getLarger());
    }
```

Comparing child nodes is a little more involved because not only can either or both of the children be `null`, you must also check the children's children and their children, and so on, all the way to the leaf nodes. For this, you created two helper methods: `equalsSmaller()` and `equalsLarger()`.These methods compare the children of the current node with the corresponding child of the other node. For example, `equalsSmaller()` compares the current node's smaller child with the smaller child of the other node. If both children are `null`, the nodes are considered equal. If only one child is `null`, they can't possibly be equal. If, however, both the current node and the other node have a smaller child, then you recursively call `equals()` to continue checking down the tree:

```
    private boolean equalsSmaller(Node other) {
        return getSmaller() == null && other == null
                || getSmaller() != null && getSmaller().equals(other);
    }

    private boolean equalsLarger(Node other) {
        return getLarger() == null && other == null
                || getLarger() != null && getLarger().equals(other);
    }
```

That's it for the node class. In the next Try it Out section, you create some tests in preparation for your final binary search tree implementation.

Try It Out Testing a Binary Search Tree

Create the test class as follows:

```
package com.wrox.algorithms.bstrees;

import com.wrox.algorithms.sorting.NaturalComparator;
import junit.framework.TestCase;

public class BinarySearchTreeTest extends TestCase {
    private Node _a;
    private Node _d;
    private Node _f;
    private Node _h;
    private Node _i;
    private Node _k;
    private Node _l;
    private Node _m;
    private Node _p;
```

```
    private Node _root;
    private BinarySearchTree _tree;

    protected void setUp() throws Exception {
        super.setUp();

        _a = new Node("A");
        _h = new Node("H");
        _k = new Node("K");
        _p = new Node("P");
        _f = new Node("F", null, _h);
        _m = new Node("M", null, _p);
        _d = new Node("D", _a, _f);
        _l = new Node("L", _k, _m);
        _i = new Node("I", _d, _l);
        _root = _i;

        _tree = new BinarySearchTree(NaturalComparator.INSTANCE);
        _tree.insert(_i.getValue());
        _tree.insert(_d.getValue());
        _tree.insert(_l.getValue());
        _tree.insert(_a.getValue());
        _tree.insert(_f.getValue());
        _tree.insert(_k.getValue());
        _tree.insert(_m.getValue());
        _tree.insert(_h.getValue());
        _tree.insert(_p.getValue());
    }

    public void testInsert() {
        assertEquals(_root, _tree.getRoot());
    }

    public void testSearch() {
        assertEquals(_a, _tree.search(_a.getValue()));
        assertEquals(_d, _tree.search(_d.getValue()));
        assertEquals(_f, _tree.search(_f.getValue()));
        assertEquals(_h, _tree.search(_h.getValue()));
        assertEquals(_i, _tree.search(_i.getValue()));
        assertEquals(_k, _tree.search(_k.getValue()));
        assertEquals(_l, _tree.search(_l.getValue()));
        assertEquals(_m, _tree.search(_m.getValue()));
        assertEquals(_p, _tree.search(_p.getValue()));

        assertNull(_tree.search("UNKNOWN"));
    }

    public void testDeleteLeafNode() {
        Node deleted = _tree.delete(_h.getValue());
        assertNotNull(deleted);
        assertEquals(_h.getValue(), deleted.getValue());

        _f.setLarger(null);
        assertEquals(_root, _tree.getRoot());
    }
```

```
    public void testDeleteNodeWithOneChild() {
        Node deleted = _tree.delete(_m.getValue());
        assertNotNull(deleted);
        assertEquals(_m.getValue(), deleted.getValue());

        _l.setLarger(_p);
        assertEquals(_root, _tree.getRoot());
    }

    public void testDeleteNodeWithTwoChildren() {
        Node deleted = _tree.delete(_i.getValue());
        assertNotNull(deleted);
        assertEquals(_i.getValue(), deleted.getValue());

        _i.setValue(_k.getValue());
        _l.setSmaller(null);
        assertEquals(_root, _tree.getRoot());
    }

    public void testDeleteRootNodeUntilTreeIsEmpty() {
        while (_tree.getRoot() != null) {
            Object key = _tree.getRoot().getValue();
            Node deleted = _tree.delete(key);
            assertNotNull(deleted);
            assertEquals(key, deleted.getValue());
        }
    }
}
```

How It Works

All of our tests use the `BinarySearchTree` class to manipulate a tree so that it looks like the one shown in Figure 10-1. Then, as you did with your node tests, you compare this tree with one you have hand-crafted. If they match, then you know your code works as expected.

The `BinarySearchTreeTest` class defines some nodes for comparison and constructs a `BinarySearchTree` with the same values as the nodes. Notice that you have inserted the values in a very specified, yet non-alphabetical, order. Remember that your tree performs no balancing. If you were to insert the values in alphabetical order, you would end up with a degenerate tree — one that looks like a linked list (refer to Figure 10-7). Instead, you insert the values in an order specifically designed to produce a balanced tree that looks like the one in Figure 10-1. Can you see why this works? You've inserted the values pre-order. That is, the order of insertion is such that the parent node of each subtree is added to the tree before either of its children:

```
package com.wrox.algorithms.bstrees;

import com.wrox.algorithms.sorting.NaturalComparator;
import junit.framework.TestCase;

public class BinarySearchTreeTest extends TestCase {
    private Node _a;
    private Node _d;
```

```
        private Node _f;
        private Node _h;
        private Node _i;
        private Node _k;
        private Node _l;
        private Node _m;
        private Node _p;
        private Node _root;
        private BinarySearchTree _tree;

        protected void setUp() throws Exception {
            super.setUp();

            _a = new Node("a");
            _h = new Node("h");
            _k = new Node("k");
            _p = new Node("p");
            _f = new Node("f", null, _h);
            _m = new Node("m", null, _p);
            _d = new Node("d", _a, _f);
            _l = new Node("l", _k, _m);
            _i = new Node("i", _d, _l);
            _root = _i;

            _tree = new BinarySearchTree(NaturalComparator.INSTANCE);
            _tree.insert(_i.getValue());
            _tree.insert(_d.getValue());
            _tree.insert(_l.getValue());
            _tree.insert(_a.getValue());
            _tree.insert(_f.getValue());
            _tree.insert(_k.getValue());
            _tree.insert(_m.getValue());
            _tree.insert(_h.getValue());
            _tree.insert(_p.getValue());
        }
```

Having set up your initial state, the next thing you do is ensure that the tree you built looks exactly like the one you're going to use for comparison.

In `testInsert()`, you assume there is a method `getRoot()` on `BinarySearchTree` that enables you to get at the root node. You then take advantage of the `equals()` method on `Node` to check them for structural equality:

```
        public void testInsert() {
            assertEquals(_root, _tree.getRoot());
        }
```

Now that you have a tree in a known state (and have tested `insert()` in the process), you test the remaining behavior of the `BinarySearchTree` class, starting with `search()`.

You expect `search()` to return the node corresponding to a specified value if found; or `null` if not. Therefore, in `testSearch()`, you perform a lookup for each of the known values, comparing the resulting node with the appropriate node in your handmade tree. Notice the check to ensure that an unknown value results in `null`:

```
public void testSearch() {
    assertEquals(_a, _tree.search(_a.getValue()));
    assertEquals(_d, _tree.search(_d.getValue()));
    assertEquals(_f, _tree.search(_f.getValue()));
    assertEquals(_h, _tree.search(_h.getValue()));
    assertEquals(_i, _tree.search(_i.getValue()));
    assertEquals(_k, _tree.search(_k.getValue()));
    assertEquals(_l, _tree.search(_l.getValue()));
    assertEquals(_m, _tree.search(_m.getValue()));
    assertEquals(_p, _tree.search(_p.getValue()));

    assertNull(_tree.search("UNKNOWN"));
}
```

The only other method you tested was `delete()`. As you know, there are a number of different scenarios to test: leaf nodes, nodes with one child, and those with two children.

Starting with the simple deletion of a leaf node, you see what happens when you delete the value H, as shown in Figure 10-8. The method `testDeleteLeafNode()` first deletes the value from the tree and records the deleted node. You then ensure that a node was actually returned after the call and that the value of the deleted node was indeed H. Finally, the test node structure is modified so that the parent of M — the F — no longer has a larger child, just as you expect the delete algorithm to have done. You can then compare the test node structure with the root of the tree; both should be equal:

```
public void testDeleteLeafNode() {
    Node deleted = _tree.delete(_h.getValue());
    assertNotNull(deleted);
    assertEquals(_h.getValue(), deleted.getValue());

    _f.setLarger(null);
    assertEquals(_root, _tree.getRoot());
}
```

Next, you deleted a node with one child — the 'M', as shown in Figure 10-9. This time, `testDeleteNodeWithOneChild()` deletes the value 'M' from the tree; and, after verifying the return value, you again modify the test node structure so that it resembles the expected structure of the tree. The two are then compared for equality. Note that you have made 'P' the larger child of 'L', thereby splicing out the 'M', just as the tree should have done:

```
public void testDeleteNodeWithOneChild() {
    Node deleted = _tree.delete(_m.getValue());
    assertNotNull(deleted);
    assertEquals(_m.getValue(), deleted.getValue());

    _l.setLarger(_p);
    assertEquals(_root, _tree.getRoot());
}
```

Lastly, you tried deleting a node with two children — the root node 'I' — as shown Figure 10-10 and Figure 10-11. Having deleted the 'I' from the tree, `testDeleteNodeWithTwoChildren()` updates the expected structure as appropriate and compares this to the root of the tree:

```
public void testDeleteNodeWithTwoChildren() {
    Node deleted = _tree.delete(_i.getValue());
    assertNotNull(deleted);
    assertEquals(_i.getValue(), deleted.getValue());

    _i.setValue(_k.getValue());
    _l.setSmaller(null);
    assertEquals(_root, _tree.getRoot());
}
```

Confident that you have the behavior of your tree tested, you implement the binary search tree class itself in the next Try It Out section.

Try It Out Implementing a Binary Search Tree

Create the `BinarySearchTree` class as follows:

```
package com.wrox.algorithms.bstrees;

import com.wrox.algorithms.sorting.Comparator;

public class BinarySearchTree {
    private final Comparator _comparator;
    private Node _root;

    public BinarySearchTree(Comparator comparator) {
        assert comparator != null : "comparator can't be null";
        _comparator = comparator;
    }

    public Node search(Object value) {
        assert value != null : "value can't be null";

        Node node = _root;

        while (node != null) {
            int cmp = _comparator.compare(value, node.getValue());
            if (cmp == 0) {
               break;
            }

            node = cmp < 0 ? node.getSmaller() : node.getLarger();
        }

        return node;
    }
```

```
    public Node insert(Object value) {
        Node parent = null;
        Node node = _root;
        int cmp = 0;

        while (node != null) {
            parent = node;
            cmp = _comparator.compare(value, node.getValue());
            node = cmp <= 0 ? node.getSmaller() : node.getLarger();
        }

        Node inserted = new Node(value);
        inserted.setParent(parent);

        if (parent == null) {
            _root = inserted;
        } else if (cmp < 0) {
            parent.setSmaller(inserted);
        } else {
            parent.setLarger(inserted);
        }

        return inserted;
    }

    public Node delete(Object value) {
        Node node = search(value);
        if (node == null) {
            return null;
        }

        Node deleted = node.getSmaller() != null && node.getLarger() != null ?
node.successor() : node;
        assert deleted != null : "deleted can't be null";

        Node replacement = deleted.getSmaller() != null ? deleted.getSmaller() :
deleted.getLarger();
        if (replacement != null) {
            replacement.setParent(deleted.getParent());
        }

        if (deleted == _root) {
            _root = replacement;
        } else if (deleted.isSmaller()) {
            deleted.getParent().setSmaller(replacement);
        } else {
            deleted.getParent().setLarger(replacement);
        }

        if (deleted != node) {
            Object deletedValue = node.getValue();
            node.setValue(deleted.getValue());
            deleted.setValue(deletedValue);
        }
```

```
        return deleted;
    }

    public Node getRoot() {
        return _root;
    }
}
```

How It Works

The BinarySearchTree class holds a comparator to use for comparing values; the root node, which may be null if the tree is empty; and a method for providing access to the root node that you used in your tests. Notice that you haven't implemented any interface, nor have you extended any base class. This binary search tree implementation is not really intended for use in its present form (Chapters 12 and 13 will attend to that):

```
package com.wrox.algorithms.bstrees;

import com.wrox.algorithms.sorting.Comparator;

public class BinarySearchTree {
    private final Comparator _comparator;
    private Node _root;

    public BinarySearchTree(Comparator comparator) {
        assert comparator != null : "comparator can't be null";
        _comparator = comparator;
    }

    public Node getRoot() {
        return _root;
    }

    ...
}
```

The simplest method you implemented was search(). This method looks for a value in the tree and returns the corresponding node, or null if the value wasn't found. It starts at the root node and continues until it either finds a match or runs out of nodes. At each pass through the while loop, the search value is compared with the value held in the current node. If the values are equal, you've found the node you're looking for and can exit the loop; otherwise, you follow the smaller or larger link as appropriate:

```
    public Node search(Object value) {
        assert value != null : "value can't be null";

        Node node = _root;

        while (node != null) {
            int cmp = _comparator.compare(value, node.getValue());
            if (cmp == 0) {
                break;
            }
```

```
            node = cmp < 0 ? node.getSmaller() : node.getLarger();
        }

        return node;
    }
```

The first half of `insert()` simply searches through the tree looking for the appropriate leaf node to which the new value will be attached, following the smaller or larger link as appropriate. When the `while` loop terminates, the variable `parent` will either be `null`, in which case the tree was empty and you can set the new node as the root node, or it will hold the parent for the new node. Then, once you have determined the parent for the new node, you set it as either the smaller or larger child as appropriate—the variable `cmp` still has the result from the last value comparison.

Do you notice anything different in the `while` loop between the `insert()` and `search()` code? In `search()`, you exit the loop if you find a matching value (`cmp == 0`). In `insert()`, however, you treat an equal value as if it was smaller (though you could just as easily have treated it as if it was larger). What do you think would happen if you added the same value twice? You end up with an unbalanced tree.

```
    public Node insert(Object value) {
        Node parent = null;
        Node node = _root;
        int cmp = 0;

        while (node != null) {
            parent = node;
            cmp = _comparator.compare(value, node.getValue());
            node = cmp <= 0 ? node.getSmaller() : node.getLarger();
        }

        Node inserted = new Node(value);
        inserted.setParent(parent);

        if (parent == null) {
            _root = inserted;
        } else if (cmp < 0) {
            parent.setSmaller(inserted);
        } else {
            parent.setLarger(inserted);
        }

        return inserted;
    }
```

Last but not least, use `delete()`. As you can imagine, deleting a value from a binary search tree is rather more complicated than either searching or insertion, as you need to consider a number of different situations. Having said that, it's actually not too difficult to combine the cases into a fairly straightforward piece of code.

The `delete()` method starts out with a search to find the node to be removed. If the value isn't found (`node == null`), there is clearly nothing to do and you can return immediately. If you do find one, however, there is still a bit of work to be done.

Once you have a node to delete, you need to determine whether the node itself can be removed or if you need to find its successor. Remember that if a node has zero or one child, it can be removed straightaway. If, conversely, a node has both its children, you need to swap it with its successor and remove that node instead.

Having decided which node to *actually* remove, the next step is to find its replacement. At this point, you know that, given the previous step, the node to be removed will have at most one child, or possibly none. Therefore, you simply get the child (if one exists) and make its parent the same as that of the deleted node.

Having chosen a replacement, you now need to fix up the link from the parent. If the deleted node was the root node, you make the replacement the new root. Otherwise, you set the replacement as the smaller or larger child as appropriate.

Finally, a bit of cleanup. If the node you removed from the tree is not the one you originally found—due to swapping with its successor—you need to also swap the values before returning the deleted node to the caller:

```
public Node delete(Object value) {
    Node node = search(value);
    if (node == null) {
        return null;
    }

    Node deleted = node.getSmaller() != null && node.getLarger() != null ?
                        node.successor() : node;
    assert deleted != null : "deleted can't be null";

    Node replacement = deleted.getSmaller() != null ?
                        deleted.getSmaller() : deleted.getLarger();
    if (replacement != null) {
        replacement.setParent(deleted.getParent());
    }

    if (deleted == _root) {
        _root = replacement;
    } else if (deleted.isSmaller()) {
        deleted.getParent().setSmaller(replacement);
    } else {
        deleted.getParent().setLarger(replacement);
    }

    if (deleted != node) {
        Object deletedValue = node.getValue();
        node.setValue(deleted.getValue());
        deleted.setValue(deletedValue);
    }

    return deleted;
}
```

Assessing Binary Search Tree Performance

Up until now, we've only talked about the performance of binary search trees, so in the next Try it Out section, you write some code that actually demonstrates the characteristics of binary search trees. For this you create some tests that measure the number of comparisons performed when inserting data. You can then compare the results of inserting randomly generated data with those of inserting ordered data.

Try It Out Implementing and Running Performance Tests

Create the performance test class as follows:

```
package com.wrox.algorithms.bstrees;

import com.wrox.algorithms.lists.ArrayList;
import com.wrox.algorithms.lists.List;
import com.wrox.algorithms.sorting.CallCountingComparator;
import com.wrox.algorithms.sorting.NaturalComparator;
import junit.framework.TestCase;

public class BinarySearchTreeCallCountingTest extends TestCase {
    private static final int TEST_SIZE = 1000;

    private CallCountingComparator _comparator;
    private BinarySearchTree _tree;

    protected void setUp() throws Exception {
        super.setUp();

        _comparator = new CallCountingComparator(NaturalComparator.INSTANCE);
        _tree = new BinarySearchTree(_comparator);
    }

    public void testRandomInsertion() {
        for (int i = 0; i < TEST_SIZE; ++i) {
            _tree.insert(new Integer((int) (Math.random() * TEST_SIZE)));
        }

        reportCalls();
    }

    public void testInOrderInsertion() {
        for (int i = 0; i < TEST_SIZE; ++i) {
            _tree.insert(new Integer(i));
        }

        reportCalls();
    }

    public void testPreOrderInsertion() {
        List list = new ArrayList(TEST_SIZE);

        for (int i = 0; i < TEST_SIZE; ++i) {
            list.add(new Integer(i));
        }
```

```
        preOrderInsert(list, 0, list.size() - 1);

        reportCalls();
    }

    private void preOrderInsert(List list, int lowerIndex, int upperIndex) {
        if (lowerIndex > upperIndex) {
            return;
        }

        int index = lowerIndex + (upperIndex - lowerIndex) / 2;

        _tree.insert(list.get(index));
        preOrderInsert(list, lowerIndex, index - 1);
        preOrderInsert(list, index + 1, upperIndex);
    }

    private void reportCalls() {
        System.out.println(getName() + ": " + _comparator.getCallCount() + "
calls");
    }
}
```

How It Works

For convenience, you wrapped the `BinarySearchTreeCallCountingTest` class up as a standard JUnit test class. Like the performance tests from Chapter 9 on binary searching, these tests aren't actually "real" tests—they make no assertions—but your familiarity with JUnit is a compelling enough reason to take this approach.

The class defines a binary tree into which you insert some values, a comparator to use for comparing values, and a constant that defines the number of values—`TEST_SIZE`—to insert. You have also added a method, `reportCalls()`, that will be used to print the number of calls made to the comparator, in the form `test-name: #### calls`.

```
package com.wrox.algorithms.bstrees;

import com.wrox.algorithms.sorting.CallCountingComparator;
import com.wrox.algorithms.sorting.NaturalComparator;
import junit.framework.TestCase;

public class BinarySearchTreeCallCountingTest extends TestCase {
    private static final int TEST_SIZE = 1000;

    private CallCountingComparator _comparator;
    private BinarySearchTree _tree;

    protected void setUp() throws Exception {
        super.setUp();

        _comparator = new CallCountingComparator(NaturalComparator.INSTANCE);
        _tree = new BinarySearchTree(_comparator);
    }
```

```
    private void reportCalls() {
        System.out.println(getName() + ": "
                                 + _comparator.getCallCount() + " calls");
    }
    ...
}
```

In `testRandomInsert()`, you insert `TEST_SIZE` randomly generated numbers, building what you imagine will be a relatively balanced tree:

```
    public void testRandomInsertion() {
        for (int i = 0; i < TEST_SIZE; ++i) {
            _tree.insert(new Integer((int) (Math.random() * TEST_SIZE)));
        }

        reportCalls();
    }
```

Then, in `testInOrderInsertion()`, you insert (in order) the values between `0` and `TEST_SIZE` to produce what you think will be a seriously unbalanced tree:

```
    public void testInOrderInsertion() {
        for (int i = 0; i < TEST_SIZE; ++i) {
            _tree.insert(new Integer(i));
        }

        reportCalls();
    }
```

If you run these tests, depending on your environment, you should see some output similar to the following:

```
testRandomInsertion: 11624 calls
testInOrderInsertion: 499500 calls
```

Table 10-2 summarizes what's going on.

Table 10-2: Performance Comparison for 1,000 Inserts into a Binary Search Tree

Insertion Type	Comparisons*
Random Insertion	11,624
In-order Insertion	499,500

* Actual results will vary due to the random nature of the test data.

As you can see, insertion performs best when the data is unordered — in fact, as Table 10-2 quite clearly shows, significantly better: The average time to perform the random insertion was `11,624 / 1000 = 11` comparisons, or `O(log N)`; for in-order, it was `499,500 / 1000 = 499`, or `O(N)`.

Summary

This chapter provided an explanation of how binary search trees work. You should now have a solid foundation for understanding some of the more practical examples in later chapters (sets in Chapter 12 and maps in Chapter 13).

This chapter demonstrated the following:

- Binary search trees hold some data and refer to a left and a right child.
- Left children are always smaller than their parent.
- Right children are always larger than their parent.
- Trees are either balanced or unbalanced.
- All binary search trees have an average search time of `O(h)`.
- Balanced trees have a height `h = O(log N)`.
- In the worst case, unbalanced trees will have a height `h = O(N)`.
- Inserting and deleting random data generally produces relatively balanced trees.
- Inserting and deleting ordered data leads to unbalanced trees.
- A simple technique that considers nothing more than the relative height of child nodes can be used to restore a tree to a relatively balanced state.

Exercises

1. Write a recursive form of `minimum()`.
2. Write a recursive form of `search()`.
3. Write a method that takes a root node and recursively prints all the values of the tree in order.
4. Write a method that takes a root node and iteratively prints all the values of the tree in order.
5. Write a method that takes a root node and recursively prints all the values of the tree pre-order.
6. Write a method that takes a root node and recursively prints all the values of the tree post-order.
7. Write a method(s) that inserts values from a sorted list into a binary search tree in such a way as to maintain balance yet require no explicit balancing.
8. Add method(s) to `Node` to recursively calculate its size.
9. Add method(s) to `Node` to recursively calculate its height.

Hashing

Hashing is a technique that promises to achieve `O(1)` data lookup. This doesn't mean that only one comparison will be made, but rather that the number of comparisons will remain the same, no matter how large the data set. Compare this with the `O(N)` search time of simple linked lists or even `O(log N)` for binary search trees, and hashing starts to look very attractive.

This chapter discusses the following:

- Understanding hashing
- Working with hash functions
- Assessing performance
- Comparing the results

Understanding Hashing

You may not even realize it, but chances are good you use concepts similar to hashing all the time. When you walk into a bookstore and head straight for the computer book section, you've just used a kind of hashing algorithm. When you are looking for a music CD by a particular artist, you no doubt go straight to the section containing CDs by artists with the same first letter of that artist's surname. Both these processes involve taking some property of the thing you are looking for — a book category or an artist's name — and using that to narrow down the search. In the case of the book, you know it is a computer book so you head straight for that section; in the case of the CD, you know the artist's name.

Hashing begins with a hash function. A *hash function* takes one value — a string, an object, a number, and so on — and produces a *hash value*, usually an integer or some other numeric value. This hash value is then used to locate a position within a *hash table* — a special kind of array.

To give you an idea of how hashing works, the following example first shows you how to produce a hash value for strings; then it proceeds to use the hash value to store and locate the strings.

One of the simplest string hashing techniques involves adding letters. The resulting hash value can then be used as a position within the hash table for storing the string. The following code example shows the results of hashing the strings "elvis," "madonna," and "sting," assuming the letters of the alphabet are assigned the values 1 for a through 26 for z:

```
e + l + v + i + s = 5 + 12 + 22 + 9 + 19
                  = 67

m + a + d + o + n + n + a = 13 + 1 + 4 + 15 + 14 + 14 + 1
                          = 62

s + t + i + n + g = 19 + 20 + 9 + 14 + 7
                  = 69
```

Looking at the generated values, you can see that the string "elvis" would be placed into an array at position 67, "madonna" at position 62, and "sting" at position 69. Notice that the strings aren't stored in any particular order. The positions seem random, and in fact hashing is sometimes referred to as *randomizing*. This is quite different from all of the previously covered data structures and algorithms, which relied on some kind of ordering to achieve adequate performance.

The hash function appears to be working satisfactorily. You can easily store values into unique locations and just as easily check for their existence. However, there are two major problems with this approach.

Take another look at the generated values. If these were used as index positions within an array, then it would need to big enough to accommodate the largest position, 69. Having filled only 3 of the 70 positions available—that is, 0 to 69—you would still have 67 empty ones. Now imagine that the values had been 167, 162, and 169 instead—you'd end up with 167 empty slots. It would seem that this very simplistic hashing scheme is pretty inefficient in terms of storage.

One way to solve this problem is to modify the hash function to produce only values within a certain range. Given the previous example, if the size of the hash table was restricted to, for example, ten positions, then the hash function could be modified to take the original result and use a modulus—the remainder after division—to find the remainder after division by 10, as shown in the following example:

```
e + l + v + i + s = 5 + 12 + 22 + 9 + 19
                  = 67 % 10
                  = 7

m + a + d + o + n + n + a = 13 + 1 + 4 + 15 + 14 + 14 + 1
                          = 62 % 10
                          = 2

s + t + i + n + g = 19 + 20 + 9 + 14 + 7
                  = 69 % 10
                  = 9
```

Now the addresses fall within the range 0 to 9 and can be stored in a hash table of size 10. So far so good.

Unfortunately, there is still one more problem with the hash function as described: It suffers from a high rate of *collisions*—different values hashing to the same address. To illustrate what is meant by collision, the following code hashes the string "lives". Notice that the result is the same address that was generated for "elvis" and therefore collides with an existing value:

```
l + i + v + e + s = 5 + 12 + 22 + 9 + 19
                  = 67 % 10
                  = 7
```

You've already seen one way to reduce the number of collisions: Increase the address space. By increasing the address space, you reduce the likelihood of a collision while at the same time increasing the amount of wasted memory. Most hashing algorithms are therefore a trade-off between efficiencies of space and time.

Another way to reduce collisions is to be more selective in the choice of hash table size. It turns out that prime numbers give better results than nonprime numbers. By choosing a prime number close to the desired size, you reduce the amount of clustering and consequently the number of collisions. How and why this works is beyond the scope of this book.

Ideally, though, you would like a *perfect hashing algorithm*—one that produces no collisions at all. Unfortunately, finding a perfect hashing algorithm is much harder than it might at first seem. For small sets of well-known input data, it may be possible to find one, but even with a very good hashing algorithm, the likelihood of finding one that produces no collisions at all is very small. A better solution is to try to reduce the number of collisions to something manageable and deal with them.

The hash function discussed thus far is actually particularly poor when it comes to collisions. For one thing, the order of letters makes no difference. As you have seen already, "elvis" and "lives" both hash to the same address. In fact, anagrams—words with the same letters but in a different order—will always hash to the same value. What you need is an algorithm that somehow considers the order of the letters to be significant.

An example of a fairly simple yet effective hashing algorithm is the one used in the `String` class of the JDK. The algorithm itself is grounded in very sound mathematics, but a proof is certainly beyond the scope of this book. Nonetheless, the actual implementation is pretty easy to understand.

Most good hashing algorithms, like the one used in the JDK String class, are based on sound mathematics. One such algorithm is the cyclic redundancy check (CRC). Many applications that compress or transmit files over networks use a CRC to ensure the integrity of the data. The CRC algorithm takes a stream of data and computes an integer hash value. One of the properties of a CRC calculation is that the ordering of the data is significant. This means that the two strings "elvis" and "lives" are almost guaranteed to hash to different values. We say "almost" here because the standard CRC isn't perfect, and hence, there is still a nonzero (yet very small) chance of a collision.

The idea is to add each letter just as you did before. This time, however, the working value is multiplied by 31 before adding each letter. The following equation shows what's involved in calculating the hash value for the string "elvis":

```
(((e * 31 + l) * 31 + v) * 31 + i) * 31 + s
```

Applying the same algorithm across all the example strings is demonstrated in the following code:

```
"elvis" = (((5 * 31 + 12) * 31 + 22) * 31 + 9) * 31 + 19
        = 4996537

"madonna" = (((((13 * 31 + 1) * 31 + 4) * 31 + 15) * 31 + 14) * 31 + 14) * 31 + 1
          = 11570331842

"sting" = (((19 * 31 + 20) * 31 + 9) * 31 + 14) * 31 + 7
        = 18151809

"lives" = (((12 * 31 + 9) * 31 + 22) * 31 + 5) * 31 + 19
        = 11371687
```

The values are wildly different from each other, and note that "elvis" and "lives" no longer collide. In addition, note how large the values are. Obviously, you aren't going to have a hash table containing 11,570,331,843 slots just to hold four strings, so just as before, you take the remainder after dividing the hash value by the hash table size (the modulus)—in this case, you'll use 11, the nearest prime number to 10—to generate the final address, as shown in the following code sample:

```
"elvis" = 4996537 % 11
        = 7

"madonna" = 11570331842 % 11
          = 3

"sting" = 18151809 % 11
        = 5

"lives" = 11371687 % 11
        = 8
```

The hash function now performs markedly better for the sample data. There are no longer any collisions, so the values can be safely stored into individual positions. At some point, though, the hash table will fill up and collisions will begin to occur. Even before it fills up, however, a collision is still very likely; this particular algorithm isn't perfect.

As an example, imagine you want to add `"fred"` to the existing hash table. The hash value for this string is calculated: `196203 % 11 = 7`, which collides with `"elvis"`. The first option available to you is simply to increase (or possibly even decrease) the size of the hash table and recompute all the addresses using the new size. The following code shows the new hash values after resizing the hash table to 17 to store the new string `"fred"`:

```
"elvis" = 4996537 % 17
        = 16

"madonna" = 11570331842 % 17
          = 7

"sting" = 18151809 % 17
        = 8
```

```
"lives" = 11371687 % 17
        = 13

"fred" = 196203 % 17
       = 6
```

Now all of the strings have unique addresses and can be stored and retrieved successfully. However, a substantial price has been paid to maintain the uniqueness of addresses. In the preceding example, the size of the hash table was increased by 6 just to accommodate one more value. The hash table now has space for 17 strings, but only 5 have actually been stored. That's a utilization of only `(5/17) * 100 = 29%`. Not very impressive, and the problem can only get worse. The more strings you add, the larger the hash table needs to be in order to prevent collisions, resulting in more wasted space. As you can see, although resizing is partially useful to reduce the number of collisions, they still occur. Therefore, some other technique is required to manage the problem.

The first solution to the problem of collision resolution is known as *linear probing*. Linear probing is a very simple technique that, on detecting a collision, searches linearly for the next available slot. Figure 11-1 shows the three steps needed to add the string `"fred"`.

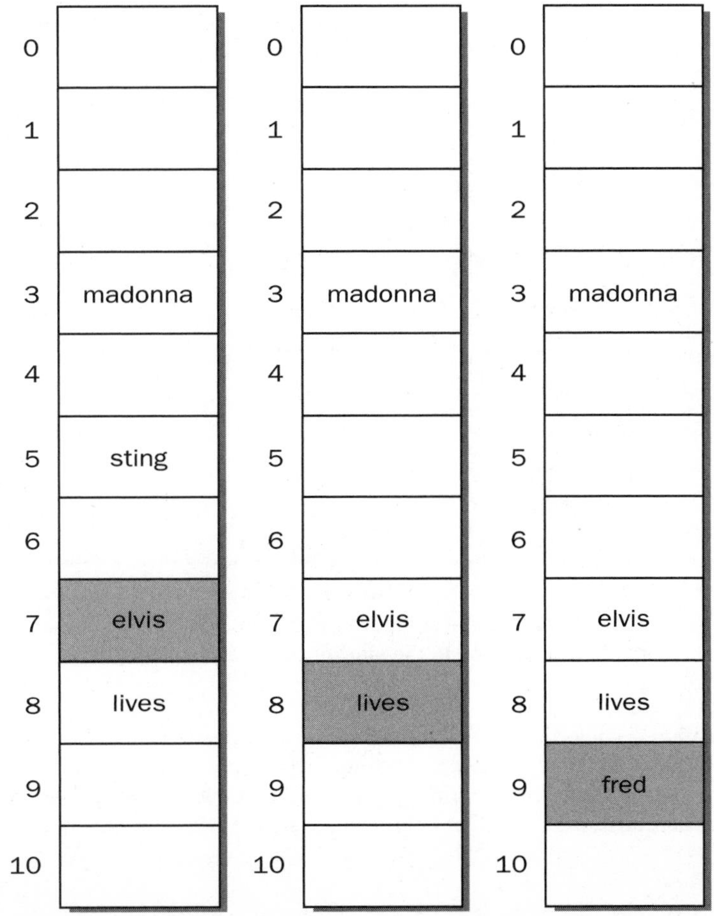

Figure 11-1: Linear probing to find a free slot into which the string "fred" can be placed.

The search starts at position 7 — the original hash value and the one that caused the collision. As this position is already occupied, the search continues to 8, also occupied, and eventually finds a free slot at position 9.

What happens when a search reaches the end of the table without finding a free slot? Instead of just giving up, it wraps around and continues from the start of the table. Figure 11-2 shows the search involved when adding the string `"tim"` (hash value 9) assuming you've already added `"mary"` (hash value 10).

0		0		0	tim
1		1		1	
2		2		2	
3	madonna	3	madonna	3	madonna
4		4		4	
5	sting	5		5	
6		6		6	
7	elvis	7	elvis	7	elvis
8	lives	8	lives	8	lives
9	fred	9	fred	9	fred
10	mary	10	mary	10	mary

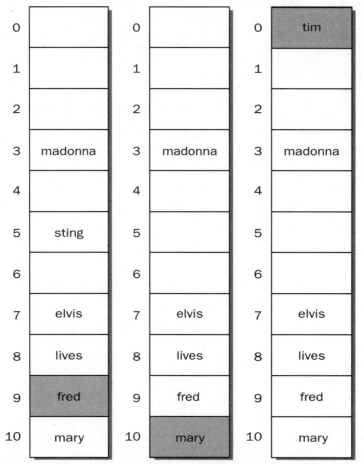

Figure 11-2: Adding the string "mary" followed by "tim" causes the search to wrap around to the start of the array.

The original position (as determined by the hash value) has already been filled, as has the next position. On reaching the end of the table, the search continues from the start and, in this case, immediately finds an available slot in which to place the string. In the event that the table is full — that is, there are no free slots — resizing is required, but until that point a linear search will work just fine.

Linear probing is simple to implement and works fairly well for sparsely populated hash tables—that is., the number of free slots is relatively large compared with the number of filled ones—but as the population density increases, searching and performance rapidly degrade from `O(1)` to `O(N)` —no better than a brute-force approach.

Another approach to collision resolution involves the use of *buckets* to store more than one item at each position. Each bucket holds zero or more items that hash to the same value. Figure 11-3 shows a hash table of size 11 populated with 16 different strings.

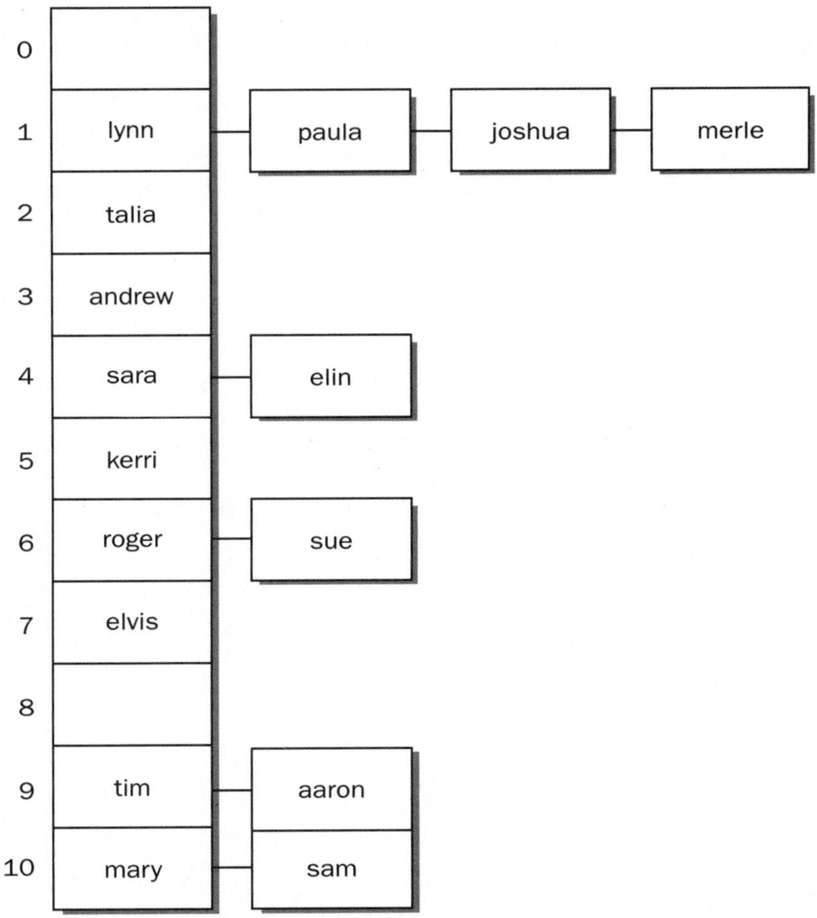

Figure 11-3: Each bucket holds items sharing the same hash value.

In this example, the strings `"lynn"`, `"paula"`, `"joshua"`, and `"merle"` all hash to the same value, `1`, and so all of them are held in the same bucket. From this example, you can see that having buckets enables the hash table to store more items than the simple linear probing could.

Of course, this flexibility isn't free. As the hash table fills and the size of each bucket increases, so too will the time required to find an item, though generally not as markedly as with linear probing. Even so, at some point, the cost of searching the buckets becomes too costly. When this happens, the solution is to increase the number of buckets available. Given a good hash function, the items will be redistributed relatively evenly between the greater number of buckets, leading to a decrease in the size of each individual bucket. The challenge is knowing when to resize.

One way to decide when to resize the hash table is to monitor the *load factor*—the ratio of stored values to available buckets. The idea is to set some threshold load factor that, when reached, will trigger a resize. In the case of Figure 11-3, the total number of buckets is 11 and the number of values stored is 16, so the load is currently `16 / 11 = 1.45 or 145%` of notional capacity (and as a result, some of the buckets are beginning to get quite large); it's probably a good time to resize.

Again, a balance needs to be found between space and performance efficiency. Making the load factor too low leads to a lot of wasted space. If it is too high, then the size of the buckets increases, resulting in more collisions. A load factor of around 0.75 or 75% of capacity is a fairly good trade-off between space and time.

Working with Hashing

In the following Try It Out section, you turn the concepts just covered into working code. You start by defining some unit tests followed by the two hash table implementations—linear probing and buckets—and finish with some more tests that compare the relative performance of each.

In all of these tests, you will store strings, so you will need a hash function that works on strings. Thankfully, the Java language already defines a method—`hashCode()`—that any class can implement to do just this. Moreover, the JDK implementation of `hashCode()` for the `String` class closely follows the example provided previously in this chapter, meaning you don't have to create one yourself. Still, it's probably worthwhile to consider how you might go about implementing one, so here is an example of what an implementation of `hashCode()` for strings might look like:

```
    public int hashCode() {
int hash = 0;
        for (int i = 0; i < length(); ++i) {
            hash = 31 * hash + charAt(i);
        }
        return hash;
    }
```

The code starts by initializing the hash to zero. It then adds in each character, making sure to multiply the result by 31 each time.

Try It Out — Creating a Generic Hash Table Interface

In order to test the linear probing and bucketing implementations, you create an interface that defines the methods common to each:

```
package com.wrox.algorithms.hashing;

public interface Hashtable {
    public void add(Object value);
    public boolean contains(Object value);
    public int size();
}
```

How It Works

The `Hashtable` interface defines three methods: `add()`, `contains()`, and `size()`. You will need to implement each of these later when you create a linear probing and bucketing version. These methods are probably familiar to you, as they are very similar to the methods of the same name defined on the `List` interface. The one difference is that whereas lists allow duplicates, hash tables don't, so calling `add()` multiple times with the same value will have no effect.

Try It Out Creating the Tests

Before developing the actual hash table implementations, you first need to write some test cases in order to ensure that the code you write later functions correctly. To take advantage of the fact that the outward behavior of any hash table will be identical, you can create a generic suite of tests that can be extended and re-used as follows:

```
package com.wrox.algorithms.hashing;

import junit.framework.TestCase;

public abstract class AbstractHashtableTestCase extends TestCase {
    private static final int TEST_SIZE = 1000;

    private Hashtable _hashtable;

    protected abstract Hashtable createTable(int capacity);

    protected void setUp() throws Exception {
        super.setUp();

        _hashtable = createTable(TEST_SIZE);

        for (int i = 0; i < TEST_SIZE; ++i) {
            _hashtable.add(String.valueOf(i));
        }
    }

    public void testContains() {
        for (int i = 0; i < TEST_SIZE; ++i) {
            assertTrue(_hashtable.contains(String.valueOf(i)));
        }
    }

    public void testDoesntContain() {
        for (int i = 0; i < TEST_SIZE; ++i) {
            assertFalse(_hashtable.contains(String.valueOf(i + TEST_SIZE)));
```

```
        }
    }

    public void testAddingTheSameValuesDoesntChangeTheSize() {
        assertEquals(TEST_SIZE, _hashtable.size());

        for (int i = 0; i < TEST_SIZE; ++i) {
            _hashtable.add(String.valueOf(i));
            assertEquals(TEST_SIZE, _hashtable.size());
        }
    }
}
```

How It Works

The AbstractHashtableTestCase class defines a single variable for holding the hash table instance currently under test, which is initialized in the setUp() method by calling the abstract method createTable. As you will see later, the createTable() method is implemented by subclasses to return an instance of a specific Hashtable implementation. Notice how the setUp() method adds data to the hash table. If you had used the integers directly as numbers (0, 1, 2, and so on), then each would likely hash to its own position in the underlying table, thereby possibly eliminating any chance of collisions occurring (which, while clearly the ideal, doesn't really reflect reality). Instead, the numbers are converted to strings in order to exercise a more complex hash function—namely, the hashCode() method defined in the String class:

```
public abstract class AbstractHashtableTestCase extends TestCase {
    private static final int TEST_SIZE = 1000;

    private Hashtable _hashtable;

    protected abstract Hashtable createTable(int capacity);

    protected void setUp() throws Exception {
        super.setUp();

        _hashtable = createTable(TEST_SIZE);

        for (int i = 0; i < TEST_SIZE; ++i) {
            _hashtable.add(String.valueOf(i));
        }
    }

    ...
}
```

Having added a number of strings to the hash table in setUp(), the first thing you did was check that contains could actually find them again. Values would be rather useless if all we could do is store them without the ability to find them again:

```
    public void testContains() {
        for (int i = 0; i < TEST_SIZE; ++i) {
            assertTrue(_hashtable.contains(String.valueOf(i)));
        }
    }
```

The next test checked that values you know don't exist aren't found by mistake:

```
public void testDoesntContain() {
    for (int i = 0; i < TEST_SIZE; ++i) {
        assertFalse(_hashtable.contains(String.valueOf(i + TEST_SIZE)));
    }
}
```

Finally, you made sure that adding the same value more than once doesn't result in the hash table growing in size:

```
public void testAddingTheSameValuesDoesntChangeTheSize() {
    assertEquals(TEST_SIZE, _hashtable.size());

    for (int i = 0; i < TEST_SIZE; ++i) {
        _hashtable.add(String.valueOf(i));
        assertEquals(TEST_SIZE, _hashtable.size());
    }
}
```

Here the size is checked both before and after the addition of duplicate values to ensure that the size remains constant.

Linear Probing

In the next Try It Out, you create a hash table that uses linear probing. The nice thing about linear probing is that the implementation is very simple and therefore relatively easy to understand.

Try It Out Testing and Implementing a Hash Table That Uses Linear Probing

Start by creating the test class:

```
package com.wrox.algorithms.hashing;

public class LinearProbingHashtableTest extends AbstractHashtableTestCase {
    protected Hashtable createTable(int capacity) {
        return new LinearProbingHashtable(capacity);
    }
}
```

Follow with the hash table implementation itself:

```
package com.wrox.algorithms.hashing;

public class LinearProbingHashtable implements Hashtable {
    private Object[] _values;

    private int _size;

    public LinearProbingHashtable(int initialCapacity) {
        assert initialCapacity > 0 : "initialCapacity can't be < 1";
        _values = new Object[initialCapacity];
    }
```

```
    public void add(Object value) {
        ensureCapacityForOneMore();

        int index = indexFor(value);

        if (_values[index] == null) {
            _values[index] = value;
            ++_size;
        }
    }

    public boolean contains(Object value) {
        return indexOf(value) != -1;
    }

    public int size() {
        return _size;
    }

    private int indexFor(Object value) {
        int start = startingIndexFor(value);

        int index = indexFor(value, start, _values.length);
        if (index == -1) {
            index = indexFor(value, 0, start);
            assert index == -1 : "no free slots";
        }

        return index;
    }

    private int indexFor(Object value, int start, int end) {
        assert value != null : "value can't be null";

        for (int i = start; i < end; ++i) {
            if (_values[i] == null || value.equals(_values[i])) {
                return i;
            }
        }

        return -1;
    }

    private int indexOf(Object value) {
        int start = startingIndexFor(value);

        int index = indexOf(value, start, _values.length);
        if (index == -1) {
            index = indexOf(value, 0, start);
        }
        return index;
    }
```

```
    private int indexOf(Object value, int start, int end) {
        assert value != null : "value can't be null";

        for (int i = start; i < end; ++i) {
            if (value.equals(_values[i])) {
                return i;
            }
        }

        return -1;
    }

    private int startingIndexFor(Object value) {
        assert value != null : "value can't be null";
        return Math.abs(value.hashCode() % _values.length);
    }

    private void ensureCapacityForOneMore() {
        if (size() == _values.length) {
            resize();
        }
    }

    private void resize() {
        LinearProbingHashtable copy =
                                    new LinearProbingHashtable(_values.length * 2);

        for (int i = 0; i < _values.length; ++i) {
            if (_values[i] != null) {
                copy.add(_values[i]);
            }
        }

        _values = copy._values;
    }
}
```

How It Works

All the actual test cases have been defined in `AbstractHashtableTestCase`, so all you needed to do was extend this and implement the `createTable()` method to return an instance of the yet to be defined `LinearProbingHashtable`. When this class is executed, all the test cases from the base class will be included and run against a hash table that uses linear probing:

```
package com.wrox.algorithms.hashing;

public class LinearProbingHashtableTest extends AbstractHashtableTestCase {
    protected Hashtable createTable(int capacity) {
        return new LinearProbingHashtable(capacity);
```

```
        }
    }
```

As for the implementation code, linear probing is very straightforward, which is reflected in the class definition.

The `LinearProbingHashtable` class has an array for holding values, and in the single constructor you can specify the maximum number of values that can initially be stored — the capacity:

```
    package com.wrox.algorithms.hashing;

    public class LinearProbingHashtable implements Hashtable {
        private Object[] _values;

        public LinearProbingHashtable(int initialCapacity) {
            assert initialCapacity > 0 : "initialCapacity can't be < 1";
            _values = new Object[initialCapacity];
        }

        ...
    }
```

Speaking of capacity, the hash table needs to resize at various times to accommodate more values. For this you have the method `ensureCapacityForOneMore()`, which, as you may well imagine, ensures that the hash table can hold at least one more value. If not, then a resize is required:

```
        private void ensureCapacityForOneMore() {
            if (size() == _values.length) {
                resize();
            }
        }
```

The `resize()` method uses a neat but effective technique for increasing the number of available slots: A temporary table is created with twice the capacity. Into this is added all the values, and the array from the new table is used to replace the existing array:

```
        private void resize() {
            LinearProbingHashtable copy =
                    new LinearProbingHashtable(_values.length * 2);

            for (int i = 0; i < _values.length; ++i) {
                if (_values[i] != null) {
                    copy.add(_values[i]);
                }
            }

            _values = copy._values;
        }
```

The `startingIndexFor()` method is central to the operation of the hash table. This method takes a value and returns the index into the array at which it would be stored. It uses the hash code as defined by the value itself — all objects in Java define a `hashCode()` method — and then takes the remainder after dividing by the capacity of the table. This ensures you end up with an index that falls within the bounds of the array of values:

```
private int startingIndexFor(Object value) {
    assert value != null : "value can't be null";
    return Math.abs(value.hashCode() % _values.length);
}
```

The two `indexFor()` methods work together to find a slot into which a new value can be placed.

The first method searches from the "natural" starting point until the end of the array. If a slot can't be found there, then a further search is made from the start of the array up to the initial starting point:

```
private int indexFor(Object value) {
    int start = startingIndexFor(value);

    int index = indexFor(value, start, _values.length);
    if (index == -1) {
        index = indexFor(value, 0, start);
        assert index == -1 : "no free slots";
    }

    return index;
}
```

The second method performs the actual search within the bounds specified by the first method. Look closely at the actual check that is made. Notice that a slot is chosen not only if it is empty (`_values[i]== null`), but also if it already contains the value (`value.equals(_values[i])`). There is little point in allowing the same value to be stored twice, as the second occurrence will likely never be found:

```
private int indexFor(Object value, int start, int end) {
    assert value != null : "value can't be null";

    for (int i = start; i < end; ++i) {
        if (_values[i] == null || value.equals(_values[i])) {
            return i;
        }
    }

    return -1;
}
```

Implementing the `add()` method is made very simple: It first ensures that there is room for another value before storing it at the appropriate position:

```
public void add(Object value) {
    ensureCapacityForOneMore();
    _values[indexFor(value)] = value;
}
```

The two `indexOf()` methods work together with the two `indexFor()` methods to find a slot into which a new value can be placed.

The first method coordinates the search, beginning with the position calculated by `startIndexFor()`, and, if necessary, another search is attempted in the lower portion of the array. If a matching value is found, then its position is returned; otherwise, a value of `-1` is used to indicate that no such value exists:

```
private int indexOf(Object value) {
    int start = startingIndexFor(value);

    int index = indexOf(value, start, _values.length);
    if (index == -1) {
        index = indexOf(value, 0, start);
    }
    return index;
}
```

The second method performs a brute-force search through the array—constrained by the specified start and end positions—in search of the value:

```
private int indexOf(Object value, int start, int end) {
    assert value != null : "value can't be null";

    for (int i = start; i < end; ++i) {
        if (value.equals(_values[i])) {
            return i;
        }
    }

    return -1;
}
```

Once the index of a value can be found, implementing `contains()` is a one-liner:

```
public boolean contains(Object value) {
    return indexOf(value) != -1;
}
```

The only other method required by the `Hashtable` interface is `size()`, which simply iterates over the array, incrementing the size each time a value is found. (As an exercise, you could try tracking the size instead of calculating it.)

```
public int size() {
    int size = 0;
    for (int i = 0; i < _values.length; ++i) {
        if (_values[i] != null) {
            ++size;
        }
    }
    return size;
}
```

Bucketing

In the next Try It Out section, you develop a hash table that uses buckets to store values. As always, you start with the tests before moving on to the implementation.

Try It Out Testing and Implementing a Hash Table That Uses Bucketing

Start by creating a test class as follows:

```
package com.wrox.algorithms.hashing;

public class BucketingHashtableTest extends AbstractHashtableTestCase {
    protected Hashtable createTable(int capacity) {
        return new BucketingHashtable(capacity, 0.75f);
    }
}
```

Now add the implementation class:

```
package com.wrox.algorithms.hashing;

import com.wrox.algorithms.iteration.Iterator;
import com.wrox.algorithms.lists.LinkedList;
import com.wrox.algorithms.lists.List;

public class BucketingHashtable implements Hashtable {
    private final float _loadFactor;
    private List[] _buckets;
    private int _size;

    public BucketingHashtable(int initialCapacity, float loadFactor) {
        assert initialCapacity > 0 : "initialCapacity can't be < 1";
        assert loadFactor > 0 : "loadFactor can't be <= 0";

        _loadFactor = loadFactor;
        _buckets = new List[initialCapacity];
    }

    public void add(Object value) {
        List bucket = bucketFor(value);

        if (!bucket.contains(value)) {
            bucket.add(value);
            ++_size;
            maintainLoad();
        }
    }

    public boolean contains(Object value) {
        List bucket = _buckets[bucketIndexFor(value)];
        return bucket != null && bucket.contains(value);
    }
```

```
    public int size() {
        return _size;
    }

    private List bucketFor(Object value) {
        int bucketIndex = bucketIndexFor(value);

        List bucket = _buckets[bucketIndex];
        if (bucket == null) {
            bucket = new LinkedList();
            _buckets[bucketIndex] = bucket;
        }

        return bucket;
    }

    private int bucketIndexFor(Object value) {
        assert value != null : "value can't be null";
        return Math.abs(value.hashCode() % _buckets.length);
    }

    private void maintainLoad() {
        if (loadFactorExceeded()) {
            resize();
        }
    }

    private boolean loadFactorExceeded() {
        return size() > _buckets.length * _loadFactor;
    }

    private void resize() {
        BucketingHashtable copy =
                          new BucketingHashtable(_buckets.length * 2, _loadFactor);

        for (int i = 0; i < _buckets.length; ++i) {
            if (_buckets[i] != null) {
                copy.addAll(_buckets[i].iterator());
            }
        }

        _buckets = copy._buckets;
    }

    private void addAll(Iterator values) {
        assert values != null : "values can't be null";

        for (values.first(); !values.isDone(); values.next()) {
            add(values.current());
        }
    }
}
```

How It Works

Once again, you re-used the tests defined in `AbstractHashtableTestCase`, this time implementing `createTable()` to return an instance of a `BucketingHashtable`. Notice the extra constructor parameter — `0.75f`. This is the load factor, which in this case specifies that the hash table should increase in size anytime the number of values stored reaches 75% of the number of available buckets:

```
package com.wrox.algorithms.hashing;

public class BucketingHashtableTest extends AbstractHashtableTestCase {
    protected Hashtable createTable(int capacity) {
        return new BucketingHashtable(capacity, 0.75f);
    }
}
```

Bucketing is a little more complex than linear probing, so the implementation class requires a little more explanation.

The `BucketingHashtable` class records the load factor, for later use, and an array of buckets. You may have noticed in the "Understanding Hashing" section that the buckets looked a lot like linked lists, and that's exactly what you've used for your buckets here. The number of buckets to use — `initialCapacity` — is specified at construction time along with the desired load factor:

```
package com.wrox.algorithms.hashing;

import com.wrox.algorithms.iteration.Iterator;
import com.wrox.algorithms.lists.LinkedList;
import com.wrox.algorithms.lists.List;

public class BucketingHashtable implements Hashtable {
    private final float _loadFactor;
    private List[] _buckets;

    public BucketingHashtable(int initialCapacity, float loadFactor) {
        assert initialCapacity > 0 : "initialCapacity can't be < 1";
        assert loadFactor > 0 : "loadFactor can't be <= 0";

        _loadFactor = loadFactor;
        _buckets = new List[initialCapacity];
    }

    ...
}
```

The method `maintainLoad()` simply checks the current load. If the desired load has been exceeded, then a resize is necessary to spread the values over a larger number of buckets. The `resize()` method works in a similar way to the method of the same name in `LinearProbingHashtable`: A new hash table is created into which all the values are added, and then the new bucket array is used to replace the existing one. Each time a resize is performed, the capacity doubles. You could choose any value for this, but it always comes down to a trade-off between space and time. The smaller the increment, the more often a resize will be required; the larger the increment, the more wasted space.

```
    private void maintainLoad() {
        if (loadFactorExceeded()) {
            resize();
        }
    }

    private boolean loadFactorExceeded() {
        return size() > _buckets.length * _loadFactor;
    }

    private void resize() {
        BucketingHashtable copy =
                new BucketingHashtable(_buckets.length * 2, _loadFactor);

        for (int i = 0; i < _buckets.length; ++i) {
            if (_buckets[i] != null) {
                copy.addAll(_buckets[i].iterator());
            }
        }

        _buckets = copy._buckets;
    }

    private void addAll(Iterator iterator) {
        assert iterator != null : "iterator can't be null";

        for (iterator.first(); !iterator.isDone(); iterator.next()) {
            add(iterator.current());
        }
    }
```

The method `bucketIndexFor()` determines which bucket a given value should be stored in. Just like you did for `LinearProbingHashtable`, the `hashCode()` method is called, and the remainder after dividing by the number of buckets is taken. This ensures you have an index that falls within the bounds of the bucket array:

```
    private int bucketIndexFor(Object value) {
        assert value != null : "value can't be null";
        return Math.abs(value.hashCode() % _buckets.length);
    }
```

The `bucketFor()` method obtains the appropriate bucket for a specified value. Ordinarily you would just use a direct array lookup, but the `bucketFor()` method also guarantees that if no bucket exists yet at the appropriate position, then one is created:

```
    private List bucketFor(Object value) {
        int bucketIndex = bucketIndexFor(value);

        List bucket = _buckets[bucketIndex];
        if (bucket == null) {
            bucket = new LinkedList();
            _buckets[bucketIndex] = bucket;
```

```
        }

        return bucket;
    }
```

The add() method obtains the appropriate bucket and the value added only if it doesn't already exist. Again, this ensures that two equal values—those for which equals would return true—can't exist in the hash table simultaneously:

```
    public void add(Object value) {
        List bucket = bucketFor(value);

        if (!bucket.contains(value)) {
            bucket.add(value);
            maintainLoad();
        }
    }
```

The contains() method is also very simple. First find the appropriate bucket and then return true if a bucket exists and contains the specified value:

```
    public boolean contains(Object value) {
        List bucket = _buckets[bucketIndexFor(value)];
        return bucket != null && bucket.contains(value);
    }
```

Finally, the size() method adds the number of values in each bucket to calculate the total size:

```
    public int size() {
        int size = 0;
        for (int i = 0; i < _buckets.length; ++i) {
            if (_buckets[i] != null) {
                size += _buckets[i].size();
            }
        }
        return size;
    }
```

Assessing Performance

Now that you have two hash table implementations, it's time to see how well they perform, not only individually, but also against one another. To evaluate the performance of each, in the next Try It Out section you develop tests that exercise the add() and contains() methods to see how many times equals() is called on the stored values: The smaller the number, the more efficiently the implementation finds a suitable location for the value.

Try It Out Creating the Tests

Create a test class as follows:

```
package com.wrox.algorithms.hashing;

import junit.framework.TestCase;

public class HashtableCallCountingTest extends TestCase {
    private static final int TEST_SIZE = 1000;
    private static final int INITIAL_CAPACITY = 17;

    private int _counter;
    private Hashtable _hashtable;

    public void testLinearProbingWithResizing() {
        _hashtable = new LinearProbingHashtable(INITIAL_CAPACITY);
        runAll();
    }

    public void testLinearProbingNoResizing() {
        _hashtable = new LinearProbingHashtable(TEST_SIZE);
        runAll();
    }

    public void testBucketsLoadFactor100Percent() {
        _hashtable = new BucketingHashtable(INITIAL_CAPACITY, 1.0f);
        runAll();
    }

    public void testBucketsLoadFactor75Percent() {
        _hashtable = new BucketingHashtable(INITIAL_CAPACITY, 0.75f);
        runAll();
    }

    public void testBuckets50Percent() {
        _hashtable = new BucketingHashtable(INITIAL_CAPACITY, 0.50f);
        runAll();
    }

    public void testBuckets25Percent() {
        _hashtable = new BucketingHashtable(INITIAL_CAPACITY, 0.25f);
        runAll();
    }

    public void testBuckets150Percent() {
        _hashtable = new BucketingHashtable(INITIAL_CAPACITY, 1.50f);
        runAll();
    }

    public void testBuckets200Percent() {
        _hashtable = new BucketingHashtable(INITIAL_CAPACITY, 2.0f);
        runAll();
    }
```

```
    private void runAll() {
        runAdd();
        runContains();
    }

    private void runAdd() {
        _counter = 0;
        for (int i = 0; i < TEST_SIZE; ++i) {
            _hashtable.add(new Value(i));
        }
        reportCalls("add");
    }

    private void runContains() {
        _counter = 0;
        for (int i = 0; i < TEST_SIZE; ++i) {
            _hashtable.contains(new Value(i));
        }
        reportCalls("contains");
    }

    private void reportCalls(String method) {
        System.out.println(getName() + "(" + method + "): " + _counter + " calls");
    }

    private final class Value {
        private final String _value;

        public Value(int value) {
            _value = String.valueOf(Math.random() * TEST_SIZE);
        }

        public int hashCode() {
            return _value.hashCode();
        }

        public boolean equals(Object object) {
            ++_counter;
            return object != null && _value.equals(((Value) object)._value);
        }
    }
}
```

How It Works

The `HashtableCallCountingTest` extends `TestCase`, making it easy to run. The class holds a hash table instance for the current test, and a counter for recording the number of times the `equals()` method is called:

```
package com.wrox.algorithms.hashing;

import junit.framework.TestCase;

public class HashtableCallCountingTest extends TestCase {
    private static final int TEST_SIZE = 1000;
```

```
        private static final int INITIAL_CAPACITY = 17;

        private int _counter;
        private Hashtable _hashtable;

        ...
    }
```

The `Value` inner class enables you to intercept and count calls to `equals()`. If you were to store simple strings, there would be no way to know when the `equals()` method had been called. Moreover, the `String` class is marked `final`, so there is no way to extend it and override the `equals()` method directly. Instead, you created your own class, which wraps a string and increments `_counter` anytime `equals()` is called. Notice how the constructor randomly assigns an underlying value to ensure that the results aren't skewed due to the insertion of ordered data:

```
    private final class Value {
        private final String _value;

        public Value() {
            _value = String.valueOf(Math.random() * TEST_SIZE);
        }

        public int hashCode() {
            return _value.hashCode();
        }

        public boolean equals(Object object) {
            ++_counter;
            return object != null && _value.equals(((Value) object)._value);
        }
    }
```

The method `reportCalls()` enables you to report the number of times `equals()` has been called, in the form `test-name(method): #### calls` (where *method* will be either `"add"` or `"contains"`, depending on which part of the test is being reported at the time):

```
    private void reportCalls(String method) {
        System.out.println(getName() + "(" + method + "): " + _counter + " calls");
    }
```

The methods `runAdd()` and `runContains()` reset the counter before running `TEST_SIZE` iterations of the `add()` and `contains()` methods, respectively, and finally reporting the results:

```
    private void runAdd() {
        _counter = 0;
        for (int i = 0; i < TEST_SIZE; ++i) {
            _hashtable.add(new Value());
        }
        reportCalls("add");
    }

    private void runContains() {
        _counter = 0;
```

```
        for (int i = 0; i < TEST_SIZE; ++i) {
            _hashtable.contains(new Value());
        }
        reportCalls("contains");
    }
```

The method `runAll()` is a convenience to enable the test cases to run both parts with a single call:

```
    private void runAll() {
        runAdd();
        runContains();
    }
```

Now we get into the actual test cases. The first set of test cases is for linear probing. There aren't that many different configurations to try — only two, in fact — as the only configurable option for `LinearProbingHashtable` is the initial capacity: The first creates a hash table with an initial capacity that is smaller than the data set's size, hopefully leading to a number of resize operations. The second test has exactly the right capacity to ensure that no resizing occurs at all:

```
    public void testLinearProbingWithResizing() {
        _hashtable = new LinearProbingHashtable(INITIAL_CAPACITY);
        runAll();
    }

    public void testLinearProbingNoResizing() {
        _hashtable = new LinearProbingHashtable(TEST_SIZE);
        runAll();
    }
```

The next set of tests exercises the bucketing version. These not only demonstrate the performance relative to linear probing, but also give you an idea of how performance varies depending on the initial configuration. Each case creates a hash table with an initial capacity small enough to guarantee that a number of resize operations will be performed. The difference between each lies in when that resize will occur. Notice the varying load factor values for each test:

```
    public void testBucketsLoadFactor100Percent() {
        _hashtable = new BucketingHashtable(INITIAL_CAPACITY, 1.0f);
        runAll();
    }

    public void testBucketsLoadFactor75Percent() {
        _hashtable = new BucketingHashtable(INITIAL_CAPACITY, 0.75f);
        runAll();
    }

    public void testBuckets50Percent() {
        _hashtable = new BucketingHashtable(INITIAL_CAPACITY, 0.50f);
        runAll();
    }

    public void testBuckets25Percent() {
        _hashtable = new BucketingHashtable(INITIAL_CAPACITY, 0.25f);
        runAll();
    }
```

```
public void testBuckets150Percent() {
    _hashtable = new BucketingHashtable(INITIAL_CAPACITY, 1.50f);
    runAll();
}

public void testBuckets200Percent() {
    _hashtable = new BucketingHashtable(INITIAL_CAPACITY, 2.0f);
    runAll();

}
```

Running the performance comparison should produce output similar to the following. Keep in mind that the actual results will be slightly different due to the random nature of the tests.

```
testLinearProbingWithResizing(add): 14704 calls
testLinearProbingWithResizing(contains): 1088000 calls
testLinearProbingNoResizing(add): 18500 calls
testLinearProbingNoResizing(contains): 1000000 calls
testBucketsLoadFactor100Percent(add): 987 calls
testBucketsLoadFactor100Percent(contains): 869 calls
testBucketsLoadFactor75Percent(add): 832 calls
testBucketsLoadFactor75Percent(contains): 433 calls
testBuckets50Percent(add): 521 calls
testBuckets50Percent(contains): 430 calls
testBuckets25Percent(add): 262 calls
testBuckets25Percent(contains): 224 calls
testBuckets150Percent(add): 1689 calls
testBuckets150Percent(contains): 903 calls
testBuckets200Percent(add): 1813 calls
testBuckets200Percent(contains): 1815 calls
```

In this form, the numbers are a bit hard to interpret, so they have been summarized in Table 11-1.

Table 11-1: Calls to equals() for 1,000 Iterations Each of add() and contains()*

Configuration	add	contains	Total	Average
Linear Probing - Resizing	14,704	1,088,000	1,102,704	551.35
Linear Probing – No resizing	18,500	1,000,000	1,018,500	509.25
Buckets – 100% Load	987	869	1,856	0.93
Buckets – 75% Load	832	433	1,265	0.63
Buckets – 50% Load	521	430	951	0.48
Buckets – 25% Load	262	224	486	0.24
Buckets – 150% Load	1,689	903	2,592	1.30
Buckets – 200% Load	1,813	1,815	3,628	1.81

* Actual results may vary due to the random nature of the tests

The most striking thing about these results is the obvious difference between linear probing and buckets. The last column in the table — Average — shows that linear probing performs generally no better than a linked list — `O(N)`. Using buckets, however, appears to work remarkably well. Even in the worst case, where the hash table didn't resize until the load reached 200%, the number of calls to `equals()` still averaged under 2! In the best case, the average was 0.24, or one call for every four values. Of course, in this case, the hash table is only ever 25% populated, leading to a lot of wasted space. In all cases, though, the buckets clearly outperform linear probing by several orders of magnitude.

There also seems to be a direct correlation between the bucket load factor and the number of calls: 100% load leads to around one call per value; 75% load results in a call for around 60% of the values, and so on. The really interesting feature, though, is that no matter what the load factor, performance still remains amazingly close to `O(1)`.

From this, you can conclude that a hash table implementation that uses buckets provides excellent overall performance, possibly the best so far, for storing and retrieving values. However, achieving such performance is contingent on finding a good hash function.

Summary

In this chapter, you learned the following:

- Hashing acts as a kind of randomizing function, destroying any sense of order within the data.
- A perfect hash function is one that causes no collisions; however, this is hard to achieve.
- The particular hashing function to use is largely determined by the nature and characteristics of the input data, which in many cases is difficult, if not impossible, to know in advance. Therefore, finding a hash function that minimizes the number of collisions, rather than eliminates them altogether, is more attainable.
- Increasing the table size can reduce the number of collisions at the expense of wasted memory, as can using a prime number for the table size.
- Linear probing degenerates into a linked list.
- Buckets coupled with a good hash function can achieve `O(1)` search times.

Exercises

1. Modify `BucketingHashtable` to always use a prime number of buckets. What effect (if any) does this have on performance?
2. Modify `LinearProbingHashtable` to maintain the number of values in the table, rather than calculate it every time.
3. Modify `BucketingHashtable` to maintain the number of values in the table, rather than calculate it every time.
4. Create an iterator that provides access to all of the entries in a `BucketingHashtable`.

Sets

Sets are collections that hold only distinct values; a set guarantees that an item will not be added more than once. They are particularly useful in scientific applications but often provide a more sensible structure than lists for holding data when duplicate values are not needed. More often than not when a list is used, a set is probably what is intended.

This chapter discusses the following topics:

- The basic operations of a set
- A set implementation designed for small amounts of data, the list set
- Another implementation that efficiently manages large amounts of unordered data, the hash set
- A third type of set that has predictable iteration order, the tree set

Understanding Sets

Think of a set as an unordered pool of data containing no duplicates. This differs from a list, which, like an array, maintains the order of insertion and allows duplicates. Figure 12-1 depicts the set of letters A through K. Notice that there is no explicit ordering of the values.

Sets typically support the operations shown in Table 12-1.

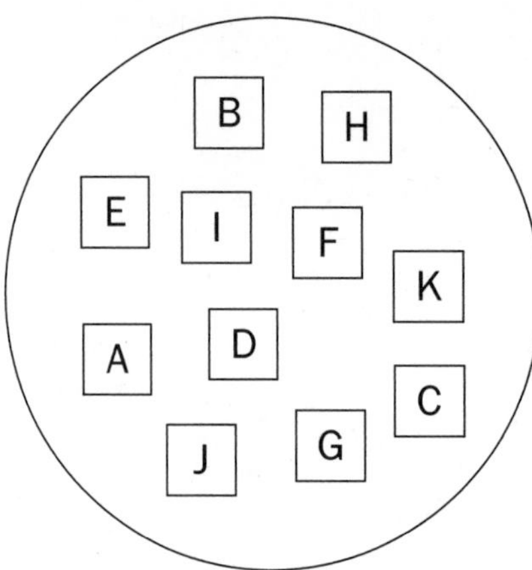

Figure 12-1: A set is a pool of distinct, unordered values.

Table 12-1: Set Operations

Operation	Description
add	Adds a value to the set. If added, the size of the set is increased by one and returns `true`; otherwise, returns `false` if the value already existed.
delete	Deletes a value from the set. If deleted, the size of the set is decreased by one and returns `true`; otherwise, returns `false` if the value didn't exist.
contains	Determines whether a specified value exists in the set.
iterator	Obtains an `Iterator` over all values in a set.
size	Obtains the number of values in the set.
isEmpty	Determines whether the set is empty. Returns `true` if the set is empty (`size() == 0`); otherwise, returns `false`.
clear	Deletes all values from the set. The size of the set is reset to zero.

Because a set may contain any given value only once, adding a value may not always be successful; if the value already exists, it won't be added again. For this reason, the `add()` operation indicates whether the value was added. Similarly, `delete()` indicates whether the value was deleted — that is, whether it existed or not.

In addition to adding and deleting values, you can query a set to determine whether a value is contained, check the size of the set, and iterate through all the values. Iterating over a set differs from iterating through a list in that lists guarantee an explicit ordering of values, whereas sets make no such promise; although ordering is not prohibited — ordered set implementations are entirely possible — in general, sets treat all values equally and make no guarantees as to the order of iteration.

Sets can be combined in various interesting and useful ways.

Assume you have the two sets shown in Figure 12-2.

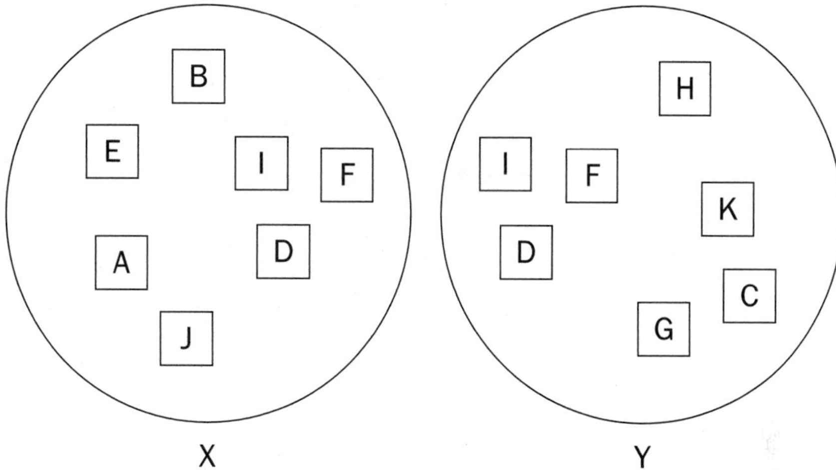

Figure 12-2: Two sets: X = {A, B, D, E, F, I, J} and Y = {C, D, F, G, H, I, K}.

The union of two sets is another set containing all the values from both, remembering of course that a set has no duplicates. You can also think of this as adding two sets together. Figure 12-3 shows the union of the two sets X and Y. Notice that even though both sets contain some overlapping values—D, I, and F—the resulting set contains no duplicates.

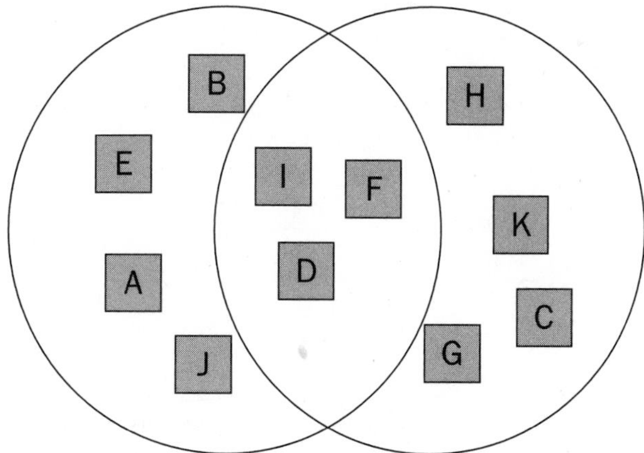

Figure 12-3: The union of two sets: X + Y.

The intersection of two sets is another set that contains only those values that are common to both, again remembering that a set can contain no duplicate values. Figure 12-4 shows the intersection of the two sets X and Y. Notice that the result contains only those values that exist in both X and Y.

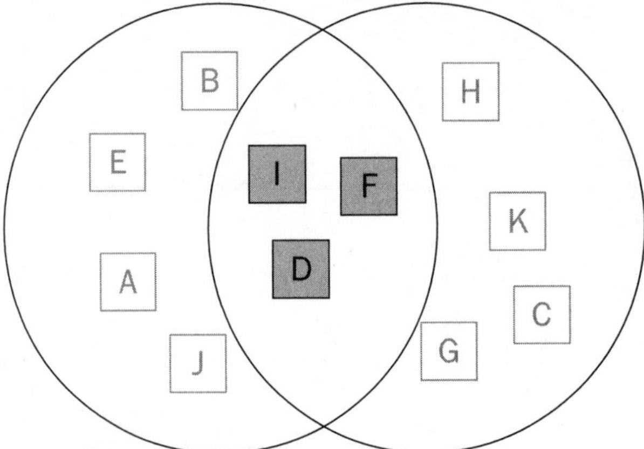

Figure 12-4: The intersection of two sets: X ∩ Y.

The difference between two sets is all elements from one set that are not also members of another. You can think of this as subtracting one set from another. Figure 12-5 shows what happens when set Y is subtracted from set X. Notice that the result contains only those values from X that aren't also contained in Y.

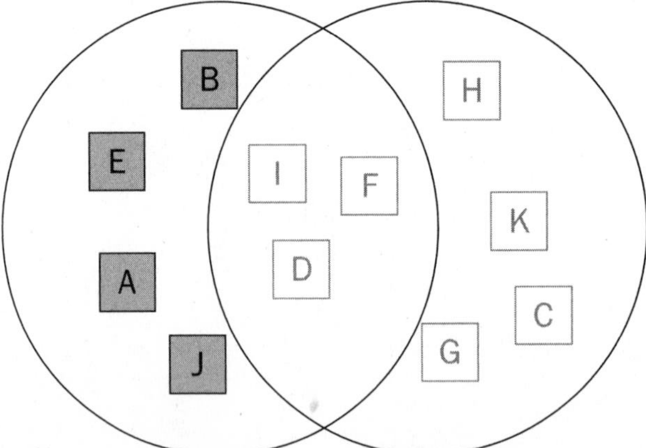

Figure 12-5: The difference between two sets: X – Y.

So that you can easily plug in different set implementations depending on the needs of your application, and, just as important, so that you can easily test each type of set, in the next Try It Out section you create an interface that defines all of the required methods.

Try It Out — Creating a Generic Set Interface

Create the `Set` interface as follows:

```
package com.wrox.algorithms.sets;

public interface Set extends Iterable {
    public boolean add(Object value);
    public boolean delete(Object value);
    public boolean contains(Object value);
    public void clear();
    public int size();
    public boolean isEmpty();
}
```

How It Works

The `Set` interface has all of the operations listed in Table 12-1 converted directly into methods on a Java interface. In addition, you've extended the `Iterable` interface, which defines the `iterator()` method, enabling a set to be used anywhere an `Iterable` is required.

Testing Set Implementations

So that you can be sure that every set implementation you create behaves correctly, in the next Try It Out section you develop a suite of tests that will work for any type of set.

Try It Out — Creating a Generic Suite of Set Tests

Create the abstract test class as follows:

```
package com.wrox.algorithms.sets;

import com.wrox.algorithms.iteration.Iterator;
import com.wrox.algorithms.iteration.IteratorOutOfBoundsException;
import com.wrox.algorithms.iteration.ReverseIterator;
import com.wrox.algorithms.lists.LinkedList;
import com.wrox.algorithms.lists.List;
import junit.framework.TestCase;

public abstract class AbstractSetTestCase extends TestCase {
    private static final Object A = "a";
    private static final Object B = "b";
    private static final Object C = "c";
    private static final Object D = "d";
    private static final Object E = "e";
    private static final Object F = "f";

    private Set _set;

    protected void setUp() throws Exception {
        _set = createSet();
```

```
        _set.add(C);
        _set.add(A);
        _set.add(B);
        _set.add(D);
    }

    protected abstract Set createSet();

    public void testContainsExisting() {
        assertTrue(_set.contains(A));
        assertTrue(_set.contains(B));
        assertTrue(_set.contains(C));
        assertTrue(_set.contains(D));
    }

    public void testContainsNonExisting() {
        assertFalse(_set.contains(E));
        assertFalse(_set.contains(F));
    }

    public void testAddNewValue() {
        assertEquals(4, _set.size());

        assertTrue(_set.add(E));
        assertTrue(_set.contains(E));
        assertEquals(5, _set.size());

        assertTrue(_set.add(F));
        assertTrue(_set.contains(F));
        assertEquals(6, _set.size());
    }

    public void testAddExistingValueHasNoEffect() {
        assertEquals(4, _set.size());
        assertFalse(_set.add(C));
        assertEquals(4, _set.size());
    }

    public void testDeleteExisting() {
        assertTrue(_set.delete(B));
        assertFalse(_set.contains(B));
        assertEquals(3, _set.size());

        assertTrue(_set.delete(A));
        assertFalse(_set.contains(A));
        assertEquals(2, _set.size());

        assertTrue(_set.delete(C));
        assertFalse(_set.contains(C));
        assertEquals(1, _set.size());

        assertTrue(_set.delete(D));
        assertFalse(_set.contains(D));
```

```
        assertEquals(0, _set.size());
    }

    public void testDeleteNonExisting() {
        assertEquals(4, _set.size());
        assertFalse(_set.delete(E));
        assertEquals(4, _set.size());
        assertFalse(_set.delete(F));
        assertEquals(4, _set.size());
    }

    public void testClear() {
        assertEquals(4, _set.size());
        assertFalse(_set.isEmpty());

        _set.clear();

        assertEquals(0, _set.size());
        assertTrue(_set.isEmpty());

        assertFalse(_set.contains(A));
        assertFalse(_set.contains(B));
        assertFalse(_set.contains(C));
        assertFalse(_set.contains(D));
    }

    public void testIteratorForwards() {
        checkIterator(_set.iterator());
    }

    public void testIteratorBackwards() {
        checkIterator(new ReverseIterator(_set.iterator()));
    }

    private void checkIterator(Iterator i) {
        List values = new LinkedList();

        for (i.first(); !i.isDone(); i.next()) {
            values.add(i.current());
        }

        try {
            i.current();
            fail();
        } catch (IteratorOutOfBoundsException e) {
        }

        assertEquals(4, values.size());
        assertTrue(values.contains(A));
        assertTrue(values.contains(B));
        assertTrue(values.contains(C));
        assertTrue(values.contains(D));
    }
}
```

How It Works

The class AbstractSetTestCase extends TestCase in order to make it a proper JUnit-compatible test class. It also defines some sample entries and a map for testing. The set is assigned a value in the setUp() method—which runs just prior to each test case—and the first four sample values are added:

```
package com.wrox.algorithms.sets;

import com.wrox.algorithms.iteration.Iterator;
import com.wrox.algorithms.iteration.ReverseIterator;
import com.wrox.algorithms.iteration.IteratorOutOfBoundsException;
import com.wrox.algorithms.lists.LinkedList;
import com.wrox.algorithms.lists.List;
import junit.framework.TestCase;

public abstract class AbstractSetTestCase extends TestCase {
    private static final Object A = "a";
    private static final Object B = "b";
    private static final Object C = "c";
    private static final Object D = "d";
    private static final Object E = "e";
    private static final Object F = "f";

    private Set _set;

    protected void setUp() throws Exception {
        _set = createSet();

        _set.add(C);
        _set.add(A);
        _set.add(B);
        _set.add(D);
    }

    protected abstract Set createSet();

    ...
}
```

The contains() method should return true for any value that is contained within the set, or false otherwise. You know that four of the sample values do exist, so in testContainsExisting(), you check to ensure that contains() returns true for each one:

```
public void testContainsExisting() {
    assertTrue(_set.contains(A));
    assertTrue(_set.contains(B));
    assertTrue(_set.contains(C));
    assertTrue(_set.contains(D));
}
```

Conversely, testContainsNonExisting() ensures that contains() returns false for values that are known not to exist:

```
public void testContainsNonExisting() {
    assertFalse(_set.contains(E));
    assertFalse(_set.contains(F));
}
```

The `testAddNewKey()` method first checks the initial size of the set before adding two values. Each time `add()` is called, the return value is checked to ensure it is `true`, indicating there was no existing value; `contains()` is then called to ensure that the new value exists, and the size is checked to ensure it has increased by one:

```
public void testAddNewValue() {
    assertEquals(4, _set.size());

    assertTrue(_set.add(E));
    assertTrue(_set.contains(E));
    assertEquals(5, _set.size());

    assertTrue(_set.add(F));
    assertTrue(_set.contains(F));
    assertEquals(6, _set.size());
}
```

The method `testAddExistingValueHasNoEffect()` simply attempts to add all the values again. Each time a duplicate is added, the return value and size are checked to ensure that the call has had no effect:

```
public void testAddExistingValueHasNoEffect() {
    assertEquals(4, _set.size());

    assertFalse(_set.add(A));
    assertEquals(4, _set.size());

    assertFalse(_set.add(B));
    assertEquals(4, _set.size());

    assertFalse(_set.add(C));
    assertEquals(4, _set.size());

    assertFalse(_set.add(D));
    assertEquals(4, _set.size());
}
```

Next, `testDeleteExisting()` removes each of the four values that were used to populate the set initially. Each time `delete()` is called, the return value and size of the set are checked to ensure they reflect the deletion:

```
public void testDeleteExisting() {
    assertEquals(4, _set.size());

    assertTrue(_set.delete(B));
    assertFalse(_set.contains(B));
    assertEquals(3, _set.size());

    assertTrue(_set.delete(A));
```

```
        assertFalse(_set.contains(A));
        assertEquals(2, _set.size());

        assertTrue(_set.delete(C));
        assertFalse(_set.contains(C));
        assertEquals(1, _set.size());

        assertTrue(_set.delete(D));
        assertFalse(_set.contains(D));
        assertEquals(0, _set.size());
    }
```

Naturally, you also test what happens when trying to delete a non-existing value. After checking the size of the set, `testDeleteNonExisting()` calls `delete()` to remove two values known not to exist. Each time, the size is checked to ensure it hasn't changed:

```
    public void testDeleteNonExisting() {
        assertEquals(4, _set.size());

        assertFalse(_set.delete(E));
        assertEquals(4, _set.size());

        assertFalse(_set.delete(F));
        assertEquals(4, _set.size());
    }
```

The method `testClear()` first ensures that the set is not empty. Then `clear()` is called and the set is once again checked to ensure that it no longer contains any values:

```
    public void testClear() {
        assertEquals(4, _set.size());
        assertFalse(_set.isEmpty());

        _set.clear();

        assertEquals(0, _set.size());
        assertTrue(_set.isEmpty());

        assertFalse(_set.contains(A));
        assertFalse(_set.contains(B));
        assertFalse(_set.contains(C));
        assertFalse(_set.contains(D));
    }
```

Finally, you verify that iterating through the contents of a set—both forwards and backwards—returns all the expected values. The method `checkIterator()` does most of the work. It first iterates over all the values in the set, adding them to a list. Then, after ensuring the iterator throws the appropriate exception once it has completed, the list is checked to ensure that it contains all the expected values:

```
    private void checkIterator(Iterator i) {
        List values = new LinkedList();

        for (i.first(); !i.isDone(); i.next()) {
```

```
            values.add(i.current());
        }

        try {
            i.current();
            fail();
        } catch (IteratorOutOfBoundsException e) {
            // expected
        }

        assertEquals(4, values.size());
        assertTrue(values.contains(A));
        assertTrue(values.contains(B));
        assertTrue(values.contains(C));
        assertTrue(values.contains(D));
    }
```

Then, to test forwards iteration, `testIteratorForwards()` simply obtains an iterator from the set and hands it off to `checkIterator()`:

```
    public void testIteratorForwards() {
        checkIterator(_set.iterator());
    }
```

Finally, to test reverse iteration, `testIteratorBackwards()` wraps the iterator in a `ReverseIterator` (see Chapter 2) before calling `checkIterator()`. In this way, all calls to `first()` and `next()` are redirected to `last()` and `previous()`, respectively, meaning you don't have to write a separate set of tests:

```
    public void testIteratorBackwards() {
        checkIterator(new ReverseIterator(_set.iterator()));
    }
```

A List Set

In the next Try It Out section, you create a set that uses a list as the underlying storage mechanism. The implementation is very straightforward and easy to follow, and although it isn't particularly efficient, it is useful for small data sets.

Try It Out Testing and Implementing a List Set

Start by creating the list set tests:

```
package com.wrox.algorithms.maps;

public class ListMapTest extends AbstractMapTestCase {
    protected Map createMap() {
        return new ListMap();
    }
}
```

Follow those with the list set class itself:

```
package com.wrox.algorithms.sets;

import com.wrox.algorithms.iteration.Iterator;
import com.wrox.algorithms.lists.LinkedList;
import com.wrox.algorithms.lists.List;

public class ListSet implements Set {
    private final List _values = new LinkedList();

    public boolean contains(Object value) {
        return _values.contains(value);
    }

    public boolean add(Object value) {
        if (contains(value)) {
            return false;
        }

        _values.add(value);
        return true;
    }

    public boolean delete(Object value) {
        return _values.delete(value);
    }

    public void clear() {
        _values.clear();
    }

    public int size() {
        return _values.size();
    }

    public boolean isEmpty() {
        return _values.isEmpty();
    }

    public Iterator iterator() {
        return _values.iterator();
    }
}
```

How It Works

The `ListSetTest` class simply extends `AbstractSetTestCase`, and in doing so inherits all the test cases. The only other thing you did was implement the `createSet()` method to return an instance of the `ListSet` class to be used by the test cases themselves.

Implementing the `ListSet` class itself is fairly straightforward. For the most part, you delegate the methods on the `Set` interface directly to equivalent methods on the underlying list.

A linked list is used as the underlying storage mechanism, though technically any list implementation will suffice. Almost all the methods are one-liners, delegating directly to methods on the underlying list — the exception, of course, being, `add()`.

The `add()` method first determines whether the value to be added already exists in the underlying list. If it does, `false` is returned to indicate that the set has not been changed; otherwise, the new value is added:

```
public boolean add(Object value) {
    if (contains(value)) {
        return false;
    }

    _values.add(value);
    return true;
}
```

As you can see, a list-based set is very simple. The `add()`, `delete()`, and `contains()` methods all perform in `O(N)` time, which is probably sufficient for handling small numbers of values.

A Hash Set

If you are storing a relatively large number of values and ordering is not important, then a set implementation based on hash tables (covered in Chapter 11) is a good choice. In the next Try It Out section, you implement a hash set, so you may wish to briefly go over hashing again to familiarize yourself with the concepts, especially the implementation of hash tables that use buckets.

Try It Out — Testing and Implementing a Hash Set

Start by creating the test class:

```
package com.wrox.algorithms.sets;

public class HashSetTest extends AbstractSetTestCase {
    protected Set createSet() {
        return new HashSet();
    }
}
```

Then create the hash set class:

```
package com.wrox.algorithms.sets;

import com.wrox.algorithms.hashing.HashtableIterator;
import com.wrox.algorithms.iteration.ArrayIterator;
import com.wrox.algorithms.iteration.Iterator;

public class HashSet implements Set {
    public static final int DEFAULT_CAPACITY = 17;
    public static final float DEFAULT_LOAD_FACTOR = 0.75f;
```

```
private final int _initialCapacity;
private final float _loadFactor;
private ListSet[] _buckets;
private int _size;

public HashSet() {
    this(DEFAULT_CAPACITY, DEFAULT_LOAD_FACTOR);
}

public HashSet(int initialCapacity) {
    this(initialCapacity, DEFAULT_LOAD_FACTOR);
}

public HashSet(int initialCapacity, float loadFactor) {
    assert initialCapacity > 0 : "initialCapacity can't be < 1";
    assert loadFactor > 0 : "loadFactor can't be <= 0";

    _initialCapacity = initialCapacity;
    _loadFactor = loadFactor;
    clear();
}

public boolean contains(Object value) {
    ListSet bucket = _buckets[bucketIndexFor(value)];
    return bucket != null && bucket.contains(value);
}

public boolean add(Object value) {
    ListSet bucket = bucketFor(value);

    if (bucket.add(value)) {
        ++_size;
        maintainLoad();
        return true;
    }

    return false;
}

public boolean delete(Object value) {
    int bucketIndex = bucketIndexFor(value);
    ListSet bucket = _buckets[bucketIndex];
    if (bucket != null && bucket.delete(value)) {
        --_size;
        if (bucket.isEmpty()) {
            _buckets[bucketIndex] = null;
        }
        return true;
    }

    return false;
}

public Iterator iterator() {
    return new HashtableIterator(new ArrayIterator(_buckets));
```

```
    }

    public void clear() {
        _buckets = new ListSet[_initialCapacity];
        _size = 0;
    }

    public int size() {
        return _size;
    }

    public boolean isEmpty() {
        return size() == 0;
    }

    private ListSet bucketFor(Object value) {
        int bucketIndex = bucketIndexFor(value);

        ListSet bucket = _buckets[bucketIndex];
        if (bucket == null) {
            bucket = new ListSet();
            _buckets[bucketIndex] = bucket;
        }

        return bucket;
    }

    private int bucketIndexFor(Object value) {
        assert value != null : "value can't be null";
        return Math.abs(value.hashCode() % _buckets.length);
    }

    private void maintainLoad() {
        if (loadFactorExceeded()) {
            resize();
        }
    }

    private boolean loadFactorExceeded() {
        return size() > _buckets.length * _loadFactor;
    }

    private void resize() {
        HashSet copy = new HashSet(_buckets.length * 2, _loadFactor);

        for (int i = 0; i < _buckets.length; ++i) {
            if (_buckets[i] != null) {
                copy.addAll(_buckets[i].iterator());
            }
        }

        _buckets = copy._buckets;
    }
```

```
    private void addAll(Iterator values) {
        assert values != null : "values can't be null";

        for (values.first(); !values.isDone(); values.next()) {
            add(values.current());
        }
    }
}
```

How It Works

Once again, the HashSetTest class extends AbstractSetTestCase, and you implement the createSet() method to return an instance of a HashSet to be tested.

For the most part, the implementation of HashSet is a direct copy of the BucketingHashtable code from Chapter 11, so we confine the discussion of the code to only the differences between it and the original BucketingHashtable implementation, which are required to fulfill the Set interface.

Besides actually implementing the Set interface, the first major difference between HashSet and BucketingHashtable is that instead of using a List for the buckets, you've instead used a ListSet. In a sense, a bucket really is a set—it cannot contain duplicate values—and the hash set merely distributes values among the different sets (based on the hash code) in order to reduce lookup times. Therefore, by using a set instead of a list for your buckets, you not only simplify the code, but more importantly, you clarify the overall intent of the code. This is reflected in the add() method by removing the need to call contains() on the bucket before adding the new value:

```
public boolean add(Object value) {
    ListSet bucket = bucketFor(value);

    if (bucket.add(value)) {
        ++_size;
        maintainLoad();
        return true;
    }

    return false;
}
```

The next difference is that you've added a delete() method, as required by the Set interface. Again, as with add(), you can take advantage of the fact that the buckets are themselves sets, so that once the appropriate bucket has been found, a simple call to delete() on the bucket is all that is needed to remove the value:

```
public boolean delete(Object value) {
    int bucketIndex = bucketIndexFor(value);
    ListSet bucket = _buckets[bucketIndex];
    if (bucket != null && bucket.delete(value)) {
        --_size;
        if (bucket.isEmpty()) {
            _buckets[bucketIndex] = null;
        }
        return true;
```

```
        }

        return false;
    }
```

Lastly, you've implemented the iterator() method to allow traversal of all the contained values. Here, you've used the HashtableIterator from Chapter 11. Note that this was possible because HashtableIterator is based on the Iterable interface, rather than a List.

Other than that, the only other thing you've done is add some convenience constructors for usability, but HashSet is pretty much a carbon copy of BucketingHashtable from Chapter 11.

Given the use of a hash table based on buckets, and assuming a good hash function in the form of the hashCode method on the values being stored, you can expect to achieve fairly close to O(1) performance. Of course, as noted at the start of this section, the use of hashing necessarily precludes any notion of ordering, so an iterator will appear to return the values randomly.

A Tree Set

Sets don't usually guarantee an ordering of the data. Sometimes, though, you may need a predictable iteration order—for example, when displaying options from which a user selects, or maybe in an alphabetical list of names from an address book, all while maintaining set semantics. Binary search trees (see Chapter 10) provide exactly the data structure you need.

Before proceeding with the implementation of tree-based sets, we recommend that you revisit binary search trees to refresh your understanding of the core concepts and code because the discussion will again be limited to only the differences between the TreeSet code presented and the original BinarySearchTree code.

Try It Out Testing and Implementing a Tree Map

Start by creating the TreeSetTest class as follows:

```
package com.wrox.algorithms.sets;

public class TreeSetTest extends AbstractSetTestCase {
    protected Set createSet() {
        return new TreeSet();
    }
}
```

Follow the class with the tree set implementation:

```
package com.wrox.algorithms.sets;

import com.wrox.algorithms.iteration.Iterator;
import com.wrox.algorithms.iteration.IteratorOutOfBoundsException;
import com.wrox.algorithms.sorting.Comparator;
import com.wrox.algorithms.sorting.NaturalComparator;
```

```
public class TreeSet implements Set {
    private final Comparator _comparator;
    private Node _root;
    private int _size;

    public TreeSet() {
        this(NaturalComparator.INSTANCE);
    }

    public TreeSet(Comparator comparator) {
        assert comparator != null : "comparator can't be null";
        _comparator = comparator;
    }

    public boolean contains(Object value) {
        return search(value) != null;
    }

    public boolean add(Object value) {
        Node parent = null;
        Node node = _root;
        int cmp = 0;

        while (node != null) {
            parent = node;
            cmp = _comparator.compare(value, node.getValue());
            if (cmp == 0) {
                return false;
            }

            node = cmp < 0 ? node.getSmaller() : node.getLarger();
        }

        Node inserted = new Node(parent, value);

        if (parent == null) {
            _root = inserted;
        } else if (cmp < 0) {
            parent.setSmaller(inserted);
        } else {
            parent.setLarger(inserted);
        }

        ++_size;
        return true;
    }

    public boolean delete(Object value) {
        Node node = search(value);
        if (node == null) {
            return false;
        }

        Node deleted = node.getSmaller() != null && node.getLarger() != null ?
node.successor() : node;
```

```
        assert deleted != null : "deleted can't be null";

        Node replacement = deleted.getSmaller() != null ? deleted.getSmaller() :
deleted.getLarger();
        if (replacement != null) {
            replacement.setParent(deleted.getParent());
        }

        if (deleted == _root) {
            _root = replacement;
        } else if (deleted.isSmaller()) {
            deleted.getParent().setSmaller(replacement);
        } else {
            deleted.getParent().setLarger(replacement);
        }

        if (deleted != node) {
            Object deletedValue = node.getValue();
            node.setValue(deleted.getValue());
            deleted.setValue(deletedValue);
        }

        --_size;
        return true;
    }

    public Iterator iterator() {
        return new ValueIterator();
    }

    public void clear() {
        _root = null;
        _size = 0;
    }

    public int size() {
        return _size;
    }

    public boolean isEmpty() {
        return _root == null;
    }

    private Node search(Object value) {
        assert value != null : "value can't be null";

        Node node = _root;

        while (node != null) {
            int cmp = _comparator.compare(value, node.getValue());
            if (cmp == 0) {
                break;
            }
```

```
            node = cmp < 0 ? node.getSmaller() : node.getLarger();
        }

        return node;
    }

    private static final class Node {
        private Object _value;
        private Node _parent;
        private Node _smaller;
        private Node _larger;

        public Node(Node parent, Object value) {
            setParent(parent);
            setValue(value);
        }

        public Object getValue() {
            return _value;
        }

        public void setValue(Object value) {
            assert value != null : "value can't be null";
            _value = value;
        }

        public Node getParent() {
            return _parent;
        }

        public void setParent(Node parent) {
            _parent = parent;
        }

        public Node getSmaller() {
            return _smaller;
        }

        public void setSmaller(Node node) {
            assert node != getLarger() : "smaller can't be the same as larger";
            _smaller = node;
        }

        public Node getLarger() {
            return _larger;
        }


        public void setLarger(Node node) {
            assert node != getSmaller() : "larger can't be the same as smaller";
            _larger = node;
        }

        public boolean isSmaller() {
```

```
        return getParent() != null && this == getParent().getSmaller();
    }

    public boolean isLarger() {
        return getParent() != null && this == getParent().getLarger();
    }

    public Node minimum() {
        Node node = this;

        while (node.getSmaller() != null) {
            node = node.getSmaller();
        }

        return node;
    }

    public Node maximum() {
        Node node = this;

        while (node.getLarger() != null) {
            node = node.getLarger();
        }

        return node;
    }

    public Node successor() {
        if (getLarger() != null) {
            return getLarger().minimum();
        }

        Node node = this;

        while (node.isLarger()) {
            node = node.getParent();
        }

        return node.getParent();
    }

    public Node predecessor() {
        if (getSmaller() != null) {
            return getSmaller().maximum();
        }

        Node node = this;

        while (node.isSmaller()) {
            node = node.getParent();
        }

        return node.getParent();
    }
```

```
        }

        private final class ValueIterator implements Iterator {
            private Node _current;

            public void first() {
                _current = _root != null ? _root.minimum() : null;
            }

            public void last() {
                _current = _root != null ? _root.maximum() : null;
            }

            public boolean isDone() {
                return _current == null;
            }

            public void next() {
                if (!isDone()) {
                    _current = _current.successor();
                }
            }

            public void previous() {
                if (!isDone()) {
                    _current = _current.predecessor();
                }
            }

            public Object current() throws IteratorOutOfBoundsException {
                if (isDone()) {
                    throw new IteratorOutOfBoundsException();
                }
                return _current.getValue();
            }
        }
    }
```

How It Works

The `TreeSetTest` class extends `AbstractSetTestCase` to re-use all the tests you created earlier, with `createSet()` returning an instance of the `TreeSet` class.

The code for `TreeSet` follows very closely the code you developed for `BinarySearchTree` in Chapter 10, so the discussion of the code is confined to only the differences between it and the original `BinarySearchTree` implementation.

The first difference, of course, is that `TreeSet` implements the `Set` interface. This means that the original `insert()` method is renamed to `add()`. Along with the name change, however, is a slight change in behavior. Whereas the original `insert()` method allowed duplicate values, the set semantics do not, and the code in `add()` has to be modified accordingly. The `while` loop in the original `insert()` method looked like this:

```
while (node != null) {
    parent = node;
    cmp = _comparator.compare(value, node.getValue());
    node = cmp <= 0 ? node.getSmaller() : node.getLarger();
}
```

Notice that when a duplicate value was inserted, it would always be added as a left child of any similar value. The `add()` method, however, cannot allow duplicates:

```
while (node != null) {
    parent = node;
    cmp = _comparator.compare(value, node.getValue());
    if (cmp == 0) {
        return false;
    }

    node = cmp < 0 ? node.getSmaller() : node.getLarger();
}
```

Here, if an existing value is found (`cmp == 0`), the method returns `false` immediately to indicate that no change has been made; otherwise, it proceeds as per the original.

The next change is that the `search()` method has been made private, and in its place is the `contains()` method as required by the `Set` interface. The `contains()` method then returns `true` only if `search()` actually finds a matching node.

Apart from the addition of the `clear()`, `isEmpty()`, `size()`, and `iterator()` methods—again mandated by the `Set` interface—the only other change of note is that the `Node` class has been made an inner class, and there is an extra `ValueIterator` inner class that iterates forwards or backwards over the nodes, in order, by calling `successor()` and `predecessor()`, respectively.

There you have it: a set implementation that, as you know from Chapter 10, has an average performance of `O(log N)`, and maintains the stored values in sorted order.

Summary

This chapter demonstrated the following:

- A set is a collection that contains only distinct values.
- In general, a set makes no guarantee of the iteration order.
- List-based sets are useful for relatively small data sets, as operations run in `O(N)`.
- Hash-table-based set operations run in `O(1)` with random iteration order.
- Binary-search-tree-based sets provide `O(log N)` performance as well as predictable iteration order.

Exercises

1. Write a method that takes two sets and determines whether they are equal.
2. Write a method that takes two sets and produces a third set containing the union of the first two.
3. Write a method that takes two sets and produces a third set containing the intersection of the first two.
4. Write a method that takes two sets and produces a third set containing the difference between the first two.
5. Update the `delete()` method in `HashSet` to free the bucket if it's empty.
6. Create a set implementation that uses a sorted list.
7. Create a set implementation that is always empty and throws `UnsupportedOperationException` whenever an attempt is made to modify it.

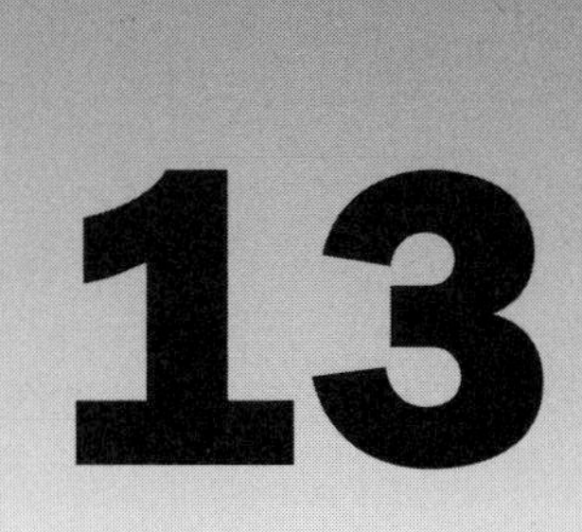

Maps

Maps — also known as dictionaries, lookup tables, and associative arrays — are especially useful for building indexes.

This chapter discusses the following topics:

- The basic operations of a map
- A map implementation designed for small amounts of data, the list map
- Another implementation that efficiently manages large amounts of unordered data, the hash map
- A third type of map that has predictable iteration order, the tree map

Understanding Maps

A map holds an association between a key and a value. Each key within a map is unique and enables you to quickly set and retrieve an associated value. This can be useful for creating lookup tables in which a code is entered and a description is obtained or for building indexes that enable you to locate information — for example, a person's record based on some pertinent details. Figure 13-1 shows a map in which the people's names represent the keys, and the values are database record numbers.

One thing to remember about maps is that while the keys in a map are guaranteed to be unique, no such promise is made about the values. This can be useful, however. Imagine an index that maps telephone numbers to database records so that you can easily find someone using his or her phone number. It's conceivable that a person might have more than one telephone number — home, business, cellular, and so on. In this case, multiple keys might map to the same record number. In Figure 13-2, you can see that Leonardo da Vinci can be contacted at two numbers: 555-123-4560 and 555-991-4511.

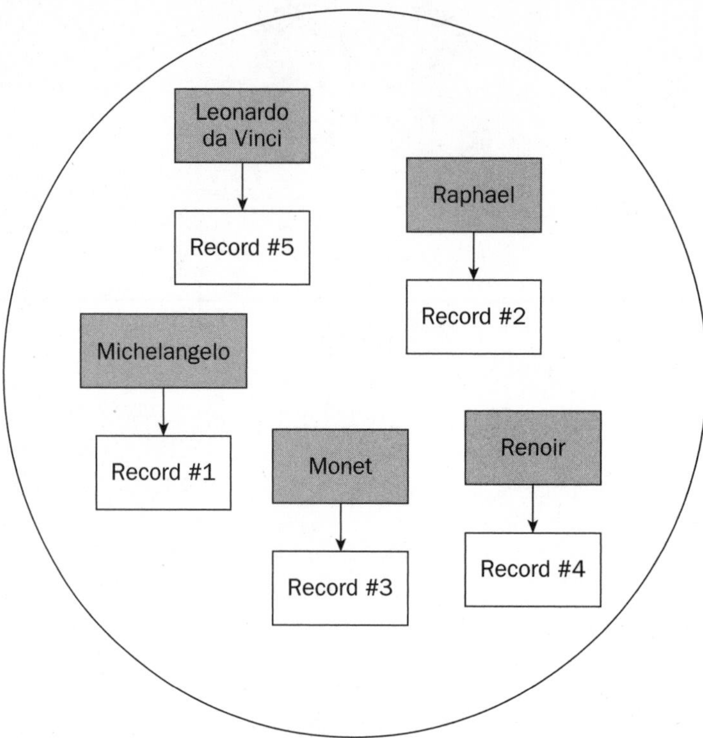

Figure 13-1: An index that maps people's names to their corresponding database record number.

Maps are also known as *dictionaries*, and it's not too hard to understand why. (In fact, the original map class in the JDK was called `Dictionary`.) A language dictionary associates a word with a definition (or, in the case of a foreign language translation dictionary, another word). In these cases, the word is the key and the definition is the value.

Lastly, another name for a map is *associative array*. In fact, it's possible to think of arrays—or lists, for that matter—as being quite similar to a map. Recall that arrays store values associated with a specific position, the index, and a map stores values associated with a specific key. Therefore, if you think of the index as being like a key, then in a sense, an array is like a specialized map.

Table 13-1 summarizes the operations provided by a map.

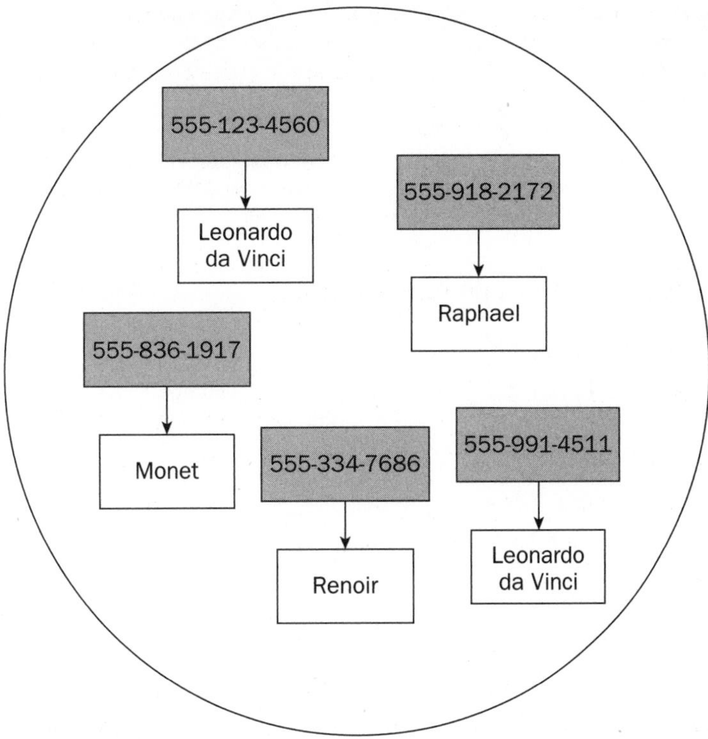

Figure 13-2: Keys are unique; values are not.

Table 13-1: Map Operations

Operation	Description
get	Obtains the value (if any) associated with a given key.
set	Sets the associated map with a given key. Returns the previous value (if any).
delete	Removes a value associated with a given key. Returns the value (if any).
contains	Determines whether a specified key exists in the map.
iterator	Obtains an `Iterator` over all key/value pairs in the map.
size	Obtains the number of key/value pairs in the map.
isEmpty	Determines whether the map is empty or not. Returns `true` if the set is empty (`size() == 0`); otherwise, returns `false`.
clear	Deletes all key/value pairs from the map. The size of the map is reset to zero.

Maps enable you to set the value for a particular key, obtain the value (if any) associated with a given key, and remove the key/value pair all together. A map also enables you to iterate over the key/value pairs—also known as *entries*—and, just like sets, maps generally make no guarantee regarding ordering.

So that you can easily plug in different map implementations depending on the needs of your application, and, just as important, so that you can easily test each type of map, in the next Try It Out section, you create an interface that defines all the required methods.

Try It Out Creating a Generic Map Interface

Create the `Map` interface as follows:

```
package com.wrox.algorithms.maps;

import com.wrox.algorithms.iteration.Iterable;

public interface Map extends Iterable {
    public Object get(Object key);
    public Object set(Object key, Object value);
    public Object delete(Object key);
    public boolean contains(Object key);
    public void clear();
    public int size();
    public boolean isEmpty();

    public static interface Entry {
        public Object getKey();
        public Object getValue();
    }
}
```

How It Works

The `Map` interface has all the operations listed in Table 13-1 translated into Java methods, and extends the `Iterable` interface so as to inherit the `iterator()` method and also be usable anywhere an `Iterable` is required. Notice the inner interface, `Entry`. This specifies a common interface for the key/value pairs contained within a map. Instances of `Map.Entry` will be returned from map iterators.

As well as the `Map.Entry` interface, in the next Try It Out section you also create a default `Map.Entry` implementation that will be used by all but one of the map classes later.

Try It Out Creating a Default Entry Implementation

Create the `DefaultEntry` class as follows:

```
package com.wrox.algorithms.maps;

public class DefaultEntry implements Map.Entry {
    private final Object _key;
    private Object _value;
```

```
    public DefaultEntry(Object key, Object value) {
        assert key != null : "key can't be null";
        _key = key;
        setValue(value);
    }

    public Object getKey() {
        return _key;
    }

    public Object setValue(Object value) {
        Object oldValue = _value;
        _value = value;
        return oldValue;
    }

    public Object getValue() {
        return _value;
    }

    public boolean equals(Object object) {
        if (this == object) {
            return true;
        }

        if (object == null || getClass() != object.getClass()) {
            return false;
        }

        DefaultEntry other = (DefaultEntry) object;

        return _key.equals(other._key) && _value.equals(other._value);
    }
}
```

How It Works

The `DefaultEntry` class holds the key and value pair and makes each available via the `getKey()` and `getValue()` methods, respectively. There is also an `equals()` method to enable you to quickly determine whether two entries are equivalent. This will be used from within the tests that follow.

Notice that the key cannot be changed after construction—it is marked as `final`—as there is no need for it to change once assigned. However, the value can be modified. Also notice that while you must always provide a key, a value may be `null`. In practice, `null` keys are rarely, if ever, useful. However, `null` values occur all the time, especially with database applications. Figure 13-3 shows a typical situation in which a database record is represented as a map.

Notice that the values for Cell Phone and Drivers License are both `null`, indicating that both have been assigned, but that the values are *unknown*.

Lastly, recall that the map interface specifies that not only may a value for a given key be updated, but also that any previously assigned value will be returned. This behavior is reflected in the fact that the `setValue()` method returns the existing value.

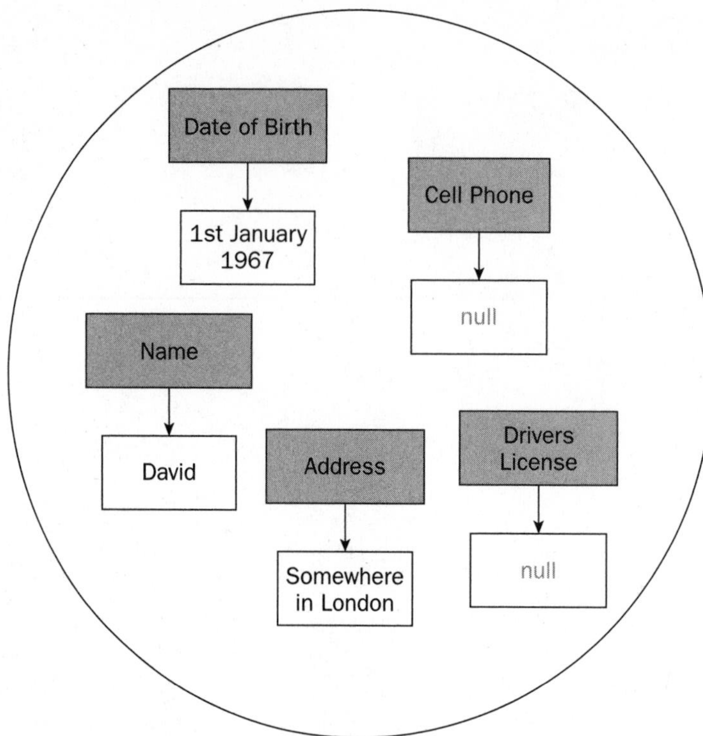

Figure 13-3: Keys in a map are mandatory, but values may be null.

You now have everything you need to start writing some generic tests: an interface with which any map implementation must conform, and a default `Map.Entry` implementation.

Testing Map Implementations

So that the tests may be re-used for any type of map, in the next Try It Out section you create an abstract test class containing all the test cases. This can then be extended with a test class specific to any map implementation that you create in the future.

Try It Out Creating a Generic Suite of Map Tests

Create the `AbstractMapTestCase` class as follows:

```
package com.wrox.algorithms.maps;

import com.wrox.algorithms.iteration.Iterator;
import com.wrox.algorithms.iteration.ReverseIterator;
import com.wrox.algorithms.iteration.IteratorOutOfBoundsException;
import com.wrox.algorithms.lists.LinkedList;
```

```
import com.wrox.algorithms.lists.List;
import junit.framework.TestCase;

public abstract class AbstractMapTestCase extends TestCase {
    private static final Map.Entry A = new DefaultEntry("akey", "avalue");
    private static final Map.Entry B = new DefaultEntry("bkey", "bvalue");
    private static final Map.Entry C = new DefaultEntry("ckey", "cvalue");
    private static final Map.Entry D = new DefaultEntry("dkey", "dvalue");
    private static final Map.Entry E = new DefaultEntry("ekey", "evalue");
    private static final Map.Entry F = new DefaultEntry("fkey", "fvalue");

    private Map _map;

    protected void setUp() throws Exception {
        super.setUp();

        _map = createMap();

        _map.set(C.getKey(), C.getValue());
        _map.set(A.getKey(), A.getValue());
        _map.set(B.getKey(), B.getValue());
        _map.set(D.getKey(), D.getValue());
    }

    protected abstract Map createMap();

    public void testContainsExisting() {
        assertTrue(_map.contains(A.getKey()));
        assertTrue(_map.contains(B.getKey()));
        assertTrue(_map.contains(C.getKey()));
        assertTrue(_map.contains(D.getKey()));
    }

    public void testContainsNonExisting() {
        assertFalse(_map.contains(E.getKey()));
        assertFalse(_map.contains(F.getKey()));
    }

    public void testGetExisting() {
        assertEquals(A.getValue(), _map.get(A.getKey()));
        assertEquals(B.getValue(), _map.get(B.getKey()));
        assertEquals(C.getValue(), _map.get(C.getKey()));
        assertEquals(D.getValue(), _map.get(D.getKey()));
    }

    public void testGetNonExisting() {
        assertNull(_map.get(E.getKey()));
        assertNull(_map.get(F.getKey()));
    }

    public void testSetNewKey() {
        assertEquals(4, _map.size());

        assertNull(_map.set(E.getKey(), E.getValue()));
```

```
        assertEquals(E.getValue(), _map.get(E.getKey()));
        assertEquals(5, _map.size());

        assertNull(_map.set(F.getKey(), F.getValue()));
        assertEquals(F.getValue(), _map.get(F.getKey()));
        assertEquals(6, _map.size());
    }

    public void testSetExistingKey() {
        assertEquals(4, _map.size());
        assertEquals(C.getValue(), _map.set(C.getKey(), "cvalue2"));
        assertEquals("cvalue2", _map.get(C.getKey()));
        assertEquals(4, _map.size());
    }

    public void testDeleteExisting() {
        assertEquals(4, _map.size());

        assertEquals(B.getValue(), _map.delete(B.getKey()));
        assertFalse(_map.contains(B.getKey()));
        assertEquals(3, _map.size());

        assertEquals(A.getValue(), _map.delete(A.getKey()));
        assertFalse(_map.contains(A.getKey()));
        assertEquals(2, _map.size());

        assertEquals(C.getValue(), _map.delete(C.getKey()));
        assertFalse(_map.contains(C.getKey()));
        assertEquals(1, _map.size());

        assertEquals(D.getValue(), _map.delete(D.getKey()));
        assertFalse(_map.contains(D.getKey()));
        assertEquals(0, _map.size());
    }

    public void testDeleteNonExisting() {
        assertEquals(4, _map.size());
        assertNull(_map.delete(E.getKey()));
        assertEquals(4, _map.size());
        assertNull(_map.delete(F.getKey()));
        assertEquals(4, _map.size());
    }

    public void testClear() {
        assertEquals(4, _map.size());
        assertFalse(_map.isEmpty());

        _map.clear();

        assertEquals(0, _map.size());
        assertTrue(_map.isEmpty());

        assertFalse(_map.contains(A.getKey()));
        assertFalse(_map.contains(B.getKey()));
```

```
        assertFalse(_map.contains(C.getKey()));
        assertFalse(_map.contains(D.getKey()));
    }

    public void testIteratorForwards() {
        checkIterator(_map.iterator());
    }

    public void testIteratorBackwards() {
        checkIterator(new ReverseIterator(_map.iterator()));
    }

    private void checkIterator(Iterator i) {
        List entries = new LinkedList();

        for (i.first(); !i.isDone(); i.next()) {
            Map.Entry entry = (Map.Entry) i.current();
            entries.add(new DefaultEntry(entry.getKey(), entry.getValue()));
        }

        try {
            i.current();
            fail();
        } catch (IteratorOutOfBoundsException e) {
            // expected
        }

        assertEquals(4, entries.size());
        assertTrue(entries.contains(A));
        assertTrue(entries.contains(B));
        assertTrue(entries.contains(C));
        assertTrue(entries.contains(D));
    }
}
```

How It Works

The class `AbstractMapTestCase` extends `TestCase` in order to make it a proper JUnit-compatible test class. It also defines some sample entries and a map for testing. The map is assigned a value in the `setUp()` method, which runs just prior to each test case, and the first four keys from the sample entries are associated with their corresponding value in the map.

The abstract `createMap()` method is to be implemented in each concrete subclass of `AbstractMapTestCase`, and is where you will create the specific instance of the map to be tested:

```
package com.wrox.algorithms.maps;

import com.wrox.algorithms.iteration.Iterator;
import com.wrox.algorithms.iteration.ReverseIterator;
import com.wrox.algorithms.lists.LinkedList;
import com.wrox.algorithms.lists.List;
import junit.framework.TestCase;
```

```
public abstract class AbstractMapTestCase extends TestCase {
    private static final Map.Entry A = new DefaultEntry("akey", "avalue");
    private static final Map.Entry B = new DefaultEntry("bkey", "bvalue");
    private static final Map.Entry C = new DefaultEntry("ckey", "cvalue");
    private static final Map.Entry D = new DefaultEntry("dkey", "dvalue");
    private static final Map.Entry E = new DefaultEntry("ekey", "evalue");
    private static final Map.Entry F = new DefaultEntry("fkey", "fvalue");

    private Map _map;

    protected void setUp() throws Exception {
        super.setUp();

        _map = createMap();

        _map.set(C.getKey(), C.getValue());
        _map.set(A.getKey(), A.getValue());
        _map.set(B.getKey(), B.getValue());
        _map.set(D.getKey(), D.getValue());
    }

    protected abstract Map createMap();

    ...
}
```

The `contains()` method should return `true` for any key that is contained within the map and `false` otherwise. You know that four of the sample keys do exist, so in `testContainsExisting()` you check to ensure that `contains()` returns `true` for each one:

```
    public void testContainsExisting() {
        assertTrue(_map.contains(A.getKey()));
        assertTrue(_map.contains(B.getKey()));
        assertTrue(_map.contains(C.getKey()));
        assertTrue(_map.contains(D.getKey()));
    }
```

Conversely, `testContainsNonExisting()` ensures that `contains()` returns `false` for keys that are known not to exist:

```
    public void testContainsNonExisting() {
        assertFalse(_map.contains(E.getKey()));
        assertFalse(_map.contains(F.getKey()));
    }
```

Next, `testGetExisting()` verifies that `get()` returns the correct value for each key that was assigned in the `setUp()` method:

```
    public void testGetExisting() {
        assertEquals(A.getValue(), _map.get(A.getKey()));
        assertEquals(B.getValue(), _map.get(B.getKey()));
        assertEquals(C.getValue(), _map.get(C.getKey()));
        assertEquals(D.getValue(), _map.get(D.getKey()));
    }
```

Similarly, `testGetNonExisting()` verifies that `null` is returned for a few keys known not to exist in the map:

```
public void testGetNonExisting() {
    assertNull(_map.get(E.getKey()));
    assertNull(_map.get(F.getKey()));
}
```

The `testSetNewKey()` method verifies whether you can successfully retrieve stored values. After first checking the initial size of the map, two key/value pairs are added. Each time `set()` is called, the return value is checked to ensure it is `null`, indicating there was no existing value; `get()` is called to ensure that the value is associated with the new key, and the size is checked to ensure it has increased by one:

```
public void testSetNewKey() {
    assertEquals(4, _map.size());

    assertNull(_map.set(E.getKey(), E.getValue()));
    assertEquals(E.getValue(), _map.get(E.getKey()));
    assertEquals(5, _map.size());

    assertNull(_map.set(F.getKey(), F.getValue()));
    assertEquals(F.getValue(), _map.get(F.getKey()));
    assertEquals(6, _map.size());
}
```

The `testSetExistingKey()` method first checks the initial size of the map. Then `set()` is called to associate a new value with an existing key, and the return value is checked to ensure that it matches the original value. A lookup is then performed to ensure that the new value is associated with the key. Finally, the size is checked against the original to verify that it hasn't changed:

```
public void testSetExistingKey() {
    assertEquals(4, _map.size());
    assertEquals(C.getValue(), _map.set(C.getKey(), "cvalue2"));
    assertEquals("cvalue2", _map.get(C.getKey()));
    assertEquals(4, _map.size());
}
```

Next, the `testDeleteExisting()` method calls `delete()` to remove each of the keys added in `setUp()`, and the return value is checked to ensure that it is correct. The `contains()` method is then called to verify that the key no longer exists, and the size is checked to ensure it has been decremented:

```
public void testDeleteExisting() {
    assertEquals(4, _map.size());

    assertEquals(B.getValue(), _map.delete(B.getKey()));
    assertFalse(_map.contains(B.getKey()));
    assertEquals(3, _map.size());

    assertEquals(A.getValue(), _map.delete(A.getKey()));
    assertFalse(_map.contains(A.getKey()));
    assertEquals(2, _map.size());
```

```
        assertEquals(C.getValue(), _map.delete(C.getKey()));
        assertFalse(_map.contains(C.getKey()));
        assertEquals(1, _map.size());

        assertEquals(D.getValue(), _map.delete(D.getKey()));
        assertFalse(_map.contains(D.getKey()));
        assertEquals(0, _map.size());
    }
```

After first checking the size of map, the `testDeleteNonExisting()` method calls `delete()` to remove a key known not to exist. The return value is then tested to make sure it is `null`, and the size is checked once again to ensure there has been no change:

```
    public void testDeleteNonExisting() {
        assertEquals(4, _map.size());
        assertNull(_map.delete(E.getKey()));
        assertEquals(4, _map.size());
        assertNull(_map.delete(F.getKey()));
        assertEquals(4, _map.size());
    }
```

The `testClear()` method first ensures that the map isn't already empty. The `clear()` method is then called and the size is rechecked to confirm that it has been reset to zero. Finally, `contains()` is called for each of the original keys to verify that none still exist:

```
    public void testClear() {
        assertEquals(4, _map.size());
        assertFalse(_map.isEmpty());

        _map.clear();

        assertEquals(0, _map.size());
        assertTrue(_map.isEmpty());

        assertFalse(_map.contains(A.getKey()));
        assertFalse(_map.contains(B.getKey()));
        assertFalse(_map.contains(C.getKey()));
        assertFalse(_map.contains(D.getKey()));
    }
```

Almost all of the work for testing `iterator()` is done in `checkIterator()`. This method iterates over all the entries in the map. Each time an entry is returned, the key and value are used to create a `DefaultEntry`, which is then added to the list. The list is then checked to ensure that the size matches the expected number of entries; and that each of the expected entries exists. Why not just add the entries as they are returned from the map itself? The answer is rather subtle, and something to be aware of, not only in this instance but when working with interfaces in general.

The `contains()` method is called to determine whether the expected entries exist in the list, which in turn calls `equals()` to determine whether the entry being searched for matches any in the list. Now recall that `Map.Entry` is an interface, so the entries returned from the iterator may be of any class that implements `Map.Entry`, not necessarily `DefaultEntry`. This means that there is no guarantee that the equals() method has been implemented or that it will even work as needed when comparing itself with a DefaultEntry. (For the authoritative discussion on equals(), see *Effective Java* [Block, 2001].) Therefore, rather than cross your fingers and hope for the best, you've instead taken the key/value pairs and added them to the list as instances of DefaultEntry, which you know implements the equals() method and is the same class as the expected entries:

```
private void checkIterator(Iterator i) {
    List entries = new LinkedList();

    for (i.first(); !i.isDone(); i.next()) {
        Map.Entry entry = (Map.Entry) i.current();
        entries.add(new DefaultEntry(entry.getKey(), entry.getValue()));
    }

    try {
        i.current();
        fail();
    } catch (IteratorOutOfBoundsException e) {
        // expected
    }

    assertEquals(4, entries.size());
    assertTrue(entries.contains(A));
    assertTrue(entries.contains(B));
    assertTrue(entries.contains(C));
    assertTrue(entries.contains(D));
}
```

Then, to test forwards iteration, testIteratorForwards() simply obtains an iterator from the map and hands it off to checkIterator():

```
public void testIteratorForwards() {
    checkIterator(_map.iterator());
}
```

Finally, to test reverse iteration, testIteratorBackwards() wraps the iterator in a ReverseIterator (from Chapter 2) before calling checkIterator(). In this way, all calls to first() and next() will be redirected to last() and previous(), respectively—meaning you don't have to write a separate set of tests:

```
public void testIteratorBackwards() {
    checkIterator(new ReverseIterator(_map.iterator()));
}
```

A List Map

In the next Try It Out section you create a map that uses a list as the underlying storage mechanism. The implementation is very straightforward and easy to follow; and although it isn't particularly efficient, it is useful for small data sets.

Try It Out — Testing and Implementing a List Map

Start by creating the `ListMapTest` as follows:

```
package com.wrox.algorithms.maps;

public class ListMapTest extends AbstractMapTestCase {
    protected Map createMap() {
        return new ListMap();
    }
}
```

Then create the `ListMap` class itself:

```
package com.wrox.algorithms.maps;

import com.wrox.algorithms.iteration.Iterator;
import com.wrox.algorithms.lists.LinkedList;
import com.wrox.algorithms.lists.List;

public class ListMap implements Map {
    private final List _entries = new LinkedList();

    public Object get(Object key) {
        DefaultEntry entry = entryFor(key);
        return entry != null ? entry.getValue() : null;
    }

    public Object set(Object key, Object value) {
        DefaultEntry entry = entryFor(key);
        if (entry != null) {
            return entry.setValue(value);
        }

        _entries.add(new DefaultEntry(key, value));
        return null;
    }

    public Object delete(Object key) {
        DefaultEntry entry = entryFor(key);
        if (entry == null) {
            return null;
        }

        _entries.delete(entry);
        return entry.getValue();
    }

    public boolean contains(Object key) {
        return entryFor(key) != null;
    }

    public void clear() {
        _entries.clear();
```

```
    }

    public int size() {
        return _entries.size();
    }

    public boolean isEmpty() {
        return _entries.isEmpty();
    }

    public Iterator iterator() {
        return _entries.iterator();
    }

    private DefaultEntry entryFor(Object key) {
        Iterator i = iterator();
        for (i.first(); !i.isDone(); i.next()) {
            DefaultEntry entry = (DefaultEntry) i.current();
            if (entry.getKey().equals(key)) {
                return entry;
            }
        }

        return null;
    }
}
```

How It Works

Because the test cases themselves have already been created, all you do for `ListMapTest` is extend `AbstractMapTest` and implement `createMap()` to return an instance of your `ListMap` class:

```
package com.wrox.algorithms.maps;

public class ListMapTest extends AbstractMapTestCase {
    protected Map createMap() {
        return new ListMap();
    }
}
```

With the tests in place, you then move on to the map implementation itself in the form of the `ListMap` class. This class holds nothing more than the list that will be used for storing the contained entries. The `clear()`, `size()`, `isEmpty()`, and `iterator()` methods all just delegate to the methods of the same name:

```
package com.wrox.algorithms.maps;

import com.wrox.algorithms.iteration.Iterator;
import com.wrox.algorithms.lists.LinkedList;
import com.wrox.algorithms.lists.List;

public class ListMap implements Map {
    private final List _entries = new LinkedList();

    public void clear() {
```

```
            _entries.clear();
        }

        public int size() {
            return _entries.size();
        }

        public boolean isEmpty() {
            return _entries.isEmpty();
        }

        public Iterator iterator() {
            return _entries.iterator();
        }

        ...
    }
```

The private `entryFor()` method obtains an entry (if any exists) for a given key. This method simply iterates through all the entries in the list, comparing the key of the entry to the search key. If a matching entry is found, it is returned; otherwise, `null` is returned to indicate that no such entry exists:

```
        private DefaultEntry entryFor(Object key) {
            Iterator i = iterator();
            for (i.first(); !i.isDone(); i.next()) {
                DefaultEntry entry = (DefaultEntry) i.current();
                if (entry.getKey().equals(key)) {
                    return entry;
                }
            }

            return null;
        }
```

Based on this, you implement `get()` to return the associated value. In this method, `entryFor()` is called to find the appropriate entry for the given key. If one is found (`entry != null`), then the value is returned; otherwise, `null` is returned to indicate that no such key exists:

```
        public Object get(Object key) {
            DefaultEntry entry = entryFor(key);
            return entry != null ? entry.getValue() : null;
        }
```

You also implement `contains()` in a similar manner by attempting to find an entry for a given key and returning `true` only if one exists:

```
        public boolean contains(Object key) {
            return entryFor(key) != null;
        }
```

The `set()` method first calls `entryFor()` to determine whether an entry already exists for the given key. If an entry is found, then its value is updated and the old value returned. If no matching entry was found, however, then a new one is added to the end of the underlying list, and `null` is returned accordingly:

```
    public Object set(Object key, Object value) {
        DefaultEntry entry = entryFor(key);
        if (entry != null) {
            return entry.setValue(value);
        }

        _entries.add(new DefaultEntry(key, value));
        return null;
    }
```

Lastly, `delete()` is called to remove a key/value pair from the map. As with the previous methods, `delete()` starts by calling `entryFor()`. In this case, however, if no entry is found, `null` is returned to indicate that the key did not exist; otherwise, the entry is deleted from the underlying list and the value is returned to the caller:

```
    public Object delete(Object key) {
        DefaultEntry entry = entryFor(key);
        if (entry == null) {
            return null;
        }

        _entries.delete(entry);
        return entry.getValue();
    }
```

There you have it—your first map implementation. The code for the `ListMap` class is very simple, and most of the work is performed by the underlying list. In this case, the simplicity comes at a price: The performance of `ListMap` is dependent on the performance of the underlying list, which is `O(N)`. This isn't particularly efficient, but for relatively small data sets, a list-based map may be enough.

A Hash Map

The next type of map you will create is based on a hash tables (covered in Chapter 11). At this point, you might like to refresh your understanding of hashing concepts—in particular, hash tables that use buckets—and the code for the `BucketingHashtable` class.

In the next Try It Out section, you start by creating the tests that will ensure the correct behavior before creating the hash map implementation proper.

Try It Out Testing and Implementing a Hash Map

Create the test class as follows:

```
package com.wrox.algorithms.maps;

public class HashMapTest extends AbstractMapTestCase {
    protected Map createMap() {
        return new HashMap();
    }
}
```

Then create the hash map implementation:

```
package com.wrox.algorithms.maps;

import com.wrox.algorithms.hashing.HashtableIterator;
import com.wrox.algorithms.iteration.ArrayIterator;
import com.wrox.algorithms.iteration.Iterator;

public class HashMap implements Map {
    public static final int DEFAULT_CAPACITY = 17;
    public static final float DEFAULT_LOAD_FACTOR = 0.75f;

    private final int _initialCapacity;
    private final float _loadFactor;
    private ListMap[] _buckets;
    private int _size;

    public HashMap() {
        this(DEFAULT_CAPACITY, DEFAULT_LOAD_FACTOR);
    }

    public HashMap(int initialCapacity) {
        this(initialCapacity, DEFAULT_LOAD_FACTOR);
    }

    public HashMap(int initialCapacity, float loadFactor) {
        assert initialCapacity > 0 : "initialCapacity can't be < 1";
        assert loadFactor > 0 : "loadFactor can't be <= 0";

        _initialCapacity = initialCapacity;
        _loadFactor = loadFactor;
        clear();
    }

    public Object get(Object key) {
        ListMap bucket = _buckets[bucketIndexFor(key)];
        return bucket != null ? bucket.get(key) : null;
    }

    public Object set(Object key, Object value) {
        ListMap bucket = bucketFor(key);

        int sizeBefore = bucket.size();
        Object oldValue = bucket.set(key, value);
        if (bucket.size() > sizeBefore) {
            ++_size;
            maintainLoad();
        }

        return oldValue;
    }

    public Object delete(Object key) {
        ListMap bucket = _buckets[bucketIndexFor(key)];
```

```
        if (bucket == null) {
            return null;
        }

        int sizeBefore = bucket.size();
        Object value = bucket.delete(key);
        if (bucket.size() < sizeBefore) {
            --_size;
        }

        return value;
    }

    public boolean contains(Object key) {
        ListMap bucket = _buckets[bucketIndexFor(key)];
        return bucket != null && bucket.contains(key);
    }

    public Iterator iterator() {
        return new HashtableIterator(new ArrayIterator(_buckets));
    }

    public void clear() {
        _buckets = new ListMap[_initialCapacity];
        _size = 0;
    }

    public int size() {
        return _size;
    }

    public boolean isEmpty() {
        return size() == 0;
    }

    private int bucketIndexFor(Object key) {
        assert key != null : "key can't be null";
        return Math.abs(key.hashCode() % _buckets.length);
    }

    private ListMap bucketFor(Object key) {
        int bucketIndex = bucketIndexFor(key);
        ListMap bucket = _buckets[bucketIndex];
        if (bucket == null) {
            bucket = new ListMap();
            _buckets[bucketIndex] = bucket;
        }
        return bucket;
    }

    private void maintainLoad() {
        if (loadFactorExceeded()) {
            resize();
```

```
        }
    }

    private boolean loadFactorExceeded() {
        return size() > _buckets.length * _loadFactor;
    }

    private void resize() {
        HashMap copy = new HashMap(_buckets.length * 2, _loadFactor);

        for (int i = 0; i < _buckets.length; ++i) {
            if (_buckets[i] != null) {
                copy.addAll(_buckets[i].iterator());
            }
        }

        _buckets = copy._buckets;
    }

    private void addAll(Iterator entries) {
        assert entries != null : "entries can't be null";

        for (entries.first(); !entries.isDone(); entries.next()) {
            Map.Entry entry = (Map.Entry) entries.current();
            set(entry.getKey(), entry.getValue());
        }
    }
}
```

How It Works

The `HashMapTest` class extends `AbstractMapTestCase` in order to re-use all the tests you created earlier. Other than that, all that you need to do is implement `createMap()` to return an instance of the `HashMap` class.

For the most part, the `HashMap` class is a copy of the code for `BucketingHashtable` introduced in Chapter 11. For this reason, the discussion concentrates only on the differences between the `HashMap` and the original `BucketingHashtable` code.

In addition to implementing the `Map` interface, probably the first thing you'll notice—besides a few constants and convenience constructors—is that you've used a `ListMap` for the buckets instead of a `List` as in the original `BucketingHashtable` code. You can think of the hash map as distributing (hopefully, fairly evenly) the key/value pairs between list maps. You know from Chapter 11 that the buckets will be kept relatively small, so the list-based maps will perform just fine. Therefore, by using a map instead of a list for your buckets, you simplify the code—once the appropriate bucket has been found, all the work of adding the key/value pair is delegated to it. This can be seen in the code for `get()`, `set()`, `delete()`, and `contains()`, where most of the work is carried out by the bucket, leaving the hash map code to perform the housekeeping duties, such as resizing, and so on.

The other obvious difference between `HashMap` and `BucketingHashtable` is that the buckets store entries. Therefore, when resizing, `addAll()` iterates through each of the key/value pairs, rather than just the values, as was the case in the original.

Lastly, because a Map is also an Iterable—and therefore so is ListMap—you can re-use the HashtableIterator from Chapter 11 to iterate over the entries.

Assuming a good hash function for the keys, you can expect to achieve fairly close to O(1) performance for the HashMap.

A Tree Map

As previously mentioned, maps don't generally guarantee any particular ordering of the keys: A ListMap, for example, will present the entries in order of insertion, whereas entries from a HashMap iterator will appear somewhat randomly. Sometimes, however, you may want a predictable ordering of the keys. In this case, a map implementation based on binary search trees is ideal.

Before proceeding with the implementation of tree-based maps, we recommend that you revisit binary search trees (see Chapter 10) to refresh your understanding of the core concepts and code, as once again, the discussion will be limited to only the differences between the TreeMap code presented here and the original BinarySearchTree code.

Try It Out Testing and Implementing a Tree Map

Starting by creating the TreeMapTest class as follows:

```
package com.wrox.algorithms.maps;

public class TreeMapTest extends AbstractMapTestCase {
    protected Map createMap() {
        return new TreeMap();
    }
}
```

Follow with the tree map implementation:

```
package com.wrox.algorithms.maps;

import com.wrox.algorithms.iteration.Iterator;
import com.wrox.algorithms.iteration.IteratorOutOfBoundsException;
import com.wrox.algorithms.sorting.Comparator;
import com.wrox.algorithms.sorting.NaturalComparator;

public class TreeMap implements Map {
    private final Comparator _comparator;
    private Node _root;
    private int _size;

    public TreeMap() {
        this(NaturalComparator.INSTANCE);
    }

    public TreeMap(Comparator comparator) {
        assert comparator != null : "comparator can't be null";
```

```
        _comparator = comparator;
    }

    public boolean contains(Object key) {
        return search(key) != null;
    }

    public Object get(Object key) {
        Node node = search(key);
        return node != null ? node.getValue() : null;
    }

    public Object set(Object key, Object value) {
        Node parent = null;
        Node node = _root;
        int cmp = 0;

        while (node != null) {
            parent = node;
            cmp = _comparator.compare(key, node.getKey());
            if (cmp == 0) {
                return node.setValue(value);
            }

            node = cmp < 0 ? node.getSmaller() : node.getLarger();
        }

        Node inserted = new Node(parent, key, value);

        if (parent == null) {
            _root = inserted;
        } else if (cmp < 0) {
            parent.setSmaller(inserted);
        } else {
            parent.setLarger(inserted);
        }

        ++_size;
        return null;
    }

    public Object delete(Object key) {
        Node node = search(key);
        if (node == null) {
            return null;
        }

        Node deleted = node.getSmaller() != null && node.getLarger() != null ?
node.successor() : node;
        assert deleted != null : "deleted can't be null";

        Node replacement = deleted.getSmaller() != null ? deleted.getSmaller() :
deleted.getLarger();
        if (replacement != null) {
            replacement.setParent(deleted.getParent());
```

```
        }

        if (deleted == _root) {
            _root = replacement;
        } else if (deleted.isSmaller()) {
            deleted.getParent().setSmaller(replacement);
        } else {
            deleted.getParent().setLarger(replacement);
        }

        if (deleted != node) {
            Object deletedValue = node.getValue();
            node.setKey(deleted.getKey());
            node.setValue(deleted.getValue());
            deleted.setValue(deletedValue);
        }

        --_size;
        return deleted.getValue();
    }

    public Iterator iterator() {
        return new EntryIterator();
    }

    public void clear() {
        _root = null;
        _size = 0;
    }

    public int size() {
        return _size;
    }

    public boolean isEmpty() {
        return _root == null;
    }

    private Node search(Object value) {
        assert value != null : "value can't be null";

        Node node = _root;

        while (node != null) {
            int cmp = _comparator.compare(value, node.getKey());
            if (cmp == 0) {
                break;
            }

            node = cmp < 0 ? node.getSmaller() : node.getLarger();
        }

        return node;
    }

    private static final class Node implements Map.Entry {
```

```
        private Object _key;
        private Object _value;
        private Node _parent;
        private Node _smaller;
        private Node _larger;

        public Node(Node parent, Object key, Object value) {
            setKey(key);
            setValue(value);
            setParent(parent);
        }

        public Object getKey() {
            return _key;
        }

        public void setKey(Object key) {
            assert key != null : "key can't be null";
            _key = key;
        }

        public Object getValue() {
            return _value;
        }

        public Object setValue(Object value) {
            Object oldValue = _value;
            _value = value;
            return oldValue;
        }

        public Node getParent() {
            return _parent;
        }

        public void setParent(Node parent) {
            _parent = parent;
        }

        public Node getSmaller() {
            return _smaller;
        }

        public void setSmaller(Node node) {
            assert node != getLarger() : "smaller can't be the same as larger";
            _smaller = node;
        }

        public Node getLarger() {
            return _larger;
        }


        public void setLarger(Node node) {
```

```
        assert node != getSmaller() : "larger can't be the same as smaller";
        _larger = node;
    }

    public boolean isSmaller() {
        return getParent() != null && this == getParent().getSmaller();
    }

    public boolean isLarger() {
        return getParent() != null && this == getParent().getLarger();
    }

    public Node minimum() {
        Node node = this;

        while (node.getSmaller() != null) {
            node = node.getSmaller();
        }

        return node;
    }

    public Node maximum() {
        Node node = this;

        while (node.getLarger() != null) {
            node = node.getLarger();
        }

        return node;
    }

    public Node successor() {
        if (getLarger() != null) {
            return getLarger().minimum();
        }

        Node node = this;

        while (node.isLarger()) {
            node = node.getParent();
        }

        return node.getParent();
    }

    public Node predecessor() {
        if (getSmaller() != null) {
            return getSmaller().maximum();
        }

        Node node = this;

        while (node.isSmaller()) {
            node = node.getParent();
```

```
            }

            return node.getParent();
        }
    }

    private final class EntryIterator implements Iterator {
        private Node _current;

        public void first() {
            _current = _root != null ? _root.minimum() : null;
        }

        public void last() {
            _current = _root != null ? _root.maximum() : null;
        }

        public boolean isDone() {
            return _current == null;
        }

        public void next() {
            if (!isDone()) {
                _current = _current.successor();
            }
        }

        public void previous() {
            if (!isDone()) {
                _current = _current.predecessor();
            }
        }

        public Object current() throws IteratorOutOfBoundsException {
            if (isDone()) {
                throw new IteratorOutOfBoundsException();
            }
            return _current;
        }
    }
}
```

How It Works

The `TreeMapTest` class extends `AbstractMapTestCase` to re-use all of the tests you created earlier with `createMap()`, returning an instance of the `TreeMap` class.

The code for `TreeMap` follows very closely the code you developed for `BinarySearchTree` in Chapter 10. Besides the fact that this class implements the `Map` interface, the most obvious difference you'll see if you browse the code is that almost everywhere the original code referenced a value, `TreeMap` uses the key. To this end, the comparator is used to compare keys, not values, and thus the tree is ordered by key.

You'll also notice that `Node` has been made an inner class; and, instead of having each node hold an entry, you've instead made `Node` implement `Map.Entry` directly. The original node implementation already held a value, so all you needed to do was add a key and modify `setValue()` slightly to return the original value, just as you did with the `DefaultEntry` earlier.

Next, the original `insert()` method has been renamed to `set()`. Whereas the original `insert()` method worked off values and allowed duplicates, the map uses keys, all of which must be unique. Additionally, `set()` returns any value previously associated with the key.

The `while` loop in the original `insert()` method looked like this:

```
while (node != null) {
    parent = node;
    cmp = _comparator.compare(value, node.getValue());
    node = cmp <= 0 ? node.getSmaller() : node.getLarger();
}
```

Notice that when a duplicate value was inserted, it would always be added as a left child of any similar value. The `set()` method now looks like this:

```
while (node != null) {
    parent = node;
    cmp = _comparator.compare(key, node.getKey());
    if (cmp == 0) {
        return node.setValue(value);
    }

    node = cmp < 0 ? node.getSmaller() : node.getLarger();
}
```

Here, if an existing key is found (`cmp == 0`), the method updates the value and returns the old value immediately; otherwise, the code proceeds as per the original.

The next change is that the `search()` method has been made private, and instead there is the `contains()` method as required by the `Map` interface. The `contains()` method then returns `true` only if `search` actually finds a matching node.

Apart from the addition of the `clear()`, `isEmpty()`, `size()`, and `iterator()` methods—again mandated by the `Map` interface—the only other change of note is the `EntryIterator` inner class, which iterates forwards or backwards over the nodes in order—and therefore the entries—by calling `successor()` and `predecessor()`, respectively.

That's it: a map implementation that, as you know from Chapter 10, has an average performance of `O(log N)` as well as the added bonus of maintaining the entries in order, sorted by key.

Summary

This chapter demonstrated the following:

- Maps store values associated with a key.
- Each key within a map is unique and enables you to quickly locate its associated value.

- Maps are also known as associative arrays, dictionaries, indexes, and lookup tables.
- In general, a map makes no guarantee of the iteration order.
- Three common map implementations are the list map, the hash map, and the tree map.
- List-based maps are useful for relatively small data sets, as operations run in `O(N)`.
- Hash table–based map operations run in `O(1)` with random iteration order.
- Binary search tree–based sets provide `O(log N)` performance as well as predictable iteration order.

Exercises

1. Create an iterator that returns only the keys contained within a map.
2. Create an iterator that returns only the values contained within a map.
3. Create a set implementation that uses a map as the underlying storage mechanism for the values.
4. Create an empty map that throws `UnsupportedOperationException` anytime an attempt is made to modify it.

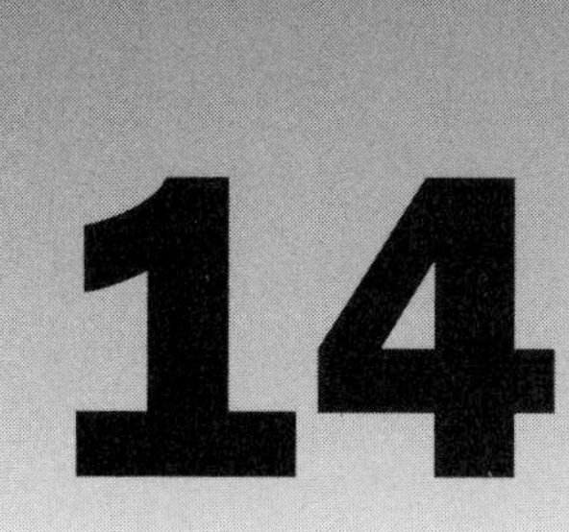

Ternary Search Trees

So far, you've learned a number of ways to store data — from simple, unordered lists to sorted lists, binary search trees, and even hash tables. All of these are great for storing objects of arbitrary types. You're about to learn one last data structure for storing strings. It's not only fast to search, it also enables you to perform some quite different and interesting forms of searching.

This chapter discusses the following topics:

- General properties of ternary search trees
- How words are stored
- How words can be looked up
- How ternary search trees can be used for creating a dictionary
- How to implement a simple application to help solve crossword puzzles

Understanding Ternary Search Trees

Ternary search trees are specialized structures for storing and retrieving strings. Like a binary search tree, each node holds a reference to the smaller and larger values. However, unlike a binary search tree, a ternary search tree doesn't hold the entire value in each node. Instead, a node holds a single letter from a word, and another reference — hence ternary — to a subtree of nodes containing any letters that follow it in the word.

Figure 14-1 shows how you could store "cup," "ape," "bat," "map," and "man" in a ternary search tree. Notice that we have depicted the siblings — smaller and larger letters — as solid links, and the children — letters that follow — as dashed links.

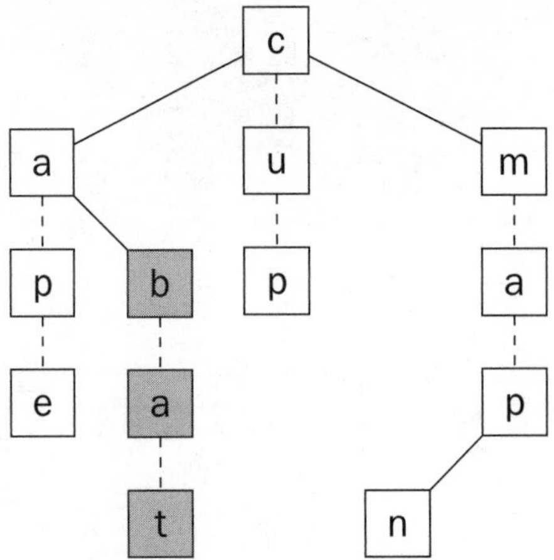

Figure 14-1: A sample ternary search tree with "c" as the root. The highlighted nodes trace out a path for "bat."

Although it doesn't look much like one, if you take out the child links at the first level, then you'd have a perfectly valid binary search tree containing the values `a`, `b`, `c`, and `m`. You've just added an extra reference from each node to its child.

At each level, just like a binary search tree, each left node is smaller — `b` is larger than `a`, which is smaller than `c`, which is smaller than `m` — and each child node represents the next letter in a word — a comes after `b`, followed by `t`, in "bat."

Searching for a Word

At each level in the tree, you perform a binary search starting with the first letter of the word for which you are looking. Just like searching a binary search tree, you start at the root and follow links left and right as appropriate. Once you find a matching node, you move down one level to its child and start again, this time with the second letter of the word. This continues until you either find all the letters — in which case, you have a match — or you run out of nodes.

To get a better idea of how a ternary search tree works, the following example searches for the word "bat" in the tree shown in Figure 14-1.

The search starts at the root node, `c`, looking for the first letter of the search word, a, as shown in Figure 14-2.

Because you don't yet have a match, you need to visit one of the siblings — if there are any — and try again. In this case, your search letter, `a`, sorts before the current node, `c`, so you try the left sibling (see Figure 14-3).

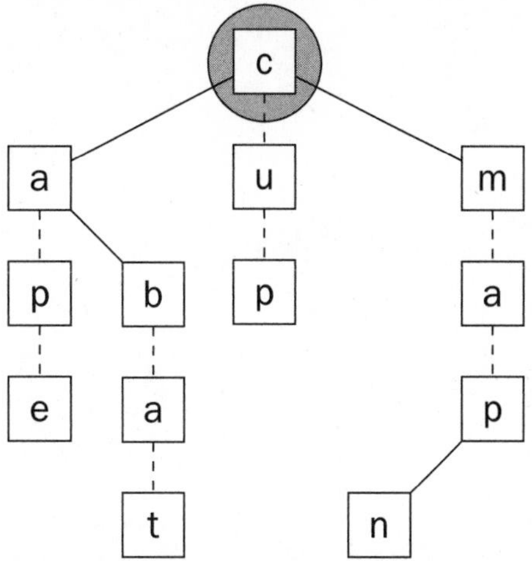

Figure 14-2: A search for the first letter at the root of the tree.

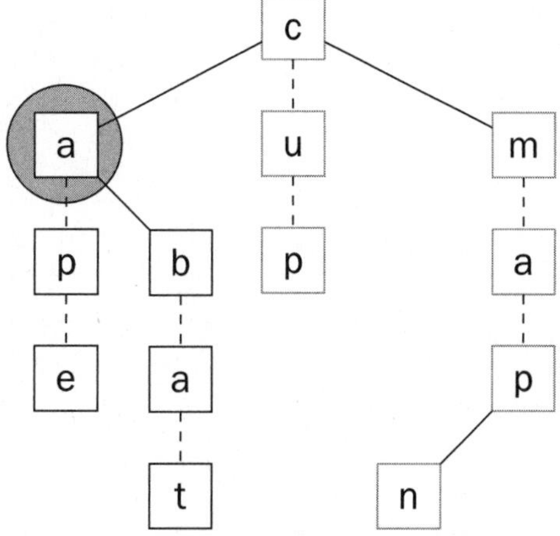

Figure 14-3: The letter b sorts before c, so you follow the left link.

Next, you compare your search letter with the letter at the next node, but again you find a mismatch. However, because `b` sorts after `a`, this time you need to follow a right link (see Figure 14-4).

Finally, you have a match for the first letter of the word, so you can move on to the second letter, `a`, starting with the first child of `b`, as shown in Figure 14-5.

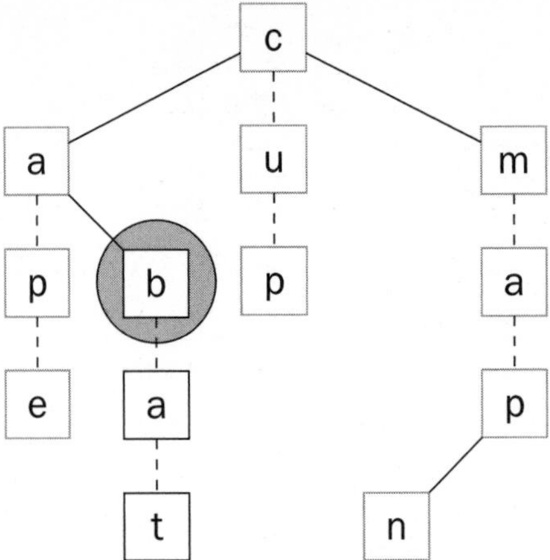

Figure 14-4: The letter b sorts after a, so you follow the right link.

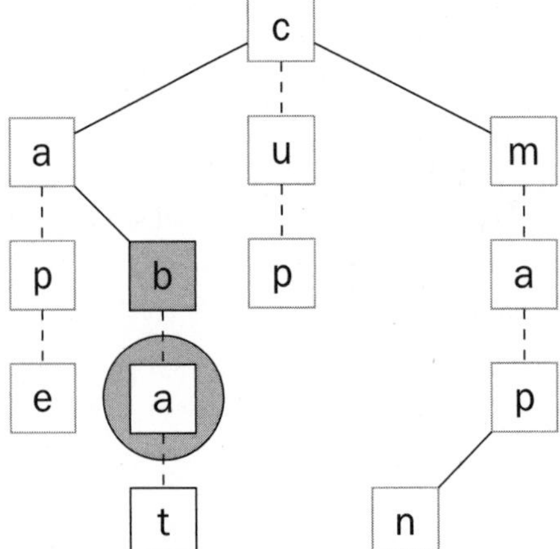

Figure 14-5: A search for the next letter starts at the first child.

This time, you get a hit straightaway, so repeating the process, you move on to the third letter, `t`, and continue searching at the next child node (see Figure 14-6).

Once again you find a matching letter and, because there are no more letters in the search word, a matching word, and you did so in a total of five individual character comparisons.

At each level, you're looking for a letter in a binary search tree. Once found, you move down a level and perform another search in a binary search tree for the next letter. This is done for all the letters of the word you are looking for. From this, you can deduce the run time for performing a lookup in your ternary search tree. You might guess that ternary search trees are at least as efficient as binary search trees. It turns out, however, that ternary search trees can actually be more efficient than simple binary search trees.

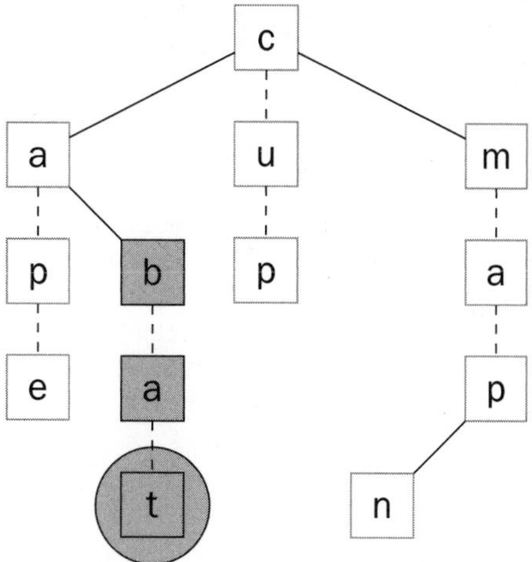

Figure 14-6: The search ends when the last letter is found.

Imagine you were looking for the word "man" in the tree from Figure 14-1. Count the character comparisons. First you would compare "m" with "c" (one). Next, you compare "m" with "m" (two), followed by "a" with "a" (three). You're now at the last letter, so you compare "n" with "p" (four) and eventually "n" with "n" (five).

Now compare the same search in an binary search tree that stores the same words, as shown in Figure 14-7. First you compare "man" with "cup," but as you get a mismatch on the first letter, you can move to the next node having performed only one letter comparison. Next you compare "man" with "map"; that's an extra three comparisons. Finally, you compare "man" with "man" for another three comparisons, giving you a grand total of `1 + 3 + 3 = 7` single-letter comparisons.

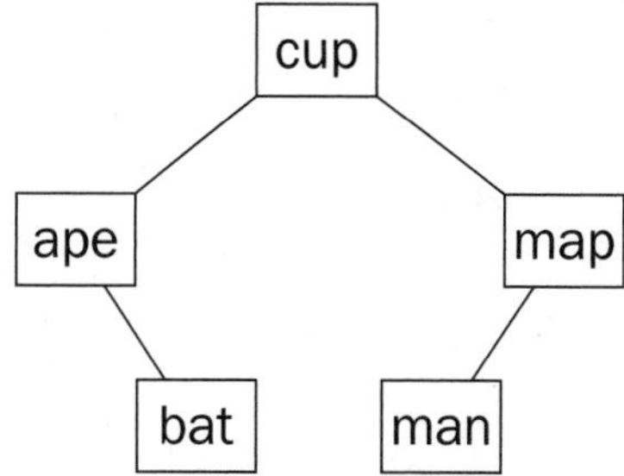

Figure 14-7: An equivalent binary search tree.

Even in such a simple tree as the one used here, you can see that a ternary search tree performs far fewer individual character comparisons compared with an equivalent binary search tree. This is because words that share a common prefix are *compressed*. Having traversed those common letters, you need never compare them again. Compare this with a binary search tree, in which you continually compare all the letters from each node, as shown previously.

In addition to being efficient at finding positive results, ternary search trees particularly excel at quickly discarding words that don't exist in the tree. Whereas a binary search tree continues searching until it runs out of nodes at the leaves, a ternary search tree will terminate as soon as no matching prefix is found.

Now that you understand how searching works, you can work out the general performance characteristics for ternary search trees. Imagine that every level contained all the letters from the alphabet arranged as nodes in a binary search tree. If the size of the alphabet (for example, A to Z for English) is represented by `M`, then you know that a search at any given level will take on average `O(log M)` comparisons. Of course, that's just for one letter. To find a word of length `N`, you would need to perform one binary search for each letter, or `O(N log M)` comparisons. In practice, however, the performance turns out to be much better due to common prefixes and the fact that not every letter of the alphabet appears at each level of each branch in the tree.

Inserting a Word

Inserting a word into a ternary search tree isn't much more difficult than performing a search; you simply add extra leaf nodes for any letters that don't already exist. In Figure 14-8, you can see that inserting the word "bats" requires the addition of a single child node, tacked onto the end of the existing word "bat," whereas inserting the word "mat" adds a single node as a sibling of the letter "p" in "map."

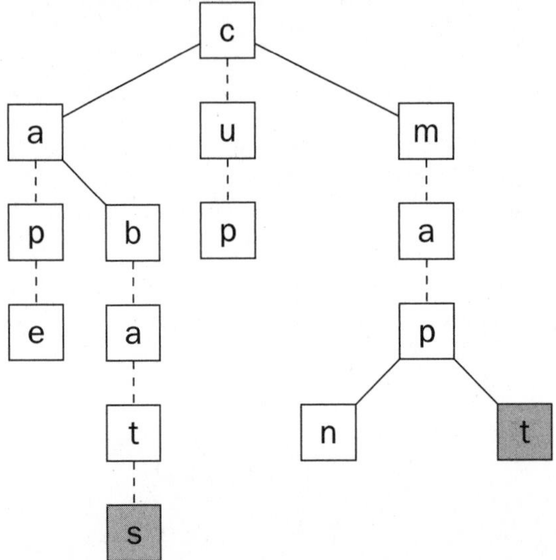

Figure 14-8: Inserting "bats" or "mat" requires the addition of only one extra node.

Of course, you now have a situation in which multiple words—"bat" and its plural, "bats"—share a common prefix. How can you tell them apart? How do you determine that "bat" is a word and so is "bats," but that "ba," "b," or even "ap" aren't?

The answer is simple: You store some associated information along with each node that tells you when you have found the end of a word, as shown in Figure 14-9. This associated information might take the form of a simple Boolean yes or no flag if all you needed was to determine whether a given search word was valid or not; or it might be the definition of the word if you were to implement a dictionary, for example. It doesn't really matter what is used — the important point is that you mark, in some way, only those nodes that represent the last letter in a word.

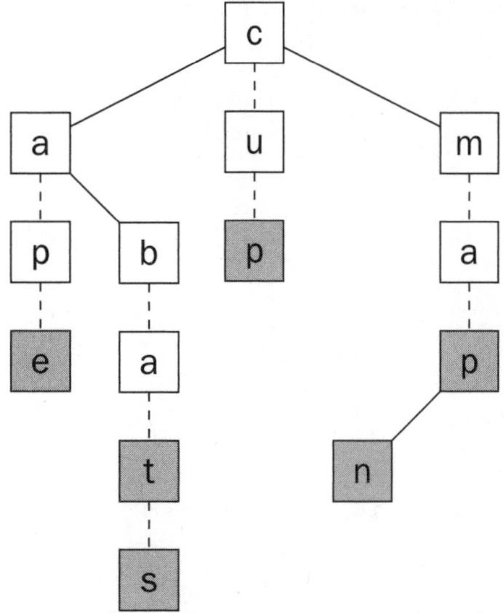

Figure 14-9: Nodes are marked to show they represent the end of a word.

So far, you've only shown balanced trees, but just like binary search trees, ternary search trees can become unbalanced. The tree shown in Figure 14-9 is the result of inserting words in the order "cup," "ape," "bat," "map," and "man," but what would happen if you inserted the words in sorted order: "ape," "bat," "cup," "man," and "map" instead? Unfortunately, in-order insertion of words leads to an unbalanced tree, as shown in Figure 14-10.

While searching a balanced ternary search tree runs in `O(N log M)` comparisons, searching an unbalanced tree requires `O(NM)` comparisons. The difference could be quite substantial for very large values of M, although in practice you typically see much better performance due to prefix-sharing and the fact that not every letter of the alphabet is represented on each level.

Prefix Searching

Perhaps you have used an application or a website that allowed you to select a value from a list by typing the first couple of letters from a word. As you type, the list of possibilities narrows until eventually it contains only a handful of values.

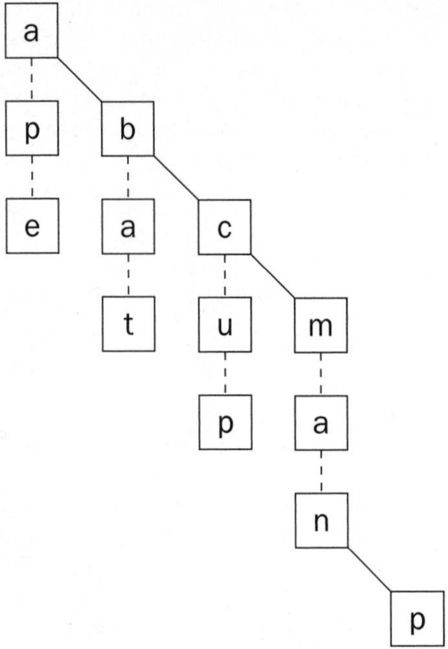

Figure 14-10: In-order insertion leads to an unbalanced tree.

One interesting use for a ternary search tree is finding all words with a common prefix. The trick is to perform a standard search of the tree using only the prefix. Then perform an in-order traversal looking for every end-of-word marker in every subtree of the prefix.

An in-order traversal of a ternary search tree is very similar to that of a binary search tree except, of course, you need to include traversal of the child node. Having found the last node in the prefix, follow these steps:

1. Traverse the left subtree of the node.
2. Visit the node itself.
3. Traverse the node's children.
4. Traverse the right subtree.

Figure 14-11 shows the first match for the prefix "ma."

Having found the prefix, you start by traversing the left subtree, which in this case returns "man." Next you traverse the node itself: "ma." However, it doesn't mark the end of a word. You would now traverse any children if there were any. Finally, you traverse the right subtree as shown in Figure 14-12, resulting in a match with "map."

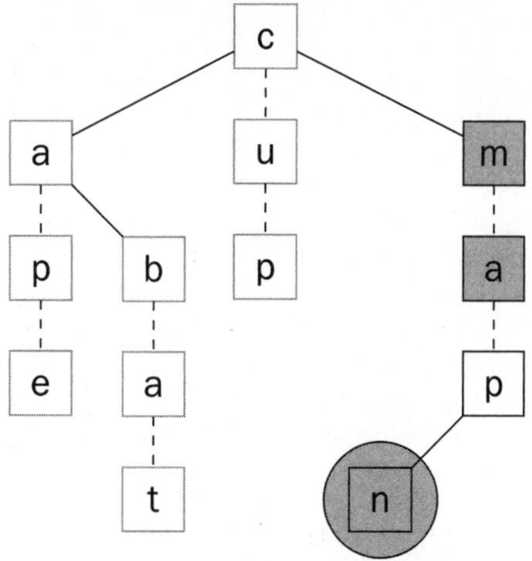

Figure 14-11: The first end-point for prefix "ma" is for "man."

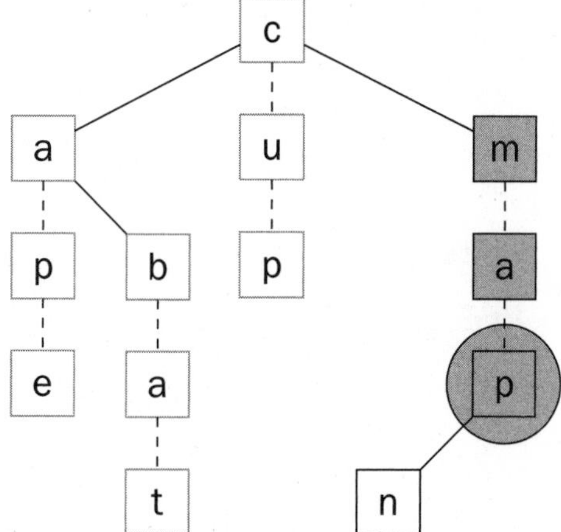

Figure 14-12: The next end-point for the prefix "ma" is for "map."

As you traverse the tree, you can either print out the words as you find them or collect them and use them in another way — for example, displaying them in a list to a user.

Pattern Matching

Have you ever been doing a crossword puzzle or playing a game of Scrabble and racked your brain to think of a word that would fit between the existing letters? There in front of you are the letters: "a-r---t" — but not a single possibility springs to mind.

One rather novel way in which ternary search trees can be used is for solving just such a problem: finding all the words that match a given pattern. A pattern is made up of a combination of regular word letters—a to z—and a special wildcard that matches anything. In the example just shown, you have used the hyphen (-) as the wildcard, but you could just as easily use a period (.) or even a question mark (?). The important thing is to choose something that won't appear as part of a normal word.

You should already be familiar with how basic searching in a ternary search tree works. Possibly the simplest way to perform a pattern match would be to use brute force: Take the pattern and construct a search word by substituting the wildcards with every possible combination of letters. Therefore, given our previous example, you might start with "aaraaat" followed by "aaraabt" and then "aaraact," and so on, all the way up to "azrzzzt." While this would work, it would be extremely slow, with a large proportion of obviously fruitless searches. Instead, you can take a more sophisticated and efficient approach by using the structure of the ternary search tree to your advantage.

Pattern matching is similar to a straight word search except that anytime you come across a wildcard, rather than look for a node with a matching letter (you won't find one), you instead visit each node as if it was a match.

Imagine you are looking for the pattern "-a-" in the tree shown in Figure 14-1. Just like a regular word search, you start at the root node. In this case, though, the first character is a wildcard, so you visit each node at the current level in sorted order. Figure 14-13 shows the search beginning at the smallest node, `a`.

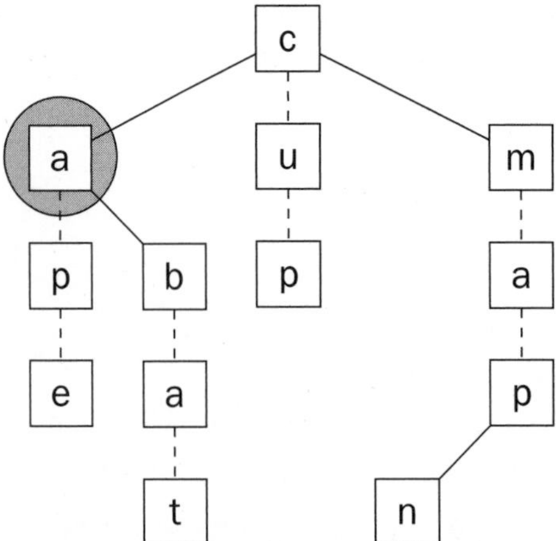

Figure 14-13: A wildcard forces a visit to each node at the current level, starting with the smallest.

Because you are searching for a wildcard, you "pretend" that each node at the current level is a match, so you proceed to match the next letter in the pattern, starting at the child of the current node.

Figure 14-14 shows that, in this instance, the next pattern character—`a`—fails to match the child node—`p`—so this branch of the tree is ignored completely.

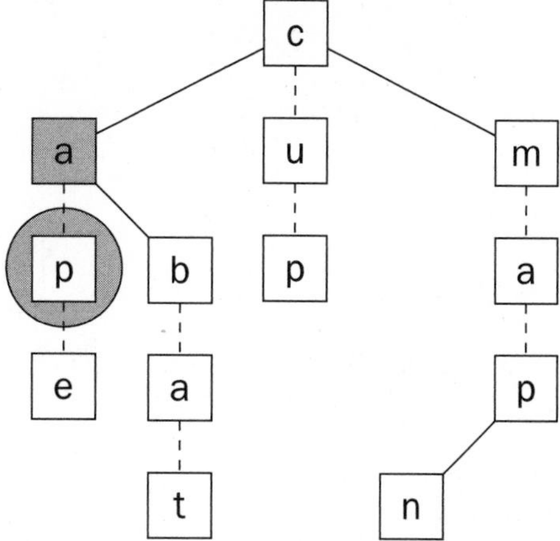

Figure 14-14: A nonmatching character terminates the search for the current branch.

Having decided there can be no possible matches down this path, the search goes back to the previous level to continue searching at the next largest node (see Figure 14-15).

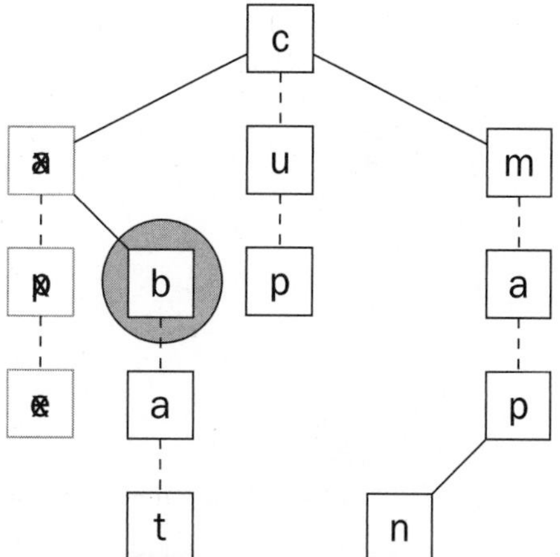

Figure 14-15: The wildcard search continues at the higher level, visiting the next largest node.

Again, because you are looking for a wildcard, you assume a match has been found and proceed to the next letter in the pattern, starting at the child node as shown in Figure 14-16.

This time, the "a" from the pattern matches the "a" in the tree, but there is still more pattern to match, so you continue searching at the child node for the next letter (see Figure 14-17).

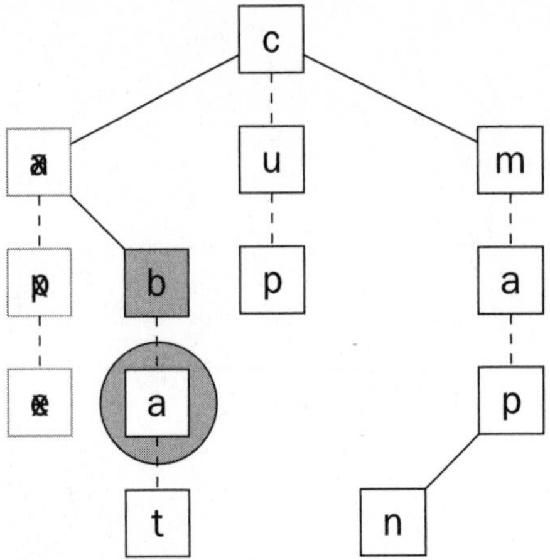

Figure 14-16: This time, you find a match with the next pattern character.

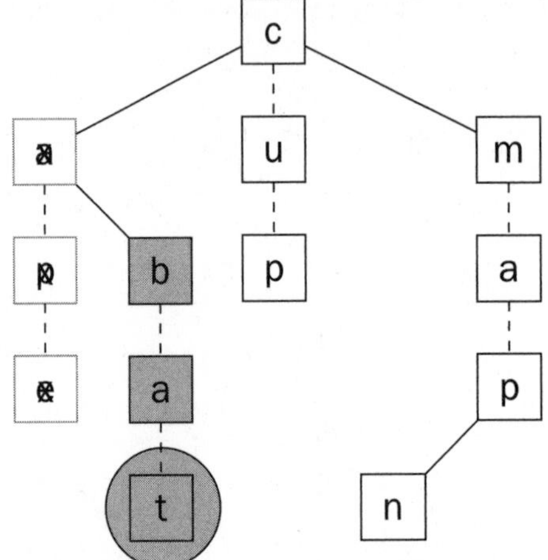

Figure 14-17: You find the first matching word.

Once again, you are looking for a wildcard, so all of the nodes will match, but you've now run out of pattern and have reached a word at the same time (see Figure 14-18)—you've found your first complete match: "bat."

This process continues until all matching words have been found. Figure 14-19 shows all matching and nonmatching words in the tree.

Here you can see that three words matched the pattern "-a-": "bat," "man," and "map." Better still, you will find them all with only 11 character comparisons. Compare that with the brute-force approach that would have attempted to find all the words from "aaa" through "zaz." In the latter case, there are `26 * 26 = 676` possible combinations, meaning you would need to perform at least that many character comparisons!

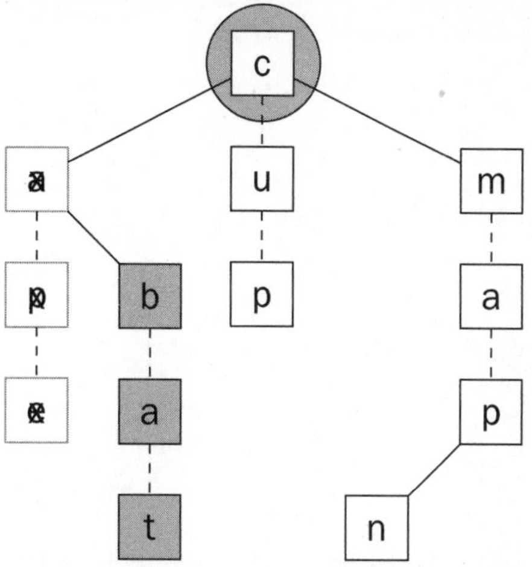

Figure 14-18: The search continues at the higher level with the next largest node.

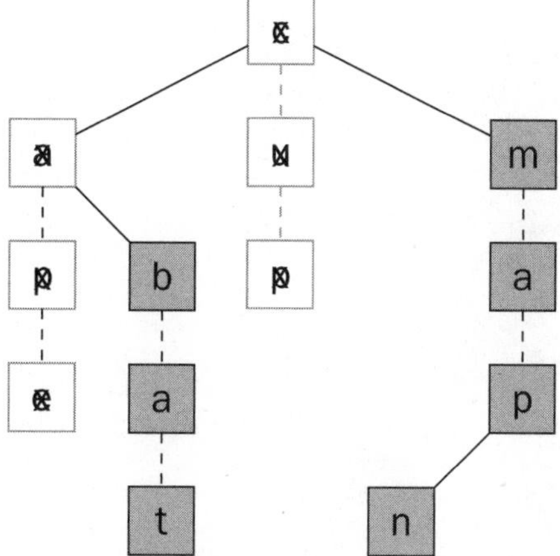

Figure 14-19: The completed search showing the matching and nonmatching words.

Putting Ternary Search Trees into Practice

Now that you understand the various ways in which ternary search trees can be used, it's time to try your hand at creating a real one. As always, you will start by creating some test cases to ensure that your implementation works correctly. Then you'll move on to creating the actual ternary search tree itself, and finally develop a simple application for helping you solve crossword puzzles.

Try It Out — Testing a Ternary Search Tree

Create the aptly named `TernarySearchTreeTest` class as follows:

```
package com.wrox.algorithms.tstrees;

import com.wrox.algorithms.lists.LinkedList;
import com.wrox.algorithms.lists.List;
import junit.framework.TestCase;

public class TernarySearchTreeTest extends TestCase {
    private TernarySearchTree _tree;

    protected void setUp() throws Exception {
        super.setUp();

        _tree = new TernarySearchTree();

        _tree.add("prefabricate");
        _tree.add("presume");
        _tree.add("prejudice");
        _tree.add("preliminary");
        _tree.add("apple");
        _tree.add("ape");
        _tree.add("appeal");
        _tree.add("car");
        _tree.add("dog");
        _tree.add("cat");
        _tree.add("mouse");
        _tree.add("mince");
        _tree.add("minty");
    }

    public void testContains() {
        assertTrue(_tree.contains("prefabricate"));
        assertTrue(_tree.contains("presume"));
        assertTrue(_tree.contains("prejudice"));
        assertTrue(_tree.contains("preliminary"));
        assertTrue(_tree.contains("apple"));
        assertTrue(_tree.contains("ape"));
        assertTrue(_tree.contains("appeal"));
        assertTrue(_tree.contains("car"));
        assertTrue(_tree.contains("dog"));
        assertTrue(_tree.contains("cat"));
        assertTrue(_tree.contains("mouse"));
        assertTrue(_tree.contains("mince"));
        assertTrue(_tree.contains("minty"));

        assertFalse(_tree.contains("pre"));
        assertFalse(_tree.contains("dogs"));
        assertFalse(_tree.contains("UNKNOWN"));
    }

    public void testPrefixSearch() {
```

```
        assertPrefixEquals(new String[] {"prefabricate", "prejudice",
"preliminary", "presume"}, "pre");
        assertPrefixEquals(new String[] {"ape", "appeal", "apple"}, "ap");
    }

    public void testPatternMatch() {
        assertPatternEquals(new String[] {"mince", "mouse"}, "m???e");
        assertPatternEquals(new String[] {"car", "cat"}, "?a?");
    }

    private void assertPrefixEquals(String[] expected, String prefix) {
        List words = new LinkedList();

        _tree.prefixSearch(prefix, words);

        assertEquals(expected, words);
    }

    private void assertPatternEquals(String[] expected, String pattern) {
        List words = new LinkedList();

        _tree.patternMatch(pattern, words);

        assertEquals(expected, words);
    }

    private void assertEquals(String[] expected, List actual) {
        assertEquals(expected.length, actual.size());

        for (int i = 0; i < expected.length; ++i) {
            assertEquals(expected[i], actual.get(i));
        }
    }
}
```

How It Works

The `TernarySearchTreeTest` class holds an instance of a ternary search tree for use by each of the individual test cases and is initialized in `setUp()` by adding a number of words:

```
package com.wrox.algorithms.tstrees;

import com.wrox.algorithms.lists.LinkedList;
import com.wrox.algorithms.lists.List;
import junit.framework.TestCase;

public class TernarySearchTreeTest extends TestCase {
    private TernarySearchTree _tree;

    protected void setUp() throws Exception {
        super.setUp();

        _tree = new TernarySearchTree();

        _tree.add("prefabricate");
```

```
            _tree.add("presume");
            _tree.add("prejudice");
            _tree.add("preliminary");
            _tree.add("apple");
            _tree.add("ape");
            _tree.add("appeal");
            _tree.add("car");
            _tree.add("dog");
            _tree.add("cat");
            _tree.add("mouse");
            _tree.add("mince");
            _tree.add("minty");
        }

        ...
    }
```

The method `testContains()` verifies that each word added in `setUp()` exists in the tree. In addition, you've checked for a few words that shouldn't exist. Notice that the words have been chosen very carefully: The sequence of letters `"pre"` and `"dog"` will actually be found in the tree but only as prefixes to other words, so `contains()` should return `false`; `"UNKNOWN"` shouldn't exist at all:

```
        public void testContains() {
            assertTrue(_tree.contains("prefabricate"));
            assertTrue(_tree.contains("presume"));
            assertTrue(_tree.contains("prejudice"));
            assertTrue(_tree.contains("preliminary"));
            assertTrue(_tree.contains("apple"));
            assertTrue(_tree.contains("ape"));
            assertTrue(_tree.contains("appeal"));
            assertTrue(_tree.contains("car"));
            assertTrue(_tree.contains("dog"));
            assertTrue(_tree.contains("cat"));
            assertTrue(_tree.contains("mouse"));
            assertTrue(_tree.contains("mince"));
            assertTrue(_tree.contains("minty"));

            assertFalse(_tree.contains("pre"));
            assertFalse(_tree.contains("dogs"));
            assertFalse(_tree.contains("UNKNOWN"));
        }
```

There are only two other publicly accessible methods in your ternary search tree implementation: one for finding words with a common prefix, and another for finding words matching a pattern. Both of these return a list of search results, so you created a simple method to help you verify whether the search results match those expected.

The custom `assertEquals()` compares an array of expected words to a list of words actually returned from a search, element by element. If the size and contents of the list match the array, then you can be confident that the search was successful:

```
        private void assertEquals(String[] expected, List actual) {
            assertEquals(expected.length, actual.size());
```

```
        for (int i = 0; i < expected.length; ++i) {
            assertEquals(expected[i], actual.get(i));
        }
    }
```

To test prefix searching, you created the method `testPrefixSearch()`. This method assembles a list of expected values and a prefix and then delegates most of the work to yet another helper method, `assertPrefixEquals()`:

```
    public void testPrefixSearch() {
        assertPrefixEquals(
            new String[] {"prefabricate", "prejudice", "preliminary", "presume"},
            "pre");

        assertPrefixEquals(
            new String[] {"ape", "appeal", "apple"},
            "ap");
    }
```

The method `assertPrefixEquals()` then creates a list to hold the results and calls the tree's `prefixSearch()` method to populate the list. The expected and actual results are then passed to your custom `assertEquals()` method for validation:

```
    private void assertPrefixEquals(String[] expected, String prefix) {
        List words = new LinkedList();

        _tree.prefixSearch(prefix, words);

        assertEquals(expected, words);
    }
```

The method `testPatternMatch()` assembles an array of expected results along with a pattern, and delegates to another helper method, `assertPatternEquals()`:

```
    public void testPatternMatch() {
        assertPatternEquals(new String[] {"mince", "mouse"}, "m???e");

        assertPatternEquals(new String[] {"car", "cat"}, "?a?");
    }
```

The method `assertPatternEquals()` calls `patternMatch()` on the tree and validates the results. Notice the use of the question mark (`?`) as the wildcard character. The choice of character is largely arbitrary, but a question mark can't possibly appear in a word by mistake, and it looks very obvious that it means "something, anything, goes here":

```
    private void assertPatternEquals(String[] expected, String pattern) {
        List words = new LinkedList();

        _tree.patternMatch(pattern, words);

        assertEquals(expected, words);
    }
```

Tests in place, in the next Try It Out section, you create the actual ternary search tree class.

Try It Out Implementing a Ternary Search Tree

Create the `TernarySearchTree` class as follows:

```
package com.wrox.algorithms.tstrees;

import com.wrox.algorithms.lists.List;

public class TernarySearchTree {
    public static final char WILDCARD = '?';
    private Node _root;

    public void add(CharSequence word) {
        assert word != null : "word can't be null";
        assert word.length() > 0 : "word can't be empty";

        Node node = insert(_root, word, 0);
        if (_root == null) {
            _root = node;
        }
    }

    public boolean contains(CharSequence word) {
        assert word != null : "word can't be null";
        assert word.length() > 0 : "word can't be empty";

        Node node = search(_root, word, 0);
        return node != null && node.isEndOfWord();
    }

    public void patternMatch(CharSequence pattern, List results) {
        assert pattern != null : "pattern can't be null";
        assert pattern.length() > 0 : "pattern can't be empty";
        assert results != null : "results can't be null";

        patternMatch(_root, pattern, 0, results);
    }

    public void prefixSearch(CharSequence prefix, List results) {
        assert prefix != null : "prefix can't be null";
        assert prefix.length() > 0 : "prefix can't be empty";

        inOrderTraversal(search(_root, prefix, 0), results);
    }

    private Node search(Node node, CharSequence word, int index) {
        assert word != null : "word can't be null";

        if (node == null) {
            return null;
```

```
        }

        char c = word.charAt(index);

        if (c == node.getChar()) {
            if (index + 1 < word.length()) {
                node = search(node.getChild(), word, index + 1);
            }
        } else if (c < node.getChar()) {
            node = search(node.getSmaller(), word, index);
        } else {
            node = search(node.getLarger(), word, index);
        }

        return node;
    }

    private Node insert(Node node, CharSequence word, int index) {
        assert word != null : "word can't be null";

        char c = word.charAt(index);

        if (node == null) {
            node = new Node(c);
        }

        if (c == node.getChar()) {
            if (index + 1 < word.length()) {
                node.setChild(insert(node.getChild(), word, index + 1));
            } else {
                node.setWord(word.toString());
            }
        } else if (c < node.getChar()) {
            node.setSmaller(insert(node.getSmaller(), word, index));
        } else {
            node.setLarger(insert(node.getLarger(), word, index));
        }

        return node;
    }

    private void patternMatch(Node node, CharSequence pattern, int index, List
results) {
        assert pattern != null : "pattern can't be null";
        assert results != null : "results can't be null";

        if (node == null) {
            return;
        }

        char c = pattern.charAt(index);

        if (c == WILDCARD || c < node.getChar()) {
            patternMatch(node.getSmaller(), pattern, index, results);
```

```
        }

        if (c == WILDCARD || c == node.getChar()) {
            if (index + 1 < pattern.length()) {
                patternMatch(node.getChild(), pattern, index + 1, results);
            } else if (node.isEndOfWord()) {
                results.add(node.getWord());
            }
        }

        if (c == WILDCARD || c > node.getChar()) {
            patternMatch(node.getLarger(), pattern, index, results);
        }
    }

    private void inOrderTraversal(Node node, List results) {
        assert results != null : "results can't be null";

        if (node == null) {
            return;
        }

        inOrderTraversal(node.getSmaller(), results);
        if (node.isEndOfWord()) {
            results.add(node.getWord());
        }
        inOrderTraversal(node.getChild(), results);
        inOrderTraversal(node.getLarger(), results);
    }

    private static final class Node {
        private final char _c;
        private Node _smaller;
        private Node _larger;
        private Node _child;
        private String _word;

        public Node(char c) {
            _c = c;
        }

        public char getChar() {
            return _c;
        }

        public Node getSmaller() {
            return _smaller;
        }

        public void setSmaller(Node smaller) {
            _smaller = smaller;
        }

        public Node getLarger() {
            return _larger;
```

```
        }

        public void setLarger(Node larger) {
            _larger = larger;
        }

        public Node getChild() {
            return _child;
        }

        public void setChild(Node child) {
            _child = child;
        }

        public String getWord() {
            return _word;
        }

        public void setWord(String word) {
            _word = word;
        }

        public boolean isEndOfWord() {
            return getWord() != null;
        }
    }
}
```

How It Works

The class definition for `TernarySearchTree` is rather bare, containing a single instance variable for holding the root node and defining a constant to be used as the wildcard character when pattern matching:

```
package com.wrox.algorithms.tstrees;

import com.wrox.algorithms.lists.List;

public class TernarySearchTree {
    public static final char WILDCARD = '?';

    private Node _root;

    ...
}
```

You also defined the `Node` class that makes up the structure of the tree, a very simple class for holding and retrieving a character value and references to the smaller and larger siblings as well as any children. Notice the strange variable `_word`. Recall that you needed some way to mark the end of a word. You could have used a Boolean, but for the purposes of this exercise we've instead chosen to store the actual word itself. Although that obviously consumes more memory, it makes the business of collecting words when performing a search much easier. There is also a convenience method, `isEndOfWord()`, that returns `true` only if there is a word stored in the node:

```
    private static final class Node {
        private final char _c;
        private Node _smaller;
```

```
        private Node _larger;
        private Node _child;
        private String _word;

        public Node(char c) {
            _c = c;
        }

        public char getChar() {
            return _c;
        }

        public Node getSmaller() {
            return _smaller;
        }

        public void setSmaller(Node smaller) {
            _smaller = smaller;
        }

        public Node getLarger() {
            return _larger;
        }

        public void setLarger(Node larger) {
            _larger = larger;
        }

        public Node getChild() {
            return _child;
        }

        public void setChild(Node child) {
            _child = child;
        }

        public String getWord() {
            return _word;
        }

        public void setWord(String word) {
            _word = word;
        }

        public boolean isEndOfWord() {
            return getWord() != null;
        }
    }
```

One thing to note before getting into the remainder of the code is that because the algorithms that operate on ternary search trees lend themselves easily to recursion, all the methods in this class have been coded as such.

The `contains()` method returns `true` if and only if the word exists in the tree (ignoring prefixes); otherwise, it returns `false`. After first validating the input, you then call `search()`, passing in the root node (if any), the word for which to search, and the position of the first character. Finally, `true` is returned only if a node marking the end of a word was found; otherwise, `false` is returned to indicate the word was not found:

```
public boolean contains(CharSequence word) {
    assert word != null : "word can't be null";
    assert word.length() > 0 : "word can't be empty";

    Node node = search(_root, word, 0);
    return node != null && node.isEndOfWord();
}
```

The private `search()` method takes a node from which to start looking, the word to search for, and the position within the word from which to start. In return, `search()` provides the node containing the last character in the word, or `null` if the word was not found.

If there is no current node (`node == null`), the search can terminate immediately. Otherwise, the character at the current position is retrieved and the search begins.

If the current search character matches the one at the current node and there are more characters in the string (`index + 1 < word.length()`), the search progresses to the next letter, starting at the child node.

If the characters don't match, the search character must exist either before or after the current node. If the character you are looking for sorts before the current node, then the search continues starting with the smaller sibling; otherwise, it must sort after the current node—in which case, the search continues with the larger sibling.

Eventually, either the letters in the search word run out or you run out of nodes. At this point, whichever node you are currently at (if any) is returned as the result:

```
private Node search(Node node, CharSequence word, int index) {
    assert word != null : "word can't be null";

    if (node == null) {
        return null;
    }

    char c = word.charAt(index);

    if (c == node.getChar()) {
        if (index + 1 < word.length()) {
            node = search(node.getChild(), word, index + 1);
        }
    } else if (c < node.getChar()) {
        node = search(node.getSmaller(), word, index);
    } else {
        node = search(node.getLarger(), word, index);
    }

    return node;
}
```

The methods `add()` and `insert()` work together to add new words to the tree.

After checking the arguments to the method, `add()` calls `insert`, passing in the root node (if any), the word to be added, and the position of the first character in the word. The only other thing that needs to be done is update the root node if necessary, with the node returned by `insert()`:

```
public void add(CharSequence word) {
    assert word != null : "word can't be null";
    assert word.length() > 0 : "word can't be empty";

    Node node = insert(_root, word, 0);
    if (_root == null) {
        _root = node;
    }
}
```

The `insert()` method starts by obtaining the current character from the word. Then, if there is no current node, one is created—you are, after all, adding.

The current character is then compared with the character for the current node. If it matches, then there are two possibilities: If there are still more characters to insert, then you recurse with the next character starting from the child node; otherwise, you can set the word in the current node to indicate you're done.

If the character doesn't match, then there are an additional two possibilities: either the character sorts lower than the current node or it sorts higher. In either case, you need to recurse using the same character but with the smaller or larger node, respectively.

Notice how the return value is used to update the reference to the appropriate child or sibling node. This works because the `insert()` method always returns the node just inserted (or the appropriate existing node). This means that the node eventually returned to `add()` is for the first character in the word, not the last, as you may have assumed:

```
private Node insert(Node node, CharSequence word, int index) {
    assert word != null : "word can't be null";

    char c = word.charAt(index);

    if (node == null) {
        node = new Node(c);
    }

    if (c == node.getChar()) {
        if (index + 1 < word.length()) {
            node.setChild(insert(node.getChild(), word, index + 1));
        } else {
            node.setWord(word.toString());
        }
    } else if (c < node.getChar()) {
        node.setSmaller(insert(node.getSmaller(), word, index));
    } else {
        node.setLarger(insert(node.getLarger(), word, index));
    }

    return node;
}
```

The method `prefixSearch()` first performs a general search to find the node containing the last letter of the prefix. This node is then passed to `inOrderTraversal()` along with the list for storing the results:

```
public void prefixSearch(CharSequence prefix, List results) {
    assert prefix != null : "prefix can't be null";
    assert prefix.length() > 0 : "prefix can't be empty";

    inOrderTraversal(search(_root, prefix, 0), results);
}
```

The method `inOrderTraversal()` recursively traverses first the smaller sibling, then the node's child, and finally the large sibling. Each time a word is encountered (`node.isEndOfWord()`), it is added to the results:

```
private void inOrderTraversal(Node node, List results) {
    assert results != null : "results can't be null";

    if (node == null) {
        return;
    }

    inOrderTraversal(node.getSmaller(), results);
    if (node.isEndOfWord()) {
        results.add(node.getWord());
    }
    inOrderTraversal(node.getChild(), results);
    inOrderTraversal(node.getLarger(), results);
}
```

The first `patternMatch()` method calls the private method of the same name, passing the root node, the pattern to match, the position of the first character in the pattern, and, of course, the list into which the results will be stored:

```
public void patternMatch(CharSequence pattern, List results) {
    assert pattern != null : "pattern can't be null";
    assert pattern.length() > 0 : "pattern can't be empty";
    assert results != null : "results can't be null";

    patternMatch(_root, pattern, 0, results);
}
```

The second `patternMatch()` method looks rather like an in-order traversal of the tree, with some restrictions.

First, instead of always traversing the left and right siblings, a check is first performed to determine whether the traversal is actually required. If the current pattern character sorts before the current node, then a traversal of the smaller sibling is made; if it sorts after the node, then a traversal of the larger sibling is made; and if it is the same as the current node, a recursive call is made, with the next character in the pattern starting at the first child.

Second, at each point, if the current pattern character is `WILDCARD`, then you traverse no matter what. This way, a wildcard character matches all other characters.

Finally, the search will only consider words of the same length as the pattern — for example, a pattern of length five will only match words of length five:

```
private void patternMatch(Node node, CharSequence pattern, int index,
                          List results) {
    assert pattern != null : "pattern can't be null";
    assert results != null : "results can't be null";

    if (node == null) {
        return;
    }

    char c = pattern.charAt(index);

    if (c == WILDCARD || c < node.getChar()) {
        patternMatch(node.getSmaller(), pattern, index, results);
    }

    if (c == WILDCARD || c == node.getChar()) {
        if (index + 1 < pattern.length()) {
            patternMatch(node.getChild(), pattern, index + 1, results);
        } else if (node.isEndOfWord()) {
            results.add(node.getWord());
        }
    }

    if (c == WILDCARD || c > node.getChar()) {
        patternMatch(node.getLarger(), pattern, index, results);
    }
}
```

Crossword Helper Example

Armed with your fully tested and implemented pattern matching code, you can turn your hand to a sample application that demonstrates a novel use of ternary search trees: crossword solving. In this section, you'll develop a very small command-line application that takes as its arguments a file containing words — one word per line — and a pattern to match, optionally containing wildcard characters.

Try It Out — Creating the Crossword Helper Application

Create the `CrosswordHelper` class as follows:

```
package com.wrox.algorithms.tstrees;

import com.wrox.algorithms.iteration.Iterator;
import com.wrox.algorithms.lists.LinkedList;
import com.wrox.algorithms.lists.List;

import java.io.BufferedReader;
```

```
import java.io.FileReader;
import java.io.IOException;

public final class CrosswordHelper {
    private CrosswordHelper() {
    }

    public static void main(String[] args) throws IOException {
        assert args != null : "args can't be null";

        if (args.length < 2) {
            System.out.println("Usage CrosswordHelper <word-list> <pattern>
[repetitions]");
            System.exit(-1);
        }

        int repetitions = 1;
        if (args.length > 2) {
            repetitions = Integer.parseInt(args[2]);
        }

        searchForPattern(loadWords(args[0]), args[1], repetitions);
    }

    private static void searchForPattern(TernarySearchTree tree, String pattern,
int repetitions) {
        assert tree != null : "tree can't be null";

        System.out.println("Searching for pattern '" + pattern + "'..." +
repetitions + " times");

        List words = null;

        for (int i = 0; i < repetitions; ++i) {
            words = new LinkedList();
            tree.patternMatch(pattern, words);
        }

        Iterator iterator = words.iterator();

        for (iterator.first(); !iterator.isDone(); iterator.next()) {
            System.out.println(iterator.current());
        }
    }

    private static TernarySearchTree loadWords(String fileName) throws IOException
{
        TernarySearchTree tree = new TernarySearchTree();

        System.out.println("Loading words from '" + fileName + "'...");

        BufferedReader reader = new BufferedReader(new FileReader(fileName));

        try {
```

```
            String word;

            while ((word = reader.readLine()) != null) {
                tree.add(word);
            }
        } finally {
            reader.close();
        }

        return tree;
    }
}
```

How It Works

The `CrosswordHelper` class defines the application entry point `main()`. This method first verifies that there are at least two arguments on the command line—one for the file containing the word list and another for the pattern. The filename, `args[0]`, is then passed to `loadWords()`, which, as you will see in a moment, returns a ternary search tree that is then passed along with the pattern, `args[1]`, to `searchForPattern()` to do the actual matching:

```
package com.wrox.algorithms.tstrees;

import com.wrox.algorithms.iteration.Iterator;
import com.wrox.algorithms.lists.LinkedList;
import com.wrox.algorithms.lists.List;

import java.io.BufferedReader;
import java.io.FileReader;
import java.io.IOException;

public final class CrosswordHelper {
    private CrosswordHelper() {
    }

    public static void main(String[] args) throws IOException {
        assert args != null : "args can't be null";

        if (args.length < 2) {
            System.out.println("Usage CrosswordHelper <word-list> <pattern>");
            System.exit(-1);
        }

        searchForPattern(loadWords(args[0]), args[1]);
    }

    ...
}
```

The method `loadWords()` takes the name of a file containing words—one each per line—and returns a fully populated ternary search tree. It starts by creating a ternary search tree into which the words will be stored. It then opens the file, reading each line and adding the word to the tree. The file is then closed and the newly populated tree is returned to the caller:

```
private static TernarySearchTree loadWords(String fileName)
        throws IOException {
    TernarySearchTree tree = new TernarySearchTree();

    System.out.println("Loading words from '" + fileName + "'...");

    BufferedReader reader = new BufferedReader(new FileReader(fileName));

    try {
        String word;

        while ((word = reader.readLine()) != null) {
            tree.add(word);
        }
    } finally {
        reader.close();
    }

    return tree;
}
```

Finally, you have the method that actually performs the search: `searchForPattern()`. This method simply creates a list for holding the results, calls `patternMatch()`, passing the pattern and the list, and then iterates over the results printing each one to the console:

```
private static void searchForPattern(TernarySearchTree tree, String pattern) {
    assert tree != null : "tree can't be null";

    System.out.println("Searching for pattern '" + pattern + "'...");

    List words = new LinkedList();
    tree.patternMatch(pattern, words);

    Iterator iterator = words.iterator();

    for (iterator.first(); !iterator.isDone(); iterator.next()) {
        System.out.println(iterator.current());
    }
}
```

Running the crossword helper with a list of around 114,000 English words for the pattern `"a?r???t"` produced the following results:

```
Loading words from 'words.txt'...
Searching for pattern 'a?r???t'...
abreact
abreast
acrobat
aeriest
airboat
airiest
airlift
airport
```

```
airpost
alright
apricot
```

Pretty handy the next time you're stuck while trying to solve a crossword or even when playing Scrabble.

Summary

This chapter demonstrated the following about ternary search trees and associated behavior:

- They are most useful for storing strings.
- Aside from a regular lookup, they can be used for prefix searching.
- They can also be used for pattern matching, such as for solving crossword puzzles.
- They are like binary search trees with an extra child node.
- Instead of holding the entire word, nodes contain one letter each.
- Like binary search trees, ternary search trees can become unbalanced.
- They are generally more time efficient than binary search trees, performing on average fewer numbers of character comparisons.

Exercise

1. Create an iterative form of `search()`.

B-Trees

So far, everything we've covered has been designed to work solely with in-memory data. From lists (Chapter 3) to hash tables (Chapter 11) and binary search trees (Chapter 10), all of the data structures and associated algorithms have assumed that the entire data set is held only in main memory, but what if the data exists on disk — as is the case with most databases? What if you wanted to search through a database for one record out of millions? In this chapter, you'll learn how to handle data that isn't stored in memory.

This chapter discusses the following topics:

- Why the data structures you've learned so far are inadequate for dealing with data stored on disk
- How B-Trees solve the problems associated with other data structures
- How to implement a simple B-Tree-based map implementation

Understanding B-Trees

You've already seen how you can use binary search trees to build indexes as maps. It's not too much of a stretch to imagine reading and writing the binary tree to and from disk. The problem with this approach, however, is that when the number of records grows, so too does the size of the tree. Imagine a database table holding a million records and an index with keys of length ten. If each key in the index maps to a record in the table (stored as integers of length four), and each node in the tree references its parent and child nodes (again each of length four), this would mean reading and writing `1,000,000` × `(10 + 4 + 4 + 4 + 4)` = `1,000,000` × `26` = `26,000,000` or approximately 26 megabytes (MB) each time a change was made!

That's a lot of disk I/O and as you are probably aware, disk I/O is very expensive in terms of time. Compared to main memory, disk I/O is thousands, if not millions, of times slower. Even if you can achieve a data rate of 10MB/second, that's still a whopping 2.6 seconds to ensure that any updates to the index are saved to disk. For most real-world applications involving tens if not hundreds of concurrent users, 2.6 seconds is going to be unacceptable. One would hope that you could do a little better than that.

You already know that a binary search tree is composed of individual nodes, so maybe you could try reading and writing the nodes individually instead of all in one go. While this sounds like a good idea at first, in practice it turns out to be rather less than ideal. Recall that even in a perfectly balanced binary search tree, the average number of nodes traversed to find a search key will be `O(log N)`. For our imaginary database containing a million records, this would therefore be $\log_2 1{,}000{,}000 = 20$. This is fine for in-memory operations for which the cost of accessing a node is very small, but not so great when it means performing 20 disk reads. Even though each node is quite small—in our example, only 26 or so bytes—data is stored on disks in much larger *blocks*, sometimes referred to as *pages*, so the cost of reading one node is no more or less expensive than reading, for example, 20 nodes. That's great, you say, you only need to read 20 nodes, so why not just read them all at once?

The problem is that given the way a binary search tree is built, especially if some kind of balancing is occurring, it's highly unlikely that related nodes will be located anywhere near each other, let alone in the same sector. Even worse, not only will you incur the cost of making the 20 or so disk reads, known as *transfer time*, but before each disk read is performed, the heads on the disks need to be repositioned, known as *seek time*, and the disks must be rotated into position, known as *latency*. All of this adds up. Even if you employed some sophisticated caching mechanisms in order to reduce the number of physical I/Os performed, the overall performance would still be unacceptable. You clearly need something better than this.

B-Trees are specifically designed for managing indexes on secondary storage such as hard disks, compact discs, and so on, providing efficient insert, delete, and search operations.

> *There are many variations on the standard B-Tree, including B+Trees, B×Trees, and so on. All are designed to solve other aspects of searching on external storage. However, each of these variations has its roots in the basic B-Tree. For more information on B-Trees and their variations, see [Cormen, 2001], [Sedgewick, 2002], and [Folk, 1991].*

Like binary search trees, B-Trees contain nodes. Unlike binary search trees, however, the nodes of a B-Tree contain not one, but multiple, keys, up to some defined maximum—usually determined by the size of a disk block. The keys in a node are stored in sorted order, with an associated child node holding keys that sort lower than it—every nonleaf node containing *k* keys must have *k*+1 children.

Figure 15-1 shows a B-Tree holding the keys A through K. Each node holds at most three keys. In this example, the root node is only holding two keys—D and H—and has three children. The leftmost child holds all keys that sort lower than D. The middle child holds all keys that sort between D and H. The rightmost child holds all other keys greater than H.

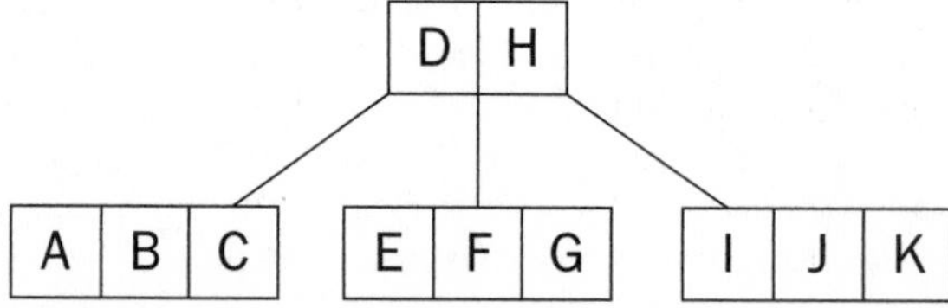

Figure 15-1: A B-Tree with a maximum of three keys per node, holding the keys A through K.

Looking for a key in a B-Tree is similar to looking for a key in a binary search tree, but each node contains multiple keys. Therefore, instead of making a choice between two children, a B-Tree search must make a choice between multiple children.

As an example, to search for the key G in the tree shown in Figure 15-1, you start at the root node. The search key, G, is first compared with D (see Figure 15-2).

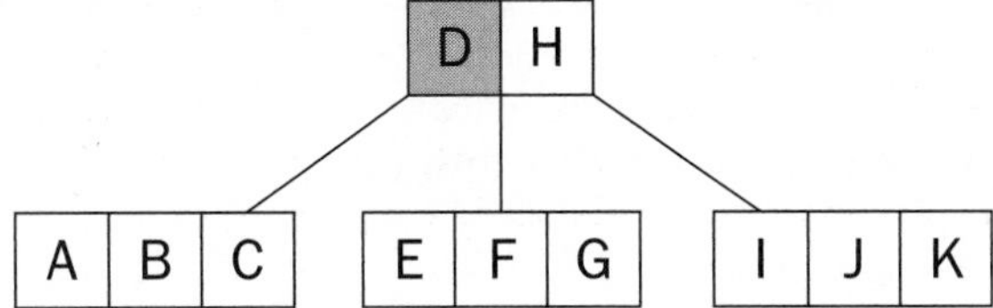

Figure 15-2: A search starts at the first key in the root node.

Because G sorts after D, the search continues to the next key, H (see Figure 15-3).

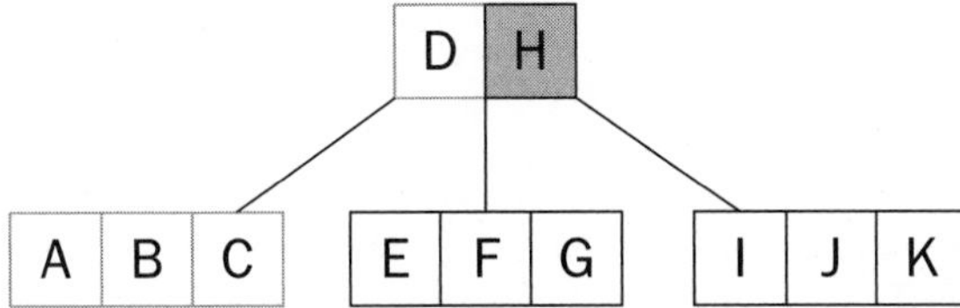

Figure 15-3: The search continues at the next key in the node.

This time, the search key sorts before the current key in the node, so you follow the link to the left child (see Figure 15-4).

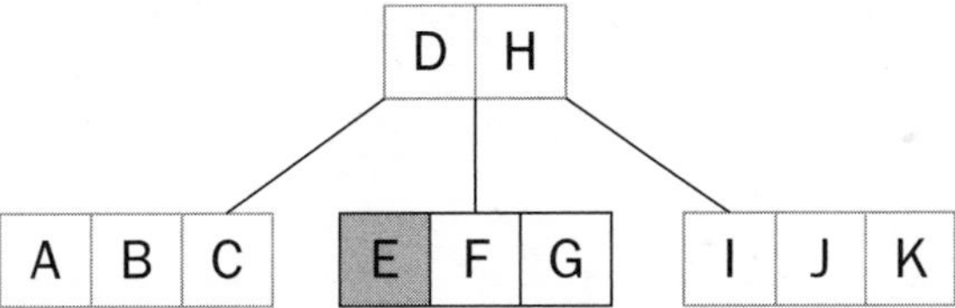

Figure 15-4: The search key falls below the current key so the search continues by following the left child link.

This continues until eventually you find the key for which you are searching (see Figure 15-5).

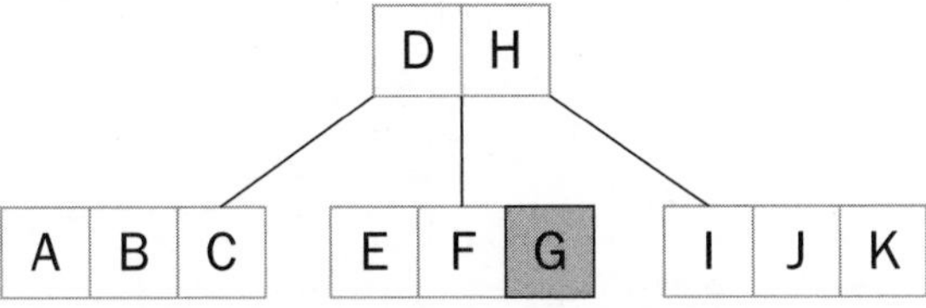

Figure 15-5: The search ends with a match.

Even though the search performed five key comparisons, only two nodes were traversed in the process. Like a binary search tree, the number of nodes traversed is related to the height of the tree. However, because each node in a B-Tree contains multiple keys, the height of the tree remains much lower than in a comparable binary search tree, resulting in fewer node traversals and consequently fewer disk I/Os.

Going back to our original example, if we assume that our disk blocks hold 8,000 bytes each, this means that each node can contain around 8,000 / 26 = 300 or so keys. If you have a million keys, this translates into 1,000,000 / 300 = 3,333 nodes. You also know that, like a binary search tree, the height of a B-Tree is `O(log N)`, where `N` is the number of nodes. Therefore, you can say that the number of nodes you would need to traverse to find any key would be in the order of `log300 3,333 = 2`. That's an order of magnitude better than the binary search tree.

To insert a key into a B-Tree, start at the root and search all the way down until you reach a leaf node. Once the appropriate leaf node has been found, the new value is inserted in order. Figure 15-6 shows the B-Tree from Figure 15-1 after the key L has been inserted.

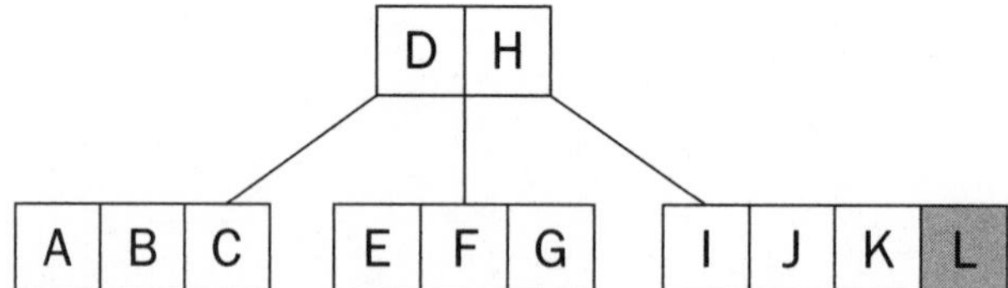

Figure 15-6: Insertion always occurs at the leaf nodes.

Notice that the node into which the new key was inserted has now exceeded the maximum allowed— the maximum number of keys allowed in this example was set at three. When a node becomes "full," it is split into two nodes, each containing half the keys from the original, as shown in Figure 15-7.

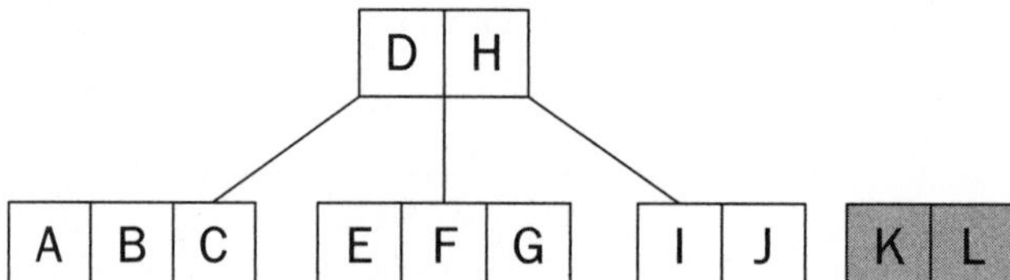

Figure 15-7: Nodes that become "full" are split in two.

Next, the "middle" key from the original node is then moved up to the parent and inserted in order with a reference to the newly created node. In this case, the J is pushed up and added after the H in the parent node, and references the node containing the K and L, as shown in Figure 15-8.

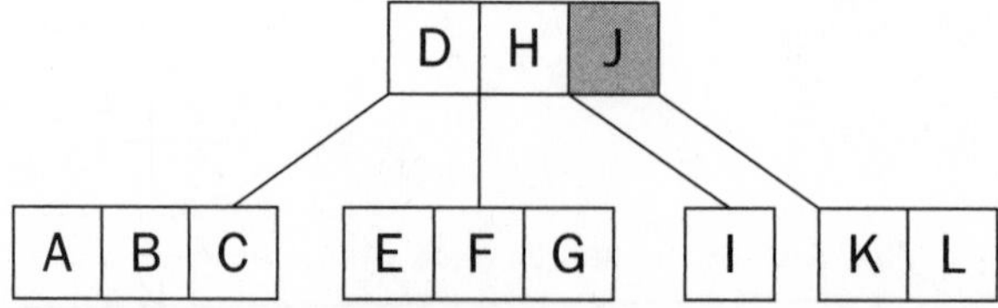

Figure 15-8: The middle key from the original node moves up the tree.

In this way, the tree spreads out, rather than increasing in height; B-Trees tend to be broader and shallower than most other tree structures, so the number of nodes traversed tends to be much smaller. In fact, the height of a B-Tree never increases until the root node becomes full and needs to be split.

Figure 15-9 shows the tree from Figure 15-8 after the keys M and N have been inserted. Once again, the node into which the keys have been added has become full, necessitating a split.

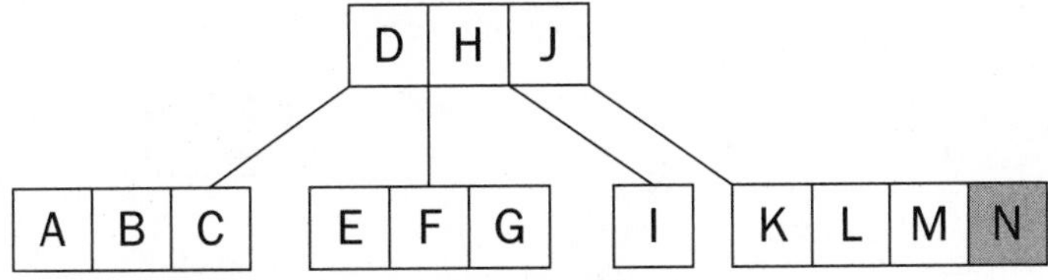

Figure 15-9: A leaf node requiring a split.

Once again, the node is split in two and the "middle" key—the L—is moved up to the root, as shown in Figure 15-10.

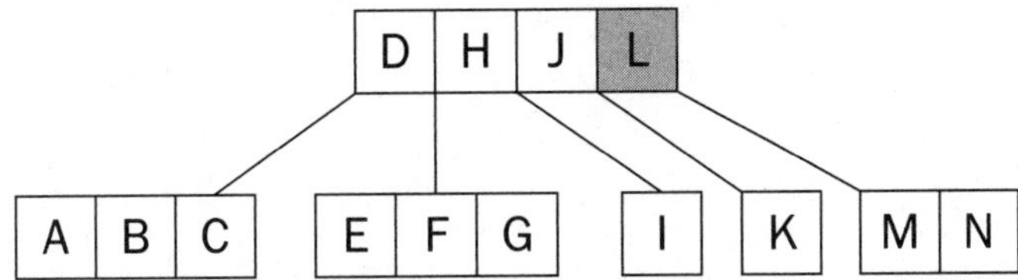

Figure 15-10: The root node has become full.

This time, however, the root node has also become full—it contains more than three keys—and therefore needs to be split. Splitting a node usually pushes one of the keys into the parent node, but of course in this case it's the root node and as such has no parent. Whenever the root node is split, a new node is created and becomes the new root.

Figure 15-11 shows the tree after the root node has been split and a new node is created above it, increasing the height of the tree. A new node containing the key H is created as the parent of the two nodes split from the original root node.

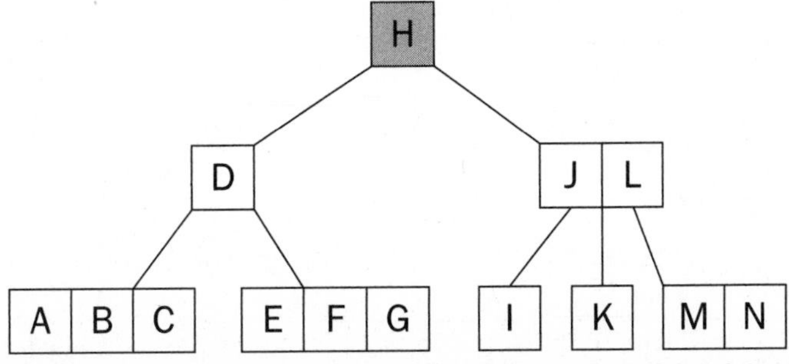

Figure 15-11: Splitting the root node increases the height of the tree.

Deletion from a B-Tree is rather more complicated than both search and insert as it involves the merging of nodes. For example, Figure 15-12 shows the tree after deleting the key K from the tree shown in Figure 15-11. This is no longer a valid B-Tree because there is no longer a middle child (between the keys J and L). Recall that a nonleaf node with *k* keys must always have *k*+1 children.

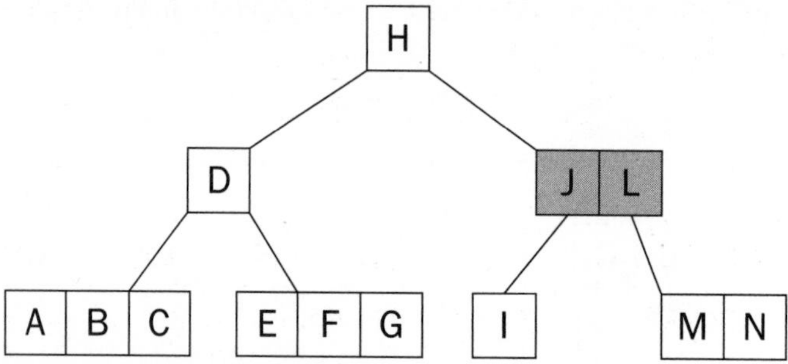

Figure 15-12: Deleting the key K produces an invalid B-Tree.

To correct the structure, it is necessary to redistribute some of the keys among the children — in this case, the key J is pushed down to the node containing the single key I, shown in Figure 15-13.

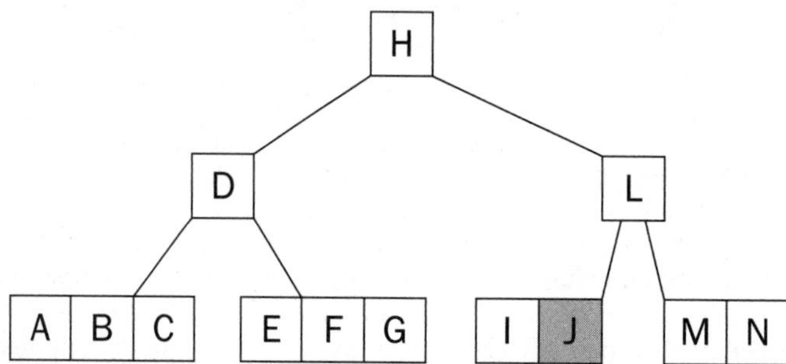

Figure 15-13: Keys are redistributed among the children to correct the tree structure.

This is only the simplest situation. If, for example, the keys I and J were deleted, then the tree would look like the one shown in Figure 15-14.

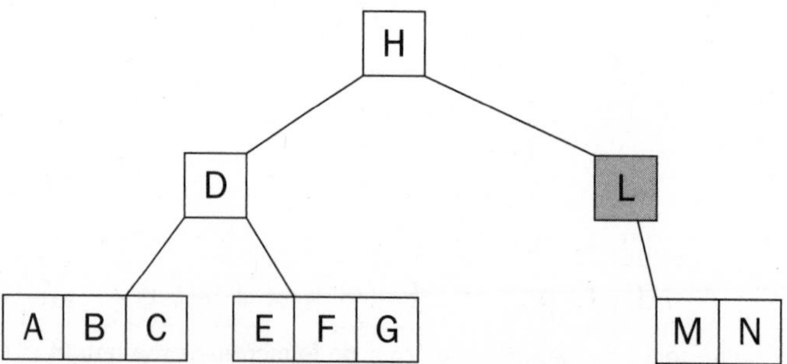

Figure 15-14: Redistribution is required to correct the tree structure.

Again, a redistribution of keys is required to correct the imbalance in the tree. You can achieve this in several ways. No matter how the keys are redistributed, however, keys from parent nodes are merged with those of child nodes. At some point, the root node must be pulled down (or removed, for that matter). When this happens, the height of the tree is reduced by one.

For the purposes of this example, you'll merge the L into its child and pull down the root node, H, as the parent (see Figure 15-15).

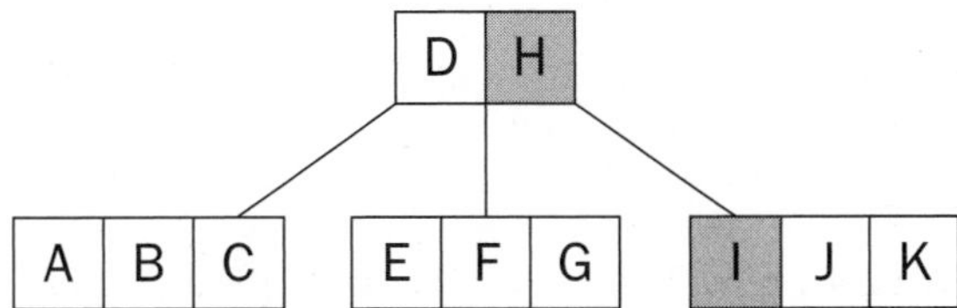

Figure 15-15: The height of the tree drops whenever the root node is either merged into a child or deleted completely.

As you can see, deletion is a rather complicated process and involves many different scenarios. (For a more in-depth explanation, refer to [Cormen, 2001].)

Putting B-Trees into Practice

Now that you understand how B-Trees work and why they are useful, it's time to try your hand at implementing one. As mentioned earlier, B-Trees are usually used as indexes, so in this simple example you'll create an implementation of the `Map` interface from Chapter 13, based on a B-Tree. However, to avoid detracting from the underlying workings of the algorithms involved, the class you create will be purely in-memory, rather than on disk.

You'll implement all the methods from the `Map` interface using your understanding of B-Trees as the basis of the underlying data structure. To this end, you'll implement the `get()`, `contains()`, and `set()` methods based on the search and insertion algorithms discussed earlier. For the `delete()` method, however, you're going to cheat a little. Because the algorithm for deleting from a B-Tree is extremely complicated — involving at least three different scenarios requiring entries to be redistributed among nodes — rather than actually delete the entries, you'll instead simply mark them as deleted. While this does have the rather unfortunate side-effect that the B-Tree will never release any memory, it is sufficient for the purposes of this example. For a more detailed explanation of B-Tree deletion, see [Cormen, 2001].

In the next Try It Out section, you create the tests to ensure that your B-Tree map implementation works correctly.

Try It Out — Testing B-Trees

Create the `BTreeMapTest` class as follows:

```
package com.wrox.algorithms.btrees;

import com.wrox.algorithms.maps.AbstractMapTestCase;
import com.wrox.algorithms.maps.Map;
```

```
import com.wrox.algorithms.sorting.NaturalComparator;

public class BTreeMapTest extends AbstractMapTestCase {
    protected Map createMap() {
        return new BTreeMap(NaturalComparator.INSTANCE, 2);
    }
}
```

How It Works

You already developed the test cases in Chapter 13, so all you needed to do was extend `AbstractMapTestCase`. The only other thing you need to do is implement the method `createMap()` and return an instance of the `BTreeMap` class. The `BTreeMap` constructor takes two parameters: a comparator for ordering the keys and the maximum number of keys per node. In this case, you force the number of keys per node to be as small as possible, ensuring the maximum number of nodes possible. Although this would seem to defeat the purpose of a B-Tree — the whole point being to keep the height and number of nodes as small as possible — by doing so in the test, you'll ensure that all the special cases, such as leaf-node and root-node splitting, are exercised.

Tests in place, in the next Try It Out section you create the actual B-Tree map implementation.

Try It Out Implementing a B-Tree Map

Create the `BTreeMap` class as follows:

```
package com.wrox.algorithms.btrees;

import com.wrox.algorithms.iteration.Iterator;
import com.wrox.algorithms.lists.ArrayList;
import com.wrox.algorithms.lists.EmptyList;
import com.wrox.algorithms.lists.List;
import com.wrox.algorithms.maps.DefaultEntry;
import com.wrox.algorithms.maps.Map;
import com.wrox.algorithms.sorting.Comparator;

public class BTreeMap implements Map {
    private static final int MIN_KEYS_PER_NODE = 2;

    private final Comparator _comparator;
    private final int _maxKeysPerNode;
    private Node _root;
    private int _size;

    public BTreeMap(Comparator comparator, int maxKeysPerNode) {
        assert comparator != null : "comparator can't be null";
        assert maxKeysPerNode >= MIN_KEYS_PER_NODE : "maxKeysPerNode can't be < " +
MIN_KEYS_PER_NODE;

        _comparator = comparator;
        _maxKeysPerNode = maxKeysPerNode;
        clear();
    }

    public Object get(Object key) {
```

```
        Entry entry = _root.search(key);
        return entry != null ? entry.getValue() : null;
    }

    public Object set(Object key, Object value) {
        Object oldValue = _root.set(key, value);

        if (_root.isFull()) {
            Node newRoot = new Node(false);
            _root.split(newRoot, 0);
            _root = newRoot;
        }

        return oldValue;
    }

    public Object delete(Object key) {
        Entry entry = _root.search(key);
        if (entry == null) {
            return null;
        }

        entry.setDeleted(true);
        --_size;

        return entry.setValue(null);
    }

    public boolean contains(Object key) {
        return _root.search(key) != null;
    }

    public void clear() {
        _root = new Node(true);
        _size = 0;
    }

    public int size() {
        return _size;
    }

    public boolean isEmpty() {
        return size() == 0;
    }

    public Iterator iterator() {
        List list = new ArrayList(_size);

        _root.traverse(list);

        return list.iterator();
    }

    private final class Node {
```

```
        private final List _entries = new ArrayList(_maxKeysPerNode + 1);
        private final List _children;

        public Node(boolean leaf) {
            _children = !leaf ? new ArrayList(_maxKeysPerNode + 2) : (List)
EmptyList.INSTANCE;
        }

        public boolean isFull() {
            return _entries.size() > _maxKeysPerNode;
        }

        public Entry search(Object key) {
            int index = indexOf(key);
            if (index >= 0) {
                Entry entry = (Entry) _entries.get(index);
                return !entry.isDeleted() ? entry : null;
            }

            return !isLeaf() ? ((Node) _children.get(-(index + 1))).search(key) :
null;
        }

        public Object set(Object key, Object value) {
            int index = indexOf(key);
            if (index >= 0) {
                return ((Entry) _entries.get(index)).setValue(value);
            }

            return set(key, value, -(index + 1));
        }

        private Object set(Object key, Object value, int index) {
            if (isLeaf()) {
                _entries.insert(index, new Entry(key, value));
                ++_size;
                return null;
            }

            Node child = ((Node) _children.get(index));
            Object oldValue = child.set(key, value);

            if (child.isFull()) {
                child.split(this, index);
            }

            return oldValue;
        }

        private int indexOf(Object key) {
            int lowerIndex = 0;
            int upperIndex = _entries.size() - 1;

            while (lowerIndex <= upperIndex) {
```

```
                int index = lowerIndex + (upperIndex - lowerIndex) / 2;

                int cmp = _comparator.compare(key, ((Entry)
_entries.get(index)).getKey());

                if (cmp == 0) {
                    return index;
                } else if (cmp < 0) {
                    upperIndex = index - 1;
                } else {
                    lowerIndex = index + 1;
                }
            }

            return -(lowerIndex + 1);
        }

        public void split(Node parent, int insertionPoint) {
            assert parent != null : "parent can't be null";

            Node sibling = new Node(isLeaf());

            int middle = _entries.size() / 2;

            move(_entries, middle + 1, sibling._entries);
            move(_children, middle + 1, sibling._children);

            parent._entries.insert(insertionPoint, _entries.delete(middle));

            if (parent._children.isEmpty()) {
                parent._children.insert(insertionPoint, this);
            }
            parent._children.insert(insertionPoint + 1, sibling);
        }

        public void traverse(List list) {
            assert list != null : "list can't be null";

            Iterator children = _children.iterator();
            Iterator entries = _entries.iterator();

            children.first();
            entries.first();

            while (!children.isDone() || !entries.isDone()) {
                if (!children.isDone()) {
                    ((Node) children.current()).traverse(list);
                    children.next();
                }

                if (!entries.isDone()) {
                    Entry entry = (Entry) entries.current();
                    if (!entry.isDeleted()) {
                        list.add(entry);
```

```
                    }
                    entries.next();
                }
            }
        }

        private void move(List source, int from, List target) {
            assert source != null : "source can't be null";
            assert target != null : "target can't be null";

            while (from < source.size()) {
                target.add(source.delete(from));
            }
        }

        private boolean isLeaf() {
            return _children == EmptyList.INSTANCE;
        }
    }

    private static final class Entry extends DefaultEntry {
        private boolean _deleted;

        public Entry(Object key, Object value) {
            super(key, value);
        }

        public boolean isDeleted() {
            return _deleted;
        }

        public void setDeleted(boolean deleted) {
            _deleted = deleted;
        }
    }
}
```

How It Works

The `BTreeMap` class holds a comparator to use for ordering the keys, the maximum number of keys per node, the root node, and the number of entries in the map. Notice that the minimum number of keys allowed per node is two. Because a node is split, there needs to be at least one key in the left child, one in the right, and one to move into the parent node. If the minimum number of keys was set at one, a node would be considered full with only two keys and therefore there would be too few to perform a split:

```
package com.wrox.algorithms.btrees;

import com.wrox.algorithms.iteration.Iterator;
import com.wrox.algorithms.lists.ArrayList;
import com.wrox.algorithms.lists.EmptyList;
import com.wrox.algorithms.lists.List;
import com.wrox.algorithms.maps.DefaultEntry;
import com.wrox.algorithms.maps.Map;
```

```
import com.wrox.algorithms.sorting.Comparator;

public class BTreeMap implements Map {
    private static final int MIN_KEYS_PER_NODE = 2;

    private final Comparator _comparator;
    private final int _maxKeysPerNode;
    private Node _root;
    private int _size;

    public BTreeMap(Comparator comparator, int maxKeysPerNode) {
        assert comparator != null : "comparator can't be null";
        assert maxKeysPerNode >= MIN_KEYS_PER_NODE : "maxKeysPerNode can't be < "
                                                    + MIN_KEYS_PER_NODE;

        _comparator = comparator;
        _maxKeysPerNode = maxKeysPerNode;
        clear();
    }

    ...
}
```

There are also two inner classes — `Entry` and `Node` — that represent a `Map.Entry` and a B-Tree node, respectively.

In addition to extending `DefaultEntry`, the `Entry` inner class also holds a Boolean flag indicating whether it has been deleted or not. This flag can be switched on and off as appropriate and is used for deleting entries:

```
    private static final class Entry extends DefaultEntry {
        private boolean _deleted;

        public Entry(Object key, Object value) {
            super(key, value);
        }

        public boolean isDeleted() {
            return _deleted;
        }

        public void setDeleted(boolean deleted) {
            _deleted = deleted;
        }
    }
```

The `Node` inner class is where most of the work is performed, so we'll discuss this class first, before the methods on the main `BTreeMap` class.

Each node is constructed with a Boolean to indicate whether it is to be a leaf node or not. Recall that leaf nodes have no children, which is reflected in the constructor: If the node is a leaf, the list of children is set to the empty list; otherwise, a new array list is allocated to hold the children. This is reflected in the method `isLeaf()`, which is used to determine whether a node is a leaf or not. In addition, there is a method, `isFull()`, for determining whether a node contains more than the maximum allowable number of keys:

```
private final class Node {
    private final List _entries = new ArrayList();
    private final List _children;

    public Node(boolean leaf) {
        _children = !leaf ? new ArrayList() : (List) EmptyList.INSTANCE;
    }

    public boolean isFull() {
        return _entries.size() > _maxKeysPerNode;
    }

    private boolean isLeaf() {
        return _children == EmptyList.INSTANCE;
    }

    ...
}
```

The first thing you need is a method for searching the entries to find a key. The `indexOf()` method performs a simple linear search of the entries to find a matching key. If found, the position within the list (0, 1, 2, . . .) is returned; otherwise, a negative index is returned to indicate where the key would have been, had it existed. (If you're interested in a more in-depth discussion of how linear searching works, refer to Chapter 9, as the code is identical to the `search()` method of `LinearListSearcher` except that it first retrieves the key from the entry before calling `compare()`.)

```
private int indexOf(Object key) {
    int index = 0;
    Iterator i = _entries.iterator();

    for (i.first(); !i.isDone(); i.next()) {
        int cmp = _comparator.compare(key, ((Entry) i.current()).getKey());
        if (cmp == 0) {
            return index;
        } else if (cmp < 0) {
            break;
        }

        ++index;
    }

    return -(index + 1);
}
```

Now that you can find a key within a node, searching through the nodes to find an entry is fairly straightforward.

The `search()` method first searches for a matching key. If one is found (`index >= 0`), it is returned immediately. Otherwise, if the node is not a leaf, the search continues recursively in the appropriate child; otherwise, it terminates without finding a matching entry—leaf nodes have no children. Notice that the `search()` method ignores entries that are marked as deleted. This is an important point to remember later:

```
public Entry search(Object key) {
    int index = indexOf(key);
    if (index >= 0) {
        Entry entry = (Entry) _entries.get(index);
        return !entry.isDeleted() ? entry : null;
    }

    return !isLeaf() ? ((Node) _children.get(-(index + 1))).search(key)
                                                              : null;
}
```

Next, you want to be able to insert keys into a node, but before doing so, it will be necessary to implement some code to split a node.

The `split()` method takes a reference to the parent node and a position into which the newly created node will be inserted. The first thing `split()` does is create a new node as its sibling—hence, the leaf flag is also copied (a sibling of a leaf is also a leaf). Next, all the entries and children from the midpoint on are moved from the node into the sibling. Then, the middle entry is inserted into the parent, followed by the reference to the sibling. A reference to the node being split is only ever inserted into the parent when the parent is a newly created root node, i.e., it has no children:

```
public void split(Node parent, int insertionPoint) {
    assert parent != null : "parent can't be null";

    Node sibling = new Node(isLeaf());

    int middle = _entries.size() / 2;

    move(_entries, middle + 1, sibling._entries);
    move(_children, middle + 1, sibling._children);

    parent._entries.insert(insertionPoint, _entries.delete(middle));

    if (parent._children.isEmpty()) {
        parent._children.insert(insertionPoint, this);
    }
    parent._children.insert(insertionPoint + 1, sibling);
}

private void move(List source, int from, List target) {
    assert source != null : "source can't be null";
    assert target != null : "target can't be null";

    while (from < source.size()) {
        target.add(source.delete(from));
    }
}
```

Now that you can split a node, you can go about adding new entries, remembering that a map guarantees uniqueness of keys. For this reason, entries are not always inserted. Instead, if an entry with a matching key already exists, the associated value is updated.

The first `set()` method starts by obtaining the position to the key within the node. If the key was found (`index >= 0`), the corresponding entry is retrieved, the value updated, and the old value returned. If the key wasn't found, then it might need to be inserted, but then again it might also exist within a child node. This logic is handled by the second `set()` method.

The second `set()` method first determines whether the node is a leaf. If it is, then the key doesn't exist anywhere in the tree and is therefore inserted along with the value as a new entry, and the size of the map is incremented accordingly. If the node has children, however, the appropriate child is found and a recursive call is made to the first `set()` method. In this case, if after insertion the child becomes full, it will need to be split:

```
public Object set(Object key, Object value) {
    int index = indexOf(key);
    if (index >= 0) {
        return ((Entry) _entries.get(index)).setValue(value);
    }

    return set(key, value, -(index + 1));
}

private Object set(Object key, Object value, int index) {
    if (isLeaf()) {
        _entries.insert(index, new Entry(key, value));
        ++_size;
        return null;
    }

    Node child = ((Node) _children.get(index));
    Object oldValue = child.set(key, value);

    if (child.isFull()) {
        child.split(this, index);
    }

    return oldValue;
}
```

The only other method on the node — `traverse()` — is used for iteration. This method adds all the entries in the tree into a list. It starts by adding all nondeleted entries in the current node. It then recursively calls each of its children to do the same. This is essentially a pre-order traversal (it is also possible to implement an in-order traversal, an exercise left to the reader):

```
public void traverse(List list) {
    assert list != null : "list can't be null";

    Iterator entries = _entries.iterator();
    for (entries.first(); !entries.isDone(); entries.next()) {
        Entry entry = (Entry) entries.current();
        if (!entry.isDeleted()) {
            list.add(entry);
        }
    }

    Iterator children = _children.iterator();
```

```
            for (children.first(); !children.isDone(); children.next()) {
                ((Node) children.current()).traverse(list);
            }
        }
```

Now that you've covered the `Node` inner class, you can proceed to the remaining `BTreeMap` methods required by the `Map` interface.

The `get()` method returns the value associated with a key. The `search()` method of the root node is called with the specified key. If an entry is found, the associated value is returned; otherwise, `null` is returned to indicate that the key doesn't exist in the tree:

```
    public Object get(Object key) {
        Entry entry = _root.search(key);
        return entry != null ? entry.getValue() : null;
    }
```

The `contains()` method determines whether a key exists within the tree. Again, the `search()` method is called on the root node and `true` is returned if an entry is found:

```
    public boolean contains(Object key) {
        return _root.search(key) != null;
    }
```

The `set()` method adds or updates the value associated with a specified key. Here, the `set()` method on the root node is called to do most of the work. After the method returns, the root node is checked to determine whether it is now full. If so, a new root node is created and the existing one is split. If not, no special handling is required. In either case, the old value associated with the key (if any) is returned to the caller as required by the `Map` interface:

```
    public Object set(Object key, Object value) {
        Object oldValue = _root.set(key, value);

        if (_root.isFull()) {
            Node newRoot = new Node(false);
            _root.split(newRoot, 0);
            _root = newRoot;
        }

        return oldValue;
    }
```

The `delete()` method removes a specified key—and its associated value—from the map. Again, the `search()` method is called on the root node to find the entry for the specified key. If no entry is found, then `null` is returned to indicate that the key didn't exist. Otherwise, the entry is marked as deleted, the size of the map is decremented accordingly, and the associated value is returned to the caller:

```
    public Object delete(Object key) {
        Entry entry = _root.search(key);
        if (entry == null) {
            return null;
        }

        entry.setDeleted(true);
```

```
        --_size;

        return entry.setValue(null);
    }
```

The `iterator()` method returns an iterator over all the entries in the map, in no particular order. The `traverse()` method on the root node is called, passing in a list to populate with all the entries in the tree, from which an iterator is returned and passed back to the caller:

```
    public Iterator iterator() {
        List list = new ArrayList(_size);

        _root.traverse(list);

        return list.iterator();
    }
```

The `clear()` method removes all entries from the map. To empty the tree, the root node is set to a leaf node—as it has no children—and the size is reset to 0:

```
    public void clear() {
        _root = new Node(true);
        _size = 0;
    }
```

Finally, the `size()` and `isEmpty()` methods complete the interface:

```
    public int size() {
        return _size;
    }

    public boolean isEmpty() {
        return size() == 0;
    }
```

The implementation you've just created only works in memory. Creating a version that can be saved to and restored from some external medium such as a hard disk requires a little work, but it's relatively straightforward. See [Cormen, 2001] for more information.

Summary

This chapter demonstrated the following key points:

- B-Trees are ideally suited for searching on external storage such as hard disks, compact discs, and so on.
- B-Trees grow from the leaves up.
- Each nonroot node is always at least half full.
- Nodes split whenever they become "full."

- When a node splits, one of the keys is pushed up into the parent.
- The height of a B-Tree only increases when the root node splits.
- B-Trees remain "balanced," guaranteeing `O(log N)` search times.

Exercises

1. Re-implement the `traverse()` method on `Node` to return the entries in key order.
2. Re-implement the `indexOf()` method on `Node` to perform a binary search instead of a linear search.

String Searching

The problem of finding one string within another comes up quite often: Searching through files on disk, DNA searches, and even Google rely on strategies for efficiently searching through text. If you've ever used a word processor or text editor or even the editor used for writing code, you have at some stage or another performed a *string search*. You may know it as the `Find` function.

There are many string searching algorithms — and no doubt many more will be discovered over time — each with its own optimizations for handling specific types of data. Some algorithms work better for plain text, while others work better for text and/or patterns containing a lot of repetition, such as DNA fragments.

This chapter covers two algorithms for plain-text searching. We start with an obvious brute-force algorithm and move on to the more sophisticated Boyer-Moore. Each is described in detail, and then you will see how a relatively simple twist on the brute-force approach enables the Boyer-Moore algorithm to perform significantly faster.

After reading this chapter you should be able to do the following:

- ❑ Describe and implement a brute-force string searching algorithm
- ❑ Describe and implement the Boyer-Moore string searching algorithm
- ❑ Understand the performance characteristics of each algorithm
- ❑ Describe and implement a generic string match iterator
- ❑ Describe and implement a simple file searching application

A Generic String Searcher Interface

Because we want to be able to implement various types of string search algorithms and implement our own variations as the need arises, it will be useful to conceive an interface that remains the same no matter what type of underlying mechanism is used. Additionally, because all of the string searches will conform to a single API, we will be able to write a single suite of tests that can be applied to all of them in order to assert their correctness.

Try It Out Creating the Interface

Start by creating this simple interface:

```
package com.wrox.algorithms.ssearch;

public interface StringSearcher {
    public StringMatch search(CharSequence text, int from);
}
```

You also need to create the `StringMatch` class that is used as the return type from `search()`:

```
package com.wrox.algorithms.ssearch;

public class StringMatch {
    private final CharSequence _pattern;
    private final CharSequence _text;
    private final int _index;

    public StringMatch(CharSequence pattern,
                       CharSequence text,
                       int index) {
        assert text != null : "text can't be null";
        assert pattern != null : "pattern can't be null";
        assert index >= 0 : "index can't be < 0";

        _text = text;
        _pattern = pattern;
        _index = index;
    }

    public CharSequence getPattern() {
        return _pattern;
    }

    public CharSequence getText() {
        return _text;
    }

    public int getIndex() {
        return _index;
    }
}
```

How It Works

The `StringSearcher` class defines a single `search()` method. This method takes two arguments, the text within which to search and an initial starting position, and returns an object that represents the match (if any), which you will learn more about in just a moment. It is assumed that the pattern to search for will be fixed at construction time—for any concrete implementation—and is therefore not required to be passed as a parameter to `search`.

Notice that you have used `CharSequence` instead of `String` for the text. If you were implementing a word processor, you would most likely use a `StringBuffer` to hold the text of any edited document. There may be times, however, when you also wish to search through a plain `String`. Ordinarily, these two classes — `String` and `StringBuffer` — have nothing in common, meaning you would need to write two different implementations of each algorithm: one for handling `Strings` and another version for `StringBuffers`. Thankfully, the standard Java library provides an interface, `CharSequence`, that is implemented by both the `String` and `StringBuffer` classes, and provides all the methods you need for the two search algorithms.

Each call to `search()` will return either an instance of `StringMatch` or `null` if no match was found. This class encapsulates the concept of a match in a class all of its own, holding not only the position of the match (0, 1, 2, . . .) but also the text and the pattern itself. This way, the result of the search is independent of any other object for its context.

A Generic Test Suite

Even though string searching is conceptually quite simple, the algorithms contain subtleties that can easily trip things up. As always, the best defense against this is to have tests. These tests will serve as our guarantee of correctness — our safety net to ensure that no matter how sophisticated our algorithms become, the outward behavior is always the same.

You will create several test cases, including tests to do the following: find a pattern at the start of some text; find a pattern at the end of some text; find a pattern in the middle of some text; and find multiple, overlapping occurrences of a pattern. Each one will test some aspect of a string searcher in order to prove its correctness.

Try It Out — Creating the Test Class

All the string searchers in this chapter share common behavior, so you can use our tried and trusted method for creating a generic test suite with hooks for subclassing:

```
package com.wrox.algorithms.ssearch;

import junit.framework.TestCase;

public abstract class AbstractStringSearcher extends TestCase {
    protected abstract StringSearcher createSearcher(CharSequence pattern);

    ...
}
```

The first test case is really the simplest of all possible scenarios: searching within an empty string. Anytime `search()` is called with a pattern that doesn't exist within the text, it should return `null` to indicate that no match has been found. Testing boundary conditions like this is a very important part of writing good-quality code:

```
    public void testNotFoundInAnEmptyText() {
        StringSearcher searcher = createSearcher("NOT FOUND");
        assertNull(searcher.search("", 0));
    }
```

The next scenario searches for a pattern at the very beginning of some text:

```
    public void testFindAtTheStart() {
        String text = "Find me at the start";
        String pattern = "Find";

        StringSearcher searcher = createSearcher(pattern);

        StringMatch match = searcher.search(text, 0);
        assertNotNull(match);
        assertEquals(text, match.getText());
        assertEquals(pattern, match.getPattern());
        assertEquals(0, match.getIndex());

        assertNull(searcher.search(text, match.getIndex() + 1));
    }
```

Having searched for a pattern at the beginning of some text, you next look for one at the end:

```
    public void testFindAtTheEnd() {
        String text = "Find me at the end";
        String pattern = "end";

        StringSearcher searcher = createSearcher(pattern);

        StringMatch match = searcher.search(text, 0);
        assertNotNull(match);
        assertEquals(text, match.getText());
        assertEquals(pattern, match.getPattern());
        assertEquals(15, match.getIndex());

        assertNull(searcher.search(text, match.getIndex() + 1));
    }
```

Next, you test that a pattern in the middle of some text is correctly identified:

```
    public void testFindInTheMiddle() {
        String text = "Find me in the middle of the text";
        String pattern = "middle";

        StringSearcher searcher = createSearcher(pattern);

        StringMatch match = searcher.search(text, 0);
        assertNotNull(match);
        assertEquals(text, match.getText());
        assertEquals(pattern, match.getPattern());
        assertEquals(15, match.getIndex());

        assertNull(searcher.search(text, match.getIndex() + 1));
    }
```

Finally, you want to verify that overlapping matches are found. Not that this occurs very often in plain text, but you do need to ensure that the algorithm is working correctly. Besides, it will also test the searcher's ability to find multiple matches—something you haven't done until now:

```
    public void testFindOverlapping() {
        String text = "abcdefffff-fedcba";
        String pattern = "fff";

        StringSearcher searcher = createSearcher(pattern);

        StringMatch match = searcher.search(text, 0);
        assertNotNull(match);
        assertEquals(text, match.getText());
        assertEquals(pattern, match.getPattern());
        assertEquals(5, match.getIndex());

        match = searcher.search(text, match.getIndex() + 1);
        assertNotNull(match);
        assertEquals(text, match.getText());
        assertEquals(pattern, match.getPattern());
        assertEquals(6, match.getIndex());

        match = searcher.search(text, match.getIndex() + 1);
        assertNotNull(match);
        assertEquals(text, match.getText());
        assertEquals(pattern, match.getPattern());
        assertEquals(7, match.getIndex());

        assertNull(searcher.search(text, match.getIndex() + 1));
    }
```

How It Works

All of the string searches you create will encapsulate the pattern for which they are looking — think of them as being a kind of pattern with "smarts," so `createSearcher()` declares the pattern as its one and only argument. Then, in each test method, you create a searcher by calling `createSearcher()` before performing the rest of the test.

The first test searches for an empty string, the result of which should be `null` to indicate that it wasn't found.

In the next test, you expect to find a match at the start of the string and therefore ensure that `search()` returns a non-`null` value. You then ensure that the details of the match are correct, including importantly, verifying the position — in this case, of the first character. Looking at the text, you can see that there should be no more matches. This needs to be tested as well, so you initiate a further search, starting one character position to the right of the previous match, and make sure that it returns `null`.

The third test looks almost identical to the previous one only this time the single occurrence of the pattern exists all the way on the right-hand side of the text, instead of at the left (beginning).

The last test is somewhat more involved than the previous ones, as this time there are multiple occurrences of the pattern — three, to be precise — all slightly overlapping. The test confirms that the searcher finds all of them and in the correct order.

That's it for the test cases. You could have written many more tests, but the ones you implement here will give you reasonably good coverage and enable you to turn your attention to the actual business of searching.

A Brute-Force Algorithm

The simplest and most obvious solution is to perform a brute-force scan through the text. This algorithm is quite widely used and actually performs pretty well in most cases. It is also very easy to describe and code.

The brute-force algorithm is very straightforward and can thus be defined in a few simple steps. Imagine overlaying the text with the pattern, starting from the left-hand side and continuing to slide the pattern right one character until a match is found:

1. Start at the first (leftmost) character in the text.
2. Compare, from left-to-right, each character in the pattern to those in the text.

   If all of the characters are the same, you have found a match.

   Otherwise, if you have reached the end of the text, there can be no more matches, and you are done.

   If neither of the preceding results occur, move the pattern along one character to the right and repeat from step 2.

The following example shows the brute-force search algorithm in action, looking for the pattern `ring` in the text `String Searching`. First `ring` is compared with the substring `Stri`—clearly not a match—followed by `ring` with `trin`, and eventually a match is found on the third attempt. Note the sliding pattern; the brute force approach must compare every character:

```
    String Search
1   ring
2    ring
3     ring
```

Now suppose you wanted to continue searching for additional occurrences of `ring`. You already know the pattern exists at the third character, so there is no point starting from there. Instead, start one character to the right—the fourth character—and follow the same process as before. The following example shows the remaining steps in the search, sliding the pattern across, one position at a time:

```
    String Search
4      ring
5       ring
6        ring
7         ring
8          ring
9           ring
10           ring
```

In this example, there are no more occurrences of `"ring"` within `"String Search"`, so you eventually run out of text before finding a match. Notice that you didn't need to move the pattern all the way to the last character; in fact, you can't move too far or you run out of text. You can see that if you attempt to move beyond the tenth character, you would end up comparing `"ring"` with `"rch"`. You know these two strings could never match because they are different sizes (one is four characters long and the other is three); therefore, you only ever need to move the pattern until it lines up with the end of the text.

It's quite easy to determine how far you need to search before you run out of text characters to compare: For any pattern of length `M` and text of length `M`, you never need move beyond the character at position `N - M + 1`. In the case of our example, the length of the text is `13`, and the pattern is `4`, giving us `13 - 4 + 1 = 10`—just what you saw in the example.

Now that you understand how the algorithm works, you can go ahead and implement it in code. You also want to create some tests to make sure you get your algorithm right.

Try It Out Creating the Test Class

You've already done the hard work of creating the actual test case earlier in the chapter. At that time, we described how you might go about re-using the test cases you created. Now is your chance to try it out:

```
package com.wrox.algorithms.ssearch;

public class BruteForceStringSearcherTest extends AbstractStringSearcherTestCase {
    protected StringSearcher createSearcher(CharSequence pattern) {
        return new BruteForceStringSearcher(pattern);
    }
}
```

How It Works

By extending `AbstractStringSearcherTestCase`, the test class inherits all the predefined test methods, meaning you don't have to do much at all besides construct an instance of your specific searcher class—in this case, `BruteForceStringSearcher`—with the specified pattern.

Try It Out Implementing the Algorithm

Next you create the `BruteForceStringSearcher` class as shown here:

```
package com.wrox.algorithms.ssearch;

public class BruteForceStringSearcher implements StringSearcher {
    private final CharSequence _pattern;

    public BruteForceStringSearcher(CharSequence pattern) {
        assert pattern != null : "pattern can't be null";
        assert pattern.length() > 0 : "pattern can't be empty";
        _pattern = pattern;
    }

    public StringMatch search(CharSequence text, int from) {
        assert text != null : "text can't be null";
        assert from >= 0 : "from can't be < 0";

        int s = from;

        while (s <= text.length() - _pattern.length()) {
            int i = 0;

            while (i < _pattern.length()
                    && _pattern.charAt(i) == text.charAt(s + i)) {
```

```
                ++i;
            }

            if (i == _pattern.length()) {
                return new StringMatch(_pattern, text, s);
            }

            ++s;
        }

        return null;
    }
}
```

How It Works

The `BruteForceStringSearcher` class implements the `StringSearcher` interface you defined earlier. The constructor performs a bit of sanity checking, such as ensuring that a pattern was actually passed, and if so, that it contains at least one character, and then it stores a reference to the pattern for later use.

The `search()` method contains two nested loops that control the algorithm: The outer `while` loop controls how far the algorithm proceeds through the text, and the inner `while` loop performs the actual left-to-right character comparison between the pattern and the text.

When the inner loop terminates, if all the characters in the pattern compared successfully, then a match is returned. Conversely, if a mismatch was encountered, the current position within the text is incremented by one and the outer loop continues. This process repeats until either a match is found or there is no more text to process, in which case `null` is returned to indicate there are no further matches.

As discussed earlier, this algorithm is called brute-force for a reason: There are no tricks, no shortcuts, and no optimizations that you have made to try to reduce the number of comparisons made. In the worst case, you would compare every character of the pattern with (almost) every character of the text, making the worst-case running time `O(NM)`! In practice, however, the performance is much better, as demonstrated toward the end of the chapter.

The Boyer-Moore Algorithm

Although the brute-force approach works fairly well, you have seen that it is far from optimal. Even in the average case, there are numerous false starts and partial matches. However, with a few simple enhancements, you can do much better.

Two men — R. S. Boyer and J. S. Moore — came up with an algorithm that has become the basis for some of the fastest string searching algorithms currently available. They observed that many of the moves made in the brute-force algorithm were redundant. In many cases, the characters in the text don't even exist within the pattern, in which case it should be possible to skip them entirely.

The following example shows the original search, this time using the Boyer-Moore algorithm. Note how large portions of the text have been skipped, reducing the total number of string comparisons to `4`. Compare this with the brute-force algorithm, which performed a total of `10`!

```
    String Search
1   ring
3     ring
4      ring
8          ring
```

The secret is in knowing how many places to shift when you find a mismatch. You can determine this by analyzing the pattern itself. Each time you encounter a failed match, you search the pattern for the last (rightmost) occurrence of the offending character and proceed according to the *bad-character* heuristic:

The original Boyer-Moore algorithm actually makes use of another — good-suffix — heuristic. However, it has been shown by most papers on the subject that this can safely be ignored, as it only improves performance for very long or repetitive patterns. For the purposes of this discussion, we focus purely on the simplified version.

1. If the character exists within the pattern, you shift right enough places to align the character in the pattern with the one in the text. In the example, after an unsuccessful first comparison of a `g` with an `i`, you determine that `i` exists within the pattern, so you move right two places until they meet.
2. If the character doesn't exist within the pattern, you shift right enough places to move just beyond it. Position 4 in our example compares a `g` with a space. The pattern itself contains no spaces at all, so you move right four places to skip past it completely.
3. Whenever the heuristic proposes a negative shift, and in this case only, you resort to the naive approach of moving right one position before returning to the Boyer-Moore algorithm proper.

This last point probably needs a little more explanation. Imagine you were searching for the pattern `over` in the text `everything`:

```
everything
over------
```

Starting from right to left in the pattern, you first compare `r` and then `e` and then `v` until you eventually encounter a mismatch between `o` and `e`. If you were to blindly follow the heuristic, you would discover that in this case the heuristic proposes a move backwards:

```
--everything
over--------
```

The pattern does contain an "e" but it is to the right of the mismatch. Clearly, this isn't what you want. Therefore, given our example, you would shift the pattern one position to the right and continue by comparing, right-to-left, the characters in "over" with "very", and so on:

```
everything
-over-----
-----over-
```

There are actually slightly more efficient ways to handle this case, rather than simply moving one character position to the right, but we have tried to keep the algorithm as simple as possible. Unfortunately, it does mean that in the worst case, our Boyer-Moore implementation performs no better than brute-force, but in practice it performs considerably better.

As demonstrated a little later, this capability to skip entire sections of text leads to some pretty amazing performance improvements over the brute-force search. In fact, although highly unlikely, if the text is such that no character from the pattern ever occurs, then the entire length of the pattern can be skipped each time, leading to a best-case running time of `O(N/M)`, where `N` is the length of the text to search and `M` is the length of the pattern.

Following along the same lines as the previous implementation, you can now create both a test class and a searcher named after the algorithm.

Creating the Tests

Again, you can make use of the tests defined in our abstract test case. This time, however, you will define an additional test specific to the Boyer-Moore implementation.

Try It Out Creating the Test Class

Create a test class as shown here:

```
package com.wrox.algorithms.ssearch;

public class BoyerMooreStringSearcherTest
        extends AbstractStringSearcherTestCase {
    protected StringSearcher createSearcher(CharSequence pattern) {
        return new BoyerMooreStringSearcher(pattern);
    }

    public void testShiftsDontErroneouslyIgnoreMatches() {
        String text = "aababaa";
        String pattern = "baba";

        StringSearcher searcher = createSearcher(pattern);

        StringMatch match = searcher.search(text, 0);
        assertNotNull(match);
        assertEquals(text, match.getText());
        assertEquals(pattern, match.getPattern());
        assertEquals(2, match.getIndex());

        assertNull(searcher.search(text, match.getIndex() + 1));
    }
}
```

How It Works

Because the Boyer-Moore algorithm can shift more than one position at a time, you need to ensure that it shifts the correct number of places. The pattern in this case contains two occurrences of each character. If there was a bug in your calculation of the last occurrence, you might shift too many or too few places.

Implementing the Algorithm

There are several steps involved in implementing the Boyer-Moore algorithm. You must create a string searcher code, compute the last occurrence table, and finally perform the search.

Try It Out Creating the BoyerMooreStringSearcher Class

Start with the basic class definition:

```
package com.wrox.algorithms.ssearch;

public class BoyerMooreStringSearcher implements StringSearcher {
    private final CharSequence _pattern;
    private final short[] _lastOccurrence;

    public BoyerMooreStringSearcher(CharSequence pattern) {
        assert pattern != null : "pattern can't be null";
        assert pattern.length() > 0 : "pattern can't be empty";

        _pattern = pattern;
        _lastOccurrence = computeLastOccurrence(pattern);
    }

    ...
}
```

How It Works

So far, this class looks very similar to the brute-force code except for the presence of the array `_lastOccurrence` and the call to `computeLastOccurrences` to initialize it. If you recall, the Boyer-Moore algorithm needs to know the position of the last occurrence of each character in the pattern. You could calculate this repeatedly by scanning the pattern as needed, but this would certainly add significant overhead, or you could calculate the values once, store them, and look them up as needed.

The construction of the lookup table does incur a once-off overhead proportional to the length of the pattern and size of the character set used. For small character sets such as ASCII, the overhead is minimal. However, larger character sets, such as those required to represent Asian and Middle-Eastern languages, may require more sophisticated techniques, which are beyond the scope of this book.

Try It Out Computing the Last Occurrence Table

The method `computeLastOccurrences()` takes the pattern and returns an array containing the position (0, 1, 2, . . .) of the last occurrence of each character. This is then stored in the `_lastOccurrence` variable for later use:

```
    private static short[] computeLastOccurrence(CharSequence pattern) {
        short[] lastOccurrence = new short[CHARSET_SIZE];

        for (int i = 0; i < lastOccurrence.length; ++i) {
            lastOccurrence[i] = -1;
        }

        for (int i = 0; i < pattern.length(); ++i) {
            lastOccurrence[pattern.charAt(i)] = (short) i;
        }

        return lastOccurrence;
    }
```

How It Works

Here you have assumed the use of the ASCII character set, so you first construct an array containing 256 elements—one for each character—and initialize each with a value of `-1` to indicate that, by default, it doesn't exist within the pattern.

You then iterate from left to right over each character in the pattern, using its character code as an index to the element at which to record the position. Processing the pattern in this way ensures that the position of each character will be overwritten by that of any duplicate that follows, thereby guaranteeing that the array always holds the position of the last (rightmost) occurrence.

Imagine you have a very simplistic character set containing only five characters: `A` , `B`, `C`, `D`, and `E`. From this, you can define a pattern, `DECADE`, and construct a corresponding last occurrence table, as shown in Figure 16-1.

A	B	C	D	E
3	-1	2	4	5

Figure 16-1: A last occurrence table.

The pattern contains one `A` at position `3` and one `C` at position `2`, but no `B`, which has consequently been set to `-1`. Both `D` and `E`, however, occur twice and have been assigned the rightmost position—`4` and `5`, respectively.

Try It Out Performing the Search

As with the brute-force approach, you could simply increment the current position within the text by one each time, but the Boyer-Moore algorithm calls for something more sophisticated:

```
public StringMatch search(CharSequence text, int from) {
    assert text != null : "text can't be null";
    assert from >= 0 : "from can't be < 0";

    int s = from;

    while (s <= text.length() - _pattern.length()) {
        int i = _pattern.length() - 1;

        char c = 0;
        while (i >= 0
                && _pattern.charAt(i) == (c = text.charAt(s + i))) {
            --i;
        }

        if (i < 0) {
            return new StringMatch(_pattern, text, s);
```

```
            }

            s += Math.max(i - _lastOccurrence[c], 1);
        }

        return null;
    }
```

How It Works

The `search()` method itself is structurally very similar to the brute-force version, with two notable differences:

- The pattern is compared backwards, i.e., from right-to-left.
- Determining the shift involves an array lookup and a calculation.

Here is the code that performs the shift calculation:

```
s += Math.max(i - _lastOccurrence[c], 1);
```

Performing the calculation is quite straightforward: You take the mismatched character from the text and use it to look up its *last known* position (0, 1, 2, . . .) within the pattern. This is then subtracted from the *current* position within the pattern. As an example, imagine you were to compare the pattern `abcd` with the text `bdaaedccda`:

```
bdaaedccda
abcd------
```

The first mismatch occurs immediately when `d` (position 3 within the pattern) is compared with `a`. The last occurrence of `a` within the pattern is at position 0, so subtracting one from the other results in a shift of `3 - 0 = 3`. Moving three place to the right, you next compare `abcd` with `aaed`:

```
bdaaedccda
--abcd----
```

Although the two `d`s match, the previous two characters (position 2 within the pattern) do not, and as there is no `e` within the pattern, the table lookup yields a value of `-1`; when used in our calculation, this gives us a shift of `2 - -1 = 3`. Moving right another three places leads to a comparison of `abcd` with `dccd`:

```
bdaaedccda
-----abcd-
```

Here you find a mismatch between the `b` (position 1 within the pattern) and the `c` from the text. The last place a `c` occurs within the pattern is at position 2, giving us a shift of `1 - 2 = -1`; you certainly don't want to be sliding backwards.

Recall, however, that the last part of our three-part heuristic deals with negative shifts. In such cases, the procedure is to resort to the naive approach of shifting right by one. Thus, the call to `Math.max(..., 1)` ensures that no matter what value is calculated, you always end up with an increment of at least one.

A String Match Iterator

If you take a look at the test cases, you may notice that anytime you wanted to iterate through a number of matches, you needed to remember your current location. This approach, though good enough for our needs so far, would ultimately force a duplication of coding effort: Every time you want to perform a search, you need to remember not only the text you are searching through, but also the current position. What you really need is another class to sit on top of a searcher and encapsulate this behavior.

Try It Out   Creating a StringMatchIterator Class

Chapter 2 introduced the `Iterator`, and throughout this book you have made good use of it. Create the following class, which demonstrates yet again the power and flexibility of the iterator and of our string searcher design by encapsulating the behavior and state required to perform multiple, successive searches:

```
package com.wrox.algorithms.ssearch;

import com.wrox.algorithms.iteration.Iterator;
import com.wrox.algorithms.iteration.IteratorOutOfBoundsException;

public class StringMatchIterator implements Iterator {
    private final StringSearcher _searcher;
    private final CharSequence _text;
    private StringMatch _current;

    public StringMatchIterator(StringSearcher searcher, CharSequence text) {
        assert searcher != null : "searcher can't be null";
        assert text != null : "text can't be null";

        _searcher = searcher;
        _text = text;
    }

    public void last() {
        throw new UnsupportedOperationException();
    }

    public void previous() {
        throw new UnsupportedOperationException();
    }

    public boolean isDone() {
        return _current == null;
    }

    public void first() {
        _current = _searcher.search(_text, 0);
    }

    public void next() {
        if (!isDone()) {
            _current = _searcher.search(_text, _current.getIndex() + 1);
```

```
            }
        }

        public Object current() throws IteratorOutOfBoundsException {
            if (isDone()) {
                throw new IteratorOutOfBoundsException();
            }
            return _current;
        }
    }
```

How It Works

The `StringMatchIterator` class holds the string searcher to use; the text to search; and, of course, the current match (if any). It is therefore assumed that you will already have created a string searcher before constructing the string match iterator.

Both `last()` and `previous()` throw `UnsupportedOperationException`. This is because the `StringSearcher` interface provides only for searching forwards through the text.

Implementing `isDone()` is simple, as the string searcher always returns `null` when no more matches are found.

Finding the first match is a matter of calling the string searcher with an initial character position of `0` — the start of the string.

Finding the next and subsequent matches is where you gain most from having the iterator. Because you always hold on to the result of any previous match, you can easily calculate the character position that is one to the right of it in order to continue the search.

Finally, you make the current match accessible via the `current()` method, again making sure to throw `IteratorOutOfBoundsException` if there isn't one.

Comparing the Performance

Now that you have your working string searching algorithms, you probably want to see how they compare with each other. We are pretty confident that the Boyer-Moore algorithm will outperform the brute-force algorithm, but how do we prove it? Usually you would come up with a suite of tests for calculating the best, worst, and average case times. Instead, we thought a more practical example would be of interest: searching a file.

This section develops a simple application that exercises our string searchers by looking for patterns within a file. In the process, you'll demonstrate a simple technique to enable measuring the relative performance of each search implementation.

Measuring Performance

There are many ways to measure the performance of algorithms. The most obvious, of course, is to record elapsed running time. Unfortunately, running times are often susceptible to unpredictable interference from operating system functions such as virtual memory swapping, task switching, network interrupts, and so on. You really need to find a more predictable measure.

Most of the performance-related discussion so far has centered around the number of comparisons made. In fact, the entire basis for deviating from the brute-force algorithm is to reduce not only the number of string comparisons, but also the number of character comparisons—by reducing the number of character comparisons, you reduce the amount of work; by reducing the amount of work, you should in theory reduce the overall running time. Therefore, if you could count the number of comparisons performed, you should be able to measure the performance of each algorithm.

Reviewing the code, it becomes apparent that in both implementations, for each comparison made, there are two character lookups: one to obtain a character from the text, and another from the pattern. From this, you can infer a direct relationship between character lookups and comparisons: If you can count the number of lookups, you can measure the relative performance.

Try It Out A Class for Counting Character Lookups

You may recall that instead of using `String`s for the text and pattern, you used the interface `CharSequence`. Another reason to use the interface is because it becomes trivial to create a wrapper (see Decorator [Gamma, 1995]) that can intercept and count every call to `charAt()`—yet another good reason to use interfaces over concrete classes.

Here is a class that does exactly what you need—namely, count character lookups:

```
package com.wrox.algorithms.ssearch;

public class CallCountingCharSequence implements CharSequence {
    private final CharSequence _charSequence;
    private int _callCount;

    public CallCountingCharSequence(CharSequence charSequence) {
        assert charSequence != null : "charSequence can't be null";
        _charSequence = charSequence;
    }

    public int getCallCount() {
        return _count;
    }

    public char charAt(int index) {
        ++_count;
        return _charSequence.charAt(index);
    }

    public int length() {
        return _charSequence.length();
    }

    public CharSequence subSequence(int start, int end) {
        return _charSequence.subSequence(start, end);
    }
}
```

How It Works

Besides implementing `CharSequence`, the class `CallCountingCharSequence` wraps and eventually delegates all method calls to another underlying `CharSequence`. Notice how each call to `charAt()` increments a counter. This counter is then made accessible via the `getCallCount()` method. In this way, it is very easy to determine how many character comparisons have been made.

Try It Out — A Class That Searches a File

Now that you have a way to count character lookups, you need a way to search through files:

```
import com.wrox.algorithms.iteration.Iterator;

import java.io.FileInputStream;
import java.io.IOException;
import java.nio.ByteBuffer;
import java.nio.CharBuffer;
import java.nio.channels.FileChannel;
import java.nio.charset.Charset;

public final class ComparativeStringSearcher {
    private static final int NUMBER_OF_ARGS = 2;
    private static final String CHARSET_NAME = "8859_1";

    private final String _filename;
    private final String _pattern;

    public ComparativeStringSearcher(String filename, String pattern) {
        assert filename != null : "filename can't be null";
        assert pattern != null : "pattern can't be null";

        _filename = filename;
        _pattern = pattern;
    }

    public void run() throws IOException {
        FileChannel fc = new FileInputStream(_filename).getChannel();
        try {
            ByteBuffer bbuf =
                 fc.map(FileChannel.MapMode.READ_ONLY, 0, (int) fc.size());

            CharBuffer file =
                   Charset.forName(CHARSET_NAME).newDecoder().decode(bbuf);

            System.out.println("Searching '" + _filename + "' ("
                        + file.length() + ") for '" + _pattern + "'...");

            search(new BruteForceStringSearcher(_pattern), file);
            search(new BoyerMooreStringSearcher(_pattern), file);
        } finally {
            fc.close();
        }
    }

    private void search(StringSearcher searcher, CharSequence file) {
```

```
        CallCountingCharSequence text = new CallCountingCharSequence(file);
        Iterator i = new StringMatchIterator(searcher, text);

        int occurrence = 0;

        long startTime = System.currentTimeMillis();

        for (i.first(); !i.isDone(); i.next()) {
            ++occurrence;
        }

        long elapsedTime = System.currentTimeMillis() - startTime;

        System.out.println(searcher.getClass().getName()
                + ": occurrences: " + occurrence
                + ", comparisons: " + text.getCallCount()
                + ", time: " + elapsedTime);
    }

    public static void main(String[] args) throws IOException {
        assert args != null : "args can't be null";

        if (args.length < NUMBER_OF_ARGS) {
            System.err.println(
                    "Usage: ComparativeStringSearcher <file> <pattern>");
            System.exit(-1);
        }

        ComparativeStringSearcher searcher =
                        new ComparativeStringSearcher(args[0], args[1]);

        searcher.run();
    }
}
```

How It Works

Most modern operating systems enable you to open memory-mapped files — instead of reading them as a stream, you can address them as if they were a contiguous array of bytes in memory. You can take advantage of memory-mapped files in your Java programs by using, among others, the `java.nio.CharBuffer` class. What does this have to do with what we're talking about? Well, the truly great thing about `CharBuffer` is that it implements `CharSequence`, which, if you haven't already guessed, means you can use a file as input to the searching algorithms, which is exactly what this class does.

The `run()` method opens the file specified in the constructor and creates a `CharBuffer` that enables you to read from the file using memory-mapped I/O. This is then passed along with a string searcher to the `search()` method, twice: once for each of the two string searcher implementations you created earlier.

The `search()` method first wraps the file with a `CallCountingCharSequence` — a `CharBuffer` is a `CharSequence` — to count the number of character lookups, and then uses a `StringMatchIterator` to find all occurrences of the pattern.

Finally, the `main()` method is called when this program is run. It simply ensures that the correct number of arguments have been passed — one for the file in which to search and another for the pattern — before calling `search()`, where all the real work will be performed.

You may also have noticed the strange `"8859_1"`. This is a character set name and is necessary when using `CharBuffers`; otherwise, there would be no way of knowing how to decode the text in the file. The character set `"8859_1"` corresponds to ISO Latin-1, used for any Western European languages, including English. (See `www.unicode.org` for more information on character sets and character encoding.)

Now the big questions are: How efficient are the two algorithms? Which one is faster? More important, by how much?

How They Compare

To give you a good idea of how each performs, we thought we'd give them a good workout by searching through some large text files looking for various patterns. For this, we used Leo Tolstoy's *War and Peace* — just a little over 3MB in size — available in plain-text format from the Gutenberg Projects website at `www.gutenberg.org`. Table 16-1 shows some of the results.

Table 16-1: Pattern Searching *War and Peace*

Pattern	Occurrences	Brute-Force	Boyer-Moore*	Relative number of comparisons (%)
a	198,999	3,284,649	3,284,650	100.00%
the	43,386	3,572,450	1,423,807	39.86%
zebra	0	3,287,664	778,590	23.68%
military	108	3,349,814	503,199	15.02%
independence	8	3,500,655	342,920	9.80%

*The figures for Boyer-Moore include one extra lookup for each character due to the building of the last occurrence table.

As you can see, the Boyer-Moore algorithm performs consistently better than the naive algorithm — in almost all cases, more than twice as fast; and in most cases, more than four times faster! In fact, if you look carefully, you will notice that the longer the pattern, the greater the improvement. This is because the Boyer-Moore algorithm is often able to skip over large chunks of text — the longer the pattern, the more characters to skip, and consequently the better the performance.

Summary

This chapter covered a few commonly used and well understood string searching algorithms — brute-force and Boyer-Moore — and an iterator that sits on top of the common string searcher interface that removes the coding burden of making multiple, successive searches. Highlights of this chapter include the following main points:

- The brute-force algorithm works by scanning from left to right one position at a time until a match is found. Given that in the worst case you must compare every character of the pattern with almost every character of the text, the worst-case running time is O(NM) — particularly nasty! The ideal scenario for the brute-force approach is a scenario in which the first character comparison fails every time, right up until a successful match at the end of the text. The running time of this best case is therefore O(N + M).
- The Boyer-Moore algorithm performs character comparisons from the right to the left of the pattern, and skips multiple character positions each time. It has a worst-case running time that is as bad as or slightly worse than (due to the overhead of the initial pattern processing) the brute-force algorithm. In practice, however, it performs remarkably better than the brute-force algorithm and can achieve a best-case running time of O(N/M) when it can continually skip the entire pattern right up until the end.
- You can implement an iterator that avoids the cumbersome state management associated with performing repeated searches. Because the iterator depends only on the `StringSearcher` interface, you can use it with any string searcher you use. For example, if you need to search through different types of text with characteristics that required some sophisticated and varied string searching algorithms, the iterator enables you to use it, assuming your new algorithm conforms to the `StringSearcher` interface while leaving all your application code as is, oblivious to the change in search technique.
- You compared the two algorithms by searching for various English words in a relatively large (~3MB) text file. Obviously, real-world results will vary depending on the type of text to search, the make-up and length of the pattern, and so on. Overall, it is hoped that you can see how, with a little thinking and a little effort, you can achieve almost an order of magnitude improvement in performance between the brute-force and the Boyer-Moore search algorithms.

There are many other well-known string searching algorithms that we haven't discussed — Rabin-Karp [Cormen, 2001] and Knuth-Morris-Pratt [Cormen, 2001] being the first to spring to mind. Neither of these perform nearly as well as Boyer-Moore in most applications, and they can often be no better than the brute-force approach for plain-text searching. Rabin-Karp, which uses a clever hashing scheme, is useful for searching multiple patterns at once. Whatever the application, the important thing is to analyze the type of text you are searching through and identify the characteristics that will enable you to avoid many of the obviously unnecessary comparisons.

String Matching

Chapter 16 concentrated on efficient techniques for finding one string within another. This chapter focuses on matching whole strings, and, in particular, attempting to find matches between non-identical yet similar strings. This can be very useful for detecting duplicate entries in a database, spell-checking documents, and even searching for genes in DNA.

This chapter discusses the following topics:

- Understanding Soundex
- Understanding Levenshtein word distance

Understanding Soundex

Soundex encoding is one of a class of algorithms known as *phonetic encoding algorithms*. Phonetic encoding takes strings and converts similar sounding words into the same encoded value (much like a hash function).

Soundex, developed by R. C. Russell to process data collected from the 1980 census, is also known as the Russell Soundex algorithm and has been used in its original form and with many variations in numerous applications — ranging from human resource management to genealogy, and, of course, census taking — in an attempt to eliminate data duplication that occurs because of differences in the spelling of people's surnames.

In 1970, Robert L. Taft, working as part of the New York State Identification and Intelligence project (NYSII), published a paper titled "Name Search Techniques," in which he presented findings on two phonetic encoding schemes. One of these was Soundex, the other an algorithm developed by the NYSII based on extensive statistical analysis of real data. The NYSII project concluded that Soundex was 95.99% accurate with a selectivity of 0.213% per search, whereas the new system (not presented here) was 98.72% accurate with a selectivity of 0.164% per search.

Other phonetic encoding schemes include Metaphone, Double-Metaphone, and many variations on the original Soundex.

The Soundex algorithm is quite straightforward and fairly simple to understand. It involves a number of rules for processing an input string. The input string, usually a surname or the like, is processed from left to right, with a transformation applied to each character to produce a four-character code of the form *LDDD*, where *L* represents a letter and *D* represents a decimal digit in the range 0 to 6.

Each input character is transformed according to one or more of the following rules (look for the relationships within each group of letters):

1. All characters are processed as if they were uppercase.
2. Always use the first letter.
3. Drop all other characters if they are A, E, I, O, U, H, W, or Y.
4. Translate the remaining characters as follows:
    - B, F, P, and V to 1
    - C, G, J, K, Q, S, X, and Z to 2
    - D and T to 3
    - L to 4
    - M and N to 5
    - R to 6
5. Drop consecutive letters having the same code.
6. Pad with zeros if necessary

After taking the first letter, you drop all the vowels. In English, it is often still possible to read most words after all of the vowels have been removed. Notice also that H, W, and Y are also ignored, as their pronunciation is often the same as a vowel sound.

The letters B, F, P, and V are also similar, not only in pronunciation but also in the shape of your mouth when making the sound. Try saying B followed by P. The same can be said for T and D as well as M and N, and so on.

Also notice that you ignore consecutive letters with the same code. This makes sense because double letters in English often sound the same as a single letter.

To give you an idea of how the encoding works in practice, take the surnames Smith and Smythe and see how you would encode them using the Soundex algorithm.

Start by initializing a result buffer with space for four characters — the maximum length of a Soundex code is four — as shown in Figure 17-1. You then start processing the input string one character at a time from left to right.

You know from rule 2 that you always copy the first character from the input string into the first character of the result buffer, so you copy across the S as shown in Figure 17-2.

The next character in the input string is m. Rule 4 says this should be encoded as a 5. Figure 17-3 shows the 5 being placed into the second character position of the result.

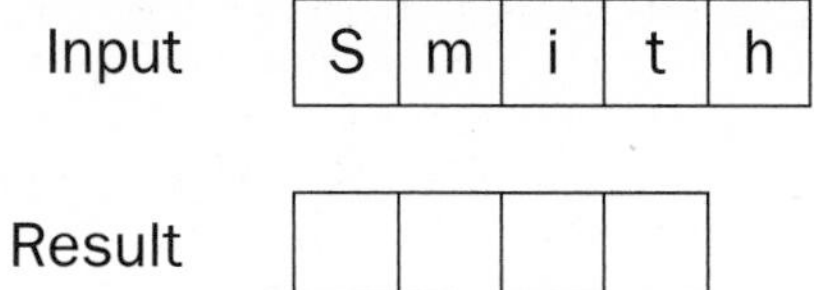

Figure 17-1: Start by initializing a result buffer with space for four characters.

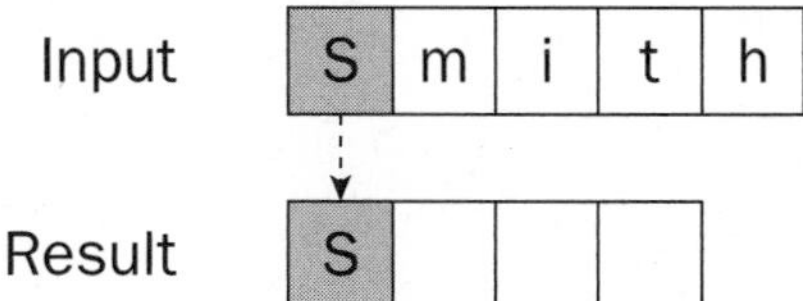

Figure 17-2: The first input string character is always used as the first character in the result.

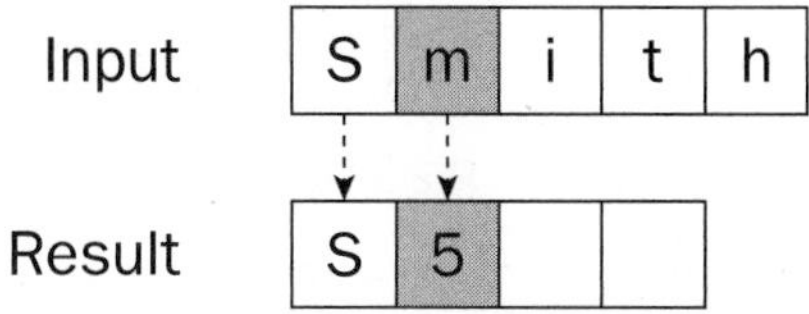

Figure 17-3: An m is encoded as a 5.

The third input string character position contains an `i`, which according to rule 3 should be ignored (along with any other vowels), and therefore does not contribute to the result (see Figure 17-4).

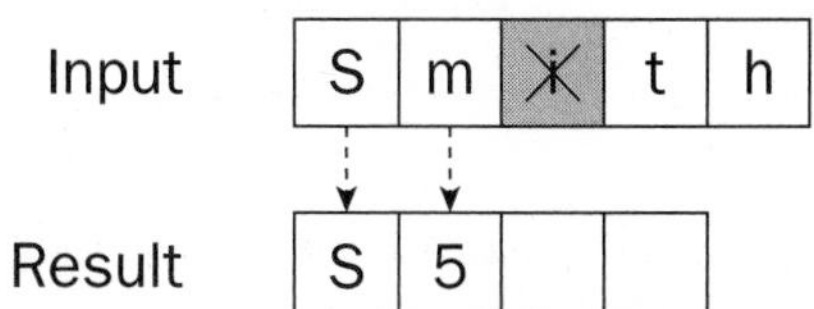

Figure 17-4: All vowels are ignored.

Following the i is the letter t, which according to the algorithm is encoded as a 3. In this example, it goes into the result at position 3, as shown in Figure 17-5.

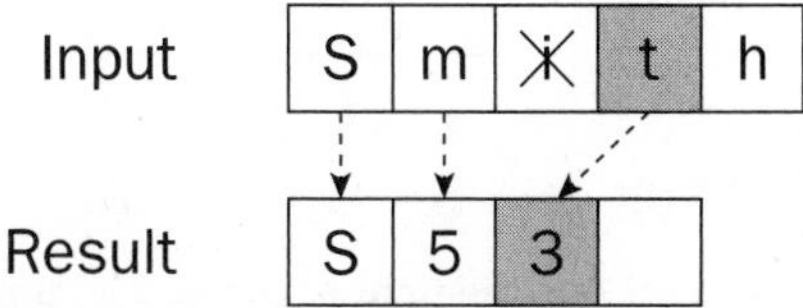

Figure 17-5: A t is encoded as a 3.

The last character, h, is a special character that is treated as if it was a vowel and is therefore ignored (see Figure 17-6).

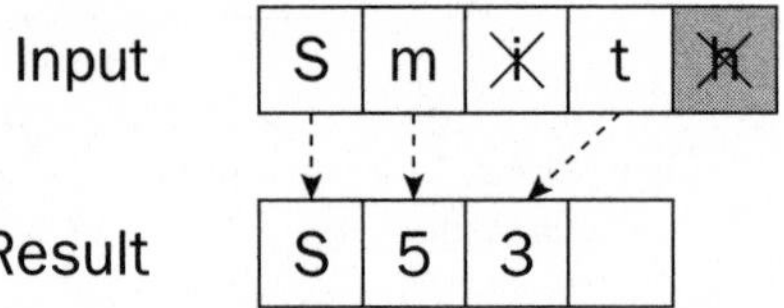

Figure 17-6: H, W, and Y are all treated as vowels and hence ignored.

You've run out of input characters but you haven't filled the result buffer, so following rule 6, you pad the remainder with zeros. Figure 17-7 shows that the Soundex value for the character string Smith is S530.

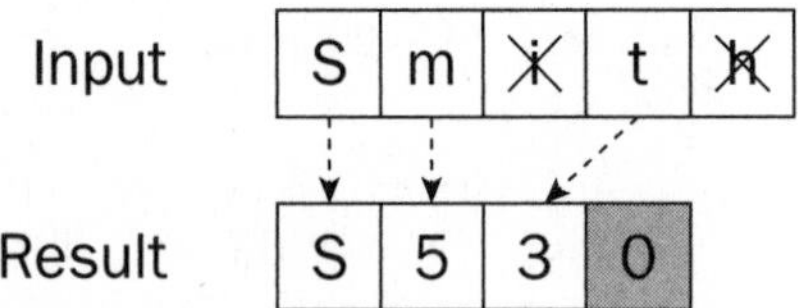

Figure 17-7: The result is padded with zeros to achieve the required four characters.

Now take a quick look at encoding `Smythe`. You start off as you did previously, with a result buffer of length four, as shown in Figure 17-8.

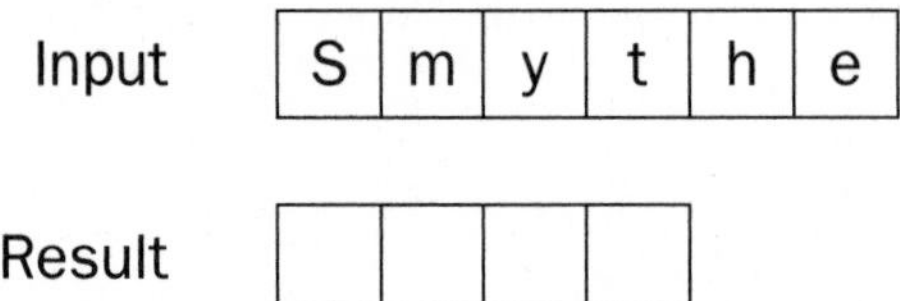

Figure 17-8: Again, begin by initializing a result buffer with space for four characters.

We're not going to show you each step in the process this time; you can do this easily enough for yourself. Instead, we've summarized the result, shown in Figure 17-9.

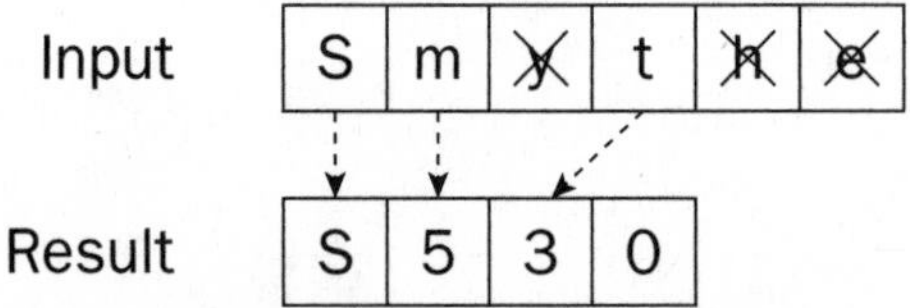

Figure 17-9: The final encoding for "Smythe".

Figure 17-9, shows that `Smythe` encodes as `S530`, as did `Smith`. If you were creating a database index using the Soundex for surnames, then a search for `Smith` would also return any records with `Smythe` and vice-versa, exactly what you would hope for in a system designed to catch spelling mistakes and find people with similar names.

Although not a huge concern in this particular instance, the algorithm clearly runs in `O(N)` time, as only one pass over the string is ever made.

Now that you have a feel for how the Soundex algorithm works in theory, in the next Try It Out section you write some tests to ensure you get your actual implementation right.

Try It Out Testing the Soundex Encoder

Create the test class as follows (there are quite a few rules and you want to cover as many as possible to ensure that you implement the algorithm correctly):

```
package com.wrox.algorithms.wmatch;

import junit.framework.TestCase;

public class SoundexPhoneticEncoderTest extends TestCase {
    private SoundexPhoneticEncoder _encoder;

    protected void setUp() throws Exception {
        super.setUp();

        _encoder = SoundexPhoneticEncoder.INSTANCE;
    }

    public void testFirstLetterIsAlwaysUsed() {
        for (char c = 'A'; c <= 'Z'; ++c) {
            String result = _encoder.encode(c + "-");

            assertNotNull(result);
            assertEquals(4, result.length());

            assertEquals(c, result.charAt(0));
        }
    }

    public void testVowelsAreIgnored() {
        assertAllEquals('0', new char[] {'A', 'E', 'I', 'O', 'U', 'H', 'W', 'Y'});
    }

    public void testLettersRepresentedByOne() {
        assertAllEquals('1', new char[] {'B', 'F', 'P', 'V'});
    }

    public void testLettersRepresentedByTwo() {
        assertAllEquals('2', new char[] {'C', 'G', 'J', 'K', 'Q', 'S', 'X', 'Z'});
    }

    public void testLettersRepresentedByThree() {
```

```
        assertAllEquals('3', new char[] {'D', 'T'});
    }

    public void testLettersRepresentedByFour() {
        assertAllEquals('4', new char[] {'L'});
    }

    public void testLettersRepresentedByFive() {
        assertAllEquals('5', new char[] {'M', 'N'});
    }

    public void testLettersRepresentedBySix() {
        assertAllEquals('6', new char[] {'R'});
    }

    public void testDuplicateCodesAreDropped() {
        assertEquals("B100", _encoder.encode("BFPV"));
        assertEquals("C200", _encoder.encode("CGJKQSXZ"));
        assertEquals("D300", _encoder.encode("DDT"));
        assertEquals("L400", _encoder.encode("LLL"));
        assertEquals("M500", _encoder.encode("MNMN"));
        assertEquals("R600", _encoder.encode("RRR"));
    }

    public void testSomeRealStrings() {
        assertEquals("S530", _encoder.encode("Smith"));
        assertEquals("S530", _encoder.encode("Smythe"));
        assertEquals("M235", _encoder.encode("McDonald"));
        assertEquals("M235", _encoder.encode("MacDonald"));
        assertEquals("H620", _encoder.encode("Harris"));
        assertEquals("H620", _encoder.encode("Harrys"));
    }

    private void assertAllEquals(char expectedValue, char[] chars) {
        for (int i = 0; i < chars.length; ++i) {
            char c = chars[i];
            String result = _encoder.encode("-" + c);

            assertNotNull(result);
            assertEquals(4, result.length());

            assertEquals("-" + expectedValue + "00", result);
        }
    }
}
```

How It Works

The `SoundexPhoneticEncoderTest` class holds an instance of a `SoundexPhoneticEncoder` that is initialized in `setUp()` and used by the test cases:

```
package com.wrox.algorithms.wmatch;

import junit.framework.TestCase;

public class SoundexPhoneticEncoderTest extends TestCase {
```

```
        private SoundexPhoneticEncoder _encoder;

        protected void setUp() throws Exception {
            super.setUp();

            _encoder = SoundexPhoneticEncoder.INSTANCE;
        }

        ...
    }
```

Rule 2 says that you must always use the first letter under any circumstances, so you start by testing this assumption. The `testFirstLetterIsAlwaysUsed()` method cycles through each character from `A` to `Z`, encoding it as the first character of a string. Once encoded, you then ensure that the return string is not `null` and that the length is four—all Soundex values must be four characters in length. You then verify that the first character of the result is the same as the one used in the input string:

```
        public void testFirstLetterIsAlwaysUsed() {
            for (char c = 'A'; c <= 'Z'; ++c) {
                String result = _encoder.encode(c + "-");

                assertNotNull(result);
                assertEquals(4, result.length());

                assertEquals(c, result.charAt(0));
            }
        }
```

The tests for the remaining rules all look pretty much the same, and use a helper method to do most of the work. The method `assertAllEquals()` accepts an expected value and an array of characters to use. Each character is used as the second letter in a two-letter input string, which is encoded. Again the return value is checked for `null` and to ensure it has the correct length. The encoded value is then compared with the expected result. In all cases, the first character should have remained unchanged, and because we only encoded a two-character string, the last two digits will always be padded with zeros. This leaves only the second character from the result to be checked, and in this case the expected value is 0, indicating that the input character was ignored:

```
        private void assertAllEquals(char expectedValue, char[] chars) {
            for (int i = 0; i < chars.length; ++i) {
                char c = chars[i];
                String result = _encoder.encode("-" + c);

                assertNotNull(result);
                assertEquals(4, result.length());

                assertEquals("-" + expectedValue + "00", result);
            }
        }
```

Rule 3 says that you must drop all vowels, including some special letters that sound like vowels. The method `testVowelsAreIgnored()` checks this by constructing a string containing nothing but an arbitrary first character—which is always copied as is—followed by a single vowel. After encoding, you expect the last three characters of the encoded value to be "000", indicating that the vowel has been ignored and the result was therefore padded to fill the remaining character spaces:

```
public void testVowelsAreIgnored() {
    assertAllEquals('0', new char[] {'A', 'E', 'I', 'O', 'U', 'H', 'W', 'Y'});
}
```

You also tested each of the six cases for rule 4. In each case, you called assertAllEquals(), passing in the expected value and the set of input characters:

```
public void testLettersRepresentedByOne() {
    assertAllEquals('1', new char[] {'B', 'F', 'P', 'V'});
}

public void testLettersRepresentedByTwo() {
    assertAllEquals('2', new char[] {'C', 'G', 'J', 'K', 'Q', 'S', 'X', 'Z'});
}

public void testLettersRepresentedByThree() {
    assertAllEquals('3', new char[] {'D', 'T'});
}

public void testLettersRepresentedByFour() {
    assertAllEquals('4', new char[] {'L'});
}

public void testLettersRepresentedByFive() {
    assertAllEquals('5', new char[] {'M', 'N'});
}

public void testLettersRepresentedBySix() {
    assertAllEquals('6', new char[] {'R'});
}
```

Rule 5 specifies that we should drop consecutive letters having the same code, although how testDuplicateCodesAreDropped() checks this may not be as obvious as with the other tests.

Essentially, you take each group of letters and use them to form a string. You know, of course, that the first letter will be used directly. You also know that the second letter will be encoded—none of the letters in the test are vowels—but because the third and subsequent letters all code the same as the second, you expect them to be ignored, ensuring that the last two digits of the encoded string will be zeros:

```
public void testDuplicateCodesAreDropped() {
    assertEquals("B100", _encoder.encode("BFPV"));
    assertEquals("C200", _encoder.encode("CGJKQSXZ"));
    assertEquals("D300", _encoder.encode("DDT"));
    assertEquals("L400", _encoder.encode("LLL"));
    assertEquals("M500", _encoder.encode("MNMN"));
    assertEquals("R600", _encoder.encode("RRR"));
}
```

Finally, testSomeRealStrings() takes three pairs of names that encode to the same and validates the result:

```
    public void testSomeRealStrings() {
        assertEquals("S530", _encoder.encode("Smith"));
        assertEquals("S530", _encoder.encode("Smythe"));
        assertEquals("M235", _encoder.encode("McDonald"));
        assertEquals("M235", _encoder.encode("MacDonald"));
        assertEquals("H620", _encoder.encode("Harris"));
        assertEquals("H620", _encoder.encode("Harrys"));
    }
```

Now that you're confident you have a test suite sufficient to ensure the correctness of your implementation, in the next Try It Out section you write the actual Soundex encoder.

Try It Out Implementing the Soundex Encoder

Starting by creating an interface definition common to any phonetic encoder:

```
package com.wrox.algorithms.wmatch;

public interface PhoneticEncoder {
    public String encode(CharSequence string);
}
```

Then create the Soundex encoder class as follows:

```
package com.wrox.algorithms.wmatch;

public final class SoundexPhoneticEncoder implements PhoneticEncoder {
    public static final SoundexPhoneticEncoder INSTANCE =
            new SoundexPhoneticEncoder();

    private static final char[] CHARACTER_MAP =
            "01230120022455012623010202".toCharArray();

    private SoundexPhoneticEncoder() {
    }

    public String encode(CharSequence string) {
        assert string != null : "string can't be null";
        assert string.length() > 0 : "string can't be empty";

        char[] result = {'0', '0', '0', '0'};

        result[0] = Character.toUpperCase(string.charAt(0));

        int stringIndex = 1;
        int resultIndex = 1;

        while (stringIndex < string.length() && resultIndex < result.length) {
            char c = map(string.charAt(stringIndex));

            if (c != '0' && c != result[resultIndex - 1]) {
                result[resultIndex] = c;
                ++resultIndex;
```

```
            }

            ++stringIndex;
        }

        return String.valueOf(result);
    }

    private static char map(char c) {
        int index = Character.toUpperCase(c) - 'A';
        return isValid(index) ? CHARACTER_MAP[index] : '0';
    }

    private static boolean isValid(int index) {
        return index >= 0 && index < CHARACTER_MAP.length;
    }
}
```

How It Works

By defining the `PhoneticEncoder` interface, you will be able to develop other variations that can be used in your own applications without depending directly on the specific implementation presented here:

```
package com.wrox.algorithms.wmatch;

public interface PhoneticEncoder {
    public String encode(CharSequence string);
}
```

The `SoundexPhoneticEncoder` class then implements the `PhoneticEncoder` interface to ensure plug-gability with different encoding schemes if you so desire.

Notice that the constructor is marked as `private`, which prevents instantiation. Recall that earlier we mentioned we would only ever need a single instance of the class, so all access to the class must be via the publicly available constant `INSTANCE`.

Notice also the character array `CHARACTER_MAP`. This is crucial to the algorithm and provides a mapping between characters and coded digits. The map is assumed to start at `A` and continue on through the alphabet until `Z`. Obviously, this limits the implementation to working only with the English language, but as the algorithm only really works for English names, this isn't much of a problem:

```
package com.wrox.algorithms.wmatch;

public final class SoundexPhoneticEncoder implements PhoneticEncoder {
    public static final SoundexPhoneticEncoder INSTANCE =
            new SoundexPhoneticEncoder();

    private static final char[] CHARACTER_MAP =
            "01230120022455012623010202".toCharArray();

    private SoundexPhoneticEncoder() {
    }

    ...
}
```

Before getting into the core of the algorithm, we'll first cover two simple helper methods: `map()` and `isValid()`. Together, these methods take a character from the input string and translate it according to the Soundex rules. The character is first converted into an index that can be used for looking up values in the array `CHARACTER_MAP`. If the index falls within the bounds of the array, the character is translated; otherwise, a `0` is returned to indicate that it should be ignored—just as for vowels:

```
private static char map(char c) {
    int index = Character.toUpperCase(c) - 'A';
    return isValid(index) ? CHARACTER_MAP[index] : '0';
}

private static boolean isValid(int index) {
    return index >= 0 && index < CHARACTER_MAP.length;
}
```

Finally, you get to the actual Soundex encoding algorithm: `encode()`. This method starts by initializing a four-character array with all zeros. This is actually a shortcut method of padding the final encoded value—you already know the result must be four characters in length, so why not start off with all zeros? Next, the first character of the input string is used as the first character of the result—and converted to uppercase just in case—as per rule 1. The method then loops over each character of the input string. Each character is passed through `map()` and the return value is stored in the result buffer—unless it is `0` or the same as the last value stored, in which case it is ignored. This continues until either the result buffer is full—four characters have been stored—or there are no more input characters to process. The result buffer is then converted to a string and returned to the caller:

```
public String encode(CharSequence string) {
    assert string != null : "string can't be null";
    assert string.length() > 0 : "string can't be empty";

    char[] result = {'0', '0', '0', '0'};

    result[0] = Character.toUpperCase(string.charAt(0));

    int stringIndex = 1;
    int resultIndex = 1;

    while (stringIndex < string.length() && resultIndex < result.length) {
        char c = map(string.charAt(stringIndex));

        if (c != '0' && c != result[resultIndex - 1]) {
            result[resultIndex] = c;
            ++resultIndex;
        }

        ++stringIndex;
    }

    return String.valueOf(result);
}
```

Understanding Levenshtein Word Distance

While phonetic coding such as Soundex is excellent for fuzzy-matching misspelled English names and even some minor spelling mistakes, it isn't very good at detecting large typing errors. For example, the Soundex values for "mistakes" and "msitakes" are the same, but the values for "shop" and "sjop" are not, even though transposing a "j" for an "h" is a common mistake—both letters are next to each other on a standard QWERTY keyboard.

The Levenshtein *word distance* (also known as *edit distance*) algorithm compares words for similarity by calculating the smallest number of insertions, deletions, and substitutions required to transform one string into another. You can then choose some limit—say, 4—below which the distance between two words is short enough to consider. Thus, the algorithm presented often forms the basis for a number of other techniques used in word processor spell-checking, DNA matching, and plagiarism detection.

The algorithm uses an effective yet rather brute-force approach that essentially looks at every possible way of transforming the source string to the target string to find the least number of changes.

Three different operations can be performed. Each operation is assigned a *cost,* and the smallest distance is the set of changes with the smallest total cost. To calculate the Levenshtein distance, start by creating a grid with rows and columns corresponding to the letters in the source and target word. Figure 17-10 shows the grid for calculating the edit distance from "msteak" to "mistake".

		m	i	s	t	a	k	e
	0	1	2	3	4	5	6	7
m	1							
s	2							
t	3							
e	4							
a	5							
k	6							

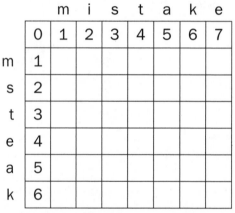

Figure 17-10: Initialized grid for comparing msteak with mistake.

Notice we've also included an extra row with the values 1–7 and an extra column with the values 1–6. The row corresponds to an empty source word and the values represent the cumulative cost of inserting each character. The column corresponds to an empty target word and the values represent the cumulative cost of deletion.

The next step is to calculate the values for each of the remaining cells in the grid. The value for each cell is calculated according to the following formula:

```
min(left diagonal + substitution cost, above + delete cost, left + insert cos)
```

For example, to calculate the value for the first cell (m, m), you apply the following formula:

```
min(0 + 0, 1 + 1, 1 + 1) = min(0, 2, 2) = 0
```

The cost for insertion and deletion is always one, but the cost for substitution is only one when the source and target characters don't match.

> *You might want to vary the cost for some operations—specifically, insertion and deletion—as you may consider the substitution of one character for another to be less costly than inserting or deleting a character.*

Calculating the value for the cell leads to the grid shown in Figure 17-11.

		m	i	s	t	a	k	e
	0	1	2	3	4	5	6	7
m	1	0						
s	2							
t	3							
e	4							
a	5							
k	6							

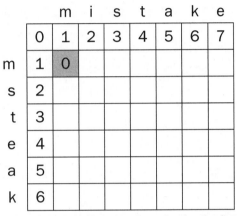

Figure 17-11: Calculating the value for the first cell (m, m).

For the next cell (m, i), it would be as follows:

```
min(1 + 1, 2 + 1, 0 + 1) = min(2, 3, 1) = 1
```

This would result in the grid shown in Figure 17-12.

		m	i	s	t	a	k	e
	0	1	2	3	4	5	6	7
m	1	0	1					
s	2							
t	3							
e	4							
a	5							
k	6							

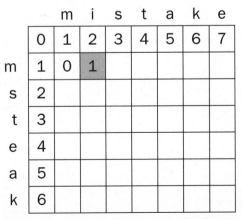

Figure 17-12: Calculating the value for the next cell (m, i).

This process continues until every cell has been assigned a value, as shown in Figure 17-13.

		m	i	s	t	a	k	e
	0	1	2	3	4	5	6	7
m	1	0	1	2	3	4	5	6
s	2	1	1	1	2	3	4	5
t	3	2	2	2	1	2	3	4
e	4	3	3	3	2	2	3	3
a	5	4	4	4	3	2	3	4
k	6	5	5	5	4	3	2	3

Figure 17-13: A completed grid. The last cell (k, e) has the minimum distance.

The value in the bottom-right cell of the grid shows that the minimum distance between "msteak" and "mistake" is 3. The grid actually provides a set of operations (or alignments) that you can apply to transform the source to the target. Figure 17-14 shows just one of the many paths that make up a set of transformations.

		m	i	s	t	a	k	e
	0	1	2	3	4	5	6	7
m	1	0	1	2	3	4	5	6
s	2	1	1	1	2	3	4	5
t	3	2	2	2	1	2	3	4
e	4	3	3	3	2	2	3	3
a	5	4	4	4	3	2	3	4
k	6	5	5	5	4	3	2	3

Figure 17-14: One of many possible paths through the grid showing the order of operations for transforming "msteak" into "mistake".

You can interpret Figure 17-14 as follows"

1. Substitute "m" with "m" at no cost.
2. Insert an "i" at a cost of 1.
3. Substitute "s" with "s" at no cost.

4. Substitute “t” with “t” at no cost.
5. Delete the “e” at a cost of 1.
6. Substitute “a” with “a” at no cost.
7. Insert an “e” at a cost of 1.

From this, you can deduce that a move diagonally down is a substitution; to the right an insertion; and straight down a deletion.

The algorithm as just defined performs in a time relative to `O(MN)`, as each character from the source, `M`, is compared with each character in the target, `N`, to produce a fully populated grid. This means that the algorithm as it stands couldn't really be used for producing a spell-checker containing any appreciable number of words, as the time to calculate all the distances would be prohibitive. Instead, word processors typically use a combination of techniques similar to those presented in this chapter.

In the following Try It Out, you build some tests that ensure that your implementation of the algorithm runs correctly.

Try It Out Testing the Distance Calculator

Create the test class as follows:

```
package com.wrox.algorithms.wmatch;

import junit.framework.TestCase;

public class LevenshteinWordDistanceCalculatorTest extends TestCase {
    private LevenshteinWordDistanceCalculator _calculator;

    protected void setUp() throws Exception {
        super.setUp();

        _calculator = LevenshteinWordDistanceCalculator.DEFAULT;
    }

    public void testEmptyToEmpty() {
        assertDistance(0, "", "");
    }

    public void testEmptyToNonEmpty() {
        String target = "any";
        assertDistance(target.length(), "", target);
    }

    public void testSamePrefix() {
        assertDistance(3, "unzip", "undo");
    }

    public void testSameSuffix() {
        assertDistance(4, "eating", "running");
    }

    public void testArbitrary() {
```

```
        assertDistance(3, "msteak", "mistake");
        assertDistance(3, "necassery", "neccessary");
        assertDistance(5, "donkey", "mule");
    }

    private void assertDistance(int distance, String source, String target) {
        assertEquals(distance, _calculator.calculate(source, target));
        assertEquals(distance, _calculator.calculate(target, source));
    }
}
```

How It Works

The `LevenshteinWordDistanceCalculatorTest` class holds an instance of a `LevenshteinWordDistanceCalculator` to be used by the tests. This is then initialized with the default instance described earlier:

```
package com.wrox.algorithms.wmatch;

import junit.framework.TestCase;

public class LevenshteinWordDistanceCalculatorTest extends TestCase {
    private LevenshteinWordDistanceCalculator _calculator;

    protected void setUp() throws Exception {
        super.setUp();

        _calculator = LevenshteinWordDistanceCalculator.DEFAULT;
    }

    ...
}
```

The method `assertDistance()` is used in all of the tests to ensure that the calculated distance is as expected. It takes a source string and a target string and runs them through the calculator, comparing the result with the expected value. The thing to note about this method—and the reason you have created it—is that it runs the calculation twice, swapping the source and target the second time around. This ensures that no matter which way the strings are presented to the calculator, the same distance value is always produced:

```
    private void assertDistance(int distance, String source, String target) {
        assertEquals(distance, _calculator.calculate(source, target));
        assertEquals(distance, _calculator.calculate(target, source));
    }
```

The method `testEmptyToEmpty()` ensures that the distance between two empty strings is zero—even though they are empty, both strings are effectively the same:

```
    public void testEmptyToEmpty() {
        assertDistance(0, "", "");
    }
```

The method `testEmptyToNonEmpty()` compares an empty string with an arbitrary non-empty string: The distance should be the length of the non-empty string itself:

```
public void testEmptyToNonEmpty() {
    String target = "any";
    assertDistance(target.length(), "", target);
}
```

Next, `testSamePrefix()` tests strings sharing a common prefix: The distance should be the length of the longer string minus the prefix:

```
public void testSamePrefix() {
    assertDistance(3, "unzip", "undo");
}
```

Conversely, `testSamePrefix()` test strings sharing a common suffix: This time, the distance should be the length of the longer string minus the suffix:

```
public void testSameSuffix() {
    assertDistance(4, "eating", "running");
}
```

Finally, you tested various combinations with known distances:

```
public void testArbitrary() {
    assertDistance(3, "msteak", "mistake");
    assertDistance(3, "necassery", "neccessary");
    assertDistance(5, "donkey", "mule");
}
```

Now that you have some tests to back you up, in the following Try It Out section, you create the actual distance calculator.

Try It Out Implementing the Distance Calculator

Create the distance calculator as follows:

```
package com.wrox.algorithms.wmatch;

public class LevenshteinWordDistanceCalculator {
    public static final LevenshteinWordDistanceCalculator DEFAULT =
            new LevenshteinWordDistanceCalculator(1, 1, 1);

    private final int _costOfSubstitution;
    private final int _costOfDeletion;
    private final int _costOfInsertion;

    public LevenshteinWordDistanceCalculator(int costOfSubstitution,
                                             int costOfDeletion,
                                             int costOfInsertion) {
        assert costOfSubstitution >= 0 : "costOfSubstitution can't be < 0";
        assert costOfDeletion >= 0 : "costOfDeletion can't be < 0";
```

```
        assert costOfInsertion >= 0 : "costOfInsertion can't be < 0";

        _costOfSubstitution = costOfSubstitution;
        _costOfDeletion = costOfDeletion;
        _costOfInsertion = costOfInsertion;
    }

    public int calculate(CharSequence source, CharSequence target) {
        assert source != null : "source can't be null";
        assert target != null : "target can't be null";

        int sourceLength = source.length();
        int targetLength = target.length();

        int[][] grid = new int[sourceLength + 1][targetLength + 1];

        grid[0][0] = 0;

        for (int row = 1; row <= sourceLength; ++row) {
            grid[row][0] = row;
        }

        for (int col = 1; col <= targetLength; ++col) {
            grid[0][col] = col;
        }

        for (int row = 1; row <= sourceLength; ++row) {
            for (int col = 1; col <= targetLength; ++col) {
                grid[row][col] = minCost(source, target, grid, row, col);
            }
        }

        return grid[sourceLength][targetLength];
    }

    private int minCost(CharSequence source, CharSequence target,
                        int[][] grid, int row, int col) {
        return min(
                substitutionCost(source, target, grid, row, col),
                deleteCost(grid, row, col),
                insertCost(grid, row, col)
        );
    }

    private int substitutionCost(CharSequence source, CharSequence target,
                                 int[][] grid, int row, int col) {
        int cost = 0;
        if (source.charAt(row - 1) != target.charAt(col - 1)) {
            cost = _costOfSubstitution;
        }
        return grid[row - 1][col - 1] + cost;
    }

    private int deleteCost(int[][] grid, int row, int col) {
        return grid[row - 1][col] + _costOfDeletion;
```

```
    }

    private int insertCost(int[][] grid, int row, int col) {
        return grid[row][col - 1] + _costOfInsertion;
    }

    private static int min(int a, int b, int c) {
        return Math.min(a, Math.min(b, c));
    }
}
```

How It Works

The `LevenshteinWordDistanceCalculator` class has three instance variables for storing the unit cost associated with each of the three operations: substitution, deletion, and insertion. The class also defines a `DEFAULT` whereby all three operations have a unit cost of one, as was the case in the discussion earlier. There is also a public constructor that enables you to play with different weightings:

```
package com.wrox.algorithms.wmatch;

public class LevenshteinWordDistanceCalculator {
    public static final LevenshteinWordDistanceCalculator DEFAULT =
            new LevenshteinWordDistanceCalculator(1, 1, 1);

    private final int _costOfSubstitution;
    private final int _costOfDeletion;
    private final int _costOfInsertion;

    public LevenshteinWordDistanceCalculator(int costOfSubstitution,
                                             int costOfDeletion,
                                             int costOfInsertion) {
        assert costOfSubstitution >= 0 : "costOfSubstitution can't be < 0";
        assert costOfDeletion >= 0 : "costOfDeletion can't be < 0";
        assert costOfInsertion >= 0 : "costOfInsertion can't be < 0";

        _costOfSubstitution = costOfSubstitution;
        _costOfDeletion = costOfDeletion;
        _costOfInsertion = costOfInsertion;
    }

    ...
}
```

Before getting into the core of the algorithm, let's start by examining some of the intermediate calculations. The first such calculation is `substitutionCost()`. As the name implies, this method calculates the cost of substituting one character for another. Recall that the substitution cost is 0 if the two letters are the same, or 1 + the value in the diagonally left cell.

The method starts off by assuming the characters will match, therefore initializing the cost to 0. You then compare the two characters, and if they differ, the cost is updated accordingly. Finally, you add in the cumulative value stored in the diagonally left cell of the grid before returning the value to the caller:

```
    private int substitutionCost(CharSequence source, CharSequence target,
                                 int[][] grid, int row, int col) {
        int cost = 0;
```

```
        if (source.charAt(row - 1) != target.charAt(col - 1)) {
            cost = _costOfSubstitution;
        }
        return grid[row - 1][col - 1] + cost;
    }
```

The method deleteCost() calculates the cost of deletion by adding the cumulative value from the cell directly above to the unit cost of deletion:

```
    private int deleteCost(int[][] grid, int row, int col) {
        return grid[row - 1][col] + _costOfDeletion;
    }
```

Lastly, insertCost() calculates the cost of insertion. This time, you add the cumulative value from the cell directly to the left of the unit cost of insertion and return that to the caller:

```
    private int insertCost(int[][] grid, int row, int col) {
        return grid[row][col - 1] + _costOfInsertion;
    }
```

The method minimumCost calculates the cost of each of the three operations and passes these to min() — a convenience method for finding the minimum of three values:

```
    private int minimumCost(CharSequence source, CharSequence target,
                            int[][] grid, int row, int col) {
        return min(
                substitutionCost(source, target, grid, row, col),
                deleteCost(grid, row, col),
                insertCost(grid, row, col)
        );
    }

    private static int min(int a, int b, int c) {
        return Math.min(a, Math.min(b, c));
    }
```

Now we can get into the algorithm proper. For this, you defined the method calculate(), which takes two strings — a source and a target — and returns the edit distance between them.

The method starts off by initializing a grid with enough rows and columns to accommodate the calculation, and the top-left cell of the grid is initialized to 0. Then, each column in the first row and each row in the first column are initialized, with the resulting grid looking something like the one shown in Figure 17-11.

Next, you iterate over each combination of source and target character, calculating the minimum cost and storing it in the appropriate cell. Eventually, you finish processing all character combinations, at which point you can select the value from the cell at the very bottom-right of the grid (as we did in Figure 17-13) and return that to the caller as the minimum distance:

```
    public int calculate(CharSequence source, CharSequence target) {
        assert source != null : "source can't be null";
```

```
        assert target != null : "target can't be null";

        int sourceLength = source.length();
        int targetLength = target.length();

        int[][] grid = new int[sourceLength + 1][targetLength + 1];

        grid[0][0] = 0;

        for (int row = 1; row <= sourceLength; ++row) {
            grid[row][0] = row;
        }

        for (int col = 1; col <= targetLength; ++col) {
            grid[0][col] = col;
        }

        for (int row = 1; row <= sourceLength; ++row) {
            for (int col = 1; col <= targetLength; ++col) {
                grid[row][col] = minimumCost(source, target, grid, row, col);
            }
        }

        return grid[sourceLength][targetLength];
    }
```

Summary

- So-called phonetic coders such as Soundex can efficiently find similar sounding words.
- Soundex values are often used to find duplicate entries and misspelled names in databases.
- Soundex calculates a four-character code in `O(N)` time.
- Levenshtein word distance calculates the number of operations necessary to transform one word into another — the smaller the distance, the more similar the words.
- The Levenshtein algorithm forms the basis for spell-checkers, DNA searches, plagiarism detection, and other applications.
- The Levenshtein algorithm runs in the time and space complexity of `O(MN)`.

Computational Geometry

This chapter gives you a taste of a fascinating area of algorithm design known as *computational geometry*. This topic could fill dozens of books on its own, so we will only be scratching the surface here. If you want to know more, check out the references or search the Internet for more material.

Computational geometry is one of the foundations of computer graphics, so if you intend to pursue an interest in developing software for games or other graphical areas, you'll need a solid understanding of computational geometry.

> *All topics covered in this chapter are limited to two-dimensional geometry. You will need to grasp the concepts in two dimensions before understanding three dimensions, a topic beyond the scope of this chapter. There are many excellent books that specialize in the explanation of the algorithms used in three-dimensional graphics. Check the references section in Appendix A or a good computer bookstore.*

This chapter discusses the following topics:

- A quick geometry refresher
- Finding the intersection point of two straight lines
- Finding the closest pair of points among a large set of scattered points

A Quick Geometry Refresher

This section saves you the trouble of digging out your high school mathematics textbook by quickly recapping some of the concepts you'll need to understand to make sense of the rest of the chapter.

Coordinates and Points

Two-dimensional spatial concepts are usually described using an *x-y coordinate system*. This system is represented by two straight lines called *axes* that are perpendicular to each other, as shown in Figure 18-1.

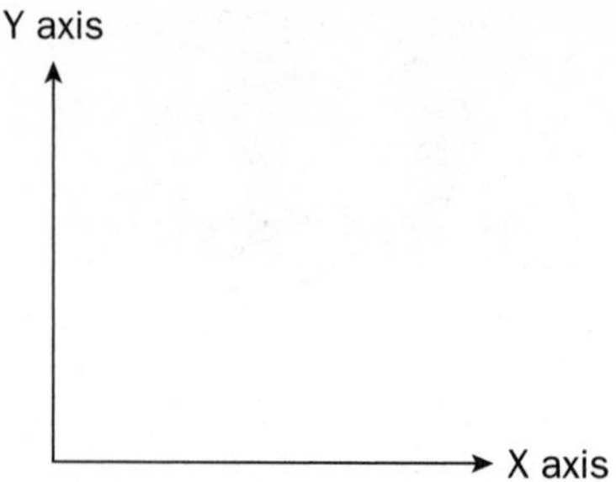

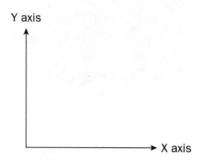

Figure 18-1: The x-y coordinate system is made up of two axes.

The horizontal axis is called the *x axis* and the vertical axis is called the *y axis*. Positions along the x axis are numbered from left to right with increasing values. Positions on the y axis have values that increase as they move upwards.

A *point* is a position in two-dimensional space that is defined by two numbers in the form (x, y), where x is the value on the x axis directly below the point, and y is the value on the y axis directly to the left of the point. For example, Figure 18-2 shows the point (3, 4) in the coordinate system.

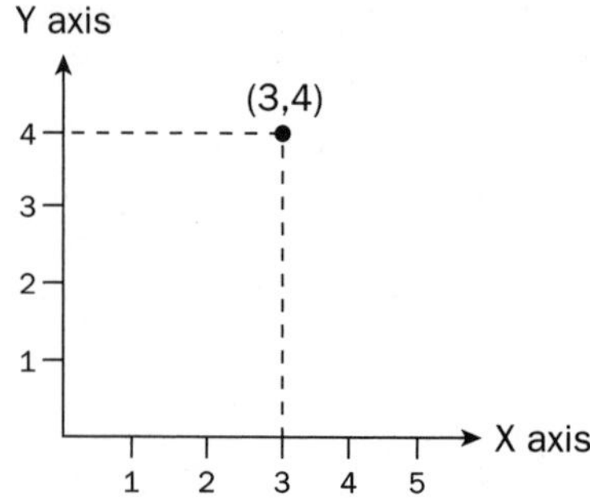

Figure 18-2: The point (3, 4) in the x-y coordinate system.

The x-y coordinate system also extends to the left and below the axes shown. Positions along these ends of the axes are defined by negative coordinates, as shown in Figure 18-3, which has points plotted in various regions.

Lines

A line is simply a straight path between two points. The two end-points are all that is needed to define a line. From that, you can determine its length, its slope, and other interesting things, but we'll get to that soon enough. Figure 18-4 shows the line (1, 1) – (5, 4).

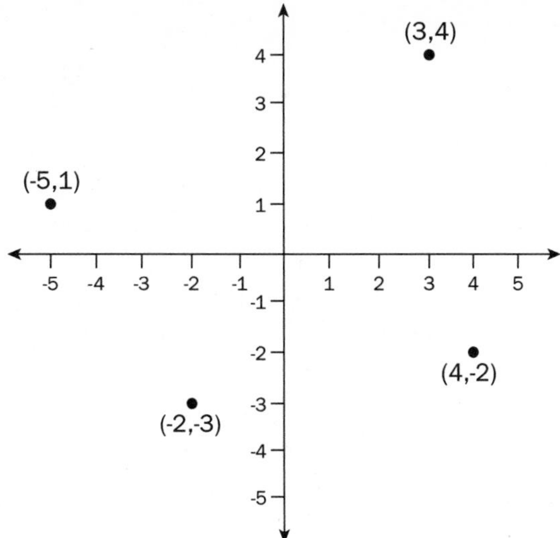

Figure 18-3: Coordinates can also be negative on both the x and y axes.

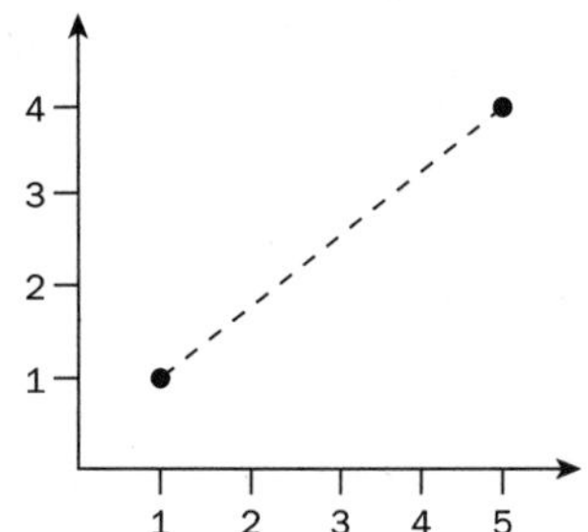

Figure 18-4: A line in the x-y coordinate system.

Triangles

We won't insult you by telling you what a triangle is (apologies if we did so when describing what a line is in the preceding section). You are mainly interested in *right-angled triangles* in this chapter; they're the ones with one 90-degree angle, as shown in Figure 18-5.

The best thing about right-angled triangles is that if you know the lengths of two of the sides, you can use *Pythagoras' theorem* to figure out the length of the third side. In Figure 18-5, the sides are labeled a, b, and c. Pythagoras' theorem states that

$$a^2 + b^2 = c^2$$

as long as c refers to the longest side, or *hypotenuse*. The usual example is a triangle like the one shown in Figure 18-6, with side lengths of 3, 4, and 5.

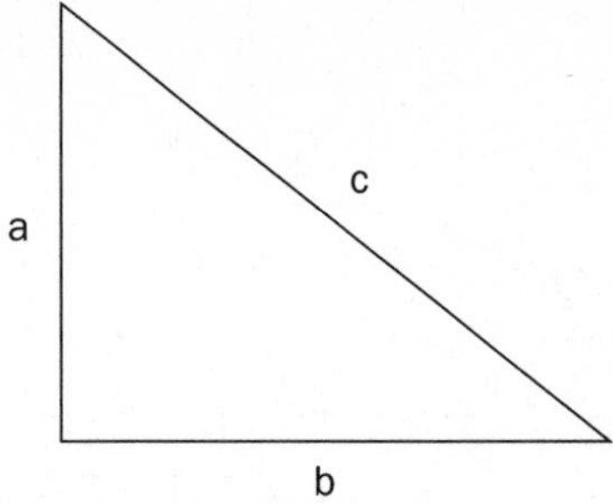

Figure 18-5: A right-angled triangle.

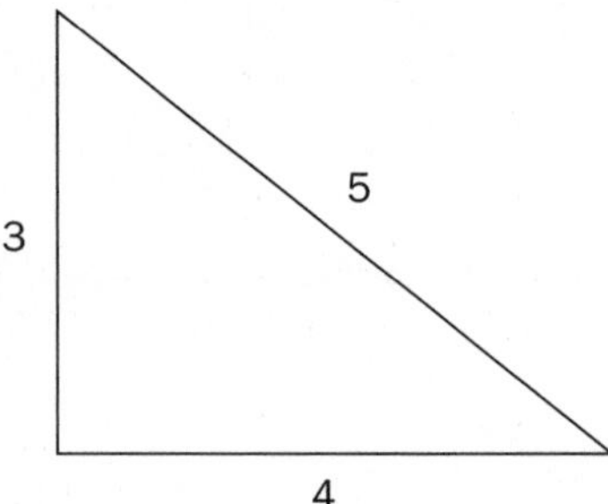

Figure 18-6: A right-angled triangle with side lengths specified.

Looking at the figure, it's easy to see that . . .

$$3^2 + 4^2 = 5^2$$

Or . . .

```
9 + 16 = 25
```

That's about all the background you need before you explore the first computational geometry problem: determining where two lines intersect.

Finding the Intersection of Two Lines

This section walks you through a computational geometry problem that finds the point where two lines intersect. Figure 18-7 shows two lines intersecting at the point marked P.

If all you know are the four points that define the end-points of the two lines, how do you figure out where (and if) the two lines intersect? The first thing you need to be comfortable with is the algebraic formula for a line, which is

```
y = mx + b
```

where y and x are the coordinates you're already familiar with, m is the slope of the line, and b is the point at which the line cuts the y axis. Don't worry, we'll explain these concepts next.

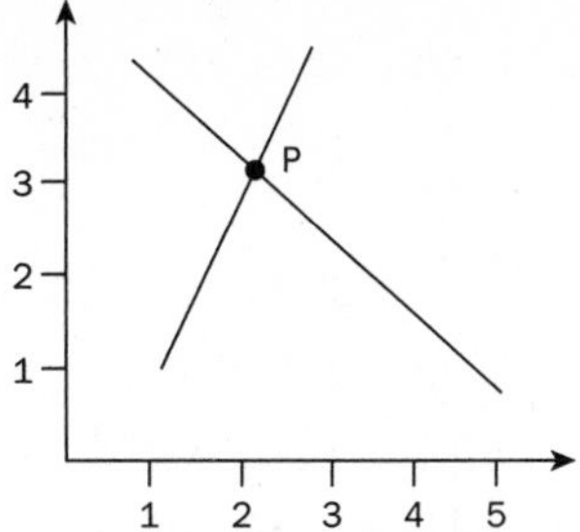

Figure 18-7: Two intersecting lines.

Slope

The *slope* of a line is simply how steep it is. You use a simple method to describe this, depicted in Figure 18-8.

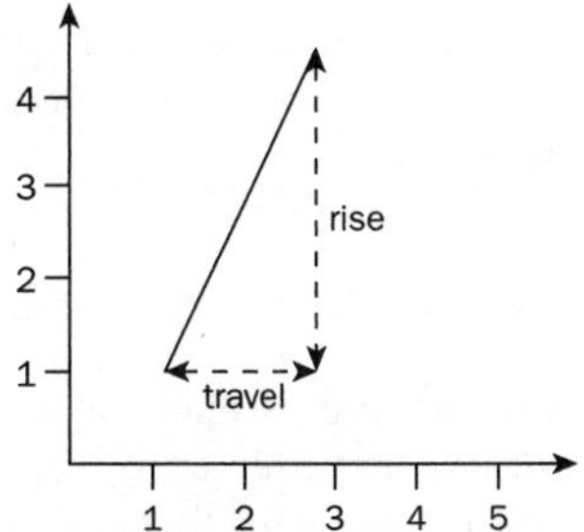

Figure 18-8: The slope of a line expressed as the ratio of rise to travel.

The *rise* is the vertical distance (amount of y axis) covered by the line. The *travel* is the horizontal distance (amount of x axis) covered by the line. Finally, the *slope* is the ratio of rise to travel. For example, a line that has the same rise as travel has a slope of 1, as shown in Figure 18-9.

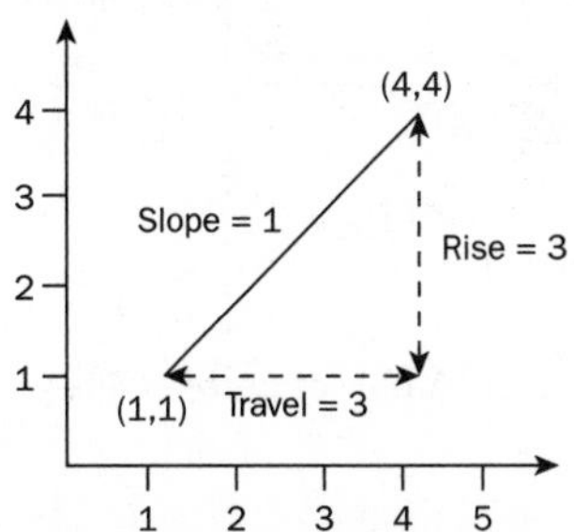

Figure 18-9: A line with a slope of 1.

Slopes can be negative. Figure 18-10 shows a line with a slope of –2, as its rise (or fall!) from the first point to the second point is downward, or negative, and is twice as large as its travel.

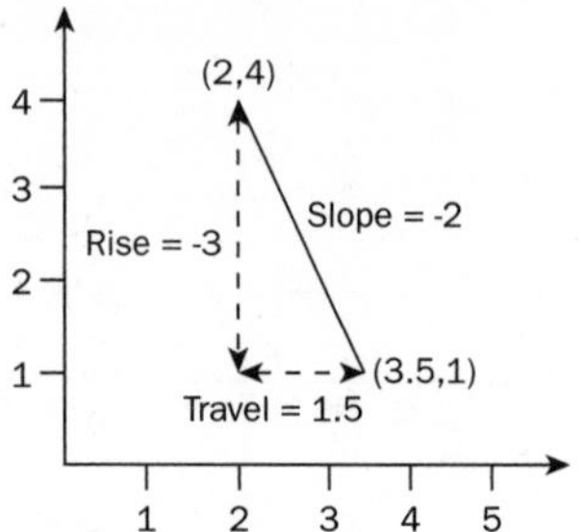

Figure 18-10: A line with a negative slope.

There are a couple of special cases to note also. Horizontal lines have a slope of zero, because no matter how large their travel, their rise is zero. More of an issue is the vertical line, which has a travel of zero no matter how much rise it has. Recall that slope is the ratio of rise to travel, which means you divide rise by travel to derive the slope. Of course, dividing by zero is impossible, so vertical lines have an infinite slope, which is of little meaning to a computer. You have to be very careful when coding to avoid issues with vertical lines, as you will see later.

Crossing the y Axis

Lines that have the same slope as each other are parallel. Two lines with the same slope differ in the point at which they cross the y axis (unless they are vertical, but don't worry about that for now). Figure 18-11 shows two parallel lines with a slope of 0.5 that cross the y axis at two different points.

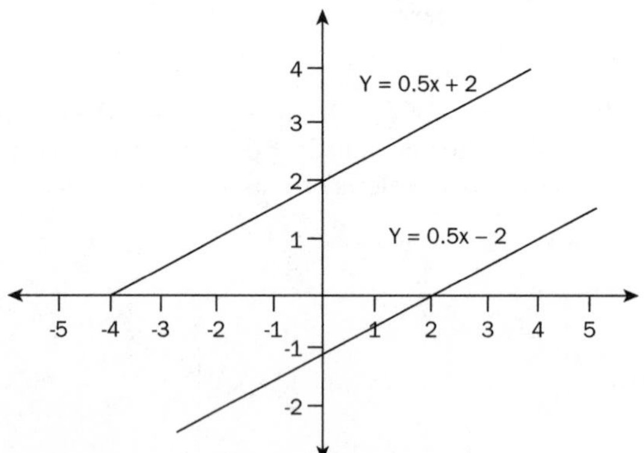

Figure 18-11: A pair of parallel lines.

Note how the higher line crosses the y axis at the y value of 2, so its formula is

```
y = 0.5x + 2
```

The lower line crosses the y axis at the y value –1, so its formula is

```
y = 0.5x - 1
```

Finding the Intersection Point

You now have enough background to work through an example of finding the intersection point of two lines. Use Figure 18-12 for this purpose.

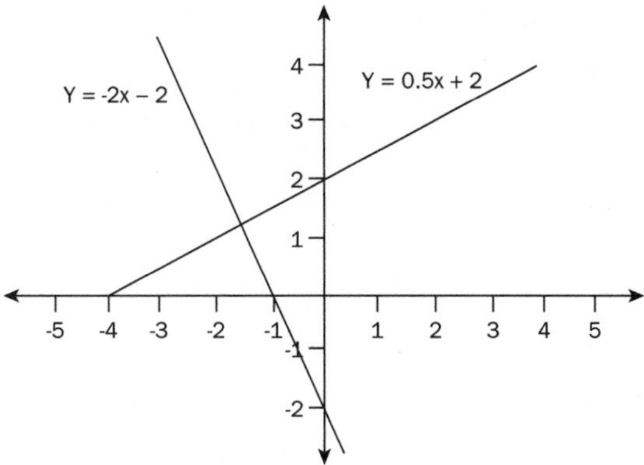

Figure 18-12: A sample pair of intersecting lines.

The trick is that the coordinates of the point of intersection will make sense in either of the formulas for the two lines. In other words, if the formula for the first line is as follows:

```
y = mx + b
```

And the formula for the second line is as follows:

```
y = nx + c
```

To find the point of intersection, use the following:

```
mx + b = nx +c
```

Rearrange that as follows:

```
mx - nx = c - b
```

Rearrange again:

```
x = (c - b) / (m - n)
```

This means that if you know the formulas for the two lines, you can find the x coordinate of the point of intersection by the formula just shown. In this example, the formula would be as follows:

```
x = (-2 - 2) / (0.5 - -2)
```

This becomes the following:

```
x = -4 / 2.5
```

Or it becomes the following:

```
x = -1.6
```

If you refer to Figure 18-12, this looks about right for the x coordinate of the point of intersection. Figuring out the y coordinate is trivial; put the just discovered x coordinate back into the formula for either line. For example:

```
y = 0.5x + 2

y = 0.5 x -1.6 + 2

y = -0.8 + 2

y = 1.2
```

The point of intersection is therefore (–1.6, 1.2) for the example lines.

The method varies slightly when one of the lines is vertical. The steps to find the x coordinate of the point of intersection do not apply, because the x coordinate of the point of intersection when one of the lines is vertical will simply be the x coordinate of the vertical line itself. Solving the nonvertical line's equation for this value of x will finish the job. It's now time to put all the theory discussed in the previous sections to work in some code. In the following Try It Out exercise, many of the concepts map directly to objects in Java, so the effort spent getting the concepts clear is worthwhile. You will begin by creating a class to represent points.

Try It Out Testing and Implementing the Point Class

Start by defining what you want the `Point` class to do in the form of a JUnit test case. You only need two behaviors from `Point`: to determine whether a point is the same as another (that is, it has the same coordinates), and to determine the distance from one point to another.

Here is the code:

```
package com.wrox.algorithms.geometry;

import junit.framework.TestCase;

public class PointTest extends TestCase {
    public void testEquals() {
        assertEquals(new Point(0, 0), new Point(0, 0));
```

```
        assertEquals(new Point(5, 8), new Point(5, 8));
        assertEquals(new Point(-4, 6), new Point(-4, 6));

        assertFalse(new Point(0, 0).equals(new Point(1, 0)));
        assertFalse(new Point(0, 0).equals(new Point(0, 1)));
        assertFalse(new Point(4, 4).equals(new Point(-4, 4)));
        assertFalse(new Point(4, 4).equals(new Point(4, -4)));
        assertFalse(new Point(4, 4).equals(new Point(-4, -4)));
        assertFalse(new Point(-4, 4).equals(new Point(-4, -4)));
    }

    public void testDistance() {
        assertEquals(13d, new Point(0, 0).distance(new Point(0, 13)), 0);
        assertEquals(13d, new Point(0, 0).distance(new Point(13, 0)), 0);
        assertEquals(13d, new Point(0, 0).distance(new Point(0, -13)), 0);
        assertEquals(13d, new Point(0, 0).distance(new Point(-13, 0)), 0);

        assertEquals(5d, new Point(1, 1).distance(new Point(4, 5)), 0);
        assertEquals(5d, new Point(1, 1).distance(new Point(-2, -3)), 0);
    }
}
```

To begin the implementation of `Point`, declare an instance variable to hold each of the x and y coordinates, and a constructor to initialize them. Note that both fields are final, making objects of this class immutable:

```
package com.wrox.algorithms.geometry;

public class Point {
    private final double _x;
    private final double _y;

    public Point(double x, double y) {
        _x = x;
        _y = y;
    }
    ...
}
```

Then provide simple accessors for the coordinates:

```
    public double getX() {
        return _x;
    }

    public double getY() {
        return _y;
    }
```

Use Pythagoras' theorem to calculate the distance between this point and another supplied to the `distance()` method:

```
    public double distance(Point other) {
        assert other != null : "other can't be null";

        double rise = getY() - other.getY();
        double travel = getX() - other.getX();

        return Math.sqrt(rise * rise + travel * travel);
    }
```

All that is left is to implement `equals()` and `hashCode()`, as follows:

```
    public int hashCode() {
        return (int) (_x * _y);
    }

    public boolean equals(Object obj) {
        if (this == obj) {
            return true;
        }

        if (obj == null || obj.getClass() != getClass()) {
            return false;
        }

        Point other = (Point) obj;

        return getX() == other.getX() && getY() == other.getY();
    }
```

How It Works

The `Point` class holds a value for each of its x and y coordinates as member variables. These variables are initialized in the constructor and cannot be changed. To determine the distance from a point to another point, the code treats the two points as the corners of a right-angled triangle, using Pythagoras' theorem to determine the length of the hypotenuse of the triangle, which is the distance between the points.

The code also determines whether two points are equal. All that is required for two points to be considered equal is that they have matching coordinates, so the code simply compares the x and y coordinates of the two points and returns `true` if they are both the same.

That's all there is to the `Point` class. In the next Try It Out, you model the slope of a line.

Try It Out — Testing the Slope of a Line

Begin by writing a test case that proves a slope knows when it's vertical:

```
package com.wrox.algorithms.geometry;

import junit.framework.TestCase;

public class SlopeTest extends TestCase {
    public void testIsVertical() {
        assertTrue(new Slope(4, 0).isVertical());
```

```
        assertTrue(new Slope(0, 0).isVertical());
        assertTrue(new Slope(-5, 0).isVertical());
        assertFalse(new Slope(0, 5).isVertical());
        assertFalse(new Slope(0, -5).isVertical());
    }
    ...
}
```

Next you create a test to prove that a slope can determine whether it is parallel to another slope. Use the standard `equals()` method for this:

```
    public void testEquals() {
        assertTrue(new Slope(0, -5).equals(new Slope(0, 10)));
        assertTrue(new Slope(1, 3).equals(new Slope(2, 6)));
        assertFalse(new Slope(1, 3).equals(new Slope(-1, 3)));
        assertFalse(new Slope(1, 3).equals(new Slope(1, -3)));
        assertTrue(new Slope(5, 0).equals(new Slope(9, 0)));
    }
```

Create a test method to ensure that a nonvertical slope can calculate its value as a Java `double`:

```
    public void testAsDoubleForNonVerticalSlope() {
        assertEquals(0, new Slope(0, 4).asDouble(), 0);
        assertEquals(0, new Slope(0, -4).asDouble(), 0);
        assertEquals(1, new Slope(3, 3).asDouble(), 0);
        assertEquals(1, new Slope(-3, -3).asDouble(), 0);
        assertEquals(-1, new Slope(3, -3).asDouble(), 0);
        assertEquals(-1, new Slope(-3, 3).asDouble(), 0);
        assertEquals(2, new Slope(6, 3).asDouble(), 0);
        assertEquals(1.5, new Slope(6, 4).asDouble(), 0);
    }
```

Finally, you need to verify what happens were someone silly enough to try to calculate the slope of a vertical line as a `double` value. You make sure that an exception is thrown with an appropriate message:

```
    public void testAsDoubleFailsForVerticalSlope() {
        try {
            new Slope(4, 0).asDouble();
            fail("should have blown up!");
        } catch (IllegalStateException e) {
            assertEquals("Vertical slope cannot be represented as double",
e.getMessage());
        }
    }
```

How It Works

The code assumes that a `Slope` object can be instantiated by providing two integer values that describe the rise and travel of the slope. It is important to remember that this does not represent a fixed point in two-dimensional space. Likewise, a slope does not have a length either. You are purely interested in representing only the slope itself. Many lines between different points can share the same slope. Lines that share the same slope are parallel. This is represented in the code by the test that proves that a slope can determine whether it is equal to another slope. This is achieved by providing both positive and negative test cases to ensure that the implementation is robust.

Recall from the description of the formula of a line (`y = mx + b`) that the value *m* is a floating-point value that is the ratio of the rise of the line to its travel. The preceding test code provides several assertions to establish that the implementation can correctly calculate this value. You need to separate the tests that deal with vertical lines from those that deal with nonvertical lines, as attempting to calculate this value for a vertical line is impossible; the tests prove that trying to do so will raise an exception.

Passing this set of tests will give you a robust implementation, so we'll build that in the next Try It Out.

Try It Out Implementing Slope

Begin the slope implementation with the pair of final member variables and a constructor to initialize them, as shown here:

```
package com.wrox.algorithms.geometry;

public class Slope {
    private final double _rise;
    private final double _travel;

    public Slope(double rise, double travel) {
        _rise = rise;
        _travel = travel;
    }
    ...
}
```

Implement `isVertical()`, which is trivial indeed:

```
    public boolean isVertical() {
        return _travel == 0;
    }
```

Implement `hashCode()` and `equals()` to determine whether two slopes are the same:

```
    public int hashCode() {
        return (int) (_rise * _travel);
    }

    public boolean equals(Object object) {
        if (this == object) {
            return true;
        }

        if (object == null || object.getClass() != getClass()) {
            return false;
        }

        Slope other = (Slope) object;

        if (isVertical() && other.isVertical()) {
            return true;
        }

        if (isVertical() || other.isVertical()) {
```

```
            return false;
        }

        return (asDouble()) == (other.asDouble());
    }
```

Finally, you calculate the numerical representation of the slope, being careful to avoid vertical lines:

```
    public double asDouble() {
        if (isVertical()) {
            throw new IllegalStateException("Vertical slope cannot be represented
as double");
        }

        return _rise / _travel;
    }
```

How It Works

You have previously seen classes that have member variables that are final and are initialized in the constructor like the `Slope` class just described, so the basic structure of the class should be familiar.

Determining whether two slopes are equal is a little more challenging. You implement a simple `hashCode()` and then build the `equals()` implementation with three cases in mind: first is the case when both slopes are vertical, in which case they are equal; next is the case when *one* of the slopes is vertical, in which case they are not equal. Finally is the general case, in which two slopes are equal if their representation as a Java `double` ratio is the same. The code has to eliminate all cases involving vertical slopes before attempting to calculate the numerical representation of either slope.

The final method calculates the ratio of the slope's rise to its travel as a `double` value. The only trick is to avoid dividing by zero when the slope is vertical. The code deals with this issue by throwing an exception.

In the next Try It Out, you set up the tests to determine several qualities of a line, including whether a given point falls on it, whether it is vertical or parallel to another line, and so on.

Try It Out Testing the Line Class

The final class in the line intersection problem is `Line`. You begin by writing a series of test cases to define the functionality you want `Line` to provide. Start with a test that proves you can ask `Line` whether it contains a specified `Point` — that is, whether `Point` falls on the line:

```
package com.wrox.algorithms.geometry;

import junit.framework.TestCase;

public class LineTest extends TestCase {
    public void testContainsForNonVerticalLine() {
        Point p = new Point(0, 0);
        Point q = new Point(3, 3);

        Line l = new Line(p, q);

        assertTrue(l.contains(p));
```

```
            assertTrue(l.contains(q));

            assertTrue(l.contains(new Point(1, 1)));
            assertTrue(l.contains(new Point(2, 2)));
            assertTrue(l.contains(new Point(0.5, 0.5)));

            assertFalse(l.contains(new Point(3.1, 3.1)));
            assertFalse(l.contains(new Point(3, 3.1)));
            assertFalse(l.contains(new Point(0, 1)));
            assertFalse(l.contains(new Point(-1, -1)));
        }
        ...
    }
```

You separately test the functionality for a vertical line, just to make sure that the special case is covered, as shown here:

```
        public void testContainsForVerticalLine() {
            Point p = new Point(0, 0);
            Point q = new Point(0, 3);

            Line l = new Line(p, q);

            assertTrue(l.contains(p));
            assertTrue(l.contains(q));

            assertTrue(l.contains(new Point(0, 1)));
            assertTrue(l.contains(new Point(0, 2)));
            assertTrue(l.contains(new Point(0, 0.5)));

            assertFalse(l.contains(new Point(0, 3.1)));
            assertFalse(l.contains(new Point(0.1, 1)));
            assertFalse(l.contains(new Point(1, 0)));
            assertFalse(l.contains(new Point(-1, -1)));
        }
```

You want a line to indicate whether it is parallel to another line. You need to be careful and treat vertical lines as a special case. The first test proves the correct behavior when the two lines are parallel but not vertical:

```
        public void testIsParallelForTwoNonVerticalParallelLines() {
            Point p = new Point(1, 1);
            Point q = new Point(6, 6);
            Point r = new Point(4, -2);
            Point s = new Point(6, 0);

            Line l = new Line(p, q);
            Line m = new Line(r, s);

            assertTrue(l.isParallelTo(m));
            assertTrue(m.isParallelTo(l));
        }
```

Next, you test the behavior for two nonvertical and nonparallel lines:

```
public void testIsParallelForTwoNonVerticalNonParallelLines() {
    Point p = new Point(1, 1);
    Point q = new Point(6, 4);
    Point r = new Point(4, -2);
    Point s = new Point(6, 0);

    Line l = new Line(p, q);
    Line m = new Line(r, s);

    assertFalse(l.isParallelTo(m));
    assertFalse(m.isParallelTo(l));
}
```

In the following test, you address some of the edge cases — first, when both lines are vertical (and therefore by definition parallel):

```
public void testIsParallelForTwoVerticalParallelLines() {
    Point p = new Point(1, 1);
    Point q = new Point(1, 6);
    Point r = new Point(4, -2);
    Point s = new Point(4, 0);

    Line l = new Line(p, q);
    Line m = new Line(r, s);

    assertTrue(l.isParallelTo(m));
    assertTrue(m.isParallelTo(l));
}
```

The final test of the `isParallel()` method is for the case when one of the lines is vertical and the other is not:

```
public void testIsParallelForOneVerticalAndOneNonVerticalLine() {
    Point p = new Point(1, 1);
    Point q = new Point(1, 6);
    Point r = new Point(4, -2);
    Point s = new Point(6, 0);

    Line l = new Line(p, q);
    Line m = new Line(r, s);

    assertFalse(l.isParallelTo(m));
    assertFalse(m.isParallelTo(l));
}
```

Now you define some tests for determining the point of intersection of two lines. You create a method on `Line` called `intersectionPoint()` that will be passed another `Line` object. This method will be allowed to return `null` if the lines do not intersect, or a `Point` object that defines the point of intersection if they do. Again, you need to take extra care to cover cases involving vertical lines.

First prove that two nonvertical lines that are parallel are correctly determined to have no intersection, as shown in the following test method:

```
    public void testParallelNonVerticalLinesDoNotIntersect() {
        Point p = new Point(0, 0);
        Point q = new Point(3, 3);
        Point r = new Point(5, 0);
        Point s = new Point(8, 3);

        Line l = new Line(p, q);
        Line m = new Line(r, s);

        assertNull(l.intersectionPoint(m));
        assertNull(m.intersectionPoint(l));
    }
```

Now establish the same behavior for a pair of vertical lines:

```
    public void testVerticalLinesDoNotIntersect() {
        Point p = new Point(0, 0);
        Point q = new Point(0, 3);
        Point r = new Point(5, 0);
        Point s = new Point(5, 3);

        Line l = new Line(p, q);
        Line m = new Line(r, s);

        assertNull(l.intersectionPoint(m));
        assertNull(m.intersectionPoint(l));
    }
```

Now test a case in which the two lines do have an easily determined point of intersection and prove that it works as expected:

```
    public void testIntersectionOfNonParallelNonVerticalLines() {
        Point p = new Point(0, 0);
        Point q = new Point(4, 4);
        Point r = new Point(4, 0);
        Point s = new Point(0, 4);

        Line l = new Line(p, q);
        Line m = new Line(r, s);

        Point i = new Point(2, 2);

        assertEquals(i, l.intersectionPoint(m));
        assertEquals(i, m.intersectionPoint(l));
    }
```

Next cover the case in which one of the lines is vertical, as shown here:

```
    public void testIntersectionOfVerticalAndNonVerticalLines() {
        Point p = new Point(0, 0);
        Point q = new Point(4, 4);
        Point r = new Point(2, 0);
        Point s = new Point(2, 4);

        Line l = new Line(p, q);
        Line m = new Line(r, s);

        Point i = new Point(2, 2);

        assertEquals(i, l.intersectionPoint(m));
        assertEquals(i, m.intersectionPoint(l));
    }
```

Finally, consider when the two lines are arranged such that they have a theoretical point of intersection, but the lines themselves are not long enough to include that point in one or other of the lines. Such lines are called *disjoint* lines. Figure 18-13 shows a pair of disjoint lines with their theoretical point of intersection marked:

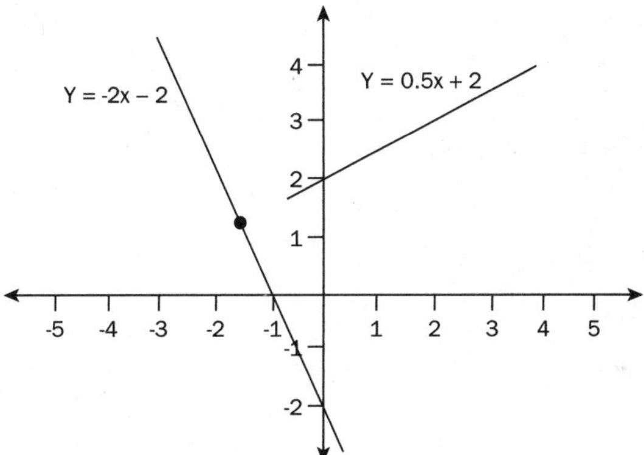

Figure 18-13: A pair of disjoint lines.

Here is the code to ensure the correct behavior in this case:

```
    public void testDisjointLinesDoNotIntersect() {
        Point p = new Point(0, 0);
        Point q = new Point(0, 3);
        Point r = new Point(5, 0);
        Point s = new Point(-1, -3);

        Line l = new Line(p, q);
        Line m = new Line(r, s);

        assertNull(l.intersectionPoint(m));
        assertNull(m.intersectionPoint(l));
    }
}
```

How It Works

The preceding test cases work by considering many examples of lines that may or may not intersect, and may or may not be vertical. When using tests to drive the implementation, it is important to cover all such cases and not just assume that the cases are covered. It may seem like a lot of test cases, but remember that you are testing for a lot of behaviors. If you require many more tests than this, you should think of ways to break up the functionality into multiple classes. This is actually why the `Slope` class was created!

In the next Try It Out, you implement the `Line` class itself and pass these tests.

Try It Out Implementing the Line Class

The `Line` class has three instance members: the two `Point` objects that define its end-points, and a `Slope` object to encapsulate its slope. Create the fields and constructor as shown here:

```
package com.wrox.algorithms.geometry;

public class Line {
    private final Point _p;
    private final Point _q;
    private final Slope _slope;

    public Line(Point p, Point q) {
        assert p != null : "point defining a line cannot be null";
        assert q != null : "point defining a line cannot be null";

        _p = p;
        _q = q;
        _slope = new Slope(_p.getY() - _q.getY(), _p.getX() - _q.getX());
    }
    ...
}
```

You implement the `isParallelTo()` method by relying on the `Slope`'s ability to determine whether it is equal to another `Slope`:

```
    public boolean isParallelTo(Line line) {
        return _slope.equals(line._slope);
    }
```

Implement the `contains()` method to determine whether a line contains the supplied point:

```
    public boolean contains(Point a) {
        if (!isWithin(a.getX(), _p.getX(), _q.getX())) {
            return false;
        }

        if (!isWithin(a.getY(), _p.getY(), _q.getY())) {
            return false;
        }

        if (_slope.isVertical()) {
            return true;
```

```
        }

        return a.getY() == solveY(a.getX());
    }
```

Create a method to calculate the y coordinate of a point on the line, given the x coordinate:

```
    private double solveY(double x) {
        return _slope.asDouble() * x + base();
    }
```

You also create a method to determine the value of b in the formula $y = mx + b$:

```
    private double base() {
        return _p.getY() - _slope.asDouble() * _p.getX();
    }
```

Create a simple utility to determine whether one number is within the range specified by two other numbers:

```
    private static boolean isWithin(double test, double bound1, double bound2) {
        return test >= Math.min(bound1, bound2)
            && test <= Math.max(bound1, bound2);
    }
```

Now you create the method that determines the intersection point of two lines:

```
    public Point intersectionPoint(Line line) {
        if (isParallelTo(line)) {
            return null;
        }

        double x = getIntersectionXCoordinate(line);
        double y = getIntersectionYCoordinate(line, x);

        Point p = new Point(x, y);

        if (line.contains(p) && this.contains(p)) {
            return p;
        }

        return null;
    }
```

To support the preceding code, create a method to determine the x coordinate of the theoretical point of intersection of the two lines:

```
    private double getIntersectionXCoordinate(Line line) {
        if (_slope.isVertical()) {
            return _p.getX();
        }

        if (line._slope.isVertical()) {
```

```
            return line._p.getX();
        }

        double m = _slope.asDouble();
        double b = base();

        double n = line._slope.asDouble();
        double c = line.base();

        return (c - b) / (m - n);
    }
```

Finally, create a method to determine the y coordinate of the point of intersection:

```
    private double getIntersectionYCoordinate(Line line, double x) {
        if (_slope.isVertical()) {
            return line.solveY(x);
        }

        return solveY(x);
    }
```

How It Works

The `Line` class has three instance members: the two `Point` objects that define its end-points, and a `Slope` object to encapsulate its slope. Much of the functionality of the `Line` class is actually provided by these encapsulated member objects. For example, to determine whether a line is parallel to another line, you simply need to determine whether their respective slopes are equal.

To determine whether a point falls within a line, you see whether the point's x coordinate falls within the range of x coordinates defined by its end-points. If not, you know the line cannot possibly contain the point. You then repeat the process for the y coordinate span of the line. Having made it that far, you know that the point in question is a candidate for being on the line. In fact, if the line is vertical, you can conclude that the point is actually on the line. However, consider Figure 18-14, which shows a point that has passed all of these tests but is still not on the line.

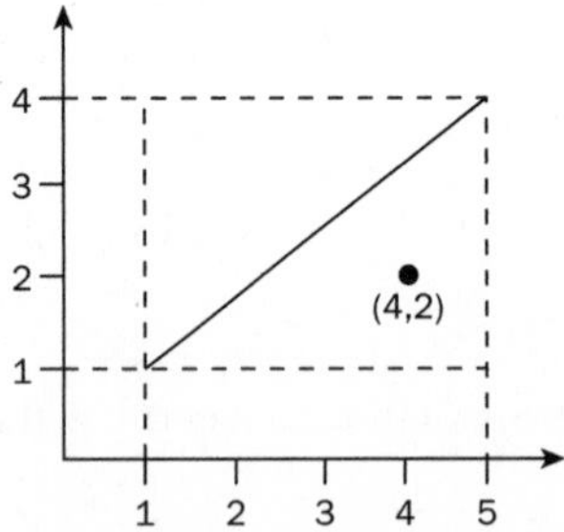

Figure 18-14: A point that is not part of the line, but which has x and y coordinates within the span of the line.

You have to do a final check to determine whether this point's coordinates make sense when plugged into the formula for the line ($y = mx + b$). For this, you create a call to `solveY()`. Given a value for the x coordinate, it calculates the corresponding y coordinate. If the point's coordinates evaluate correctly, the point lies on the line.

Now you come to the heart of the matter: determining the intersection point of two lines. The basic idea is this: If the lines are parallel, there is no intersection point; if they aren't, first determine the x coordinate of the (theoretical) intersection point, and then use this value to determine the y coordinate of the (theoretical) intersection point. Finally, you need to confirm that both lines actually contain the theoretical intersection point before returning it.

To determine the x coordinate of the intersection point, you first need to determine whether either line in question is vertical. If one is, the answer is just the x coordinate of either end-point of the vertical line. If not, you use the formula described earlier to determine the x coordinate of the intersection point.

The final method determines the y coordinate of the point of intersection. Again, you have to be on guard for the case where one of the lines is vertical (you won't be doing this if both are vertical). This means that you simply use a nonvertical line to calculate the y coordinate of the point of intersection.

If you run the tests, you will see that all of them work. You now have a nicely abstracted set of classes representing geometrical concepts, with some well-tested and valuable functionality. You can now move on to your next challenge, finding the closest pair among an arbitrary set of points.

Finding the Closest Pair of Points

Imagine a large set of scattered points such as those shown in Figure 18-15.

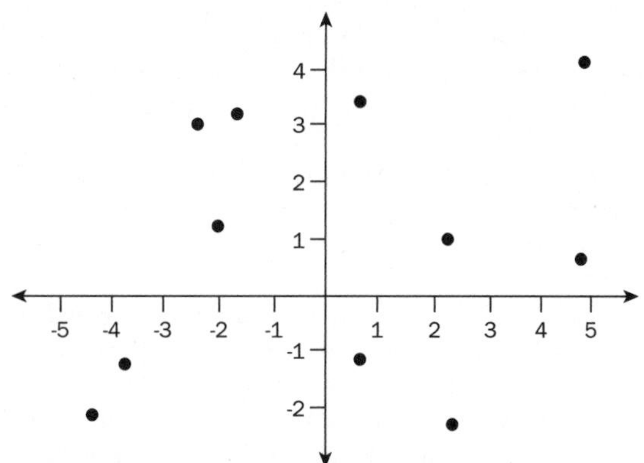

Figure 18-15: A number of scattered points.

Can you find the pair of points that are closest to each other? You might think that's pretty easy—just compare every point with every other point, compute the distance between them, and remember the pair of points with the minimum distance. While that would work, by now you should be forming an allergy to brute-force solutions that are `O(N²)` because they process every item in relation to every other item. We won't bother implementing such a naive solution for this problem. Instead, this section looks at an algorithm known as the *plane sweep* algorithm.

The plane sweep algorithm considers each point in order from left to right in the coordinate system. It makes a single pass, or sweep, across the two-dimensional plane containing the points, remembering the currently known smallest distance and the two points that are separated by that minimum distance.

It's easier to understand this algorithm with an example that has progressed a little. Figure 18-16 shows the state of the algorithm when the fifth point (from left to right) is about to be processed (the x and y axes have been removed to avoid cluttering the diagram).

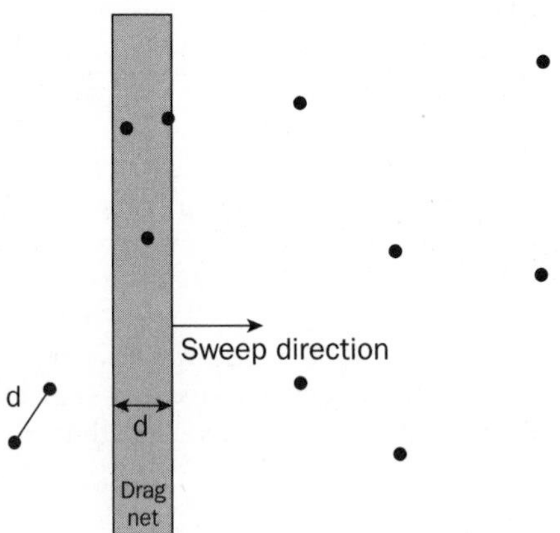

Figure 18-16: The plane sweep algorithm in progress.

Notice in the figure that the currently identified closest pair of points is separated by a distance *d*. The point currently being considered as the sweep progresses is treated as if it was at the right edge of a r ectangular box referred to as the *drag net*. The key thing to notice about the drag net is that its width is also *d*—that is, you create an imaginary box *behind* the current point that is no wider than the distance between the current closest pair of points. That's quite a mouthful, but it will make sense soon enough.

The idea is that if the point being considered is to be part of a pair (with a point to its left) that is a closer pair than the current closest pair, then the second point in that new pair *must* lie within the drag net. If not, it could hardly form a closer pair than the currently identified pair. Therefore, the algorithm checks the distance between the point under the sweep line with all other points in the drag net to determine whether any combination forms a closer pair than the one currently identified. If a closer pair is found, the algorithm proceeds with a smaller drag net until every point has been processed. In this way, depending on the distribution of the points, relatively few comparisons are required. A more advanced form of the algorithm can ignore points in the drag net that are farther away than *d* from the point being considered in the y direction as well, restricting the number of comparisons even further.

Figure 18-17 shows the situation after almost all the points have been processed.

There are two main aspects to implementing the plane sweep algorithm just described. The points need to be sorted according to their coordinates, and then they have to be scanned in the algorithm itself. The first thing you need to be able to do is sort the points into logical order. This involves creating a comparator that can be plugged into a sorting algorithm. In the following Try It Out, you write tests for this comparator.

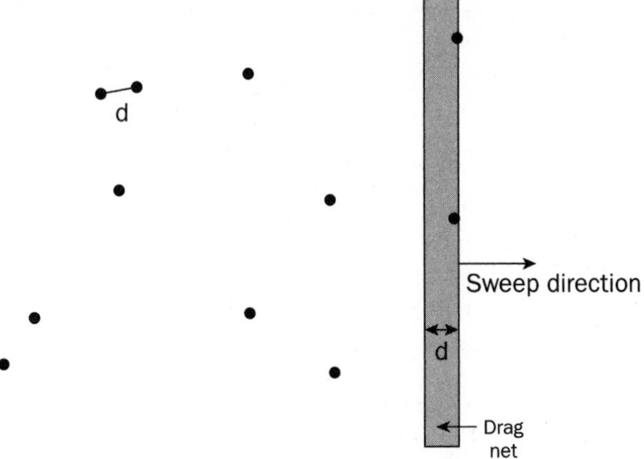

Figure 18-17: The algorithm is almost complete.

Try It Out Testing the XY Point Comparator

You start with a simple test that proves that two points that are equal are correctly handled by our comparator — that is, the result is zero:

```
package com.wrox.algorithms.geometry;

import junit.framework.TestCase;

public class XYPointComparatorTest extends TestCase {
    private final XYPointComparator _comparator = XYPointComparator.INSTANCE;

    public void testEqualPointsCompareCorrectly() {
        Point p = new Point(4, 4);
        Point q = new Point(4, 4);

        assertEquals(0, _comparator.compare(p, q));
        assertEquals(0, _comparator.compare(p, p));
    }
    ...
}
```

You then need a test to prove that the points sort according to their x coordinate as you expect. You do this by setting up three points and testing them relative to each other, as shown here:

```
    public void testXCoordinateIsPrimaryKey() {
        Point p = new Point(-1, 4);
        Point q = new Point(0, 4);
        Point r = new Point(1, 4);

        assertEquals(-1, _comparator.compare(p, q));
        assertEquals(-1, _comparator.compare(p, r));
        assertEquals(-1, _comparator.compare(q, r));

        assertEquals(1, _comparator.compare(q, p));
```

```
        assertEquals(1, _comparator.compare(r, p));
        assertEquals(1, _comparator.compare(r, q));
    }
```

Finally, you need a test to establish that the points will take their y coordinates into account when their x coordinates are the same. Here's the code for this test:

```
    public void testYCoordinateIsSecondaryKey() {
        Point p = new Point(4, -1);
        Point q = new Point(4, 0);
        Point r = new Point(4, 1);

        assertEquals(-1, _comparator.compare(p, q));
        assertEquals(-1, _comparator.compare(p, r));
        assertEquals(-1, _comparator.compare(q, r));

        assertEquals(1, _comparator.compare(q, p));
        assertEquals(1, _comparator.compare(r, p));
        assertEquals(1, _comparator.compare(r, q));
    }
```

How It Works

You need a comparator that can sort points according to their x coordinates. This obviously means that negative x coordinates will precede positive ones, but what about when two points share the same x coordinate? You need to sort them somehow, so you arbitrarily choose to sort them by their y coordinate in this circumstance. You might be wondering how to handle points that have the same x *and* y coordinates. The answer is that you won't allow that—by simply using a `Set` to contain the points under consideration. Recall that the semantics of a `Set` do not allow duplicate items, and that `Point` objects are considered equal if both their coordinates are the same.

The immediately previous tests work by creating a sufficiently broad set of cases and asserting that the comparator provides the expected behavior. That should be enough to get your comparator going. You implement it in the next Try It Out.

Try It Out Implementing the XYPointComparator

Start by declaring a singleton instance and a private constructor, as this object has no state of its own:

```
package com.wrox.algorithms.geometry;

import com.wrox.algorithms.sorting.Comparator;

public final class XYPointComparator implements Comparator {
    public static final XYPointComparator INSTANCE = new XYPointComparator();

    private XYPointComparator() {
    }
    ...
}
```

Implement `compare()`, which delegates to a strongly typed version by casting its parameters to `Point` objects:

```
public int compare(Object left, Object right) throws ClassCastException {
    return compare((Point) left, (Point) right);
}
```

Finally, create the strongly typed version of `compare()`:

```
public int compare(Point p, Point q) throws ClassCastException {
    int result = new Double(p.getX()).compareTo(new Double(q.getX()));
    if (result != 0) {
        return result;
    }
    return new Double(p.getY()).compareTo(new Double(q.getY()));
}
```

How It Works

Don't be concerned that the comparator itself takes fewer lines of code than the accompanying unit test— it's perfectly normal! The only method you need to implement is `compare()`, which delegates to a strongly typed version by casting its parameters to `Point` objects. This will throw a `ClassCastException` when objects other than points are passed in, but that is explicitly allowed by the `Comparator` interface.

The implementation of the `compare()` method, which knows the objects are of class `Point`, is where the real logic lives. The return value is based on the x coordinates of the respective objects, and only if they are equal does the method take their y coordinates into account.

With your comparator in place, you are ready to implement the plane sweep algorithm itself, which you do in the next Try It Out. You assume that there will be other algorithms that solve the problem of finding the closest pair (see the exercises at the end of this chapter), so you create an abstract test that can be used to prove the behavior of various implementations. You then extend this test with a specific version for our algorithm.

Try It Out Testing the Plane Sweep Algorithm

Define an abstract factory method to allow specific implementations to instantiate the appropriate algorithm class, as shown here:

```
package com.wrox.algorithms.geometry;

import com.wrox.algorithms.sets.ListSet;
import com.wrox.algorithms.sets.Set;
import junit.framework.TestCase;

public abstract class AbstractClosestPairFinderTestCase extends TestCase {
    protected abstract ClosestPairFinder createClosestPairFinder();
    ...
}
```

The first test case simply proves that if you supply an empty set of points, you get `null` in return:

```
public void testEmptySetOfPoints() {
    ClosestPairFinder finder = createClosestPairFinder();
    assertNull(finder.findClosestPair(new ListSet()));
}
```

It's pretty hard to find the closest pair when there's only a single point, so you also prove that in this case you get `null` as a return value:

```
public void testASinglePointReturnsNull() {
    ClosestPairFinder finder = createClosestPairFinder();

    Set points = new ListSet();
    points.add(new Point(1, 1));

    assertNull(finder.findClosestPair(points));
}
```

Obviously, the next case occurs when only two points are provided in the input set. In this case, it's easy to determine the closest pair, so test it with the following code:

```
public void testASinglePairOfPoints() {
    ClosestPairFinder finder = createClosestPairFinder();

    Set points = new ListSet();
    Point p = new Point(1, 1);
    Point q = new Point(2, 4);

    points.add(p);
    points.add(q);

    Set pair = finder.findClosestPair(points);

    assertNotNull(pair);
    assertEquals(2, pair.size());
    assertTrue(pair.contains(p));
    assertTrue(pair.contains(q));
}
```

Now we come to an interesting case. Imagine there are three points in a line, evenly spaced. Which pair should be the closest pair? You'd like your algorithm to take the first pair it encounters in the sweep, which will depend on the comparator you created to sort the points. You need to make sure this is what happens, so here is the test:

```
public void testThreePointsEquallySpacedApart() {
    ClosestPairFinder finder = createClosestPairFinder();

    Set points = new ListSet();
    Point p = new Point(1, 0);
    Point q = new Point(1, 4);
```

```
        Point r = new Point(1, -4);

        points.add(p);
        points.add(q);
        points.add(r);

        Set pair = finder.findClosestPair(points);

        assertNotNull(pair);
        assertEquals(2, pair.size());
        assertTrue(pair.contains(p));
        assertTrue(pair.contains(r));
    }
```

A similar case occurs when you have a larger set of points in which two pairs have the same distance. Again, you decide you want the algorithm to return the pair it encounters first, so you prove it with the following test case:

```
    public void testLargeSetOfPointsWithTwoEqualShortestPairs() {
        ClosestPairFinder finder = createClosestPairFinder();

        Set points = new ListSet();

        points.add(new Point(0, 0));
        points.add(new Point(4, -2));
        points.add(new Point(2, 7));
        points.add(new Point(3, 7));
        points.add(new Point(-1, -5));
        points.add(new Point(-5, 3));
        points.add(new Point(-5, 4));
        points.add(new Point(-0, -9));
        points.add(new Point(-2, -2));

        Set pair = finder.findClosestPair(points);

        assertNotNull(pair);
        assertEquals(2, pair.size());
        assertTrue(pair.contains(new Point(-5, 3)));
        assertTrue(pair.contains(new Point(-5, 4)));
    }
```

Finally, you extend your abstract test case, making a version that is specific to your plane sweep algorithm, as shown here:

```
package com.wrox.algorithms.geometry;

public class PlaneSweepClosestPairFinderTest extends
AbstractClosestPairFinderTestCase {
    protected ClosestPairFinder createClosestPairFinder() {
        return PlaneSweepClosestPairFinder.INSTANCE;
    }
}
```

How It Works

As with many test cases, the preceding code works by considering a number of unusual cases, such as an empty set of points, a set of points with only one item in it, a set of points with only two items in it, and items that have exactly the same distance between them. Sometimes the number of test cases can be higher than you might expect, but that is an indication of the complexity of the problem you're trying to solve. Each individual test method is quite simple on its own.

In the next Try It Out, you implement the algorithm, and get all these tests to pass.

Try It Out — Creating the ClosestPairFinder Interface

The interface that defines your algorithm is very simple indeed. It has a single method that accepts a `Set` of `Point` objects, and returns another `Set` containing the two `Point` objects that make up the closest pair in the original set of points. It can also return `null` if it is not possible to determine the closest pair (for example, if there is only one `Point` provided).

```
package com.wrox.algorithms.geometry;

import com.wrox.algorithms.sets.Set;

public interface ClosestPairFinder {
    public Set findClosestPair(Set points);
}
```

Try It Out — Implementing the Plane Sweep Algorithm

Create the declaration of the class, including a binary inserter that will enable you to turn the `Set` of points you receive into a sorted `List`:

```
package com.wrox.algorithms.geometry;

import com.wrox.algorithms.bsearch.IterativeBinaryListSearcher;
import com.wrox.algorithms.bsearch.ListInserter;
import com.wrox.algorithms.iteration.Iterator;
import com.wrox.algorithms.lists.ArrayList;
import com.wrox.algorithms.lists.List;
import com.wrox.algorithms.sets.ListSet;
import com.wrox.algorithms.sets.Set;

public final class PlaneSweepClosestPairFinder implements ClosestPairFinder {
    public static final PlaneSweepClosestPairFinder INSTANCE = new
                        PlaneSweepClosestPairFinder();

    private static final ListInserter INSERTER = new ListInserter(
            new IterativeBinaryListSearcher(XYPointComparator.INSTANCE));

    private PlaneSweepClosestPairFinder() {
    }
    ...
}
```

The algorithm to find the closest pair is shown in the following code:

```
public Set findClosestPair(Set points) {
    assert points != null : "points can't be null";

    if (points.size() < 2) {
        return null;
    }

    List sortedPoints = sortPoints(points);

    Point p = (Point) sortedPoints.get(0);
    Point q = (Point) sortedPoints.get(1);

    return findClosestPair(p, q, sortedPoints);
}
```

Create the following method (explained in more detail below):

```
private Set findClosestPair(Point p, Point q, List sortedPoints) {
    Set result = createPointPair(p, q);
    double distance = p.distance(q);
    int dragPoint = 0;

    for (int i = 2; i < sortedPoints.size(); ++i) {
        Point r = (Point) sortedPoints.get(i);
        double sweepX = r.getX();
        double dragX = sweepX - distance;

        while (((Point) sortedPoints.get(dragPoint)).getX() < dragX) {
            ++dragPoint;
        }

        for (int j = dragPoint; j < i; ++j) {
            Point test = (Point) sortedPoints.get(j);
            double checkDistance = r.distance(test);
            if (checkDistance < distance) {
                distance = checkDistance;
                result = createPointPair(r, test);
            }
        }
    }

    return result;
}
```

The preceding code relies on the following method to arrange the points according to their x and y coordinates, using the comparator you defined earlier in this chapter:

```
private static List sortPoints(Set points) {
    assert points != null : "points can't be null";

    List list = new ArrayList(points.size());

    Iterator i = points.iterator();
```

```
        for (i.first(); !i.isDone(); i.next()) {
            INSERTER.insert(list, i.current());
        }

        return list;
    }
```

The last utility method is a simple one to create a `Set` to represent the closest pair, given two `Point` objects:

```
    private Set createPointPair(Point p, Point q) {
        Set result = new ListSet();
        result.add(p);
        result.add(q);
        return result;
    }
}
```

How It Works

This plane sweep algorithm implements the `ClosestPairFinder` interface defined in the preceding section. It is also implemented as a singleton with a private constructor, as it has no state of its own.

An early exit is taken if there are not enough points to comprise even a single pair. You sort the points according to their coordinates. After you have a sorted list, you can extract the first two `Point` objects and assume they are the closest pair to begin with. You then delegate to another method that sweeps through the remaining points to determine whether any pairs are closer than this initial pair.

The following method is the heart of the plane sweep algorithm. It's a little more complex than the other methods in this class, so you might want to examine it carefully. Refer to Figure 18-16 and Figure 18-17, which illustrate the algorithm earlier in this chapter, if you need to confirm your understanding of how it works in principle:

```
    private Set findClosestPair(Point p, Point q, List sortedPoints) {
        Set result = createPointPair(p, q);
        double distance = p.distance(q);
        int dragPoint = 0;

        for (int i = 2; i < sortedPoints.size(); ++i) {
            Point r = (Point) sortedPoints.get(i);
            double sweepX = r.getX();
            double dragX = sweepX - distance;

            while (((Point) sortedPoints.get(dragPoint)).getX() < dragX) {
                ++dragPoint;
            }

            for (int j = dragPoint; j < i; ++j) {
                Point test = (Point) sortedPoints.get(j);
                double checkDistance = r.distance(test);
                if (checkDistance < distance) {
                    distance = checkDistance;
                    result = createPointPair(r, test);
                }
```

```
            }
        }

        return result;
    }
```

Note the following key points when looking at the code:

- `result` contains the `Point` objects that make up the closest pair.
- `distance` represents the currently identified distance between the closest pair. Of course, this is also the width of the drag net.
- `dragpoint` is the index of the leftmost `Point` within the drag net.
- `sweepx` is the x coordinate of the `Point` under the sweep line.
- `dragx` is the x coordinate representing the left edge of the drag net.

This algorithm ignores the first two points in the sorted list, starting the sweep line at the third point, as the first two have already been assumed to make the closest pair for now. It then ignores points that have slipped behind the drag net by advancing the `dragpoint` variable. Finally, it checks the distance from the point under the sweep line to each of the points in the drag net, updating the resulting closest pair and the distance between them if a closer pair is found than that currently identified.

That wraps up your implementation of the plane sweep algorithm. If you now run all the tests defined for this algorithm, you'll see that they all pass.

Summary

- This chapter covered some of the theory behind two-dimensional geometry, including the coordinate system, points, lines, and triangles.
- We covered two geometric problems in detail: finding the intersection point of two straight lines, and finding the closest pair among a set of points.
- You implemented solutions to these problems with fully tested Java code.

We barely had time to scratch the surface of the subject of computational geometry. It is a fascinating field that covers areas including trilateration (the mechanism behind the Global Positioning System), 3D graphics, and computer-aided design. We hope that we have stimulated an interest you will pursue in the future.

Exercises

1. Implement a brute-force solution to the closest pair problem.
2. Optimize the plane sweep algorithm so that points too distant in the vertical direction are ignored.

Pragmatic Optimization

You might be wondering what the chapter about optimization is doing way at the back of the book. Its placement here reflects our philosophy that optimization does not belong at the forefront of your mind when building your applications. This chapter describes the role of optimization, including when and how to apply it, and demonstrates some very practical techniques to get great performance improvements in the software you build. You'll be encouraged to keep your design clean and clear as the first order of business, and use hard facts to drive the optimization process. Armed with this knowledge, you will be able to measure your progress and identify when the optimization effort has stopped adding value.

In this chapter, you learn the following:

- How optimization fits into the development process
- What profiling is and how it works
- How to profile an application using the standard Java virtual machine mechanism
- How to profile an application using the free Java Memory Profiler tool
- How to identify performance issues related to both the CPU and memory usage
- How to achieve huge performance increases with small and strategic alterations to code

Where Optimization Fits In

Optimization is an important part of software development, but not as important as you might think. We recommend that you take time to accumulate an awareness of the types of issues that affect performance in your particular programming environment, and keep them in mind as you code. For example, using a `StringBuffer` to build a long character sequence is preferable to multiple concatenations of `String` objects in Java, so you should do that as a matter of course.

However, you will stray into dangerous territory if you let this awareness cause you to change your design. This is called *premature optimization*, and we strongly encourage you to resist the temptation to build an implementation that is faster but harder to understand. In our experience, we are always surprised at the performance bottlenecks in our applications. It is only by measuring the behavior of your system and locating the real issue that you can make changes that will have the greatest benefit. It is simply not necessary to have optimized code throughout your system. You only need to worry about the code that is on the critical path, and you might be surprised to find out which code that is, even when you've written it yourself! This is where profiling comes in, which is the topic of the next section.

The key thing to remember is that a clean and simple design is much, much easier to optimize than one that the original developers thoughtfully optimized while writing it. It is also very important to choose the right algorithm initially. You should always be aware of the performance profile of your chosen implementation before trying to optimize it — that is, be conscious of whether your algorithm is `O(N)`, `O(log N)`, and so on. Choosing the wrong class of algorithm for the problem at hand will put a hard limit on the benefits that optimization is able to provide. That's another reason why this chapter is at the back of the book!

Experience shows that the first cut of a program is very unlikely to be the best performing. Unfortunately, experience also shows that it is unlikely that you can guess the exact reason why performance is suffering in any nontrivial application. When first writing a given program, you should make it work before making it fast. In fact, it is a good idea to separate these two activities very clearly in your development projects. By now, you know that we suggest using test-driven development to ensure the correct functioning of your programs. This is the "make it work" part. We then recommend the approach outlined in this chapter to "make it fast." The tests will keep your code on track while you alter its implementation to get better performance out of it. Just as unit tests remove the guesswork out of the functional success of your program, the techniques you learn in this chapter take the guesswork out of the performance success of your program.

The good news is that most programs have a very small number of significant bottlenecks that can be identified and addressed. The areas of your code you need to change are typically not large in number. The techniques described here enable you to quickly find them, fix them, and prove that you have achieved the benefits you want. We recommend that you avoid guessing how to make your code faster and relying on subjective opinions about the code's performance. In the same way that you should avoid refactoring without first creating automated unit tests, you should avoid optimizing without automated performance measurements.

Every program that takes a nontrivial amount of time to run has a bottleneck constraining its performance. You need to remember that this will still be true even when the program is running acceptably fast. You should begin the optimization process with a goal to meet some objective performance criteria, not to remove all performance bottlenecks. Be careful to avoid setting yourself impossible performance targets, of course. Nothing you do will enable a 2MB photo to squeeze down a 56K modem line in 3 seconds! Think of optimization as part of your performance toolkit, but not the only skill you'll need to make your applications really fast. Good design skills and a knowledge of the trade-offs you make when choosing particular data structures and algorithms are much more important skills to have at your disposal.

Understanding Profiling

Profiling is the process of measuring the behavior of a program. Java lends itself to profiling because support for it is built right into the virtual machine, as you'll see later in this chapter. Profiling other languages varies in its difficulty but is still a very popular technique. Three major areas are measured when profiling a program: CPU usage, memory usage, and concurrency, or threading behavior.

Concurrency issues are beyond the scope of this chapter, so be sure to check Appendix A for further reading if you need more information on the topic.

A profiler measures CPU usage by determining how long the program spends in each method while the program is running. It is important to be aware that this information is typically gathered by sampling the execution stack of each thread in the virtual machine at regular intervals to determine which methods are active at any given moment. Better results are obtained from longer-running programs. If your program is very fast, then the results you get might not be accurate. Then again, if your program is already that fast, you probably don't need to optimize it too much!

A profiler will report statistics such as the following:

- How many times a method was called
- How much CPU time was consumed in a given method
- How much CPU time was consumed by a method and all methods called by it
- What proportion of the running time was spent in a particular method

These statistics enable you to identify which parts of your code will benefit from some optimization. Similarly for memory usage, a profiler will gather statistics on overall memory usage, object creation, and garbage collection, and provide you with information such as the following:

- How many objects of each class were instantiated
- How many instances of each class were garbage collected
- How much memory was allocated to the virtual machine by the operating system at any given time (the heap size)
- How much of the heap was free and how much was in use at a given time

This kind of information will give you a deeper insight into the runtime behavior of your code, and is often the source of many informative surprises, as you'll see later in this chapter when we optimize an example program. Again, the profiler gives you a lot of evidence on which to base your optimization efforts.

The following section shows you how to profile a Java program using two different techniques. The first uses the profiling features built into the Java virtual machine itself. These features are simple in nature, but readily available for you to try. The second technique involves an open-source tool known as the Java Memory Profiler (JMP). This provides much more helpful information in a nice graphical interface, but requires you to download and install the software before you can get started. The next section explains the sample program used in the profiling exercises.

The FileSortingHelper Example Program

You will use a contrived example program for the purposes of profiling and optimization. This program will be a simple Unix-style filter that takes input from standard input, assuming each line contains a word, and then sorts the words and prints them out again to standard output in sorted order. To put a twist on things, the comparator used to sort the words will sort words according to their alphabetical order were the words printed backwards. For example, the word "ant" would sort before the word "pie" because when printed backwards, "tna" ("ant" backwards) sorts after "eip" ("pie" backwards). This is simply to make the program work a little harder and make the profiling more interesting, so don't worry if it seems pointless — it probably is!

If you used this sample program to sort the following list of words:

```
test
driven
development
is
one
small
step
for
programmers
but
one
giant
leap
for
programming
```

then you'd get the following output:

```
one
one
programming
small
driven
leap
step
for
for
is
programmers
giant
development
test
but
```

Here is the code for the comparator:

```
package com.wrox.algorithms.sorting;

public final class ReverseStringComparator implements Comparator {
    public static final ReverseStringComparator INSTANCE = new
                        ReverseStringComparator();

    private ReverseStringComparator() {
    }

    public int compare(Object left, Object right) throws ClassCastException {
        assert left != null : "left can't be null";
```

```
        assert right != null : "right can't be null";

        return reverse((String) left).compareTo(reverse((String) right));
    }

    private String reverse(String s) {
        StringBuffer result = new StringBuffer();

        for (int i = 0; i < s.length(); i++) {
            result.append(s.charAt(s.length() - 1 - i));
        }

        return result.toString();
    }
}
```

There's no need to go into great detail about how this code works, as you won't be using it in any of your programs. It implements the standard `Comparator` interface, assumes both its arguments are `String` objects, and compares them after first creating a reversed version of each.

Try It Out — Implementing the FileSortingHelper Class

The `FileSortingHelper` class is shown here:

```
package com.wrox.algorithms.sorting;

import com.wrox.algorithms.iteration.Iterator;
import com.wrox.algorithms.lists.LinkedList;
import com.wrox.algorithms.lists.List;

import java.io.BufferedReader;
import java.io.IOException;
import java.io.InputStreamReader;

public final class FileSortingHelper {
    private FileSortingHelper() {
    }

    public static void main(String[] args) throws Exception {
        sort(loadWords());

        System.err.println("Finished...press CTRL-C to exit");

        Thread.sleep(100000);
    }
    ...
}
```

How It Works

As you can see, this class has a private constructor to prevent instantiation by other code, and a `main()` method that delegates most of the work to two other methods, `loadWords()` and `sort()`. It then does an apparently strange thing — it prints a message advising you to kill the program and puts itself to sleep for a while using the `Thread.sleep()` call. This is simply to give you more time to look at the results of the profiling in JMP when the program finishes, so don't worry about it.

Following is the code for the `sort()` method. It accepts a list of words, using the comparator just defined, and a shell sort implementation to sort them. Finally, it simply prints out the sorted list of words one by one:

```
    private static void sort(List wordList) {
        assert wordList != null : "tree can't be null";

        System.out.println("Starting sort...");

        Comparator comparator = ReverseStringComparator.INSTANCE;
        ListSorter sorter = new ShellsortListSorter(comparator);

        List sorted = sorter.sort(wordList);

        Iterator i = sorted.iterator();
        i.first();
        while (!i.isDone()) {
            System.out.println(i.current());
            i.next();
        }
    }
```

The final method in our sample program is `loadWords()`, which simply drains standard input, adding each line to a `List` that is returned to the caller when no more input is available. The only issue here is that you need to catch any `IOException` that may arise:

```
    private static List loadWords() throws IOException {
        List result = new LinkedList();

        BufferedReader reader = new BufferedReader(new
InputStreamReader(System.in));

        try {
            String word;

            while ((word = reader.readLine()) != null) {
                result.add(word);
            }
        } finally {
            reader.close();
        }

        return result;
    }
```

If you compile and run the program, then you will need to direct it to read its input from a file, as shown by the following command line:

```
java com.wrox.algorithms.sorting.FileSortingHelper <words.txt
```

To run this command, you need to be in the directory that contains the compiled Java class files for the sample program. You also need to create or obtain a file called `words.txt` with a large number of lines of text in it. A quick Internet search for dictionary files will lead you to files with many thousands of words in them for this purpose. Appendix B contains the URL of the one we used when developing this book.

On our Pentium 4 laptop, running this program with a file containing 10,000 words took about a minute, with the CPU running at 100 percent. This is much longer than we are prepared to wait, so some optimization is in order. Let's take a look at what's going on by profiling this program.

Profiling with hprof

The standard Sun Java virtual machine supports basic profiling out of the box. To determine whether your Java environment has this support, try the following command:

```
java -Xrunhprof:help
```

The -Xrun command-line option loads extra modules into the virtual machine when it starts. In this case, you're running the hprof module. You're also passing that module a command — in this case, help — to get some instructions on how to use it. The following listing shows the output from this command:

```
Hprof usage: -Xrunhprof[:help]|[:<option>=<value>, ...]

Option Name and Value  Description              Default
---------------------  ----------------------   -------
heap=dump|sites|all    heap profiling           all
cpu=samples|times|old  CPU usage                off
monitor=y|n            monitor contention       n
format=a|b             ascii or binary output   a
file=<file>            write data to file       java.hprof(.txt for ascii)
net=<host>:<port>      send data over a socket  write to file
depth=<size>           stack trace depth        4
cutoff=<value>         output cutoff point      0.0001
lineno=y|n             line number in traces?   y
thread=y|n             thread in traces?        n
doe=y|n                dump on exit?            y
gc_okay=y|n            GC okay during sampling  y

Example: java -Xrunhprof:cpu=samples,file=log.txt,depth=3 FooClass

Note: format=b cannot be used with cpu=old|times
```

The preceding output shows that several different parameters can be passed to hprof to tailor its behavior. The parameter for this example is cpu=samples, which provides you with sample-based profiling of your application. The following command uses this profiling option on our sample application, and redirects both input and output to files in the current directory:

```
java -Xrunhprof:cpu=samples com.wrox.algorithms.sorting.FileSortingHelper
<words.txt >sorted.txt
```

When you run the program with profiling turned on, it will run noticeably slower than before, but that is understandable because quite a bit of work is required to collect the statistics. All profilers have a big impact on performance, but the idea is that the relative measures of time spent in various parts of the program will be quite accurate.

After the program finishes, you will see the following message:

```
Dumping CPU usage by sampling running threads ... done.
```

Although it doesn't tell you, this has created a file in the working directory called `java.hprof.txt` that contains the information gathered during profiling. If you open this file in a text editor, then you will see contents like the following (after some boilerplate text at the top of the file):

```
THREAD START (obj=2b76bc0, id = 1, name="Finalizer", group="system")
THREAD START (obj=2b76cc8, id = 2, name="Reference Handler", group="system")
THREAD START (obj=2b76da8, id = 3, name="main", group="main")
THREAD START (obj=2b79bc0, id = 4, name="HPROF CPU profiler", group="system")
...
```

This gives you information about the threads that were running in the virtual machine. As you can see, `hprof` creates a thread of its own to do its work. After the thread information, you will see a series of small Java stack traces like the following:

```
TRACE 23:
 java.lang.StringBuffer.<init>(<Unknown>:Unknown line)
 java.lang.StringBuffer.<init>(<Unknown>:Unknown line)
 com.wrox.algorithms.sorting.ReverseStringComparator.reverse
            (ReverseStringComparator.java:48)
 com.wrox.algorithms.sorting.ReverseStringComparator.compare
            (ReverseStringComparator.java:44)

TRACE 21:
 com.wrox.algorithms.sorting.ReverseStringComparator.reverse
            (ReverseStringComparator.java:51)
 com.wrox.algorithms.sorting.ReverseStringComparator.compare
            (ReverseStringComparator.java:44)
 com.wrox.algorithms.sorting.ShellsortListSorter.sortSublist
            (ShellsortListSorter.java:79)
 com.wrox.algorithms.sorting.ShellsortListSorter.hSort
            (ShellsortListSorter.java:69)
```

You will see many of these stack traces occupying the bulk of the contents of the output file. They are simply all the different stack contents encountered during the sampling effort. The idea is that each time a sample is taken, `hprof` looks at the top of the stack to determine whether that combination of method calls has been encountered before. If so, the statistics are updated, but another `TRACE` record is not created. The number after `TRACE` (for example, `TRACE 21` above) is simply an identifier that is used farther down in the profiling output, as you will see shortly.

The final section of the output is the most interesting because it indicates where the program is spending most of its time. Here are the first few lines of the final section:

```
CPU SAMPLES BEGIN (total = 1100) Wed Jun 22 21:54:20 2005
rank   self  accum   count trace method
   1 29.55% 29.55%     325    16 ReverseStringComparator.reverse
   2 17.18% 46.73%     189    15 LinkedList.getElementBackwards
   3 16.00% 62.73%     176    18 LinkedList.getElementForwards
   4 13.09% 75.82%     144    17 LinkedList.getElementBackwards
   5 11.55% 87.36%     127    14 LinkedList.getElementForwards
   6  2.55% 89.91%      28    19 LinkedList.getElementBackwards
   7  2.09% 92.00%      23    29 LinkedList.getElementBackwards
   8  1.91% 93.91%      21    24 LinkedList.getElementForwards
...
```

The most important columns here are the `self` and `accum` columns, as well as the final column that identifies which method is being described by each row. The `self` column indicates the percentage of execution time spent in the method itself, while the `accum` column defines the percentage of time spent in that method and all methods called by it. As you can see, this list is ordered by the `self` column in descending order, on the assumption that you are most interested in finding out which individual method is consuming the most time. The `trace` column is the identifying number that enables you to refer back to the trace section of the file to see more detail about the execution stack for the method in question.

Before trying to improve this situation, you'll first try profiling the same program with the Java Memory Profiler.

Profiling with JMP

The Java Memory Profiler is a free tool that you can download from the following URL:

```
http://www.khelekore.org/jmp/
```

The JMP comes with great documentation to get you started, so you'll need to follow the instructions carefully. Bear in mind that the JMP is not itself a Java program, so the installation may not be familiar to you if Java is your main programming environment. For example, on a Windows system, you need to copy a DLL into your Windows system directory to get it going.

To determine whether you have the JMP installed correctly, the test is very similar to the `hprof` example in the preceding section. Type the following at the command line:

```
java -Xrunjmp:help
```

This will ask the JMP to give you some instructions on its use, as shown here:

```
jmp/jmp/0.47-win initializing: (help):...
help wanted..
java -Xrunjmp[:[options]] package.Class
options is a comma separated list and may include:
help      - to show this text.
nomethods - to disable method profiling.
noobjects - to disable object profiling.
nomonitors - to disable monitor profiling.
allocfollowsfilter - to group object allocations into filtered methods.
nogui     - to run jmp without the user interface.
dodump    - to allow to be called with signals.
dumpdir=<directoryr> - to specify where the dump-/heapdumpfiles go.
dumptimer=<n> - to specify automatic dump every n:th second.
filter=<somefilter> - to specify an initial recursive filter.
threadtime - to specify that timing of methods and monitors
           should use thread cpu time instead of absolute time.
simulator - to specify that jmp should not perform any jni tricks.
           probably only useful if you debug jmp.

An example may look like this:
java -Xrunjmp:nomethods,dumpdir=/tmp/jmpdump/ rabbit.proxy.Proxy
```

As you can see, the JMP has many options that you can use to tailor its behavior. For our purposes, we'll simply use the default configuration and run it against our sample program with the following command line:

```
java -Xrunjmp com.wrox.algorithms.sorting.FileSortingHelper <words.txt >sorted.txt
```

Three windows will appear with statistics, as shown in Figure 19-1.

The main JMP window (shown at the bottom of Figure 19-1) provides a graphical view of the memory being used by the running application. This shows two values changing over time: the total heap size allocated to the virtual machine, and the amount that is currently allocated for object use. You can see from the fluctuating shape of the graph that the amount of memory being used changes constantly as objects are created and garbage is collected. If the amount of memory needed exceeds the current total heap size allocated to the virtual machine, more will be requested from the operating system and the extra space will be used to store more objects.

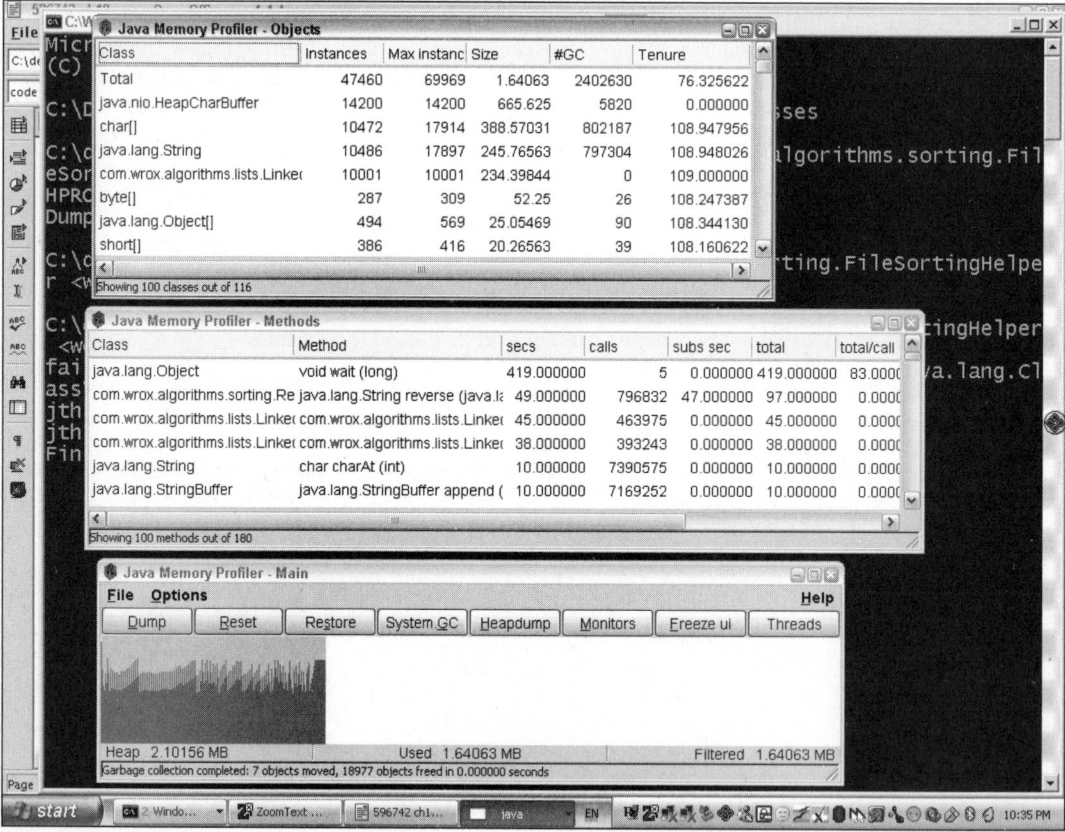

Figure 19-1: JMP windows during profiling.

The JMP Objects window, shown at the top of Figure 19-1, lists many interesting statistics about the instances in the virtual machine. The first column shows the class name, followed by the current number of instances of the class, the maximum number of instances that have been active at any point during the running of the program, the amount of memory used by the current instances, and the number of instances that have been garbage collected during the execution. This is a column you'll have some interest in when you optimize this program shortly.

The JMP Methods window, shown in the middle of Figure 19-1, contains statistics about the methods called during the program's execution, such as the class and method name, the number of calls, how long those calls took (in seconds), and how long the methods called by the method took (in seconds). This information will also prove extremely useful when you attempt to speed up the sample program.

Understanding Optimization

Before you attempt to optimize a program, be aware that if you have chosen the wrong algorithm, you will be absolutely wasting your time attempting to optimize it. For example, if you are wondering why a sorting program is slow when sorting a million records using a bubble sort, don't turn to optimization for the answer. No amount of tweaking will change the fact that an `O(N²)` algorithm on a large data set is going to give you plenty of time to go for a coffee while it's running. You could probably have lunch as well. This is why optimization is not the first chapter of this book; it really is not as important as you might think. We'll assume for the rest of this chapter that you have chosen the most appropriate algorithm for your purposes and that you just need to get the most out of it with your optimization efforts.

Another good way to waste time is to optimize a part of your program that is not a bottleneck on its performance. That may sound obvious, but it is extremely common for developers to twist themselves into knots to create a faster version of some code that is rarely called, or is called only at application startup, for example. These efforts inevitably result in code that is harder to understand and harder to maintain, and contributes nothing to the overall performance of the application, even though it runs faster than it previously did.

If you only remember one thing from this chapter, remember this: Don't *guess* why your program is slow. Find out the facts about its performance via profiling or some other means, so that you can take a targeted approach to improving it. Our recommended approach to program optimization is as follows:

1. Measure the performance of your program with a profiler.
2. Identify the significant contributors to the performance problem.
3. Fix *one* of the problems, preferably the most significant, but go for an easier one if it is also significant.
4. Measure the performance again.
5. Ensure that the change effected the desired result. If not, undo the change.
6. Repeat these steps until the benefits are no longer worth the effort or the performance is acceptable.

There is really no mystery to this method. It is simply a targeted approach based on some hard facts, ensuring that each change you make has a measurable benefit. The next section uses this technique to optimize our sample program.

Putting Optimization into Practice

You've already profiled the sample application using the JMP, and now you're interested in why it is so slow. Take a closer look at the JMP Methods window shown in Figure 19-2 to see where all the time is going.

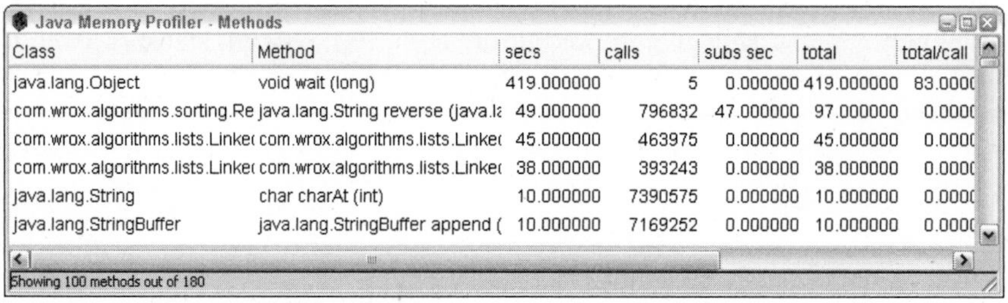

Java Memory Profiler - Methods

Class	Method	secs	calls	subs sec	total	total/call
java.lang.Object	void wait (long)	419.000000	5	0.000000	419.000000	83.000(
com.wrox.algorithms.sorting.Re	java.lang.String reverse (java.la	49.000000	796832	47.000000	97.000000	0.000(
com.wrox.algorithms.lists.Linke(	com.wrox.algorithms.lists.Linke(	45.000000	463975	0.000000	45.000000	0.000(
com.wrox.algorithms.lists.Linke(	com.wrox.algorithms.lists.Linke(	38.000000	393243	0.000000	38.000000	0.000(
java.lang.String	char charAt (int)	10.000000	7390575	0.000000	10.000000	0.000(
java.lang.StringBuffer	java.lang.StringBuffer append (	10.000000	7169252	0.000000	10.000000	0.000(

Showing 100 methods out of 180

Figure 19-2: The JMP Methods window.

You'll notice that you're spending a lot of time reversing `String` objects, and you're spending a lot of time doing `LinkedList` manipulations as well. (You can ignore the top item in this list because that's just the time you spent looking at the screen before you pressed Ctrl+C to kill the application.)

So what do you do? You could try to figure out a more efficient way of reversing `String` objects, but it seems easier to deal with the `LinkedList` issue for now. You initially used a `LinkedList`, as you didn't know how many words were going to be coming in as input, but you knew it would be a lot, so you thought adding them to the back of a `LinkedList` would be the way to go. However, now you recall that the sorting needs a lot of index-based access to items in the list, and that's where you seem to be losing out according to the profiler. If you look at the `calls` column in Figure 19-2, you'll see that the two `LinkedList` operations are being called several hundred thousand times, with only ten thousand words to sort. This leads to the conclusion that you made the wrong choice of data structure here; building the initial list will only involve ten thousand calls to `add()`, so you should choose the data structure that supports the operations you need most. In this case, that's index-based access to items after the list has been built, so you need to use an `ArrayList` instead.

Try It Out — Implementing an ArrayList

It's extremely simple to replace the `LinkedList` with an `ArrayList` in the `loadWords()` method of our sample `FileSortingHelper`, as shown here:

```
private static List loadWords() throws IOException {
    List result = new ArrayList();

    BufferedReader reader = new BufferedReader(new InputStreamReader
                                  (System.in));

    try {
        String word;

        while ((word = reader.readLine()) != null) {
            result.add(word);
        }
```

```
        } finally {
            reader.close();
        }

        return result;
    }
```

The next step is to recompile the program and profile it again with the following command:

```
java -Xrunjmp com.wrox.algorithms.sorting.FileSortingHelper <words.txt >sorted.txt
```

This time, the JMP profiler produces the results shown in Figure 19-3.

How It Works

Take a closer look at the JMP Methods window again, as shown in Figure 19-4.

There's no sign of the `LinkedList` anymore, and, just as important, there's no sign of the `ArrayList` you just added. Although it often happens that a change you make will just move the problem, or even make it worse, that isn't the case here. However, this is why it is so important to measure after each change you make to ensure that your optimization efforts are moving you forward.

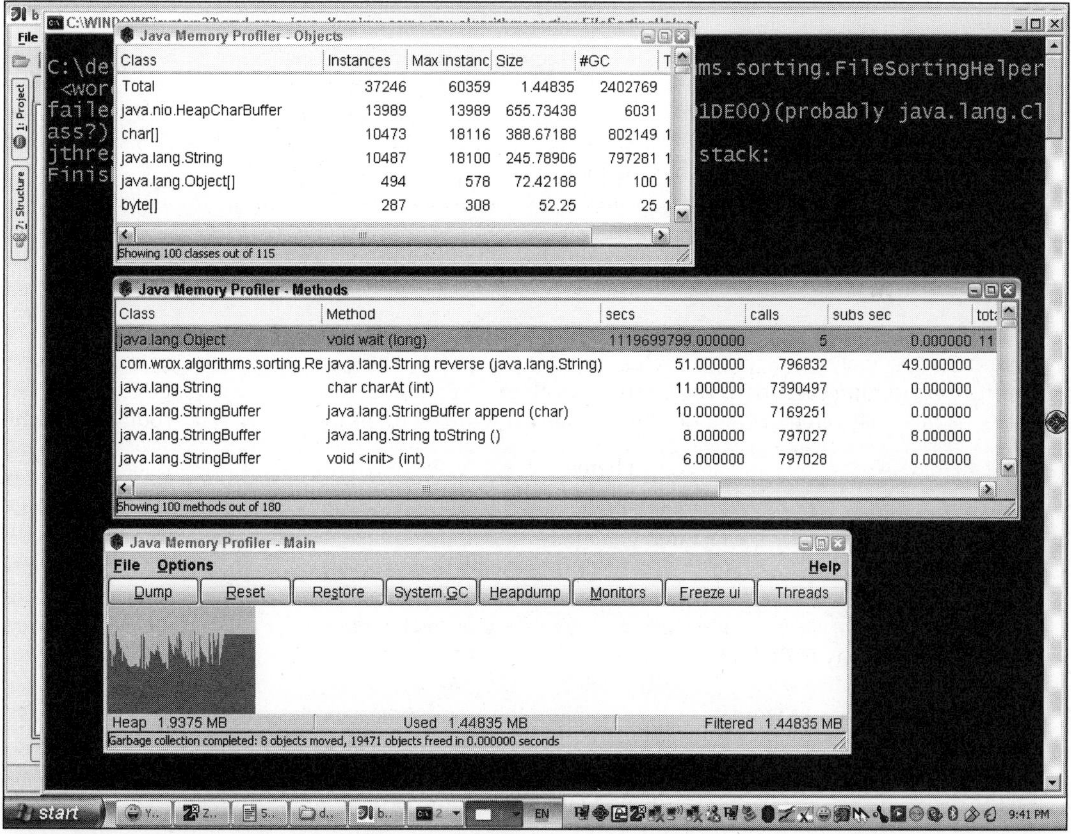

Figure 19-3: Profiling after switching to an ArrayList.

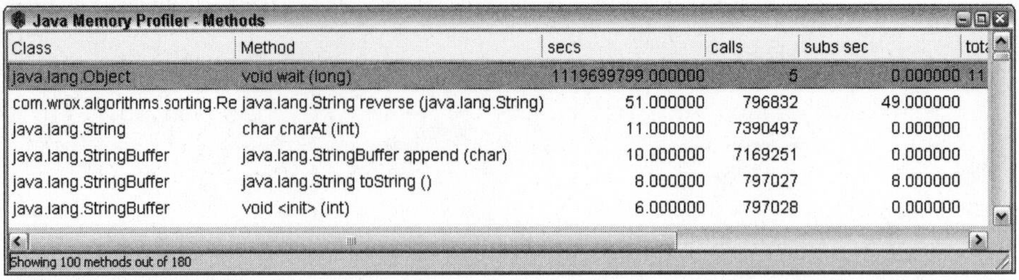

Java Memory Profiler - Methods

Class	Method	secs	calls	subs sec	tot:
java.lang.Object	void wait (long)	1119699799.000000	5	0.000000	11
com.wrox.algorithms.sorting.Re	java.lang.String reverse (java.lang.String)	51.000000	796832	49.000000	
java.lang.String	char charAt (int)	11.000000	7390497	0.000000	
java.lang.StringBuffer	java.lang.StringBuffer append (char)	10.000000	7169251	0.000000	
java.lang.StringBuffer	java.lang.String toString ()	8.000000	797027	8.000000	
java.lang.StringBuffer	void <init> (int)	6.000000	797028	0.000000	

Showing 100 methods out of 180

Figure 19-4: The JMP Methods window with the ArrayList implementation.

Notice in Figure 19-4 that the `reverse()` method in the `ReverseStringComparator` is taking 51 seconds, while the next largest method only takes 11 seconds. It's time to think about all this `String` reversing business if you're going to make the next big step forward. Take a look at how many times the `reverse()` method is called—almost 800,000 times! This is important information. If it took 51 seconds and was only called once, that would mean it was a fairly poorly written method indeed. As it is, it's more of an issue that it's being called so often. The situation is made even clearer by the JMP Objects window, shown in Figure 19-5.

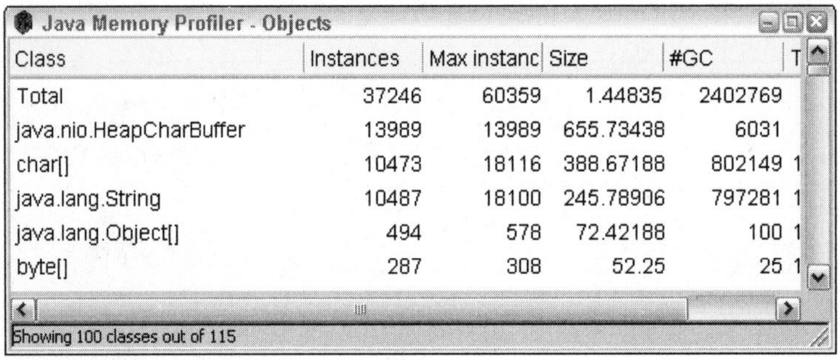

Java Memory Profiler - Objects

Class	Instances	Max instanc	Size	#GC	T
Total	37246	60359	1.44835	2402769	
java.nio.HeapCharBuffer	13989	13989	655.73438	6031	
char[]	10473	18116	388.67188	802149	1
java.lang.String	10487	18100	245.78906	797281	1
java.lang.Object[]	494	578	72.42188	100	1
byte[]	287	308	52.25	25	1

Showing 100 classes out of 115

Figure 19-5: The JMP Objects window.

Look at the `#GC` column, which indicates how many objects of the given class were garbage collected during the program execution. The total shows almost 2.5 million objects were garbage collected. Surely that's ridiculous given that you only created one list with ten thousand words in it, wouldn't you think?

The clue is the number of `String` objects that are garbage collected. It's also around 800,000, about the same number of calls to the `reverse()` method in the Methods window. You can now feel confident that the issue is caused by the fact that you are reversing the `String` objects you are comparing every time pairs of `String` objects are evaluated during the sorting process. Given that each `String` will be involved in multiple pairwise comparisons, you're reversing the same `String` objects repeatedly, creating new `String` objects each time and spinning off thousands of objects for garbage collection. There must be a better way to do this.

If you have 10,000 input words, you could reduce the amount of work the program is doing by only reversing each `String` once. If you reversed them before putting them into the list for sorting, you would not even need our `ReverseStringComparator` at all! You could just use a natural comparator on the reversed `String` objects. This would eliminate all the tedious work being done during the current sorting routine, and drastically reduce the number of temporary objects you create. At least we think so; you'll have to try it and measure it, of course.

There will be the problem of printing out the sorted list at the end of the sorting process; you'll have to reverse all the `String` objects again to put them back into their original correct character sequences; otherwise, the output won't be what the user expects. That will be another 10,000 reverse operations, but even so, it should be a lot more effective than what you have now. Again, you won't know until you make the change and measure its effect.

Try It Out Optimizing the FileSortingHelper

Our `FileSortingHelper` is going to have to change a little, so you create a new class in our sample code base called `OptimizedFileSortingHelper` to keep the two different implementations available for quick reference. The start of the `OptimizedFileSortingHelper` class is shown here:

```
package com.wrox.algorithms.sorting;

import com.wrox.algorithms.iteration.Iterator;
import com.wrox.algorithms.lists.ArrayList;
import com.wrox.algorithms.lists.List;

import java.io.BufferedReader;
import java.io.IOException;
import java.io.InputStreamReader;

public final class OptimizedFileSortingHelper {

    private OptimizedFileSortingHelper() {
    }
    ...
}
```

Like the `FileSortingHelper`, this optimized version has a private constructor to prevent it from being inadvertently instantiated by other programs. The `main()` method is shown below:

```
    public static void main(String[] args) throws Exception {
        List words = loadWords();
        reverseAll(words);

        System.out.println("Starting sort...");

        Comparator comparator = NaturalComparator.INSTANCE;
        ListSorter sorter = new ShellsortListSorter(comparator);

        List sorted = sorter.sort(words);
        reverseAll(sorted);
        printAll(sorted);

        System.err.println("Finished...press CTRL-C to exit");

        Thread.sleep(100000);
    }
```

The `main()` method delegates much of the work to methods that will be shown later. Note that after the words are loaded from the input stream, the `reverseAll()` method is called to—you guessed it—reverse all the words. The list of reversed words is then sorted using a `NaturalComparator` that treats them like normal strings. The strings in the resulting sorted list are then reversed again and printed out.

Next is the `loadWords()` method. It is unchanged from the `FileSortingHelper` class shown previously:

```
    private static List loadWords() throws IOException {
        List result = new ArrayList();

        BufferedReader reader = new BufferedReader(new InputStreamReader
                                     (System.in));

        try {
            String word;

            while ((word = reader.readLine()) != null) {
                result.add(word);
            }
        } finally {
            reader.close();
        }

        return result;
    }
```

The `reverse()` method, shown here, was all that was salvaged out of the now redundant `ReverseStringComparator` that you created earlier in the chapter:

```
    private static String reverse(String s) {
        StringBuffer result = new StringBuffer();

        for (int i = 0; i < s.length(); i++) {
            result.append(s.charAt(s.length() - 1 - i));
        }

        return result.toString();
    }
```

The `reverseAll()` method simply iterates over the `List` provided to it, treating each element as a `String` that is reversed and placed back into the `List`:

```
    private static void reverseAll(List words) {
        for (int i = 0; i < words.size(); ++i) {
            words.set(i, reverse((String) words.get(i)));
        }
    }
```

The `printAll()` method is also a simple list iteration routine to print out the elements in the `List` supplied to it:

```
    private static void printAll(List stringList) {
        Iterator iterator = stringList.iterator();
        iterator.first();
        while (!iterator.isDone()) {
            String word = (String) iterator.current();
            System.out.println(word);
            iterator.next();
        }
    }
```

How It Works

It's now time to try running our optimized version of the sample application. The following command will use the JMP to profile our `OptimizedFileSortingHelper`:

```
java -Xrunjmp com.wrox.algorithms.sorting.OptimizedFileSortingHelper <words.txt
>sorted.txt
```

The JMP output for this run is shown in Figure 19-6.

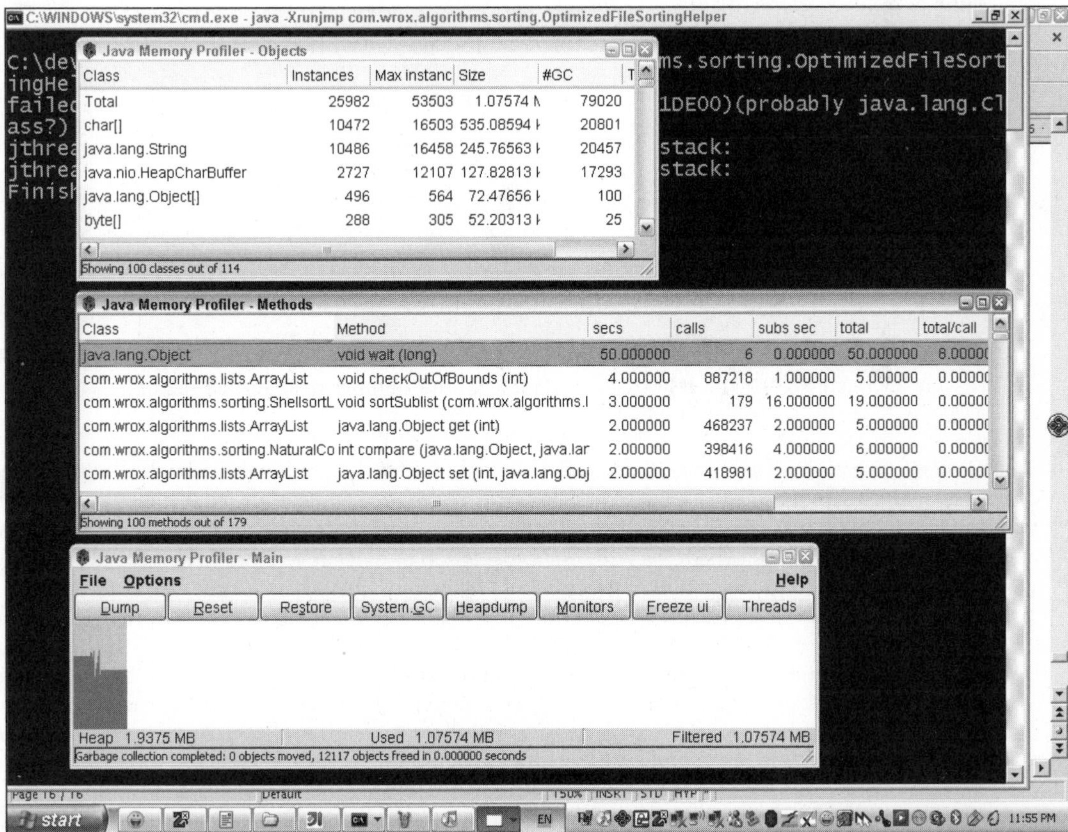

Figure 19-6: JMP output from the OptimizedFileSortingHelper.

Take a closer look at the JMP Methods window, shown in Figure 19-7, to determine whether you have eliminated the 50 seconds of effort you spent doing all that string reversing.

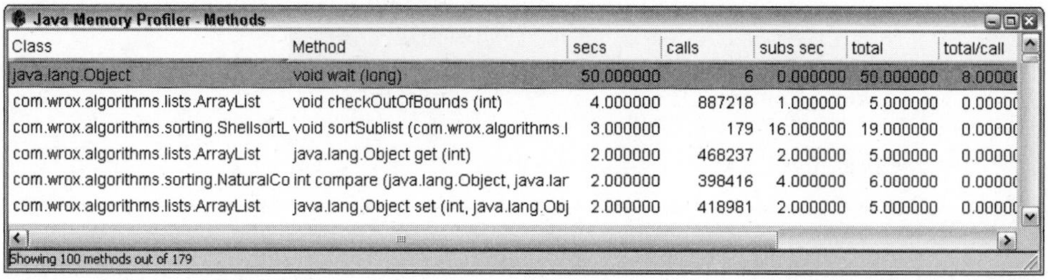

Java Memory Profiler - Methods

Class	Method	secs	calls	subs sec	total	total/call
java.lang.Object	void wait (long)	50.000000	6	0.000000	50.000000	8.0000
com.wrox.algorithms.lists.ArrayList	void checkOutOfBounds (int)	4.000000	887218	1.000000	5.000000	0.0000
com.wrox.algorithms.sorting.ShellsortL	void sortSublist (com.wrox.algorithms.l	3.000000	179	16.000000	19.000000	0.0000
com.wrox.algorithms.lists.ArrayList	java.lang.Object get (int)	2.000000	468237	2.000000	5.000000	0.0000
com.wrox.algorithms.sorting.NaturalCo	int compare (java.lang.Object, java.lar	2.000000	398416	4.000000	6.000000	0.0000
com.wrox.algorithms.lists.ArrayList	java.lang.Object set (int, java.lang.Obj	2.000000	418981	2.000000	5.000000	0.0000

Showing 100 methods out of 179

Figure 19-7: The JMP Methods window for the OptimizedFileSortingHelper.

You can see that there is no sign of the `reverse()` method in this list of bottleneck methods. Note also that the biggest contributor is only taking four seconds anyway! This is looking like a huge improvement.

Now take a closer look at the JMP Objects window, shown in Figure 19-8, to determine whether your prediction of reduced garbage collection panned out as you hoped.

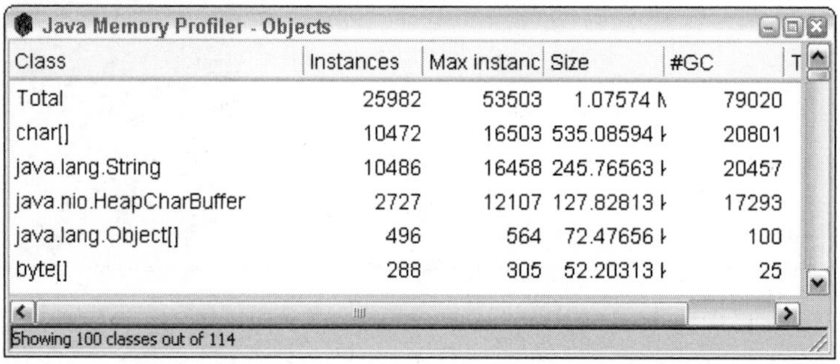

Java Memory Profiler - Objects

Class	Instances	Max instanc	Size	#GC
Total	25982	53503	1.07574 M	79020
char[]	10472	16503	535.08594 K	20801
java.lang.String	10486	16458	245.76563 K	20457
java.nio.HeapCharBuffer	2727	12107	127.82813 K	17293
java.lang.Object[]	496	564	72.47656 K	100
byte[]	288	305	52.20313 K	25

Showing 100 classes out of 114

Figure 19-8: The JMP Objects window for the OptimizedFileSortingHelper.

There is also a dramatic change here. Look at the `#GC` column for the top line, which is the total number of objects of all classes that were garbage collected during the program execution. It is less than 80,000, whereas previously it was over 2 million! Also note that the number of `String` objects that were garbage collected was around 20,000, which fits with our expectation of twice reversing each of the 10,000 input words. It is very important to verify that the numbers make sense to you in the context of the change you have made, so make sure you check each time you make a change and re-profile your application.

You have done two rounds of optimization for our sample application, dramatically reducing the time taken by the bottleneck execution methods. The final thing you need to do is leave the profiling and go back to normal execution to see how well it runs. Recall that this program originally took over a minute to run on our machine. Run without the JMP command-line switch:

```
java com.wrox.algorithms.sorting.OptimizedFileSortingHelper <words.txt >sorted.txt
```

How It Works

The program now runs in under two seconds! That's around 50 times faster than our first version. This is quite typical of the real-world experience we have had optimizing Java code. The important thing is that we didn't have to give any thought to performance while writing the code, other than to carefully select an algorithm with the right characteristics for our needs. Well-designed code that is clear and simple lends itself to later optimization very well. For example, the fact that you were able to unplug implementations of the `List` and `Comparator` interfaces in the example program was key to achieving the performance you wanted.

Summary

In this chapter, you learned that . . .

- Optimization is an important aspect of software development, but not as important as a good understanding of algorithms.
- Profiling is a technique to gather hard facts about the runtime behavior of your Java code.
- The Java Virtual Machine supports profiling with a simple command-line argument syntax.
- The free Java Memory Profiler provides a graphical view of the memory usage of your application, allowing you to quickly find the problem areas that you need to address.
- You can make an example of a slow-running program run 50 times faster with a targeted and methodical approach to optimization.

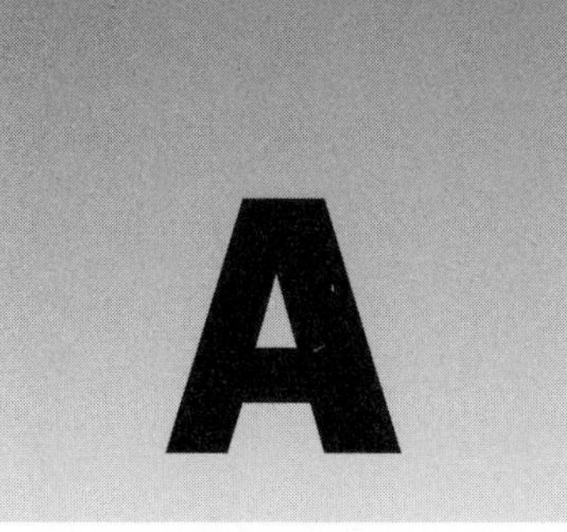

Further Reading

It is hoped that this book has inspired you to delve further into the world of algorithms. Of course, we also hope you'll take with you some of the design patterns and ideas from test-driven development as well! Here are some books on these topics that you might want to peruse next time you're in the bookstore. There is also a wealth of resources on the Internet that you can easily find by typing a few keywords into your favorite search engine, so we'll leave that to you.

Algorithms in Java, Third Edition, Parts 1–4: Fundamentals, Data Structures, Sorting, Searching, by Robert Sedgewick. Addison Wesley, 2002.

Design Patterns, by Erich Gamma et al. Addison-Wesley, 1995.

File Structures, by Michael Folk and Bill Zoellick. Addison-Wesley, 1991.

Introduction to Algorithms, Second Edition, by Thomas H. Cormen et al. The MIT Press, 2001.

Java Performance Tuning, Second Edition, by Jack Shirazi. O'Reilly Associates, 2003.

JUnit in Action, by Vincent Massol with Ted Husted. Manning, 2004.

Test-Driven Development: By Example, by Kent Beck. Addison-Wesley, 2002.

Test-Driven Development: A Practical Guide, by David Astels. Prentice Hall PTR, 2003.

The Art of Computer Programming, Volume 1: Fundamental Algorithms (Second Edition), by Donald E. Knuth. Addison-Wesley, 1973.

The Art of Computer Programming, Volume 3: Sorting and Searching (Second Edition), by Donald E. Knuth. Addison-Wesley, 1998.

Resources

Apache Jakarta Commons: `http://jakarta.apache.org/commons`

Java Memory Profiler home page: `www.khelekore.org/jmp/`

JUnit: `www.junit.org`

National Institute of Standards and Technology: `www.nist.gov`

Project Gutenberg: `www.gutenberg.org`

Unicode home page: `www.unicode.org`

University of Southern Denmark Department of Mathematics and Computer Science: `http://imada.sdu.dk`

University of Calgary Department of Computer Science: `www.cpsc.ucalgary.ca`

Wikipedia: `www.wikipedia.org`

Word Lists: `http://wordlist.sourceforge.net/`

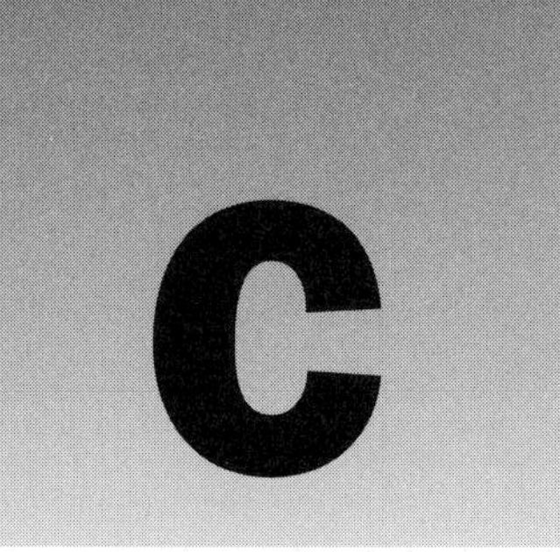

Bibliography

[Astels, 2003] Astels, David. *Test-Driven Development: A Practical Guide*. Prentice Hall PTR, 2003.

[Beck, 2000] Beck, Kent. *Extreme Programming Explained*. Boston: Addison-Wesley, 2000.

[Beck, 2002] Beck, Kent. *Test-Driven Development: By Example*. Addison Wesley Longman, 2002.

[Bloch, 2001] Bloch, Joshua. *Effective Java*. Addison-Wesley, 2001.

[Cormen, 2001] Cormen, Thomas H., et al. *Introduction to Algorithms, Second Edition*. The MIT Press, 2001.

[Crispin, 2002] Crispin, Lisa, and Tip House. *Testing Extreme Programming*. Addison Wesley, 2002.

[Fowler, 1999] Fowler, Martin. *Refactoring*. Addison-Wesley, 1999.

[Gamma, 1995] Gamma, Erich, Richard Helm, Ralph Johnson, and John Vlissides. *Design Patterns*. Addison-Wesley, 1995.

[Hunt, 2000] Hunt, Andy, and Dave Thomas. *The Pragmatic Programmer*. Addison-Wesley, 2000.

[Knuth, 1973] Knuth, Donald E. *Fundamental Algorithms,* Volume 1 of *The Art of Computer Programming, Second Edition*. Addison-Wesley, 1973.

[Knuth, 1998] Knuth, Donald E. *Sorting and Searching,* Volume 3 of *The Art of Computer Programming, Second Edition*. Addison-Wesley, 1998.

[Massol, 2004] Massol, Vincent. *JUnit in Action*. Manning, 2004.

[Sanchez, 2003] Sánchez-Crespo Dalmau, Daniel. *Core Techniques and Algorithms in Game Programming*. New Riders Publishing, 2003.

[Sedgewick, 2002] Sedgewick, Robert. *Algorithms in Java, Third Edition, Parts 1–4: Fundamentals, Data Structures, Sorting, Searching*. Addison Wesley, 2002.

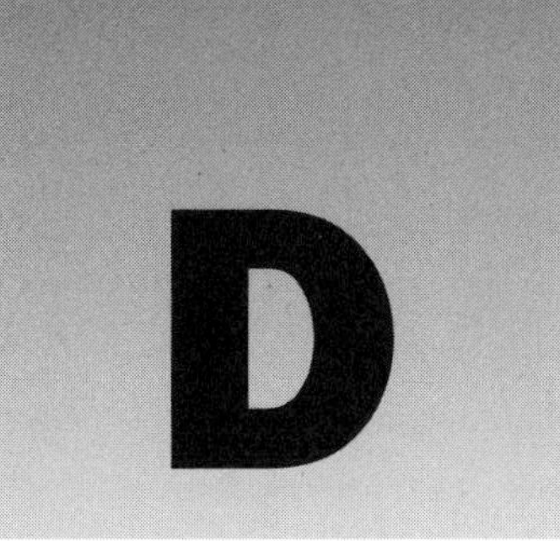

Answers to Exercises

The solutions provided in this appendix are sample answers. Not every chapter had exercises at the end, but it is hoped that the ones provided will give you ample opportunity to put what you've learned into practice. We encourage you to experiment with each chapter's concepts.

Chapter 2

Exercises

1. Create an iterator that only returns the value of every n^{th} element, where n is any integer greater than zero.
2. Create a predicate that performs a Boolean AND (&&) of two other predicates.
3. Re-implement `PowerCalculator` using recursion instead of iteration.
4. Replace the use of arrays with iterators in the recursive directory tree printer.
5. Create an iterator that holds only a single value.
6. Create an empty iterator that is always done.

Exercise 1 Solution

```
package com.wrox.algorithms.iteration;

public class SkipIterator implements Iterator {
    private final Iterator _iterator;
    private final int _skip;

    public SkipIterator(Iterator iterator, int skip) {
        assert iterator != null : "iterator can't be null";
        assert skip > 0 : "skip can't be < 1";
        _iterator = iterator;
        _skip = skip;
    }

    public void first() {
        _iterator.first();
```

```
        skipForwards();
    }

    public void last() {
        _iterator.last();
        skipBackwards();
    }

    public boolean isDone() {
        return _iterator.isDone();
    }

    public void next() {
        _iterator.next();
        skipForwards();
    }

    public void previous() {
        _iterator.previous();
        skipBackwards();
    }

    public Object current() throws IteratorOutOfBoundsException {
        return _iterator.current();
    }

    private void skipForwards() {
        for (int i = 0; i < _skip && !_iterator.isDone(); _iterator.next());
    }

    private void skipBackwards() {
        for (int i = 0; i < _skip && !_iterator.isDone(); _iterator.previous());
    }
}
```

Exercise 2 Solution

```
package com.wrox.algorithms.iteration;

public final class AndPredicate implements Predicate {
    private final Predicate _left;
    private final Predicate _right;

    public AndPredicate(Predicate left, Predicate right) {
        assert left != null : "left can't be null";
        assert right != null : "right can't be null";

        _left = left;
        _right = right;
    }

    public boolean evaluate(Object object) {
        return _left.evaluate(object) && _right.evaluate(object);
    }
}
```

Exercise 3 Solution

```
package com.wrox.algorithms.iteration;

public final class RecursivePowerCalculator implements PowerCalculator {
    public static final PowerCalculator INSTANCE = new PowerCalculator();

    private RecursivePowerCalculator() {
    }

    public int calculate(int base, int exponent) {
        assert exponent >= 0 : "exponent can't be < 0";

        return exponent > 0 ? base * calculate(base, exponent - 1) : 1;
    }
}
```

Exercise 4 Solution

```
package com.wrox.algorithms.iteration;

import java.io.File;

public final class RecursiveDirectoryTreePrinter {
    private static final String SPACES = "  ";

    public static void main(String[] args) {
        assert args != null : "args can't be null";

        if (args.length != 1) {
            System.err.println("Usage: RecursiveDirectoryTreePrinter <dir>");
            System.exit(4);
        }

        System.out.println("Recursively printing directory tree for: " + args[0]);
        print(new File(args[0]), "");
    }

    private static void print(Iterator files, String indent) {
        assert files != null : "files can't be null";

        for (files.first(); !files.isDone(); files.next()) {
            print((File) files.current(), indent);
        }
    }

    private static void print(File file, String indent) {
        assert file != null : "file can't be null";
        assert indent != null : "indent can't be null";

        System.out.print(indent);
        System.out.println(file.getName());

        if (file.isDirectory()) {
```

```
                print(new ArrayIterator(file.listFiles()), indent + SPACES);
            }
        }
    }
```

Exercise 5 Solution

```
package com.wrox.algorithms.iteration;

public class SingletonIterator implements Iterator {
    private final Object _value;
    private boolean _done;

    public SingletonIterator(Object value) {
        assert value != null : "value can't be null";
        _value = value;
    }

    public void first() {
        _done = false;
    }

    public void last() {
        _done = false;
    }

    public boolean isDone() {
        return _done;
    }

    public void next() {
        _done = true;
    }

    public void previous() {
        _done = true;
    }

    public Object current() throws IteratorOutOfBoundsException {
        if (isDone()) {
            throw new IteratorOutOfBoundsException();
        }
        return _value;
    }
}
```

Exercise 6 Solution

```
package com.wrox.algorithms.iteration;

public final class EmptyIterator implements Iterator {
    public static final EmptyIterator INSTANCE = new EmptyIterator();

    private EmptyIterator() {
```

```
        // Nothing to do
    }

    public void first() {
        // Nothing to do
    }

    public void last() {
        // Nothing to do
    }

    public boolean isDone() {
        // We're always done!
        return true;
    }

    public void next() {
        // Nothing to do
    }

    public void previous() {
        // Nothing to do
    }

    public Object current() throws IteratorOutOfBoundsException {
        throw new IteratorOutOfBoundsException();
    }
}
```

Chapter 3

Exercises

1. Write a constructor for `ArrayList` that accepts a standard Java array to initially populate the `List`.
2. Write an `equals()` method that will work for any `List` implementation.
3. Write a `toString()` method that will work for any `List` implementation that prints the contents as a single line with values surrounded by square brackets and separated by commas. For example, "`[A, B, C]`" or "`[]`" for an empty `List`.
4. Create an `Iterator` that will work for any `List` implementation. What are the performance implications?
5. Update `LinkedList` to traverse backwards if, when inserting and deleting, the desired index is more than halfway along the list.
6. Rewrite `indexOf()` so that it will work for any `List`.
7. Create a `List` implementation that is always empty and throws `UnsupportedOperationException` if an attempt is made to modify it.

Exercise 1 Solution

```
public ArrayList(Object[] array) {
    assert array != null : "array can't be null";

    _initialCapacity = array.length;
    clear();

    System.arraycopy(array, 0, _array, 0, array.length);
    _size = array.length;
}
```

Exercise 2 Solution

```
public boolean equals(Object object) {
    return object instanceof List ? equals((List) object) : false;
}

public boolean equals(List other) {
    if (other == null || size() != other.size()) {
        return false;
    }

    Iterator i = iterator();
    Iterator j = other.iterator();

    for (i.first(), j.first();
        !i.isDone() && !j.isDone(); i.next(),
        j.next()) {

        if (!i.current().equals(j.current())) {
            break;
        }
    }

    return i.isDone() && j.isDone();
}
```

Exercise 3 Solution

```
public String toString() {
    StringBuffer buffer = new StringBuffer();

    buffer.append('[');

    if (!isEmpty()) {
        Iterator i = iterator();
        for (i.first(); !i.isDone(); i.next()) {
            buffer.append(i.current()).append(", ");
        }

        buffer.setLength(buffer.length() - 2);
```

```
        }

        buffer.append(']');

        return buffer.toString();
    }
```

Exercise 4 Solution

```
package com.wrox.algorithms.lists;

import com.wrox.algorithms.iteration.Iterator;
import com.wrox.algorithms.iteration.IteratorOutOfBoundsException;

public class GenericListIterator implements Iterator {
    private final List _list;
    private int _current;

    public GenericListIterator(List list) {
        assert list != null : "list can't be null";
        _list = list;
    }

    public void first() {
        _current = 0;
    }

    public void last() {
        _current = _list.size() - 1;
    }

    public boolean isDone() {
        return _current < 0 || _current >= _list.size();
    }

    public void next() {
        ++_current;
    }

    public void previous() {
        --_current;
    }

    public Object current() throws IteratorOutOfBoundsException {
        if (isDone()) {
            throw new IteratorOutOfBoundsException();
        }
        return _list.get(_current);
    }
}
```

Exercise 5 Solution

```
    private Element getElement(int index) {
        if (index < _size / 2) {
            return getElementForwards(index);
        } else {
            return getElementBackwards(index);
        }
    }

    private Element getElementForwards(int index) {
        Element element = _headAndTail.getNext();

        for (int i = index; i > 0; --i) {
            element = element.getNext();
        }

        return element;
    }

    private Element getElementBackwards(int index) {
        Element element = _headAndTail;

        for (int i = _size - index; i > 0; --i) {
            element = element.getPrevious();
        }

        return element;
    }
```

Exercise 6 Solution

```
    public int indexOf(Object value) {
        assert value != null : "value can't be null";

        int index = 0;
        Iterator i = iterator();

        for (i.first(); !i.isDone(); i.next()) {
            if (value.equals(i.current())) {
                return index;
            }

            ++index;
        }

        return -1;
    }
```

Exercise 7 Solution

```
package com.wrox.algorithms.lists;

import com.wrox.algorithms.iteration.EmptyIterator;
import com.wrox.algorithms.iteration.Iterator;

public final class EmptyList implements List {
```

```
    public static final EmptyList INSTANCE = new EmptyList();

    private EmptyList() {
    }

    public void insert(int index, Object value)
            throws IndexOutOfBoundsException {
        throw new UnsupportedOperationException();
    }

    public void add(Object value) {
        throw new UnsupportedOperationException();
    }

    public Object delete(int index) throws IndexOutOfBoundsException {
        throw new UnsupportedOperationException();
    }

    public boolean delete(Object value) {
        throw new UnsupportedOperationException();
    }

    public void clear() {
    }

    public Object set(int index, Object value)
            throws IndexOutOfBoundsException {
        throw new UnsupportedOperationException();
    }

    public Object get(int index) throws IndexOutOfBoundsException {
        throw new UnsupportedOperationException();
    }

    public int indexOf(Object value) {
        return -1;
    }

    public boolean contains(Object value) {
        return false;
    }

    public int size() {
        return 0;
    }

    public boolean isEmpty() {
        return true;
    }

    public Iterator iterator() {
        return EmptyIterator.INSTANCE;
    }
}
```

Chapter 4

Exercises

1. Implement a thread-safe queue that performs no waiting. Sometimes all you need is a queue that will work in a multi-threaded environment without the blocking.

2. Implement a queue that retrieves values in random order. This could be used for dealing cards from a deck or any other random selection process.

Exercise 1 Solution

```
package com.wrox.algorithms.queues;

public class SynchronizedQueue implements Queue {
    private final Object _mutex = new Object();
    private final Queue _queue;

    public SynchronizedQueue(Queue queue) {
        assert queue != null : "queue can't be null";
        _queue = queue;
    }

    public void enqueue(Object value) {
        synchronized (_mutex) {
            _queue.enqueue(value);
        }
    }

    public Object dequeue() throws EmptyQueueException {
        synchronized (_mutex) {
            return _queue.dequeue();
        }
    }

    public void clear() {
        synchronized (_mutex) {
            _queue.clear();
        }
    }

    public int size() {
        synchronized (_mutex) {
            return _queue.size();
        }
    }

    public boolean isEmpty() {
        synchronized (_mutex) {
            return _queue.isEmpty();
        }
    }
}
```

Exercise 2 Solution

```
package com.wrox.algorithms.queues;

import com.wrox.algorithms.lists.LinkedList;
import com.wrox.algorithms.lists.List;

public class RandomListQueue implements Queue {
    private final List _list;

    public RandomListQueue() {
        this(new LinkedList());
    }

    public RandomListQueue(List list) {
        assert list != null : "list can't be null";
        _list = list;
    }

    public void enqueue(Object value) {
        _list.add(value);
    }

    public Object dequeue() throws EmptyQueueException {
        if (isEmpty()) {
            throw new EmptyQueueException();
        }
        return _list.delete((int) (Math.random() * size()));
    }

    public void clear() {
        _list.clear();
    }

    public int size() {
        return _list.size();
    }

    public boolean isEmpty() {
        return _list.isEmpty();
    }
}
```

Chapter 6

Exercises

1. Write a test to prove that each of the algorithms can sort a randomly generated list of `double` objects.
2. Write a test to prove that the bubble sort and insertion sort algorithms from this chapter are stable.

3. Write a comparator that can order strings in dictionary order, with uppercase and lowercase letters considered equivalent.
4. Write a driver program to determine how many objects are moved by each algorithm during a sort operation.

Exercise 1 Solution

```
public class ListSorterRandomDoublesTest extends TestCase {
    private static final int TEST_SIZE = 1000;

    private final List _randomList = new ArrayList(TEST_SIZE);
    private final NaturalComparator _comparator = NaturalComparator.INSTANCE;

    protected void setUp() throws Exception {
        super.setUp();

        for (int i = 1; i < TEST_SIZE; ++i) {
            _randomList.add(new Double((TEST_SIZE * Math.random())));
        }
    }

    public void testsortingRandomDoublesWithBubblesort() {
        ListSorter listSorter = new BubblesortListSorter(_comparator);
        List result = listSorter.sort(_randomList);
        assertSorted(result);
    }

    public void testsortingRandomDoublesWithSelectionsort() {
        ListSorter listSorter = new SelectionSortListSorter(_comparator);
        List result = listSorter.sort(_randomList);
        assertSorted(result);
    }

    public void testsortingRandomDoublesWithInsertionsort() {
        ListSorter listSorter = new InsertionSortListSorter(_comparator);
        List result = listSorter.sort(_randomList);
        assertSorted(result);
    }

    private void assertSorted(List list) {
        for (int i = 1; i < list.size(); i++) {
            Object o = list.get(i);
            assertTrue(_comparator.compare(list.get(i - 1), list.get(i)) <= 0);
        }
    }
}
```

Exercise 2 Solution

```
import com.wrox.algorithms.lists.ArrayList;
import com.wrox.algorithms.lists.List;
import junit.framework.TestCase;

public class ListSorterStabilityTest extends TestCase {
```

```
private static final int TEST_SIZE = 1000;

private final List _list = new ArrayList(TEST_SIZE);
private final Comparator _comparator = new FractionComparator();

protected void setUp() throws Exception {
    super.setUp();

    for (int i = 1; i < TEST_SIZE; ++i) {
        _list.add(new Fraction(i % 20, i));
    }
}

public void testStabilityOfBubblesort() {
    ListSorter listSorter = new BubblesortListSorter(_comparator);
    List result = listSorter.sort(_list);
    assertStableSorted(result);
}

public void testStabilityOfInsertionsort() {
    ListSorter listSorter = new InsertionSortListSorter(_comparator);
    List result = listSorter.sort(_list);
    assertStableSorted(result);
}

private void assertStableSorted(List list) {
    for (int i = 1; i < list.size(); i++) {
        Fraction f1 = (Fraction) list.get(i - 1);
        Fraction f2 = (Fraction) list.get(i);
        if(!(f1.getNumerator() < f2.getNumerator()
                || f1.getDenominator() < f2.getDenominator())) {
            fail("what?!");
        }
    }
}

private static class Fraction {
    private final int _numerator;
    private final int _denominator;

    public Fraction(int numerator, int denominator) {
        _numerator = numerator;
        _denominator = denominator;
    }

    public int getNumerator() {
        return _numerator;
    }

    public int getDenominator() {
        return _denominator;
    }
}

private static class FractionComparator implements Comparator {
```

```
        public int compare(Object left, Object right) throws ClassCastException {
            return compare((Fraction) left, (Fraction) right);
        }

        private int compare(Fraction l, Fraction r) throws ClassCastException {
            return l.getNumerator() - r.getNumerator();
        }
    }
}
```

Exercise 3 Solution

```
public final class CaseInsensitiveStringComparator implements Comparator {
    public int compare(Object left, Object right) throws ClassCastException {
        assert left != null : "left can't be null";
        assert right != null : "right can't be null";

        String leftLower = ((String) left).toLowerCase();
        String rightLower = ((String) right).toLowerCase();
        return leftLower.compareTo(rightLower);
    }
}
```

Exercise 4 Solution

```
public class ListSorterCallCountingListTest extends TestCase {
    private static final int TEST_SIZE = 1000;

    private final List _sortedArrayList = new ArrayList(TEST_SIZE);
    private final List _reverseArrayList = new ArrayList(TEST_SIZE);
    private final List _randomArrayList = new ArrayList(TEST_SIZE);

    private Comparator _comparator = NaturalComparator.INSTANCE;

    protected void setUp() throws Exception {
        super.setUp();

        for (int i = 1; i < TEST_SIZE; ++i) {
            _sortedArrayList.add(new Integer(i));
        }

        for (int i = TEST_SIZE; i > 0; --i) {
            _reverseArrayList.add(new Integer(i));
        }

        for (int i = 1; i < TEST_SIZE; ++i) {
            _randomArrayList.add(new Integer((int)(TEST_SIZE * Math.random())));
        }
    }

    public void testWorstCaseBubblesort() {
        List list = new CallCountingList(_reverseArrayList);
        new BubblesortListSorter(_comparator).sort(list);
        reportCalls(list);
```

```
    }

    public void testWorstCaseSelectionSort() {
        List list = new CallCountingList(_reverseArrayList);
        new SelectionSortListSorter(_comparator).sort(list);
        reportCalls(list);
    }

    public void testWorstCaseInsertionSort() {
        List list = _reverseArrayList;
        List result = new CallCountingList(new ArrayList());
        new InsertionSortListSorter(_comparator).sort(list, result);
        reportCalls(result);
    }

    public void testBestCaseBubblesort() {
        List list = new CallCountingList(_sortedArrayList);
        new BubblesortListSorter(_comparator).sort(list);
        reportCalls(list);
    }

    public void testBestCaseSelectionSort() {
        List list = new CallCountingList(_sortedArrayList);
        new SelectionSortListSorter(_comparator).sort(list);
        reportCalls(list);
    }

    public void testBestCaseInsertionSort() {
        List list = _sortedArrayList;
        List result = new CallCountingList(new ArrayList());
        new InsertionSortListSorter(_comparator).sort(list, result);
        reportCalls(result);
    }

    public void testAverageCaseBubblesort() {
        List list = new CallCountingList(_randomArrayList);
        new BubblesortListSorter(_comparator).sort(list);
        reportCalls(list);
    }

    public void testAverageCaseSelectionSort() {
        List list = new CallCountingList(_randomArrayList);
        new SelectionSortListSorter(_comparator).sort(list);
        reportCalls(list);
    }

    public void testAverageCaseInsertionSort() {
        List list = _randomArrayList;
        List result = new CallCountingList(new ArrayList());
        new InsertionSortListSorter(_comparator).sort(list, result);
        reportCalls(result);
    }

    private void reportCalls(List list) {
```

```
            System.out.println(getName() + ": " + list);
        }
    }
```

Chapter 7

Exercises

1. Implement mergesort iteratively, rather than recursively.
2. Implement quicksort iteratively, rather than recursively.
3. Count the number of list manipulations (for example, `set()`, `add()`, `insert()`) during quicksort and shellsort.
4. Implement an in-place version of insertion sort.
5. Create a version of quicksort that uses insertion sort for sublists smaller than five items.

Exercise 1 Solution

```
public class IterativeMergesortListSorter implements ListSorter {
    private final Comparator _comparator;

    public IterativeMergesortListSorter(Comparator comparator) {
        assert comparator != null : "comparator cannot be null";
        _comparator = comparator;
    }

    public List sort(List list) {
        assert list != null : "list cannot be null";

        return mergeSublists(createSublists(list));
    }

    private List mergeSublists(List sublists) {
        List remaining = sublists;
        while (remaining.size() > 1) {
            remaining = mergeSublistPairs(remaining);

        }
        return (List) remaining.get(0);
    }

    private List mergeSublistPairs(List remaining) {
        List result = new ArrayList(remaining.size() / 2 + 1);

        Iterator i = remaining.iterator();
        i.first();
        while (!i.isDone()) {
            List left = (List) i.current();
            i.next();
            if (i.isDone()) {
```

```
                result.add(left);
            } else {
                List right = (List) i.current();
                i.next();
                result.add(merge(left, right));
            }
        }

        return result;
    }

    private List createSublists(List list) {
        List result = new ArrayList(list.size());

        Iterator i = list.iterator();
        i.first();
        while (!i.isDone()) {
            List singletonList = new ArrayList(1);
            singletonList.add(i.current());
            result.add(singletonList);
            i.next();
        }

        return  result;
    }

    private List merge(List left, List right) {
        List result = new ArrayList();

        Iterator l = left.iterator();
        Iterator r = right.iterator();

        l.first();
        r.first();

        while (!(l.isDone() && r.isDone())) {
            if (l.isDone()) {
                result.add(r.current());
                r.next();
            } else if (r.isDone()) {
                result.add(l.current());
                l.next();
            } else if (_comparator.compare(l.current(), r.current()) <= 0) {
                result.add(l.current());
                l.next();
            } else {
                result.add(r.current());
                r.next();
            }
        }

        return result;
    }
}
```

Exercise 2 Solution

```
public class IterativeQuicksortListSorter implements ListSorter {
    private final Comparator _comparator;

    public IterativeQuicksortListSorter(Comparator comparator) {
        assert comparator != null : "comparator cannot be null";
        _comparator = comparator;
    }

    public List sort(List list) {
        assert list != null : "list cannot be null";

        quicksort(list);

        return list;
    }

    private void quicksort(List list) {
        Stack jobStack = new ListStack();

        jobStack.push(new Range(0, list.size() - 1));

        while (!jobStack.isEmpty()) {
            Range range = (Range) jobStack.pop();
            if (range.size() <= 1) {
                continue;
            }

            int startIndex = range.getStartIndex();
            int endIndex = range.getEndIndex();

            Object value = list.get(endIndex);

            int partition = partition(list, value, startIndex, endIndex - 1);
            if (_comparator.compare(list.get(partition), value) < 0) {
                ++partition;
            }

            swap(list, partition, endIndex);

            jobStack.push(new Range(startIndex, partition - 1));
            jobStack.push(new Range(partition + 1, endIndex));
        }
    }

    private int partition(List list, Object value, int leftIndex, int rightIndex) {
        int left = leftIndex;
        int right = rightIndex;

        while (left < right) {
            if (_comparator.compare(list.get(left), value) < 0) {
                ++left;
                continue;
            }

            if (_comparator.compare(list.get(right), value) >= 0) {
```

```
                --right;
                continue;
            }

            swap(list, left, right);
            ++left;
        }

        return left;
    }

    private void swap(List list, int left, int right) {
        if (left == right) {
            return;
        }
        Object temp = list.get(left);
        list.set(left, list.get(right));
        list.set(right, temp);
    }

    private static final class Range {
        private final int _startIndex;
        private final int _endIndex;

        public Range(int startIndex, int endIndex) {
            _startIndex = startIndex;
            _endIndex = endIndex;
        }

        public int size() {
            return _endIndex - _startIndex + 1;
        }

        public int getStartIndex() {
            return _startIndex;
        }

        public int getEndIndex() {
            return _endIndex;
        }
    }
}
```

Exercise 3 Solution

```
public class AdvancedListSorterCallCountingListTest extends TestCase {
    private static final int TEST_SIZE = 1000;

    private final List _sortedArrayList = new ArrayList(TEST_SIZE);
    private final List _reverseArrayList = new ArrayList(TEST_SIZE);
    private final List _randomArrayList = new ArrayList(TEST_SIZE);

    private Comparator _comparator = NaturalComparator.INSTANCE;

    protected void setUp() throws Exception {
```

```
        super.setUp();

        for (int i = 1; i < TEST_SIZE; ++i) {
            _sortedArrayList.add(new Integer(i));
        }

        for (int i = TEST_SIZE; i > 0; --i) {
            _reverseArrayList.add(new Integer(i));
        }

        for (int i = 1; i < TEST_SIZE; ++i) {
            _randomArrayList.add(new Integer((int)(TEST_SIZE * Math.random())));
        }
    }

    public void testWorstCaseQuicksort() {
        List list = new CallCountingList(_reverseArrayList);
        new QuicksortListSorter(_comparator).sort(list);
        reportCalls(list);
    }

    public void testWorstCaseShellSort() {
        List list = new CallCountingList(_reverseArrayList);
        new ShellsortListSorter(_comparator).sort(list);
        reportCalls(list);
    }

    public void testBestCaseQuicksort() {
        List list = new CallCountingList(_sortedArrayList);
        new QuicksortListSorter(_comparator).sort(list);
        reportCalls(list);
    }

    public void testBestCaseShellSort() {
        List list = new CallCountingList(_sortedArrayList);
        new ShellsortListSorter(_comparator).sort(list);
        reportCalls(list);
    }

    public void testAverageCaseQuicksort() {
        List list = new CallCountingList(_randomArrayList);
        new QuicksortListSorter(_comparator).sort(list);
        reportCalls(list);
    }

    public void testAverageCaseShellSort() {
        List list = new CallCountingList(_randomArrayList);
        new ShellsortListSorter(_comparator).sort(list);
        reportCalls(list);
    }

    private void reportCalls(List list) {
        System.out.println(getName() + ": " + list);
    }
```

```
}

public class CallCountingList implements List {
    private final List _list;

    private int _insertCount;
    private int _addCount;
    private int _deleteCount;
    private int _getCount;
    private int _setCount;

    public CallCountingList(List list) {
        assert list != null : "list can't be null";
        _list = list;
    }

    public void insert(int index, Object value) throws IndexOutOfBoundsException {
        _list.insert(index, value);
        ++_insertCount;
    }

    public void add(Object value) {
        _list.add(value);
        ++_addCount;
    }

    public Object delete(int index) throws IndexOutOfBoundsException {
        ++_deleteCount;
        return _list.delete(index);
    }

    public Object delete(Object value) {
        ++_deleteCount;
        return _list.delete(value);
    }

    public Object get(int index) throws IndexOutOfBoundsException {
        ++_getCount;
        return _list.get(index);
    }

    public Object set(int index, Object value) throws IndexOutOfBoundsException {
        ++_setCount;
        return _list.set(index, value);
    }


    public void clear() {
        _list.clear();
    }

    public int indexOf(Object value) {
        return _list.indexOf(value);
    }

    public boolean contains(Object value) {
```

```
        return _list.contains(value);
    }

    public boolean isEmpty() {
        return _list.isEmpty();
    }

    public Iterator iterator() {
        return _list.iterator();
    }

    public int size() {
        return _list.size();
    }

    public String toString() {
        return new StringBuffer("Call-counting List: ")
                .append("add: " + _addCount)
                .append(" insert: " + _insertCount)
                .append(" delete: " + _deleteCount)
                .append(" set: " + _setCount)
                .append(" get: " + _getCount).toString();
    }
}
```

Exercise 4 Solution

```
public class InPlaceInsertionSortListSorter implements ListSorter {
    private final Comparator _comparator;

    public InPlaceInsertionSortListSorter(Comparator comparator) {
        assert comparator != null : "comparator cannot be null";
        _comparator = comparator;
    }

    public List sort(List list) {
        assert list != null : "list cannot be null";

        for (int i = 1; i < list.size(); ++i) {
            Object value = list.get(i);
            int j;
            for (j = i; j > 0; --j) {
                Object previousValue = list.get(j - 1);
                if (_comparator.compare(value, previousValue) >= 0) {
                    break;
                }
                list.set(j, previousValue);
            }
            list.set(j, value);
        }

        return list;
    }
}
```

Exercise 5 Solution

```
public class HybridQuicksortListSorter implements ListSorter {
    private final Comparator _comparator;

    public HybridQuicksortListSorter(Comparator comparator) {
        assert comparator != null : "comparator cannot be null";
        _comparator = comparator;
    }

    public List sort(List list) {
        assert list != null : "list cannot be null";

        quicksort(list, 0, list.size() - 1);

        return list;
    }

    private void quicksort(List list, int startIndex, int endIndex) {
        if (startIndex < 0 || endIndex >= list.size()) {
            return;
        }
        if (endIndex <= startIndex) {
            return;
        }

        if (endIndex - startIndex < 5) {
            doInsertionSort(list, startIndex, endIndex);
        } else {
            doQuicksort(list, startIndex, endIndex);
        }
    }

    private void doInsertionSort(List list, int startIndex, int endIndex) {
        for (int i = startIndex + 1; i <= endIndex; ++i) {
            Object value = list.get(i);
            int j;
            for (j = i; j > startIndex; --j) {
                Object previousValue = list.get(j - 1);
                if (_comparator.compare(value, previousValue) >= 0) {
                    break;
                }
                list.set(j, previousValue);
            }
            list.set(j, value);
        }
    }

    private void doQuicksort(List list, int startIndex, int endIndex) {
        Object value = list.get(endIndex);

        int partition = partition(list, value, startIndex, endIndex - 1);
        if (_comparator.compare(list.get(partition), value) < 0) {
            ++partition;
```

```
        }

        swap(list, partition, endIndex);

        quicksort(list, startIndex, partition - 1);
        quicksort(list, partition + 1, endIndex);
    }

    private int partition(List list, Object value, int leftIndex, int rightIndex) {
        int left = leftIndex;
        int right = rightIndex;

        while (left < right) {
            if (_comparator.compare(list.get(left), value) < 0) {
                ++left;
                continue;
            }

            if (_comparator.compare(list.get(right), value) >= 0) {
                --right;
                continue;
            }

            swap(list, left, right);
            ++left;
        }

        return left;
    }

    private void swap(List list, int left, int right) {
        if (left == right) {
            return;
        }
        Object temp = list.get(left);
        list.set(left, list.get(right));
        list.set(right, temp);
    }
}
```

Chapter 8

Exercises

1. Use a priority queue to implement a `Stack`.
2. Use a priority queue to implement a `FIFO Queue`.
3. Use a priority queue to implement a `ListSorter`.
4. Write a priority queue that provides access to the smallest item, rather than the largest.

Exercise 1 Solution

```
package com.wrox.algorithms.stacks;

import com.wrox.algorithms.queues.EmptyQueueException;
import com.wrox.algorithms.queues.HeapOrderedListPriorityQueue;
import com.wrox.algorithms.sorting.Comparator;

public class PriorityQueueStack extends HeapOrderedListPriorityQueue
                                implements Stack {
    private final static Comparator COMPARATOR = new StackItemComparator();
    private long _count = 0;

    public PriorityQueueStack() {
        super(COMPARATOR);
    }

    public void enqueue(Object value) {
        super.enqueue(new StackItem(++_count, value));
    }

    public Object dequeue() throws EmptyQueueException {
        return ((StackItem) super.dequeue()).getValue();
    }

    public void push(Object value) {
        enqueue(value);
    }

    public Object pop() throws EmptyStackException {
        try {
            return dequeue();
        } catch (EmptyQueueException e) {
            throw new EmptyStackException();
        }
    }

    public Object peek() throws EmptyStackException {
        Object result = pop();
        push(result);
        return result;
    }

    private static final class StackItem {
        private final long _key;
        private final Object _value;

        public StackItem(long key, Object value) {
            _key = key;
            _value = value;
        }

        public long getKey() {
            return _key;
        }

        public Object getValue() {
```

```
            return _value;
        }
    }

    private static final class StackItemComparator implements Comparator {
        public int compare(Object left, Object right) throws ClassCastException {
            StackItem si1 = (StackItem) left;
            StackItem si2 = (StackItem) right;

            return (int) (si1.getKey() - si2.getKey());
        }
    }
}
```

Exercise 2 Solution

```
package com.wrox.algorithms.queues;

import com.wrox.algorithms.sorting.Comparator;

public class PriorityQueueFifoQueue extends HeapOrderedListPriorityQueue {
    private static final Comparator COMPARATOR = new QueueItemComparator();
    private long _count = Long.MAX_VALUE;

    public PriorityQueueFifoQueue() {
        super(COMPARATOR);
    }

    public void enqueue(Object value) {
        super.enqueue(new QueueItem(--_count, value));
    }

    public Object dequeue() throws EmptyQueueException {
        return ((QueueItem) super.dequeue()).getValue();
    }

    private static final class QueueItem {
        private final long _key;
        private final Object _value;

        public QueueItem(long key, Object value) {
            _key = key;
            _value = value;
        }

        public long getKey() {
            return _key;
        }

        public Object getValue() {
            return _value;
```

```
        }
    }

    private static final class QueueItemComparator implements Comparator {
        public int compare(Object left, Object right) throws ClassCastException {
            QueueItem si1 = (QueueItem) left;
            QueueItem si2 = (QueueItem) right;

            return (int) (si1.getKey() - si2.getKey());
        }
    }
}
```

Exercise 3 Solution

```
public class PriorityQueueListSorter implements ListSorter {
    private final Comparator _comparator;

    public PriorityQueueListSorter(Comparator comparator) {
        assert comparator != null : "comparator cannot be null";
        _comparator = comparator;
    }

    public List sort(List list) {
        assert list != null : "list cannot be null";

        Queue queue = createPriorityQueue(list);

        List result = new ArrayList(list.size());

        while (!queue.isEmpty()) {
            result.add(queue.dequeue());
        }

        return result;
    }

    private Queue createPriorityQueue(List list) {
        Comparator comparator = new ReverseComparator(_comparator);
        Queue queue = new HeapOrderedListPriorityQueue(comparator);

        Iterator i = list.iterator();
        i.first();
        while (!i.isDone()) {
            queue.enqueue(i.current());
            i.next();
        }

        return queue;
    }
}
```

Exercise 4 Solution

```
public class MinimumOrientedHeapOrderedListPriorityQueue
        extends HeapOrderedListPriorityQueue {
    public MinimumOrientedHeapOrderedListPriorityQueue(Comparator comparator) {
        super(new ReverseComparator(comparator));
    }
}
```

Chapter 10

Exercises

1. Write a recursive form of `minimum()`.
2. Write a recursive form of `search()`.
3. Write a method that takes a root node and recursively prints all the values of the tree in order.
4. Write a method that takes a root node and iteratively prints all the values of the tree in order.
5. Write a method that takes a root node and recursively prints all the values of the tree pre-order.
6. Write a method that takes a root node and recursively prints all the values of the tree post-order.
7. Write a method(s) that inserts values from a sorted list into a binary search tree in such a way as to maintain balance yet require no explicit balancing.
8. Add method(s) to `Node` to recursively calculate its size.
9. Add method(s) to `Node` to recursively calculate its height.

Exercise 1 Solution

```
    public Node minimum() {
        return getSmaller() != null ? GetSmaller() : this;
    }
```

Exercise 2 Solution

```
    public Node search(Object value) {
        return search(value, _root);
    }

    private Node search(Object value, Node node) {
        if (node == null) {
            return null;
        }

        int cmp = _comparator.compare(value, node.getValue());
        if (cmp == 0) {
            return node;
        }

        return search(value, cmp < 0 ? node.getSmaller() : node.getLarger());
    }
```

Exercise 3 Solution

```
public void inOrderPrint(Node node) {
    if (node == null) {
        return;
    }

    inOrderPrint(node.getSmaller());
    System.out.println(node.getValue());
    inOrderPrint(node.getLarger()));
}
```

Exercise 4 Solution

```
public void inOrderPrint(Node root) {
    for (Node node = root.minimum(); node != null; node = node.successor()) {
        System.out.println(node.getValue());
    }
}
```

Exercise 5 Solution

```
public void preOrderPrint(Node node) {
    if (node == null) {
        return;
    }

    System.out.println(node.getValue());
    preOrderPrint(node.getSmaller());
    preOrderPrint(node.getLarger()));
}
```

Exercise 6 Solution

```
public void postOrderPrint(Node node) {
    if (node == null) {
        return;
    }

    postOrderPrint(node.getSmaller());
    postOrderPrint(node.getLarger()));
    System.out.println(node.getValue());
}
```

Exercise 7 Solution

```
public void preOrderInsert(BinarySearchTree tree, List list) {
    preOrderInsert(tree, list, 0, list.size() - 1);
}

private void preOrderInsert(BinarySearchTree tree, List list,
                            int lowerIndex,int upperIndex) {
    if (lowerIndex > upperIndex) {
```

```
            return;
        }

        int index = lowerIndex + (upperIndex - lowerIndex) / 2;

        tree.insert(list.get(index));
        preOrderInsert(tree, list, lowerIndex, index - 1);
        preOrderInsert(tree, list, index + 1, upperIndex);
    }
```

Exercise 8 Solution

```
    public int size() {
        return size(this);
    }

    private int size(Node node) {
        if (node == null) {
            return 0;
        }

        return 1 + size(node.getSmaller()) + size(node.getLarger());
    }
```

Exercise 9 Solution

```
    public int height() {
        return height(this) - 1;
    }

    private int height(Node node) {
        if (node == null) {
            return 0;
        }

        return 1 + Math.max(height(node.getSmaller()), height(node.getLarger()));
    }
```

Chapter 11

Exercises

1. Modify `BucketingHashtable` to always use a prime number of buckets. What effect (if any) does this have on performance?
2. Modify `LinearProbingHashtable` to maintain the number of values in the table, rather than calculate it every time.
3. Modify `BucketingHashtable` to maintain the number of values in the table, rather than calculate it every time.
4. Create an iterator that provides access to all of the entries in a `BucketingHashtable`.

Exercise 1 Solution

```
package com.wrox.algorithms.hashing;

public final class SimplePrimeNumberGenerator {
    public static final SimplePrimeNumberGenerator INSTANCE =
                                                   new SimplePrimeNumberGenerator();

    private SimplePrimeNumberGenerator() {
    }

    public int generate(int candidate) {
        int prime = candidate;

        while (!isPrime(prime)) {
            ++prime;
        }

        return prime;
    }

    private boolean isPrime(int candidate) {
        for (int i = candidate / 2; i >= 2; --i) {
            if (candidate % i == 0) {
                return false;
            }
        }
        return true;
    }
}
```

```
package com.wrox.algorithms.hashing;

import com.wrox.algorithms.iteration.Iterator;
import com.wrox.algorithms.lists.LinkedList;
import com.wrox.algorithms.lists.List;

public class BucketingHashtable implements Hashtable {
    ...

    public BucketingHashtable(int initialCapacity, float loadFactor) {
        assert initialCapacity > 0 : "initialCapacity can't be < 1";
        assert loadFactor > 0 : "loadFactor can't be <= 0";

        _loadFactor = loadFactor;
        _buckets = new Bucket[
                SimplePrimeNumberGenerator.INSTANCE.generate(initialCapacity)];
    }

    ...
}
```

Exercise 2 Solution

```
package com.wrox.algorithms.hashing;

public class LinearProbingHashtable implements Hashtable {
    ...

    private int _size;

    public void add(Object value) {
        ensureCapacityForOneMore();

        int index = indexFor(value);

        if (_values[index] == null) {
            _values[index] = value;
            ++_size;
        }
    }

    public int size() {
        return _size;
    }
}
```

Exercise 3 Solution

```
package com.wrox.algorithms.hashing;

import com.wrox.algorithms.iteration.Iterator;
import com.wrox.algorithms.lists.LinkedList;
import com.wrox.algorithms.lists.List;

public class BucketingHashtable implements Hashtable {
    ...

    private int _size;

    public void add(Object value) {
        List bucket = bucketFor(value);

        if (!bucket.contains(value)) {
            bucket.add(value);
            ++_size;
            maintainLoad();
        }
    }

    public int size() {
        return _size;
    }
}
```

Exercise 4 Solution

```
package com.wrox.algorithms.hashing;

import com.wrox.algorithms.iteration.EmptyIterator;
import com.wrox.algorithms.iteration.Iterable;
import com.wrox.algorithms.iteration.Iterator;
import com.wrox.algorithms.iteration.IteratorOutOfBoundsException;

public class HashtableIterator implements Iterator {
    private final Iterator _buckets;
    private Iterator _values = EmptyIterator.INSTANCE;

    public HashtableIterator(Iterator buckets) {
        assert buckets != null : "buckets can't be null";
        _buckets = buckets;
    }

    public void first() {
        _buckets.first();
        _values = EmptyIterator.INSTANCE;
        next();
    }

    public void last() {
        _buckets.last();
        _values = EmptyIterator.INSTANCE;
        previous();
    }

    public boolean isDone() {
        return _values.isDone() && _buckets.isDone();
    }

    public void next() {
        for (_values.next();
             _values.isDone() && !_buckets.isDone();
             _buckets.next()) {
            Iterable bucket = (Iterable) _buckets.current();
            if (bucket != null) {
                _values = bucket.iterator();
                _values.first();
            }
        }
    }

    public void previous() {
        for (_values.previous();
             _values.isDone() && !_buckets.isDone();
             _buckets.previous()) {
            Iterable bucket = (Iterable) _buckets.current();
            if (bucket != null) {
                _values = bucket.iterator();
                _values.last();
            }
```

```
            }
        }

        public Object current() throws IteratorOutOfBoundsException {
            if (isDone()) {
                throw new IteratorOutOfBoundsException();
            }
            return _values.current();
        }
    }
```

Chapter 12

Exercises

1. Write a method that takes two sets and determines whether they are equal.
2. Write a method that takes two sets and produces a third set containing the union of the first two.
3. Write a method that takes two sets and produces a third set containing the intersection of the first two.
4. Write a method that takes two sets and produces a third set containing the difference between the first two.
5. Update the `delete()` method in `HashSet` to free the bucket if it's empty.
6. Create a set implementation that uses a sorted list.
7. Create a set implementation that is always empty and throws `UnsupportedOperationException` whenever an attempt is made to modify it.

Exercise 1 Solution

```
        public boolean equals(Set a, Set b) {
            assert a != null : "a can't be null";
            assert b != null : "b can't be null";

            Iterator i = a.iterator();
            for (i.first(); !i.isDone(); i.next()) {
                if (!b.contains(i.current())) {
                    return false;
                }
            }

            return a.size() == b.size();
        }
    }
```

Exercise 2 Solution

```
        public Set union(Set a, Set b) {
            assert a != null : "a can't be null";
```

```
        assert b != null : "b can't be null";

        Set result = new HashSet();

        Iterator i = a.iterator();
        for (i.first(); !i.isDone(); i.next()) {
            result.add(i.current());
        }

        Iterator j = b.iterator();
        for (j.first(); !j.isDone(); j.next()) {
            result.add(j.current());
        }

        return result;
    }
```

Exercise 3 Solution

```
    public Set intersection(Set a, Set b) {
        assert a != null : "a can't be null";
        assert b != null : "b can't be null";

        Set result = new HashSet();

        Iterator i = a.iterator();
        for (i.first(); !i.isDone(); i.next()) {
            if (b.contains(i.current())) {
                result.add(i.current());
            }
        }

        return result;
    }
```

Exercise 4 Solution

```
    public Set difference(Set a, Set b) {
        assert a != null : "a can't be null";
        assert b != null : "b can't be null";

        Set result = new HashSet();

        Iterator i = a.iterator();
        for (i.first(); !i.isDone(); i.next()) {
            if (!b.contains(i.current())) {
                result.add(i.current());
            }
        }

        return result;
    }
```

Exercise 5 Solution

```
public boolean delete(Object value) {
    int bucketIndex = bucketIndexFor(value);
    ListSet bucket = _buckets[bucketIndex];
    if (bucket != null && bucket.delete(value)) {
        --_size;
        if (bucket.isEmpty()) {
            _buckets[bucketIndex] = null;
        }
        return true;
    }

    return false;
}
```

Exercise 6 Solution

```
package com.wrox.algorithms.sets;

import com.wrox.algorithms.bsearch.IterativeBinaryListSearcher;
import com.wrox.algorithms.bsearch.ListSearcher;
import com.wrox.algorithms.iteration.Iterator;
import com.wrox.algorithms.lists.ArrayList;
import com.wrox.algorithms.lists.List;
import com.wrox.algorithms.sorting.Comparator;
import com.wrox.algorithms.sorting.NaturalComparator;

public class SortedListSet implements Set {
    private final List _values = new ArrayList();
    private final ListSearcher _searcher;

    public SortedListSet() {
        this(NaturalComparator.INSTANCE);
    }

    public SortedListSet(Comparator comparator) {
        _searcher = new IterativeBinaryListSearcher(comparator);
    }

    public boolean contains(Object value) {
        return indexOf(value) >= 0;
    }

    public boolean add(Object value) {
        int index = indexOf(value);
        if (index < 0) {
            _values.insert(-(index + 1), value);
            return true;
        }

        _values.set(index, value);
        return false;
    }

    public boolean delete(Object value) {
```

```
        int index = indexOf(value);
        if (index >= 0) {
            _values.delete(index);
            return true;
        }

        return false;
    }

    public Iterator iterator() {
        return _values.iterator();
    }

    public void clear() {
        _values.clear();
    }

    public int size() {
        return _values.size();
    }

    public boolean isEmpty() {
        return _values.isEmpty();
    }

    private int indexOf(Object value) {
        return _searcher.search(_values, value);
    }
}
```

Exercise 7 Solution

```
package com.wrox.algorithms.sets;

import com.wrox.algorithms.iteration.EmptyIterator;
import com.wrox.algorithms.iteration.Iterator;

public final class EmptySet implements Set {
    public static final EmptySet INSTANCE = new EmptySet();

    private EmptySet() {
    }

    public boolean contains(Object value) {
        return false;
    }

    public boolean add(Object value) {
        throw new UnsupportedOperationException();
    }

    public boolean delete(Object value) {
        throw new UnsupportedOperationException();
    }

    public void clear() {
```

```
    }

    public int size() {
        return 0;
    }

    public boolean isEmpty() {
        return true;
    }

    public Iterator iterator() {
        return EmptyIterator.INSTANCE;
    }
```

Chapter 13

Exercises

1. Create an iterator that returns only the keys contained within a map.
2. Create an iterator that returns only the values contained within a map.
3. Create a set implementation that uses a map as the underlying storage mechanism for the values.
4. Create an empty map that throws `UnsupportedOperationException` anytime an attempt is made to modify it.

Exercise 1 Solution

```
package com.wrox.algorithms.maps;

import com.wrox.algorithms.iteration.Iterator;
import com.wrox.algorithms.iteration.IteratorOutOfBoundsException;

public class MapKeyIterator implements Iterator {
    private final Iterator _entries;

    public MapKeyIterator(Iterator entries) {
        assert entries != null : "entries can't be null";
        _entries = entries;
    }

    public void first() {
        _entries.first();
    }

    public void last() {
        _entries.last();
    }

    public boolean isDone() {
        return _entries.isDone();
```

```
    }

    public void next() {
        _entries.next();
    }

    public void previous() {
        _entries.previous();
    }

    public Object current() throws IteratorOutOfBoundsException {
        return ((Map.Entry) _entries.current()).getKey();
    }
}
```

Exercise 2 Solution

```
package com.wrox.algorithms.maps;

import com.wrox.algorithms.iteration.Iterator;
import com.wrox.algorithms.iteration.IteratorOutOfBoundsException;

public class MapValueIterator implements Iterator {
    private final Iterator _entries;

    public MapValueIterator(Iterator entries) {
        assert entries != null : "entries can't be null";
        _entries = entries;
    }

    public void first() {
        _entries.first();
    }

    public void last() {
        _entries.last();
    }

    public boolean isDone() {
        return _entries.isDone();
    }

    public void next() {
        _entries.next();
    }

    public void previous() {
        _entries.previous();
    }

    public Object current() throws IteratorOutOfBoundsException {
        return ((Map.Entry) _entries.current()).getValue();
    }
}
```

Exercise 3 Solution

```
package com.wrox.algorithms.maps;

import com.wrox.algorithms.iteration.Iterator;
import com.wrox.algorithms.sets.Set;

public class MapSet implements Set {
    private static final Object PRESENT = new Object();

    private final Map _map;

    public MapSet(Map map) {
        assert map != null : "map can't be null";
        _map = map;
    }

    public boolean contains(Object value) {
        return _map.contains(value);
    }

    public boolean add(Object value) {
        return _map.set(value, PRESENT) == null;
    }

    public boolean delete(Object value) {
        return _map.delete(value) == PRESENT;
    }

    public Iterator iterator() {
        return new MapKeyIterator(_map.iterator());
    }

    public void clear() {
        _map.clear();
    }

    public int size() {
        return _map.size();
    }

    public boolean isEmpty() {
        return _map.isEmpty();
    }
}
```

Exercise 4 Solution

```
package com.wrox.algorithms.maps;

import com.wrox.algorithms.iteration.EmptyIterator;
import com.wrox.algorithms.iteration.Iterator;

public final class EmptyMap implements Map {
```

```
    public static final EmptyMap INSTANCE = new EmptyMap();

    private EmptyMap() {
    }

    public Object get(Object key) {
        return null;
    }

    public Object set(Object key, Object value) {
        throw new UnsupportedOperationException();
    }

    public Object delete(Object key) {
        throw new UnsupportedOperationException();
    }

    public boolean contains(Object key) {
        return false;
    }

    public void clear() {
    }

    public int size() {
        return 0;
    }

    public boolean isEmpty() {
        return true;
    }

    public Iterator iterator() {
        return EmptyIterator.INSTANCE;
    }
}
```

Chapter 14

Exercise

1. Create an iterative form of `search()`.

Exercise 1 Solution

```
    private Node search(Node node, CharSequence word, int index) {
        assert word != null : "word can't be null";

        while (node != null) {
            char c = word.charAt(index);
            if (c == node.getChar()) {
                if (index + 1 < word.length()) {
                    node = node.getChild();
                } else {
                    break;
```

```
                }
            } else {
                node = c < node.getChar() ? node.getSmaller() : node.getLarger();
            }
        }

        return node;
    }
```

Chapter 15

Exercises

1. Re-implement the `traverse()` method on `Node` to return the entries in key order.
2. Re-implement the `indexOf()` method on `Node` to perform a binary search instead of a linear search.

Exercise 1 Solution

```
        public void traverse(List list) {
            assert list != null : "list can't be null";

            Iterator children = _children.iterator();
            Iterator entries = _entries.iterator();

            children.first();
            entries.first();

            while (!children.isDone() || !entries.isDone()) {
                if (!children.isDone()) {
                    ((Node) children.current()).inOrderTraversal(list);
                    children.next();
                }

                if (!entries.isDone()) {
                    Entry entry = (Entry) entries.current();
                    if (!entry.isDeleted()) {
                        list.add(entry);
                    }
                    entries.next();
                }
            }
        }
```

Exercise 2 Solution

```
        private int indexOf(Object key) {
            int lowerIndex = 0;
            int upperIndex = _entries.size() - 1;

            while (lowerIndex <= upperIndex) {
                int index = lowerIndex + (upperIndex - lowerIndex) / 2;

                int cmp = _comparator.compare(key,
```

```
                                    ((Entry) _entries.get(index)).getKey());

            if (cmp == 0) {
                return index;
            } else if (cmp < 0) {
                upperIndex = index - 1;
            } else {
                lowerIndex = index + 1;
            }
        }

        return -(lowerIndex + 1);
    }
```

Chapter 18

Exercises

1. Implement a brute-force solution to the closest pair problem.
2. Optimize the plane sweep algorithm so that points too distant in the vertical direction are ignored.

Exercise 1 Solution

```
package com.wrox.algorithms.geometry;

import com.wrox.algorithms.iteration.Iterator;
import com.wrox.algorithms.lists.ArrayList;
import com.wrox.algorithms.lists.List;
import com.wrox.algorithms.sets.ListSet;
import com.wrox.algorithms.sets.Set;
import com.wrox.algorithms.bsearch.ListInserter;
import com.wrox.algorithms.bsearch.IterativeBinaryListSearcher;

public final class BruteForceClosestPairFinder implements ClosestPairFinder {
    public static final BruteForceClosestPairFinder INSTANCE = new
BruteForceClosestPairFinder();

    private BruteForceClosestPairFinder() {
    }

    public Set findClosestPair(Set points) {
        assert points != null : "points can't be null";

        if (points.size() < 2) {
            return null;
        }

        List list = sortPoints(points);

        Point p = null;
```

```
        Point q = null;
        double distance = Double.MAX_VALUE;

        for (int i = 0; i < list.size(); i++) {
            Point r = (Point) list.get(i);
            for (int j = 0; j < list.size(); j++) {
                Point s = (Point) list.get(j);
                if (r != s && r.distance(s) < distance) {
                    distance = r.distance(s);
                    p = r;
                    q = s;
                }
            }
        }

        return createPointPair(p, q);
    }

    private static List sortPoints(Set points) {
        assert points != null : "points can't be null";

        List list = new ArrayList(points.size());

        Iterator i = points.iterator();
        for (i.first(); !i.isDone(); i.next()) {
            INSERTER.insert(list, i.current());
        }

        return list;
    }

    private Set createPointPair(Point p, Point q) {
        Set result = new ListSet();
        result.add(p);
        result.add(q);
        return result;
    }
}
```

Exercise 2 Solution

```
package com.wrox.algorithms.geometry;

import com.wrox.algorithms.bsearch.IterativeBinaryListSearcher;
import com.wrox.algorithms.bsearch.ListInserter;
import com.wrox.algorithms.iteration.Iterator;
import com.wrox.algorithms.lists.ArrayList;
import com.wrox.algorithms.lists.List;
import com.wrox.algorithms.sets.ListSet;
import com.wrox.algorithms.sets.Set;

public final class PlaneSweepOptimizedClosestPairFinder implements
ClosestPairFinder {
```

```
    public static final PlaneSweepOptimizedClosestPairFinder INSTANCE = new
PlaneSweepOptimizedClosestPairFinder();

    private static final ListInserter INSERTER = new ListInserter(
            new IterativeBinaryListSearcher(XYPointComparator.INSTANCE));

    private PlaneSweepOptimizedClosestPairFinder() {
    }

    public Set findClosestPair(Set points) {
        assert points != null : "points can't be null";

        if (points.size() < 2) {
            return null;
        }

        List sortedPoints = sortPoints(points);

        Point p = (Point) sortedPoints.get(0);
        Point q = (Point) sortedPoints.get(1);

        return findClosestPair(p, q, sortedPoints);
    }

    private Set findClosestPair(Point p, Point q, List sortedPoints) {
        Set result = createPointPair(p, q);
        double distance = p.distance(q);
        int dragPoint = 0;

        for (int i = 2; i < sortedPoints.size(); ++i) {
            Point r = (Point) sortedPoints.get(i);
            double sweepX = r.getX();
            double dragX = sweepX - distance;

            while (((Point) sortedPoints.get(dragPoint)).getX() < dragX) {
                ++dragPoint;
            }

            for (int j = dragPoint; j < i; ++j) {
                Point test = (Point) sortedPoints.get(j);
                if (Math.abs(r.getY() - test.getY()) > distance) {
                    continue;
                }
                double checkDistance = r.distance(test);
                if (checkDistance < distance) {
                    distance = checkDistance;
                    result = createPointPair(r, test);
                }
            }
        }

        return result;
    }

    private static List sortPoints(Set points) {
```

```
        assert points != null : "points can't be null";

        List list = new ArrayList(points.size());

        Iterator i = points.iterator();
        for (i.first(); !i.isDone(); i.next()) {
            INSERTER.insert(list, i.current());
        }

        return list;
    }

    private Set createPointPair(Point p, Point q) {
        Set result = new ListSet();
        result.add(p);
        result.add(q);
        return result;
    }
}
```

Index

Index

NUMBERS

A

B

D

M

T